Ref. 12/8/92 EHD

AMERICAN WOMEN PLAYWRIGHTS, 1900–1930

"AMERICAN WOMEN PLAYWRIGHTS, 1900–1930"

A Checklist

Compiled by
Frances Diodato Bzowski

Bibliographies and Indexes in Women's Studies, Number 15

GREENWOOD PRESS
Westport, Connecticut • London

Library of Congress Cataloging-in-Publication Data

Bzowski, Frances Diodato.
    American women playwrights, 1900-1930 : a checklist / compiled by
Frances Diodato Bzowski.
        p. cm.—(Bibliographies and indexes in women's studies,
ISSN 0742-6941 ; no. 15)
    Includes bibliographical references (p.   )
    ISBN 0-313-24238-0 (alk. paper)
    1. American drama—Women authors—Bio-bibliography. 2. American
drama—Women authors—Stories, plots, etc. 3. Women dramatists,
American—20th century—Registers. 4. American drama—20th century—
Bio-bibliography. 5. Women and literature—United States.
I. Title. II. Series.
Z1231.D7B95 1992
[PS338.W6]
016.812'52099287—dc20   92-12301

British Library Cataloguing in Publication Data is available.

Library of Congress Catalog Card Number: 92-12301
ISBN: 0-313-24238-0
ISSN: 0742-6941

First published in 1992

Greenwood Press, 88 Post Road West, Westport, CT 06881
An imprint of Greenwood Publishing Group, Inc.

Printed in the United States of America

The paper used in this book complies with the
Permanent Paper Standard issued by the National
Information Standards Organization (Z39.48-1984).

10 9 8 7 6 5 4 3 2 1

Contents

Preface

About ten years ago I took an undergraduate course called "Women in Drama." Half of the course was spent studying female characters in plays written by men; the other half, in reading plays written by women. In that second half, along with works by such well-known playwrights as Lillian Hellman and Lorraine Hansberry, we read "Trifles," a one-act play by Susan Glaspell. At the time I had never heard of Glaspell, but her play captivated me. It was such a perfectly constructed play, revelatory of the ways in which women view events differently from men. I began to wonder how many other plays had been written by women, how many other treasures lay buried in the obscurity of library special collections or out of print anthologies. I casually began to do a "little research" on the subject, never realizing that my initial brief list would grow like some Alice in Wonderland, eventually becoming so immense that I could barely contain it within the confines of one book.

Along the way, I enrolled at Brown University as a graduate student with a concentration in women's studies and began to research a particular period of history—the time of the New Woman in the early twentieth century. I started a search for plays that specifically dealt with issues that were important to the New Woman—suffrage, world peace, marriage and career conflicts, social issues.

The beginning of the twentieth century was a unique time for women interested in writing, performing and directing plays. As New Women, they found their voice in an era that accepted a woman's right to express herself. And this new personal freedom occurred at the same time that the little theatre movement provided countless opportunities for women to write plays and to see them performed. Hardly any sizable community was without some kind of amateur theatre at this time. Also, it was an age of pageantry, when cities and communities, as well as the women's movement itself, utilized spectacle and drama. Community, college and church dramatics were acceptable forums for women, providing them with the chance not only to write plays, but also to direct and produce them.

At this point in my research my focus broadened. As I looked for socially significant plays of the New Woman, I found that I could not fairly separate the chaff from the grain. A woman writing a health play for a neighborhood settlement house, or a children's play for the classroom, or a musical performance to express her religious views, or a farce for a little theatre group, or a commemorative celebration for her college, or a pageant for her city, was also a part of this great movement allowing women so much more freedom in life and in theatre. So I began to record any and all plays that I found written by women during the era of the New Woman.

I was obliged to put some kind of time limit on this growing checklist. Although the phenomenon of the New Woman began in the late nineteenth century, I felt that for the sake of convenience I would begin with 1900. I closed with 1930 as the end date because the Depression, beginning in 1929, changed the theme of drama. The 1920s was a decade that allowed women less restricted roles in society. Like their counterparts in the 1970s and 1980s, women of the flapper generation felt that they could have it all—marriage and career, freedom and responsibility. The Depression ended this somewhat naive attitude, which did not surface again until the contemporary women's movement of the 1970s, when it was enlightened by the awareness of the limits that society places on women's expanded roles.

Most of the plays included in this checklist are not notable as literature and probably deserve the anonymity which they have received. But there could be some "treasures" like "Trifles" included in the list. And even without a classic or outstanding play, the sheer volume of women's drama for the thirty years I researched is noteworthy. My greatest wish is that this checklist will prove useful for future scholars of women's history who are searching for some kind of written testimony of women's lives and interests at the beginning of the century.

In this checklist I have tried to be as accurate and as inclusive as possible, stretching the boundaries of the word "play" to include all kinds of dramatic presentations—plays, pageants, stunts, exercises, musical comedies, masques, operas, cantatas and dialogues. I have listed not only adult drama, but also the countless little plays written by women for children and for the celebration of holidays.

Since my basic research was done at the John Hay Library at Brown University, most of the published works that I include can be found there and are designated by the code RPB, which is the coding used by the National Union Catalog to represent Brown University libraries. However, this code after the title of a play does not mean that the work can be found *only* at Brown. A play with no location code after it was probably published, but I cannot locate where a copy can be found.

Furthermore, I included works that were never published but exist only in typed manuscripts in college and university libraries. Also, some of the plays that I listed were produced but not published, and I gave that information wherever I had it. In most cases I indicated how many acts a play has. Unless otherwise noted, plays are three acts. One-act plays are shown with a (1). Also, I included any information about awards that the play received. Plays which were printed only in periodicals were also included in the checklist.

Whenever I had any doubt if a name was a woman, I did include it, and I included names that could be either gender, such as Marion. Whenever I found more than one spelling of a woman's name, I listed both, including hyphenated versions of last names. In many cases I listed both single and married names as a cross reference, if a woman published under both names. One of the great difficulties of doing research on women is this problem of changing last names.

In some cases I could not be sure if a woman was British or American. Whenever there was any doubt, I listed the name, although in some cases I noted that she might be British. Also, when I was not sure whether or not a title was a dramatic work of some kind, I designated (play?) after the title. As long as a woman wrote at least one play between 1900 and 1930 I included her in the checklist, even if the rest of her plays did not fall in that time period.

I did not do extensive biographical research, but whenever I could, I did include a woman's birth and death dates. Also, I checked four major biographical sources, and I noted with a letter code if a woman was included in any of them.

Following this preface are two listings that decode abbreviated notations in the entries:

1. play anthologies and library collections
   (library codes taken from the National Union Catalog – NUC)
2. biographical sources (These codes are listed immediately after the woman's name, rather than in the right-hand column where the other two codes are found.)

The following sample provides a guide for understanding my notations (numbers in brackets [ ] refer to the explanations below):

[1] **ZOE AKINS**   [2](1886-1958)   [3]AWW   NWAT
   [4]Daddy's Gone A-Hunting, [5]1923, prod. 1921, in [7]Everybody's   [9]RPB
   Magazine, 45, December, 1921, 93-100.
   [4]Such a Charming Young Man, [5]1924, [6]comedy, [9]OPS-I, CLU, CSmH
   in [7]Smart Set, 48. April, 1916, 67-78   [8](1)

1. name, including alternate spellings and additional surnames
2. birth and death dates where known
3. coded biographical sources
4. play title
5. publication and/or production dates
6. description of type of play
7. other information about the play, including other locations
8. number of acts
9. coded collections of plays or library collections in which the play can be found.

Finally, I would like to acknowledge the help of many people in the completion of this book. First, I thank my husband, Edward, and my sons for their understanding and patience while I spent many hours of many days at the Hay Library. Furthermore, I wish to thank Dr. Carolyn Swift of Rhode Island College for first introducing me to the wonder of women's drama; Dr. Don Wilmeth of Brown University for encouraging me to conduct my independent study of women playwrights and to publish my findings; Dr. Mari Jo Buhle of Brown University for reaffirming in my mind the importance of women's history; the librarians and staff of the John Hay Library for their immeasurable patience in finding and re-shelving the thousands of plays I checked at the library; Karon Dionne and Janet D'Alesandre, without whose help in formatting the text on the computer this book would probably have remained nothing more than a stack of papers in my den. I accept all responsibility for any errors which exist, for I know that there must be some errors in a work of such length and complexity.

Codes for Play Anthologies
and Library Collections

[Libraries indicated by *]

AAP   The Appleton Little Theatre Plays, New York, 1924.

AGW   Alexander, R. C. and O. P. Goslin, Worship Through Drama, New York, Harper, 1930.

An-C-VU*   University of British Columbia, Vancouver, Canada

APS   Auditorium Plays and Stunts for High School, Franklin, Ohio, Eldridge Entertainment House, 1930.

AU*   University of Alabama, University

AzU*   University of Arizona, Tuscon

BAO   The Banner Anthology of One-Act Plays by American Authors, compiled by Leslie H. Carter, ed. by Ellen M. Gall, San Francisco Banner Play Bureau, Inc., 1929.

BAW   Barlow, Judith E., Plays By American Women: the Early Years, New York, Avon Books, 1981.

BCC   Brings, Lawrence M., Choice Comedies for Junior High Schools, Minneapolis, Minn.: The Northwestern Press, 1934.

BCE   Brings, Lawrence M., The Christmas Entertainment Book, Minneapolis, Minn., The Northwestern Press, 1937.

BCF   Clever Comedies for Female Characters, Boston, Walter H. Baker, 1915.

BHP   Bullivant, Cecil H., Home Plays, London, T. C. & E. C. Jack, 1911, New York, Dodge Publishing Co., 1912.

BMC   Merry Christmas Plays and Entertainments by Various Authors, Boston, W. H. Baker and Co., 1916.

BPC   Bailey, Carolyn S., Plays for the Children's Hour, Springfield, Mass., Milton Bradley Co., 1931.

BPD   Drama League of America, Dickon Goes to the Fair and Other Plays, New York, George H. Doran Co., 1927.

BPH   Baker, George Pierce, Plays of the Harvard Dramatic Club, New York, Brentano's, first series, 1918; second series, 1919; third series, Harvard Plays.

BPP   Plays in Pinafore, Boston, Walter H. Baker, 1916.

BPW   Baker, George Pierce, Plays of the 47 Workshop, New York, Brentano's, first series, 1918; second series, 1920; third series, 1922; fourth series, 1925.

BTG   Boston Theatre Guild Plays, Boston, Walter H. Baker Co., 1924.
           Buffalo, New York
BYP   Baker, George Pierce, Yale One-Act Plays, New York, Samuel
           French, I-1930, edited by Baker; II-1930, edited by W. P. Eaton; III-
           1937.
C*   California State Library, Sacramento
CaOTP*   Toronto Public Library, Toronto, Canada
CCF   Cartmell, Van H. and Bennett A. Cerf, Famous Plays of Crime and
           Detection, Philadelphia, The Blakistone Co., 1946.
CCO   Clark, Barrett H. and Thomas R. Cook, One-Act Plays, Boston, D.C.
           Heath & Co., 1929.
CCP   Cordell, Kathryn and William H. Cordell, The Pulitzer Prize Plays,
           New York, Random House, 1935, 1938, 1940.
CCS   Cerf, Bennett A. and Van H. Cartmell, SRD: The Most Successful
           Plays in the History of the American Stage, New York, Doubleday,
           1944.
CCS-2   Cerf, Bennett and Van H. Cartmell, Sixteen Famous American
           Plays, New York, Garden City Publishing Co., 1941.
CCT   Cerf, Bennett and Van H. Cartmell, Twenty-four Favorite One-Act
           Plays, Garden City, New York, Dolphin Books, 1963.
CCT-2   Chandler, Frank W. and Richard A. Cordell, Twentieth Century
           Plays, New York, T. Nelson and Sons, 1934.
CCT-3   Cerf, Bennett and Van H. Cartmell, Thirty Famous One-Act Plays,
           New York, Modern Library, 1943.
CD   Community Drama, prepared by the Playground and Recreation
           Assoc. of America, New York: The Century Co., 1926.
CJB   The Christmas Joy Book, Syracuse, N. Y., Willis N. Bugbee Co.,
           1930.
CJP   Cohen, Helen, The Junior Play Book, New York, Harcourt Brace
           Co., 1923.
CLM   Cohen, Helen L. Longer Plays By Modern Authors, New York,
           Harcourt Brace Co., 1922.
CLP   Clark, Barrett H., America's Lost Plays, Bloomington, Indiana
           University Press, 1940.
CLP-1   Clark, Ada and others, Little Plays for Christmas, Chicago, Beckley-
           Caudy Co., 1928.
CLSU*   University of Southern California at Los Angeles
CLU*   University of California at Los Angeles
CMO   Cohen, Helen L., More One-Act Plays by Modern Authors, New
           York, Harcourt Brace and Co., 1927.
CNA   Clark, Barrett H. and Kenyon Nicholson, The American Scene, New
           York, Appleton Co., 1930.
CNM   Clark, Barrett & William H. Davenport, Nine Modern American
           Plays, New York, Appleton-Century-Crofts, 1951.
Co*   Colorado State Library, Denver
CoD*   Denver Public Library, Denver, Colorado
COP   Cohen, Helen, One-Act Plays by Modern Authors, New York,
           Harcourt Brace, 1921.

CP	Christmas Plays, Boston, The Pilgrim Press, 1927.
CPE	Church Plays and Entertainments for Young People, Franklin, Ohio, Eldridge Entertainment House, 1924.
CPR	Catchy Plays and Recitations, Syracuse, N. Y., Willis N. Bugbee Co., 1929.
CPR-1	Catchy Plays and Recitations, No. 2, Syracuse, N. Y., Willis N. Bugbee, 1930.
CRM	Cordell, Richard A., Representative Modern Plays: British and American, New York, Nelson and Sons, 1929.
CSdS*	San Diego State College, San Diego, California
CSmH*	Henry Huntington Library, San Marino, California
CSP	Cook, George Cram and Frank Shay, The Provincetown Plays, Cincinnatti, Stewart Kidd, 1921.
CSP-1	Clements, Colin C., Sea Plays, Boston, Small, Maynard, 1923.
CSS	Cole, Josephine R. and Grace Silver, comp., Socialist Dialogues and Recitations, Chicago, Charles H. Kerr & Co., 1913.
CSt*	Stanford University, Stanford, California
CStoC*	University of the Pacific, Stockton, California
CTC	Chandler, Frank Wadleigh, Twentieth Century Plays, New York, Nelson and Sons, 1934.
CTM	Clark, Ada and others, Tributes to Mother and Dad, Syracuse, Willis N. Bugbee, 1937.
CtY*	Yale University, New Haven, Connecticut
CU*	University of California, Berkeley
DCC	Dickinson, Thomas H. and Jack R. Crawford Jr., Contemporary Plays, Boston, Houghton Mifflin, 1935.
DCC-2	Dickinson, T. H., Chief Contemporary Drama, 2nd series, Boston, Houghton Mifflin, 1921.
DCU	Drummond, Alexander M., Cornell University Plays, New York, Samuel French, 1932.
DDP	Double Demon and Other One-Act Plays, New York, Appleton, 1924.
DFP	Deseo, Lydia Glover, Four Peace Plays, New York, The Methodist Book Concern, 1929.
DGL	Drummond, Alexander M. and Robert E. Gard, The Lake Guns of Seneca and Cayuga and Eight Other Plays of Upstate New York, Ithaca, New York, Cornell University Press, 1942.
DHEW*	United States Dept. of Health, Education and Welfare Library
DHU*	Howard University, Washington, D. C.
DLC*	Library of Congress, Washington, D. C.
DPC	Drama League, Playwriting Contest for 1928, New York, Longman's Green and Co., 1929.
DPP	Dakota Playmaker Plays, Boston, Walter H. Baker Co., 1923.
DSS	Dean, Alexander, Seven to Seventeen, plays for School and Camp, New York, Samuel French, 1931.
DWP	Dickinson, Thomas H., Wisconsin Plays, New York, P. W. Huebsch, 1914.
ECO	Emerson College of Oratory, Vol. 1, The Cathedral Clock and Other

One-Act Plays, Boston, Expression Co., 1927.

EEY   Easy Entertainments for Young People, Philadelphia, Penn Pub. Co., 1920.

EMR   Eastman, Fred., Modern Religious Dramas, New York, Harper and Bros., 1928.

ETO   Eastman, Fred, Ten One-Act Plays, New York, Clark and Co., 1937.

ETP   Eaton, Walter P., Twelve One-Act Plays, New York, Longmans Green and Co., 1926.

FBP   Fifty Best Plays of the American Theatre, New York, Crown Publishers, Inc., 1969, 4 volumes.

FCP   France, Rachel, A Century of Plays by Women, New York, Richards Rosen Press, Inc., 1979.

FDD   Fish, Helen R., Drama and Dramatics, New York, Macmillan, 1930.

FFP   The First Flag and Other Patriotic Plays and Exercises for Children, Boston, Educational Publishing Corp., 1917.

FKC   Freeman, Carolyn and others, The Kiddies' Christmas Book, Syracuse, N. Y., Willis N. Bugbee Co., 1925.

FMC   Faxon, Grace B., Many a Way to Closing Day, Boston, Walter H Baker Co.,1926.

FMM   Faxon, Grace B., Many a Way for Memorial Day, Boston, Walter H. Baker Co.,1926.

FOA   Funny One-Act Christmas Plays, Dayton, Ohio, Paine Publishing Co., 1935.

FON   Finney, Stella B., Plays Old and New, New York, Allyn and Bacon, 1928.

FOV   Friedl, Bettina, Ed., On to Victory: Propaganda Plays of the Woman Suffrage Movement, Boston: Northeastern University Press, 1987.

FP   Famous Plays of 1936, London, V. Gollancz Ltd., 1936. (?? series of plays in l930s by this company).

FPP   Faxon, Grace B., Pieces and Plays for Washington's Birthday, Dansville, N. Y., F. A. Owen Pub. Co., 1916.

FRD   Federal Council of Churches of Christ in America, Religious Dramas, New York, Century, 1923, I and II.

FSP   Flying Stag Plays for the Little Theatre, no. 1-9, 1918-1920.

FTaSU*   Florida State University, Tallahassee

FU*   University of Florida, Gainesville

FWP   Flaurier, Noel and others, Winning Plays and Dialogues, Chicago, Beckley-Cardy Co., 1930.

GEU*   Emory University, Atlanta, Georgia

GHP   Goin' Home and Other Plays of the 1927 Contest, London and New York, Longmans Green and Co., 1928.

GJY   Garrigus, Fred and Theodore Johnson, You're On the Air, plays adapted for radio, Boston, Walter H. Baker Co., 1946.

GLL   Greenlaw, Edwin and others, Literature and Life, Chicago, Scott Foresman, 1929, II and III.

GMO   Griffith, Francis J. and Joseph Mersand, One Act Plays for Today, New York, Globe Book Co., 1945.

GOP   Goldstone, George A., One-Act Plays, New York, Allyn and Bacon, 1926.

GP	Grange plays.
GPD	Gaw, Alison and Ethelean, Eds., Pharaoh's Daughter and Other Biblical Plays of the Contest, 1927, New York, Longmans Green and Co., 1928.
GPF	Galbraith, Esther E., Ed., Plays Without Footlights, New York, Harcourt Brace and Co., 1945.
GTB	Gassner, John, Twenty Best Plays of the Modern American Theatre, New York, Crown Publishers, 1941.
GTP	Gassner, John, Twenty-five Best Plays of the American Theatre, New York, Crown Publishers, 1949.
GU*	University of Georgia, Athens
HBP	Harper's Book of Little Plays, New York and London, Harper and Bros., 1910.
HDC	Hallock, Grace T., Dramatized Child Health, New York, American Child Health Association, 1925.
HFP	Hughes, Hatcher, et. al., Four Full Length Plays, New York, D. Appleton Co., 1928.
HNM	Hampden, John, Nine Modern Plays, London, Thomas Nelson and Sons, 1926.
HPC	Hamilton, Dorothy T., Primary Christmas Programs, Chicago, A. Flanagan Co., 1928.
HPP	Hale, Florence, Spring Plays and Programs, a Collection of Entertainment Material for Classroom and Auditorium Use, New York, Educational Publishing Co., 1934.
HPY	Heron, Henrietta, comp., Pageants For the Year, Cincinnati, Ohio, The Standard Publishing Co., 1928.
HQC	Hendrie, Ernest, Quite a Nice Cat and Other Sketches, for Women's Institutes, Girl Guides, etc., New York and London, Samuel French Co., 1927.
HRE	Heywood, Delia A. and others, The Red Entertainment Book, Chicago, A. Flanagan Co., 1930.
HSB	Hatch, James V. and Ted Shine, Black Theatre U.S.A.: 45 Plays by Black Americans, 1847-1974, New York, Free Press, 1974.
HSP	Hughes, Glenn, Short Plays for Modern Players, New York, D. Appleton and Co., 1931.
HTM	Hampden, John, Ten Modern Plays, London, Thomas Nelson and Sons, 1928.
HUW	Hughes, Glenn, University of Washington Plays, Seattle, University of Washington Press, 1921; 2nd series, 1924; 3rd series, 1927.
IaU*	University of Iowa, Iowa City
ICIU*	University of Illinois, Chicago
ICJ*	John Crerar Library, Chicago, Illinois
ICN*	Newberry Library, Chicago, Illinois
ICU*	University of Chicago, Chicago, Illinois
IdPI*	Idaho State University, Pocatello, Idaho
IEG*	Garrett Theological Seminary, Evanston, Illinois
IFSchs*	Stephenson County Historical Society, Freeport, Illinois
InI*	Indianapolis Public Library, Indianapolis, Indiana

InU*   Indiana University, Bloomington
IP   International Plays, Chicago, Dramatic Publishing Co., 1936.
IPA   Isaacs, Edith J. R., Plays of American Life and Fantasy, New York,
            Coward McCann, 1929.
IPP   Indiana Prize Plays, Indianapolis, Bobbs-Merrill Co., 1924.
IshdL*   Iowa State Historical Department Library
IU*   University of Illinois, Urbana
JAB   Johnson, Theodore, Another Book of Miniature Plays, Boston,
            Walter H. Baker Co., 1934.
JDC   Johnson, Theodore, Diminutive Comedies, Boston, Walter H. Baker
            Co., 1931.
JEC   Johnson, Theodore, The Easy Christmas Book, Boston, Walter H.
            Baker Co., 1939.
JEL   Johnson, Theodore, Easy Plays for Lincoln's Birthday, Boston,
            Walter H. Baker Co., 1939.
JEM   Johnson, Theodore, Easy Entertaining Monologues, Boston, Walter
            H. Baker Co., 1938.
JEM-2   Johnson, Theodore, Easy Programs for Mother's Day, Boston,
            Walter H. Baker Co., 1939.
JEP   Johnson, Theodore, Easy Programs for Christmas, Boston, Walter
            H. Baker Co., 1945.
JET   Johnson, Theodore, Easy Plays for Teen Age Girls, New York, The
            Amateurs' Playshop, 1938.
JGH   Johnson, Theodore, The Gingerbread House and Eight Other Plays
            for Children, Boston, Walter H. Baker Co., 1928.
JMP   Johnson, Theodore, More Plays in Miniature, Boston, Walter H.
            Baker, 1929.
JMS   Johnson, Theodore, Miniature Plays for Stage or Study, Boston,
            Walter H. Baker Co., 1930.
JNS   Jagendorf, Moritz A., Nine Short Plays, written for young people,
            New York, Macmillan Co., 1937.
JOP   Jagendorf, Moritz A., One-Act Plays for Young Folks, New York,
            Brentanos, 1924.
JPG   Johnson, Theodore, Plays About George Washington, Boston,
            Walter H. Baker Co., 1931.
JPM   Johnson, Theodore, Plays in Miniature, Boston, Walter H. Baker
            Co., n.d.
JPP   The Jester's Purse and Other Plays for Boys and Girls, New York,
            Harcourt Brace and Co., 1926.
JPP-1   Johnson, Marie W., Plays and Pageants for the Church School,
            Boston, The Beacon Press. 1929.
JPR   Juvenile Plays and Readings, Hot Springs National Park, Arkansas,
            J. M. Connelly Publishers, 1929.
JPW   Johnson, Theodore, Prize Plays for Women and Girls, Boston,
            Walter H. Baker Co., 1935.
JTC   Jagendorf, Moritz A., Twenty-five Non Royalty Plays for Children,
            New York, Greenberg Publishers, 1942.
JTF   Johnson, Theodore, Ten Fantasies for Stage and Study, Boston,

	Walter H. Baker Co., 1932.
JTN	Jagendorf, Moritz A., <u>Twenty-five Non Royalty Holiday Plays</u>, New York, Greenberg Publishers, 1944.
JWA	Johnson, Theodore, <u>Washington Anniversary Plays</u>, Boston, Walter H. Baker Co., 1931.
KAF	Koch, Frederick, <u>American Folk Plays</u>, New York, D. Appleton-Century Co., 1937.
KC	Kampmeier, Roland, <u>Contemporaries!</u> current forms of composition from L. C. Woodman's College Freshman English Classes, Vinton, Iowa, Kruse Publishing Co., 1928.
KCC	Koch, Frederick, <u>Carolina Folk Comedies</u>, New York, Samuel French, 1931.
KCF	Koch Frederick H., <u>Carolina Folk Plays</u>, New York, Henry Holt Co., I-1922; II-1924; III-1928; IV-1931.
KFA	Kozelka, Paul, <u>Fifteen American One-Act Plays</u>, New York, Washington Square Press, 1961.
KMK*	Kansas State University, Manhattan
KPC	Knickerbocker, Edwin Van B., <u>Plays for Class Room Interpretation</u>, New York, Henry Holt and Co., 1921.
KSP	Knickerbocker, Edwin Van B., <u>Short Plays</u>, New York, Henry Holt Co., 1931.
KTN	Kozlenko, William, <u>Twenty-five Non Royalty One-Act American Comedies</u>, New York, Greenberg Publishers, 1943.
KTP	Knickerbocker, Edwin Van B., <u>Twelve Plays,</u> New York, Holt, 1924.
KU*	University of Kansas, Lawrence
KWD	Kriegel, Harriet, <u>Women in Drama</u>, New York, New American Library, 1975.
LAM	Leonard, Sterling Andrus, <u>Atlantic Book of Modern Plays</u>, Boston, Atlantic Monthly Press, 1921.
LCO	Lewis, Roland B., <u>Contemporary One-Act Plays</u>, New York, Scribners, 1922.
LGP	Locke, Alain and Montgomery Gregory, <u>Plays of Negro Life</u>, Westport, Conn., Negro University Press, 1927.
LMS	Law, Frederick Houk, <u>Modern Plays Short and Long</u>, New York, The Century Co., 1924.
LNarc*	Amistad Research Center, New Orleans, Louisiana
LNP	Lutkenhaus, Anna M., Margaret Knox and others, <u>New Plays for School Children,</u> New York, Century, 1929.
LOL	Lowe, Orton, <u>Our Land and Its Literature</u>, New York, Harper, 1936.
LPS	Lutkenhaus, Mrs. Anna May, <u>Plays for School Children</u>, New York, D. Appleton Co., 1915.
LU*	Louisiana State University, Baton Rouge
LUU	Lewis, B. R., <u>University of Utah Plays</u>, Boston, Walter H. Baker Co., 1928.
MAT	Moses, Montrose, <u>Another Treasury of Plays for Children</u>, Boston, Little Brown Co., 1926.
MB*	Boston Public Library, Boston, Massachusetts
MDeeP*	Pocumtuck Valley Library, Deerfield, Massachusetts

MeBa*   Bangor Public Library, Bangor, Maine
MH*   Harvard University, Cambridge, Massachusetts
Mi*   Michigan State Library, Lansing
MiD*   Detroit Public Library, Detroit, Michigan
MiU*   University of Michigan, Ann Arbor
MnHi*   Minnesota Historical Society, St. Paul
MNS*   Smith College, Northampton, Massachusetts
MoKU*   University of Missouri, Kansas City
MOP   Marriott, Joseph, One Act Plays Today, New York, Dodd, Mead,
             1929.
MoU*   University of Missouri, Columbia
MP   Morningside Plays, New York, Frank Shay and Co., 1917.
MPD   Mayorga, Margaret, Plays of Democracy, New York, Dodd, Mead,
             1945.
MPP   McGraw, H. W. and J. N. Perry, Prose and Poetry for the Twelfth
             Year, Syracuse, NewYork, L. W. Singer Co., 1930.
MRA   Moses, Montrose, Representative American Dramas—National and
             Local, Boston, Little Brown Co., 1933.
MRC   Moses, Montrose, Ring Up the Curtain, Boston, Little Brown and
             Co., 1932,
MRO   Mayorga, Margaret, Representative One-Act Plays by American
             Authors, Boston, Little, Brown, 1919.
MsSM*   Mississippi State University, State College
MsU*   University of Mississippi, University
MTP   Moses, Montrose, A Treasury of Plays for Children, Boston, Little,
             Brown and Co., 1927.
MTS   Mayorga, Margaret, Twenty Short Plays on a Royalty Holiday,
             New York, Samuel French Co., 1937.
MWA*   American Antiquarian Society, Worcester, Massachusetts
MWS   Mayorga, Margaret, The World's a Stage: Short Plays for Juniors,
             New York, Samuel French Co., 1944.
N*   New York State Library, Albany
NAB   Nicholson, Kenyon, Appleton Book of Short Plays, New York,
             Appleton, First series, 1926, 1928, 1937; Second series, 1927, 1938.
NBuG*   Grosvenor Reference Division, Buffalo and Erie County Public
             Library,
NBuHi*   Buffalo and Erie County Historical Society, Buffalo, New York
NBuU*   State University of New York at Buffalo
Nc*   North Carolina State University at Raleigh
NcC*   Charlotte, North Carolina Public Library and Mecklenburg County
NcD*   Duke University, Durham, North Carolina
NcGU*   University of North Carolina, Greensboro
NcU*   University of North Carolina, Chapel Hill
NhD*   Dartmouth College, Hanover, New Hampshire
NHi*   New York Historical Society, New York
NHP   Nicholson, Kenyon, Hollywood Plays, Twelve One-act Plays from
             the Repertory of the Writers' Club of Hollywood, Calif., 1930.
NIC*   Cornell University, Ithaca, New York

NjP*	Princeton University, New Brunswick, New Jersey
NjR*	Rutgers University, Brunswick, New Jersey
NN*	New York Public Libary, New York
NNC*	Columbia University, New York, New York
NPM	New Plays for Men and Boys, New York, Samuel French Co., 1939.
NPW	New Plays for Women and Girls, New York, Samuel French Co., 1932.
NRB	Nicholson, Kenyon, Revues: A Book of Short Sketches, New York, D. Appleton and Co., 1926.
NRU*	University of Rochester, Rochester, New York
OAT	The One Act Theater, New York, Samuel French, 9 volumes, I-1936, II-1936.
OC*	Cincinnatti Public Library, Cincinnati, Ohio
OCH*	Hebrew Union College, Cincinnati, Ohio
OCl*	Cleveland Public Library, Cleveland, Ohio
OClW*	Case Western Reserve University, Cleveland, Ohio
ODW*	Ohio Wesleyan University, Delaware, Ohio
OKentC*	Kent State University, Kent, Ohio
OO*	Oberlin College, Oberlin, Ohio
OPS	One Act Plays for Stage and Study, New York, Samuel French Co., 10 volumes: I-1924, II-1925, III-1927, IV-1928, V-1929, VI-1931, VII-1932, VIII-1934, IX-1938, X-1949
OPW	Oneal, Billie (Mrs. Ben G. Oneal), Prize Winning One Act Plays, Dallas, Southwest Press, 1930.
Or*	Oregon State Library, Salem
OrCS*	Oregon State University Library, Corvallis
OrHi*	Oregon Historical Society, Portland
OrP*	Library Association of Portland, Oregon
OrU*	University of Oregon, Eugene
OU*	Ohio State University, Columbus
OWibiU*	Wilberforce University, Carnegie Library, Wilberforce, Ohio
PBa*	Academy of the New Church, Byrn Athyn, Pennsylvania
PBL*	Lehigh University, Bethlehem, Pennsylvania
PBm*	Bryn Mawr College, Bryn Mawr, Pennsylvania
PCW	Plays of the University of California Little Theatre Workshop.
PDP	Pence, Raymond Woodbury, Ed., Dramas by Present-day Writers, New York, C. Scribner's Sons, 1927.
PJB	Phillips, Le Roy and Theodore Johnson, Baker's Anthology of One-Act Plays, Boston, The Baker International Play Bureau, 1925.
PLP	Playshop Laboratory Plays, Mount Holyoke College, S. Hadley, Mass., 1932.
PP	Prize Plays of 1927-1928, Philadelphia, The Penn Publishing Co., 1930.
PP*	Free Library of Philadelphia, Philadelphia, Pennsylvania
PPBC*	Union Library Catalogue of Pennsylvania, Philadelphia, Pennsylvania
PPC*	College of Physicians of Philadelphia, Philadelphia, Pennsylvania
PPDrop*	Dropsie College for Hebrew Cognate Learning, Philadelphia, Penn.

PPT*	Temple University, Philadelphia, Pennsylvania
PSS	Phelps, Pauline and Marion Short, Sixteen Two-Character Plays, New York, E. S. Werner and Co., 1906.
PST	Pulling the Show Together, New York, Samuel French Co., 1928.
PSt*	Pennsylvania State University, University Park
PTM	Philips, LeRoy, Types of Modern Dramatic Composition: An Anthology of One-Act Plays for Schools and Colleges, New York, Ginn and Co., 1927.
PTS	Pearson, Paul M., The Speaker: A Collection of the Best Orations, Poems, Stories, Debates and One-Act Plays for Public Speaking and Voice Training, New York, Noble and Noble, 1925, eight volumes
PU*	University of Pennsylvania, Philadelphia
PWP	Plays With a Punch, Boston, Walter H. Baker Co., 1916.
QCP	Quinn, Arthur H. Contemporary American Plays, New York, C. Scribner's Sons, 1923.
QRA	Quinn, Arthur Hobson, Representative American Plays, New York, Appleton-Century Crofts,1953.
RCT	Rich, Mabel I., Classified Types of Literature, New York, Century, 1926.
RMN	Richardson, Willis and May Miller, Negro History in Thirteen Plays, Washington, The Associated Publishers Inc., 1935.
RMP	Richardson, Willis and May Miller, Plays and Pageants from the Life of the Negro, Washington, The Associated Publishers, Inc., 1930.
RPB*	Brown University, Providence, Rhode Island
RPB-M*	Brown University, Providence, Rhode Island—Music only
RSS	Rohrbough, Katherine F., Successful Stunts, Garden City, New York, Doran, 1929.
RUM	Rowe, Kenneth, University of Michigan Plays, Ann Arbor, Michigan, 3 volumes, I-1929; II-1930; III-1932.
SAC	Shay, Frank, Appleton Book of Christmas Plays, New York, D. Appleton and Co., 1929.
SAH	Shay, Frank, Appleton Book of Holiday Plays, New York, D. Appleton Co., 1930.
SAP	Sanford, Anne P., American Patriotic Plays, New York, Dodd, Mead & Co., 1937.
SAR	Sanford, Anne P., Assembly Room Plays, New York, Dodd, Mead & Co., 1936.
SBC	Sindelar, Joseph C., The Best Christmas Book, Chicago, Beckley-Cardy Co., 1913.
SBE	Sindelar, Joseph, Bright Entertainments for Christmas, Chicago, Beckley-Cardy Co., 1922.
SBO	Schafer, Barbara Louise, A Book of One-Act Plays, Indianapolis, Bobbs-Merrill Co., 1922.
SBP	Strutton, Rebecca and others, Best Primary Plays, Chicago, Beckley-Cardy, 1930.
SBT	Sindelar, Joseph C., The Best Thanksgiving Book, Chicago, Beckley-Cardy, 1918.

SCC	Sindelar, Joseph C., <u>Christmas Celebrations</u>, Chicago, A. Flanagan Co., 1906.
SCO	Shay, Frank, <u>Contemporary One-Act Plays of 1921</u>, Cincinnatti, Stewart Kidd, 1922.
SCS	Skinner, Ada M., <u>Christmas Stories and Plays</u>, New York, Rand McNally & Co., 1915.
SCS-1	Snook, Lee Owen, Ed., <u>Comedies Seven</u>, New Non-Royalty Plays for General Community Use, New York, Row, Peterson & Co., 1933.
SCT	<u>Smith College Theatre Workshop Plays</u>, Northampton, Mass., The Theatre Workshop, Smith College, 1921.
ScU*	University of South Carolina, Columbia
SFM	Shay, Frank, <u>Fifty More Contemporary One-Act Plays</u>, New York, D. Appleton and Co., 1928.
SGW	Sanford, Anne P., <u>George Washington Plays</u>, New York, Dodd, Mead & Co., 1931.
SH	Schauffler, Robert H., <u>Halloween</u>, New York, Dodd, Mead & Co., 1938.
SHP	Sullivan, Victoria and James Hatch, <u>Plays By and About Women</u>, New York, Vintage Books, 1974.
SKS	<u>Short Plays</u>, Stewart Kidd.
SLC	Shay, Frank and Pierre Loving, <u>Fifty Contemporary One-Act Plays</u>, Cincinnatti, Stewart Kidd Co., 1920.
SLP	Sturgis, Granville F., <u>Little Plays for All Occasions</u>, Boston, The Cornhill Publishing Co., 1923.
SLP-1	Sanford, Anne Putnam, Ed., <u>Lincoln Plays</u>, New York, Dodd, Mead & Co., 1933.
SNB	<u>St. Nicholas Book of Plays and Operettas</u>, New York, The Century Co., 1916.
SNC	Sindelar, Joseph, <u>The New Christmas Book</u>, Chicago, A. Flanagan Co., 1910.
SNC-2	Sanford, Anne P., <u>New Plays for Christmas</u>, New York, Dodd Mead & Co., 1935.
SNP	Sanford, Anne P., <u>New Plays for Children</u>, New York, Dodd, Mead & Co., 1936.
SOP	Sanford, Anne P., <u>One Act Plays for Women</u>, New York, Dodd, Mead & Co., 1934.
SOP-1	Sanford, Anne P., <u>Outdoor Plays for Boys and Girls</u>, New York, Dodd Mead & Co., 1930.
SP	<u>Six Plays</u>, London, Victor Gollancz, 1933.
SP-2	<u>Seven Plays</u>, London, Heineman, 1935.
SPA	Sanford, Anne P., <u>Plays for Autumn and Winter Holidays</u>, New York, Dodd, Mead & Co., 1938.
SPC	Sanford, Anne P., <u>Plays for Civic Days</u>, New York, Dodd, Mead & Co., 1931.
SPD	<u>Sunshine Plays and Dialogues</u>, by Marie Irish and others, Syracuse, New York, Willis N. Bugbee Co., 1920.
SPE	Sanford, Anne P., <u>Little Plays for Everybody</u>, New York, Dodd,

	Mead & Co., 1939.
SPG	Sanford, Anne P., <u>Plays for Graduation Days</u>, New York, Dodd, Mead & Co., 1930.
SPN	Sanford, Anne Putnam, Ed., <u>Pageants of Our Nation</u>, New York, Dodd, Mead & Co., 1929.
SPP	Sanford, Anne P., <u>Peace Plays,</u> New York, Dodd, Mead & Co., 1932.
SPS	Sanford, Anne P., <u>Plays of Story and Legend,</u> New York, Dodd, Mead & Co., 1937.
SPS-2	Sanford, Anne P., <u>Plays for Spring and Summer Holidays</u>, New York, Dodd, Mead & Co., 1938.
SSA	Sanford, Anne P. and R. H. Schauffler, <u>Armistice Day</u>, New York, Dodd, Mead & Co., 1927.
SSC	Sanford, Anne P. and Robert H. Schauffler, <u>Christmas Plays,</u> New York, Dodd, Mead & Co., 1932.
SSH	Schauffler, R. and Anne P. Sanford, <u>Plays for Our American Holidays</u>, New York, Dodd, Mead & Co., 1928. Volumes I-IV.
SSL	Sanford, Anne P. and Robert H. Schauffler, <u>Little Plays for Little People,</u> New York, Dodd, Mead & Co., 1929.
SSM	Sanford, Anne P. and Robert H. Schauffler, <u>The Magic of Books, an Anthology for Book Week</u>, New York, Dodd, Mead & Co., 1929.
SSP	Smith, Alice M., <u>Short Plays by Representative Authors</u>, New York, Macmillan Co., 1921.
SSV	Smith, Milton, <u>Short Plays of Various Types</u>, New York, Charles E. Merrill, 1924.
STC	Shay, Frank, <u>Twenty Contemporary One-Act Plays—American</u>, Cincinnatti, Stewart Kidd, 1920.
STE	Sindelar, Joseph C., <u>Thanksgiving Entertainments</u>, Chicago, A. Flanagan Co., 1906.
STM	Shay, Frank, <u>A Treasury of Plays for Men,</u> Boston, Little Brown and Co., 1923.
STN	Smith, Betty, <u>Twenty-five Non-Royalty Plays for All-Girl Casts</u>, New York, Greenberg Publishers, 1942.
STP	Sanford, Anne P., <u>Thanksgiving Plays,</u> New York, Dodd, Mead & Co., 1935.
STS	Shay, Frank, <u>Twenty-five Short Plays—International</u>, New York, D. Appleton and Co., 1926.
STW	Shay, Frank, <u>A Treasury of Plays for Women,</u> Boston, Little Brown and Co., 1923.
SWD	Sindelar, Joseph C., <u>Washington Day Entertainments</u>, Chicago, A. Flanagan Co., 1910.
TAJ	Thomas, Charles Swain, <u>Atlantic Book of Junior Plays</u>, Boston, Little Brown and Co., 1924.
TDF	<u>Three Drills and a Farce, by three teachers who have used them,</u> Chicago, A. Flanagan Co., 1901.
TGA	<u>The Theatre Guild Anthology,</u> New York, Random House, 1936.
TMA	Tucker, Samuel Marion, <u>Modern American and British Plays</u>, New York, Harper and Brothers, 1931.
TMC	Thornton, E. W., <u>More Christian Endeavor Playlets,</u> Cincinnati,

	Ohio, The Standard Publishing Co., 1929.
TMP	Tucker, Samuel Marion, <u>Modern Plays,</u> New York, Macmillan Co., 1932.
TP	<u>Tournament Plays,</u> New York, Samuel French Co., 1937.
TTM	Tucker, Samuel Marion, <u>Twenty-five Modern Plays,</u> New York, Harper and Brothers, 1931.
TTO	Tucker, Samuel Marion, <u>Twelve One-Act Plays</u>, New York, Ginn and Co., 1929.
TU*	University of Tennessee, Knoxville
TxCM*	Texas A & M University, College Station
TxFS*	Southwestern Baptist Theological Seminary, Fort Worth, Texas
TxU*	University of Texas, Austin
UU*	University of Utah, Salt Lake City
VET	<u>Vassar Experimental Theater Plays</u>, Poughkeepsie, New York, n.d.
ViU*	University of Virginia, Charlottesville
VP	<u>Vagabond Plays,</u> Baltimore, Norman Remington, first series, 1921.
VTml*	Thetford Memorial Library, Thetford, Vermont
WaPS*	Washington State University, Pullman
WaS*	Seattle Public Library, Seattle, Washington
WaSp*	Spokane Public Library, Spokane, Washington
WaT*	Tacoma Public Library, Tacoma, Washington
WCP	<u>Wisconsin Community Plays,</u> Chicago, Dramatic Publishing Co., 1935.
WHi*	Wisconsin State Historical Society, Madison
WPP	Whiting, Margaret A., <u>Educational Plays and Pageants for Children,</u> New York, Educational Publishing Co., 1925.
WRP	<u>Wisconsin Rural Plays,</u> Chicago, Dramatic Publishing Co., 1931.
WSP	<u>Washington Square Plays,</u> Garden City, New York, Doubleday Page and Co., 1916.
WTP	Weiss, Morton Jerome, <u>Ten Short Plays,</u> New York, Dell Publishing Co., 1963.
WU*	University of Wisconsin, Madison
WWO	Webber, James P. and Hanson Hart Webster, <u>One-Act Plays for Secondary Schools,</u> New York, Houghton-Mifflin Co., 1923.
WWS	Webber, James P. and Hanson Hart Webster, <u>Short Plays for Junior and Senior High School</u>, New York, Houghton-Mifflin , Co., 1925.
WWT	Webber, James P. and Hanson Hart Webster, <u>Typical Plays for Secondary Schools,</u> New York, Houghton Mifflin, 1929.
WWY	Webber, James P. and Hanson Hart Webster, <u>Short Plays for Young People,</u> Boston and New York, Houghton Mifflin Co., 1925.
YSP	<u>The Yearbook of Short Plays,</u> first series edited by Claude Merton Wise, New York, Row Peterson and Co., 1931. <u>The Second Yearbook of Short Plays,</u> edited by Lee Owen Snook, Evanston, Illinois, Row Peterson and Co., 1934. 3rd series-1936; 4th series-1938; 5th series-1939.
ZKP	Zachar, Irwin J. and Rodney A. Kimball, <u>Plays of Experience</u>, New York, The Odyssey Press, 1944.

Biographical and Miscellaneous Codes

AWW   American Women Writers: A Critical Reference Guide from Colonial Times to the Present in Four Volumes. Ed. by Lina Mainiero. New York: Frederick Unger Pub. Co., 1979-81.

NAW   Notable American Women, 1607-1950: A Biographical Dictionary. Ed. by Edward T. James. Cambridge, Mass.: Harvard University Press, 1971.

          Notable American Women: The Modern Period. Ed. by Barbara Sicherman and Carol Hurd Green. Cambridge, Mass.: Harvard University Press, 1980.

NUC   National Union Catalog.

NWAT   Notable Women in the American Theatre: A Biograhpical Dictionary. Ed. by Alice M. Robinson, Vera Mowry Roberts and Milly S. Barranger. Westport, Conn.: Greenwood Press, 1989.

SBAA   Selected Black American Authors. Compiled by James A. Page. Boston: G.K. Hall and Co., 1977.

A Checklist of Plays

A

ELEANOR HALLOWELL ABBOTT (COBURN) (1872-1958) AWW
Man's Place, 193? coll. This is a 32 volume collection of plays.   RPB

ETHELYN ABBOTT
Cinderella, 1918, 3 acts, young   RPB

JANE LUDLOW DRAKE ABBOTT (1881- ?)
Lightheart, 1918, 2 act allegorical play for children   RPB
The Wonder Gate, 1918, for children   RPB

BARBARA ABEL
Finance Behind the Footlights, 1930 "finance campaign in five dramatic   RPB
    flavors"
Follow the Leadership and Other Skits, 1938
"Gym and Jerry," 1924, health skit
Here We Are! 1930, six scenes and three prospects, YWCA play   RPB
Lights Up, 1942, "playlet that gives glimpses of the war service program   RPB
    of the YWCA"
Mother Earth and Her Children, 1931 (as given at the conference on the   RPB
    cause and cure of war, Jan., 1931)
Tell It to Venus, 1926, comic health play   RPB
Two Weeks with Pay, 1924, "midsummer daydream"   RPB
A Word to the Y's, 1925, stunt

REBECCA P. ABRAHAMSON
Hooverizing Internationalle, 1918, encouraging thrift during the war (1)   RP

MRS. JACOB J. ABT
Awakening, masque, typewritten ms.   PU, DLC
Duna, the spirit of the dunes, masque presented by the Prairie Club in   RPB
    the dunes near Tremont, Ind., Oct. 19, 1913

DOROTHY LYON ACKERMAN
Outside This Room, 1929   RUM-I

BERTHA DEVEREUX ADAMS
Love's Embassy, 1909, 4 act romantic comedy (scenario)   RPB

CARRIE BELLE WILSON ADAMS (1859-1940)

The Angelic Choir, 1910, Christmas cantata	RPB-M
The Christmas Adoration, 1920, Christmas cantata	RPB-M
Easter Praise, 1908, cantata	NN, Or
Fall in Line, 1915, rally day exercise	Or
The Harbor of Home, 1915, Mother's Day exercise	Or
The Heavenly Light, 1926, general cantata for church choirs	
The Herald Angels, 1924, Christmas cantata	Or
Joyous Bells of Easter, 1928, Easter cantata	Or
The Lowly King, 1916, Christmas exercise	Or, OrP
Loyal Service, 1917, Children's Day exercise	Or
Mother and Home, 1920, Mother's Day exercise	Or, OrP
Mother Mine, 1917, exercise for Mother's Day	Or
The National Flower, 1893, operetta	RPB-M
The New Fangled Baby Show, 1928, evening of fun for church choirs, schools and clubs	OrP
Now Is Christ Risen, 1918, Easter cantata	RPB-M
Old Cabin Home Minstrels, 1921, 3 act minstrel entertainment	Or
Praise and Thanksgiving, 1919, Thanksgiving cantata	Or, OrP
Redeemer and King, 1902, Christmas cantata	Or, OrP
The Rejuvenation of Santa Claus, 1912, humorous Christmas cantata	Or
The Resurrection Hope, 1913, cantata	Or, OrP
The Resurrection Story, 1923, Easter cantata	
See America First, 1924, musical comedy	
The Star of Bethlehem, 1917, Christmas cantata	Or, OrP
A Tale of a Hat, 1913, musical comedy	
Tidings of the Morning, 1915, missionary exercise	RPB
Tubal Cain, 1925, cantata	Or
Under the Stars and Stripes, 1917, patriotic operetta for schools, clubs and churches	Or
The Wonderful Birthday, 1915, Christmas exercise	Or, OrP
Working for the Master, 1920, rally day exercise	

ESTELLA ADAMS

Indiana for Little Children, covering 3 episodes in early Indiana history, 1915	InI

LAURA MERRIHEW ADAMS

Aunt Deborah's First Luncheon, 1913, comedy (1)	RPB
The Great Idea, 1922, comedy	RPB
How They Ran the Church Bazaar, 1923, comedy (1)	RPB
The Polly-William Club, 1922, 3 act comedy	RPB
Sniffling Hiram—Widower, 1927, 3 act comedy	RPB

MAY ADDY

Southold Pageant,1915, Southold, New York

RUTH ADKINSON

The Christmas Story, 1936, miracle play	
The Holiday Recitation Book for Lower Grades, 1928	RPB
Humorous Recitations for Children, 1927, with others	RPB
Station X-M-A-S, 1929 (1)	RPB
When Santa Claus Was Sick, 1931, operetta in 3 scenes, music by Pearl Booth	RPB

HELEN ELISE ADLER

Puppets, 1929	RUM-I

GERTINE AHRENS
  Ah, Togetherness, 1959, for women (also under title, The Quitters) (1)   RPB
  Advice to Movie Aspirants, 1930, mimeographed monologue   RPB
  Age Rebels, 1939, comedy for women (1)   RPB
  Background, 1938, comedy for women (1)   RPB
  The Bargain Hunters, 1932, duolog for women   RPB
  The Doctor's Bride Plays Bridge, 1930, mimeographed monologue   RPB
  Far Above Rubies, 1940, comedy for women (1)   RPB
  The Lady and the Cop, 1930, mimeographed comic monologue   RPB
  Mother's Cooking, 1934, comedy for women   RPB
  Oo! la! la! 1930, mimeographed comic monlogue   RPB
  Original Monologues and Recitations, 1928, with Bessie Rainer Ford   RPB
  Real Life Readings, 1927, collection of 18 clever readings for platform work

ALMA W. AIKEN
  The Chocolate Wedding, 1929, black dialect comedy   RPB

EDNAH ROBINSON AIKEN (1872- ?)
  The Hate Breeders, 1916, drama of war and peace   RPB

MRS. J. S. AIKEN
  The Suffragettes' Convention, 1914   RPB

MARY AINSWORTH
  Nance and George Listen In, 1928, Christmas play for jr. high school   RPB

IRENE M. AITKEN
  The Meaning of America   LNP
  Our Country and Its Flag   LNP
  A Tribute to America   LNS

ULLIE R. AKERSTROM
  A Doctor by Courtesy; or, a Jolly Mixup, 1906, 3 act farce   RPB
  The Eleventh Hour; or, Two Sisters, 1911, sketch, typewritten ms.   DLC

BERTHA AKIN
  Emily's Revolt, 1929, comedy (1)   RPB

MARIAN AKINS
  Below Par, 1927, farce (1)   UWP,HUW-3

ZOE AKINS (1886-1958) AWW   NWAT
  Another Darling, prod. 1950, typescript   OU, CLU,CSmH
  Anybody's Woman or The Better Way, screenplay based on story by   CSmH
    Gouveneur Morris
  An Attic in Paris, alternate title for First Love   CSmH,CLU
  Babylonian Lullaby, never prod.   CSmH,CLU
  Bitter Waters, 1956, adapt. from Louise Gallant by Henry James   CSmH
  Bright Shadows   CSmH
  Camille, 1936, screenplay
  Careers, adapt. from German of Alfred Kauer and   CSmH,CLU
    Paul Rosenhayn
  Castle on the Sand, prod. 1949, adapt. of Rings and Chains,   CSmH
    a short story by Akins
  Cock Robin, incomplete   CSmH
  Clemence, 1911, psychological study (1)
  The Crown Prince, prod. 1927, adapted from Hungarian of Ernest Vajdo

ZOE AKINS (continued)

Daddy's Gone A-Hunting, 1923, prod. 1921, Everybody's Magazine,   RPB
    45, December, 1921, 93-100 (later made into a film)
Declasse´, 1923, prod. 1919 (later made into a film)   RPB
Desire Me (See A Woman of His Own)
Devil's Bargain, verse tragedy   CSmH
Did It Really Happen? in Smart Set, 52, May, 1917, 343-52 (1)   CSmH,CLU
Discretion, screenplay (also titled The False Front and Facade)   CSmH
The End of the Strike, 1903
Eve's Secret, 1925, screenplay
Facade (See Discretion)
The False Front (See Discretion)
First Love, prod. 1926, adapted from French of Louis Verneuil   CSmH
Food of Love, screenplay   CSmH,CLU
Foot Loose, prod. 1919, adapted from Forget-Me-Not by H. C. Merivale
    and F. C. Groves
The Furies, prod. 1928   CSmH, CLU
The Furious Bride, screenplay (also titled Prepared for Peace)   CSmH
Girls About Town, screenplay   CSmH
Gray Gardens, teleplay, adapt. of By the Water of Paradise by   CSmH
    F. Marion Crawford
Greatness, 1923, prod. 1922 as The Texas Nightingale   RPB
The Greeks Had a Word for It, prod. 1930 (later a film)   CSmH,CLU
Green Hat, 1934, screenplay, released as Outcast Lady   CSmH
The Happy Days, prod. 1941, adapted from French of   RPB
    Claude Andre Puget
Hatter's Castle, 1932, never prod., adapt. and dialogue   CSmH,CLU
Hazard (See Thou Desperate Pilot)
Hearken to the Evidence, adapt. of novel by H. Russell Wakefield   CSmH
    (title later changed to The Law's Delay) incomplete copy
His Famous Wife, screenplay   CSmH
The Human Element, 1933, from short story by W.   RPB,CLU, CSmH
    Somerset Maugham, typed copy
I Am Different, prod. 1938, comedy, adapt. from Hungarian of   CSmH,CLU
    Lili Hatvany
Intermezzo, screenplay   CSmH
Iseult, the Fair, 1905, verse drama
Kitty's Claws (Later converted into a novelette, Cake Upon   CSmH
    the Waters)
Lady of the Camellias, 1936, screenplay   CSmH
The Last Kiss, adapt. of play by Ludwig Bire, prod. under title of The   CSmH
    Moon Flowers, also a screenplay
The Law's Delay, (See Hearken to the Evidence)
The Learned Lady, 1910, comedy
The Little Miracle, 1936, Ladies Home Journal, 53, April, 1936, for   RPB
    women (1)
The Love Duel, prod. 1929, adapted from a play by Lili Hatvany   CSmH,CLU
Madame Butterfly, screenplay   SCmH
Mademoiselle Frou-Frou, screenplay, prod. under title of   CSmH
    The Toy Wife
The Magical City, prod. 1916, in Forum, 55, May, 1916, 507-50,   CSmH
    free verse tragedy
The Meddler, 1909, about anarchism
The Moon-Flower, prod. 1924, from Hungarian of Lajos Biro, ms.   DLC
The Morning Glory, 1933, screenplay by Howard J. Green,   NN,CSmH
    adapt. of play by Akins, (1951, radio script by Arthur Arent, NN)   CLU
Mrs. January and Mr. Ex, 1948, prod 1942 (See also Plans for Tomorrow   RPB
    the orig. title)

ZOE AKINS (continued)

My Lady's Dress, 1930, screenplay, adapt. from story   CSmH
    by Edward Knoblock

New York Nocturne, from The Magical City   CSmU

No Pity Please or The Wedding Present, adapt. of story by Lynne   CSmH
    Sherman

No Regrets, screenplay   CSmH,CLU

O Evening Star, prod. 1935   CSmH

The Old Maid, 1935, dram. of novel by Edith Wharton, won Pulitzer   RPB
    Prize

Outcast Lady (See The Green Hat)

Papa, 1913, prod. 1919, "an amorality in three acts"   RPB

Papa's Jewels, prod. 1919, adapt. of German play by Franz Blei   CSmH

Pardon My Glove, prod. 1926

Phaethon, 3 act drama   CLU

Plans for Tomorrow, 3 act comedy, 193?, typescript   DLC,NN,CSmH,CLU
    (See Mrs. January and Mr. Ex)

The Portrait of Tiero, 1924, Theatre Arts Mag., 4, October, 1920, 316-37,
    tragedy (1)   CSmH,CLU

Prepared for Peace, screenplay, also titled The Furious Bride   CSmH

Pride and Prejudice, screenplay of novel by Jane Austen   CSmH,CLU

The Pursuit of Love, screenplay of novel by Nancy Mitford   CSmH

Reprise, adapt. of novel, Return Engagement, by Swen Davenport,   CSmH
    revision of The Swallow's Nest

The Romance of Robert and Clara Schumann, screenplay   CLU

A Royal Fandango, prod. 1923   CSmH

Saint Ursula, based on a synopsis by Edward Sheldon   CSmH

Sarah and Son, screenplay   CSmH

Showboat, 1931, screenplay   CSmH

The Sin, 1909, modern drama on theme of heredity

The Singing Swans   CSmH.CLU

Sleeping Dogs, never prod., early play   CSmH

South of Siam, adapt. of German of Alfred Schirokauer and Paul   CSmH
    Rosehayn

The Starling, a play, holograph, unfinished   CLU

Starvation on Red River, 19??, 3 acts, typescript   NN , CLU, CSmH,DLC

Strangers and Lovers, screenplay, adapt. of novel by   CSmH
    Edwin Granberry

Such a Charming Young Man,1924, comedy, Smart Set,   OPS-1,CSmH,CLU
    48, April, 1916, 67-78, (1)

Swallow in the Chimney, teleplay   CSmH

The Swallow's Nest, 1951, adapt. of novel, Return Engagement,   CSmH,CLU
    by Gwen Davenport

The Texas Nightingale, prod. 1922, (See Greatness)   CSmH,CLU

Thou Desperate Pilot, prod. 1927 (also titled Hazard)   CSmH

Three O'Clock Dinner, screenplay of novel   CSmH

The Toy Wife, adapt. of French play, Frou Frou (See His Famous Wife)

The Trojan Pony, sequel to How to Marry a Millionaire   CSmH,CLU

The Varying Shore, prod. 1921, incomplete prompt book,   NN, CSmH
    (musical version at CSmH)   CLU

A Very Rich Man, comedy, never produced   CSmH

Victoria Grandelet, adapt. of novel, never prod.   CSmH

The Voice, 1907 (1)

The Wandering Shepherd, 1907, masque

A Woman of His Own, screenplay, adapt. from German novel, Carl   CSmH
    and Anne, by Bruno Frank, prod. as Desire Me

Working Girls, 1931, screenplay, adapt. from play, Blind Mice,   InU, CSmH
    by Vera Caspary and Winifred Lenihan, mimeo film script

ZOE AKINS (continued)
    World War I Masque   CSmH
    Zaza, screenplay from French of Pierre Berton   CSmH

ROSE ALBERT (PORTER??) NUC lists (See Rose Albert Porter (1903- ?)
    Chrysalis, n.d., (listed in NUC as prod. by Lawrence Langner and
        Theresa Helburn, 1932)
    Release, 1928   HFP

LILLIE H. VANDERVEER ALBRECHT (See LILLIE H. VANDERVEER)

ALICE WIGHT ALDEN (1865- ?)
    Dickon Goes to the Fair, 1927, young   BPD
    Dickon Goes to the Fair and Other Plays, 1927, pub. by Drama League of RPB
        America
    The Duchess and the Dancer, prod.? 1917-26, Pasadena Community
        Playhouse
    The Grandmother of Susan, 1932 for junior h. s. girls (1)   RPB
    The House in the Wood, 1926, young   RPB

"RUTH ALDEN" (real name possibly Alice Armstrong)
    The Sniggles Family, 1909, for women, "humorous entertainment"   EEY

BEATRICE ALDERMAN
    A Fairy Conspiracy, 1914, operetta for children   RPB
    On Midsummer's Day 1915, operetta for children   RPB

HILDA DOOLITTLE ALDINGTON (See HILDA DOOLITTLE "H.D.")

MARY REYNOLDS ALDIS (MRS. ARTHUR TAYLOR ALDIS) (1872-1949)
                (She was director of The Playhouse at Lake Forest, Ill.)
    An Heir at Large, 1926, from a cartoon story by John T. McCutcheon,   RPB
        pub. in Chicago Tribune, 1921-22, romantic comedy
    The Bachelor
    Case No. 34
    The Drama Class of Tan-kaha Nevada, comedy, with Harriet Calhoun
        Moss (1) (in Plays for Small Stages)
    Extreme Unction, in Plays for Small Stages and in Little Review, 2,
        April,1915, 31-71, drama
    Flying Blind, prod. 1930
    The Grasshopper
    The Letter, in Plays for Small Stages, drama
    Mrs. Pat and the Law, 1923, comedy, also   RPB, MRO,SSH-I
        in Plays for Small Stages
    No Curtain; Suggested Themes for Impromptu Plays, 1935   RPB
    Plays for Small Stages, 1915, five plays   RPB
    The Princess Jack
    Temperament, "musical tragedy in 2 scenes," in Plays for Small Stages
    Ten P. M., problem play, in Drama, 11, March, 1921, 187-8
    Two Plus Two, or Two and Two Make Four, 1929, comedy   RPB
    What About Katie? in Journal of Home Economics, 9, Nov., 1917, 515-19

AZELLE M. ALDRICH
    The Pawn, prod. 1917, with Joseph Noll

CECILE ALEXANDER
 Dance of the Chanukah Candles, 1929, young   RPB
 The Night of the Eighth Candle, 1935, young   RPB
 A Purimdige Birthday, 1935, young (1)   RPB

LOIS AMY ALEXANDER
 A Football Fan, 193? comedy   RPB
 Gladys Goes in For Baseball, 1931, comedy   RPB
 The Red Hot Stuff, 1927, comedy   RPB
 Revenge on a Stingy Beau, 1928, comedy   RPB

ESTHER MARION ALGER
 In'ependence, in Poet Lore, 41, Spring, 1930, 140-9,   RPB
  "black dialect play"(1)

CADDIE BOLTON ALLBRITAIN
 Mr. and Mrs. Santa's Christmas Party, 1915   RPB

DOROTHY C. ALLAN
 About Candle-Light Times (1)

ALICE E. ALLEN
 Broadcast from Bookland   FMC
 December School-room Plays and Exercises, 1906   RPB
 The Fairy Cakes, little play of Early England and the Puritans WPP
 The Flower of Cheer, about Pilgrims   WPP
 The Night Before Christmas, 1906, young, music by Archibald RPB
  Humboldt
 Pete in Flowerland, 1902, operetta   RPB
 School Days   FMC
 The Three Bears, 1908, music by L. E. Orth   RPB

EDNA MAY ALLEN (1887- ?)
 America Remembers, 1928, Armistice Day play   RPB

JEAN ALLEN
 The Village Dressmaker, 1928, "humorous monolog for girl or woman" RPB

LYDIA ALLEN
 Put On Your Thinking Cap, 1927, young "nonsense play"   RPB
 Story Book Pals, 1927, young   RPB

MARGARET F. ALLEN
 The Happy Prince, with Lou Wall Moore, dram. of story by Oscar Wilde,
  in Poet Lore, 27, Vacation, 1916, 406-10 (1)

MARY MOSHER ALLEN
 Maisie, 1905, melodrama (1)   RPB

OLIVE ALLEN
 Aunt Grundy   BHP
 Peter Grief   BHP

MABEL CONKLIN ALLYN
 Big Brother, 1934, 3 act comedy-drama   RPB
 Business—Merely Business, 1936, 3 act comedy for women RPB
 Diamonds, 1931, 3 act farce   RPB
 Elizabeth's Holiday, 1932, comedy (1)   RPB

MABEL CONKLIN ALLYN (continued)
Grand Girl, 1938, 3 act comedy   RPB
A Greater Vision, 1931, 3 act missionary play for women   RPB
It's a Woman's Privilege, 1932, for women (1)   RPB
Joyce Helps Herself, 1932, for women (1)   RPB
Let Mary Do It, 1929, for women (1)   RPB
Maggie Fixes It, 1929, 3 act comedy   RPB
The Man From Nowhere, 1932, 3 act comedy   RPB
Matrimony Limited, 1935, farce (1)   RPB
The Mission Barrel, 1931, religious comedy (1)   RPB
Mystery at Midnight, 1935, 3 act mystery   RPB
Mystery at World's End, 1937, 3 act mystery   RPB
The Poor Fish, 1933, comedy (1)   RPB
Porch Pussies, 1936, comedy (1)   RPB
A Retrieved Christmas, 1941 (1)   RPB
Saving Dad, 1929 (1)   RPB
Sweet Adeline; or, the Cowboy Minstrels, 1935   RPB
That Younger Generation, 1934 (1)   RPB
This Thing Called Happiness, 1934, 3 act romantic comedy   RPB
Tommy Takes a Wife, 1938, comedy (1)   RPB
Tourists Welcome, 1938, comedy   RPB
Town Tattlers, 1935 (1)   RPB
Wagging Tongues, 1929, comedy for women (1)   RPB

JOAN ARMSTRONG ALQUIST
The Wooing of Mary Magdela, 1921, religious drama (1)   RPB

BESSIE M. ALSTON
A Lesson from Birdland, 1924, playlet, young   RPB

BESSIE MIRIAM ALTHEIMER (1875- ?)
Albion and Rosamund, 1930, tragedy   RPB

JULIA COOLEY ALTROCCHI (1893- ?)
The Dance of Youth, 1917, pageant, Hanover, N. H.

ADA TULLY AMMERMAN
The Reader, 1915, comedy (1)   RPB

OLIVIA DONALDSON CUSHING ANDERSEN (1871- ?)
Creation and Other Biblical Plays, 1929   RPB
Emperor and Pope
First in Peace
Ten Plays, a synopsis, 19??

A. HELEN ANDERSON
To the Rising Sun, masque in two episodes, Denver, Col., June 7, 1929,   RPB
    graduating exercise for South High School

CONSTANCE POWELL ANDERSON (SEE CONSTANCE POWELL-ANDERSON)

EMILY L. ANDERSON
The Fairy Mirror, 1904, "children's spectacular play in 3 acts"   RPB

ISABEL WELD PERKINS ANDERSON (MRS. LARZ ANDERSON) (1876-1948)
<u>A City Built in a Night</u>, "first produced under the auspices of the   DLC
    Boston University Women's Council, December 18, 1937"
<u>Dick Whittington</u>, 1932, "musical extravaganza," music by Mrs. M. H.   RPB
    Gulesian; lyrics by Pierre de Reeder
<u>Everyboy and Other Plays for Children</u>, 1914   RPB
<u>Freedom</u>, 1933, historical biography of episodes in life of her father   RPB
<u>The Green Turban and Under the Bo Tree</u>, 1937 (two one-acts)   RPB
<u>Little Madcap's Journey</u>, 1931 "fairy extravaganza," music by Julia   RPB
    Ward Howe
<u>The Magic Bough</u>, 1937   RPB
<u>Princess Marina</u>, 1932, music and lyrics by Grace Warner Gulesian,   RPB-M
    musical fantasy
<u>Sir Frog Goes a-traveling</u>, 1935   RPB

JESSIE YSOBEL CALHOUN ANDERSON
<u>The Masque of the Seasons</u>, 1921   RPB

MADGE ANDERSON
<u>The Fairy Ring</u>, "the tale of a night"   JNS

MARY ANDERSON (1859-1940) NAW
<u>The Garden of Allah</u>, prod. 1911, with Robert Hichens and based on his novel

EULALIE ANDREAS
<u>Four One-Act Comedies</u>, 1924, Hollywood, Cal., the Playworkers Studio
<u>Yes, Yes! Go On</u>, 1928, with Jane Hurrle, 3 act comedy   RPB

ANNABEL ANDREWS
<u>The Standard Juvenile Speaker</u>, 1926, coll. of recitations, dialogues, etc.   RPB

JANE VIRGINIA HAWKINS ANDREWS (1913- ?)
Revenge, 1928, melodramatic period piece she wrote for creative   RPB
    English class in high school (1)

JULIA LINCOLN ANDREWS (MRS. JAMES D. ANDREWS) (1867- ?)
<u>An Ancestral Quintet</u>, 1902   RPB
<u>Golf</u>, 1902, 2 acts   RPB

MARIETTA MINNEGERODE ANDREWS (1869-1931)
<u>The Cross Triumphant</u>, 1921, pageant of the church in England and   NcD
    America
<u>Many Waters</u>, 1931, George Washington pageant, music arr. by Lyman   MB
    McCrary
<u>The Master-Builders</u>, 1923? pageant of patriotism and Freemasonry,
    Washington, D. C.
<u>The Voice of the Wild Flowers</u>, 1922, fantasy written for the benefit of   RPB
    the Wildflower Preservation Society

MARY RAYMOND SHIPMAN ANDREWS (1860-1936) AWW, NAW
<u>The Ditch</u>, 1918, World War I play, pub. in <u>Scribner's</u>, 63, April, 1918,
    405-14, and in <u>Joy in the Morning</u>, collection of her works—at RPB
<u>West Point Regulation</u>, in <u>McClure's</u>, 23, Aug., 1904, 385-94 (1)

ANCELLA ANSLEE
<u>Six Month's Option</u>, prod. 1917

EVA ANSTRUTHER (may be British)
Bon Secours,1903, Little Miracle play, in Fortnightly, 79, Feb., 1903, 358-64 (1)

MARY EMILY APLIN
By Chance, 1918, "musical conglomeration in 3 acts" by class of 1918   RPB-M
Mt. Holyoke
Overtown Freddy, 1917

FLORENCE APPEL
Self Surrender, 1909   RPB

DAISY R. APPELL
Poems and Playlets for School Use, 1929   RPB

MARGARET TYSON APPLEGARTH (1886- ?)
Color Blind, 1923, 3 act missionary play
Fare, Please; New Americans, 1924, in Short Missionary Plays
The Girl Who Fell Through the Earth, 1923, Chinese play, in Short
Missionary Plays
More Short Missionary Plays, 1923   RPB
The Pill Bottle, 1924, medical missionary play   RPB
Short Missionary Plays, 1923   RPB

ALLITA EMERY APPLEGATE (1887- ?)
The Choice of Giannetta, in Poet Lore, 36, Autumn, 1925, 504-14 (1)

JEAN ARCHIBALD
"Call the Doctor," 1917, prod. 1920, typewritten ms. and promptbook   NN
Marry the Man, prod. 1929

ETHEL MARIE ARMES
"Behold the Pioneers!" historical pageants of Michigan, Playground, 16,
July, 1922, 171

ANNA REBECCA ARMSTRONG
The Epiphany, 1920 "religious service in the nature of a mystery play"   RPB

MRS. INGRAM L. ARMSTRONG
How Farmer Jones Was Won, 1914, suffrage play   RPB

LOUISE VAN VOORHIS ARMSTRONG (1889- ?)
Ali Baba and the Forty Thieves, pantomime
The Doctor of Lonesome Folk, 1928, Christmas pantomime   RPB
Dolls, 1926, "Christmas nonsense play," in Drama, 11, Nov., 1920,   RPB
52-7 (1)
The Gold Altar, 1929, comedy, based on a pirate tale (1)   RPB
Good Roads, 1929, adapt. of a story by Rose Wilder Lane (1)   RPB
The Late Captain Crow, "comic tragedy of the Spanish Main"   OPS-V
The Mouse, 1928, " pirate play with a moral but no morals" (1)   RPB
Naiya-Janam (Reincarnation) 1915, written for and first production by   RPB
the Girls' Life Class Association at Art Institute of Chicago, April 14, 1915,
music by Frederick P. Hart
The Old History Book, 1928, Americanization pageant, in Drama, 12,   RPB
Jan., 1922, 125-9, 137, presented by Neighborhood Guild of
Northwestern Un. Settlement
The Waning Moon, 1929, pirate adventure tale (1)   RPB

STELLA MORSE ARMSTRONG
The Bride Maid, 1927, farce (1)   RPB
Uninvited Guests, 1929, comedy (1)   RPB

ZELLA ARMSTRONG
Tennessee's Dream of Fair Women, 1931 "pageant in miniature,"   RPB
    presented at Thirtieth Annual Convention of Tenn. Woman's
    Press and Authors Club, Knoxville, Tenn., 1930

ANNA (ANNE) WILLIAMS ARNETT
The King's Choice   CLP-I
Little Plays for Christmas, 1928, with others   RPB

ESTHER WATKINS ARNOLD
Cherry Pie, 1929 (1)   RPB
I Don't Want To! 1929, young, 3 acts   RPB
Jerry the Jock; The Mystery of the One S-cent; Her Wedding   RPB
    Mo(u)rning, 1931, three plays for camp or club
A Juliet for Jim, 1934, rural sketch in one scene   RPB
King Quarrel and the Beggar, 1927, Christmas play (1)   RPB
The Magic Pills, 1931, fairy play   RPB
Much Ado About Miriam, 1932, "nonsensical playlet"   RPB
The Pet Show, 1932 (1)   RPB
Thanksgiving Dinner in Person, 1935   RPB
The Tooth Fairy, 1927, young   RPB
Twinkle, Twinkle Christmas Star, 1945 (1)   RPB
The Witch and the Christmas Story, 1934, young (1)   RPB

LUCY EDITH ARNOLD (1862- ?)
Mrs. Buttermilk's Dolls, 1902   RPB

KARIN ASBRAND (See KARIN SUNDELOF-ASBRAND)

RUTH ASHMORE
Bombs and Balloons, 1907, musical comedy, book by Ashmore, Gillian NBuG
    Barr, Emily Gurgen and others; music and lyrics by Grace Hollingsworth

FRANCES ELIZABETH ATCHINSON (BACON) (1903- ?)
Phantoms, pantomime for Halloween   SPE
Story Terrace (1)   SSL

MARY MEEK ATKESON
The Crossroads Meetin' House, 1918, "country play for country people   RPB
    dealing with some of the problems of the church in rural communities"
Don't, 1922 (1)
The Good Old Days, 1922, pageant of country life
The Will, 1922, farce (1)

GRACE JEWETT AUSTIN (1872-1948)
Abigail, 1924, 5 acts, Biblical drama   RPB

HELEN ATWOOD AUSTIN
A Sketch From Life, 1912, 5 act melodrama   RPB

HELEN H. AUSTIN
"Almost Everyman," 1929, in Quarterly Journal of Speech Education, 5,   RPB
    Jan., 1919, 45-53, "better English play"

MARY HUNTER AUSTIN (1868-1934) AWW, NAW

The Arrow Maker, 1911	RPB
The Astrol Experiences of J. Emery Pottle (1)	CSmH
Bilkins and Wilkins, scenario	CSmH
The Blue Moon, scenario	CSmH
The Briar, 3 acts	CSmH
Bride of the Sun, 1929, scenario	CLU
Camp-Afraid-of-a-Bear (1)	CSmH
Children of the Evening Star, play written on scenario by Elliot Schuck?	CSmH
The Coyote Doctor, with Elmer Harris	CSmH
The Defiance, 4 acts	CSmH
Don, scenario	CSmH
The Emperor Celebrates (1)	CSmH
The Faun and the Lady, scenario	CSmH
Fire, 1914, in The Playbook, Oct.-Dec., 1914, 1-25	RPB,CSmH
The Flock, 1932, scenario	CLU
The Golden Bough	CSmH
How Christmas Came to the Colonies	CSmH
The Island of Desire, incomplete scenario	CSmH
Like a Gentleman	CSmH
The Man Who Didn't Believe in Christmas, pub. 1969, in St. Nicholas, 45, Dec., 1917, 156-62	RPB
Mazouka, scenario	CSmH
Merry Christmas Daddy! prod. 1916	CSmH
The Potato Patriot, 1917, scenario	CSmH
Powers, scenario	CSmH
The Realist, scenario	CSmH
Sekala Ka'ajma, dance drama, in Theatre Arts Monthly, 13, April, 1929, 267-78(1)	
Sekala Ka' Ajnia: Plains Man's Hunting Ceremony, two Indian plays	CSmH
The Sword, scenario	CSmH
Thinking White, scenario	CSmH
The Time Machine, scenario	CSmH
The Vacuum, 3 acts	CSmH
The White Cockatoo, scenario	CSmH
The White Hour, scenario	CSmH

CLARA ROSE AVERELL

Bill's Wife, 1931, comedy (1)	RPB
The Ghost's Return, 1927, mystery play	RPB
Just Bluff, 1927 (1)	RPB
The Magic Spectacles, 1937, comedy (1)	
Off the Main Road, 1927, comedy (1)	RPB
Out To Win, 1929, two act comedy	RPB
Pot Luck, 1930, 3 act comedy	RPB
Snap Judgment, 1936, 3 acts	RPB
Stolen Apples, 1937 (1)	
Ted's Family, 1931	RPB
Two Week's Vacation, 1935	RPB
A Will and a Way, 1930, 3 act comedy	RPB
Youth Rebels, 1928, 2 act comedy	RPB

ESTHER CUNNINGHAM AVERILL (1895- ?)

Answered Prayer, 1939, dramatized sermon	RPB
Be a Good Neighbor, 1941, dramatized sermon (1)	RPB
Christian Endeavor Playlets, 1928, ed. by Henrietta Heron, a contributor	RPB
Church Bells, 1940	RPB
Church Spires, 1938	

ESTHER CUNNINGHAM AVERILL (continued)

Conversion, 1939, dramatized sermon (1)	
The Father of His Country, 1931, George Washington pageant	RPB
The Front Door Salesman, 1931, monologue	
The Heirs Get the Air, 1931, comedy (1)	RPB
Hen Peck at the Hitching Post, 1929, "mock wedding"	RPB
The Home the Star Shone On, 1937, Christmas (1)	RPB
I Made Christ's Cross, 1949, Easter	RPB
John the Beloved Disciple, 1934, Easter	RPB
Joseph and Mary, 1934, Christmas	RPB
The Junky Man, 1934 (1)	RPB
The Love Clinic, 1944, "novelty entertainment" for women	RPB
The Man on the Road, 1940, comedy drama	RPB
Marks of a Good Citizen, (1)	TMC
The Message of the Christmas Angels, 1944	RPB
More Christian Endeavor Playlets, 1929, ed. by E. W. Thornton, a	RPB
contributor	
My House of Dreams, 1931, 3 act comedy	RPB
The Old Home Road, 1933, 3 act comedy	RPB
Salute to the Flag, 1942, dramatic presentation of patriotism	RPB
The Seamless Robe, 1944, Easter	RPB
Take a Chance, 1937, 3 act comedy	RPB
Vacations Are Like That! 1939, for women (1)	RPB
When the Minutes Drag, 1939, monologue	RPB
The Word, 1931, pageant of the books of the Holy Bible	RPB
The World Tomorrow, 1943, young (1)	
Your Church and Mine, 1939, religious drama	RPB

RUTH AWKWRIGHT

Baby New Year (1)	SSH-II
Brownikins and Other Fancies, n. d., one-acts	

B

MRS. BERNIE SMADE BABCOCK (1868- ?)
Mammy, 1915, drama   RPB

LOUISE FRANKLIN BACHE
The Fountain that Lived in a Pitcher, n. d., play of ancient Greece, from   RPB
   "The Miraculous Pitcher" by Nathaniel Hawthorne
How the Alps Got Their Name, 1928, 2 acts   RPB
The Italian Twins and Nona, the Goat, 1928, 2 acts, pub. by the
   Dairymen's League
Mr. Cold , You Can't Catch Me, 1937, mimeographed health play for   RPB
   children, for National Service Bureau, Federal Theatre Project, WPA
The Most Wicked Pirate that Ever Sailed the Seas, 1937, health play for   RPB
   children, for Nat. Service Bureau, Federal Theatre Project, WPA
When Junior Meets Junior in a History Book   SPC

EMMA HENRIETTA SCHERMEYER BACKUS
(MRS. HENRY W. BACKUS) (1876- ?)
The Singing Soul, 1920, Chinese play (1)   RPB

HELENE B. BACKUS
Listen Officer, 1928, 3 act farce   RPB
Signing Off, 1932 (1)   RPB

"DOLORES MARBOURG BACON" (See MARY SCHELL (HOKE) BACON)

EVA M. BACON
In the Olden Golden Days, 1928, novelty minstrel   RPB
The Journey of Life, 1926, morality play (1)   RPB
The Princess of Moonbeam Castle, 1926, young (1)
Tony and Maryooch, 1928, vaudeville sketch   RPB
The Try Outs, 1929, novel entertainment   RPB
The Wooing of Spring, 1930, entertainment for child or adults   RPB

HAZEL BACON
Hats, 1926, entertainment in 3 acts   RPB
Some Little Mother, 1929, novel sketch for little folks (1)   RPB
Something for Nothing, 1920, with Mary G. Taylor   RPB

JOSEPHINE BACON (ADKINS) (1906- ?)
Angel Face, 1937, comedy, with Jack D. Keller (1)
Backfire, 1934, comedy (1)
The Ballyhoo, 1929, monologue, mimeographed copy   RPB
A Bear Deception, 1936, 3 act comedy, by Margaret Waite, ed. by Bacon
A Cafeteria Queen, 1918, monologue, mimeographed copy   RPB
The Christmas Carol, 1937, dram. of Dickens, by "Ann Lee"
The Christmas Waif, 1938
Crosspatch, 1934, fantasy for children
Dinner Bell, 1935, comedy (1)
Domestic Science versus Aunt Matilda, 1926, mimeographed copy
The Instincts of a Lady, 1936, comedy, with George Milton Savage
   ("Fairfax Kerry") (1)
The Last Page, 1937, drama (1)
Low Ebb, 1926, reading by L. S. Sonderegger, arr, by Bacon, mimeo copy DLC
Maybe It's a Murder, 1935, mystery comedy (1)

JOSEPHINE BACON (continued)
    Snaps, 1935, collection of stunts and short sketches for every occasion,   RPB
        compiled and edited by her
    The Tinklebutton, 1934, play for children by Kathryn Lace, ed. by Bacon
    Willie's First Contest, 1926, mimeographed

JOSEPHINE DODGE DASKAM BACON (1876-1961)
    At Commencement, 1915, in her Smith College Stories   RPB
    The Bouquet, 1916, anniversary play written for Mr. and Mrs. Robinson   RPB
        Smith
    The First of October, comedy, in Harper's, 109, Oct., 1904, 721-33 (1)
    The Twilight of the Gods, in Forum, 57, Jan., 1915, 7-20 (1)
    The Wanderers, in Century, 62, Aug., 1901, 583-9 (1)

MARY SCHELL HOKE BACON (1870- ?) ("Dolores Marbourg Bacon")
    A King's Favorite, 1902, 3 act comedy by "Dolores Marbourg Bacon"   RPB

GLADYS BAGG (TABER) (1899- ?)
    La Gitana, 1920, 3 act operetta, written for Barnswallows, Wellesley   RPB-M
        College, lyrics and book by Bagg and others, music by Marjorie
        Perkins and others
    Lady of the Moon, 1928, 3 act comedy
    Miss Manda in Poet Lore, 38, 1927, 412-21 (1)

HELEN F. BAGG
    Amusing Mimi, 1925, 3 act comedy   RPB
    Behind the Lines, 1918, "war comedy" (1)   RPB
    Clever Carola, 1932, 3 act farce   RPB
    The Delegates, 1923, 3 act farce   RPB
    Dry Weather, 1929, 3 act comedy   RPB
    The Fascinating Fanny Brown, 1912, 2 act farce   RPB
    First Aid, 1918, "war time comedy" (1)   RPB
    For Rent, Furnished, 1927, 3 act comedy   RPB
    A Game of Bridge, 1911, monologue
    Good Evening, Uncle Ben, 1929, comedy (1)   RPB
    His Model Wife, 1908, comedy (1)   RPB
    A Hot Day, 1920, 2 act comedy   RPB
    If Morning Glory Wins, 1906, "racing play," comedy (1)   RPB
    The Lady in the Kimono; or, Mrs. Ainslie's Front Door, 1906, farce
    The Leftovers, 1927, 3 act comedy   RPB, PP-1
    "Lest We Forget"; or, the Victory Loan, 19??
    Let's All Get Married, 1914, 2 act comedy   RPB
    Looking for Mary Jane, 1915, 3 act farce   RPB
    The Man Outside, 1918, farce (1)   RPB
    The Missing Link, 1944, comedy (1)
    Mrs. Beverly's Bifocals, 1931, 3 act farce   RPB
    Pirate of the Gulf, 1915, music by Lulu Jones Downing   CLU
    Promoting Romeo, 1922, 3 act farce   RPB
    The Scheming Six, 1925, comedy (1)   RPB
    The Spoken Word; or The Better Speech Child, 1918, play?
    The Superior Sex, 1905, farce (1)   RPB
    The Telephone Man, 1928, 3 act comedy   RPB
    That Blonde Person, 1912, farce (1)   RPB
    Through Mocking Bird Gap, 1921, by "Jarvis Hall," play?
    Unlucky Bill Crawford, 1935, play?
    Untangling Tony, 1908, 2 act comedy   RPB
    Up the Rito, 1925, by "Jarvis Hall," play?

HELEN F. BAGG (continued)
Ways and Means, 1924, comedy for women (1)   RPB
Whiskers, 1912, farce (1)   RPB
Why Not Jim? 1911, farce (1)   RPB

ALICE WARD BAILEY (1857- ?)
The Great Experiment, 1909, Shakespearean fantasy, with Anna Morgan RPB

ANNA (ANNIE) ELIZA CLAY BAILEY
The Last Chance, 1916, 2 act comedy   RPB

CAROLYN SHERWIN BAILEY (1875-1961) AWW
A Christmas Party   BPC
The Foolish Mouse, in Delineator, 75, June, 1910, 557 (1)
The Home-Coming, with W. E. Howe   BPC
The Maypole   BPC
Plays for the Children 's Hour, 1931   RPB
The Rabbit Who Wanted Wings   BPC
The Search for Santa Claus   BPC
Why Jack-O'-Lantern Keeps Halloween   BPC

ETHEL MC CASLIN BAILEY
Johnson County Centennial Pageant, 1923, Franklin, Ind.   InI

ETHEL V. BAILEY
Damon and Pythias

HELEN BAILEY
The Young Folks' Clubs at the County Fair, 1930, young   RPB

HELEN CHENEY (CHEYNEY) BAILEY
The Demigod , in Drama, 8, Nov., 1918, 505-14 (1)

KATE BAILEY
Aunt Polly's Weddin', 1921, comedy   RPB

LORETTO CARROLL BAILEY (1908- ?)
Black Water, prod. 1929, in Carolina Playbook, 2, March, 1929, 16-32 (1)
Cloey "play of North Carolina folk," Carolina Playbook4, March, 1931,   KCC
   15-31; also in Samuel Selden, A Player's Handbook, 1934
Job's Kinfolk, 1930 (3 acts) "play of the mill people,"   KFC-III
   Carolina Playbook, 1, June, 1928, 24-38 (one-act)
Roads and Rain, 1926 Little Theatre Tournament, under name Loretto
   Carroll
Strike Song, 1931, with James Osler Bailey, typewritten ms. 1933   PU, PPBC

ETHEL BAIN
By the Water and the Word, 1931, pageant of mission
Come Ye to Bethlehem, 1930, Christmas mystery drama
The Glowing Cross, 1931, miracle playlet for Easter   RPB
He Is Risen, 1929, Easter   RPB
"It Is Finished," 1933, vesper service for Good Friday   RPB
Rogation Days Across the Years, 1930?, historical pageant and prayer
   service
The Road to Bethlehem, 1929, first pub. 1927, Christmas, young   RPB
The Spirit of the Church, 1942, pageant

EVA R. BAIRD
   Alphabet Antics, 1933, young   RPB
   Christian Endeavor Playlets, 1928, ed. by Henrietta Heron, a contributor
   Harvest Home   HPY
   The Mission of Midas   SPD
   More Christian Endeavor Playlets, 1929, ed. by E. W. Thornton, a contributor
   Mother Dear, 1927, Mother's Day (1)   RPB
   The New Mother Goose, in Primary Educator, 45, Jan., 1928
   The Number Children, 1933, young   RPB
   The Vision (in the Interest of Missions)   HPY

ANNA G. BAKER
   Queen of the Night, 1902, cantata, music by William Berwald   DLC
   A Rustic Life, 1902, cantata, music by William Berwald   RPB-M

BESSIE BAKER
   The Brightville Indoor Chautaqua, 1921, entertainment in 5 parts, with   RPB
      Nellie Hanna (entertainments for 5 nights)

EDITH ELLIS BAKER (See EDITH ELLIS)

ELEANOR BAKER
   A Batch of Cookies; or, Fifty Days of Europe, 1910, with Barber Baker   RPB

ELIZABETH BAKER
   Faithful Admirer, 1930   SFM

IDA EMMA FITCH BAKER (1858-1948)
   The Story of Canada, 1927, Canadian historical play   RPB

JESSIE M. BAKER
   The Crowning of the Queen, in St. Nicholas, 42, May, 1915, 634-7 (1)   RPB

JOSEPHINE TURCK BAKER
   The Apache, prod. 1923
   Madame De Stael, 1922, drama   RPB

RACHEL E. BAKER (See RACHEL E. GALE)

IDA M. BALCH
   Christian Endeavor Playlets, 1928, ed. by Henrietta Heron, a contributor

MARY GERTRUDE BALCH
   Johnny's New Suit, 1917, 2 act comedy   RPB

ETTA BALDWIN
   In Sixteen Twenty-one   SBT

WINNIE BALDWIN
   Divided Honors, prod. 1929

EFFIE SAMMOND BALPH
   Princess Rosy Cheeks, 1921, good health play for children (1)   RPB

MRS. GEORGE F. BANCROFT (ELIZABETH DAVIS BANCROFT)
   The Trouble of Bethesda Pool, 1917, 2 act comedy, based on story by
      Laura Elizabeth Howe Richards

CARRIE WYATT BANKS
With Eyes of Love, 1912   RPB

HELEN WARD BANKS
The Black Knight, 191?, with Anne Selleck, paraphrased from Scott's   RPB
    Ivanhoe

MARGARET CULKIN BANNING (1891- ?) AWW
Her Sacred Duty, (won $50 prize for best play by a local dramatist, Little
    Theatre of Duluth)

LINDSEY BARBEE (1876- ?)
After the Game, 1907, 2 act college comedy   RPB
All Aboard, 1934, comedy (1)
All For the Cause, 1918, Red Cross play (1)   RPB
All In a Day, 1937   RPB
All On a Saturday Morning, 1946, comedy (1)
All on a Summer's Day, 1916, comedy   RPB
Anything Can Happen, 1947, comedy (1)   RPB
Artichokes for Dinner, 1930, 3 acts, for women   RPB
Assembly Skits, 1941, "collection of short novelty skits aimed to   RPB
    promote an educational idea"
At the End of the Rainbow, 1910, 3 act college comedy   RPB
A Bandit of the Mist, 1936, jr. h. s. mystery comedy (1)   RPB
Barbara Puts It Over, 1931, 3 act comedy   RPB
Beggars Can't Be Choosers, 1925, missionary play   RPB
The Boston Tea Party, in Plays, 5, May, 1946, 42-7 (1)
By Way of the Secret Passage, 1916, 3 act comedy drama   RPB
The Call of the Colors, 1918, 2 act patriotic play   RPB
The Call of Wohela, 1917, 3 act campfire girls play, comedy drama   RPB
The Camouflage of Shirley, 1918, 3 act comedy drama   RPB
Campus Deadline, 1944, 3 act comedy
"Christmas Gift," 1938, comedy (1)   RPB
Cinderella and Five Other Fairy Plays, 1922   RPB
"Clever Caddy," 1935, comedy (1)   RPB
Columbus Sails the Sea, in Plays, 4, Oct., 1944, 44-51 (1)
Comrades Courageous, 1921, 2 acts, 8th grade   RPB
Contents Unknown, 1922, 3 act "comedy drama of mystery"   RPB
Dolly Saves the Picture, in Plays, 5, Feb., 1946, 49-57 (1)
"Dorsey Disappears," 1935, comedy (1)   RPB
The Dream Comes True, in Plays, 3, May, 1944, 56-7 (1)
The Dream That Came True, 1913, 3 act comedy drama   RPB
East of the Morning Star, 1931, 3-act comedy   RPB
The Emergency Trio, 1940, 3 act comedy
The Empty House, 1930, 3 act comedy drama   RPB
Fanciful Plays for Children; or, Let's Pretend, 1917   RPB
Fashions in Love, 1930, 3 act comedy   RPB
The Fifteenth of January, 1911, 3 act college comedy   RPB
First! in Plays, 4, April, 1945, 72-6
The First Day of April, in Plays, 27, April, 1968, 45-50 (1)
Five Short Acts for High School Girls, 1931   RPB
The Flag of the United States, in Plays, 4, Feb., 1945, 42-6 (1)
The Four Extra Valentines, in Plays, 5, Feb., 1946, 42-6 (1)
Four in a Tower, 1941, comedy (1)   RPB
The Four of Us Meet Again, 1944, mystery comedy (1)
"Freddy," 1937, comedy (1)   RPB
Freshman Coed, 1941, 3 act college comedy
From Dusk to Dawn, 1925   RPB

LINDSEY BARBEE (continued)

From Ten to Two, 1940, comedy for women (1)	
Gay Youth, 1936, 3 act comedy	RPB
Glorifying Gloria, 1936, for jr. h. s.	
Hands Up! 1933, 2 act jr. h. s. comedy	RPB
Happy New Year, in Plays, 4, Jan., 1945, 60-3 (1)	
Have You Seen the Queen? 1928, 3 act school and college comedy	RPB
Helen's Sixth Sense, 1934, young	RPB
Her First Scoop, 1917, comedy (1)	RPB
His Best Investment, 1924, 3 act comedy drama	RPB
Hollister Wins, 1938, 2 act comedy	
The Holly Hangs High, in Plays, 5, Dec., 1945, 34-40 (1)	
How Beth Won the Camp Fire Honor, 1920, comedy drama	RPB
How Many Marys Have We Here? 1922	RPB
How the Race Was Won, 1927, 2 acts for upper grammar grades	RPB
Hunt for the Violet, in Plays, 4, May, 1945, 36-40 (1)	
In the College Days, 1914, group of monologues	
In the Corner Cupboard, 1932	RPB
In the Light of the Moon, 1932, 3 act comedy	RPB
It's a Magic Time, in Plays, 5, Oct., 1945, 53-5 (1)	
Janey on the Spot, 1938, for jr. h. s.	
"Just Before the Prom," 1935, comedy (1)	RPB
The Kingdom of Heart's Content, 1909, 3 act college comedy	RPB
The Lady in Gray, 1942, 3 act comedy	RPB
"The Lady's Slipper," 1935, comedy (1)	RPB
The Last of the Ruthuens, 1936, mystery	
"Let's Have Some Excitement," 1930, 3 act comedy	RPB
Let's Pretend, 1917, children's plays (See Fanciful Plays)	RPB
A Letter to Lincoln, in Plays, 5, Jan., 1946, 45-50 (1)	
A Light-Fingered Lady, 1931 mystery comedy for women (1)	RPB
Listen in on the Campus, 1930, 3 act school and college comedy	RPB
The Luck of Derryveraugh, 1924, Irish play	RPB
Magic For Three, 1946 (1)	
The Making of a King, Biblical drama	GPD
The Mallory Case, 1937, 3 act mystery	
The Man in the Shadow, 1930, 3 act comedy drama	RPB
Martha Has a Vision, in Plays, 3, Feb., 1944, 43-6 (1)	
Melissa's Muffins, in Plays, 10, Jan., 1951, 48-52 (1)	
Midsummer Madness, 1934, 3 act comedy for jr. h. s.	RPB
Molly Rushes In, 1935, 3 act comedy	RPB
The Moon Rides High, 1939, 3 act romantic comedy	RPB
The Mysterious Rosalind, 1930, comedy for 8th grade and lower	RPB
Mystery Island, 1927, 3 acts for women	RPB
The Mystery of the Third Gable, 1926, 3 act mystery drama	RPB
No References Required, 1935, 3 act comedy drama	
Out of the Stillness, 1920, 3 act comedy drama	RPB
Paging John Brown, 1940, comedy (1)	RPB
Patty Saves the Day, 1918, 2 acts for 8th grade	RPB
Permanently Engaged, 1937, 3 act comedy	
Peter Pops In, 1933, 3 act comedy	RPB
A Prince of Adventure, 1927, 3 act romantic drama	RPB
Rainbow Cottage, 1935, 3 acts	RPB
Reach for the Moon, 1933, 3 act comedy	RPB
The Real Thing After All, 1919, "after the war comedy drama," 3 acts	RPB
Rescued By Radio, 1923, 2 acts 8th grade	RPB
Ruth in a Rush, 1919, 3 act comedy	RPB
Salad a La Trizie, 1933, jr. h. s. (1)	RPB
Sally Ann Finds Herself, 1920, 2 acts for 8th grade	RPB

LINDSEY BARBEE (continued)

Sally Pulls the Strings, 1950, 3 act jr. h. s. comedy	RPB
Sapphira, Incorporated, 1938	RPB
Sing a Song of Seniors, 1915, comedietta for girls	RPB
So Proud to Serve, in Plays, 5, Dec., 1945, 65-9 (1)	
The Spell of the Image, 1917, 3 act comedy	
The Stranger, 1940, mystery comedy (1)	RPB
Sword in Hand, in Plays, 5, Feb., 1946, 23-32 (1)	
Take Off Your Mask, 1949, jr. h. s. mystery comedy	RPB
Tea Toper Tavern, 1925, 3 act comedy drama	RPB
Ten Days Before the Wedding, 1929, romantic adventure for women	RPB
"Thanksgiving Adventure," 1938, comedy (1)	RPB
Then Greek Met Greek, 1917, comedy	RPB
Thirteen and Halloween, in Plays, 4, Oct., 1944, 52-3 (1)	
The Thread of Destiny, 1914, 3 act comedy drama	RPB
Three Short Stunts, 1927	RPB
"Three Taps on a Wall," 1935, mystery comedy (1)	RPB
Tomorrow at Ten, 1916, comedy	RPB
Top O' the World, 1934, 3 act comedy	RPB
A Trial of Hearts, 1915, 4 act college comedy	RPB
Twelve Hours by the Clock, 1935, 2 act comedy for women	RPB
The Unexpectedness of Catherine Henry, 1924, for 8th grade girls, 2 acts	RPB
A Valentine Dance, in Plays, 4, Feb., 1945, 39-42 (1)	
Wander Inn, 1940, 3 act comedy	RPB
A Watch, a Wallet, and a Jack of Spades, 1917, comedy (1)	RPB
Wedding Cake, 1929, 3 act comedy for women	RPB
What an Image! 1941, farce (1)	
What Happened at Brent's? 1921, young	RPB
When the Clock Strikes Twelve, 1921, 3 act comedy drama	RPB
When the Homeland Calls, 1918	RPB
The Whole Truth, 1917, comedy (1)	RPB
Why Shouldn't I? 1932, 3 act comedy	RPB

MARY E. BARBER

Mechanical Jane, 1910, comedy for women (1)	RPB

MARY FOSTER BARBER

The Squealer, prod. 1919 by Provincetown Players (1)	DLC

RHODA S. BARCLAY

Jane Wins by a Hobby, 1926, comedy (1)	RPB
Mrs. Swatten Attends the Convention, 1921, monologue	RPB
Oh! What a Family, 1923	RPB
Spinsterhood of Mary, 1926 or earlier, monologue	
Starting Something, 1926, 2 act comedy	RPB
The Transformation of Sarah Maria, 1934, comedy (1)	RPB

CORRINNE LOCKE BARCUS

Historic Pageant of Long Island, 1927, with Bernice Gallup Tucker	RPB

MYRTLE L. BARGER

"Eating Milk," n.d., "a short health play that you or I, or anyone can produce"	RPB
"Following the Milk Can," n. d., short health play	RPB
How Milk Is Made, n.d., short health play, with Robert W. Balderston, dance arranged by C. Ellwood Carpenter	RPB
"Milk for the Whole World," 1922, "a short health play that you or I, or anyone can produce"	RPB

ADRIA D. BARKULOO
My America, 192? pageant by The Woman's Home Missionary Society   RPB

KITTY BARNE (MRS. ERIC STREATFIELD) (1883- ?)
Susie Pays a Visit (1)

BESS BARNES
Old Pipés and the Dryad, in Primary Educator, 33, Sept., 1925, 476-8+

CARMAN DEE BARNES (1912-   ) AWW
A Passionate Victorian, with Hamilton Fish Armstrong (about Fanny Kemble)
Schoolgirl, prod. 1930, with A. W. Pezet, based on her novel

DJUNA BARNES ("LYDIA STEPTOE") (1892-1982)   AWW   NWAT
An Irish Triangle; A Play in One Act, prod. 1919-20, in Playboy, 7,
     May, 1921, 3-5
The Antiphon, 1943, prod. 1958, also in Selected Works   RPB
At the Root of the Stars; A Play in One Act, in New York Morning
     Telegraph Sunday Magazine, Feb. 11, 1917, 8
The Beauty
A Book, 1923, collection includes plays
The Death of Life; 'Death Is the Poor Man's Purse'—Baudelaire, New York
     Morning Telegraph Sunday Magazine, December 17, 1916, 8
The Dove, in Little Theatre Tournament, 1926 (in A Book) (1)
Five Thousand Miles; A Moral Homily Inspired by All the Current Talk
     About the Wild Free Life in the South Seas, in Vanity Fair, 20, March,
     1923, 50
Kurzy of the Sea, prod. 1919-20, typescript (1)   DLC
Little Drops of Rain; Wherein is Discussed the Advantages of XIXth
     Century Storm Over XXth Century Sunshine, by "Lydia Steptoe,"
     in Vanity Fair, 19, Sept., 1922, 50+
Madame Collects Herself, in Parisienne, 6, June, 1918, 89-91
Maggie of the Saints, in New York Morning Telegraph Sunday Magazine,
     Oct. 28, 1917, 4
A Night Among the Horses, 1929, reissue of A Book with added stories   RPB
A Passion Play, in Others, 4, Feb., 1918, 5-17 (1)
Selected Works, 1962   RPB
She Tells Her Daughter, in Smart Set, 72, Nov., 1923, 77-80 (1)
Ten Minute Plays II: Two Ladies Take Tea, in Shadowland, 8, April, 1923, 17+
Ten Minute Plays VI: The Beauty, by "Lydia Steptoe," in Shadowland, 9,
     October, 1923, 43+
Three From the Earth in Little Review, 6, Nov., 1919, 3-15, also in   FCP
     A Book and A Night Among the Horses (1)
To the Dogs, She Tells her Daughter
Two Ladies Take Tea
Water—Ice; Wherein the Wintry Lady Fiora Silvertree is Unexpectedly
     Thawed, in Vanity Fair, 20, July, 1923, 59

ELEANOR A. BARNES
Close to the Wind, in Poet Lore, 40, Winter, 1929, 588-96 (1)

IDA M. BARNES
Rooms to Rent Lit and Het, 1930 (1)   RPB

MARGARET AYER BARNES (1886-1967) AWW
 The Age of Innocence, prod. 1928, dramatization of novel by Edith Wharton
 (Dishonest) Dishonored Lady, prod. 1930, with Edward Sheldon, ms.   PBm
      (microfilm copies of typed ms. at CU)
 Jenny, prod. 1929, with Edward Sheldon, typescript   NN
 Johnny, ms.   PBm

MARY EMELIA CLARK BARNES
 Who Is My Neighbor? 1917, Americanization drama pub. by   RPB
      Missionary Education Movement of the U. S. and Canada

ANNA LOUISE BARNEY (1857?-1931)
 The Grasshopper at the Home of the Ants, 1930, trans. from French of   RPB
      Legouve and Labiche (1)
 Make It Five, 1933, farce (1)   RPB
 Rainbow Gold, 1930, with Hildreth Kotsch, springtime fantasy (1)   RPB

MADALENE DEMAREST BARNUM (1874- ?)
 A Book of Plays for Little Actors, 1907, with Emma L. Johnston   RPB
 The French Maid and the Phonograph, 1911 (1)   RPB
 How Sleep the Brave (1)
 Lady Bird (1)
 A Mother Goose Play, 1912
 Our Aunt from California, 1903, farce (1)   RPB
 School Plays for All Occasions, 1922   RPB
 The Spirit of Progress, 19??, pageant given at Brooklyn Training School
      for Teachers in honor of William H. Maxwell, city superintendent
      of schools, 1887-1912

AMELIA E. BARR
 Thanksgiving   STE

CAROLYN BARR
 Be Careful Doctor, 1928, comedy (1)   RPB
 Benny's Halloween, 1933   RPB
 Goody's Invitation, 1934, written for and presented by Children's Civic   RPB
      Theatre of Chicago
 Jimmie or Ned, 1926, comedy (1)   RPB
 Katherine Decides, 1928, college comedy (1)   RPB
 Mary's Lesson, 1934, for Children's Civic Theatre of Chicago   RPB
 Renouncement, 1926 (1)   RPB
 Six Plays for Six Grades, 1930   RPB
 Suzanne Skids, 1931, comedy for women (1)   RPB

HENRIETTA C. BARR
 Bedtime Stories, 1931, comedy (1)   RPB
 The Party of the Second Part, 1929, with Maude Fealy, 3 acts, "modern   RPB
      comedy"

LOUISE BASCOM BARRATT
 The Book of Entertainments and Theatricals, 1923, with Helena Smith   RPB
      Dayton
 Hot Water, prod. 1923, with Helen Dayton

LILLIAN BARRETT
 The Dice of the Gods, prod. 1923

LUCILE J. BARRETT
  Right About Face, 1922, 3 act operetta for Wellesley Barnswallows, lyrics
    and libretto with Beatrice W. Jefferson, Hildegarde E. Churchill and
    others; music by Mary Zweizig, Rebecca Stickney and others

PAULINE B. BARRINGTON
  When the Young Birds Go, 1915, won first prize in Los Angeles Drama   RPB
    League Play Contest (1)

MABEL HAY BARROWS (MUSSEY) (1873- ?)
  The Flight of Aeneas, 1898, Latin tragedy in 3 acts, arr. by Barrows
  The Return of Odysseus, 1899, arr. by Barrows
  The White Butterfly, 1903, 3 acts, 16th century romance   RPB

(RUTH) MARJORIE BARROWS
  The Clown of Doodle Doo   JNS
  The Enchanted Door, n.d., for children's book week
  The Golden Key, n. d., for children's book week
  Jack O'Lantern Inn   SPE
  Magic Windows   SSL
  Marching Home   SSL
  Pan's Secret   SOP-I
  The Pink Parrot   SPE
  Santa and Son   SSC
  The Surprise Christmas   SSC
  The Teddy Bear Cave   SNP
  The Wistful Witch   SOP I

GERTRUDE BARRY
  Shakespeare Pageant, 1916, Newark, Del.

BLANCHE MARIE LOUISE OELRICHS BARRYMORE
  (See MRS. BARRYMORE TWEED)

BELLE BARSKY
  As We Like It, 1930, play on manners, with Eleanor F. Naughton   RPB

"JEAN BART" (See MARIE ANTOINETTE SARLABOUS)

ALICE HUNT BARTLETT (1870- ?)
  Caesar—The Undefeated, 1929, poetic drama (also in Six Historic   RPB
    Romantic Leaders)
  The Freedom of the Mediterranean, 1938,"historic documentary drama"
  Six Historic Romantic Leaders Who Envisioned World Peace, 1946,   RPB
    poetic dramas
  Washington Pre-Eminent, 1931 (also in Six Historic Romantic Leaders)   RPB

ELIZABETH M. BARTLETT
  Honor at the Bar, 1922, civic drama   RPB

ALICE L. BARTON
  Cleopas, also in Eleven Short Biblical Plays   DPC

DOROTHEA BARTON
  Running Water, 1930, pub. by American Farm Bureau Fed.   RPB

LUCY BARTON (1891- ?)
Arabian Gold (1)   SAR
The Frenchman (1)   SAP
The Garden, children's play for Arbor Day   SPS-2
The General Goes Home , in The Playground, 20, Jan., 1927, 568-71, for   SGW
   girls (1)
Jimmy, the Irish Snake, children's St. Patrick's Day play   SPS-2
The Kerry Dance   SNP
The Lake   SOP-I
The Magic Crystal, 1926, masque for schools and playgrounds
The Minute Man   SPS
New Loves For Old   SNP
New Salem Days   JEL, SLP-1
New Under the Sun (1)   SAP
Some Witch! Halloween   SPA
Somehow Thanksgiving (1)   STP
Susan Should Marry, 1936 (1)   RPB, SOP
The Sword with the Golden Hilt (1)   SPS
Three Christmas Eves   SNC-2
Toward Liberty, n.d., pageant
What Is Home?, in Playground and Recreation Assoc. of Am.   JEM-2
   Community
 A Mother's Day Program, drama service, 1931? playlet for   SPS-2
   Mother's Day
The Witch, n.d., in Playground and Recreation Assoc. of Am., How to
   Celebrate Halloween

LOUISE RAND BASCOM
The Bachelor Club's Baby, 1912   RPB
The Boy Who Found Christmas (in Bright Ideas for Christmas, 1920)   RPB
Catching Clara, 1914, commencement play   RPB
The Golden Goblet, 1911, 3 act farce   RPB
Look Out for Hezikah, 1912, farce (1)   RPB
The Lunatic, or the Professor, 1912, farce   RPB
The Masonic Ring, or the Adventures of a College Bride, 1910, 3 act farce   RPB
Molly's Aunt, 1916, 3 act farce   RPB
One on the Agent, 1912, farce   RPB
Petite Plays, 1912, collection
The Posy Pots' Mission, or A Realy (sic) Truly Hero, 1917
"Scat," 1912, farce   RPB
The Train Leaves in Ten Minutes, 1912, farce (1)   RPB
Vera's Vacation, 1912, 3 act drama   RPB

CLARA BURBANK BATCHELDER ("BARBARA BURBANK")
Anne of Old Salem, 1906, 3 act romantic drama   RPB
Billy's Chorus Girl, 1907, comedietta (1)   RPB
Little Miss Van Winkle, 1902, young, 2 act comedy, by "Barbara Burbank" RPB
The Postman's Knock, 1902, by "Barbara Burbank," in Comedies for
   Young Folks, 1902
The Revenge of Shari-Hot-Su, 1904, by "Barbara Burbank," 2 act   RPB
   Japanese comedy
The Separation of the Browns, 1907, comedy (1)   RPB
A Symphony in Black, 1901, by "Barbara Burbank," 2 acts for women   RPB
The Wings of Mignonette, 1905, young, 2 acts   RPB

SABRA F. BATCHELDER
> Gentleman Jack, musical comedy, music by Rosamund Batchelder;   RPB-M
> > book by Grace R. Henry; lyrics by Sabra and Rosamund Batchelder;
> > given by Spence Alumnae Society, April 18-9, 1917

ELLA SKINNER BATES
> The Convention of the Muses, 1891, classical play for parlor and school   RPB
> > for 9 females
> Greek Costume Plays for School or Lawn Performance, 1914, with others RPB

ESTHER WILLARD BATES (1884- ?)
> Be Your Age, prod. 1929, with Thomas P. Robinson, won the Richard
> > Herndon Prize at Harvard
> Bridal Shower, 1946, for women (1)   RPB
> The Children's Vision, 1935, Easter pageant, music by Lyman R. Bayard   RPB
> The Christmas Cradle, 1926   RPB
> The Christmas Flowers, 1924, mystery play for children   RPB
> Christopher Columbus, 1917, trans. and adapt. by George La Piana,   RPB
> > given under auspices of the Woman's Educational Assoc. of Boston
> > (in English and Italian)
> The City of God, 1926, dramatic allegory   RPB
> A Cloud of Witnesses, 1946, Easter   RPB
> Colonial Pageant, 1909, Springfield, Mass., pub. in Pageants and Pageantry
> Columbus Discovers America, 1930, with music   RPB
> Daniel Boone, 1930, 3 acts, "play of the wilderness road"   RPB
> Engaging Janet, 1908, farce (1)   RPB
> The Evacuation of Boston (1)   JWA
> Garafelia's Husband, 1919 (1)   BHP-II
> George Washington of Young America, 1931, pageant   RPB
> The Guiding Star, 1933, nativity play   RPB
> Heart of the World, 1914, pageant, Springvale, Maine
> Little Brother of the Blest, 1938, Christmas   RPB
> Medway Pageant, 1913, Medway, Mass.   RPB
> A Pageant of Pilgrims, 1920   RPB
> A Pageant of the League of Free Nations, 1919   RPB
> Pageants and Pageantry, 1912   RPB
> Parade of Nations, 1908, pageant, Springfield, Mass.
> The Prodigal and the Shepherd, 1939   RPB
> The Promise of Peace, 1927, Christmas   RPB
> A Puritan Pageant on the Founding of the Massachusetts Bay Colony,   RPB
> > 1930
> The Saints Return, 1940, Christmas fantasy (1)   RPB
> Saugus Centennial Pageant, 1915, Saugus, Mass.
> The Shadow of a Great Man, 1930 (about Lincoln)   RPB
> The Three Gifts, 1945, Christmas (1)   RPB
> The Tree of Life, 1922, Easter pageant (1)   RPB, SSH-I
> The Tree of Paradise, 1933, Christmas fantasy   RPB
> The Two Thieves, 1925, Easter (1)   RPB,FRD-II
> Washington at Valley Forge, 1931 (1)   RPB
> The Wing is on the Bird, 1942, with Thomas P. Robinson, 3 act comedy   RPB
> The Wise Men at the Well, 1937, Christmas   RPB

KATHARINE LEE BATES (1859-1929) AWW
> The Light of the World, 1921, program for children's day
> Little Robin Stay-behind and Other Plays in Verse for Children, 1923   RPB
> The New Crusade, 1919, "flag exercise for the schools of the nation"   RPB

LILYBELL BATES
The Word Made Flesh, 1929, Christmas pageant, music by Horace B.   RPB
          Blackmer

RUTH L. BAUGHMAN
His Wife's Place, 1920, written by students at Un. of N. D., adapt.   RPB, DPP
          of story by Clarence Buddington Kelland
Sacrifice, 1920, tragedy, second Arneberg prize (1)   RPB, DPP

MARIE BAUMER (1905- ?)
Blind Spot
Clancy
Creeping Fire, 1934, prod. 1935, melodrama   NN
For Lack of a Nail, in Plays, 2, Oct., 1942, 63-8 (1)
House of Remsen, prod. 1934, with Nicholas Soussanin and William J.Perlman
It's An Ill Wind, 1929 (1)   OPS-V
Jobyna Steps Out, 1932, 3 act comedy
Little Brown Jug, 1946, 3 act drama
Penny Arcade, prod. 1930
Seen But Not Heard, 1937, prod. 1936, with Martin Berkeley
Town, 1930 (1)
"Town Boy," 1930, prod. 1929, first prod. at Scarborough-on-Hudson   RPB
          under title, Strength

MARTHA B. BAYLES
The Crowning of the Dryads (1)   LPS
The Thanksgiving Day, 1896, with Anna M. Lutkenhaus (1)   LPS

(BELL) BELLE BAYLESS
Georgianna's Wedding Gown, 1914, farce
Left in Charge, 1908, farce (1)

CLARA KERN BAYLISS (1848- ?)
The Camp Fire Girls, 1914, scenic reading   RPB

"MARTHA BAYLY" (See MATTIE BAYLY SHANNON)

NANCY BEACH
The Wasted Tip (1)   RSS

MAUDE STEWART BEAGLE
Alice in Bookland, pageant for Children's book week   SPE
The Awakening of Dad   SPC
The Baby's Fortune (1)   SGW
The Book Revue, 1928, pageant for Children's book week   RPB, SSM
The Fairy Isle, 1934, presented by Michigan DAR on 300th anniversary
          of the landing of Jean Nicolet at Mackinac Island
Holly's First One Hundred Years, 1938, centennial celebration, Holly,
          Michigan
Peace in No Man's Land   SPP
Prince Fairy Foot, Halloween   SP A
The Seven Ages of Washington, pageant   SGW
Tea and Gingerbread (1)   SGW
Valley Forge (1)   SGW
Washington as President (1)   SGW
Washington, the Lover (1)   SGW
The Wedding at Mount Vernon (1)   SGW

MAUDE STEWART BEAGLE (continued)
  Womanhood, 1928, pageant presented by Flint Federation of Women's   Mi
    Clubs, Flint, Mich.
  The Young General (1)   SGW

IDA HELM BEATTY
  Mrs. Willing's Busy Day, 1918, comedy   RPB

JESSICA BEATTY
  Everyday Fairies, in Woman's Home Companion, 42, May, 1915, 38+ (1)

LILLIAN STOLL BEAZLEY (1895- ?)
  Art for Heart's Sake, 1925, 3 act comedy   RPB
  A Bed of Roses, 1926, comedy (1)   RPB
  Bobbed Hair, 1926, 2 act comedy   RPB
  The Broadcaster, 1925, 2 act comedy   RPB
  The College Stick, 1924, 2 act comedy   RPB
  Courageous Men, 1925, comedy (1)   RPB
  Flap Goes the Flapper, 1923, 2 act comedy, by Lillian Stoll   RPB
  His Friend in Need, 1923, 2 act farce   RPB
  A Merry Christmas, 1924, 2 acts   RPB
  Mother Pulls the Strings, 1924, comedy by Lillian Stoll (1)   RPB
  Mother Tongue as Matchmaker, 1925, 2 act comedy   RPB
  Red Roses, 1924, comedy (1)   RPB
  Renting Jimmy, 1923, 2 act comedy   RPB
  Stylish Stouts, 1926, 2 act comedy   RPB
  Thin and Forty, 1925, 3 act comedy   RPB
  Things of Beauty, 1926 (1)   RPB
  Trying Them Out, 1921, comedy by Lillian Stoll (1)   RPB
  Virginia's New Car, 1924, 4 act comedy by Lillian Stoll   RPB
  The Way of a Man, 1926, comedy (1)   RPB

ANNE LANDSBURY BECK
  King of the Castles, 1924, 3 act operetta   RPB

BERTHA REED BECK
  All Because of a Maid; or, A Bachelor's House Party, 1924, 5 act romantic RPB
    drama
  Santa Claus' Joke, 1926, "humorous pantomime"   RPB
  Tubs and Pearls, 1931, 3 act comedy   RPB

ALTA BECKER
  Miss Nibbs Novelty Shop, 1921, comic entertainment in 2 scenes   RPB

BEATRICE BECKER
  The Open Highway, 1927, with Ethel Reed Jasspon   RPB
  Ritual and Dramatized Folkways, 1925, "for use in camps, clubs,   RPB
    religious assembly, settlement and school," with Ethel R. Jasspon

MARY PORTER BEEGLE
  Barnard Greek Pageant, 1914, New York City
  Dartmouth Festival, 1913, pageant, Hanover, N. H.
  Magic of the Hills, 1914, festival, Hanover, N. H.
  New York Shakespeare Tercentenary Celebration, 1916, New York City
    (She was director)
  Pageant of Newark, 1916, Newark, N. J., co-director with Thomas Wood
    Stevens and Sam Hume
  Pageant of Elizabeth, 1914, Elizabeth, N. J., unpublished text   MB
  Romance of Work, 1914, New York City

ADALINE HOHF BEERY
Christmas Rainbow, 1908, young (1)   RPB
A Home for the Christ, 1908, for boys   RPB
The Rostrum, 1900, collection of recitations, dialogues, motion songs,   CSt
   etc., compiled by Beery

MAXINNE BEEZLEY
Historic Pageant "Whitley County," 1927, Etna, Ind.   InI

CAROLA BELL
The Fairy Four-Leaf, 1923, outdoor play for girls   RPB

EMMA A. BELL
Her Dark Marriage Morn, 1906, melodrama   RPB

LILIAN LIDA BELL (MRS. A. H. BOGUE) (1867-1929)
Father's Talking Now, 193?   RPB
The Land of Don't Want To, 1928, with Alice Gerstenberg, based   RPB
   on book by Bell

MAY BELL (may be British)
What of the Night and Other Sketches, 1918, one-acts

FREDERICA LE FEVRE BELLAMY
A Child's Friends, playlet for little folks   SPE
Darkness and Dawn, 1925, Easter mystery play   RPB, SSH-I
"Go Ye Unto All the World," 1925, plea for missions   RPB
The Jongleur's Story, 1926, religious pageant   RPB
A Sacrifice Once Offered, 1930, Easter   RPB
Venite Adoremus, service for Christmas Eve   SSC

ALVA E. SMITH BELMONT (MRS. O. H. P. BELMONT) (1853-1933) NAW
Melinda and Her Sisters, 1916, with Elsa Maxwell, musical about   RPB, FOV
   suffrage (1)

ELEANOR ROBSON BELMONT (MRS. AUGUST BELMONT) (1879- ?)
Christopher Rand, 1929, with Harriet French Ford
The Divine Afflatus, 1931, prod. 1923, with Harriet French Ford (1)   NN
"In the Next Room," 1925, with Harriet French Ford, 3 act comedy   RPB
   mystery, based on novel by Burton Stevenson

KATHARINE ISABEL BEMIS
New Pieces for Every Day the Schools Celebrate, 1929, with Norma H.   NcC
   Deming
Pieces for Every Day the Schools Celebrate, 1922, with Norma H.   RPB
   Deming   (1931 enlarged ed. at RPB)
Special Day Pageants for Little People, 1929, with Marion Kennedy   RPB
Stories of Patriotism, 1918, with Norma Helen Deming, poetry and   RPB
   short plays

ALICE WELLES BENHAM
"Alumni Day at Hickville School," 1928, comic entertainment   RPB

KATHLEEN BERKE BENITE
The Broken Commandment, 1908, 4 act melodrama   RPB

IRMA A. BENJAMIN
Shadows of Our Past, 1924, Hanukah entertainment   RPB

CLARA MARION BENNETT
The Good Samaritan, 1907, Biblical drama   RPB

ELLEN CORRINNE BENNETT
Playing the Races, 1905, comedy (1)   RPB

MABEL KEIGHTLEY BENNETT
My Dixie Rose, 1927, 3 act comedy drama   RPB

REBECCA BENNETT
Vagabond, If You Please, 1928, 3 act comedy   RPB

MARY A. BENSON
The Fairies' Christmas, in Ladies Home Journal, 20, Nov., 1903, 32 (1)

(CAROLINE) RITA BENTON (1881- ?)
Bible Plays, 1922, one acts
Carrots May Be Golden, 1932, winning religious play in Drama League   RPB
    contest, 1931
The Christmas Story, 192? from Bible Plays   TxU
The Elf of Discontent and Other Plays, 1927   RPB
Franklin and Other Plays, 1924   RPB
Shorter Bible Plays, 1922, one acts
The Star Child and Other Plays, 1921, one acts   RPB

CLARA BERANGER
The Bedroom Window, 1924, screen play   NN, CLSU
The Blemish, 1918? by Edmund Goulding, scenario by Beranger, typed CLSU
    copy
Clarence, 1922, by Booth Tarkington, scenario by Beranger, screenplay   NN
Colonel Carter of Cartersville, n.d., by F. Hopkinson Smith, scenario by CLSU
    Beranger, typed screenplay
Dr. Jekyl and Mr. Hyde, 1920, screenplay by Beranger, typed copy   CLSU
Don't Call It Love, 1923, screenplay by Beranger from book by Julian   NN
    Street, shooting script
The Fast Set, 1923, screenplay by Beranger, shooting script   NN
The Fear Market, 1920, prod. 1916, adaptation by Beranger of a play by CLSU
    Amelie Rives
The Firing Line, 1919, by Robert W. Chambers, scenario by Beranger,   CLSU
    typed copy
The Forbidden Woman, 1927, screenplay by Beranger from story by   CLSU
    Elmer Harris, mimeo copy
Grumpy, by Horace Hodges and Wigney Percyval, photoplay by   NN
    Beranger, screenplay
His Chinese Wife, 1920, with Forrest Halsey ·
His, Hers, and Theirs, 1921, sketch   CLSU
Locked Doors, 1925, scenario   CLSU
Lost Romance, 1921, screenplay by Beranger, shooting script   NN
The Marriage Maker, 1923, screenplay from play by Edward Knoblock,   NN
    shooting script
Men and Women, 1925, screenplay from play by Henry C. de Mille and CLSU
    David Belasco, mimeo copy.
Miss Lulu Bett, 1921, photoplay from book by Zona Gale, shooting script NN
New Brooms, 1925, screenplay from play by Frank Craven,   NN,CLSU
    shooting script
Nice People, 1922, adaptation of play by Rachel Crothers,   NN,CLSU
    shooting script

CLARA BERANGER (continued)
Only 38, 1923, screenplay from play by A. E. Thomas, shooting script　　NN
Pirate Gold, 1916? with Forrest Halsey, scenario　　CLSU
Polly of the Ballet, 192? story and screenplay by Beranger, shooting script NN
Rip Van Winkle, 192? screenplay of story by Washington Irving　　NN
This Mad World, 1929, (originally titled, Inhuman Ground) picture　　CLSU
　　play with dialogue adapted from French of Francois de Curel,
　　mimeo copy
White Collars, 1928, screenplay of play by Edith Ellis, typed copy　　CLSU
White Youth, 1920, Creole love story, with Forrest Halsey　　CLSU
The World's Applause, 1923, originally titled, Notoriety, scenario　　CLSU

IRENEE BERGE
The Wondrous Cross, 1917, cantata for Eastertide or general use　　RPB-M

HELEN CORINNE BERGEN (1868- ?)
The Princess Adelaide, 1900　　RPB
When Jack Comes Late, 1893, comedy monologue for a lady　　RPB

PATTY PEMBERTON BERMANN
Familiar Quotations (1)　　HBP

EDITH HEAL BERRIEN (See EDITH HEAL)

MRS. OSCAR BERRINGER (or BERINGER)　　British?
A Bit of Old Chelsea
Holly Tree Inn, adapted from Dickens, Christmas (1)

CARRIE ADAMS BERRY
New Trails, 1926, for women's clubs (1)　　RPB

LUCILE BLACKBURN BERRY
America in Pilgrim Days, 1915, program for Thanksgiving　　RPB
A Christmas Carol, 1915, dramatization from Dickens' story　　RPB
Good English Program, 1920　　RPB
The Melting Pot; or, The Americanization of the Strangers, 1919　　RPB
Old Colony Days, 1915, dram. of Longfellow's "The Courtship of Miles
　　Standish"

FLORENCE BERSTEIN
Yoku-ki, pantomime

JOSEPHINE M. BESIO
Toys' Christmas Frolic, 1928, humorous play for children　　RPB

KATHLEEN M. H. BESLY
Anent Joan of Arc, 1920, drama (1)　　RPB

ERA BETZNER
Marenka, festival
The Mystic Flower, 1928, 3 act operetta based on Slovakian folk legend　　RPB
Three Pantomimes, 1919　　RPB

JULIE HELENE BIGELOW
The Fascinating Mrs. Osborne, in Smart Set, 35, Dec., 1911, 129-34 (1)

MARIE HEALY BIGOT (MME. CHARLES BIGOT)
("JEANNE MAIRET") (1843- ?)
The Home Theatre, 1871, collection
Our Ancestors, 1911, 2 act comedy by "Jeanne Mairet"   RPB

MATHILDE BILBRO
Belling the Cat, 1927, playlet with music (1)   RPB
The Geranium Sewing Club, 1926, musical play for little girls   RPB
The Land of Elves, 1918, musical journey for young students in   RPB
  12 episodes

ELIZABETH R. BILLS
Beauty Secrets, 1930, comedy for 5 women (1)   RPB
The Ladies Lounge, 1931, first prod. at Un. of Chicago, farce   RPB
  for women (1)

RUTH ATLAS BINSTOCK
Harvest Festival, 1925, pageant in 4 scenes   RPB

GRACE ELECTRA BIRD
Historical Plays for Children, 1912, with Maud Starling (1924 ed. at RPB) RPB

IOLA GETCHELL BISHOP
An Evening with Janice Meredith; or, A Surprise Party of the 18th   RPB
  Century, 1904, "a new way of giving an old-fashioned concert,"
  "issued under the auspices of the Ladies Aid Society of the First
  Presbyterian Church, Savannah, Ga."

MAYME RIDDLE BITNEY
Cornelia Pickle, Plaintiff, 1912, "burlesque trial for ladies"   RPB
Dialogues of Pep and Humor, 1924
The First Day of School, 1922, humorous entertainment   RPB
Fun on the Podunk Limited, 1906, comic entertainment   RPB
Humorous Monologues, 1906, "particularly suitable for ladies"   RPB
Jolly Christmas Dialogues and Recitations, 1926   RPB
The Light Brigade, 1908, "comic entertainment for ladies"   RPB
Monologues for Young Folks, 1937   RPB
Monologues Grave and Gay, 1911   RPB
Pageants and Plays for Holidays, 1926   RPB
Saved by the Royal Neighbors, 1914, 4 act comedy   RPB
Thanksgiving in the Primary Grades, 1924
The Third Degree, 1907, "burlesque for women's societies"   RPB
Valentine Gayety Book, 1926   RPB

GLADYS BLACK
The Frat Entertains, 1927, school entertainment (1)   RPB

LEOTA HULSE BLACK
Angel Wings, 1935, dramatic reading   RPB
At the Declam Contest, 1928   RPB
Beach Nuts, 1935   RPB
The Beauty Contest, 1939   RPB
Before the Banquet, 1935   RPB
Bread Upon Waters, 1934   RPB
Brotherly Love, 1929   RPB
Brothers at the Beach, 1940   RPB
Brothers at the Broadcast, 1942   RPB

LEOTA HULSE BLACK (continued)

Brothers Bereft, 1933	RPB
Brothers-in-Battle, 1935	RPB
Brothers in Bedlam, 1938	RPB
Brothers in Business, 1934	RPB
Brothers-in-Love, 1932	RPB
Brothers Prefer Blondes, 1939	RPB
Brothers Take a Bow, 1936	RPB
The Cat Came Back, 1933	RPB
Cataracts, 1933	RPB
Cave-Man Stuff, 1937	RPB
Cheese hid-bits, 1940	RPB
Choirs of God, 1936	RPB
Danny's Little Tin Soldier, 1935	RPB
The End of a Perfect Weekend, 1928	RPB
Eyes, 1933	RPB
For the Love o' Mike, 1935	RPB
Four O'clock at the "Sip 'n Bite," 1939	RPB
Gerty Gets Going, 1932	RPB
He Who Laughs Last, 1937	RPB
Honey, 1933	RPB
The Incorrigibles, 1933	RPB
Joey's Friend, 1931	RPB
A Kitty Goes Adopting, 1932	RPB
A Lack and a Lass, 1941	RPB
The Least of These, 1933	RPB
Let Brotherly Love Continue, 1931	RPB
Ma at the Baseball Game, 1930	RPB
Ma at the Homecoming, 1933	RPB
Ma at the Museum, 1934	RPB
Ma at the P.T.A., 1932	RPB
Ma at the Races, 1929	RPB
Ma By Bus, 1931	RPB
Ma Does Her Christmas Shopping, 1941	RPB
Ma Makes Merry, 1934	RPB
Ma Takes the Air, 1939	RPB
Ma Takes a Chance, 1935	RPB
Ma Turns to Tutoring, 1938	RPB
Mary Ellen's Star, 1932	RPB
Ma's Berth-night, 1931	RPB
Ma's Daily Doesn't, 1940	RPB
Ma's Dollar Day, 1936	RPB
Ma's Monday Morning, 1927	RPB
Ma's Psychological Moment, 1943	RPB
Ma's Sabbath Mourn, 1931	RPB
Mickey's Marker, 1930	RPB
Mind Over Matter, 1937	RPB
A Modern Portia, 1939	RPB
New Dishpansation, 1938	RPB
Nocturne, 1934	RPB
Of Mice and Pen, 1941	RPB
A One-man Dog, 1934	RPB
Out of the Storm, 1935	RPB
Penny, 1939	RPB
The Perfect Background, 1933	RPB
Resting Easily, 1935	RPB
Sammy's Strategy, 1928	RPB
Saturday's Child, 1933	RPB

LEOTA HULSE BLACK (continued)

Scratch, the Newsboy's Dog, 1927	RPB
September Mourn, 1938	RPB
Sisterly Sparring, 1933	RPB
Sisters in Law, 1938	RPB
Sisters in Society, 1934	RPB
The Sparrow's Fall, 1932	RPB
A Stitch in Time, 1934	RPB
Stout Fella, 1939	RPB
A Temporary Permanent, 1929	RPB
Ten-cent Blues, 1933	RPB
**Tipping Off Teacher, 1934, comedy contest selection	RPB
Two Little Pigs Went to Market, 1933	RPB
Under the Big Top, 1932	RPB
An Underhand Pass, 1934	RPB
Where There's a Will, 1931	RPB
White Lilacs, 1933	RPB
The Widow's Mites, 1933	RPB
X Marks the Spot, 1934	RPB
The Yanks Are Coming, 1935	RPB

**All but this title are "In Wetmore Declamation Bureau, Readings, plays, entertainments." Sioux City, Iowa, Vols. 3-5.

MERRY BETH BLACK

At the County Fair, 1929, monologue	RPB
Fisherman's Luck, 1929, monologue	RPB

MARY JOHNSON BLACKBURN
Folklore from Mammy Days, 1925, a speaker

BEATRICE BLACKMAR

Man's Estate, 1929, with Bruce Gould, Theatre Guild play	NN

MADELINE BLACKMORE

As the Twig is Bent, 1925 (1)	RPB
"I Am Over Forty," 1933, comedy (1)	
It's Human Nature, 1935, with Mildred Katharine Smith, 3 act comedy	
To Die With a Smile, 1929	NHP

OLGA GATES BLAGDEN

Happy Land, 1929, allegory, "graphic portrayal of truth"	RPB

MARJORIE BLAINE

The Unknown Woman, prod. 1919, melodrama, with Willard Mack, typescript	NN

AMY ELLLA BLANCHARD (1856-1926)

A Dear Little Girl, 1910? play?	OKentC
Hearts and Clubs, 1910, 3 act comedy	

DOROTHY BLANCHARD
The Bridge, 1930, in Little Theatre tournament

MARGARET BLAND
Dead Expense, 1929 (1)   RPB
First at Bethel, 1935, comedy (1)
Jinsey   MWS
Land and Larnin' 1951, comedy drama (1)   RPB
Lighted Candles, 1926, with Louisa Duls, "tragedy of the Carolina   KCF
    highlands" (1)
Pink and Patches, 1928, in Little Theatre tournament, winner of Samuel   RPB
    French prize (1)
The Princess Who Could Not Dance, 1929, young (1)   RPB
The Spinach Spitters, 1935, young (1)   RPB

M. BARBARA BLANKENHORN
How the Shoes Were Danced to Pieces, 1926, "founded on an ancient   RPB
    fairy tale by the Brothers Grimm. With appropriate places for dances."

LYN BLANNING
In Broad Daylight, 1928, comedy for women (1)   RPB

EVANGELINE WILBOUR BLASHFIELD (? -1918)
Masques of Cupid, 1901, collection of four comedies   RPB

DOROTHEA BLIEDUNG
Romance Off the Reel, 1917, 3 act musical comedy, written for   RPB-M
    Barnswallows, Wellesley College; lyrics by Bliedung and others;
    music by Winifred Allison and others

MARGUERITE BECK BLOCK (1889- ?)
The Fortune Teller, 1919, with Era Betzner, in Betzner's Three   RPB
    Pantomimes
The Pageant of Reading, 1923, Reading, Pa.

MAXINNE BLOCK
Eyes, 1930, winner of Samuel French prize in Little Theatre   RPB
    tournament, tragedy (1)

LILLIAN S. BLOOM
Tommy on Parent-Teachers, 1927, comic monologue   RPB

MAUDE MC FIE BLOOM
"Tonita of the Holy Faith," 1924, "Archeological Institute of America,   RPB
    Papers of the School of American Research"

FRANCES W. BLOSE
The Good Health Way and the Queen of May, 1929, musical   RPB
    fantasy-comedy, music by Dr. Johann M. Blose

MELESINA MARY BLOUNT ("MRS. GEORGE NORMAN")
Green Cushions, in Living Age, 256, Feb. 29, 1908, 554-7 (1)
The Young Visitors, prod. 1920, with Margaret MacKenzie, from book by
    Daisy Ashford

MRS. W. A. BOADWAY
Case of Eviction, 1918, prod. by Pasadena Comm. Players
Family Pride, 1918

ANNIE SARA BOCK
  County Centennial, 1906, comedy (1)   RPB
  The Family Reunion, 1909, 2 act comedy   RPB
  The Minstrel and Womanless Wedding, 1919   RPB
  Union Depot, 1905, comedy (1)   RPB

FLORENCE BREWER BOECKEL (1855- ?)
  Taking Stock, 1929, by "F.B.B," for Armistice Day, mimeograph copy   RPB
  Through the Gateway, 1925, collection of stories, poems and pageants for
      children, in Vol. 1 of Books of Goodwill, which is at RPB
  The Whole World's Christmas Tree, 1926, young, pub. by National   RPB, SPP
      Council for Prevention of War

MARTHA BOESE
  There Is a Way, 1927, with Alma Rupnow, pageant of Christian Ed.   RPB

MARIE BOILEAU
  When Anne Was Queen; or, a Gentleman of the Road, 1920, with
      Jonathan Erle, comedy (1)

INEZ MILHOLLAND BOISSEVAIN (See INEZ MILHOLLAND)

IVY MAY BOLTON (1879- ?)
  Guiding Light, 1927, Nativity play   RPB
  The King of Sherwood, 1924   SSH-2

BEULAH EUGENIA BOMSTEAD (also BORNSTEAD) (1896- ?)
  The Diabolical Circle, 1921, prod. by Dakota Players, first   GOP, LCO,
      Arneberg prizeplay, colonial romance (1)   JAB, DPP

OLIVE P. BOND
  Crowning of the May Queen, 1922, May Day pageant for boys and girls   RPB

AMY CLARKE BONE
  A Glorious Christmas Eve, 1930, 2 acts   RPB

MARY BONHAM
  A Christmas Pull, 1930   RPB
  Cinderella's Reception, 1926   RPB
  Co'tin' Dat Counts, 1925, comedy (1)   RPB
  The Easter Lily Garden, 1924, young   RPB
  Hollyhock Drill and Pantomime, 1929   RPB
  The Kink in Kizzie's Wedding, 1921, "mock Negro wedding"   RPB
  Malinda and the Duke, 1922 (1)   RPB
  Mandy Airs Her Views on the Modern Girl, 1926, monologue   RPB
  Mandy Broadcasts the Wedding News, 1926, monologue
  Mandy Mixes Matrimony and Mandy Plants de Switch Bush, 1927,   RPB
      "two Negro dialect readings"
  Miss Janie; or, the Curtailed Courtship, 1922, comedy drama   RPB
  Miss Milly Wins, 1926 (1)   RPB
  Outwitting Lucy Lee, 1925, comedy (1)   RPB
  Possum and Sweet Taters, 1923, "black face drill and song"   RPB
  The Rainbow Christmas, 1923   RPB
  The Scent of Roses, 1926   RPB
  Tell Us the Christmas Story, 1932, "play for all the grades"   RPB
  Trouble in Egypt, 1923   RPB
  When Do-it School Entertained, 1922, Christmas (1)   RPB

GERALDINE BONNER (1870-1930)
  Sauce for the Goose, prod. 1911, with Hutcheson Boyd
  Sham, prod. 1909, with Elmer Harris, 3 acts, typewritten copy   NN, MH

MARITA OCCOMY BONNER
  Exit an Illusion, in Crisis, 36, October, 1929 (1)
  Muddled Dream
  The Pot-Maker, in Opportunity, 5, Feb., 1927 (1)
  The Purple Flower, in Crisis, 35, Jan., 1928 (1)   HSB

ANNE BOOTH
  Shakespeare Pageant, 1916, Paducah, Ky.

HILLIARD BOOTH
  "Breakfast in Bed," 1919, with Willard Mack, from French of Georges
      Feydeau, 4 acts
  Camp Keep-Off, 1915, 2 act comedy   RPB
  The Children's Vaudeville, 1925   RPB
  Cupid in Khaki, 1918, 2 acts   RPB
  Doris and the Dinosaur, 1922, 2 acts   RPB
  Forget-me-knots, 1927, 3 act farce   RPB
  A Helping Hand, 1921, 2 act comedy   RPB
  Her Radio Romeo, 1927, 2 act comedy   RPB
  His Majesty, the Queen, 1927   RPB
  Letters, 1928, 3 act comedy   RPB
  Love's Service Flag, 1918, 2 act comedy   RPB
  Nine Points of the Law, 1928, 3 act farce   RPB
  Prexy's Proxy, 1915, 2 act comedy   RPB
  The Red Lamp, 1914, 2 acts
  The Rookie and the Rules, 1929, comedy (1)   RPB
  A Royal Spark, 1915, 2 acts
  Sally's Ship Comes In, 1927, 3 act comedy   RPB
  White Carnations, 1927, 3 act comedy   RPB

MARY BORDEN
  Jane, Our Stranger, prod. 1925, based on her novel

ONA WINANTS BORLAND (HAVERKAMP)
  (NUC lists her as ONA (WINANTS) HAVERKAMP)
  The Lamentable Tragedy of Julius Caesar, 1905, song and verse   RPB
  The Lamentable Tragedy of McLizze, 1916, in song and verse   RPB
  The Lamentable Tragedy of Omelet and Oatmealia, 1912, song and verse RPB

BEULAH BORNSTEAD (See BEULAH BOMSTEAD)

MARTHA BOSWELL
  Politicin' in Horse Cove, 1924, comedy of mountain folk (1)
  Yon Side O' Sunk Creek, 1924, tragedy of mountain folk, Carolina play (1)

SARA M. BOURKE
  The Sky Scrappers, 1906, operetta, lyrics by Bourke and Caroline   RPB-M
      Wright; book by Wright; music by Mabel Osborne; presented at
      Radcliffe College

GRACE BOUTELLE
  Pageant of Spring, 1914, festival, Minneapolis, Minn.

MARGARET ELIZABETH BOWEN
  Crude and Unrefined   OPW

SYBIL SPANDE BOWEN
Through the Gate, 1928, Salt Lake City

SUSAN THAYER BOWKER
His Lucky Day, 1902, romantic comedy (1)   RPB

MARIAN BOWLAN
City Types, 1916, " book of monologues sketching the city woman"   RPB
Elevating the Drama, 1912, monologue*   RPB
In the Life Class, 1913, monologue*   RPB
Minnie at the Movies, 1913, monologue*   RPB
Popular Music Hath Charms, 1913, monologue*   RPB
Teena Stars on Tag Day, 1911, monologue*   RPB
Up in the Air, 1912, monologue*   RPB
Why Shoe Clerks Go Insane, 1912, monologue*   RPB
    *All also in City Types.

ELLA SHANNON BOWLES (1886- ?)
Jed Settles Down, 1923, romantic comedy drama (1)   RPB

LORENE BOWMAN
Fifteen Funny Monologues, 1926   RPB

LOUISE MOREY BOWMAN
And Forbid Them Not, in Poetry, 13, March, 1919, 306-7 (1)

MARY BOYCE
Festival of Nations, 1912, pageant, Clarion, Pa.

NEITH BOYCE (1872-1951) (MRS. HUTCHINS HAPGOOD)
Constancy, 1914
Enemies, 1916, with Hutchins Hapgood   CSP-2
The Two Sons, 1916   CSP-3
Winter's Night, 1916   FCP, SFM

EVA PHILIPS BOYD
Garden Pageant: The Place Remembers, 1930, "portraying ten episodes in MB
    the history of Loring-Greenough house and neighborhood, Jamaica
    Plain, Mass."

"NANCY BOYD" (See EDNA ST. VINCENT MILLAY)

EDITH E. L. BOYER
The Spirit of Progress, 1928, praise and history of America   RPB

ELIZABETH HANCHETT BRACE ("BROWNIE BRACE")
The Capture of Mr. Static, 1934, by "Brownie Brace" (1)   RPB
Husbands Three, 1934, 3 act comedy, "winner of Drama League play   RPB
    contest in Michigan
Little Boy Blue, 1934, 2 acts by "Brownie Brace," "the Junior League   RPB
    plays"
Quite a Remarkable Person, 1930, 3 acts, "the Junior League plays" RPB
The Rescue of St. Nick, 1931, 3 acts by "Brownie Brace," "the Junior   RPB
    League plays"
Teddy Somersault; or, the Magic Birthday Cake, 1934, 2 acts by "Brownie RPB
    Brace" "the Junior League plays," music by Bessie Knott

GLADYS BRACE (See GLADYS BRACE VILSACK)

LOUISE A. BRADBURY
Game of Dominoes, 1885, adapted from French of Louis-Emile Dubry   RPB
    (1905 edition titled The Masqueraders; or, a Game of Dominoes)
My Country, 1920, school exercise for the celebration of the 4th of July   EEY

ANN WISHART BRADDY
She's Perfectly Innocent, 1930, Carolina play
Rest For My Soul, 1931, Carolina play

ALICE E. BRADEN
Overheard in Japan, 1923   RPB

ANITA BRADFORD
The Americana, 1917, Spanish American comedy drama for women in   RPB
    3 acts

ALICE BRADLEY (1875-1946) (See ALICE SHELDON in AWW)
The Governor's Lady, prod. 1912, with David Belasco, melodrama,   DLC
    typewritten copy (prompt book at NN)

BEULAH M. BRADLEY
Aladdin's Garden, 1930, with Helen L. Miller, "pageant play for   RPB
    commencement"
The Court of Revelry, 1930, with Helen L. Miller, "pageant of fun and   RPB
    frolic for the 4th of July"
The Open Sesame, 1934, with Helen L. Miller, "pageant play for   RPB
    commencement," mimeograph copy
The Quest, 1932, with Helen L. Miller, "pageant play for   RPB
    commencement," mimeograph copy
Through the Portals, 1930, with Helen L. Miller, "pageant play for   RPB
    commencement"

LILLIAN TRIMBLE BRADLEY (1875- ?) British?
As Others See Us, prod. 1917?
Beating Back, prod. 1916?
Izzy, prod. 1924, with George Broadhurst
Mr. Myd's Mystery, prod. 1915
Out Goes She, prod. 1928
The Red Falcon, prod. 1924, with George Broadhurst (also called Red Hawk)
Virtue For Sale, typescript   NN
What Happened Then? 1934, prod. 1933, 3 act melodrama
The Woman on the Index, prod. 1918, with George Broadhurst,
    melodrama spy play
The Wonderful Thing, prod. 1920, based on story by Forrest Halsey,   NN
    comedy, typescript

MARY E. BRADLEY
That Vidder, 1926, 5 act comedy   RPB

MAUD MENEFREE BRADLEY
A Mystery Play for Christmas, 1926   RPB

MARIEL BRADY
Peter Projects, 1928, arranged from "Genevieve Gertrude," a book   RPB
    by Brady

RUBY PHILLIPS BRAMWELL
From the Sidelines, 1935, with Marjorie Fredenhagen, "rollicking   RPB
    stunt"
The Magic Thrift Lamp, in Normal Instructor and Primary Plans, 35, Jan.,
    1926, 59 (1)
Mary Ann's Truce, 1927 (1)   RPB
Never Take Your Wife to a Ball Game, 1931, monologue
Not According to Schedule, 1924, dram. of short story by Mary Stewart   RPB
    Cutting (1)

ANNA (ANN) HEMPSTEAD BRANCH (1875-1937) AWW   NAW
Bubbles, by "Ann Hemstead"
Ceremony for the Bringing in of the Birthday Cake, 1926?
A Child's Ritual for the Admiration of a Single Flower, 1927?   RPB
Christadora House Papers, 192? Dramatic Series, young   NN
A Christmas Miracle and God Bless This House, 1925, ceremony for   RPB
    Christmas Eve
God Bless This House, 1917, ceremony for Christmas Eve   RPB
Green Rowan, n.d., "milk drinking ceremony" (1)   RPB, HDC
The Heart of the Road and Other Poems, 1901 (contains "Lazarus") (1)   RPB
In the Queen's Garden, 190?, "loose leaf drama"   RPB
The Rose of the Wind and Other Poems, 1910 (1)   RPB
St. Francis and the Wolf, 1928 (1)   SSH-IV
The Shoes That Danced, 1905 (1)   RPB,WWO
To Dust Returning (1)   WWS, WWY

LOUISE FENTON BRAND
Bathing the Baby, 1924, health play
City Hall Central
Getting in Step, 1930, "Christmas seal playlet in one act"

DOROTHY BRANDON
The Outsider, prod. 1924, incomplete typescript (anti-medical   NN, PU
    profession)

PAULINA BRANDRETH
Alvise, 1906, 3 act verse tragedy   RPB

CLAUDIA BRANNON
Marcelle, 1904, with Willibert Davis, 4 act tale of the Revolution   RPB

GENA BRANSCOMBE (1881- ?)
Pilgrims of Destiny, 1929, choral drama   RPB

AURA WOODIN BRANTZELL
The Resemblance, with Alice Leal Pollock, in Smart Set, 33, Feb., 1911,
    127-34 (1)

LAVINIA E. BRAUFF
Beauty and Blessing, 1908, Children's Day service, music by W. B.   RPB-M
    Judefind and A. L. Judefind; words by Brauff and Maud Frazer

LOUISE WHITEFIELD BRAY
The Harbor of Lost Ships, 1918, adapted from short story by   BPH-II
    Ellen Payne Huling (1)
Mis' Mercy, 1922 (1)   BPW-III

BERNICE BREEN
Sightseers, 1929, in Little Theatre Tournament

BESSIE SPRINGER BREENE
Gracie, 1921, comedy (1)   RPB
Sparks Divine, 1920, comedy (1)   RPB
Twelve Good Men and True, 1922, comedy (1)   RPB

KATHERINE MARIE CORNELIA BRE´GY (1888- ?)
The Little Crusaders, 1919, "drama of the Children's Crusade"   RPB

BLANCHE IRBE BREMNER (1871- ?)
The Hut in the Forest, 1917, dramatic poem in 3 episodes   RPB

EVANGELINE LENT BRETHERTON
The Minister's Messenger, 1915, comedy for girls (1)   RPB

EVE BRETHERTON
A Dash of Vanity and Other Monologues, 1933
The Ninth Day, 1933 (1)
The Rag Doll, 1934 (1)   RPB
The Sillyville School, 1928 "playlette"   RPB

HELEN D. BREWER
The Thane of Cawdor, 1914, mock grand opera in 5 acts by Helen D.   RPB
    Brewer, '14 and Alma L. Hall, '15, of the Pine River Public School,
    Pine River, Minn.

EMMA E. BREWSTER
Aunt Mehetible's Scientific Experiment, 1880, farce for women (1)   RPB
Beresford Benevolent Society, 1906, with Lizzie B. Scribner, farce (1) RPB
Cent-any-all-Centennial, 1881, 3 act charade
The Christmas Box, 1881
A Dog That Will Fetch Will Carry, 1880, farce for women   RPB
Eliza's Bona-fide Offer, 1901, farce for women (1)   RPB, BCF
How the Colonel Proposed, 1880, farce   RPB
Parlor Varieties, Plays, Pantomimes and Charades, 1881, editor   RPB
Poor Peter, 1881, farce (1)
Zerubbabel's Second Wife, 1880, farce (1)   RPB

MAY M. BREWSTER
The Angel and the Star, 1917, Christmas cantata, music by Ira B. Wilson   IU
The First Christmas Gift, 1918, Christmas service, music by Ira B. Wilson RPB
Heirs of Liberty, 1919, peace celebration for Children's Day, music by RPB
    Ira B. Wilson
Methodism Marches On, 1939, drama in 8 historical episodes
Snowbound on Christmas Eve, 1934, music by Anne Owen
We Would See Jesus, 1945, Children's Day pageant for younger children

SADIE B. BREWSTER
America's Making, 1926, patriotic pageant   RPB
The Hope of the World, 1919, patriotic pageant   RPB

MARGARET S. BRIDGE (1887- ?)
Snappy Stunts for Social Gatherings, 1920
Sorepaw and Fells Indoor Circus, 1921, with Margaret H. Hahn   RPB
What to Do Commencement Week, "a novel collection of material for
    school commencement activities"

ANN PRESTON BRIDGERS
    The Beautiful Structure, play of John S. Calhoun, 1936   NcU
    Coquette, prod. 1927, with George Abbott, pub. 1928
    Miss Sally, ms.   NcU
    The Throne of Kings, ms.   NcU

"MADELINE BRIDGES" (See MARY AINGE DE VERE)

GLADYS RUTH BRIDGHAM
    At the Sign of the Shooting Star, 1916, 3 act comedy   RPB
    Behind the Scenes, 1917, 2 act comedy   RPB
    Bobby Takes a Look, 1921, 2 act comedy   RPB
    Brown-eyed Betty, 1916   RPB
    Captain Cranberry, 1917, "Cape Cod comedy," 3 acts   RPB
    A Case for Sherlock Holmes, 1913, 2 act comedy for women   RPB
    Cupid's Partner, 1914, 3 act comedy   RPB
    Cynthia Looks Ahead, 1918, 2 acts   RPB
    Excuse Me! 1915, 2 act comedy   RPB
    Five Feet of Love, 1919, 2 act comedy   RPB
    The Girl from Upper Seven Ranch, 1915, 3 act comedy   RPB
    The Girl Upstairs, 1916, 2 act comedy   RPB
    Golden Hope, 1921, 2 acts, "for girls"   RPB
    The Heart of Maine, 1925, 3 act drama   RPB
    Her First Assignment, 1914, comedy (1)   RPB
    His Father's Son, 1916, 3 act comedy   RPB
    Hitty's Service Flag, 1918, 2 act comedy   RPB
    Honeymoon Flats, 1918, 2 act comedy, "expanded by permission from a   RPB
      sketch in one act by Hallie Hale Hassey"
    The House by the Side of the Road, 1926, 3 act comedy   RPB
    The House in Laurel Lane, 1920, 2 act comedy for women   RPB
    The Hurdy Gurdy Girl, 1918, 3 act comedy   RPB
    I Grant You Three Wishes, 1920, fantasy (1)   RPB
    Just Plain Mary, 1920, 2 act comedy   RPB
    Katy Did, 1916, 2 act comedy   RPB
    Leave It to Polly, 1914, 2 act comedy for women   RPB
    Line Busy, 1919, 2 act comedy   RPB
    Lucinda Speaks, 1919, 2 act comedy   RPB
    The Man of Yesterday, 1925   RPB
    The Man Without a Country, 1918, adapt. of the story by Edward Everett   RPB
      Hale
    Mrs. Haywood's Help, 1914, 2 act comedy   RPB
    A Modern Cinderella, 1915, 2 act comedy   RPB
    Mother Mine, 1922, 3 acts, "a play that reaches the heart"   RPB
    Not on the Programme, 1915, comedy (1)   RPB
    Oh! Oh! Deacon! 1922   RPB
    On the Quiet, 1915, 2 act comedy   RPB
    One Minute Past, 1927, play for radio (1)   RPB
    One On Dick, 1916, 2 act comedy   RPB
    Polly Lou, 1919   RPB
    Polly Wants a Cracker, 1921, 2 act comedy   RPB
    The Prince of Poppyland, 1916   BPP
    The Queen of Hearts, 1912, high school comedy (1)   RPB
    A Regular Rah! Rah! Boy, 1915, 3 act comedy   RPB
    A Regular Scream (Royal Fetters), 1913, 2 act comedy for men   RPB
    Ring-around-a-Rosie, 1914, comedy (1)   RPB
    Sally Lunn, 1914, 2 act comedy   RPB
    Short Plays for Small Players, 1915, one-acts, with Edith Burrows and   RPB
      others

GLADYS RUTH BRIDGHAM (continued)
Six Times Nine, 1914, 2 act comedy for women   RPB
Step Lively, 1917 (1925?) 2 act comedy   RPB
Sweet William, 1927, 3 act comedy   RPB
Thirteen Plus, 1922, 3 act comedy   RPB
The Thirteenth Star, 1918, 3 act comedy   RPB
This Way Out, 1921   RPB
Three of a Kind, 1913, comedy (1)   RPB
Tillie Listens In, 1926, 2 act comedy for women   RPB
The Turn in the Road, 1912 (1925?) 2 act comedy   RPB
Way Down Along, 1921, "Cape Cod comedy in prologue and 2 acts"   RPB

LILIAN CLISBY BRIDGHAM
The Famous Brown vs. Brown Separate Maintenance Case, 1912,   RPB
    "woman's suffragette mock trial"
Margery Makes Good, 1915, 2 act romantic comedy   RPB
The Marriage of Jack and Jill, 1913 "Mother Goose entertainment in RPB
    2 scenes"
A Suffragette Town Meeting, 1912 (1)   RPB

CAROLINE BRIGGS
One a Day, fantasy (about World War I) (1)   MP

CAROL RYRIE BRINK (1895-1981) AWW
Caddie Woodlawn, 1945, dramatization of her book, for young people RPB
The Queen of Dolls, 1928, pantomimed reading for young people   RPB

MARGARET SUTTON BRISCOE (HOPKINS) (1864- ?)
    (listed under Hopkins in NUC)
The Frog Fairy   HBP
An I.O.U., 2 acts, in Scribner's, 14, September, 1893, 305-13

EDITH BRISTOL
Uncle Sam's S.O.S., 1918, pageant, with Estelle Miller   RPB

MARGUERITTE HARMON BRO (1894- ?)
Al's Technique, 1931, "Negro farce" (1)   RPB
Granny, 1929
Home Rule, in Chicago University, Plays, Skits and Lyrics, 1936
Milk, 1929 (1)   RPB
Progressive Education, in Chicago University, Plays, Skits and Lyrics, 1936
The Terrible Meek, 1933? Pub. by National Council for Prevention of   NBuG
    War, typewritten copy
Within the Four Seas, "play set in China," in Chicago University, Plays,
    Skits and Lyrics, 1936

ALICE WHITNEY BROCKETT
In Music Land, 1921, young   RPB
When Troubadours Sang at the Court of England for Richard the
    Lion-Hearted, 1929, pageant of song

ELIZABETH BROOKE
Peg Lends a Hand, 1930, "Camp Fire play"   RPB

KATHARINE BARRON BROOKMAN
Interpolated, in Poet Lore, 35, Spring, 1924, 78-888 (1)

ANNIE SILLS BROOKS
　　The Discovery, playlet for a "Mother and Daughter" Meeting   HPY

HELEN LEE BROOKS
　　The Pursuit of the Parson, 1909, "mock trial in the year A.D. 1980," for   RPB
　　　　women

KATHERINE R. BROOKS
　　The Swan-song, 193? reading in Wetmore Declamation Bureau   RPB

EDITH J. BROOMHALL
　　Converting Bruce, 1919, farce (1)   RPB
　　What Rosie Told the Tailor, 1919, farce (1)   RPB

NANCY BANCROFT BROSIUS
　　Footsteps, 1931, with Marian Harvey, "breathtaking mystery play"   RPB
　　A Little Learning, 1937, domestic tragedy (1)   TP
　　Sue 'em, 1925, comedy, "the first radio play printed in America," won   RPB
　　　　first prize in WGBS radio drama contest

ALICE WILLIAMS BROTHERTON
　　The Talisman, in Poet Lore, 40, 1929, 153-7 (1)

HELEN BROUN
　　Clouds, prod. 1925

ALICE K. BROWER (BOWER)
　　A Trick of the Trade, 1920 (1)   RPB

ABBIE FARWELL BROWN (1871-1927) AWW NAW
　　The Green Trunk, 1921, "masque written for the 50th birthday of the   MH
　　　　Saturday Morning Club of Boston
　　The Lantern and Other Plays for Children, 1928   RPB
　　Quits, 1896, college girl comedy (1)   RPB

ALICE BROWN (1857-1948) AWW NAW
　　But an' Ben, 1931, made into Scotch by Margaret M. Muir from Joint   RPB
　　　　Owners of Spain (1)
　　Charles Lamb, 1924   RPB
　　Children of the Earth, 1915, winner of $10,000 Winthrop Ames prize   RPB
　　Doctor Auntie, 1929 (1)   RPB
　　The Golden Ball, 1921 (1)   RPB
　　Joint Owners of Spain, 1914   RPB, HQC
　　The Loving Cup, 1918, in Woman's Home Companion, 40, May, 1913,   RPB
　　　　11-2+ (1)
　　A March Wind, 1921 (1)   RPB
　　The Marriage Feast, 1931, fantasy   RPB
　　One-Act Plays, 1921   RPB
　　Pilgrim's Progress, 1927, 3 act comedy (RPB has 1944 edition)   RPB
　　The Sugar House, prod. 1916 by Washington Square Players

ALICE H. BROWN
　　Dora Thorne, 1906, "by Bertha M. Clay (i.e Charlotte Mary Brame)"   RPB
　　　　dram. by Brown

ANNIE K. BROWN
　　Voice on Wire, in Counselor Print, 1919

BEULAH BROWN
    A Christmas Fantasy, 1930, mimeographed copy, young   RPB
    Touring, 1930, comedy about camping, mimeographed copy (1)   RPB

ESTELLE AUBREY BROWN
    A Woman of Character, 1924, for women (1)   RPB, ETP

ESTHER BROWN
    In Poppy Land, 1926 or earlier, musical entertainment for children, with
        Edith M. Weeks

"EVE BROWN" (See MARY EUDORA NICHOLS)

GRACE OVERTON BROWN
    An Easter Play, 1927, founded on the Four Gospels   RPB

KATHARINE S. BROWN
    One Night in Bethlehem, 1925, with Glenna Smith Tinnin, play of the   RPB
        Nativity

LAURA NORTON BROWN
    Kissing Goes By Favor, in Drama, 16, Oct., 1925, 14-5+ (1)

LIDA M. BROWN
    The Man Who Left the Farm, 1928,   RPB
        "play in 3 acts for rural communities"

LUCY KENNEDY BROWN
    Another World, 1934, drama (1)   RPB
    The Duchess Bounces In, 1928, pantomime   RPB
    Remnant Day, 1929, comedy (1)   RPB
    The Right Answer, 1929, comedy (1)   RPB
    Two Tables of Bridge, 1928, comedy for women (1)   RPB

MARIAN KATHERINE BROWN
    Everychild, 1911, morality play, with Lena Dalkeith Burton
    On the Tower of the Shadows   JPP
    Power, 1915, "pageant of the inner life for children"   RPB

MARY C. BROWN
    The Knight in Poverty, 1925, 3 act operetta for Barnswallows,   RPB-M
        Wellesley College, lyrics by Mary C. Brown and others; music by
        Margaret Bixler and others; book by Mary Louise Robinson

MARY MITCHELL BROWN
    Pocahontas, the Indian Princess, 1922, forest fantasy, libretto and lyrics   RPB
        by Brown; music by John P. Campbell (comic version)

MAUDE BASS BROWN
    Aunt Abigail Speaks, 1923, comedy for women   RPB
    When Romance Lived, 1924, "phantasy in one act"   RPB

MAY BROWN
    Graduatin' at Gooseville, 1935, farcical entertainment
    Le Faker's Youth Restorer, 1920, entertainment (1)   RPB

MAY BELLEVILLE BROWN
    References Required, 1923, farce for women's clubs   RPB

MURIEL BROWN
    Ivanhoe, 1930, dram. of novel by Sir Walter Scott
    Robin Hood, 1930, comedy in 5 scenes

PATRICIA BROWN
    Gloria Mundi, 1925, in Little Theatre tournament, winner of second   RPB
        Samuel French prize; pub. in vol. 2 of National Little Theatre
        Tournament Plays (1)

MRS. R. J. BROWN
    The Upper Sash, 19?? "Christian friendliness play," 2 acts, mimeo.   RPB
        copy printed by Woman's American Baptist Home Mission Society

SHIRLEY BROWN
    Counted Out, 1932, "ten rounds of laughter and fun"   RPB
    Sandwich Glass, 1929, "drama of Cape Cod"   RPB

TERESA A. BROWN
    Today is Monday, 1923, "originally presented in New London, Conn.   RPB
        by the teachers of Saltonstall School"

VIOLA GARDNER BROWN
    Billy's Mishap, 1903, farce (1)   RPB
    Madame G. Whiliken's Beauty Parlor; or, A Man at the Bottom of It,
        1919, 2 act farce

EDITH BROWN-EVARTS
    Eighteen Dialogues and Plays for Young People, 1902
    Young Folks' Dialogues and Dramas, 1902   RPB

ALICE WILSON BROWNE
    Mr. Butte from Montana, 1903, 3 act comedy, with W. Gault   RPB

HENRIETTE BROWNE
    Over the Hills, 1929, "the greatest story of Mother-love ever written"   RPB

MABEL MONTGOMERY BROWNE
    Christian Endeavor Playlets, ed. by Henrietta Heron, 1928, a contributor   RPB
    Day By Day, 1926, "play for the women of the Eastern Star"   RPB
    Esther, 1924, dramatization of Biblical history   RPB
    Faith and What It Does (1)   TMC
    A Literary Romance, 1922, "pantomime farce for literary classes and   RPB
        clubs"
    More Christian Endeavor Playlets, ed. by E. W. Thornton, a contributor   RPB
    Peter, a Great Evangelist (1)   TMC
    Successful Evangelism in Mission   TMC

EVELYN B. BROWNELL
    The Legend of the Laurel, pageant

MARY ALICE BROWNELL
    Swimming Pageants for Outdoor Production, 1926 (pub. under   RPB
        "Pageants with a Purpose," ed. by Linwood Taft)

LESLIE CHADWICK BROWNING
    The House of a Thousand Thrills, 1926, 3 act mystery drama   RPB

MARY WILSON BROWNSON
　　Victory Through Conflict, 1920, "pageant of striving humanity,"　　RPB-M,MB
　　　　with Vanda E. Kerst; music by Walter Wild; for 50th anniversary
　　　　of Penn. College for Women, Pittsburgh

EMMA BEATRICE KAUFMAN BRUNNER
　　Bits of Background in One-Act Plays, 1919　　　　　　　　　　　　RPB

MAUD(E) BRUNTON
　　Mr. and Mrs. Santa Claus, 1922, "musical Christmas play in 4 scenes"　　RPB

JOSEPHINE VAN TASSEL BRUORTON
　　Summer Boarders; or, the Great Jewel Mystery, 1908, 4 act comedy drama RPB

DOROTHY HAMILTON BRUSH (WALMSLEY) (1894-1968)
　　One-Eye, Two-Eye and Three-Eye, 1929, 3 act puppet play for children,　　RPB
　　　　"the Junior League plays"
　　The Poor Little Turkey Girl, 1928, "play of Pueblo Indian folklore,"　　RPB
　　　　"Junior League play"

KATHERINE C. BRYAN
　　The Light, 1926, "service of worship for a white Christmas"　　　　RPB

LOUISE FRANCES STEVENS BRYANT (1885-1956?)
　　The Game, 1916, prod. by Provincetown Players (1)　　　　CSP-1st series

CATHERINE TURNER BRYCE (1871- ?)
　　Bound or Free and The Wizard of Words, 1922　　　　　　　　　RPB
　　The Charm, 1921, "play for children to teach better English"　　　RPB
　　The Child-lore Dramatic Reader, 1908　　　　　　　　　　　　RPB
　　The Flag in Birdland, 1918, patriotic play for children　　　　　RPB
　　The Light, 1920, "educational pageant"　　　　　　　　　　　　RPB
　　Story-land Dramatic Reader, 1916
　　To Arms for Liberty, 1918, "pageant of the war for schools and societies"

FANNIE REBECCA BUCHANAN (1875- ?)
　　Daughters of Freedom, 1919, patriotic ceremonial　　　　　　　RPB
　　The First Noel, masque　　　　　　　　　　　　　　　　　　SCS
　　The Lighting of the Torch, masque, in Drama, 10, July-Sept,, 1920, 350-4 (1)
　　Who Defeated Doogan? 1924, with Clara Wilson, "one-act playlet with　　DLC
　　　　prolog; being a study of election laws and a farce of election errors"
　　Yankee Doodle to the Rescue, by "F. R. Buchanan," in Normal Instructor
　　　　and Primary Plans, 34, June, 1925, 66-7

MARGARET BUCHANAN
　　A Columbus Pageant　　　　　　　　　　　　　　　　　　　WPP

GERTRUDE BUCK (1871-1922)
　　Mother Love, in Drama, 9, Feb., 1919, 1-30.
　　Poems and Plays by Gertrude Buck, 1922, ed. by Laura Johnson Wylie　　RPB

FANNIE LOUISE BUCKINGHAM
　　My Mexican Sweetheart, 1905, playlet　　　　　　　　　　　　RPB

ISABEL BUCKINGHAM
　　The Ugly Duckling, 1923, cantata for children,　　　　　　　　RPB
　　　　music by Granville English

ALICE MARY BUCKTON (may be British)
   Chorales forEager Hearts, 1909, Christmas mystery play
   The Coming of Bride, 1914, pageant play written by the students of Chalice
      Wells for the Guild of Festival Players
   Eager Heart, 1905, Christmas mystery play in verse   RPB
   The Garden of Many Waters, 1907, masque
   Kings in Babylon, 1906, 2 acts
   A Masque of Beauty and the Beast, 1904
   The Meeting in the Gate, 1916, Christmas interlude

CAROLINE H. BUDD
   The Only Girl in Sight

MARGARET A. BUELL
   The Red Mill, in Young Pegasus, Intercollegiate Literary Magazine   OU
      Conference, N. Y., Dail Press, 1926

ELIZA BUFFINGTON (? -1938)
   Star Dust Fairy, 1922, music by Carrie W. Lyon, "rhymes, illuminations, RPB
      dance and puzzle figures"

LUCY E. HANSON BUFORD
   The House of Lords: An Equal Suffrage Play, 1914 (1)

BESSIE M. BUHL
   Call of Oliver P. Morton, 1923, pageant, Centerville, Ind.   InI

CLARA DURLAND BULL
   Pageant to Commemorate the Coming of Sarah Wells to Orange   RPB
      County 200 Years Ago, 1912, music by Tannery; given at 45th
      annual Bull family reunion

KATIIERINE BULL (1903?-1918)   RPB
   White Silences, 1920, "poems, a play and a tale" (the play is titled
      "Death") (She died at age 15)

KATHARINE THOMAS JARBOE BULL ("KATE THOMAS")
   A Bit of Nonsense, 1908, by "Kate Thomas" (1)   RPB
   An Evening at Helen's, 1908, by "Kate Thomas" (1)

ABBY BULLOCK
   The Pledging of Polly, 1909, 2 act farce with Margaret Currier Lyon   RPB

FREDA GRAHAM BUNDY
   Henry's Mail-Order Wife, 1930, comedy (1)   RPB
   It Happened at Christmas, 1929   RPB
   Just For Tonight, 1941, farce (1)
   Mother Goes on a Strike, 1929, comedy   RPB
   Prairie Wife, 1952, drama (1)   RPB
   The Round-up of Minnie, 1935, play?

ANNE BUNNER
   The Professor's Daughter, 1919, 3 act romantic comedy   RPB

"BARBARA BURBANK" (See CLARA BURBANK BATCHELDER)

MAUDE BURBANK
    Maids of All Nations, 1909, "entertainment suitable for stage or parlor"   RPB
    A Pan of Fudge, 1907, boarding school comedy (1)   RPB

HELEN BURCH
    The Spirit of Roanoke, 1920, pageant of Halifax County, with A. E.   MB
        Akers and Annie M. Cherry

KATHERINE STANBERRY BURGESS
    Duetto, 1927   OPS-III
    God Winks, 1925, comedy (1)   RPB, ETP,
        SSH-III

MINNIE C. BURGESS
    Four Little Fir Trees, in Christmas Plays for Children, 1916 (1)

INEZ M. BURKE
    Riding the Goat (1)   RMP
    Two Races, pageant for 7th and 8th grades   RMP

LUCIE TOUSEY BURKHAM
    When the Land Was Young, 1909, "incident of the Revolution" (1)   RPB

LOUISE BURLEIGH (1890- ?)
    Punishment, 1916, 4 act drama, with Edward Hale Bierstadt   RPB
    Signal Fires, 1912, masque of service (Un. of Va. Record—Extension   RPB
        series, Feb.,1934, v. 8, no. 6) printed for Graduate Nurses Assoc. of
        Virginia

MABELLE P. BURNET
    Vision, 1928, 3 acts "play about P.E.O."   RPB

FRANCES ELIZA HODGSON BURNETT (1849-1924) AWW NAW NWAT
    The Dawn of a Tomorrow, prod. 1908, (prompt book at NN) filmed 1915 MH
    Editha's Burglar (her novel was dramatized by Augustus Thomas in
        1884) pub. 1932 (See Phyllis)
    Esmeralda, 1881, with William Gillette, comedy drama, in Century, 23,   RPB
        Feb., 1882, 513-53, filmed in 1915
    The First Gentleman of Europe, prod. 1897, with Julia Constance Fletcher
    Judy O'Hara, prod. 1911, with Frederick A. Stanley
    A Lady of Quality, prod. 1897, with Stephen Townsend, filmed in 1924
    The Little Hunchback Zia, 1916   RPB
    Little Lord Fauntleroy, prod. 1888, pub. 1889, 3 acts, filmed in 1921   RPB
    The Little Princess, prod. 1902 (also as A Little Fairy Princess)   RPB, MTP
        pub. in Plays, 17, Jan., 1958, 87-96—adapted by Lewy Olfson; and in
        Plays, 22, Feb., 1963, 33-4,—adapted by Adele Thane, filmed in 1939
    Nixie, 1890, with Stephen Townsend (also titled Editha's Burglar)
    Phyllis, 1889, adapt. of her novel, The Fortunes of Philippa Fairfax
    The Pretty Sister of Jose, prod. 1903, typescript   NN
    The Racketty Packetty House, prod. 1912, pub. 1926 (also in Plays,   RPB, MAT
        24, May, 1965, 75-8—adapted by Ruth Putnam Kimball)
    The Showman's Daughter, 1892, with Stephen Townsend
    That Lass o' Lowries, 1878, dram. of her novel, filmed as The Flame of
        Life, 1923
    That Man and I, prod. 1904, adapt. of her novel, In Connection with the
        De Willoughby Claim

CLARA LOUISE ROOT BURNHAM (1854-1927) AWW
Judge Santa Claus, a New Departure, 1887, Christmas cantata,   RPB-M
    music by George F. Root
Phyllis, the Farmer's Daughter, 1892, operatic cantata
The Right Princess, n.d., 3 acts, typewritten copy   MH
Santa Claus and Co. 1889, Christmas cantata, music by George Root   RPB-M
Santa Claus' Mistake; or, the Bundle of Sticks, 1885, Christmas cantata, RPB-M
    music by George Root
Snow White and the Seven Dwarfs, 1916, operetta for young folks,   RPB-M
    music by George Root

HELEN BURNHAM
The Lucky Fool, 1927, comedy (1)   RPB
Mom, 1926, 4 act comedy drama   RPB
Over the Garden Wall, 1929, 3 act comedy with music   RPB

ANNELU BURNS
Hooray for the Girls, 1919, lyrics by Burns, book by Helen Woodruff,
    music by Madelyn Sheppard, "presented by the sub-debs, debs, and
    super debs of N. Y. society for the benefit of the American Committee
    for Devastated France"

MARY MODENA BURNS
The Doo-Funny Family, 1920, humorous entertainment   RPB
Good Things for Sunday Schools, 1916 (She was compiler of the   RPB
    collection.)
Her Honor, the Mayor, 1916, 3 act comedy   RPB
Schoolroom Entertainments, 1920

NANCY M. BURNS
A Complete Holiday Program for First Grade, 1911, with May Nunney   RPB

AMELIA JOSEPHINE BURR (1878- ?)
Hearts Awake, 1919, includes the poetic drama, "The Pixy"   RPB
Judgment , tragedy, in The Poetry Journal, May, 1913, 201-17; June, 1913,
    258-78; July, 1913, 6-25 (1)
A Masque of Women Poets, in Stratford Journal, 1, March, 1917, 13-33
Plays in the Market-place, 1910, 5 poetic dramas   RPB
The Point of Life, 1907, 3 acts   RPB

BERTHA Y. BURRILL
Rich Man, Poor Man, 1927, farce, written and produced in the Town   RPB
    and Gown School of the Theatre of Northwestern Un. and the Drama
    Club of Evanston (1)

MARY (MAMIE P.) BURRILL (1879-1946)
The Aftermath, in The Crisis, Nov., 1919 and in The Liberator, 2, April, FCP
    1919, 10-4, in Little Theatre Tournament of 1928
They That Sit in Darkness, in Birth Control Review, III, Sept., 1919 (1) HSB

IDA BENJAMIN BURROUGHS
Handsome Is   YSP-I

EDITH MAIE BURROWS (1887- ?)
Anti-Aunts, 1913, young   RPB
Behind the Rain Curtain, 1921, young   RPB
Charter Oak, 1916, music by Edward Johnston, for boys   RPB

EDITH MAIE BURROWS (continued)
>Cheery Comedies for Christmas, 1915, collection of one-acts with   RPB
>>Gertrude M. Henderson and others
>
>"Dear Cyril," 1913   RPB
>A Fairy Frolic, 1919   RPB
>A Garden Cinderella, 1920, 2 acts, young   RPB,SSH-II
>In a Flower Garden, 1914, cantata for girls, music by William   RPB
>>Rhys-Herbert
>
>Jack O' Hearts, 1913, 3 act comedy   RPB
>O Hara San, 1918, with Edward Johnston   RPB
>Our Motherland, 1921, patriotic pageant   RPB
>Patriotic Pictures, 1919, tableau   RPB
>Seasons and Holidays, 1913   RPB
>Short Plays for Small Players, 1915, one-acts with Gladys R. Bridgham   RPB
>>and others
>
>"Their Lordships," 1913 (first pub. 1909)   RPB
>The Wild Rose, 1915, operetta   RPB

RUBY BOOTHE BURSCH
>The Antidote, 1927, 2 act comedy   RPB

OLIVE F. WOOLEY BURT (1894- ?)
>Dandy Drills and Dances, 1929, with Marie Irish
>The Left-over Toys, 1929, Christmas, young   RPB
>Midsummer Night   BPD
>The Wise Gifts   FKC

LENA DALKEITH BURTON
>Everychild, 1911, morality play with Marian Katherine Brown

IRENE DE REATH BYRD BUSEY
>The Yellow Tree, 1922 (1)

BERTHA EVANGELINE BUSH (1866- ?)
>Making a Flag (1)   FFP
>St. Patrick and the Druids, 1914, for boys   RPB
>Santa Claus and His Helpers, 1905, Christmas service with T. Martin   RPB
>>Towne and Charles H. Gabriel
>
>Santa Claus and His Toys, 1914, child cantata, music by J. Lincoln Hale RPB
>Soldiers of the Land, 1908, music by Ira B. Wilson, service for rally day OrP
>>and missionary occasions
>
>The Yuletide Story, 1906, Christmas service with Charles H. Gabriel   RPB

OLIVIA WARD BUSH (1869- ?)
>Memories of Calvary, 1915, Easter sketch   RPB

KATE BUSS
>Jevons Block, 1918, series of dramatic poems   RPB

TADEMA WHALEY BUSSIERE (1891- ?)
>Claudine
>Fire Daddy
>A Friendly Divorce
>Gertie
>Once Upon a Time
>The Open Gate

MRS. F. D. BUTCHART
Feeling the Hurt, 1918, Christmas   RPB

MARY BECKWITH BUTCHART
Adventuring With Jesus, 1932, pageant   RPB
The Pilgrim Way, 1934, dramatic religious play   RPB
Puck's Gift, 1919, Christmas, music by Clarice Paul   RPB

MILDRED ALLEN BUTLER
Here Comes the Bride, 1937, comedy (1)
Literature Dramatized for Classroom Use, 1926

RACHEL BARTON BUTLER
The Lap-Dog
Mama's Affair, 1919, won the $500 Oliver Morosco prize at Harvard,   RPB
   3 act comedy
"Mom," comedy, typescript   NN
Prudence in Particular, 1928, based on novel by Ethel Hueston
West of Omaha, 1909, farce (1)   RPB

EDITH HADLEY BUTTERFIELD
Humorous Recitations for Children, 1927, with Mary Harden, Ruth   RPB
   Adkinson, Bessie Ford and others
The Military Sewing School, 1927, for girls   RPB
Ten Shadow Plays for Little Folks, 1935

MARIE BUTTERFIELD
The Old Maid's Club, 1903, comic entertainment   RPB

EDNA BUTTIMER
A Fair Exchange, 1930, 3 act comedy with Anna Radke   RPB

DOROTHY BUTTS
Avenues (1)   SCT

KATHERINE BUXBAUM
In Pursuit of Her Heritage, n.d., with Bernice Ladd Halvorson   RPB

MINNIE A. BUZBEE
To Give or Not to Give, 1930, "depicting some of the problems of the   RPB
   modern banker," typewritten copy (1)

ALICE BYINGTON
Cranford Dames, 1918 or earlier, for women (1)

IRENE DE REATH BYRD (See IRENE DE REATH BYRD BUSEY)

DOLLY BYRNE (See DOROTHEA (CADOGAN) DONN-BYRNE)

C

FLORALYN CADWELL
  The Wicked Wang Pah Meets a Dragon, 1925, 3 act Chinese fantasy   RPB

CAROLINE CAFFIN (COFFIN?)
  Home Thrust, 191? comedy about suffrage (1)

ELIZABETH CALDER
  One Room, Plus, 1924, 3 act dramatic comedy with Walter Ben Hare   RPB

ANNE (ANNA) CALDWELL (1867-1936)
  The Bunch and Judy, prod. 1920, book and lyrics with Hugh Ford;   RPB-M
      music by Jerome Kern
  Chin-Chin, prod. 1914, book with R. H. Burnside; lyrics by Caldwell;   RPB-M
      music by Ivan Caryll
  The City Chap, prod. 1925
  Criss-Cross, prod. 1926, libretto with Otto Harbach; music by Jerome Kern
  Go To It, prod. 1916, with John L. Golden and John E. Hazzard, musical
      founded on Charles Hoyt's A Milk-White Flag
  Good Morning Dearie, prod. 1921, music by Jerome Kern, typescript   NN
  Hitchy Koo, prod. 1920, book and lyrics with Glen MacDonough; music by
      Jerome Kern
  A Husband by Proxy, typescript   NN
  Jack-O'-Lantern, prod. 1917, with R. H. Burnside, music by Ivan Caryll
  The Lady of the Slipper, prod. 1912, book with Lawrence McCarty; lyrics by
      James O'Dea; music by Victor Herbert
  The Lady in Red, prod. 1919, music by Robert Winterberg
  The Magnolia Lady, prod. 1924, music by Harold Levey, based on play by
      Alice Duer Miller
  A Model Girl, prod. 1912
  The Nest Egg, prod. 1910, farce, typescript   NN
  New Girl
  The Night Boat, prod. 1920, music by Jerome Kern, adapt. of farce   RPB-M
      by Alexandre Bisson
  Oh, Please!, 1926, with Otto Harbach, music by Vincent Youmans   NN
      based on story by Maurice Hennequin and Pierre Veber, typescript
  Once Upon a Time, 1921, with Lawrence McCarty and James O'Dea,   NN
      typescript (no music ever written)
  Peg -O'-My-Dreams, prod. 1924, with J. Hartley Manners,
      music by Hugo Felix
  Pom-Pom, prod. 1916, music by Hugo Felix, comic opera   RPB-M
  She's a Good Fellow, prod. 1919, music by Jerome Kern
  Stepping Stones, prod. 1923, with R. H. Burnside, music by Jerome Kern
  The Sweetheart Shop, prod. 1920, music by Hugo Felix
  Take the Air, prod. 1927, book and lyrics with Gene Buck, music by Dave
      Stamper

ANNE (ANNA) CALDWELL (continued)

Three Cheers, prod. 1928, book with R. H. Burnside, music by Raymond
  Hubbell

Tip Top, prod. 1920, book and lyrics with R. H. Burnside; music by   NN
  Ivan Caryll, typescript

The Top o' the World, musical extravaganza, music with   RPB-M
  Manuel Klein

Uncle Sam, 1911, with James O'Dea, farcical comedy, typescript and   NN
  promptbook

When Claudia Smiles, prod. 1914, comedy

Yours Truly, prod. 1927, with Clyde North, music by Raymond Hubbell

ELEANOR BAIRD CALDWELL

Tobias and the Angel, 1925, 2 acts   RPB
The Wolf Girl, 1930   DLC

DOROTHY DONNELL CALHOUN

Cupid's Column, 1918, farce (1)   RPB
The 100 Per Cent American, 1918, comedy for girls (1)   RPB
The Parlor Patriots, 1918, comedy for girls (1)   RPB
Pretties (All Her Life), in Touchstone, 6, October, 1919, 26-31 (1)

BERNICE ANDERSON CALL

Thankful At Last, 1930, Thanksgiving play for girls   RPB

EMILIE H. CALLAWAY

Miss Oliver's Dollars, 1909, farce (1)   RPB
A Widow's Wiles, 1908, 3 act comedy   RPB

ROMAINE CALLENDER

Friska; or, the Fountain of Youth, 1908, light opera in 3 acts   RPB

LURA WARNER CALLIN

Daughters of Liberty, 1923, pageant written and designed for children's RPB
  and young people's entertainments, patriotic and religious

ELEANOR CAMERON

(All * plays are listed as Baker's series of Happyland's Fairy Grotto Plays)
*The Little Gray Lady, 1922, with Emilie B. Stapp (1)   RPB
*The Lost Firewood, 1922, with Emilie B. Stapp (1)   RPB
Many-a-way for Christmas Day, 1929, collection   RPB
Many-a-way for Patriotic Days, 1930, collection
*Mr. February Thaw, 1922, with Emilie B. Stapp (1)   RPB
*Molly's New Year's Party, 1922, with Emilie Stapp (1)   RPB
The Mystic Numbers, 1930, young (1)   RPB
*The Tadpole School, 1922, with Emilie Stapp (1)   RPB
A Thanksgiving Dinner   STE

HELEN CAMERON
  Hot Lunch Pageant, 1923, with Christy Nichols   RPB

MARGARET CAMERON (KILVERT)
  (MARGARET CAMERON SMITH) (1867-1947)
  (All * plays are listed as Baker's series of Happyland's Fairy Grotto Plays)
  *The Burglar, 1903, "One of the most popular plays for   RPB
    girls ever written," (also in Comedies in Miniature) (1)
  *A Christmas Chime, 1910, in McClure's, 22, Dec., 1903, 174-84   RPB-micro
    (Also in Comedies in Miniature) (1)
  Comedies in Miniature, 1903, collection of seven plays   RPB
  The Committee on Matrimony, in McClure's, 21, Oct., 1903, 659-65, comedy
    (also in Comedies in Miniature) (1)
  Four Acting Monologues, 1910   RPB
  *The Kleptomaniac, 1903 (also in Comedies in Miniature)   RPB
  (A) The Loyal Renegade, 1900, by "Margaret Cameron Smith" (1)   RPB
  *Miss Doulton's Orchids, 1910 (also in Comedies in Miniature) (1)   RPB
  One of Those Days, 1931 (1)   RPB, NPW
  *A Pipe of Peace, 1900, by "Margaret Cameron Smith"   KTP,RPB-micro
    (also in Comedies in Miniature) (1)
  The Piper's Pay, 1905, comedy for women (1)   RPB
  The Teeth of the Gift Horse, 1909, (1)
  The White Elephant, 1916, with Jessie Leach Porter, comedy (1)

CONSTANCE WILLIS CAMP
  The Birthday of a King, 1929, Christmas pageant   RPB
  The Open Tomb, 1928, Easter pageant   RPB

CONSTANCE CAMPBELL
  One of the Old Guard (1)

EVANGELINE CAMPBELL
  The Husking Bee, 1910, country romance (1)   RPB

JOSEPHINE ELIZABETH CAMPBELL (MRS. VERE CAMPBELL)
  The Worth of a Man, prod. 1914

LILLIAN HAWKINS (HANKINS) CAMPBELL
  Harvest Blessings   WPP
  History's Patriotic Party (1)   FPP

MARIAN D. CAMPBELL
  A Chinese Dummy, 1899, farce for women "specially written for   RPB
    performance by the students of Radcliffe College" (1)
  An Open Secret, 1898, 2 act farce   RPB
  Sunbonnets, 1900, 2 act farce   RPB
  An Unconscious Conspirator

RACHEL HARRIS CAMPBELL
    The Potter's Field, 1939, religious drama   RPB
    An Unfinished Symphony, 1929, dramatic interpretation of   RPB
        Franz Schubert, typed copy (in El Palenque, vol. 2, Nov., 1928, 11-3, San
        Diego State College)

ROSE CAMPION (NUC lists this as a pseudonym for Arthur LeRoy Kaser,
        Jean Lee Latham, and Ruth Perry)
    Alice's Blue Gown, 1932, comedy (1)   RPB
    Ask Nancy! 1932, comedy (1)   RPB
    Betty Behave! 1930, for girls (1)   RPB
    The Christmas Pearl, 1944, (1)   DLC
    The Ghost of a Freshman, 1932, farce (1)   RPB
    Talk Costs Lives, 1942 (1)   RPB
    Ten Easy Acts for Women, 1930, her name on type page by error,   RPB
        in place of Arthur LeRoy Kaser
    Too Many Marys, 1931, comedy for girls (1)   RPB

MARY CASS CANFIELD
    "Anne of England,"1941?, with Ethel Borden, typescript   NN
    The Duchess Says Her Prayers, 1926 (1)   SFM
    Lackeys of the Moon, 1923, won prize in contest by   RPB
        San Diego Players (1)

LOUISE GEBHARD CANN
    Life Is Always the Same, in Drama, 9, May, 1919, 1-20 (1)

FANNY (or FANNIE) VENABLE CANNON (1876- ?)
    Caselda Comes Home; or, Old Maids, 1921, 3 act comedy   RPB
        (listed as Old Maids at RPB)
    The Lady of the Opera House, 1916, romantic comedy (1)
    The Love Laggard
    The Man Who Found Himself
    The Mark of the Beast, prod. 1915, with Georgia Earle
    Meow! 1914, with Alice E. Ives, comedy (1)   RPB
    Playing Fair, 1940, book of tolerance plays for h.s. students   RPB
    Rehearsal for Safety, 1939, book of safety plays   RPB
    What's In a Name? 1916, comedy (1)   RPB

LILIA MACKAY CANTELL (or MACKAY-CANTELL)
    Jephtha's Daughter, prod. 1915 at Neighborhood Playhouse,   NN
        Biblical dance drama, prompt book
    The Shadow Garden of Shut-Eye Town

ESTHER A. CANTER
    Being Beautiful, 1929, monologue for a woman   RPB

EVELYN GRAY WHITING CARD (See EVELYN GRAY WHITING)

CARA CARELLI
Go West Young Man, prod. 1923, with Fay Pulsifer

FIDELIA BURNELL CARGILL
Lydia of Philippi, n.d., Bible play (1)   NN
Nehushta, 1925, "dramatization of the fall of Jerusalem and the captivity" RPB

MABEL MASON CARLTON
The Spirit of Independence, 1926, patriotic pageant, with Henry   RPB
    Fisk Carlton

BLANCHE D. CARLYLE
The Adventure of the Saving Pennies, 1927   RPB

KATHRINE F. CARLYON
The Crowning of Columbia, 1918, patriotic fantasy (1)   RPB

MRS. HARRY A. CARPENTER
The First Independence Day, 1927, "little history lesson"   RPB

MARY E. CARPENTER
All On the King's Highway   BPC
Baucis and Philemon   BPC
Hans Who Made the Princess Laugh   BPC

MYRTLE BARBER CARPENTER
The Advent of Spring, with Florence I. Hope, in Normal Instructor and
    Primary Plans, 34, April, 1925, 76
Billy's Awakening, in Normal Instructor and Primary Plans, 36, April, 1927,
    72-3
Boy Who Knew Columbus, in Primary Educator, 45, March, 1928, 558
The Girl from Weepah, 1929, with Erma M. Stockwell, comedy for   RPB
    females (1)
Her Uncle's Boots, 1910,   farce for females (1)   RPB
Mabel's Aunt, 1926, with Florence Isbell Hope   RPB
The Sister of Pocahontas, 1927   RPB
Three Wise Old Owls, 1933, young   RPB
The Wednesday Club Entertains, 1928, comedy   RPB

MARY LUCRETIA CARR
The Budget Ghost, 1925   WU
Fools and Angels, 1926, comedy (1)   RPB
The World Circle, 1925, with Emma Knauss, "world friendship play   RPB
    for girl reserves"

SARAH PRATT CARR (1850- ?)
The Cost of Empire, 1912, operetta   Or, WaU
The Jenkins Go to the Circus, 1912, "rural romp" (1)   RPB
Narcissa, 1912, music by Mary Carr Moore, based on lives of Marcus and
  Narcissa Whitman, missionaries to the Oregon territory

ELAINE STERNE CARRINGTON (1892-1958) AWW
The Empress, 1936, with Fairfax Proudfit Walkup, typewritten ms., first   NN
  prod. at Pasadena Community Playhouse in 1936
Five Minutes from the Station, 1930 "comedy of life that comes close   HSP
  to being a tragedy"
A Good Provider, 1928 (1)   RPB, ASP
Night Sticks, 1929, by "John Ray" (according to Ferguson it was prod. 1927
  with John Wray and the Nugents)
One of the Finest, 1929, with John Wray (1)   RPB
"One Voice," 195? typescript   NN
Sins of the Mother, won first prize in a contest of the "Evening Sun"
When a Girl Marries, 1942, radio program   NN

ANNIE CARROLL
Shakespeare Pageant and Masque, 1916, Atlanta, Georgia

ELSIE C. CARROLL
Success, 1929

MRS. S. F. CARROLL
A Dress Rehearsal, 1906, parlor comedy (1)   RPB

ELLA KAISER CARRUTH
Helping Father Convalesce, 1928, monologue   RPB
Mrs. Gabby's Busy Day, 1922, monologue   RPB
The Professor's Wife Balances Her Accounts, 1922, monologue   IaU,DLC

MRS. W. M. CARRUTH
Comforting Her Patient, 1921, comedy

ALICE P. CARTER
A Sad Mistake, musical comedy (1)   BCF

EDITH CARTER
Educating a Husband, 1936, 3 acts
Lass O' Laughter, prod. 1925, with Nan Marriott Watson
The Two Mrs. Camerons, 1937, with Winifred Carter, 3 act   RPB
  mystery comedy
Wanted a Wife, 1937, with Winifred Carter, 3 act romantic comedy   RPB

ELSIE HOBART CARTER
Christmas Candles, 1915, collection of one-acts for the young

JOSEPHINE HOWELL CARTER (or HOWELL-CARTER)
Hilarion, in Poet Lore, 26, Summer, 1915, 374-92 (1)

LESLIE H. CARTER
Acting Scenes from Successful Plays, 1938, she was compiler	DLC
At the Risk of His Life, 1948, "short burlesque on the old time Meller-Drammar"	RPB
The Banner Anthology of One-act Plays by American Authors, 1929, compiled by Carter, ed. by Ellen M. Gall	RPB
Banner Victory Minstrel Book, 1944, with Arthur LeRoy Kaser	RPB
"Blitz" Hits for the Entertainment Program, 1943, compiled by Carter, ed. by Ellen Gall	DLC
Crossed Wires , with Ellen Gall, comedy (1)	
Domesticated Papas, 1931, "talking act for 2 men"	CU, MiD
The Gay Nineties Revue, 1946, "musical burlesque of Ye Olde Daze"	MiD
Goodbye Little Eva, 1948, "burlesque on the dying scene of Eva with apologies to Uncle Tom's Cabin," arranged by Carter	RPB
A Home Run, with Ellen Gall	
Hoo-haa-hee, 1925, monologue	DLC
How Do I Know, 1926, vaudeville sketch for 2 male characters	RPB
Matrimony a la Mexico, 1948, comedy (1)	RPB
Ming Toy, 1949, musical comedy with John Laurence Seymour, book by Carter	RPB
Mother Pays, 1926, comedy by Winifred Cozzens, revised by Carter (1)	RPB
Now Trixie, 1925, mystery comedy, with Ellen M. Gall (1)	RPB
Peekaboo, Lady, 1928, 3 act farce, with Ellen M. Gall	RPB
The Pepp and Pepper Steppers, 1931, "red hot minstrel," with Ellen M. Gall	RPB
The Psychological Moment, 1934, comedy for women	CU, MiD
The Razzberry, 1948, comedy (1)	RPB
Satisfying the Public, 1934, "talking act for 2 women"	CU
Scavang! She no-A Da Good, 1926 "wop monologue"	RPB
Sherman Said It, 1931, military burlesque for 3 men	MiD
Six Radio or Stage Sketches: the Adventures of Mr. and Mrs. Brown, 1940	DLC
Skits With a Punch, 1954, compiled by Carter	ScU, TU
Stray Cats, 1925, 3 act farce, with Ellen M. Gall	NN
Surprise Attacks in Bits and Skits by Various Authors, 1942, compiled by Carter, ed. by Gall	RPB
Topsy and Eva, 1934, "travesty of Uncle Tom days," for 2 women	KMK
Turnups, 1926 or earlier, "comedy in seven letters, not a cross word in it"	
Vaudeville What-nots, 1929, collection	RPB
The Womanless Wedding, 1926, farce (1)	RPB

LOUISE CARTER (may be a pseudonym for Clement Wood, a man)
Bedfellows, prod. 1929

MARGARET CARTER (may be British)
Aladdin, 1934, 2 act pantomime   DLC
The Babes in the Wood, 1937, 2 act pantomime   DLC
Beauty and the Beast, 1947, 2 act pantomime   DLC
Cinderella, 1928, 2 part pantomime   RPB
Dick Whittington, 1929, 2 act pantomime   DLC
The Dutch Doll, 1929   DLC
Griselda Married, 1929   DLC
Half Past Thirteen, 1929   DLC
Jack and the Beanstalk, 1930   DLC
The King and the Cakes, 1929   DLC
Little Red Riding Hood, 1939, 2 act pantomime   DLC
Managee and the Robbers, 1929   DLC
Mother Goose, 1951, pantomime   NN
Pedro, the Toreador, 1935, "comedy of ancient Spain"   NN
Robinson Crusoe, 1949, 2 act pantomime   DLC
Sinbad the Sailor, 1935, 2 act pantomime   DLC
Snow White and the Seven Dwarfs, 1954, 2 act pantomime   NN
The Stoway's Inheritance, 1912   NN,DLC

"LILY CARTHEW" (See LILLIAN P. HEYDEMANN)

CLAIRE CARVALHO
Lamplight, 1924, in Little Theatre Tournament
Paging Danger, 1930, prod. 1931, with Leighton Osmun, typescript   NN

ADA JACK CARVER (1890-1972) AWW
The Cajun, 1926, in Little Theatre Tournament (1)   RPB, CNA
The Clock Strikes Tomorrow, children's plays

KATE LEE CARVER
Three Foolish Bears   WPP

ALICE V. CARY
New Names for Old, 1923, "safety first play" (1)   RPB

MRS. C. WILBUR CARY
The Colrain Pageant, in The Playground, 7, June, 1913, 121-4

BEATRICE MARIE CASEY
The All-around Christmas Book, 1933, with others   RPB
All Set for Etiquette, 1933, young (1)   RPB
Beg Your Pardon? 1936, play?   DLC
A Cap and Bells, 1936, play?   DLC
The Carnival Princess, 1950, juvenile operetta, music by   RPB
    Henry Wansborough
Christmas Hijinks, 1937, juvenile operetta, music by   RPB-M, Or
    Harold Wansborough (1)

BEATRICE MARIE CASEY (continued)

The Christmas Light, 1936, juvenile operetta, music by Henry   RPB-M, Or
    S. Sawyer (1)
The Crash of the Air Mail, 1931, young   RPB
Excuse for Living, 1959? church play (1)   RPB
The Favorite Mother's Day Program, 1931   RPB
The Fickle Friend, 1931, young (1)   RPB
Fighting Through, 1934, jr. and senior h. s. (1)   RPB
Good Plays for Tiny Players, 1937   RPB
Good Primary Plays for Children of the First and Second Grades, 1934   RPB
Good Things for Closing Day, 1953, with Effa E. Preston
Good Things for Easter, 1930   RPB
Good Things for Everyday Programs, 1950
Good Things for Halloween, 1929   RPB
Good Things for Mother's Day, 1952
Good Things for Special Holidays, 1928   RPB
Intermediate Assembly Plays, 1937, with others   RPB
Intermediate Closing Day Book for the Upper and Lower Intermediate RPB
    Grades, 1939
The Little Good People, 1929, young (1)   RPB
"The Little Lamplighter," 1935,   play?   DLC
The Love of Ruth, 1955, religious play (1)   RPB
Lucky Star, 1951, juvenile operetta, music by Harold Wansborough (1)RPB-M
The Magic Thanksgiving Pie, 1927   RPB
Peppy Stunts and Games, 1938, with others   DLC
The Popular Christmas Book, 1927   RPB
The Red-lacquered Box, 1936,   play?   DLC
Ruth Comes Home, 1928, 3 act drama   RPB
Shirley Scintillates, 1927, 2 act comedy   RPB
"The Silver Arrow," 1935,   play?   DLC
Silver Wings for Christmas, 1938,   (1)   DLC
Sunny of Sunnyside, 1929, juvenile operetta, music by Harry L. Alford   RPB
Taffy Ann, 1936, juvenile operetta in 2 acts, music by Harold   RPB-M,WaSp
    Wansborough
Thanksgiving Hide and Seek, 1938,   young (1)   RPB
Too Much Varnish, 1927, 3 act comedy   RPB

VERA CASPARY (1904- ?) AWW

Bedelia, 1947, film adaptation
Blind Mice, prod. 1930, with Winifred Lenihan, 1931 film adaptation
Geraniums in My Window, prod. 1934, with Samuel Ornitz
Laura, 1945, prod. 1947, with George Sklar, based on her mystery novel   RPB
A Letter to Three Wives, 1949, screen adaptation
Three Husbands, 1950, screenplay with Edward Eliscu, script   NN
Wedding in Paris, prod. 1954, musical with H. May

INA LEON CASSILIS
Cheerful and Musical, 1920, (first pub. 1891) duologue   RPB
A Cheerful Companion, 1905, duologue by "Bob O' Link"   RPB
A Superior Person, 190?, duologue   RPB
Those Landladies, 1906, boarding house comic duologue for females RPB, PSS
The Two Misses Ibbetson, 1900 (1)   RPB

HARRIET DAVENPORT CASTLE (1843- ?)
Castle's School Entertainment, 4 volumes, 1887-1905   RPB
The Courting of Mother Goose, 1923 (first pub. 188?)   RPB, EEY
Picnic in Fairyland, 1899, children's cantata, music by E. S. Lorenz RPB
Santa's Prescription, 1911 (for Sunday Schools, Day Schools etc.),   RPB
    humorous Christmas cantata, music by Ira B. Wilson
Santa's Reception, 1913?, humorous Christmas cantata for Sunday   RPB
    schools, Day Schools, etc., music by Ira B. Wilson
The Suffragettes, 1914, music by Ira B. Wilson   RPB

HETTIE FITHIAN CATTELL
For the Love of Pete, 1925, "tragi-comedy of the affections," for 3 women RPB

FRANCES CAVANAH
The Glorious Wish   JPG
The Honorable Guest, 1928, "play about Japan for jr. girls"   RPB
Joy Time, 1929, young   RPB
King of the Bookcase (1)   JGH
The Knight of the Funnybone and Other Plays for Children, 1929   RPB
Lil' Black Heliotrope, 1932, for girls (1)   RPB
Mr. Bunny's Prize (first published in Child Life)   JOP
The Pine Tree's Blossoming, 1930, Christmas   RPB
Robin Hood's Enchanted Spring and Other One-Act Plays, 1930
Thanksgiving Wonders, 1929   RPB
The Transfiguration of the Gifts, 1923, pageant for Christmas   RPB
When the Moon Learned to Smile (1)   JGH

MILLIS CAVERLY
Christmas Revels, 1928, Christmas festival in 3 parts   RPB
In a Mission Garden, 1930, "play of Spanish California in 3 acts"   RPB
The Mystery of Goodacre Farm, 1946, 3 act comedy   ViU,DLC

ROSE CAYLOR
Riviera, 19?? adapt. of Molnar, typescript   NN
Uncle Vanya, prod. and pub. 1930, adaptation of Chekhov

ALICE CHADWICK
Tish, dramatization of a story by Mary Roberts Rinehart

MADELINE ANNE CHAFFEE
Business a la Mode, 1930, comedy of business   RPB
Dutch Wind and King Grisly-beard, 1929, two pantomimes   RPB
Health in a Palace, 1931, good health playlet   RPB
Memories of Ali Baba, 1931, fairy play   RPB
She Does Her Christmas Shopping Early, 1931, monologue   RPB
Spring Dreams, 1927   RPB
We Like Windmills, "play featuring Dutch child life"   HPP

AGNES CHALMERS
The King's Cupbearer, 1919, "historical morality play in 12 canticles"   RPB

MARY CHALMERS
The Making of the Constitution, with Elizabeth F. Hague, 5 acts
Nathan Hall, with Elizabeth F. Hague, 5 acts

IDA HOYT CHAMBERLAIN
Enchanted Isle, prod. 1927, musical

GRACE HILTON CHAMBERLIN
The Fortissimo Music Society, 1913, farce (1)   RPB

MARGARET CHAMPNEY
Nothing But Money

JULIA CHANDLER
The Gift, prod. 1924, with Alethea Luce

LILIAN (LILLIAN) F. CHANDLER
At the Window, 1915, comedy (1)   RPB
The Patriot Girl, 1914, 2 act patriotic comedy   RPB
When Shakespeare Struck the Town, 1913   RPB

ANNA ALICE CHAPIN (1880-1920)
The Deserters, prod. 1910, with Robert Peyton Carter (Ferguson lists Robert
    Cuitin and Robert Carten—NUC lists George C. Jenks)
The Spring Song, n.d., typescript   NN

ELIZABETH LITTLE CHAPIN
The Doll Shop, 1926, pantomime   RPB

KATHERINE GARRISON CHAPIN (1890-1977) AWW
The Lady of the Inn, Christmas play included in her collection of   RPB
    poetry, Outside of the World, 1930

R. C. CHAPIN
Pageant of Saluda, 1915, Saluda, N. C.

ALICE LOUISE WILLIAMS CHAPLIN (1887- ?)
By Hook or By Crook, 1931, 3 act comedy   RPB
Dearies, 1925, 3 act comedy for females   RPB
Her Aunt Elvira, 1931, 3 act comedy   RPB
The Hidden Name, 1920, for girls   RPB
Jack's Wife Arrives, 1922, 2 act farce   RPB
The Old Ordway House, 1931, 3 act comedy   RPB
A Play a Month for Female Characters, 1917, one-acts   RPB
Six Rehearsal-less Entertainments, 1921   RPB
Three Pegs, 1923, 3 act comedy   RPB

ALICE EUDORA CHAPMAN
Pageant of Littleton, 1914, Littleton, Mass.   RPB

CLAIRE CHAPMAN
Following the Star, 1915, Christmas pageant with Irwin Smith   RPB-M

KATHARINE LINDER CHAPMAN
The Golden Age, 1930, dramatic dance pageant of mythology
A Port of Dreams, 1928, dramatic pageant   RPB

MAXINNE CHAPMAN
The Kiddies' Recitation Book, 1926, compiled with Willis N. Bugbee
   and others   RPB

PHYLLIS CHAPMAN
Betsy Anne, 1928, New York rural life play   RPB

HELEN B. R. A. CHASE
A Child's Dream of the Bible, 1913   RPB

MARJORIE CHASE (SURDEZ)
The Man's Name, prod. 1921, with Eugene Walter
"The Whip Hand," 1928, with George S. Brooks, typed copy   NN

ESTHER H. CHEEVER
The Too Perfect Husband, 1927, comedy, 1 act and 2 scenes   RPB

ANNE CLEVELAND CHENEY
The Nameless One, 1916, 3 act poetic tragedy (pub. in 1912 as
   The Firstborn)   RPB

ANNIE M. CHERRY
The Spirit of Roanoke, 1921, pageant of Halifax County, with Helen Burch
   and A. E. Akers   MB

JEANNE YATES CHERRY (1879- ?) "LENA DALKEITH" (may be British)
Little Plays, 1907, one-acts

MYRTLE CHERRYMAN
Old Friends Together, 1905, in Clara J. Denton, Ed., All the Holidays, 1905

LILLIAN ELEANOR HAUSER CHESTER (1888- ?)
Cordelia Blossom, prod. and pub. 1914, with George Chester
It's Yours If You Can Get It, 1916, 4 act satirical farce, with George Chester

RUTH E. CHEW
The Magic Christmas Tree, 1924, "story of the first Teddy Bear"   RPB

CLARA CHILDS
The Truth Always, about George Washington (1)

IRENE M. CHILDS
Bonnie's Christmas Eve, with Jay Clay Powers   BMC

ELIZABETH A. CHIPMAN
Beverly's Triumph, 1910, 3 act mystery comedy   RPB

ALICE CHITTENDEN
Martyr, 1916, tragedy of Belgium, drama in 5 acts by Jean Lecman,   RPB
    trans. by Chittenden for the Belgium Women's War Relief Committee

CHARLOTTE BARROWS CHORPENNING (1873–1955) NWAT
Abe Lincoln—New Salem Days, 1954, historical play for children
The Adventures of Tom Sawyer, 1946   RPB
Alice in Wonderland, 1946   RPB
Between the Lines, 1916, won the Craig prize at Harvard
Cinderella, 1940
The Emperor's New Clothes, 1936, prod. 1931-2, music by   NN
    A. Lehman Engel, script
Flibberty Gibet (His Last Chance), 1952, with Nora Tully Mac Alvay
Hans Brinker and the Silver Skates, 1938
The Indian Captive, 1937
Jack and the Beanstalk, 1935
James Thurber's Many Moons, 1946   RPB
King Midas and the Golden Touch, 1950
A Letter to Santa Claus, 1938
Lincoln's Secret Messenger—boy detective to a president,   RPB
    1955, historical play
Little Black Sambo, 1939? typescript   NN
Little Black Sambo and the Tigers, 1938, prod. 1936, with Shirley Graham
    Du Bois, puppet show
Little Lincoln, 1940   MWS
Little Red Riding Hood; or, "Grandmother Slyboots," 1946

CHARLOTTE BARROWS CHORPENNING (continued)
The Magic Horn, 1954, with Anne Nicholson
Many Moons
The Prince and the Pauper, 1938 (1954 ed. at RPB)   RPB
Radio Rescue, 1938, comedy drama for young people (1954 ed. at RPB)   RPB
Rama and the Tigers, 1954, comedy-fantasy from a story by   RPB
    Helen Bannerman
The Return of Rip Van Winkle, 1938
Rhodopis, the First Cinderella, 1936, 3 acts
Rip Van Winkle, 1954, young   RPB
Robinson Crusoe, 1952
Rumpelstiltskin, 1944   UU, WU
The Secret Weapon, 1944, typewritten copy   DLC
The Sleeping Beauty, 1937, 3 acts   MCR.IdPI
The Three Bears, 1949
Tom Sawyer's Treasure Hunt, 1937

MAYME CHRISTENSEN
Christmas Week in the Intermediate Grades, 1931, poetry, plays, etc.
Christmas Week in the Primary Grades, 1930, poetry, plays, etc.   RPB
Christmas Windows, 1928, pantomime, with Flora M. Frick   RPB
Terry Had a Toothache, 1929, health play for children   RPB

FRANCES ELOISE CHRISTIAN
The Kingdom of Love, 1919, Christmas play, young   RPB

CENA BAILE CHRISTOPHER (1907- ?)
The Grand Old Man, 1931   YSP-I, MoU
The Holy Hour, poetic drama, won Longman's Green prize in   MoU
    playwriting

ALICE CHRISTY
Beefsteak and Browning, 1924

ELIZABETH FIELD CHRISTY
The Victory of Cupid, 1911   RPB

VIRGINIA WOODSON FRAME CHURCH (1880- ?)
The Bee Man (1)
Commencement Day, 1908, with Margaret Mayo, 3 act play of   IaU
    college girl life
Curtain! 1932, collection which she edited   RPB
The Heart Specialist
The Perverseness of Pamela, 1916
Pierrot by the Light of the Moon, fantasy, in Drama, 9, Feb., 1919, 139-48
The Revolt of the Dolls (1)
Shakespeare's Children, 1915, pageant, San Diego, Calif.

VIRGINIA WOODSON FRAME CHURCH (continued)
  Very Social Service, satire, in Drama, 15, Dec., 1924, 54-6+ (1)
  What Men Live By, adapt. from Tolstoy, in Drama, 12,   RPB, TAJ,EMR, LMS
    Oct.-Nov., 1921, 33-8 (also in Curtain!) (1)

HILDEGARDE E. CHURCHILL
  Right About Face, 1922, 3 act operetta for Wellesley Barnswallows, lyrics and
    libretto with Beatrice W. Jefferson, Lucile J. Barrett and others; music by
    Mary Zweizig, Rebecca Stickney and others

CARMEN CINNIRELLA
  The Unwilling Sister, 1929, first pub. 1926, melodrama   RPB

ADA CLARK
  Bouquets for Father, 1932, collection for Father's Day   RPB
  A Christmas Joke   CLP-I
  The Christmas Program Book, 1931, collection with others
  Christmas Recitations for the Grades, 1932   RPB
  Funny One-act Christmas Plays, 1935, with others   RPB
  Little Plays for Christmas, 1928, with others   RPB
  The Merry Christmas Book, 1936, with Kathryn Docter
  Mother's Day in the Primary, 1930, collection   RPB
  Next Year, 1937   CTM
  100 Christmas Recitations, 1930   RPB
  Seven Boys and Three Girls   CLP-I
  Tributes to Mother and Dad, 1937, with Lettie C. Van Derveer and   RPB
    others
  The Twins' Christmas   CLP-I
  We Believe in Santa Claus   FOA
  Your Mother and Mine, 1930, collection for Mother's Day, with others   RPB

ALICE H. CLARK
  The Church Victorious Through Love, 1921, masque, with   RPB
    Rockwell S. Brank

AUDREY CLARK
  The Quarry, 1930   CNA

CARROLLE BARBER CLARK
  The Ballad of Roaring Brook, 1908, shadow pantomime   RPB

DOROTHY CLARK
  The King's Fool, 1929, fantasy (1)   RPB
  The Vision of Sir Launfal, 1928, pageant based on poem by James R.   RPB
    Lowell, with Georgia Lyons Unverzagt

ESTELLE MERRYMAN (or MERRYMON) CLARK (may be British)
An Old Spanish Custom, 1933, 2 act operetta, with Palmer John Clark
And It Rained! 1934, operetta, music by Adele Bohling Lee, vocal score   IU
Ask the Professor, 1933, 2 act operetta, music by Adele Bohling Lee
Big Day, 1935, operetta for girls, music by Adele Bohling Lee (1)
Bittersweet Anne, 1930, 2 act operetta, with Palmer John Clark
Bugs; or, Send for Aphis! n.d., operetta, music by Adele Bohling Lee (1)
Carrie Comes to College; or, Campus Daze, 1926, 2 act operetta, with Palmer
    John Clark
Jerry of Jericho Road, 1928, 2 act operetta, music by Palmer John Clark   RPB
Lazytown, 1935, 2 act operetta, music by George A. Grant-Schaefer,   RPB
    vocal score
Magazine Princess, 1937, 2 act operetta, music by Adele Bohling Lee,   IU
    vocal score
Oh Doctor! 1931, 2 act operetta, with Palmer John Clark
Polly Make-Believe, 1932, 2 act operetta, with Carol Christopher
Top O' the World, 1940, 2 act operetta, music by Hilda Butler Farr

HEBE HALLEN CLARK
A Shoe Factory Dialogue   CSS

HELEN CLARK
At the Wishing Well, 1923, young   RPB
The Mystic Pipes, 1926, young (1)   RPB

LOTTA ALMA CLARK
Bridgewater Pageant, 1915, Bridgewater, Mass., celebrating the 75th   MB
    anniversary of Bridgewater State Normal School, prompt book
Cave Life to City Life, the pageant of a perfect city, 1915, Boston,   MB
    prompt book and scrapbook
Charlestown Pageant, 1910, 1912, Charlestown, Mass., programme-text   MB
The Ministering of the Gift, 1913, Medford, Mass. (She was director.)
National YWCA Pageant, 1913, Richmond, Va.
Old Royal House Pageant, 1915, Medford, Mass.
Pageant of American Childhood, 1913, Worcester, Mass.
Pageant of Cape Cod, 1914, Sandwich, Mass. (She was organizational
    director with William Chauncey Langdon)
Pageant of Education, 1908, Boston, Mass., with Vittoria Dallin,   MB
    programme-text (1915 version at WU) (She was director.)
Pageant of Hollis, 1916, Hollis, N. H.
Pageant of the Perfect City, 1910, Boston, Mass.   MB
Pageant of the YMCA, 1916, Boston, Mass.
The Pilgrim Pageant, pub. by Mass. Dept. of Ed., The Pilgrim   MB
    Tercentenary, 1920, pp. 74-96
Shakespeare Tercentenary Pageant, 1916, Boston, Mass.
The Torchbearers, 1917, pageant, Peterborough, N. H., Programme-text   MB
    (with Mary Cutler)
University of Wisconsin Pageant, 1914, Madison, Wisc.

MARGARET STANLEY CLARK
Wet Blanket (1)

PATTY LEE CLARK
The Admirable Miranda, 1905, "written for the Hopefully Well
    Affected Club," Westfield, Mass. (Shakespearean spoof)   RPB

PEARL FRANKLIN CLARK (See PEARL FRANKLIN)

SARAH GRAMES CLARK
At the End of the Warpath, 1929, Indian operetta for juveniles, music by MiU
    John Iroquois, vocal score
The Bamboo Box, 1933, 2 act musical comedy, music by Winifred Moore,   IU,
    vocal score   OCl
The Bandwagon, 1937, music by Arthur A. Penn   RPB
Behind the Scenes, 1926, 3 acts, young   RPB
Bobby, 1942, 2 act operetta, music by Clair Johnson   RPB
A Christmas Carol, 1936, adapted as a musical play, music by Bryceson
    Treharne
The Christmas Program Book, 1931, with others
Indian Love Charms, 1932, Amerindian choral, music by Charles   RPB
    Wakefield Cadman
It Happened in Holland, 1936, operetta for jr. h. s., music by   RPB
    Arthur A. Penn
Jewels of the Desert, 1933, 2 act musical comedy, music by Lily
    Strickland, dance by Clara Elizabeth Whips   RPB
Kathleen (The Maid of Killarney), 1939, 2 act operetta, music by Lily
    Strickland   RPB
The Lost Clown, 1933, two act juvenile operetta, music by Agnes Wright RPB
O Cho San; or, the Stolen Jade, 1928, Japanese operetta for children,   RPB
    music by Mrs. R. R. Forman
Paints and Patches, 1932, 2 act musical comedy for jr. h. s.,   IU, OCl
    music by Arthur A. Penn
Pantomime for "In the Garden"— the famous gospel song by
    C. Austin Mills, 1924
Prince of Peddlers, 1933, 2 act operetta, music by Bryceson Treharne   RPB
Ready Made Programs for Every Month, 1928
Santa Borrows Trouble, 1924, Christmas cantata, music by Ira B. Wilson   PP
The Smiling Sixpence, 1930, 2 act operetta for children, music by RPB
    Geoffrey O'Hara

SOPHIE LOUISE WEPF CLARK
Entertainments to Make Votes for Women, 1911

BENAIAH FRANKLIN CLARKE
Bless His Little Heart, 1927, 3 act farce   RPB

CHARLOTTE LOUISE KIRKLAND CLARKE (1865-1913)   RPB
 Cinderella, 1913, dramatization in 4 acts, adapted especially for
  presentation in the sign language, by Mrs. Lottie K. Clarke, Vancouver,
  Washington School for the Deaf

EDNAH PROCTOR CLARKE
 The Revolt of Santa Claus, in Ladies Home Journal, 19, Dec., 1901, 19 (1)

ELLA A. CLARKE
 Choosing a Husband
 Columbia's Army, 1901?, temperance operetta (1)   RPB

FRANCES ELIZABETH CLARKE
 Oberon and Titania, 1915, adaptation of the fairy scenes in Shakespeare's RPB
  A Midsummer Night's Dream

HELEN ARCHIBALD CLARKE (1860-1926)
 Balaustion's Euripedes, 1912, dramatic version of "Balaustion's Adventure"
  and "Aristophanes' Apology" by Robert Browning, 4 acts, pub. in Poet
  Lore, 26, New Year, 1915, 1-37
 A Little Book of Poets' Parleys, 1903, selections arranged in dialogue   RPB
  form (She also did translations with Charlotte Porter of Maeterlinck,
  which were pub. in Poet Lore.)

LOIS W. CLARKE
 Elsie's Triumph, 1928, 2 act comedy   RPB
 No Room in the Inn, 1928, Christmas   RPB
 When Day Ran Away, 1928, young (1)   RPB

VIOLET CLARKE
 The Power of Flattery, in Smart Set, 8, Oct., 1902, 143-5 (1)

KATHERINE COLES CLAY
 Home Sweet Home, 1908, "Maccabee playlet"   RPB

EDITH MARTIN CLAYES
 Pedigree, 1924, comedy   RPB

ALICE J. CLEATER
 Christmas Praises, 1909, Christmas service with Charles H. Gabriel,   RPB-M
  Edith Sanford Tillotson and Lizzie De Armond
 The Sweetest Story Ever Told, 1907, Christmas service with   RPB-M
  Charles H. Gabriel and Edith Sanford Tillotson
 Tidings of Great Joy, 1903, Christmas service, with others   RPB-M

DOROTHY CLEATHER
 A Handy Book of Plays for Girls, 1915, one acts   NN

BERTHA JOHANNA CLEMANS (1875- ?)
The Awakening of Mr. Smith, 1916, missionary play   RPB

MAUDE MOORE CLEMENT (or MOORE-CLEMENT)
The Children of Tomorrow

CLEMENTIA (Sister of Mercy, St Patrick's Academy, Chicago)
(MARY EDWARD FEEHAN) (1878- ?)
Frolic of the Bees and the Butterflies, 1910   RPB
Happy Days, 1910   RPB
Nancy, 1911   RPB
One of His Little Ones, 1910   RPB
Roses for the King, 1932, Christmas   RPB
Sic itur ad astra, 1912   RPB
There Was No Room at the Inn, 1911   RPB
Thy Kingdom Come; or, the Ninth Promise Fulfilled, 1915   RPB
The Twinkette, One of His Little Ones, Frolic of the Bees and the   RPB
   Butterflies, three plays, 1933
A Wonderful Christmas Gift, 1916   RPB
Young King Cole, 1911   RPB

CLAUDINE E. CLEMENTS
The First Nowell, 1926, " for Christmas tide"   RPB
A Troubador's Dream, "play for Christmastide in one act and 3 episodes
   and an epilogue," in Drama, 16, November, 1925, 57-8

ROSE WEAVER CLEVENGER
Christian Endeavor Playlets, ed. by Henrietta Heron, 1928, a contributor RPB
More Christian Endeavor Playlets, ed. by E. W. Thornton,   RPB
   1929, a contributor

HELEN C. CLIFFORD
Alice's Blighted Profession, 1919, sketch for girls   RPB
That Parlor Maid, 1922, 3 act comedy   RPB
Wait and See, 1919, 3 act comedy drama   RPB
We Moderns, 1926, 2 act comedy   RPB
Whose Widow, 1919, comedy (1)   RPB

LUCY LANE CLIFFORD ("MRS. W. K. CLIFFORD") (? -1929)
The Likeness of the Night, 4 acts, in Anglo-Saxon Review, 4,
   March, 1900, 38-93
A Long Duel, 1902, "serious comedy in 4 acts," in Fortnightly, 76,   RPB
   Supplement, Sept., 1901
Madeline, 1905
The Search Light, in Nineteenth Century, 53, Jan., 1903, 159-72 (1)
A Supreme Moment, in Nineteenth Century, 46, July, 1899, 153-72 (1)
Three Plays, 1910   RPB
A Woman Alone, 1915, 3 acts, in Nineteenth Century, 75, May, 1914,   RPB
   1144-1184

MARGARET ELLEN CLIFFORD
Can You Hear Their Voices? 1931, with Hallie Flanagan, "play of our times,"
    based on a story by Whittaker Chambers in New Masses   RPB, FCP
The Sleeping Beauty, 1928, "a fairy tale retold " (1)   RPB

ETHEL CLIFTON
For Value Received, 1923, melodrama

MARY A. DELANO CLIFTON
Der Two Subprises, 191? Dutch farce by M.A.D. Clifton (1)   RPB
In the Wrong Box, 1883? Ethiopian farce by M.A.D. Clifton (1)   RPB
Schnapps, 188? Dutch farce by M.A.D. Clifton (1)   RPB

INEZ FUNK CLINTON
The Resurrection of Peter, 1925, short drama for the Easter season   RPB

LYNNE FOX CLINTON
A Night at Dinner, 1914, skit   RPB

BELLE BROWN CLOKEY
Circle Three Sees a Vision, 1921   RPB
Granny of the Hills, 1915, home missionary play   RPB

MRS. J. B. CLOPTON
Let's Debate, 1930, short sketch with a purpose for high schools   RPB

FLORENCE CLOTHIER (1903- ?)
She Canna Perish, 1926, play of the Labrador Coast, mimeograph   RPB, VET
    copy (1933 ed. at RPB)

KATHARINE THATCHER CLUGSTON (1892- ?)
Barnum Returns; or the New American Museum, 1936, historical   RPB
    vaudeville show, Federal Theater Project
The Bone of Convention, 1927, with George Freedley, typescript   NN
The Colonel's Commupence
Finished, 1931, comedy, prod. in 1928 under title, These Days (1)   RPB, BYP
Tail Wags Dog, 193? satirical extravaganza, mimeo playscript   KU
These Days, prod. 1928, typescript and promptbook   NN

MRS. GEORGE C. COBB
Just Advertise, 1923, comedy drama in short episodes (1)   RPB, JMP

JOSEPHINE M. COBB
The Oxford Affair, 1924 (c. 1896) with Jennie E. Paine, 3 act comedy   RPB

LUCY M. COBB
Gaius and Gaius Jr., 1923, comedy of plantation days, pub. in The   KCF-II
    Carolina Magazine, Chapel Hill, N. C., Nov., 1927 (1)
A Gift for Penelope, 1955, tragedy of Blackbeard's time   NcD, Nc

SUSAN HARRISON COBB
Paging Mr. Tweedy, 1934, comedy (1)   RPB
Sally's Hat Shop, 1931, comedy for women (1)   RPB
Tourists Accomodated, 1927, 3 act comedy   RPB

EVE OWEN COCHRAN
A Half Hour at the Gate and Other One Act Plays, 1930   RPB
Wilderness Rose, 1914, 4 acts, "especially adapted for use of American   RPB
    historical societies and chapters of the DAR"

MAUD COCKRELL
Golliwog in Fairyland; or, How Edward the Teddy Became a Knight, 1921 (1)
The Innkeeper's Shirt, 1925, fairy play

MARIE E. COE
The Speeders, 1929, 3 act comedy with Henry B. Lister and   RPB
    Lydia Warren Lister (previously titled The Lawbreakers)

MRS. RUDOLPH COFFEE (See MINNIE SUCKERBERG JAFFA)

GERTRUDE WILSON COFFIN
Magnolia's Man, 1929, comedy of mountain people (1)   KCC
Plays
A Shotgun Splicin' 1927, mountain comedy (1)   KCF-III

LIDA LAVINIA COGHLAN (1860- ?)
The Same Man, 1909, comedy sketch (revised in 1933 by Shirley Kaye   RPB
    as "miniature one act play for two girls")

CARRIE W. COLBURN
His Last Chance; or, the Little Joker, 1895, 3 act comedy   RPB
A Romantic Rogue, 1902? comedy drama (1)   RPB

ANNE COLBY
The Last of the Courtesans, 1924, synopsis of a photographic play   RPB
    about Lola Montez

ELEANOR COLBY
A Vision of Youth, in Ladies Home Jorunal, 30, March, 1913, 91+ (1)

GERTRUDE K. COLBY
The Conflict, 1921, health masque in pantomime

GRETCHEN COLBY
The First Easter Bunny (1)   SSH-I

MARION IDA COLBY
Early Seminary Days (the senior play, "The First Days," with   RPB
      Betsey Farley, presented by the class of 1911, Mt. Holyoke College)
      typewritten copy

ALICE H. COLE
The Compromise, 1926 or earlier (1)
The Golden Will and Three Other One Act Plays, 1926 or earlier
The Return of Hope, 1926 or earlier (1)

CATHERINE COLE
The Flapper's Recital, 1927, humorous monologue   RPB

EDNA EARLE COLE
The Good Samaritan and Other Bible Stories Dramatized, 1915   RPB

ELIZABETH COLE
The Tale of the Griffin, 1909, musical comedy presented by the class RPB-M
      of 1909, Mt. Holyoke College, music by Clara Searle

IDA B. COLE
Wagner at the Smallville Woman's Club, 1906, entertainment   RPB
      in one scene

JOSEPHINE R. COLE
Cooperation, dialogue   CSS
The Red Ribbon, dialogue   CSS
Socialist Dialogues and Recitations, 1913, comp. with Grace Silver   RPB
The Snow House, dialogue   CSS

MRS. F. DOUGLAS COLEMAN
The Call to Service, 1929, "four act drama full of laughter, romance RPB
      and tears, played before the Woman's Mite Missionary Convention,
      Covington, Ky., Aug., 1929"

EDNA A. COLLAMORE
The Crowning Glory, 1924, comedy (1)   RPB

DR. MARIE GOLDMAN COLLETTI-REINA
Thoughts From the Heart, 1925 (includes "Through Darkness to   RPB
      Darkness," four act drama; and "The First Day of Aranjuez (happiness)"
      —a one-act dramatic sketch)

CONSTANCE COLLIER (1878-1955)
Peter Ibbetson, 1930, lyric drama in 3 acts from novel by George du   RPB
      Maurier; libretto by Collier and Deems Taylor; music by Deems Taylor

ANNE COLLINS
    Bottled, 1928, with Alice Timoney, prompt book   NN
    Wilderness Road, 1930, with Alice Timoney, 3 act comedy drama   RPB

LILLIAN F. COLLINS
    The Little Theatre in School, 1930, collection, includes 4 plays written with
        children

LOUISE COLLINS
    The Modern Autocrat, comedy of cross purposes, in Smart Set, 8, Dec., 1902,
        157-8 (1)

MARIE COLLINS
    The Utopians, 1913, all college operetta, Wellesley, with Ruth Van   RPB-M
        Blarcom

MARY T. COLLINS
    Out of Bounds, 1929, 3 act comedy drama   RPB

RUTH COFFIN COLLINS
    Pageant of Chicago, 1914   DLC

EMOGENE STODDARD COLMAN
    Day in Romance-land, pageant, in Playground, 18, August, 1924, 287

BERNICE E. COMEY
    Radio Complications, 1926, 3 act comedy   RPB

FLORENCE CROCKER COMFORT
    The Birthday Pie, 1941, "animated cartoon musical playlet, make-believe for
        children," music by Jessie Thomas (1)
    Golden Cornstalk Goes Home, "musical make-believe in 2 acts"   JNS
    The Kitchen Clock, 1927, "musical make-believe," music by Herbert   MiU
        E. Hyde
    The Magic Voice; America's Call for Better Speech, 1918, "make-believe" (1)
    Peter Pickers' Plight, 1933, music by Hazel Watts Cooke   RPB-M
    The Sing-a-Song Man, "make-believe for little children"   JOP
    Springtime and Summer, 1922, "suitable for both children and adults,   RPB
        make-believe of flowers, birds and butterflies, written for Chicago
        chapter of Wildlife Preservation Society of America"
    Twelve Short Plays Written for Children, 195?   MiU

ANNA OLCOTT COMMELIN
    Atala, an American idyl, 1902, poetic dramatization of the work of
        Chateaubriand   RPB

ELLA BROWN DOWNEY COMMONS (MRS. JOHN ROGERS COMMONS)
The Merman's Pipe   BPD

FANNY AMANDA COMSTOCK (1854- ?)
A Dickens Dramatic Reader, 1913
A Dramatic Version of Greek Myths and Hero Tales, 1912   RPB
A Dramatization of Longfellow's "The Courtship of Miles   RPB
    Standish," 1911
A Dramatization of Sir Walter Scott's "Lady of the Lake, 1911   RPB

ISABELLA HOWE FISKE CONANT (1874- ?)
Acropolis, 1920, masque of a city, New York   MB
An Evening Musicale, by Isabella Howe Fiske, in Smart Set, 10, July, 1903,
    111-4 (1)
Clouds of the Sun, by Isabella Howe Fiske, in Poet Lore, 15, 1904, 52-74
A Comedy of the Exile, by Isabella Howe Fiske, in Poet Lore, 17, Spring,
    1906, 51-8 (1)
Gabriel, 1912, pageant of vigil, Portland, Maine   RPB
Pageant of the Charles River, 1914   DLC
Pageant of Fellowship, 1916, Pittsfield, Mass., by Isabella Howe Fiske
The Pageant of the Tree, 1910, "presented in aid of the child welfare   MB
    work of the Fathers and Mothers Club, Boston"
Persephone, 1914, pageant at the Bishop's School, San Diego, Calif.   RPB
Will o' the World, 1916, Shakespearean tercentenary masque,   RPB
    Wellesley, Mass.

ISABEL CONDIE
Mother Goose and Her Friends   WPP

BERNICE CONE
Pageant of Fairmont, 1917, Fairmont, Minn.

MARGARET LYNCH CONGER
The Brightness of His Rising, 1926, Christmas miracle play   NN
The Brown Bull of Norway, 1924   RPB
The Festival of Proserpina, 1924   RPB
Folk Story Plays for Children, 1920, one-acts   RPB
Lake George Pageant, 1912, Lake George, New York
Night and Morning, 1925, Easter miracle play   NN
Pageant of Greenwich Village, 1912
St. Francis of Assisi, 1925, Christmas masque (1)   DLC

MARTHA MORTON CONHEIM (See MARTHA MORTON)

HARRIET N. CONNELL
At the First Tee   APS
At the Sign of the Pewter Jug, 1924, 3 act comedy   RPB
The Coming of Caroline, 1928, comedy drama   RPB
The Cousin from Coon Ridge, 1927, 3 act comedy   RPB
Ducks, 1928, 3 act comedy   RPB
Here Comes the Bride, 1927, comedy (1)   RPB
Mrs. Rushington's Rest Cure, 1926, comedy (1)   RPB
No Men Admitted, 1929, 3 act comedy for women   RPB
Oh, Didn't It Rain! 1928, 2 act farce   RPB
Parking Place for Papa, 1934, 3 act comedy for women, with Kathryn   RPB
    Wire Hammond
Petticoat Politics, 1926, comedy (1)   RPB
The Ranch on Sunset Trail, 1929, 3 act comedy   RPB
Terry the Terrible, 1931, 3 act comedy drama, with Kathyrn Wire   RPB
    Hammond
To Meet Miss Mary Dulanne, 1929, comedy (1)   RPB
Treasure Farm, 1926, 3 act comedy drama   RPB
Well, Did You Ever? 1929, 3 act comedy, with Kathyrn Wire Hammond   RPB
What Price Ancestors? 1930, 3 act comedy drama   RPB
When They Built the D. and R.G., 1924, 3 act comedy   RPB

LOUISE FOX CONNELL
Queen Bee, prod. 1929, with Ruth Hawthorne

JEAN CONOVER
The Passion Play, 1929, Chicago, dramatized and arranged by Conover RPB

FLORENCE CONVERSE (1871- ?)
The Blessed Birthday, 1917, Christmas miracle play (also in Garments RPB
    of Praise)
Garments of Praise, 1921, collection, "miracle cycle"   RPB
The Holy Night, 1922, masque to be performed by young children (with
    music by Kate Stearns Page in the 1929 edition)
The Madman and the Wrecking Crew, 1939, morality for Holy CrossDay RPB
A Masque of Sibyls, 1910   RPB
Santa's Conversazione, 1921, All Saints miracle play (also in Garments RPB
    of Praise)
Soul's Medicine, 1921, Witsuntide miracle play of healing (also in   RPB
    Garments of Praise)
The Three Gifts, 1924 (1)   RPB, BTG
Thy Kingdom Come, 1921 (also in Garments of Praise and in Atlantic   RPB
    Monthly, 127, March, 1921, 352-62, Easter play (1)

MARY PARKER CONVERSE
The Christmas Story, 192? "play in 3 scenes with a musical setting" RPB

"OLIVE CONWAY"
  Becky Sharp, 1924, adaptation of Thackeray (1)   RPB, MOP
  Costume Plays, 1926   WaU, DLC
  The King's Waistcoat, 1926 (1)   MOP, DLC
  Mimi (from "Scenes de la vie de Boheme")   MOP-3rd
  The Starlight Widow, 1929, 3 act comedy   OCl, DLC
  Tip and Run (1)   OAT-III
  Women Do Things Like That, in J. W. Marriott, Ed., The Best One Act
      Plays of 1931

ALICE CARTER COOK (1868- ?)
  Komateekay, 1936, folk play, based on a Liberian legend, in Poet Lore,   RPB
      43, no. 2, 1936, 151-60 (1)
  Michal, 1922, playlet of time of David   RPB

CORONA RAYLE COOK
  Capturing the Christmas Spirit, 1937, modern Christmas drama (1)   DLC
  The Dawn, 1937, Easter drama (1)   DLC
  The Golden Rule in Courtship, 1928   EMR

ESTELLE COOK
  "As the Twig Is Bent," 1917, rural school drama   DHEW
  The Hero of the Gridiron, 1908, 5 act college comedy   RPB
  Kindling the Hearth Fire, 1915, rural drama   RPB
  Partners; or, Building the Community Church, 1917   DLC

FRANCES A. COOK
  Seven Keys, 1920, health crusade playlet   RPB

MILDRED EMILY COOK
  The Adoration of the Kings and Shepherds, 1922, pageant of the   RPB
      Nativity, arranged by Cook

RUBY COOK
  But This Is Different, 1926, farce (1)   RPB

CONSTANCE COTTIN COOKE
  Elsie in Mother Goose Land   FMC
  Friends in Need, 2 acts   JPG
  In the Days of Robin Hood   FMC
  The Princess and the Pea   FMC

HAZEL WATTS COOKE
  Kay and Gerda; or, the Snow Queen, 1925, juvenile operetta, adapted   RPB-M
      from Hans Christian Andersen
  Peter Pickers' Plight, c1933, "musical make believe," music by Cooke;   RPB-M
      book and lyrics by Florence Crocker Comfort

MARJORIE BENTON COOKE (1876-1920)

At Mme. Newberry's, 1903, monologue	RPB
The Case of Sophronia, 1906, for girls (1)	RPB
A Christian Soldier, 1907, monologue	IaU
A Christmas Benefit, 1906 (1)	RPB
A Court Comedy, 1930 or earlier	
Cupid Plays Coach, 1903, monologue	RPB
A Dark-Brown Diplomat, 1903, monologue	RPB
Dramatic Episodes, 1904, collection of one acts	RPB
The Fairy Ring, 1906, young (1)	RPB
The Finer Shades of Honor, 1906, for 8th grade (1)	RPB
The First Thanksgiving Dinner, 1906, for grades 6-12 (1)	RPB
Her Day at Home, 1903, monologue	RPB
Heroines, 1907, monologue	NN, IU
Highly Colored Sketch, 193?	RPB
Home, 1933, 3 acts	RPB
In the Good Greenwood, 1906, for boys (1)	RPB,WWS,WWY
In the Merry Month of May, 1903, monologue	RPB
Manners and Mode, 1930 or earlier	
Modern Monologues, 1909 (c1903)	RPB
More Modern Monologues, 1907	RPB
On Woman's Rights, 1903, monologue	RPB
The Optimist, 1903, monologue	RPB
A Page From the Past, 1906, for girls (1)	RPB
The Redemption of Anthony, 1911	RPB
The Roll Call of Heroes, 1906, Decoration Day entertainment	RPB
Romeo of the Rancho (1)	
School Plays	
A Springtime Fantasy, 1900, young, Easter (1)	RPB
Tit For Tat, 1906, young (1)	RPB
When Knights Were Bold, 1906, school play (1)	RPB
When Love Is Young, 1928 (1)	MiD
When Morning Breaks, 193?	RPB

JULIA COOLEY (See JULIA COOLEY ALTROCCHI)

JANE TOY COOLIDGE (See JANE TOY)

RUTH BURLEIGH DAME COOLIDGE (1880- ?)

The Pageant of the Mystic, 1930, Medford, Mass.	RPB
The Pageant of the Royall House, 1915, Medford, Mass., typed copy	MB, MH

"SUSAN COOLIDGE" (See SARAH CHAUNCEY WOOLSEY)

KATHLEEN READ COONTZ

Christmas at the Old Lady's Shoe, 1930, young   RPB
Living Pages from Washington's Diary, 1931, "candle-time reverie"   DLC
That Blooming Boy, 1931, play of the Revolution   RPB
The View From the Window, 1931, George Washington pageant
Washington Returns, 1931, pageant

ANNA D. COOPER

The Courtin', 1906, illustrated pantomime based on poem by J. R.   RPB
    Lowell
Fedalma's Dance, 1907, illustrated pantomime, scene from "The   NN
    Spanish Gipsy," (sic) a poem by George Eliot
The Gypsy's Warning, 1907, illustrated pantomime   RPB
Hark, Hark My Soul, 1907, illustrated pantomime   RPB
Miss Huldah's Offer, 1907, illustrated pantomime   RPB
My Country 'Tis of Thee, 1907, illustrated pantomime   RPB
Paradise and the Peri, illustrated pantomime, selection from "Lalla
    Rookh," by Thomas Moore

CLARA ETTA COOPER   (1868- ?)

Tableau and Pantomime Entertainments for School or Public   RPB
    Performance, 1914, with Laura M. Parsons, Bertha Currier Porter
    and others

MIRIAM DENNESS COOPER

The Canticles of Mary, 1930, Christmas mystery play   RPB
The Gleaner Valiant, 1930, Old Testament miracle play   RPB
He Liveth, 1927, Easter mystery play   RPB
The Quest of the Flame, 1930, "play in the manner of a medieval   OO, DLC
    miracle"
The Wrestler at Jabbok, 1927, Old Testament mystery play   NN

JENNIE FREEMAN COPELAND   (1879- ?)

Pageant of Boston, in 3 parts, in New England Magazine, 54, March,   MB
    1916, 115-26

ELEANOR COPENHAVER

The Glory of the Task, 1927, "pageant of woman's growing heritage,"   RPB
    with Laura Scherer Copenhaver

LAURA SCHERER COPENHAVER

The Glory of the Task, 1927, "pageant of woman's growing heritage,"   RPB
    with Eleanor Copenhaver
The Heritage of the Child, 1923, "pageant of religious education"   RPB
Let's Be Friends, 19?? "little play of China and America and every   NN
    land," with Katharine Scherer Cronk
The Search for the Light, 19?? "pageant of man's quest for God," with   OO
    Katharine Scherer Cronk

LAURA SCHERER COPENHAVER (continued)
  Short Pageants for the Sunday School, 1929
  The Striking of America's Hour, 1925, first pub. 1919, with Katharine   RPB
    Scherer Cronk and Mathilde A. Vossler
  The Way, 1923, "pageant of Japan," with Katharine S. Cronk
  The Way of Peace, 1924, with Katharine S. Cronk and Ruth Mougrey   RPB
    Worrell, pageant

ELIZABETH COPMANN
  Waitin', 1927, Little Theatre Tournament

ELIZABETH FRANCES CORBETT (1887- ?) AWW
  The After-glow, in Poet Lore, 36, Summer, 1925, 311-6 (1)
  The Hanger Back, in Poet Lore, 41, Spring, 1930, 91-104 (1)

ELEANOR CORDE
  An American Butterfly, 1912, 4 act comedy   RPB
  Dean Swift, 1922, 4 act drama   DLC

IDA CORDY
  Love at First Sound, 1926, farce (1)   RPB

MILDRED CORELL
    (All written with Irma Liccione)
  Animated Toys (1)   SBD
  The Conscience Elf (1)   SBD
  Dr. Bluejay's Patient (1)   SBD
  A Halloween Nutting Party (1)   SBD
  The March Wind (1)   SBD
  Safety First (1)   SBD
  The Snow-man (1)   SBD
  Spare the Trees! (1)   SBD
  Thanksgiving in the Barn (1)   SBD
  William and the Sandman (1)   SBD

MAUDE S. CORNEAU
  General George Washington (1)   SGW

ELIZABETH CORNELL
  The Starter, 1930, health play, won first prize in Mass. Tuberculosis   RPB
    Assoc. Contest, 1918 (1)

MARY TAYLOR CORNISH
  Juvenile Plays and Readings, 1929
  More Mother Goose Plays, Book II, 1926   RPB
  Mother Goose Kiddie Plays, 1926, Book III   RPB
  Mother Goose Plays, 1926, Book I   RPB

MARY TAYLOR CORNISH (continued)
Three Little Runaway Trees, 1925, Christmas, 2 acts   RPB
Tommy's Thanksgiving Dinner, 1925, for young actors   RPB
When Turkes Turned the Tables   JPR

MARY CORSE
The Magnet

LOUISE CORTIS
One For All, prod. 1927, with Ernest Cortis

EDITH ISHAM COULTER
Mimi Lights the Candle, 1926 "Christmas uplift play," 2nd Samuel   RPB
    French prize in the national contest of the Gen. Fed. of Women's
    Clubs (1)

MAY ELLA COUNTRYMAN (1882- ?)
Hiram Jones' Bet, 1915, farce (1)   RPB
Miss Parkington, 1912, farce (1)   RPB
The Rebellion of Mrs. Barclay, 1912, "comedy of domestic love"   RPB
Which One Won? 1909, 2 act comedy   NcU

ZELLAH WALL COVINGTON
For Her Sister's Honor, 1907, melodrama (1)   RPB
Heads Up, prod. 1929? with Margaret Mayo
The Poor Simp, 1935, revised by Margaret Mayo and Nathaniel Edward RPB
    Reeid
Second Childhood, 1925, 3 act farce, with Jules Simonson   RPB
Some Baby! prod. 1915, with Jules Simonson

SADA COWAN (1883-1943)
Auf Wiedersehen, 1937, anti-Nazi (1)   FCP
The Ball and Chain, 1930, in Pomp and Other Plays (1)   NN
"Forbidden Heaven," shooting script from typewritten copy,   NN
    screenplay by Cowan from story by Christine Jope-Slade
In the Morgue, 1920, in Forum, 55, April, 1916, 399-407 and in Pomp SLC
    and Other Plays
The Investigation
The Moonlit Way, in Theodore Johnson, Ed. Ten International One-act
    Plays, 1937 (1)
Pomp and Other Plays, 1926   RPB
Sintram of Skagerrak, 1930, also in Pomp and Other Plays (1)   MRO,CSP-I
The State Forbids, 1915, also in Pomp and Other Plays (1)   RPB
Strangers, in Smart Set, 42, March, 1914, 115-6 (1)
A Woman's Touch, comedy   JAB

BESS SHERMAN COWDEN
Cinderella from Hong Kong, 1927, stunt for men or boys   RPB
The Garden of Happiness, 1931, instructive play for children   RPB
Oh, Hamlet, Hamlet, where have you been? 1923, "laughable burlesque" RPB
Secrets of Long Ago, 1926, " novel sketch"   RPB
Turning In on the Past, 1926, "novel sketch on the memories of the   RPB
    past (apologies to James Whitcomb Riley)"

CARRIE A. COWDEN
Uncle Sam's Pageant, in Journal of Education, 79, May 21, 1914, 579-80

JANE COWL (1883?-1950) NAW NWAT
Daybreak, prod. 1917, with Jane Murfin, 3 act melodrama, typescript   NN
    (MH has description of characters, staging, props, etc.)
Hervey House, prod. 1935, with Reginald Lawrence
Information Please, prod. 1918, with Jane Murfin, 3 acts, typed copy   DLC
The Jealous Moon, prod. 1928, with Theodore Charles, typed copy (1)   DLC
Lilac Time, 1917, with Jane Murfin, war play
Smilin' Through, 1924, prod. 1919, With Jane Murfin (original author   RPB
    listed as "Allan Langdon Martin")

FLORENCE A. COWLES
Where the Lane Turned, 1912, "rural comedy drama in 4 acts"   RPB

ETHEL LOUISE COX
Julian and Other Poems, lyrical and dramatic, 1925
Poems Lyric and Dramatic, 1904   RPB

MABEL CRAMPTON COX
Nobody's Child, 1935, Christmas pageant
The Soul of Christmas, 1932   RPB
The Sweetest Story Ever Told, 1930, Christmas pageant   RPB

NANCY BURNEY COX
It Couldn't Happen to Us, 1924, prod. Pasadena Community Playhouse
Tugging, in Drama, 15, Feb., 1925, 107-9 (1)

CLOVIS COXE
Three Ghosts Walk, in Sewanee Review, 31, July, 1923, 281-4 (1)

DELPHINE HARRIS COY
Falicity's Hope Chest, 1931, "rural comedy drama" (1)   RPB
Imperfect Peace, 1932 (1)   RPB
The Parking Place, 1931, "character comedy" (1)   RPB
The Rainbow Fountain and The Harp of Apollo, 1930, "a pool pageant   RPB
    and a Greek pastoral fete for physical education activities"

CLARA V. COYLE
  Hope, Easter play   JPP-I

WINIFRED COZZENS
  Mother Pays, 1926, with Leslie Carter, comedy (1)   RPB

MATTIE CRABTREE
  The Book of the Dicky County Pageant, 1917, pub. by Dickey County
      Leader, Ellendale, N. D., 1917 (She was director.)
  Enchanted Summer   WPP

(ANNA) ANNE ABBOT THROOP CRAIG (1869- ?)
  "Am dhord Fhiann," 1913, Irish historic pageant (Also in   NN, OC
      Book of the Irish Historic Pageant)
  Book of the Irish Historic Pageant, 1913   RPB
  The Dramatic Festival, 1912, collection of one-acts   RPB
  The Fire That Quenched Beltaire's, 1926   MH
  Passing of Dana's People, dramatic cantata, in Poet Lore, 35, Winter, 1924,
      605-11
  The Well of Hazels, allegory, in Poet Lore, 34, Autumn, 1923, 429-44 (1)

GRACE E. CRAIG
  The Spirit of Christmas, 1920   RPB

MRS. MARION CRAIG-WENTWORTH (See MRS. MARION
  CRAIG WENTWORTH)

PEARL MARY TERESA RICHARDS CRAIGIE
  ("MRS. CRAIGE") (1867-1906) AWW
  (All of her plays were published under the name of "JOHN OLIVER
      HOBBES")
  The Ambassadors, 1898, 4 act comedy   RPB
  The Bishop's Move, prod. 1903, with Murray Carson, 3 act comedy RPB
  The Fool's Hour, "the first act of a comedy," with George Moore, in
      Yellow Book, 1, April, 1894, 253-72 (1)
  Osbern and Ursyne, pub. 1900, 3 acts, in Anglo Saxon Review, 1, June,
      1899, 124-75
  A Repentance, 1899 (1)
  The Wisdom of the Wise, 1900, 3 act comedy

EDITH JANICE CRAINE (1881- ?)
  Pharaoh's Knob, 1919, comedy (1)

ROSEMARY CRAMB
  The Flapper and Her Friends, 1928, written for radio production (1) RPB
  Modern Ideas, 1928, written for radio production (1)   RPB

IRENE JEAN CRANDALL

Beyond the Gate, 1916, 2 act morality play	RPB
A Cabin Courtship, 1921, 3 act comedy	RPB
The Fairy Woods, 1920, young	RPB
The First Club Meeting, 1933 (1)	RPB
For Freedom, 1918 (1)	RPB
The Great Man, 1940 (1)	
Hands All Around, 1918, patriotic play (1)	RPB
The Last Rehearsal, 1919, comedy (1)	RPB
Memories, 1925	RPB
Milestones of Modes and Melodies, 1934, "fashion show in a prologue and 12 episodes"	
My Lady's Shawl, 1936, "pageant of the shawls of many countries"	DLC
Smile a While, 1935, 3 act comedy	DLC
Smouldering Fires, 1927, romantic comedy (1)	RPB
Sparkling Lucia, 1926 (1)	RPB
Tea and Politics, 1920, comedy (1)	
Voice and Gesture, 1926, with selections for dramatic reading	

ELEANOR MAUD CRANE

The Bachelor Maid's Reunion, 1906, entertainment (1)	RPB
The Best Man, 1910, comedy (1)	RPB
Billy's Bungalow, 1910, 3 act comedy	RPB
Encores and Extras, 1920, collection with others	RPB
Fads and Fancies, 1917, "sketch for girls" (1)	RPB
Fun in the Farm House, 1913, entertainment	RPB
Her Victory, 1920, comedy (1)	RPB
"His Soul," 1922 (1)	RPB
"The Honor of the Class," 1912, "schoolroom sketch for girls" (1)	RPB
In the Ferry House, 1906, "character sketches in one act and one scene"	RPB
Just for Fun," 1899, "up-to-date society comedy in 3 acts"	RPB
A Little Savage, 1907, "military comedy in 3 acts"	NN
The Lost New Year, 1897, 2 scenes, young	RPB
Men, Maids and Match-makers, 1901, "up-to-date comedy in 3 acts"	RPB
Next Door, 1906, "comedy of today"	RPB
A Pair of Idiots, 1902, 2 act comedy	RPB
Peggy's Predicament, 1915, farce for girls (1)	RPB
The Rainbow Kimona, 1908, 2 act comedy for women	RPB
Raps, 1911, vaudeville sketch	RPB
The Real Thing, 1911, "up-to-date comedy in 3 acts"	RPB
A Regular Flirt, 1903, "up-to-date society comedy in 5 acts"	RPB
When a Man's Single, 1905, "rural society comedy in 3 acts"	RPB
Ye Quilting Party of Long Ago, 1935	
Ye Village Skewl of Long Ago, 1904, entertainment	RPB

ELIZABETH GREEN CRANE
Are You Men? 1923, 4 act poetic drama   RPB
Berquin, 1897 (orig. pub. 1891) 5 act poetic tragedy   RPB
The Imperial Republic, 1902, " drama of the day," poetic tragedy   RPB
The Necken, 1913, poetic drama   RPB

MABEL H. CRANE
At the Milliner's, 1916, comedy (1)   RPB
The Girls, 1916, comedy (1)   RPB
Romance By Schedule, 1917, comedy for females (1)   RPB, JET
A Rumpus on Olympus, 1915, comedy (1)   RPB

MILDRED CRANK
Brass, 1928-9

ALICE CRARY
The Holy Scenes of Christmas, in Ladies Home Journal, 20, Nov., 1903, 32 (1)

BESS J. CRARY
The Boy, 1922, prod. Pasadena Community Playhouse

LILLIAN J. CRAW
Out of the Past, 1926, pageant of the Negro race   RPB

CAROLINE ALATHEA STICKNEY CREEVEY (1843-1920)
Ninepin Club; or, Flora the Queen of Summer, with Margaret   HBP
  Sangster (1)
A Thanksgiving Dream, with Margaret E. Sangster (1)   HBP

BEATRICE CREIGHTON
Little Plays for Little Folks, 1931   RPB
Runaway Clowns   BPC

HELEN COALE CREW (1866-1941)
The Door   DPC
The Password   JOP

CATHERINE CREWS
Damaging Evidence, 1924, comedy (1)   RPB

DOROTHY CRICHTON
As Ye Sew, 1921, "Talking Doll Missionary Play" (1)   RPB

AGNES LOUISE CRIMMINS

The Man Without a Country, 1918, with Elizabeth McFadden, based on   RPB
    the story by Edward Everett Hale

"Mrs. Tompkins," 1911, 3 act farce   NN

The Pride of the Family, 1918 (1)   RPB

She Knows Better Now, 1918, 3 act farce   RPB

ALICE KEENEN CRIPPS

The Hired Man's Courtship, 1921, 2 act comedy drama   NN

Pat Entertains, 1925, comedy entertainment (1)   RPB

JESSIE GERTRUDE CRISTE

The Earth Child, 1906, "fairy pantomime in one scene"   RPB

LUCILE CRITES (SLIGH) (1885- ?)

Apartment for Rent, 1932, comedy (1)   RPB

The Athletic Hero, 1928, comedy (1)   RPB

Bachelors Forever, 1924, comedy (1)   RPB

Betty Entertains the Minister, 1933   RPB

Catherine Explains, 1927 (1)   RPB

Chairs and Callers, 1925, monologue   RPB

A Child Shall Lead Them, 1938, 3 act Christmas play   DLC

The Christian Christmas Tree, 1933, young (1)   RPB

The Christmas Bouquets, 1931   RPB

Christmas Plays and Comedies, 1925, with others   RPB

The Christmas Tree Party, 1929, 3 acts   RPB

Collars, 1932, young   RPB

Colored Mandy's Cure, 1925, monologue   RPB

Curin' Hannah and New Fangled Doctors, 1925, monologues   RPB

Dad Held 'em Up, 1932   RPB

De Res' Cure, 1925, monologue   RPB

Dinner for the D. D., 1934, comedy (1)

Dorothy Dumb, Census Taker, 1951, by Lucile Crites Sligh, comedy (1)   RPB

Dorothy Dumb Monologs, 1935, 8 monologues   DLC

"Fatty Freckles," 1932   RPB

First Aid from the Ladies Aid, 1927 (1)   RPB

Five Two-some Plays, 1935

Fresh Air Fiends and A Bachelor Girl Calls on Mother of Two, 1925,   RPB
    Negro character monologues

Home Cured, 1928, "farce written especially for the Chamber of   RPB
    Commerce putting over the importance of buying home products" (1)

Hunting a Cook, 1925, monologue   RPB

In the Receiving Line, 1927, monologue   RPB

Josephine Jesebel, 1925, monologue   RPB

The Little White Ribboner, 1934, temperance reading   RPB

Lucindy on Weddin's and Funerals and De Sweat Box, 1927, Negro   RPB
    dialect recitations

LUCILE CRITES (continued)

Mandy Reads the Newspaper and Mandy Entertains the Minister, 1925,   RPB
    monologue
Mary Comes Home from College, 1928, "a bunch of fun" (1)   RPB
Mrs. Portly's Physical Culture Lesson, 1925, monologue   RPB
More Dorothy Dumb Monologues, 1951, by Lucile Crites Sligh   RPB
Parson's Spinach, 1934   RPB
Santa's Gift plus His Surprise (1)   FKC
Seeing a Style Show from Behind a Post, 1925, monologue   RPB
Selina Lou Celebrates and About Dogs, 1925, monologues   RPB
Sellin' Drugs, pub. with Myrtle Giard Elsey's Romance and   RPB
    Kid Brother, 1925
Seven Christmas Stockings, 1942   DLC
Short Stunts for Shower Parties, 1934   RPB
Take a Letter, 1942, comedy (1)   RPB
The Tale of a Mule's Tail, 1928, comedy (1)   RPB
Tempting the Court, 1934   RPB
They Went to the Game (1)   APS
Those Christmas Gifts, 1927 (1)   RPB
Trying on Hats, pub. with Myrtle Giard Elsey's Buying Shoes, 1925,   RPB
    monologue
Two Funny Monologues, 1927   RPB
When the Lining is Silver, 1932 (1)   RPB
Why Sunday School Teachers Get Gray, 1933, Easter reading   RPB
William Takes a New Degree, 1928, 3 act comedy   RPB
Yes, We Have No Baking Powder, 1929   RPB

MRS. E. G. CRONK

Thanksgiving Gates, 1924, Thanksgiving and Thank-offering program   RPB
    for boys and girls

KATHARINE SCHERER CRONK (1877- ?)

America for Americans, n.d., "play of world friendship and good will
    for boys and girls"
Let's Be Friends, 19??, "little play of China and America and every   NN
    land," with Laura Copenhaver
The Search for Light, 19?? "pageant of man's quest for God," with   OO
    Laura Copenhaver
The Striking of America's Hour, 1925, with Laura Scherer Copenhaver   RPB
    and Mathilde A. Vossler
The Way, 1923, with Laura Copenhaver, pageant of Japan   RPB
The Way of Peace, 1924, pageant, with Laura Copenhaver and Ruth   RPB
    Mougey Worrell

MARJORIE WILSON CROOKS

A Play for San Jacinto Night, 1916, also in Bulletin of Un. of Texas, RPB
    No. 72, Dec. 25, 1916

PHILOMENE CROOKS

Drills and Dances for the Grades, 1935   RPB

"Sam Learns a Lesson in Safety," 1929, "lesson play for intermediate   RPB
grades"

The Spirit of Christmas   BCE

VIVIAN CROSBY

Queen at Home, prod. 1930, with Shirley Warde

Trick for Trick, prod. 1932, with Harry Wagstaff Gribble (Grimble) and
Shirley Warde

MARGARET BESSIE CROSS

Beauty's Bloom, 1933, comedy, 2 scenes for junior high school, "good   RPB
health play for May Day"

A Lucky Trifle, 1903

Spoken Thoughts, 1903

RACHEL CROTHERS (1870-1878?-1958) AWW NAW NWAT

"As Husbands Go," 1931, comedy   RPB, CTC,CCT-2

Bill Comes Back, 1945, never produced

Bon Voyage, 1929

The Captain of the Gray Horse, c1903, with Louise M. Sill, founded on a   MH
novel by Hamlin Garland, typewritten copy

Caught Wet, 1932, prod. 1931, 3 act comedy   RPB

The Coming of Mrs. Patrick, prod. 1907, microfilm of typewritten copy   ICU

Criss-Cross, 1904, prod. 1899 (1)   RPB, FCP

Elizabeth, (1897-1902?) (1)

Every Cloud Has a Silver Lining; or, The Ruined Merchant, 1883?
juvenile venture with May Fitzwilliams

"Everyday," 1930, prod. 1921, 3 act comedy drama   RPB

Expressing Willie, 1925, 3 act comedy drama   RPB

He and She, 1917, prod. 1920 (1st prod. as The Herfords in 1911)   RPB, QRA
3 acts (RPB has1933 ed.)

The Heart of Paddy Whack, 1925, prod. 1914, 3 act comedy   RPB

The Herfords, 1912, typewritten ms. (See He and She)   NN

Katy Did, in Smart Set, 27, Jan., 1909, 129-36 (1)

Kiddies, 1909?

A Lady's Virtue, prod. 1925

Let Us Be Gay, 1929, comedy (staged and directed by Crothers)   RPB

A Little Journey, 1923, prod. 1918, 3 act comedy drama   RPB

A Man's World, 1915, prod. 1910, 4 act drama   RPB, BAW

Mary the Third, 1925, 3 act comedy   RPB, TMA,TTM, TMP,DCC

Mother Carey's Chickens, 1925, prod. 1917, with Kate Douglas Wiggin   RPB

Mrs. John Hobbs (1892-1902?) (1)

Mrs. Molly, in Smart Set, 27, March, 1909, 104-13 (1)

My South Window, 1950, never produced

"Myself Bettina," prod. 1908, typescript and promptbook   NN

RACHEL CROTHERS (continued)

Nice People, prod. 1921, in Everybody's Magazine,   MRA, QCP,NN, CLSU
   45, Nov. 1921, 87-94, motion picture script by Clara Beranger, 1922,
   shooting script

Nora, prod. 1913 at Academy of Dramatic Arts (1)

Old Lady 31, 1923, prod. 1916, based on novel by Louise Forsslund   RPB

Once Upon a Time, 1925, prod. 1918, 4 act comedy   RPB

Ourselves, prod. 1913

Peggy, 1925, also in Scribner's Magazine, 76, Aug., 1924, 175-83 (1) RPB, PTM

Point of View, prod. 1904

The Rector, 1905, prod. 1902 (1)   RPB, OPS-I

Revenge; or, The Pride of Lillian Le Mar, prod. 1913 (1)

Six One Act Plays, 1925   RPB

Susan and God, 1938, prod. 1937   RPB

Talent, prod. 1934?

39 East, 1925, prod. 1919, 3 act comedy   RPB

The Three of Us, 1916, prod. 1906, 4 acts   RPB

Three Plays by Rachel Crothers, 1924   RPB

"The Valiant One," 1937, 3 act comedy drama   RPB

Venus, prod. 1927

A Water Color (1897-1902?) (1)

We Happy Few, 1955, never prod.

What They Think, in Ladies Home Journal, 40, Feb., 1923, 12-3+ (Also in
   Six One Act Plays)

When Ladies Meet, 1932, prod. 1933, comedy drama   RPB

Which Way, 190? (1)

William Craddock, prod. 1914

Young Wisdom, prod. 1914

MABEL CROUCH

Christmas Comes to Aunt Kate, 1936, play?

Christmas in Her Eyes, 1940 (1)   RPB

Christmas Patches, 1935 play?

Christmas Without Patsy, 1936 play?

Down Cheery Lane, 1934, 3 act comedy drama   RPB

The Gift Basket, 1939, Christmas play   DLC

High Priced Happiness, 1936, "modern comedy drama in 3 acts"   NN, DLC

Howdy Folks, 1931, 3 act comedy   RPB

It's Christmas Again, 1935 play?

Keeping Christmas, 1937 (1)   DLC

The Merry Rush, 1938, Christmas (1)   DLC

On the Air, 1931, Christmas nursery playlet   RPB

Santa Claus and Co., 1939, comedy (1)   DLC

Selling Christmas, 1940 (1)   RPB

The Sunpath, 1931, 3 act comedy drama   RPB

The Surprise Package, 1930   RPB

Those Christmas Smiles, 1938 (1)   DLC

MABEL CROUCH (continued)
The Town Talkie, 1930, 3 act comedy drama   RPB
A Voice in the Wilderness, 1938, 3 act drama, Catholic play   NN
Where's Your Christmas Spirit? 1941, comedy (1)   RPB

MARTHA FOOTE CROW (1854-1924)
The World Above, 1905, duologue   RPB

ANNE CROWELL
Snow White, in The Delineator, 93, July, 1918, 32+, 3 acts
The Wild Swans, in The Delineator, 93, Oct., 1918, 27, 2 acts

JULIE GRINNELL STORROW CRUGER
("MRS. VAN RENSSELAER CRUGER") (? -1920) ("JULIEN GORDON")
The Blue Diamond, 192? 2 act musical comedy, book by "Julien   NN
    Gordon"; music by Victor Englander; lyrics by Michael Furneaux
A Modern Child, in Smart Set, 1, May, 1900, 79-85 (1).
A Modern Daughter, in Smart Set, 1, April, 1900, 77-82 (1)
A Modern Mother, in Smart Set, 1, March, 1900, 79-86 (1)
The Naughty Duchess, 1925, by "Julien Gordon" and Kathyrne Thorne,   NN
    music by Victor Englander

AGNES L. CRUMMINS
The Pride of the Family (1)

MRS. R. E. CRUMP
A Primary Book Pageant   WPP

LUCY ALSANSON CUDDY
Basket of Wishes, 1927 (1)   DLC
Blue Lupines, 1927, tragic mystery (1)   RPB
Columbus, 1927, with others, "play of perseverance for school use"   Or, DLC
"Dolores of San Juan," 1937, San Juan Bautista pageant, music by   DLC
    Francisco Vallejo McGettigan
The Green Dragon Emerald, 1928, 3 act mystery   RPB
Jack and Jill, Little Miss Muffet, Six Little Mice and Yellow Pussy, 1925, DLC
    dram. by Cuddy; music by Mary Weaver McCauley
Li Chen, 1927, Chinese comedy   DLC
Mother Goose Plays, with others
Paradise Vale, musical pantomime (1)
Pierette of the Circus Poster (1)
San Juan Bautista Pageant, 1938, music and lyrics by Francisco Vallejo   DLC
    McGettigan
The Shepherdess and the Chimney Sweep, 1923, dram. by Cuddy,   Or, DLC
    based on story by Hans Christian Andersen; music by Mary Weaver
    McCauley
The Silver Forest

LUCY ALSANSON CUDDY (continued)
Tai Chen, 1927, Chinese tragedy (1) (probably same as Li Chen)   RPB
Thanksgiving in Plymouth, 1925, 3 acts, music by Mary Weaver McCauley
   and others
A Wayside Shrine, musical pantomime (1)

ANGELA CUDMORE
We Dine at Seven, 1909, with Peter Davey, "one-act sketch for ladies"

ANNIE LAURIE CULLENS
Safety First, 1927, safety play   RPB

ELIZABETH M. CULLIS
Kill or Cure, 1927, comedy for boys (1)   RPB
The Telegram, 1927, comedy (1)   RPB

IRENE MARGARET CULLISON
Mother Goose Finger Plays, 1915   RPB

LOUISE L. G. CUMMINGS
Frankincense, Christmas program for children   CP

MAUD CUNEY-HARE (Also MAUD CUNEY HARE) (1874-1936
Antar of Araby, 1929 (1)   RMP

ELIZABETH OVERSTREET CUPPY (probably British)
Mollusk or Suffragette? in Putnam's Magazine, 7, Nov., 1909, 172-81 (1)

ELVA SAWYER CURETON
Calico Land, 1915, 4 act farce   RPB
The Tenderfoot, 1921, Boy Scout campfire play   RPB

SARAH JEFFERIS CURRY
The Devil's Gold, dramatization of Chaucer's "Pardoner's Tale" (1)   STM

AGNES BERYL CURTIS
Christmas at Mother's, 1928 (1)   RPB
Christmas Comedies, 1927, collection of one acts   RPB
The Christmas Dinner, 1930, "domestic science Christmas play" (1)   RPB
Christmas Magic, 1929, comedy (1)   RPB
Christmas Plays for One and All, 1930, with others   RPB
The Christmas Tree That Lived, 1931   RPB
Clever One-Act Comedies for Women and Girls, 1938   RPB
Clever Plays for Women, 1929   DLC
A Critical Case, 1937, comedy (1)   DLC
The Cunning Lunatic, 1937, comedy (1)   DLC
Everyday is Mother's Day, 1938, one-act program   NN

AGNES BERYL CURTIS (continued)

Glimpses of Newton's Past Told in History and Drama, 1918	RPB
Good Plays for Patriotic Holidays, 1932	RPB
Holiday Plays for Young People, 1929	DLC
If There Were No Children, 1931	RPB
Life at Any Price, 1928, 3 act comedy	RPB
Making Mother Modern, 1931, farce for 20 women	RPB
Merry Christmas in the Old Home Town, 1928 (1)	RPB
The Orange Colored Necktie, 1927, farce (1)	RPB
The Other Side of the Family, 1929, 3 act comedy drama	RPB
Prize Holiday Plays for Children, 1953	NN
Short Commencement Plays for Junior High School, 1946	RPB
Special Day Plays, 1947 (No. 2 pub. 1950)	RPB
Ten Short Plays for Women and Girls, 1928	RPB
Tit for Tat, 1937, comedy (1)	DLC
A Vigilant Santa Claus, 1929, comedy (1)	RPB
When Father Goes on a Diet, 1926, comedy (1)	RPB

ELIZABETH ALDEN CURTIS (1878- ?)

The Norseman, 1912, 4 act drama	RPB

ELIZABETH VAN OLINDA CURTIS

Gooseland, 1927, fairy operetta for boys and girls	RPB-M

JOAN CURTIS

This World and the Next, 1928-9

CATHERINE CHISHOLM CUSHING

Between the Acts, 1914, typescript (1)	NN
Edgar Allen Poe, prod. 1925, character study, typescript	ViU
Gloriana, prod. 1918, music by Rudolph Friml	
Jerry, 1930, prod. 1914, 3 act comedy (typescript at NN)	RPB
Kitty Mackaye, prod. 1914, incomplete typescript	NN
Lassie, prod. 1920, music by Hugo Felix (musical revival of Kitty Mackaye)	
Little Partners, 1915, 3 acts, typescript	NN
"Marge," 1923, prod. 1924, typescript	NN
Marjolaine, prod. 1922, with H. Felix and B. Hooker (based on Pomander Walk by L. N. Parker)	
The Master of the Inn, prod. 1925	
Miss Ananias	
Nancy Stair, 1923, prod. 1905, dramatization of book by Elinor MacCartney Lane, typescript	NN
Polyanna, the Glad Girl, 1923, prod. 1915, based on novel by Eleanor H. Porter, 4 act comedy	RPB
The Poppy Kiss, prod. 1923, character study, typescript	NN
The Princess Pretend, 1914, typescript (1)	NN
The Real Thing, prod. 1911	

CATHERINE CHISHOLM CUSHING (continued)
Sari, prod. 1914, operetta with E. P. Heath and E. Kalman, adapted from German
Topsy and Eva, prod. 1924, musical comedy
Widow by Proxy, 1930, prod. 1913, 3 act farce, (typescript and prompt   RPB
book at NN)

M. G. CUSHING
Mt. Holyoke Pageant, 1913, S. Hadley, Mass.

OLIVIA DONALDSON CUSHING
(See OLIVIA DONALDSON CUSHING ANDERSEN)

FAITH BALDWIN CUTHRELL (1893-1978) AWW
A Garden in Mitylene, in her book of poems, Sign Posts, 1924   RPB

MARY CUTLER
Pageant of Lake Minnetonka, 1916, Excelsior, Maine
The Torchbearers, 1918, with Lotta Clark, Minneapolis, Minn.

AROLYN CAVERLY CUTTING
Rosebrook Farm, 1913, 3 act rural comedy   RPB
Rosemary, 1912, 4 act comedy for girls   RPB

MARY STEWART DOUBLEDAY CUTTING (1851-1924)
A Good Dinner, in Ladies Home Journal, 22, Feb., 1905, 5+ (1)
Not According to Schedule, 1924, based on her short story, dramatized by
Ruby Phillips Bramwell

BELVA CUZZORT
The Magic Square, George Washington pageant

ELLEN M. CYR (MRS. R. P. SMITH) (? -1920)
The Dramatic First Reader, 1905   RPB

D

DORIS DABBS
Johnny and His Ma at the Picnic, 1928   RPB
The Letter from New York, 1928, monologue, typewritten copy   RPB
The Yankee, 1937, 3 act comedy   DLC

FRANCES S. DABNEY
Anne-Marie in Easter, 1926   SSH

JULIA PARKER DABNEY (1850- ?)
Children of the Sunrise, in Poet Lore, 26, Nov.-Dec., 1915, 653-93 (1)
Mademoiselle Merowska, 1907, 3 act mystery   RPB
Waters of Life, 1925, 4 act poetic drama   RPB

FRANCES MAY DADMUN (1875- ?)
The Renewal of Life, Easter pageant   JPP-1

MARION VINCENT DAILEY
The Extra Plate, 1930, farce with Frances D. Singler, mimeograph copy   RPB

ALPHABELL DAILY
The Juvenile Recitation Book, 1928, with Minnie Leona Upton, Neva   RPB
    McFarland Wadhams and others
Madonna Lilies, 1927, monologue   RPB
Mickey's Banty, 1928, reading   DLC
The Pot of Gold, 1928, reading   DLC
Twelve Splendid Monologs, 1935   DLC
White Carnations, 1927, monologue   RPB

MARGARET DAKIN
The Lady of the Lake, 1916, with Miriam Thomas, dram. of poem by   RPB
    Walter Scott

GRETCHEN DALE
Mrs. Avery, prod. 1911, with Howard Estabrook

REBECCA VAN HAMM DALE
Billboard, 1933, Junior League play (1)   RPB
Ethel's Queer Complex, 1929, comedy for girls   RPB
The Girls' Finesse, 1928, comedy for girls (1)   RPB
The King's Choice, 1928, Junior League play (1)   RPB

"LENA DALKEITH" (See JEANNE YATES CHERRY)

KATE WEAVER DALLAS
Midsummer Night's Dream, 1911, "Shakespeare arranged and   RPB
    condensed"

MARGUERITE DALLAS
Dawn of the Third Day, Easter pageant   HPY

VITTORIA DALLIN (MRS. COLONNA MURRAY DALLIN)
Arlington Pageant, 1913, with Laura Ingalls, Arlington, Mass., to   RPB
    commemorate the dedication of the new Town Hall (program text at MB)

VITTORIA DALLIN (continued)
    Pageant of Education, 1908, with Lotta Clark, Boston, Mass., program   MB
      text
    A Pageant of Progress, 1911, Lawrence, Mass.   MB, DLC

LEONA DALRYMPLE (or C. LEONA DALRYMPLE) (1884- ?)
    The Colonel's Maid, 1910, 3 act comedy   RPB
    The Land of Night, 1907, fairy comedy for young folks   RPB
    Mrs. Forrester's Crusade, 1908, farce (1)   RPB
    Surprises, 1908, farce (1)   RPB
    Tangles, 1907, farce (1)   RPB
    The Time of His Life, 1909, 3 act comedy   RPB
    While Brother Phil Was Walking, 1908, farce (1)   IU, PU
    A White Shawl, 1905, 2 act farce

STEPHANIE DAMIANAKES
    The Obstacle, in Plays of the Little Theatre Workshop, 1922 (1)

ETHEL MOSELEY DAMON (1883- ?)
    One Hundred Years of Christian Civilization in Hawaii, 1920,   RPB
      "historical pageant commemorating the arrival of the first
      missionaries on Hawaiian shores," pub. in Hawaiian Missions
      Centennial, 1820-1920, Honolulu, Hawaii, pp. 14-39, music by Jane
      Lathrop Winne
    Punahou Pageant, 1916, Honolulu, Hawaii, "for the 75th anniversary   RPB
      of Punahou School, now Oahu College"
    The Romance of Reality, 1920, historical play in 2 acts (Hawaiian   RPB
      Mission Centennial, The Mission Play)

GRETCHEN DAMROSCH (See GRETCHEN DAMROSCH FINLETTER)

SYBIL LENTNER DANIELSON
    A "P.E.O.'s" Dream, 1929, mimeograph copy   RPB

MILDRED DANNENBAUM
    Platform Hits, 1930

HELEN T. DARBY
    The Truth for a Day, 1913, play for girls for Washington's birthday (1)   RPB

OLIVE TILFORD DARGAN (1869-1968) AWW
    The Flutter of the Goldleaf and Other Plays, 1922, one-acts, with   RPB
      Frederic Peterson
    Lords and Lovers and Other Dramas, 1906, period pieces   RPB
    The Mortal Gods and Other Plays, 1912, historical period plays   RPB
    The Raven, 1904, 5 acts   ViU
    Semiramis and Other Plays, 1904, historical plays   RPB
    The Shepherd, prod. 1912 by the Neighborhood Players at Henry Street
      Settlement
    The Woods of Ida, in Century Magazine, 74, Aug., 1907, 590-604 (1)

ELLA DARLING
    Pageant of Julius Caesar, 1916, Greenville, Miss.

ANNE CHARLOTTE DARLINGTON
  Beginning at Jerusalem, 1928, 3 scenes   RPB
  The Lady Joanna and Two Other Plays, 1928, religious plays   RPB
  Spring Song, 1932, National League of American Penwomen Plays (1)   RPB
  Through the Dark, 1928, one-act play on Africa   RPB
  Where the Trails Cross, 1928, one-act play of Navajo life   RPB
  Yelenka the Wise and Other Folk Tales in Dramatic Form, 1926   RPB

HELENE D'ASALENA
  The Wishing Gate, 1929, "fantasy written for radio broadcasting" (1)   RPB

EDITH DASEKING
  Graveyard Shift, 1928-9, "play of California factory workers" (1)
  Mountain Magic, 1928, Carolina folk play
  The Pirate's Ghost Garden, 1932, 2 act comedy mystery   RPB
  Schoolin', 1932   RPB

SONIA V. M. DAUGHERTY
  Esther, 1930, 3 act drama, winning Biblical play of the 1929 Drama   RPB
    League-Longmans, Green and Co. playwriting contest

EMILY DAVID
  The Mirth-Provoking Schoolroom, 1906, farce (1)   RPB

WINIFRED M. DAVID
  Second Best, 1928, romantic comedy (1)   RPB

ELEANOR GADDIS DAVIDSON
  The Court of Wisdom, 1905, masque as it was presented by the class of   RPB
    1905 at Wells College

LILLIAN DAVIDSON
  Aunt Susan's Troubles on the Farm, 1916, monologue for woman   RPB
  Boy's Essay on Boys, 1916, monologue   RPB
  De Scrumscious Weddin', 1916, Negro dialect monologue for a woman   RPB
  Her Doubtful Patriotism, 1918, monologue   RPB

MARION LAMONT DAVIDSON
  A Bit o' Heather, 1930, comedy (1)   RPB
  Whipped Cream, comedy   JDC

MARY RICHMOND DAVIDSON
  A Christmas Party at Sir Roger's, 1927   RPB
  Christmas to Christmas, 1931, "six around-the-year plays for children"   RPB
  The Coming of William Dane, 1927, "dramatization to be used in   RPB
    connection with the study of Silas Marner"
  Joyful and Triumphant Christmas, 1933   RPB
  On the Road to Egypt, 1928, Christmas   RPB
  Sire de Maletroit's Door, 1927, dramatization of story by R. L. Stevenson RPB
  The Wandering Child, 1926 (1)   RPB

MARIA THOMPSON DAVIES
  The Melting of Molly, prod. 1918, musical based on her novel, music by
    S. Romberg; lyrics by Cyrus Wood; musical adaptation by Edgar Smith
    (music at CU)

MARY CAROLYN DAVIES
Cobweb Kings (1)   OPS-IV
Our America, 1944, patriotic operetta, book and lyrics by Davies and Don
    Wilson; music by Geoffrey O'Hara
The Slave with Two Faces, 1918, allegory, Flying Stag   RPB, SCO,PDP, SLC
    Plays, No. 6; also in John Sweet and Kenneth Lynd, Eds., Designs for
    Reading: Plays, 1969
Tables and Chairs (1)   OPS-V

MYRTA LITTLE DAVIES (1888- ?)
Sweet Christmas Time, 1929, pageant for Christmas   RPB

DOROTHY MARIE DAVIS
The Print of the Nails, 1932, Easter (1)   RPB-M
Sir Tommy's Pilgrimage, 1930   RPB-M
The Street of Hearts, 1928, Christmas fantasy for children   RPB
Wings Over the World, 1932, pageant of world friendship and youth RPB

EDNA CLARK DAVIS
I'm So Nervous, 1930, 3 act comedy   RPB
The Magic Toy Shop, 1924, 3 acts   RPB
Only Six Letters, M-O-T-H-E-R, 1934, story and song service for   RPB
    Mother's Day, music by I. H. Meredith

GEORGENE WEBBER DAVIS (1900- ?)
The Round Table, 1930, "history drawn from unreliable chronicles" RPB

LILLIE DAVIS
Another Engagement, n.d., comedietta   InU
Aunt Madge, 1898, comedietta   NcU
Bumps, 1911, farce for females (1)   RPB
"Don't Jump at Conclusions," n.d., comedietta   InU
Dorothy's Victory, n.d., for 2 females (1)   InU
The Little Performers, n.d., dialogue for children   InU
Rival Relatives, 189? "dialogue for 4 ladies"   NcU

LUCILLE DAVIS
The New Way, 1927, "one-act play for any young people's organization" RPB

MARJORIE H. DAVIS
The Patriot's Parade, 1918, patriotic play for young people (1)   RPB

MARJORIE R. DAVIS
A Roosevelt Program, 1930, birthday program as produced in the   RPB
    Roosevelt Jr.H. S. , San Diego, Calif., Oct. 21-5, 1929

MARY A. DAVIS
"The Gods Condescend," 1929, with Dorothy Gardiner, for h. s. and RPB
    college

MARY EVALYN DAVIS
Diplomatic Bridget, 1926, comedy (1)   RPB

MARY EVELYN MOORE DAVIS (also MOLLIE MOORE DAVIS) (1852-1909)
A Bunch of Roses, 1907, romantic comedy   RPB
A Bunch of Roses and Other Parlor Plays, 1903, collection of 6 plays RPB
Christmas Boxes, 1907, comedy   RPB

MARY EVELYN MOORE DAVIS (continued)
A Christmas Masque, Of Saint Roch, Pere Dagobert, and Throwing the
    Wanga, 1896
A Dress Rehearsal, 1907, comedy   RPB
His Lordship, 1907, romantic comedy   RPB
The New System, 1907, comedy   RPB
Queen Anne Cottages, 1907, romantic comedy   RPB

RUTH HELEN DAVIS (DAVIES?)
The Daughter of Helen, trans. of work by "Pierre Loti" (pseud.) and
    Judith Gautier
The Guilty Man, prod. 1916, with Charles Klein, dram. of book by   RPB
    Francois Copee
The Supreme Victory, and Yesterday and Today, 1920, two plays, lyrics   NN
    by EllaWheeler Wilcox

ADA CLARK DAVISON (1882- ?)
All Wool, a Yard Wide, 1929, 3 act comedy   RPB
A Big Depression, 1930, comedy for women (1)   RPB
Crafty Grandpa, 1930, 3 act comedy   RPB
Entertaining Ed, 1928, 2 act comedy   RPB
Information, please! 1928, monologue   RPB
'Lijah Buys a Radio, 1925, monologue   RPB
Marigold Johnsing's Yaller Dress, 1927, monologue   DLC
Meeting Matilda, 1927, monologue   RPB
Once Too Often, 1931, 3 act comedy   RPB
Over the Ironing Boards, 1926, monologue   RPB
Rosemary at the Benefit, 1926, monologue   DLC
Temptation, 1929, monologue   RPB
Uncle Henry's Suitcase, 1928, 3 act comedy   RPB
Waiting for the Groom, 1927, monologue for a woman   RPB
A Week's Trial, 1926, 2 act comedy   RPB
What Husbands Don't Know, 1928, entertainment for women's clubs   RPB
The Wrong Twin, 1929, comedy (1)   RPB

ELOISE K. DAWLEY
Little Plays from Greek Myths, 1928, with Marie Oller   RPB

ANNE MARJORIE DAY (1875- ?)
Dante and the Rose, 1928, (Auspices of Sons of Italy, May 25, 1928)   RPB
The Guiding Light, 1921, Pilgrim Tercentenary pageant play   RPB

EDITH ELEANOR DAY
I Come Third, 1929, 3 act religious play   RPB

HELENA SMITH DAYTON
The Book of Entertainment and Theatricals, 1923, with Louise Bascom   RPB
    Barratt
Hot Water, prod. 1929, with Louise B. Barratt

KATHARINE DAYTON
First Lady, prod. 1935, with George S. Kaufman, 3 act political satire   RPB
Loose Leaves, 1923, poetry and plays
Save Me the Waltz, 1937, prod. 1938, typewritten copy   DLC

ELOISE EARLE DEAN
Stockin' Money, 1929, folk play, won Drama League-Longmans   NN, DLC
    Green Contest in1928

FRANCES DEAN
  Normal School Pageant, 1911, Salem, Mass.

LENA CARSON DEAN
  A Howling Success, 1929, comedy (1)   RPB

"DORA DEANE" (See DAISY D. NICHOLS)

LIZZIE DE ARMOND
  Alive Forever More, 1895, Easter service, with W. A. Post   RPB-M
  All's Right With the World, 1916, Children's Day service   RPB-M
  Christmas Praises, 1909, Christmas service, with others   RPB-M
  Easter Sunrise, n.d., Easter cantata pageant, music by Edmund Simon   OrP
    Lorenz
  Hail! Joyful Morning, 1912, Easter cantata, with Henry Fillmore   RPB-M
  Hail the King, 1908, Christmas service, with others   RPB-M
  How Santa Came to the Home, 1908, young   RPB
  Joyful Tidings, 1906? Christmas service, with Post, Thiele and Rosche RPB-M
  The King of the World, 1914, Christmas cantata   RPB-M
  Mother Goose's Visit to Santa Claus, 1903, music by I. H. Meredith   RPB-M
  The Paramount Children's Day Book, 1930, a contributor   RPB
  The Royal Quest, 1915, Christmas, music by E. S. Lorenz   RPB-M
  The Spirit of Christmas, 1909, Christmas service, with others   RPB-M
  The Star of Hope, 1924, pageant of the nativity, music by George F.   RPB-M
    Rosche
  A Summer Song, 1919, Children's Day service, music by   RPB-M
    Fred B. Holton
  Tidings of Great Joy, 1903, Christmas service, with others   RPB-M
  To Santa's Land with the Dream Man, 1905, Christmas cantata, music   NN
    by Isaac H. Meredith
  The Tree of Promise, 1919, Christmas cantata, music by E. S. Lorenz   RPB-M
  Triumphant Morn, 1922, Easter cantata for Sunday school
  The Uncrowned King, 1922, story cantata for Christmas, music by Dr.
    Adam Geibel
  Victory, 1915, Easter service   RPB-M
  Washington's Birthday Entertainment Book, 1908, collection, with   CSmH
    others
  Why Christmas Was Late, 1908, for boys (1)   RPB
  Yuletide Promise, 1919, cantata (Sunday school edition of the   RPB-M
    Christmas cantata, The Tree of Promise)

MARY CHRISTINE DE BARDELEBEN (1881- ?)
  Amos, 1926, 2 acts, written by the students in Old Testament at the Un. RPB
    of Okla. under the direction of De Bardeleben

IRIS DECKER
  The Outlaw King, 1930, Robin Hood operetta in 3 acts, libretto by Clare RPB
    Grubb; lyrics by Decker; music by Decker and "Louis Malone" (pseud.)

MARY A. DECKER
  The Smith Family Reunion, 1905, "characteristic description in 3 acts,"   RPB
    Dunkirk, N. Y.
  The Smith Family Reunion, 1907, musical   RPB

MAUDE DE CON
  Martha Washington Tea Party, Colonial pantomime, in Schell, Stanley,   RPB
    Clever Penelope, Belmar, N. J., 1928, 17-19

MABEL CLARE CRAFT DEERING (1872- ?)
Adam Bede, 1901, dram. of George Eliot's novel   NN, DLC
The Turncoat; or, Parson Peter, 1902, 4 acts   DLC
Victory; or, On the Heights, 1903, 4 acts, based on a novel by Auerbach   RPB

MARIAN DE FOREST (1864-1935)
Barnabette, (later Erstwhile Susan) c. 1914   NBuHi
Erstwhile Susan, 1926, prod. 1916, 3 acts, based on a novel by Helen R.   RPB
  Martin, called Barnabetta
Friendship Village, 1930? character comedy founded on Zona Gale's   NBuU
  stories, typewritten copy
Little Women, 1921, prod. 1912, dram. of novel by Louisa Alcott, by   RPB
  arrangement with Jessie Bonstelle
Lovers of Yesterday, 1928?   NBuHi
Mary 39, 1928?, with John D. Wells   NBuHi
Mister Man, based on a story by Frank R. Adams   NBuHi
The Trespasser, with Jane Miller   NBuHi
Trespassing, 1930? with Jane Miller   NBuHi
The Vision of Noah, 1928?
The Zonta Zoo; or, The Vision of Noah   NBuHi

HELENA DE GUZMAN
Gold Bug Millions, 1927, 3 act comedy drama   RPB

ELSIE DE HUFF
Five Religious Education Plays, 1927   RPB
The Only Day I Have, 1927, Sabbath observance play (1)   RPB

KATHLEEN H. B. DE JAFFA
The Emperor Jones, 1932, 2 act opera after Eugene O'Neill's play, music
  by Louis Gruenberg
La Rondine, 1927, English version of opera by Puccini
Sadko, 1930, lyric legend by A. Rimsky-Korsakow, English version by   RPB
  De Jaffa
Violanta, 1927, English version of drama by Hans Mueller, music by Erich
  W. Korngold

DOROTHY DEJAGERS
Hot Waffles, 1929, comedy (1)   RPB
Little Girl Blue, 1931, prod. 1927, with Dorothy Heyward, (prod. in 1930   RPB
  as Cinderelative) romantic comedy
Oh, Papa! 1926, comedy (1)   RPB

EDITH BARNARD DELANO
Friend of the Family, 1931, comedy (1)   RPB
Grandma Pulls the Strings, 1926, with David Carb, comedy (1)   RPB
Is There a Manger Here? 1932, Christmas   RPB
Lady of Pain, 1926, with David Carb, comedy of youth (1)   RPB

RUTH B. DELANO
Friend Fritz, dram. of story by Erkmann-Chatrian

CLARISSA SCOTT DELANY (1901-1927)
Dixie to Broadway, 1924

HATTIE DELARO
The Girl from Macy's, 1904   RPB

VINA DELMAR (1905- ?)
<u>Bad Girl</u>, prod. 1930, dram. of her novel, with Brian Marlow,   CLSU
    screenplay
<u>Midsummer</u>, 1954, prod. 1953, 3 act comedy, formerly titled <u>Lily</u>   RPB
<u>The Rich Full Life</u>, 1946, 3 acts, (c. 1945 as <u>Time of Her Life</u>, a story)   RPB
<u>Warm Wednesday</u>, 1959, 3 act comedy   RPB

KATHERYN DE LUHERY
<u>A Colonial Day Program: the Spirit of Washington</u>

ADA ROSE DEMEREST
<u>The Church and Her Children</u>, 1929, pageant for Children's Day   RPB
<u>Junior Pageants</u>, 1927, pageants and programs designed for junior groups
<u>Junior Worship</u>, 1931, with programs, songs and stories
<u>Life and Love Triumphant</u>, 1926, Easter pageant   OC
<u>Stories for the Junior Hour</u>, 1926, stories and dramatizations adapted from
    Scriptures

BEATRICE DE MILLE
<u>The Greatest Thing in the World</u>, prod. 1900, with Harriet French Ford,   NN
    typescript

AIDA RODMAN DE MILT (1871- ?)
<u>Values</u>, 1927, Little Theatre Tournament

NORMA HELEN DEMING
<u>New Pieces for Every Day the Schools Celebrate</u>, 1929, with Katharine I. NcC
    Bemis
<u>Pieces for Every Day the Schools Celebrate</u>, 1921, with Katharine Isabel   RPB
    Bemis
<u>Stories of Patriotism</u>, 1918, patriotic reader for the intermediate grades,   RPB
    with Katharine Isabel Bemis, contains poetry and short plays

MARJORIE DE MOTT
<u>His Come-uppance; or, the Triumph of the Gertrude</u>, 1930, comedy (1)   RPB
<u>Keeping Nora Happy</u>, 1932, comedy (1)   RPB

EMILY D. DENBY
<u>Blackbird Pie</u>   FMC

EMILY HEREY DENISON
<u>The Little Mother of the Slums and Other Plays</u>, 1915, one-acts   RPB

GRACE ATHERTON DENNEN (1874- ?)
<u>California, the Land of Dreams</u>, 1921, pageant with Eleanor Brodie   RPB
    Jones and others

NELLIE M. DENNISON
<u>The White Indian</u>, 1907, Western melodrama   RPB

CECILIA P. DENSLOW
<u>The Offerings of the Year</u>, 1899, Christmas, young   RPB
<u>The Shamrock Minstrels</u>, 1902   RPB

CLARA JANETTA FORT DENTON

All Is Fair in Love, 1897	RPB
All Sorts of Dialogues, 1898, collection	RPB
All the Holidays, 1905	
The Best Authors' Christmas Plays, 1909, with Elizabeth Guptill and others	RPB
The Birthdays, 1910, Lincoln-Washington dialogue	RPB
Bobby's Help, 189?	RPB
The Boy Scouts, 1917, operetta, music by S. T. Paul	RPB-M
A Change of Color, 1897, drama (1)	RPB
Christmas All Over the World, 1906, juvenile cantata, music by James Henry Fillmore	IaU
Christmas at Happy Valley, 1925, 2 acts	RPB
Christmas with Mother Goose	SCC
The Commencement Treasury, 1929	
Creepy Halloween Celebrations, 1926	DLC
Denton's Best Plays and Dialogues, 1925	RPB
Denton's New Program Book, 1926	RPB
Dialogues for Closing Day, 1925	DLC
"Dot Pooty Gompliment," 19??, monologue	NcD
Entertainments for All the Year, 1912, first pub. 1910	RPB
From Tots to Teens, 1897, dialogues	RPB
Getting Track of the Mallories, 189? monologue	RPB
The Graduates' Gayety Book, 1924	
The Graduates' Own Book, 1926	
How the Fairies Play	SCC
In Bethlehem, 1917, Christmas, music by S. T. Paul	RPB-M
In the East, 1922	SBE
In Ye Olden Tyme	STE
Jack Frost's Mistake, 1907, "operetta for Thanksgiving or any time"(1)	RPB-M
The "Left-handed" Sleeve, 19??, monologue	NcD
Let Us Give Thanks	STE
Little Lines for Little Speakers, 1891	MsU
Little People's Christmas Book, 1915	RPB
Little People's Dialogues, 1912	RPB
Mademoiselle's Mistake, 1910, farce (1)	RPB
The Man Who Went to Europe, 1897, comedy (1)	RPB
Merry Christmas Celebrations, 1924	
Merry Dialogues for Country Schools, 1924	RPB
The Minister's Daughter	SBE
Old Santa's Fairies, 1917, music by S. T. Paul	RPB-M
The Old Ship, 1910, dialogue	RPB
One Little Chicken, 189? monologue	RPB
A Pair of Scissors, for girls	SWD
The Paramount Christmas Book, 1922, a contributor	RPB
Parlor Varieties, 1903, with Emma E. Brewster	
Pat and His Countryman, 1907, dialogue for boys	RPB
Petite Plays, 1912	
The Program Book, 1910	
The Red Cross, 1917, music by S. T. Paul, for girls	RPB-M
The Return	STE
Sammie's Lesson, 1910, dialogue	RPB
Seeing the Animals, 1912, farce	RPB
Seeing Uncle Jack, 1910, 2 act comedy for girls	RPB
Seen and Not Heard, and Vi'let's Troubles, 1918? two monologues	RPB
The Snowflakes and the Fairies	HPC

CLARA JANETTA FORT DENTON (continued)
"Sorry for Billy," n.d., monologue	NN
The Strike in Santa Claus Land	SBE
Surprised, 1921, comedy (1)	RPB
Thirty Christmas Dialogues and Plays, 1940, with Marie Irish, Laura R.	RPB
Smith and others	
Thirty New Christmas Dialogues and Plays, 1909	
The Three Georges, about George Washington (1)	
To Meet Mr. Thompson, 1890, farce for females (1)	RPB, BCF
Topsy on the Top Floor, 1901 play?	DLC
Trouble in the Toyroom	SNC
A True Patriot, for boys	SWD
Uncle Peter and the Widow, 189? monologue	RPB
An Unsuccessful Hunt	SNC
The Vision, 2 acts, young, about George Washington	SWD
"W. H.," 1897, farce (1)	RPB
Waiting for Oscar, 189? monologue	RPB
When the Curtain Rises, 1919 or earlier, ten juvenile plays, 8 adult	
monologues, and 7 adult plays	
When Duty Calls, about George Washington (1)	
When the Lessons Are Over, 1891, dialogues, exercises and drills	
The White Chief, 1915, playlet for Thanksgiving	RPB
The Yellow Law, 1910, young	RPB

ELEANOR DENTON
Sing-a-song-o'-Sixpence, 1927, five plays

ELVA DE PUE
Hattie, 1917, play of tenement life, in Touchstone, Aug., 1917, 361-9+ (1)	MP

LYDIA MAY GLOVER DESEO (1898- ?)
Friends of Jesus, 1923, collection, dramatizations from the New	RPB
Testament for young, by Lydia M. Glover	
Looking at Life Through Drama, 1931, with Hulda Mossberg Phipps,	RPB
includes a play by Elizabeth Yates	
Making Ends Meet, 1929, stewardship dialogue	DLC
A Morning Call, 1929	DFP
Nason, the Blind Disciple, 1927, sermon drama, by Lydia Glover	RPB
Never the Twain, in Poet Lore, 41, Summer, 1930, 272-92 (1)	
The Portrait, 1929	DFP, SPP
"These Things Shall Pass," 1924, pageant play of the church of all	RPB
nations, by Lydia Glover and G. Bromley Oxnam	
A Woman Shall Lead Them, 1929, Christian stewardship playlet, by J.	
Wesley Oborn, dram. by Deseo	

LEONIE DE SOUNY
Musk, 1920

MARY AINGE DE VERE ("MADELINE BRIDGES")
A Nowadays Call, in Smart Set, 23, Oct., 1907, 19-20 (1)
Two in a Fog, in Ladies Home Journal, 32, Aug., 1915, 8 (1)

MARY DEVEREUX (? -1914)
Pageant of Marblehead, 1912, Marblehead, Mass.

LOUISE E. DEW (1871- ?)
The Christmas Spirit Tarries, 1928 (1)	RPB
Entertainments for All Seasons, 1904	

MARTHA DEWEY
  Pageant of Education, 1917, Valley City, N. D.

LOUISE HENRY DE WOLF
  Whom Seek Ye? 1930, Easter mystery play   RPB

CAROLINE EARNEST DICKENSON
  All Round Recitations, 1928   RPB
  Roll Call of a Nation, with Stanley Schell, in Werner's Magazine, 27,
    May, 1901, young

"PENELOPE DICKERSON" (See GLADYS SIGLER HENDERSON)

MARIE PAULE DICKORE
  Learning to Eat Potatoes, 1915, in 3 scenes, Wisconsin Un. Extension   RPB
    Division

MARGARET S. DICKSON
  Being a Hero   FMC

LEOTA DIESEL
  Better Never Than Late, 1927, winner of the Wilson prize, Washington   RPB
    Un., St. Louis, Mo., comedy

LAURABELLE DIETRICK
  In the Shadow of the Desert, 1930
  The White Senorita, 1930

BLANCHE DILLAYE (? -1931)
  Masks

KATE ROSE DILLON
  Sweet Rose of Briar Gulch, 1909, 3 acts   RPB

ELISABETH DIMICK
  At the Picture Show, 1928 or earlier, monologue
  The Boy in the Carpenter Shop, 1929, religious monologue   RPB
  Her Club Business, 1924, monologue   DLC
  Mrs. Lears Joy Ride, 1924, monologue   DLC

MARTHA L. DINGMAN
  Two Monologs: The Days That Are Gone, and School Days, 1914   RPB

MARY C. DINSMORE
  The Passing of the Seasons, 1902, literary entertainment   RPB

ANNEE (or AIMEE) DIX
  Sister Celestine's Silver Jubilee, 1912, school play in 3 acts   RPB

BEULAH MARIE DIX (FLEBBE) (1876-1970) AWW
  Across the Border, 1915, "play of the present"   RPB
  Allison's Lad (1)   HNM,KSP, KCP,MRO-1929
  Allison's Lad and Other Martial Interludes, 1910, 6 one-acts   RPB
  The Arnott Will, with Evelyn Greenleaf Sutherland, typed copy   OrU
  At the Sign of the Buff Bible, 1898, typed copy   OrU
  Boy O'Carroll, 1902, with Evelyn G. Sutherland
  The Breed of the Treshams, 1902, written under pseud. "John   OrU
    Rutherford," with Evelyn G. Sutherland, typed copy

BEULAH MARIE DIX (continued)

The Captain of the Gate	LAM
Cicely's Cavalier, 1896, comedy (1)	RPB
Clemency, written for American School Peace League (1)	
The Dark of the Dawn	SSV
A Daughter of Wrath, typed copy	OrU
The Day of Defeat, romantic melodrama in 4 acts	OrU
Diccon Goodnaught, with Evelyn Greenleaf Sutherland, 4 act romantic comedy	OrU
An Easter Play, typed copy	OrU
The Enemy, 1915, written for Am. School Peace League for secondary school boys (1)	RPB
English Born	OrU
The Evil Fruit, screenplay with Bertram Millhauser, typed copy	OrU
For the King, typed copy	OrU
The Girl Comes Home, 1927, comedy (1)	RPB
The Glorious Game, written for Am School Peace League (1)	
The Hundredth Trick, romantic tragedy (1)	TTO
A Legend of St. Nicholas, in Poet Lore, 25, Autumn, 1914, 473-95 (1)	
A Legend of St. Nicholas and Other Plays, 1927, one-acts	RPB
The Lilac Room, 1902, with Evelyn G. Sutherland	OrU
The Lonely Lady, 1915 (original titles—The Imperfect Lady and Some Women Are Different)	OrU
Matt of Merrymount, 1902, with Evelyn G. Sutherland	
The Minx, 1905, comedy (1)	OrU
Moloch, 1916, prod. 1915 (anti-war)	RPB
Nan of the Killigrews, 4 act romantic comedy, typed copy	OrU
The Other Side of It, typed copy	OrU
A Pageant of Peace, 1915, written for Am School Peace League for upper elementary schools	RPB
The Pendleton Place, with Evelyn G. Sutherland	OrU
Phyllida, 4 act romantic comedy, typed copy	OrU
The Pioneer Woman, 1927, typed copy	OrU
Predestination	OrU
Ragged Army, prod. 1934, 3 acts, with Bertram Millhauser, typescript	NN, OrU
Rapparee Trooper, with Evelyn G. Sutherland	OrU
The Rapscallion, With Evelyn G. Sutherland, 3 act romantic comedy, typed copy	OrU
The Road to Yesterday, 1925, prod. 1906, with E. G. Sutherland, "comedy of fantasy"	RPB
A Rose O' Plymouth Town, 1902, with E. G. Sutherland, 4 act romantic comedy	RPB
State O' Maine, with Evelyn G. Sutherland, 4 acts	OrU
Stigmata, with Evelyn G. Sutherland and Eva Unsell, 4 act tragedy	OrU
The Substitute	OrU
Supernumeraries, with Evelyn G. Sutherland, comedy	OrU
Three Miracle Plays, adapted from the Chester Miracle Plays, typed copy	OrU
The Tide Comes In, typed copy	OrU
To Serve for Meat and Fee, 1900, 4 act romantic comedy	OrU
Two Christmas Plays, typed copy	OrU
Where War Comes, 1916, written for Am School Peace League for lower elementary schools	RPB, SPP
The Wise Woman of Hogsdon, adapt. of play by Thomas Heywood	OrU
The Woman Dotes	OrU
The Woman Wakens (1)	OrU
Young Fernald, 1902, with E. G. Sutherland, 4 act comedy, typed copy	OrU
Yule-Tide,	OrU

MAY DIXIE
  The Footlight Revue, 1922, "a colorful contrivance in five flashes,"   RPB
      devised by F. G. Johnson, ensemble numbers arranged by Dixie
  (She also did several illustrated song pantomimes.)

ANNA BOWMAN BLAKE DODD (1855- ?)
  The American Husband in Paris, 1901, comedy   RPB

NELLIE C. DODD
  Broken Chains, 1915, pub. by missionary ed. movement of U.S. and   RPB
      Canada

FLORA BEGELOW DODGE
  Mrs. Mack's Example, in Smart Set, 5, Sept., 1901, 51+ (1)

MAY HEWES DODGE
  College Days, 1921, with John Wilson Dodge, 3 act musical,   RPB-M
      "romance of American college life"
  The Crimson Eyebrows, 1922, with John Wilson Dodge, "fantastic
      romance of old China"
  Cynthia's Strategy, 1922, with John W. Dodge, (1)   RPB-M
  Daniel O'Connell, 1918, "romantic Irish musical play," with John Wilson
      Dodge, for the benefit of the Belgian Babies Relief Fund
  The Glass Slipper; or, The Adventures of the Cinder Maid, 1921, with RPB-M
      John W. Dodge, 3 act musical
  The Gypsy Rover, 1919, with John W. Dodge, 3 act musical   RPB-M
  Hulda of Holland, 1925, with John W. Dodge, 3 act musical   RPB-M
  In the Garden of the Shah, 1920, "romance of Persia," 3 act musical   CLU
      comedy
  In Old Louisiana, 1922, with John W. Dodge, 3 act musical, "romance RPB-M
      of the Old South"
  Knight of Dreams; or, A Modern Pygmalion and Galatea, 1924, with   IU
      John Wilson Dodge, 3 act musical comedy
  Miss Cherryblossom; or, a Maid of Tokyo, 1918, with John W. Dodge, RPB-M
      3 acts
  Old Crosspatch, 1938, music by John W. Dodge; book and lyrics by   RPB-M
      Cynthia Dodge; operetta for children
  Paul Revere, 1919, with John W. Dodge, 3 act musical comedy   MB, Mi
  Rose, Wonderful Rose, 1922, musical, with John W. Dodge   OCl
  The Singer of Naples, 1928, 2 act musical comedy   Or
  The Wishing Well, 1923, with John W. Dodge, romance of Old Ireland   NN

MARGARET A. DOHENY
  Play Awhile, 1916, dramatic reader for the second school year   RPB

AGNES M. DOIG
  Doig's Excellent Dialogues for Young Folks, 1901   RPB

LENORE K. DOLAN
  A Bandit Santa Claus   FOA
  The Best Halloween Book, 1931   DLC
  Big Book of Thanksgiving Entertainments, 1941, with Noel Flaurier
      and others
  Celebrating Closing Day in the Grades, 1934   NcC
  Cheery Christmas Entertainments, 1933, with Marie Irish and James Rowe
  The Children's Own Play Book, 1931   RPB
  The Christmas Program Book, 1931, with others

LENORE K. DOLAN (continued)
<u>Confusion in Santa Claus Land</u>   FOA
<u>Funny One Act Christmas Plays</u>, 1935, with others   RPB
<u>The Gladtime Christmas Book</u>, 1932
<u>The Gladtime Thanksgiving Book</u>, 1932, with Marie Irish   RPB
<u>The Good Health Treasure Book</u>, 1930   RPB
<u>Handy Helps for Halloween</u>, 1932   WaS
<u>Merry Christmas in All the Grades</u>, 1932   Or
<u>Misses and Mistletoe</u>   FOA
<u>Novelty Thanksgiving Collection for Children</u>, 1937   RPB
<u>Short Plays and Pageants for All Occasions and Grades</u>, 1930   RPB
<u>The Surprise Package</u>   FOA
<u>Thanksgiving Tidbits</u>, 1932   RPB
<u>William's Christmas Gift</u>   FOA

MRS. H. C. DOLLSON
<u>Coffin-Nails and Common Sense</u>, "In the Interest of Anti-cigarets (sic)"   HPY

EMILY DONAGHY
<u>The Paramount Children's Day Book</u>, 1930, a contributor   RPB
<u>The Paramount Mother's Day Book</u>, No. 2, 1941, a contributor   RPB

DOROTHY DONALD
<u>Desert Poison</u>, 1925, melodrama   RPB

ALICE MARIE DONLEY
<u>Grange Plays</u>, No. 3, one-acts   RPB

DOROTHEA CADOGAN DONN-BYRNE ("DOLLY BYRNE")
<u>Enter Madame</u>, 1921, prod. 1920, with Gilda Varesi, 3 acts   RPB
<u>The Land of the Stranger</u>, 192? "kindly comedy"

DOROTHY DONNELLY (1880-1928)
<u>Blossom Time</u>, prod. 1921, musical adaptation from German
<u>The Call of Life</u>, prod. 1925, English version of play by Arthur Schnitzler
<u>Fancy Free</u>, prod. 1918, with Edgar Smith, music by Augustus Barratt
<u>Flora Bella</u>, prod. 1916, book by Donnelly, Felix Doerman and Cosmo
     Hamilton; music by Charles Cuvillier and Milton Schwarzwald
<u>Forbidden</u>, prod. 1919
<u>Hello Lola!</u> prod. 1926
<u>My Golden Girl</u>, variant of <u>My Princess</u>
<u>My Maryland</u>, 1927, music by Sigmund Romberg
<u>My Princess</u>, prod. 1927, modern operetta in 3 acts, based on a play by
     Donnelly and Sheldon; music by Sigmund Romberg; book and lyrics
     by Donnelly, (music at CU)
<u>Poppy</u>, prod. 1923, music by Stephen Jones and Arthur Samuels
<u>The Proud Princess</u>, prod. 1924
<u>The Riddle Woman</u>, prod. 1918, with Charlotte E. Wells, incomplete   NN
     typescript
<u>The Student Prince</u>, prod. 1924, music by Sigmund Romberg   RPB-M

ALICE DONOVAN
<u>The Garden</u>, religious play

HILDA DOOLITTLE (ALDINGTON) "H.D." (1886-1961) AWW NAW
<u>Hippolytus Temporizers</u>, 1927, 3 act poetic drama   RPB
<u>Hymen—a Masque</u>, in her book of verse, <u>Hymen</u>, 1921

KATHARINE ELIZABETH DOPP (1863- ?)
Homer and David, 1903, from an essay by Edward E. Hale, "historical play for the use in schools" (1)

MARIE DORAN

Among the Winners, 1937, 3 act comedy	DLC
An Accusing Finger, 1929, 3 act mystery comedy	RPB
Ann Comes to Her Senses, 1932, comedy (1)	RPB
Another Angle, 1937, 3 act comedy	DLC
Betty's Bungalo, 1933, comedy (1)	RPB
Carmen, 1905, melodramatic play in one act and one scene, typed copy	MH
Cecelia, 1928, 3 act religious drama	RPB
Dorothy's Neighbors, 1917, 4 act youthful comedy	RPB
The Education of Doris, 1932, 3 act comedy	RPB
Eyes of Faith, Americanization play (1)	
Fast Colors, 1928, 3 act mystery	RPB
The Gay Coeds, 1933, 3 act comedy	RPB
(A) The Ghost of a Chance, 1933, comedy (1)	RPB
The Girls Over Here, 1917, patriotic play (1)	RPB
Grandma Gets a Job, 1936, 3 act comedy	
A Happy Surprise, 1930, 3 act comedy	RPB
The Honor Pupil, 1925, 4 act comedy	RPB
The Hope Chest, 1927, 3 act comedy	RPB
How Nellie Made Good, 1919 (1)	RPB
It's Great To Be Young, 1936, 3 act comedy	
Jane, Jessie, and Jack, 1928, 3 act comedy	RPB
June, 1917, 4 act comedy drama	RPB
Kathleen Mavourneen, 1918, 4 act romantic Irish drama	RPB
Keeping Up with Jane, 1934, 3 act comedy	
Lena Rivers, 1918, comedy drama, based on novel by Mary J. Holmes	RPB
The Liberty Thrift Girls, 1918, patriotic play (1)	RPB
Listen to This, 1934, 3 act comedy	
The Little Flower, 1925, 3 act religious drama	RPB
Molly Bawn, 1920, 4 act comedy drama, based on story by Mrs. Hungerford	RPB
Mother Puts One Over, 1931, comedy (1)	RPB
The New Coed, 1915, 4 act comedy	RPB
Our High Brow Sister, 1929, 3 act comedy	RPB
Quo Vadis, 1928, based on novel by Henry Sienkiewicz	OCl, DLC
Something to Talk About, 1935, 3 act comedy	
A Substitute for Sally, 1931, 3 act comedy	RPB
Teacher Was Right, 1931, 3 act comedy	RPB
Tempest and Sunshine, comedy drama, based on novel by Mary J. Holmes	
That Orphan, 1924, 4 act comedy	RPB
These Are Your Neighbors, 1935, 3 act comedy	
Tommy's Flivver, 1927, 3 act farce	RPB
The Trials of Mary, 1921, 4 act comedy	
While Your Mother Is Away, 1930, "comedy about sensible girls"	
Would You Believe It? 1932, 3 act comedy	
Youth Shows the Way, 1933, 3 act comedy	OCl, DLC

ELIZABETH JOHNSON WARD DOREMUS (MRS. CHARLES A. DOREMUS)

The Duchess of Devonshire, 1906? 4 act romantic comedy	NN
The Fortune of the King, 1904, with Leonidas Westervelt	
Grif, n.d., with Frank Allen, dram. of novel by B. L. Farjeon, typed copy (1)	NN
Mock Trial for Breach of Promise, n.d., with Miss H. E. Manchester	RPB

HELEN DORSEN
   The Power of Loyalty, 1918, "war-time play of today written for Young   RPB
      America—the boys and girls of our public schools" (1)

HELEN DORTCH
   Companion-Mate Maggie, Negro comedy, in Carolina Playbook, 1929   KCC

EDITH KINNEY DOTEN
   Maundy Thursday   DPC
   A Pageant of the Life of Fanny Crosby, the Blind Gospel Songwriter,   RPB
      1925

KATHARINE KINARD DOUGHTIE
   Groceries and Notions, 1931, "drama carelessly interspersed   RPB, VET
      with songs"
   Simples by Moonlight, 1930

ISODORE DOUGLAS
   Fandango Land, 1910, 2 act musical comedy, written for senior class,   RPB-M
      Barnswallows, Wellesley College; lyrics by Douglas and others; music
      by Edith Sweetser and others

JEANETTE E. DOUGLASS
   Mother Tongue's Party, good English play   WPP

ADELE NEILL DOWLING
   Aunt Betsy, 1931, "pantomimic novelty"   RPB
   The Little Bluffer, 1925, farce (1)   RPB
   Luck o' Land, 1927   RPB, ECO

MILDRED DOWLING
   Lorna Doone, 1901, 5 acts, based on the novel by R. D. Blackmore   RPB

JUNE ETTA DOWNEY (1875-1932) NAW
   The Arrow, in Poet Lore, 38, 1927, 297-306 (1)
   A Study in the Nude, tragedy, in Poet Lore, 31, Summer, 1920, 253-60

CLARA B. DRAKE
   The Doom of King Alcohol, 1903, dramatic sketch in 3 acts   RPB

EMILY H. DRAKE
   Roseberry Shrub Sec., 1928, by Frank C. Drake, rev. and ed. by Emily,   RPB
      comedy, motif of play from "The Pearl of Ohio" by Bessie Chandler

RUTH K. DRAKE
   Father's Joy Ride, 1926 or earlier

JANE DRANSFIELD ("JANE STONE") (1875-1975)
   Arshaluis; or, the Promise of a New Day, 1919, sketch   RPB
   The Baroness (1)
   Blood O' Kings, 1928 (1)   RPB, CNA,STM
   Joe, a Hudson Valley Play, 1923, tragedy (1)   RPB, STS
   The Lost Pleiad, 1918, verse drama, dream fantasy based on   RPB, STW
      Greek myth
   Mal Treloare, 1940   RPB, MTS
   Monologue Hits, 1948, by "Jane Stone"   RPB
   The Romance of Melrose Hall, 1908, "play of the revolution, founded on
      the history and traditions of Flatbush"

JANE DRANSFIELD (continued)
That's Life, 1952, monologue by "Jane Stone"   RPB
Two Women (1)
The White Window (1)

OCTAVINE LOPEZ DREEBEN (1886- ?)
The Choice, 1914, 3 acts   RPB

CAROLINE HYDE DREHER
Idle Brains, 1928, farce (1)   RPB

MARIE DRENNAN
The Anger of the Sun; or, the Wrath of Ama-Terasu, 1928, pageant   RPB
    adapted from Shintu legends
The Slippers That Broke of Themselves, in Poet Lore, 37, 1926, 258-73 (1)
The Valley of Gloom, in Poet Lore, 34, Autumn, 1923, 449-57 (1)

MARY DRESCHER
The Magic Word, 1928, 3 scene playlet based upon "Ali Baba and the   RPB
    Forty Thieves," Written by Mary Drescher and Genevieve Harper,
    students, under the supervision of Lena M. Abel, Faculty Advisor,
    Roosevelt H. S., Seattle, Washington

CLARA DRISCOLL (1881-1945) NAW
Mexicana, prod. 1906, with Robert B. Smith, musical

GERTRUDE PORTER DRISCOLL (1898- ?)
The Coming of Summer, with Clara P. Peterson, based on Am. Indian   JPP
    fairy tale

LOUISE DRISCOLL (1875- ?)
The Child of God, in Seven Arts, 1, Nov., 1916, 34-46 (1)
The Garden of the West, in Poetry, 13, Dec., 1918, 138-45, pub. 1922 (1)
The Metal -Checks, in Poetry, 5, Nov., 1914, 49-54 (1)
A Pageant of Women, in Drama, 14, May-June, 1924, 263-5 (1)
The Poor House, in Drama, 7, Aug., 1917, 448-60 (1)   CMO

MARJORIE DRISCOLL
The Song With Wings, prod. 1919 by Pasadena Comm. Players
The White Bird, prod. by Pasadena Comm. Players

SHIRLEY GRAHAM DU BOIS (See SHIRLEY GRAHAM)

THEODORA MC CORMICK DU BOIS (1890- ?)
Aladdin, 1926   MRC
Amateur and Educational Dramatics, 1917, with Evelyne Hilliard and
    Kate Oglebay
Rocks and Rills, 1932, "cartoon in 3 dimensions" (about 1929 economic   RPB
    crisis)
The Sleeping Beauty, 1919, 3 acts   RPB

ELEANOR DUBUISSON
Bonny and Billy's Christmas Dream, 1927, 2 acts   RPB, JEC
A Gift for Father Andrew, 1933, 2 acts, Christmas   RPB
It Happens Every Day, 1927, character monologue   RPB

CAROLINE KING DUER (1865- ?)
The Ambassador's Daughter (Burglar), in Smart Set, 5, Nov., 1901, 49-57 (1)
Jacqueline, 1909, with Harriet French Ford, typescript NN
Mr. Shakespeare at School, in Smart Set, 7, June, 1902, 65-73 (1)
Where Julia Rules, 1923, 4 act comedy, with Harriet French Ford

DOROTHY MANLEY DUFF
Stigma, 1927, with Donald Duff (about miscegenation)

LOUISA DULS
Lighted Candles, with Margaret Bland, "tragedy of the Carolina KCF
highlands" (1)

HETTIE JANE DUNAWAY
The Flapper Grandmother, 1924, musical comedy, including "An RPB
Automobile Romance," novelty curtain raiser

OLIVIA HOWARD DUNBAR (1873- ?)
Blockade, in Theatre Arts Magazine, 7, April, 1923, 127-42 (1) IPA
Enter Women, 1939, "America in Action play" (1) RPB

ALICE RUTH MOORE DUNBAR-NELSON
(or ALICE RUTH DUNBAR NELSON)
(MRS. PAUL LAWRENCE DUNBAR) (1875-1935) AWW NAW SBAA
The Author's Evening at Home, in Smart Set, 2, Sept., 1900, 105-6 (1)
The Dunbar Speaker and Entertainer, 1920 RPB
Mine Eyes Have Seen, 1918, in The Crisis, 15, April, 1918 (1) HSB

FRANCES DUNCAN (1877- ?)
Save the Wild Flowers, with Elsie Duncan Yale, in Woman's Home
Companion, 54, May, 1927, 49

MISS L. B. DUNCAN
Patriotic Pageant for Washington Day

SARAH L. DUNCAN
Alice Markham, Spinster, in Carolina Magazine, 41, no. 5, Feb., 1924

THELMA MYRTLE DUNCAN (1902- ?)
Black Magic, 1931 (1) YSP-I
The Death Dance, 1923, musical (1) LGP
Sacrifice (1) RMP
The Scarlet Shawl (1)

WINIFRED DUNCAN
The Classic Dancing School, in Drama, 17, May, 1927, 235-42 (1)

DORA DUNCKER (1855-1915)
The Witch's Song, 1902, 3 tragic scenes, taken from the poem, "Das RPB
hexenlied," by Ernest von Wildenbruch

GISELLE C. D'UNGER
Jack's Predicament, 1907 (1)
Pink Carnations, 1901, "monolog for a lady" RPB

HENRIETTA F. DUNLAP
Circus Day	FMC
The Flags at War	FMM
The Guarding Angels	FMM
Just Before Yorktown, 1919, ten-minute play for 7th and 8th grades,	MB
"written with a view to increasing the sale of war-savings stamps"	
The Prince of Ko-Am	FMC
The Rough Riders	FMM

NANCY D. DUNLEA
Aunt Em Hears the Symphony, 1931	RPB
Bring Up Bobby, 1926, monologue	RPB
Sewin' Out by the Day, 1925, monologue	RPB
She Made a "Punkin" Pie, 1929	RPB

ETHEL M. DUNMIRE
The Christmas Story, 1924, dram. using hymns and Scripture texts	RPB

FANNIE WYCHE DUNN (1879- ?)
Tweedledum and Tweedledee	
What Shall We Play? 1916, dramatic reader, one acts	RPB

LUELLA M. DUNNING
Elisha	DPC

EDITH KELLOGG DUNTON ("MARGARET WARDE") (1875- ?)
The Betty Wales Girls and Mr. Kidd, 1912, by "Margaret Warde"	RPB
Is Your Name Smith? 1921, comedy (1)	RPB

HELEN DURHAM (1893-1932)
Fashion Review Down Petticoat Lane, 1923, includes songs	RPB
Me For You, 1930, musical comedy with fashion review, rev. by Ethel	Or
Gesner Rockwell	
The Nativity of the Manger, 1928, Christmas tableau	

MARY EVA DUTHIE
Balanced Diet, 1928, comedy by Elizabeth Lay Green, ed. by Duthie and	RPB
Alexander M. Drummond	
Mother's Share, 1938, with Emma Dodd Nevin, 4-H Club play (1)	DLC
The Old Timers' Bureau, 1928, by John H. Munson, ed. by Duthie and	RPB
Alexander Drummond	
Out of the Night, 1928, by John Smith, ed. by Duthie and Alexander	RPB
Drummond	
That Upper Forty, by Marvin Herrick and Hoyt H. Hudson, ed. by	RPB
Duthie and Drummond	
Too Busy, 1928, by Bertha E. Wallace, ed. by Duthie and Drummond	RPB
Wedding Clothes, by Grace Kiner, ed. by Duthie and Drummond, N. Y.	RPB
State rural life play	

EMMA BARTLETT DUTTON
Around the World with Girl Scouts, 1927, international pageant for	RPB
Girl Scouts and Brownies	
Found—A Girl Scout, 1933, for jr. h. s.	RPB

MARY VIRGINIA DUVAL (1850- ?)
The Court of Fame, 1903, "play of great women " (1)	RPB
The Queen of the South, 1899	GU, MsU

ELIZABETH E. DU VERNET
    The Brown Chiny Teapot, 1928   RPB

CHARITY DYE (1849- ?)
    Pageant of New Harmony, 1914, New Harmony, Ind.   InI, DLC
    Pageant Suggestions for the Indianapolis Statehood Centennial   InI
       Celebration, 1916

CHLOE (CHLORINE) DYSART
    The Comin' Out of Mary Jane Cummins, 1911, 2 act comedy   RPB
    The Dancing Contest, 1920, comedy sketch   RPB
    July the Fourth, 1910, comedy (1)   RPB
    A Meeting of the Confidential Club, 1916, sketch   RPB

E

MARGARET MACLAREN EAGER

Boston Historic Festival, 1897, for Boston Teachers' Mutual Benefit   RPB
     Association (She was director.) program
Cornell Pageant, 1916, Ithaca, N. Y.
Duxbury Days, 1909, pageant, Duxbury, Mass., program   MDeeP
Everychild, 1915, pageant, Greenfield, Mass.
Festival of the Hills, 1915, pageant, Conway, Mass.
Historical Pageant of First Church, 1914, Pittsfield, Mass.
Historical Pageant of Newburgh-on-the Hudson, 1915, "pageant of peace   NN
     and true patriotism," Newburgh, N. Y.
Historical Pageant of Northampton at Wildwood, 1911, Northampton,   MB
     Mass., (program text at MDeeP)
Ipswich Pageant, 1910, Ipswich, Mass., program text   MDeeP, OU
More-Roxbury Pageant, 1915, Roxbury, N. Y.
Old Plymouth Days and Ways, 1897, pageant (She was director.)   RPB
     handbook
Old Worcester Ways, 1910, pageant, Worcester, Mass.
Pageant of Bennington, 1911, Bennington, Vt., program text   MDeeP
Pageant of Brattleboro, 1912, Brattleboro, Vt., program text   MDeeP, OU
Pageant of Great Barrington, 1912, Great Barrington, Mass.
Pageant of Hartford, 1911, Hartford, Vt., program text   MDeeP
Pageant of the Mohawk Trail, 1914, N. Adams, Mass.
Pageant of Old Deerfield, 1910, Deerfield, Mass., program text   MDeeP
Pageant of Plattsburgh, 1914, Plattsburgh, N. Y., program text   MDeeP
Pageant of Salem, 1913, Salem, Mass., presented under   RPB,MDeeP, OU
     management of Board of Directors of House of Gables Settlement Assoc.,
     program text
Pageant of Saratoga, 1912, 1913 Saratoga, N. Y.   RPB
Pageant of Utica, 1914, Utica, N. Y., program text   MDeeP,NN
Pageant of Warren, 1914, Warren, R. I., "in honor of 150th anniversary   RPB
     of founding of First Baptist Church of Warren, the founding of R. I.
     College (Brown Un.) and setting off of the town of Warren"
Rochester Shakespeare Pageant, 1916, Rochester, N.Y., prog. text MDeeP,DLC
Spielkartenfest, 1895, Providence, R. I., by Margaret MacLaren, under   RPB
     auspices of R. I. Exchange for Women's Work—includes tableaux,
     songs, games, frolic of the flowers and living whist
Ten Teddy Bears, 1907, operetta for children, music by   RPB-M
     Florence Maxim
Toyland; or, Nip and Tuck, the Fairy Toymakers, n.d., children's cantata   RPB
     dram. by Eager of work by William Wilberforce Newton
The Wonder-wander Man, 1908, musical play founded on poems of   RPB
     Eugene Fields, with Wendell Endicott

FLORENCE E. EAKMAN

Attic Secrets, 1935 (1)
The Badge of Honor, 1928 (1)   RPB
The Enchanted Dolls, 1928, manners and morals play for children   RPB
The Fairies Party, 1927 (1)   RPB
The Little House of Pleasant Dreams, 1927, health play for children (1)   RPB
Noel—a Gift, 1927, Christmas play for children   RPB
O-O-Oh—A Ghost! 1927, Halloween play for children   RPB
Penny Sense, 1928, thrift play for children (1)   RPB
The Stranger, 1927, library play for children (1)   RPB
The Uninvited Guest, 1927, Thanksgiving play for children (1)   RPB

DOROTHY KIRCHENER EARLE
You're Such a Respectable Person, Miss Morrison, in Smart Set, 46,
    August, 1915, 87-94 (1)

GEORGIA EARLE
Before the Play Begins, 1919, comedy (1)   RPB
Gettin' Acquainted, 1919, small-town comedy (1)   RPB
The Lie That Jack Built, 1910, comedy (1)   RPB
The Mark of the Beast, prod. 1915, with Fanny Cannon

MIRIAM LEE EARLEY (1878- ?)
The Lion and the Mouse, scene from the play by Charles Klein and   PTS-VIII
    Arthur Hornblow, arranged for reading by Earley

ELAINE GOODALE EASTMAN (1863-1953)   AWW
The Eagle and the Star, 1916, American Indian pageant play for Camp   RPB
    Fire girls, 3 acts

IDA RAUH EASTMAN
The Last Trick, suffrage (1)

EMMA FLORENCE EATON
Dramatic Studies from the Bible, 1906   RPB

MABEL E. EATON
That Boy George and The Lincoln League, 190? dialogues for young   RPB

SOPHIE B. EBB
Joseph, Biblical play, in The Jewish Home, 10, no. 4, Dec., 1903, 127-37   RPB

NELLE RICHMOND MC CURDY EBERHART (1871-1944)
The Father of Waters, 1928, American cantata, music by Charles   RPB-M
    Wakefield Cadman
The Garden of Mystery, 1925, grand opera, music by Charles   RPB-M
    Wakefield Cadman
Portland's Rose Festival, The Pageant of the Rose, 1925, story by   RPB-M
    Doris Smith; words by Eberhart; music by Charles W. Cadman
The Robin Woman (Shanewis), 1927, American opera, music by   RPB-M
    Charles W. Cadman (1)
Sayonara, 1910, Japanese romance, music by Charles W. Cadman   RPB-M
Spring Rapture, 1945, cantata, music by Harvey B. Gaul   RPB-M
A Witch of Salem, 1926, music by Charles W. Cadman   RPB-M

MERAB EBERLE
Bobby in Belgium, 1918, Jr. Red Cross play   RPB
Captain Anne of the Red Cross; or, How the Militant Ghosts Saved   RPB
    Millville, 1918, Red Cross comedy for girls
The May Dew Charm, 1918, for school performance (1)   RPB
The Spirit of Democracy, 1917, allegorical pageant   RPB

MARY S. EDGAR
The Conspiracy of Spring, 1920, (mimeograph copy at WaU) (1)   SSH-II
Everygirl, 1920, pageant of the girl reserves   OCl
The Scarlet Knight, 1920, autumn play for children, mimeograph copy   WaU
The Wayside Piper, 1915, written for commencement week of the   NN,DLC
    class of 1915, of the National Training School, won first prize in Panama-
    Pacific Exposition Contest, based on "Pied Piper of Hamlin" (1)

HARRIET EDGERTON
The Deluded Dragon, puppet play with Ellen Van Colkenburg

HELEN MARION EDGINTON (MAY EDGINTON) (1883- ?)
A Lesson in Love, prod. 1923, with Rudolph Bessier
Secrets, 1930, prod. 1922, with Rudolph Bessier

MINNIE A. G. EDINGTON
Glories of Summer, 1929, Children's Day pageant service for Sunday   RPB
    school; music by Thomas, Nevin, Martin, Nolte, and Rosche
O Little Town of Bethlehem, 1929, Christian pageant-service for Sunday DLC
    school, music by Nevin, Thomas, Nolte and others

ELISABETH EDLAND
Children of Galilee, 1935, young   RPB
Children's Dramatizations, 1926   RPB
The Children's King and Other Plays for Children, 1928   RPB
His Book, 1925, dramatic sketch for junior groups   NcD
Plum Blossom and Other Plays, 1925, young   RPB
Spring in the Brown Meadow and Other Pantomimes for Little   RPB
    Children, 1928
The Tercentenary Pageant of Reformed Church in America, 1920   NN, DLC
The Waiting Guest, 1925, play of S. American village life for h. s. age NcD

LILLY TEGGE EGGERT
Wild Rose of the West, 1912   RPB

FAY EHLERT
The Undercurrent, 1929, also in Drama, 18, Jan., 1928, 111-4 (1)   RPB, KFA

ELMA C. EHRLICH
A Peace Pageant for Children and Young People, 1915, with Cora   MB
    Mel Patten

IDA LUBLENSKI EHRLICH (1886- ?)
Changing Places (1)   OPS-III
Cured, comedy (1)   OPS-IV
The Girl from Samos, 1955, prod. 1954, "reconstructed from the   RPB
    fragment of Menander"
Helena's Boys, 1927, prod. 1924, dram. of story by Mary B. Pulver   RPB
Late Spring, 1935 (1)
Love Kills, 1934
One Hundred Dollars, 1925 (1)   RPB
Peace-Makers, farce (1)   OAT-I
Snaring the Lion, in Drama, 34, May, 1919, 60-83 (1)
Stutzpunkt, 1946, 2 acts, typescript   NN
Theme and Variations, 1937 (1)   DLC
'Twas Ever Us, farce   NAB-II
Winners All, 1928, farce (1)   SFM

BESS EHRMANN
Pageant of Prohibition, 1927, dedicated to the Rockport, Ind. WCTU   InI

LESLIE P. EICHEL
Americans, n.d., typescript   NN
Marion Surrenders, 1912   RPB

GRACE SHULL EICHMANN
   The Little City of Friendly Hearts, 1928, fantasy for children   RPB

BLANCHE GOODMAN EISENDRATH (See BLANCHE GOODMAN)

LINDA EKMAN
   The Nativity, 1922, mystery play for voices with piano and organ, with RPB-M
      Elizabeth Fyffe

DOROTHY ELDERDICE
   The Carroll County Caravan, 1937, pageant of the soil, Westminster, Md. DLC
   Demas, a play of the 1st Century, 1936, religious play   RPB
   The Good Samaritan, 19?? adapted from Dorothy Elderdice by Bessie   GEU
      Irwin, "dramatic service telling the story of the hospital movement
      of the Methodist Episcopal Church, Atlanta, Ga."
   1918 and Now, 1936, play for amateurs   RPB
   The Oyster Supper, 1937, with Howard Amos, rural church comedy   RPB
   The Sheathing of the Sword, 1922, pageant of peace   RPB
   Speak Through the Earthquake, 1937, "play for one-self, for young   DLC
      people's day"
   U-leh-lah, Pocahontas of Florida, 1926, historical play   FU

ETHEL J. ELDRIDGE
   Children's Pantomimes for Special Days, 1936   DLC
   Old Home Song Pantomimes, 1910   OCl
   Personal Liberty   JEM
   Ten Good Christmas Pantomimes, 1921   RPB-M

FLORENCE M. ELDRIDGE
   The Growth of a Nation, 1926   RPB

JOAN ELDRIDGE
   "First Aid," with Richard Eldridge (1)

SARAH B. ELDRIDGE
   Showers and Sunshine, 190? song and drill for 12-16 children   CLSU
   The Vitaphone Courtship, 1928, 2 act comedy drama   RPB

ANNIE ELIOT (See ANNIE ELIOT TRUMBULL)

CHARLOTTE CHAMPE (CHAUNCEY) STEARNS ELIOT (1843-1929) NAW
   Savonarola, 1926, dramatic poem   RPB

MARY E. ELLIOTT
   Animated Slang, 1914   RPB
   The Dark Meetin', 1924, Negro play   RPB

MAUD HOWE ELLIOTT (1854-1948) AWW
   The Man Without a Shadow, 19?? fairy piece in 4 acts from Hans   RPB
      Christian Andersen, typewritten copy

EDITH ELLIS (BAKER) (1876-1960) AWW
   Adventure
   The Amethyst Ring, 1913, operetta
   Anna Karanina
   A Batch of Blunders, 1897, musical
   Because I Love You, 1903

EDITH ELLIS (continued)

Ben of Broken Bow, 1925, prod. 1905, "an original American comedy"   RPB
Betty's Last Bet, 1921, 3 act romantic comedy   RPB
Bravo Claudia, 1919
Captives
Cleopatra
"Contrary Mary," 1912, 3 act comedy
Cupid's Ladder, 1915, 3 act operetta, lyrics by William C. Duncan, music   RPB
    by Charles J. Hambitzer
"The Devil's Garden," 1915, based on a story by William B. Maxwell,   NN
    typescript
Fields of Flax, sociological drama
He Fell in Love with His Wife, 1910
If You Think It's So, It's So, with Oliver Erlan
The Illustrious Tartarin, 1922, based on Alphonse Daudet's Tartarin   NN
    in the Alps, 3 act comedy, typescript
Incarnation; or, Plea from the Master, 1936, transcribed from a work of
    Wilfred Brandon
The Judsons Entertain, 1922, 3 act comedy   RPB
The King of Kalamazoo, before 1909
The Lady of La Paz, prod. 1936, based on novel, These Generations, by
    Elinor Mordaunt
The Last Chapter, prod. 1930, with Edward Ellis
The Last of the Crusoes, with Robert Sneddon
Leave It to Me
The Lottery Man
Love in the Afterlife, 1956, dram. of work by W. Brandon
The Love Thief
The Love Wager, 1912
Madame Is Amused, 1933, comedy   DLC
Make-Believe Man, 1915
Make Your Fortune
Making Dick Over, prod. 1915 (1916)
Man and His Mate
The Man Higher Up, prod. 1912
The Man with the Black Gloves, 1915
Mary and John, prod. 1905 (under name Edith Ellis Baker)
Mary Jane's Pa, 1914, prod. 1908, 3 acts (motion picture script 1934)   RPB
The Moon and Sixpence, 1924, after the story by Somerset Maugham,   DLC
    typescript
Mrs. B. O'Shaughnessy (Washlady), 1900
Mrs. Clancey's Car Ride, 1918, with Edward Ellis, for Federal Gov. Dept. of
    Dramatic Activities among the Soldiers
Mrs. Jimmie Thompson, prod. 1920, with Norman Rose, 3 act comedy,   RPB
    press and promotion book
My Man, prod. 1910, with Forrest Halsey
Never Too Late
New Wine
Open the Door, 1935, transcribed from the work of Wilfred Brandon KMK, N
Partners, 1911
Personality, with Arthur Shaw
The Point of View, 1904, domestic drama, prod. at Berkeley Lyceum, N. Y.
Seven Sisters, 1937, prod. 1911, farce, adapt. from Hungarian of Herczeg RPB
    (c. 1910 under title, Seven Girls, by Edith Ellis Furness)
Sonya, with Violet Heming and Otto Kruger
Storms on the Equator
"Strickland," 1923, based on Somerset Maugham's The Moon and   DLC
    Sixpence

EDITH ELLIS (continued)
The Swallow, typescript   NN
Vespers, before 1909, Canadian drama
We Knew These Men, 1942, 3 acts, transcribed from work of W. Brandon
"White Collars," 1926, prod. 1925, 3 act comedy, based on story by   RPB
    Edgar Franklin
The White Villa, 1921, based on a novel by Karen Michaelis, The
    Dangerous Age
Whose Little Bride Are You? 1919, 3 act romantic comedy   RPB
The Wrong Man, 1905

KATE FLORENCE ELLIS
The Christmas Shopper, monologue   JEC
The Family Album, 1893, "as exhibited by Mrs. Almira Pease of   RPB
    Hockanum," monologue
Fit and Suitemall, fashions, 1904, "fantastic entertainment in two   RPB
    scenes and a tableau"
Platform Monologues and Stage Entertainments, 1905   RPB
Then and Now, 1902, "an evening's entertainment"   RPB
Then and Now; or, Tea of the Past and Tea of the Present, 1929?   RPB
    specialty monologue in Scenes and Songs of Ye Olden Times,
    Boston, W. H. Baker, 1929?

MARIE STACKER ELLIS
A Lesson in Dietetics, 1923, good health play   RPB

RUTH ELMS
The Tempestuous Tale, 1916, presented by the class of 1916, Mount   RPB
    Holyoke; plot suggested by Dorothy Towle; play written by Helen
    Paschall, words and music by Elms

MYRTLE GIARD ELSEY
The Alley Daffodil, 1930, comedy   RPB
A Bargain for Cash, 1932, 3 act comedy   RPB
Beads on a String, 1927, 3 act comedy   RPB
The Beggar of Brampton Road, 1931, 3 act comedy   RPB
The Bride of the Army, 1934, 3 act comedy   RPB
Business Picks Up, 1932, 3 act comedy   RPB
Buying Shoes, 1925   RPB
Covered with Blushes, 1929, 3 act comedy   RPB
The Dark Side of Life, 1925, monologue for a boy   RPB
Drums of Fury, 1930   RPB
Fingerprints, 1928, 3 act comedy   RPB
Five or Six Hundred, 1925, 3 act comedy   RPB
Fool's Holiday, 1931, 3 act comedy   RPB
The Galloping Princess, 1928, 3 act comedy   RPB
The Girl in the Fur Coat, 1930   RPB
The Glow Lights of San Rey, 1931, 3 act comedy-drama   RPB
Governor Joe's Amen, 1935, 3 act comedy drama
He Liked Them Modern, 1931, comedy (1)   RPB
If We Did It Today, 1934, "take-off on the Declaration of Independence"   RPB
The Imperfect Past, 1934, comedy for grammar school groups   RPB
In a Burst of Glory, 1935, 3 act comedy
Jupiter Smiles, 1933, 3 act comedy   RPB
The Key to Happiness, 1924, 2 acts, Christmas   RPB
The Leopard's Paw, 1931   RPB
The Man in the Green Shirt, 1930, 3 act comedy   RPB

MYRTLE GIARD ELSEY (continued)
The Man in the Moon, 1929   RPB
Mr. Bandy's Glass Eye, 1931, 3 act comedy   RPB
Mr. Cinderella, 1935, 3 act comedy-drama
No Money Down, 1927, 3 act comedy   RPB
One Minute of Twelve, 1927, 3 act comedy   RPB
Out of the Ark Came Noah, 1931, 3 act comedy   RPB
The Pilgrim Follies, 1935, "take-off on the landing of the Pilgrims"
The Pumpkin Hill Grammar School Graduation, 1931, comedy for jr.   RPB
     high schoool
The Purple Tantrum, 1929, comedy
Red Hostage, 1932, 3 act comedy   RPB
A Reed in the Wind, 1928, 3 acts, circus drama   RPB
Romance and Kid Brother, 1925, monologue for a boy   RPB
Second Hand Smith, 1934, 3 act comedy   RPB
Short Thirty-six, 1932, 3 act comedy   RPB
The Spare Room, 1931, 3 act comedy   RPB
The Third Customer, 1929   RPB
Truth Takes a Holiday, 1933, 3 act comedy drama   RPB
Wild Ginger, 1928, 3 act comedy-drama   RPB
With the Help of Scotty, 1931, 3 act comedy   RPB
A Worthy Vagabond, 1927, 3 act comedy-drama   RPB
Zippy, 1930, comedy-drama   RPB

VERNA ELSINGER
The Court of Agriculture, 1929, play?   OCl
The Prince Comes, 1929, typed copy, allegory   RPB

MARY ELWES
Temporary Engagements and Other Plays, 1920   NN, DLC

LIZZIE MAY ELWYN
Dot, the Miner's Daughter; or, One Glass of Wine, 1888, 4 act   RPB
     temperance drama
Millie, the Quadroon; or, Out of Bondage, 189? (c. 1888) 5 act   RPB, PU
     drama (RPB has film copy, original at PU)
Murder Will Out, 1890, farce for females (1)   RPB
Rachel, the Fire Waif, 1900, 4 act drama   RPB
A Ruined Life; or, The Curse of Intemperance, 1904, 3 acts   RPB
Sweetbrier; or, the Flower Girl of New York, 1889, 6 act drama   RPB
Switched Off, 1899, temperance farce (1)   RPB
Uncle Sam's Cooks, 1904, farce (1)   RPB

BLANCHE T. ELY
A Country Romance, 1922   RPB

INEZ EMERY
Our First Thanksgiving Day   STE

EVELYN EMIG (See EVELYN EMIG MELLON)

MARGUERITE EMILIO
A Candle-Lighting Pageant   JPP-I

MYRA EMMONS
Visiting Momma, in Harper's Bazaar, 43, Sept., 1909, 860-4 (1)

JOSEPHA MURRAY EMMS
Under Suspicion, 1925, 2 act mystery comedy   RPB

HILMA LEWIS ENANDER
Three Plays, 1913   RPB

SARAH FOLSOM ENEBUSKE
A Detective in Petticoats, 1900, 3 act comedy for females, originally   RPB
    prod. as A Lover in Duplicate, by the Emanuel Club of Radcliffe College,
    May 16, 1896

MARY A. ENLOE
Year Around Primary Programs, 1928   RPB

FLORENCE WARING ERDMAN
Sparks—an Inbetween, 1929, revised and edited by Marion Short (1)   RPB

ALICE HENSON ERNST
Back Stage in Xanadu, 1938, collection   RPB
High Country, 1932, four plays from the Pacific Northwest   RPB
Nightingale; an Arabian Night's Fantasy, in Poet Lore, 37, June, 1926,
    293-314
Out Trail, 1933, typescript   NN
Spring Sluicing, 1927, in Theatre Arts, 12, Feb., 1928, 125-38 (1)   IPA, GHP
    Drama League-Longmans-Green prize
The Valley of the Lost Men, in Theatre Arts, 14, May, 1930, 430-40 (1)   NN

JESSIE ERNST
Storm Center, prod. 1927, with Max Simon

LAURIE YORKE ERSKINE (1894- ?)
The Boy Who Went, 1923, young   RPB
Three Cans of Beans, 1930, Christmas   HSP

RAGNA B. ESKIL
America in the Making, 1918, patriotic historical episodes (1)   RPB
Aunt Harriet's Night Out, 1917, comedy (1)   RPB
Betty's and Bobby's Christmas, before 1920
The Calamity Howler, 1927, comedy (1)   RPB
Egging on Egbert, 1926, comedy (1)   RPB
For the Sake of Peggy, 1920, child welfare play (1)   RPB
Good Plays for School Days, 1923, collection   RPB
In the Trenches "Over There," 1918, "a play within a play" (1)   RPB
Lottie Sees It Through, 1918 (1)   RPB
Me and Betty, 1921, comedy (1)   RPB
Propping the Triangle, 1923, Little Theatre playlet   RPB
Who's the Boss? 1918, comedy (1)   RPB

ANNE L. ESTABROOK
The Christening Robe, 1917, comedy (1)   RPB
Ladies' Delight, 1906, comedy for females (1)   RPB

ANNA CAPE EVANS
Uncle Sam's Choice, n.d., children's pageant, mimeograph copy   RPB

DELLA J. EVANS
The Skeleton in the Closet, 1927, comedy (1)   RPB
Two Plays and a Preface, 1921, one-acts   RPB

FLORENCE WILKINSON EVANS
King John Tippey, 1922, 4 acts, galley proofs   NN
The Marriage of Guineth, 1913, verse play in her collection of poetry,   RPB
    The Ride Home (1)
Two Plays of Israel, 1904   RPB

FRANCES BILLINGE EVANS
The Universal King, 1913, Christian service of story and song   RPB

GLADYS LA DUE EVANS
The Little Mortal Child, in Poet Lore, 32, Autumn, 1921, 409-15 (1)

HELENA PHILLIPS EVANS
Happy Go Lucky, prod. 1926, music by Lucien Denni

MARGARET EVANS
Faith, in Poet Lore, 33, Spring, 1922, 132-7 (1)

EDITH EVERETT (1875- ?)
Every Student, his encounters in pursuit of knowledge, 1912,   RPB, HRE
    modern morality play (1)
The Red Entertainment Book, 1941, with others, 25 plays for grade and   RPB
    high school

LEOLYN LOUISE EVERETT (1888- ?)
La Magnifica, 1924, tragedy, music by Timothy M. Spelman (1)   NN
Queen Zenobia, 1908, 4 act verse drama   RPB

MRS. TORREY EVERETT
Cinderella, 1917, prod. by Pasadena Comm. Players

CORA EVERETTE
Chester Pageant, 1914, West Chester, Pa.

JEANNIE PENDLETON EWING
The Holidays, a play, in Hints, 1906   RPB

MARGARET EWING
Reflections

ROSE EYTINGE (1835-1911) NAW NWAT
Golden Chains, 1905?

F

MARY FAGIN
  Room 222, in Poet Lore, 36, Winter, 1925, 610-4 (1)

PAULINE FAIN
  What's the Use? prod. 1926

JANET AYER FAIRBANK
  In Town and Other Conversations, 1910 (first pub. in Chicago   RPB
    Record-Herald)

MARION FAIRFAX
  Mrs. Boltay's Daughters, 1915
  The Chaperon, prod. 1909
  A Modern Girl, prod. 1914, with Ruth C. Mitchell
  Nemesis, 19?? (1)   NN
  The Talker, 1912, comedy

FRANCES FAIRFIELD
  Tableaux for Home and School, 1922   RPB

ANITA BELLE FAIRGRIEVE
  Purple and Fine Linen, with Helena Miller, 3 act comedy of Puritan
    New England, the "Lend a Hand" Smith College prize play

MARGARET C. FAIRLIE
  Making Our Flag, 2 acts   FPP
  Our Flag (1)

FLORENCE WILLIAMS FALCONER
  The Angel's Message, 1908, Sunday school service for Christmas,   RPB-M
    with Adam Geibel and others
  The Messiah, 1908, Sunday school service for Christmas, with Adam   RPB-M
    Geibel and W. A. Post

THERESE FALKENEAU
  The Crutch, 1928-9

ANITA FALLON
  The Leading Lady, 1904, farce (1)   RPB

KATE MILLS FARGO
  A Voting Demonstration; or, an Election in Primerville, 1912,   RPB, FOV
    demonstration of how to vote in California (1)

EMMA BETSEY FARLEY
  Early Seminary Days (includes "The First Day"—senior play written   RPB
    with Marion Colby) Mt. Holyoke College, 1911

VIRGINIA FARMER
  Spring Song, prod. 1927

GERALDINE FARO
  Plays and Monologues, 1906   RPB

RUTH E. FAULDS

RUTH E. FAULDS
Just a Family Affair, 1930, pub. in Two Prize Health Plays, 1930, won   RPB
        second prize in N. E. health playwriting contest, Copley Theatre,
        Boston, May, 1929

KATHERINE FAUST
Love in a Palace, 1926   RPB

HARRIET B. FAWCETT
The Circle of Life   JPP-I
Garments of Praise   JPP-I

GRACE B. FAXON (1877- ?)
The Bachelor's Reverie, 1906 (1)   RPB
Closing Day Exercises, 1917, she was compiler   Or
Favorite Songs Pantomimed and Posed, 1917   RPB
Grace B. Faxon's Book of Pantomimes, 1906   DLC
Maids and Matrons, 1906, 3 act colonial play for young women   RPB
Many a Way for Closing Day, 1926, editor   RPB
Many a Way for Memorial Day, 1926, editor   RPB
Mother Earth's Party, and A Bird Day Exercise, 1903, young   NN
Pieces and Plays for Lincoln's Birthday, 1916, editor   RPB
Pieces and Plays for October Days, 1917, editor
Pieces and Plays for Primary Pupils, 1918, editor
Pieces and Plays for Special Days, 1919, editor
Pieces and Plays for Thanksgiving Day, 1917, editor
Pieces and Plays for Washington's Birthday, 1916, editor   RPB
Popular Recitations and How to Recite Them, 1909   RPB
A Shaker Romance, 1905, recitation with lesson-talk   RPB

MAUDE FEALY
The Party of the Second Part, 1929, with Henrietta Barr, modern 3 act   RPB
        comedy
Something in the Air, 1942, with Alice Gerstenberg (originally titled,   RPB
        A Grain of Mustard,1920, and then, The Promise, 1929) comedy

FRANCES HEWITT FEARN
"Let Us Have Peace," dram. from the "Diary of a Refugee," 1910   RPB

MARY EDWARD FEEHAN (See CLEMENTIA)

JANE MAULDIN FEIGL (or FEIGEL)
The Girl Patsy, prod. 1906
Texas, 190? comedy drama of the Southern plains, typescript   NN

AUGUSTA L. FEINER
Peter Pan   WPP

ELLA FEIST
Fly-away Land, children's fantasy (1) (listed as 1812 in NUC ??)

GESINA FELDHAUS
Richard Morgan; or, When Women Hate, 1906, 4 act drama, "dram. of   RPB
        Dickens' Dombey and Son transplanted to Norfolk, Virginia"

MARION LUCY FELTON (MRS. CARL FELTON)
Goose Money, 1928 (1)   RPB, WRP
Plays
Seeing Things Right, 1930, rural comedy, prize winner in Wisconsin   RPB
  Home Talent Tournament, 1930 (1)
"This Way Out," 1931, rural comedy (1)   RPB, WCP

MARIAN WARNER WILDMAN FENNER
"Speak to the Earth and It Shall Teach Thee"   JPP-I

CORDELIA BROOKS FENNO
The Fairy Thorn, 1917, cantata, music by Henry Hadley   RPB-M
The First Christmas, 1919, cantata, music by Louis Adolphe Coerne RPB-M
The Flight of the Eagle, 1930, cantata, music by Frederick Shepherd
  Converse
The Goblin Fair, 1920, fairy operetta, music by Arthur Bergh   MB
A South Sea Holiday, 1924, children's operetta, music to be found in   RPB
  "Child Songs from Hawaii," by Ermine Cross and Elsa Cross

MARY MC NEIL FENOLLOSA
The Lady of the Hair Pins, in Smart Set, 25, August, 1908, 140-9 (1)

EDNA FERBER (1885-1968) AWW NAW NWAT
Bravo! 1949, prod. 1948, with George Kaufman, 3 act comedy   RPB
Dinner at Eight, 1935, prod. 1932, with George Kaufman, comedy   RPB
The Eldest, 1925, prod. 1919 (1)   RPB, CNA,NAB-II, FCP
The Land Is Bright, 1941, with George Kaufman   RPB
  (first pub. as Three Acts, 1941)
Minick, prod. 1924, with George Kaufman, 3 act comedy based on her   RPB
  story
Old Man Minick, 1924, with George Kaufman   RPB
Our Mrs. McChesney, prod. 1915, dram. of stories by Ferber, with NN
  George V. Hobart, typescript
The Royal Family, 1928, prod. 1927, comedy with George Kaufman,   RPB
  acting edition
Showboat, 1935, from novel by Ferber, screenplay by Oscar Hammerstein NN
Stage Door, 1936, with George Kaufman, 3 acts   RPB, CNM,GTB
$1200 a Year, 1920, with Newman Levy, 3 act farce   RPB

MRS. CHARLES F. FERNALD
The Cat and the Cherub (1)
Christmas Capers, 1901, young (1)   CLSU
Footlight Frolics, 1882, entertainment for home and school   RPB
School and Temperance Dialogues, with Olivia Lovell Wilson   BPP

LINNA M. FERRER
Bobby's Dream, 1921   RPB

ANITA BROCKWAY FERRIS (1881-1923)
Alice Through the Postal Card, missionary play
Children of the Christmas Spirit, 1914, Christmas entertainment for jr.   Or
  boys and girls, also pub. in Everland, 6, December, 1914, 33-7 (1)
Followers of the Stars, 1922, missionary play, "pageant of India's   RPB
  Christians"
The Friend of All Men, 1923   FRD-1
The Gift of Light, 1917, "missionary pageant prepared for the jubilee   DLC
  celebration of the Woman's Board of Missions"

ANITA BROCKWAY FERRIS (continued)
The Good Samaritan, 1924   FRD-1
The Lamp, 1921, pageant of religious education   ODW
Livingstone Hero Plays, 1918, dram. of stories by Susan Mendenhall   RPB
Magi of Today, 1918, Christmas, also pub. in Everyland,   NN, PPC
   November, 1918
The Pageant of Brotherhood, 1918   OrP
The Ring of Rama Krishniah, 1922, pageant of Christian stewardship   RPB
The Road to Christmas, in Everyland, 8, November, 1917, 337-42 (1)
Robert and Mary, 1918, missionary romance   RPB
Ruth's Donation Party, 1918, missionary play   RPB
Santa's Allies, in Everyland, 8, July, 1917, 198-205 (1)
The Set of the Sail, 1921, missionary play   RPB
The Slave Raiders, in Everyland, 8, August, 1917, 244-7 (1) (also in
   Livingstone Hero Plays)
The Spirit of the Fathers, 1919, "pageant of the missionary enterprise   ODW
   of the Methodist Episcopal church"
The Triumph of Peace, missionary entertainment for young, in Everyland,
   6, Sept., 1915, 223-31 (1)
Visitors from the Colonial Period, in Everyland, 7, Feb., 1919, 75-9 (1)
Why Didn't You Tell? 1917, also in Everyland, 7, March, 1916, 114-8 (1)   Or

HELEN JOSEPHINE FERRIS (1890- ?)
Extra! The Newspaper Minstrels Are Out! in Ladies Home Journal, 37,
   Sept., 1920, 142 (1)
Producing Amateur Entertainments, 1921, varied stunts and other   RPB
   numbers with program plans and directions

MABEL FERRIS
Another Man's Shoes, prod. 1918, with Laura Hinkley
"The Bridge of the Gods," 1911, from book by F. H. Balch,   RPB
   pageant-drama of the great Northwest (RPB has coll. of articles,
   pictures etc. about the prod.)

ABBY FARWELL FERRY (1851- ?)
A Christmas Phantasy, 1929   RPB

ETTA SHOCKLEY FEW
The Silver Lining, 1917, 4 act Southern drama   RPB

HELENA A. FFEIL
Bill Perkins' Proposin' Day (1)

FLO FIELD
A´ la Creole, 1952, comedy
Hunger Hall, 1928-9

RACHEL LYMAN FIELD (1894-1942) AWW NAW
At the Junction, 1942 (first pub. 1927) "fantasy for railroad stations" (1) RPB
The Bad Penny, 1931, in Scholastic, 24, March, 24, 1934, 7-10+ (1) RPB,OPS-VI
Bargains in Cathay, 1927, comedy (1)   CCO
Cinderella Married, 1924, comedy   ICU
Columbine in Business, 1924, "modern harlequinade" (1)   NN, ICU
The Cross Stitch Heart, 1927, fantasy (1)   WU
The Cross Stitch Heart and Other Plays, 1927 (dedicated to Clare   RPB
   Kummer)

RACHEL LYMAN FIELD (continued)
Everygirl, in St. Nicholas, 40, Oct., 1913, 1115-7   SNB
The Fifteenth Candle, 1921 (1)   TAJ, ZKP
First Class Matter, 1936, comedy (1)
"Greasy Luck," 1927, "fragment of the New England whaling days" (1) CNA
The Londonderry Air, 1925, "play of day before yesterday"   OPS-III,WU
   (also in Elizabeth Collette, Good Reading: American Writers, 1939)
The Magic Pawnshop, 1927, New Year's Eve fantasy,   play??
The Nine Days' Queen, 1927, historical fantasy (1)   ICU
Patchwork Plays, 1930
The Patchwork Quilt, fantasy (1) (in H. Ward McGraw, Prose   MPP, MoU
   and Poetry for Enjoyment, 1940; Luella B. Cook, et.al., Hidden
   Treasures in Literature, II; Thomas Briggs, et.al., American Literature,
   1941; and Harriet M. Lucas and Herman M. Ward, Prose and Poetry for
   Enjoyment, 1950)
Polly Patchwork, 1930, comedy
Rise Up Jenny Smith, 1918, Great War play, won prize in Drama League   RPB
   of America patriotic play competition (1)
The Sentimental Scarecrow, 1930, comedy (1)
Six Plays, 1922   RPB
Theories and Thumbs, 1924, "fantasy for museums"
Three Pills in a Bottle, 1918, in Little Theatre Tournament (1)   BPW(v-1)
Three Plays, 1924
Wisdom Teeth, 1924, comedy (1) (also in Russell A. Sharp, et. al., High
   School Anthology—Literary Types, 1938)

SARA BARD FIELD (1882- ?)
Barabbas, 1932, dramatic narrative   RPB
The Vintage Festival, 1920, "play-pageant and festivities celebrating the   RPB
   vine in the Autumn of each year at St. Helena in the Napa Valley"

ANNIE ADAMS FIELDS (MRS. JAMES T. FIELDS) (1834-1915) AWW NAW
Orpheus, 1900, masque   RPB
The Return of Persephone, 1877, dramatic sketch   RPB

DOROTHY FIELDS (1905-1974) NAW NWAT
Annie Get Your Gun, 1947, prod. 1946, book by Dorothy and Herbert   RPB
   Fields; music and lyrics by Irving Berlin
Arms and the Girl, prod. 1950, with Herbert Fields and Rouben   NN
   Mamoulian, (NWAT lists Morton Gould) typewritten prompt book
Blackbirds of 1928, prod. 1928, with Lew Leslie, music by Jimmy McHugh
By the Beautiful Sea, 1954, with Herbert Fields, music by Arthur   NN
   Schwartz, typescript
Hello Daddy, prod. 1928, lyrics by Fields; book by Dorothy and Herbert Fields
International Revue, prod. 1930, lyrics by Fields; book by Nat Dorfman
   and Lew Leslie; music by Jimmy McHugh
Joy of Living, 1936, screenplay
Let's Face It! prod. 1941, book by Dorothy and Herbert Fields; lyrics by   NN
   Fields; music by Cole Porter, shooting script for motion picture
Mexican Hayride, prod. 1944, with Herbert Fields, music by Cole Porter,   NN
   typewritten copy
Redhead, prod. 1959, book by Dorothy and Herbert Fields, Sidney   NN
   Sheldon and David Shaw; music by Albert Hague; lyrics by Fields,
   typescript
Seesaw, 1975, prod. 1973, book by Michael Bennet; lyrics by Fields; musicRPB-M
   by Cy Coleman
Singin' the Blues, 1931, songs by Jimmy McHugh and Fields

DOROTHY FIELDS (continued)
Something for the Boys, prod. 1943, book by Dorothy and Herbert Fields;
music by Cole Porter
Stars in Your Eyes, prod. 1939, book by J. P. McEvoy; lyrics by Fields; music
by Arthur Schwartz (also called Swing to the Left)
Sweet Charity, prod. 1966, book by Neil Simon; lyrics by Fields; music by   RPB
Cy Coleman
A Tree Grows in Brooklyn, prod. 1951, book by Betty Smith and George
Abbott; lyrics by Fields; music by Arthur Schwartz
Up in Central Park, 1945, book by Dorothy and Herbert Fields; music by   NN
Sigmund Romberg, typescript

EVELYN HENDERSON FIFE
We Are Three, in Drama 16, Oct., 1925, 17-8+ (1)

EFFIE WOODWARD FIFIELD   (MRS. J. C. FIFIELD)
(See EFFIE WOODWARD MERRIMAN)

CARRIE LAW MORGAN FIGGS
Select Plays, 1923

ELSIE GARRETSON FINCH
Spineless   SCT

LUCINE FINCH
At the Sign of the Silver Spoon, in Smart Set, 38, Oct., 1912, 73-7 (1)
The Butterfly, in Poet Lore, 21, Sept.-Oct., 1910, 401-14

GRETCHEN DAMROSCH FINLETTER
At 8:45, with Leopoldine "Polly" Damrosch Howard   CU
If Men Went to Matinees as Women Do, with Leopoldine "Polly"   CU
Damrosch Howard
The Life Line, prod. 1930
The Passing Present, 1927, prod. 1931, 3 acts, typescript   NN
Picnic, prod. 1934
Transatlantic, with Leopoldine "Polly" Damrosch Howard   CU
The Understudy, with Leopoldine "Polly" Damrosch Howard   CU
The Woman Pays to Advertise, with   CU
Leopoldine "Polly" Damrosch Howard

SISTER MARY PAULINA FINN ("M. S. PINE") (1842- ?)
Alma Mater; or, The Georgetown Centennial and Other Dramas, 1913,   RPB
by "M. S. Pine," pub. for Georgetown Visitation Convent

MAXINNE FINSTERWALD
From These Shores, 1935? with Lewis Fall, typescript   NN
May Moon (1)   OPS-IX
On Whitman Avenue, 1946, typescript   NN
Sandals and Golden Heels, 1948, fantasy (1)   RPB
Seven Against One, 1930, National Little Theatre Tournament, won
Samuel French Prize (1)
The Severed Cord, 1929, Samuel French prize, National Little Theatre   RPB
Tournament (1)

BLANCHE FISACKERLY
Favorite Dramatizations, 1920, with Emma Schulz, children's stories   RPB
dramatized

NELLIE L. FISCHER
Educatin' Mary, 1924, rural play (1)   RPB

BELLE FISH
Pageant of Revere, 1916, Revere, Mass.

DAISY EARLE FISH
Dramatic Missionary Sketches

ANNE FISHER
Pageant of Warwick, 1912, Warwick, Mass.

BLANCHE PROCTOR FISHER
Finding the Mayflower, 1918, young, Puritan play (1)   RPB
Santa Claus Gets His Wish, 1921, young (1)   RPB

DOROTHEA FRANCES CANFIELD FISHER (1879-1958) AWW NAW
A Family Talk About War, 1940, for use in elementary schools, written   NN
     for Children's Crusade for Children, adapt. from her story
Liberty and Union, 1940, with Sarah N. Cleghorn, written to be acted in
     the school of America as part of Children's Crusade for Children
Tourists Accommodated, 1934, some scenes from present-day summer   RPB
     life in Vermont
The Woman Who Never Gets Any Sympathy, in Harper's Bazaar, 40,
     Nov., 1906, 1002-5

MAY ISABEL FISK
An Evening Musicale, in Smart Set, 10, July, 1903, 111-4 (1)
Another Point of View, in Smart Set, 11, Nov., 1903, 115-6, monologue
The Biter Bitten, in Harper's, 145, Aug., 1922, 419-22 (1)
Buying a Hat, 1919, monologue   DLC
Desperately Ill, 1920, monologue   DLC
Dressing for the Play, in Harper's, 126, Jan., 1913, 317-20, monologue (1)
The Eternal Feminine, 1911, monologues   RPB
Little Comedies of Married Life, 1926   play?   NNC, InU
Monologues, 1903   RPB
Monologues and Duologues, 1914   RPB
Shopping, in Harper's, 133, Oct., 1916, 793-7, monologue (1)
The Silent Sex, 1923, monologue
The Talking Woman, 1907, monologues

ISABELLA HOWE FISKE (See ISABELLA HOWE FISKE CONANT)

MINNIE MADDERN DAVEY FISKE (1865-1932) NAW NWAT
Countess Ravdine
The Dream of Matthew Wayne
The Eyes of the Heart, prod. 1905
Fontenelle, with Paul Kester
John Doe
A Light from St. Agnes, 1938, prod. 1905, lyric tragedy (1)   OPS-IX,NN
     later adapted into an opera by Frank Harling
Moses
Not Guilty
The Rose, prod. 1905 (1)
Verrick

CLARA FITCH
Pioneer Days, 1911, pageant, Louisville, Ky.

CLAUDIA FITZGERALD
The Patriotic Potato, 1918? typed copy   IshdL

EDITH FITZGERALD
Five and Ten, 1931, filmscript of book by Fannie Hurst, mimeo copy   CLSU
Many a Slip, prod. 1930, with Robert Riskin

GERALDINE FITZGERALD
Cousin Charlotte's Visit, 1900, 3 acts, for girls' schools   RPB

LUTIE FITZGERALD
The Matrimonial Bureau, 1904, comedy entertainment   RPB
The Old School at Hick'ry Holler, 1904, comic entertainment   RPB

HALLIE FERGUSON FLANAGAN (DAVIS) (1890-1969) AWW NAW NWAT
American Plan, 1934, with Mary St. John, "play of our time"   RPB
Can You Hear Their Voices? 1931, with Margaret Ellen Clifford,   RPB, FCP
   "play for our time" (first pub. in New Masses)   VET
The Curtain, in Drama, 13, Feb., 1923, 167-9, prize play Little Theatre   RCT
   contest, Des Moines, Iowa (1)
Dawn Over Zero, 1947, assisted by Sylvia Gassel and Day Tuttle, "living
   newspaper about the atomic age" (See E=mc2)
The Dream of Vasavadatta, 1933, translated from Sanskrit by A. G. Shirreff
   and Panna Lall, acting version by Flanagan
E=mc2, 1948, with Sylvia Gassel and Day Tuttle, "living newspaper   RPB
   about the Atomic Age"
Fear, 1934, trans. from Russian, acting version by Flanagan
Incense, 1924
The Sky Will Be Lit Up, 1933, with Janet Hartmann, 3 acts   RPB

HILDEGARDE FLANNER (1899- ?) AWW
Mansions, 1920, drama (1)   RPB, SLC
The White Bridge, 1938 (1)   RPB

MARY H. FLANNER
Bargain Day, 1911 (1)   PU, OCl
The Christmas Burglar, 1913 (1)   RPB
In Quest of Freedom, 1916, pageant, Richmond, Ind.

"NOEL FLAURIER" (See LENORE HAZEL HETRICK)

ETHEL FLEMING
A Missionary Clinic   CPE
Entertaining Aunt Mina   CPE

"GEORGE FLEMING" (See JULIA CONSTANCE FLETCHER)

MARTHA FLEMING
Playmaking and Plays, 1930, with John Merrill

HATTIE BENNETT FLETCHER
Uncle Sam's Visit to Rhode Island, 1918, written for the State Food   RPB
   Conservation Committee (1)

JULIA CONSTANCE FLETCHER ("GEORGE FLEMING") (1858-1938)
    The Canary, 1900? by "George Fleming," 3 act farce, typescript   NN
    The First Gentleman of Europe, prod. 1897, with Frances Burnett
    A Man and His Wife, prod. 1900, by "George Fleming," 3 acts, typescript NN

ANNE CRAWFORD FLEXNER (1874-1955) AWW NWAT
    Aged 26, 1936, about John Keats   RPB
    All Soul's Eve, prod. 1920
    The Blue Pearl, prod. 1918, mystery
    Law Breakers, 194? adapt. of Die Verbrecher by "Ferdinand Bruckner" NN
       (Theodor Taggard)
    A Lucky Star, prod. 1910
    A Man's Woman, 1899
    The Marriage Game, 1916, prod. 1913, 3 act comedy   RPB
    Miranda on the Balcony, prod. 1901, dram. of novel by A.E.W. Mason,   NN
       typescript
    Mrs. Wiggs of the Cabbage Patch, 1924, prod. 1904, dram. of story by   RPB
       Alice Hegan Rice
    Wanted—An Alibi, 1917

HORTENSE FLEXNER (1885- ?)
    The Broken God, masque (1)
    The Faun, in Drama, 11, June, 1921, 311-8 (1)
    Mahogany, 1921   DLC
    The Road (1)
    Three Wise Men of Gotham (1)
    Voices, in Seven Arts Magazine, 1, Dec., 1916, 135-43, prod. at Stuart   MRO
       Walker's Portmanteau Theatre, peace theme

EVA KAY FLINT (1902- ?)
    Subway Express, prod. 1929, with Martha Madison, mystery, typed copy NN
    Under Glass, prod. 1933, with George Bradshaw, typewritten copy   NN
    The Up and Up, prod. 1930, with Martha Madison, "slice of low life in
       Bronx"

MAY HARBIN FLINT
    The Empty Stocking Elf, 1916, Christmas (1)   RPB

LYDIA STIRLING FLINTHAM
    The Queen of the Mystic Isle, 1908, 2-act musical drama for girls   RPB

PRISCILLA FLOWERS
    A Comedy
    The Forks of the Dilemma, comedy about Queen Elizabeth and the boy   DSS
       Shakespeare
    May Night, in 1926 Little Theatre Tournament, pub. in Poet Lore, 37, 1926,
       551-64
    The White Peacock, in 1928 Little Theatre Tournament

CLAIRE WALLACE FLYNN
    The String of Pearls, in Woman's Home Companion, 37, Feb., 1910, 8-9+, RPB
       comedy (1)

MARIE AGNES FOLEY

The Camel with the Wrinkled Knees, 1940, fantasy, dram. of story by   RPB
  Johnny Grevelle
The Gift, 1921, religious drama (1)   RPB
Heidi, 1945, 3 acts   NN
Love in a Fix, 1923, farce (1)   RPB
The Magic Whistle, 1945, young

BEULAH FOLMSBEE

Goblin Parade, in Plays, 2, Oct., 1942, 37-43 (1)
Guki the Moon Boy and Other Plays, 1928   RPB
Once in Bethlehem, 1930 (1)   RPB
The Princess and the Crystal Pipe, in St. Nicholas, 48, Nov., 1920, 61-5 (1)

MARY FOOTE

The Lost Camping Place, 1927   RPB
The Runaway Ball, 1925, safety play   RPB

ANNE FORD

Is Marriage Legal? 1928, for National Woman's Party

BESSIE RAINER FORD

Humorous Recitations for Children, 1927, with Edith Hadley   RPB
  Butterfield, Ruth Adkinson, Mary Harden and others
Original Monologues and Recitations, 1928, with Gertine Ahrens   RPB

GRACE FORD

The Love Pirate (1)

HARRIET FRENCH FORD (MORGAN) (1863? or 1868?-1949)   AWW NWAT

Are Men Superior? 1932, farce (1)   OPS-VII
The Argyle Case, 1927, prod. 1912, with Harvey O'Higgins, mystery   RPB
Audrey, prod. 1902, with E. F. Bodington, dram. of novel by Mary Johnston
The Beast and the Jungle, with Harvey O'Higgins
The Bride, 1924, comedy (1)
Christopher Rand, 1929, with Eleanor Robson (Mrs. August Belmont)
Cupid and Psyche   NN
The Dickey Bird, 1925, prod. 1915, with Harvey O'Higgins, "the   OPS-II, NN
  sad story of a male Nora"
The Divine Afflatus, 1931, with Eleanor Robson (1)   NN
The Dummy, 1925, prod. 1914, with Harvey O'Higgins and W. J. Burns,   RPB
  detective comedy
The Fourth Estate, prod. 1909, with Joseph M. Patterson, typescript   NN
A Gentleman from France, prod. 1901, dram. of book by Stanley   NN
  Weyman, typescript (typewritten copy at MH)
The Greatest Thing in the World, prod. 1900, with Beatrice de Mille,   NN
  typescript
The Happy Hoboes, 1928, with Althea Sprague Tucker, comedy (1)   RPB
Heroic Treatment, 1933, comedy (1)   RPB
The Hold Up, 1930, with Anna G. O'Higgins, comedy (1)   RPB
The Honor of the Humble, 1902? adapt. from French of "Pierre   NN
  Newsky" (Petr Krubovski) typewritten copy
In the Next Room, 1925, prod. 1923, with Eleanor Robson Belmont,   RPB
  melodrama mystery
In-Laws, 1928 (1)   OPS-IV
Jacqueline, 1909, with Caroline Duer, typewritten copy   NN

HARRIET FRENCH FORD (continued)

The Land of the Free, prod. 1917, with Fannie Hurst	
A Little Brother to (of) the Rich, prod. 1909, with Joseph Patterson	
Love in Livery, 192? trans. of Marivaux with Marie Louise Le Verrier	RPB
Main Street, prod. 1921, with Harvey O'Higgins, adapt. of novel by Sinclair Lewis	
Me and Methuselar and Other Episodes, 1895	RPB
Mr. Lazarus, 1926, prod. 1916, with Harvey O'Higgins, comedy	RPB
Mr. Susan Peters, 1928 (1)	
Mysterious Money, 1929, 3 act comedy	RPB
Old P.Q., 1928, with Harvey O'Higgins	
On the Hiring Line, 1923, prod. 1919, with Harvey O'Higgins, comedy (also called Wrong Number)	RPB
Orphan Aggie, 1927, with Harvey O'Higgins	RPB
Polygamy, prod. 1914, with Harvey O'Higgins	
Sweet Seventeen, prod. 1924, with Leonidas Westervelt, John Clements and Harvey O'Higgins	
Under Twenty, 1926, with Harvey O'Higgins, L. Westervelt and John Clements, comedy	RPB
Wanted—Money, 1928, with Harvey O'Higgins and Althea Sprague Tucker, comedy (1)	RPB
What Are Parents For? 1930 (1)	RPB
What Imagination Will Do, 1928, comedy (1)	
"When a Feller Needs a Friend," 1920, prod. 1918, with Harvey O'Higgins, "patriotic play for amateurs"	
Where Julia Rules, 1923, with Caroline Duer, 4 act comedy	MsSM
The Woman He Married, prod. 1917	
Youth Must Be Served, 1926, comedy (1)	OPS-III

JULIA ELLSWORTH SHAW FORD (1859- ?)

The Mist, 1912	RPB
Snickerty Nick, 1919	RPB, MRC
Snickerty Nick and the Giant, 1919 (1935 ed. at RPB)	RPB

OLIVE WHITE FORTENBACHER

Anna the Absolute, 1930, based on story by Florence Ryerson	RPB
At the Family Reunion, 1934, monologue	RPB
Babs and the Little Gray Man, 1930, based on story by Florence Ryerson	RPB
Barker's Treasure Chest, 1936, 25 platform readings	RPB
Bargain Day for Babies, 1930, based on story by Florence Ryerson	RPB
Beautiful But Young, 1932, based on story by Duncan Norton-Tayler	RPB
Big Java, 1932, based on story by Maude Woodruff Newell	RPB
Bill's Night Out, 1934, monologue	RPB
Bittersweet, 1929, based on story by Shirley L. Seiffert	RPB
Borax or Lanoil, 1929, based on story by Corinne Harris Markey	RPB
The Coming of Peter Piper, 1929, based on story by Christine Whiting Parmenter	
Contest Selections from Best Authors, 1930	RPB
Discarded: One Superfluous Wedding, 1931, based on story by Florence Ryerson	RPB
Easter Parade	JEM
The Faith That Never Falters, 1929, based on story by Margery Land May	RPB, JEM-2
Fifteen Superior Platform Readings, 1932	RPB
The Fugitive from Finley's Alley, 1929	RPB
It's Just Her Way, 1934, monologue	RPB
Jimmy and the Ultimatum, 1929, based on story by Franklyn Barrow	

OLIVE WHITE FORTENBACHER (continued)
Junior Is a Genius, 1948, comedy (1)	RPB
Looking Up Cousin Milly	JEM
Mabel Arrives	JEM
The Man Who Dreaded to Go Home, 1928, based on story by Bess Streeter Aldrich	
Mother Martin's Wing, arranged from story by Christine Whiting Parmenter	JEM-2
A Mother Who Wouldn't Give Up, arranged from story by Linda Buntyn Willie	JEM-2
On the 7:50 Express, 1929, based on story by Edwin Balmer	
Out of Order, 1930, based on story by Corinne Harris Markey	RPB
The Truthful Lies of Jimsie, 1930, based on story by Florence Ryerson	RPB
Twenty-One Good Monologues, 1933, with others	RPB
The U. S. Revolt, 1948, comedy (1)	RPB
When Queens Ride, 1932, arranged as contest selection from story by Agnes Sligh Turnbull	RPB
Willie the Worm, 1931, based on story by Florence Ryerson	RPB
Winning a Car	JEM
Women and Baseball, 1934, monologue	

JAN ISABELLE FORTUNE (1892- ?)
Flammule, 1934, 3 act comedy	RPB
Texas History Plays: the Cavalier from France, (Great Moments in Texas History), 1930	OPW

ALICE J. FOSDICK
Helpers in the Home, 1921, "Mothercraft play," pub. by Family Welfare Assoc. of Fitchburg	RPB

ALMA PRUDENCE FOSS
China Blue Eyes, 1928	RPB
Flaming Youth, 1928	RPB
Jimmy Jones at the Circus, 1928	RPB
Jimmy Jones Studies Geography, 1927	RPB

ADELAIDE RAWNSLEY FOSSARD
Near Old Cockaigne, 1905	RPB

CAREY FOSTER
The Living Fan, 1904, Japanese fancy	CLSU
The Moon Menagerie, 1903, "Mother Goose sketch"	RPB

CAROLINE HOLCOMBE WRIGHT FOSTER (1864-1929)
Little Comedies of Today in California, 1906	RPB

LAURE CLAIRE FOUCHER
Effie's Christmas Dream, 1912, adapt. of Louisa M. Alcott's "A Christmas Dream and How It Came True," on microcard (1)	MsU

CATHARINE W. FOWLER
The Message of the Star, 1904, Christmas cantata, music by Raymond Huntington Woodman	RPB-M
The Prince of Peace, 1900, text compiled from the Scriptures, music by John Spencer Camp	RPB-M

LAURA AMSDEN FOWLER
  Girl Magic, 1931, fairy play (1)   RPB
  Just Across the Road, 1927 (1)   RPB

ANCELLA M. FOX
  The Anniversary, 1908? with Herman Devries, drama (1)   RPB

FLORENCE C. FOX
  Childhood Days in Washington's Time, pageant

MARGARET L. FOX
  The Returning of Rosalia, 1920, for Camp Fire girls   RPB

VIRGINIA WOODSON FRAME
  Commencement Days, 1908, 3 act play of college girl life, with Margaret RPB
    Mayo

CELIA FRANCIS
  Junior High Varieties, 1929   RPB

MARGARET HOLMES FRANCISCO
  Lancelot and Elaine, 1902, illustrated from Tennyson's "Idyls of the   RPB
    King"
  "Scenes from Dreamland," "Christian and Christina's Journey,"   RPB
    arranged from Bunyan's Pilgrim's Progress, 1902

CAROLINE FRANCKE
  Exceeding Small, 1930, prod. 1928 (staged by Rachel Crothers)   RPB
  Father of the Bride, 1951, based on novel by Edward Streeter, comedy   RPB
  The Fighting Littles, 1943, based on novel by Booth Tarkington, 3 acts RPB
  The 49th Cousin, 1962, with Florence Lowe   RPB

DORIS FRANCKLYN
  Flora-florizel, 1915? musical play (1)   RPB
  Mrs. Shrimper's Boarders, 1905? comedy   RPB

FLORENCE KIPER FRANK (1886?- ?)
  Cinderelline; or, the Little Red Slipper, 1913, modern poetic   RPB, FOV
    drama of the new woman, by Florence Kiper
  The Garden, in Drama, 8, Nov., 1918, 471-93 (1)
  Gee-rusalem, prod. 1918-9, typescript   DLC
  The Home for the Friendly, 1928, comedy (1)   SFM
  Jael, 1914, poetic drama (1)   RPB
  Over the Hills and Far Away, in Drama, 11, Dec., 1920, 80-9, young
  The Return of Proserpine, in Drama, 11, Aug.-Sept., 1921, 432-7, young
  Three Plays for a Children's Theatre, 1926   RPB
  The Three Spinners, in Drama, 16, Feb., 1926, 179-80+, young
  Visitors, 1916, young (1)   DLC

MAUDE MORRISON FRANK (1870- ?)
  A Friend in Need; or, How "The Vicar of Wakefield" Found a Publisher,
    in St. Nicholas, 42, March, 1915, 47-51 (1)
  Miss Burney at Court (1)   WWS,WWY
  A Mistake at the Manor   WWT
  Short Plays About Famous Authors, 1915   RPB

PEARL FRANKLIN (CLARK) (MRS. WALLACE CLARK) (c1888- ?)
Cowboy Crazy, with George Abbott (by Peg Franklin?)
Following Father, 1931, 3 act comedy
"I Haven't Time," 1925
A Mountain Wedding, 1926, based on a scene from Thunder   RPB
Thunder, prod. 1919, with Elia Peattie (also called Howdy Folks) (by Peg
    Franklin?)
Young America, 1925, with Fred Ballard (1)   OPS-II

BERTHA COOPER FRASER
Two Americas, missionary play
Two Masters, missionary play   WaPS

EDITH L. FRASER
Betty Want-it-all, 1926, Christmas   RPB
Peter Pain and the Good Health Kids, 1928, 2 acts, young   RPB

MAUD FRAZER
Beauty and Blessing, 1908, Children's Day service, music by W. B.   RPB-M
    Judefind and A. L. Judefind; words by Frazer and Lavinia E. Brauff

FANNY EVELYN FREEHOF
Forever and————, 1929, Chanukah play   RPB
The Little Lost Tree, 1945, Chamisho Osor play

CAROLYN R. FREEMAN
Bright Ideas for Easter, Mother's Day and Children's Day, 1926, with others
Christmas Memories, 1923, service for Sunday schools, with others
The Christmas Strike   FKC
The Easter Challenge, 1929, pageant for juniors   DLC
The Kiddies' Christmas Book, 1925, with Ann Gladys Lloyd and others   RPB
The Paramount Children's Day Book, 1923, a contributor   RPB
The Paramount Christmas Book, 1922, a contributor   RPB
The Paramount Easter Book, 1923, a contributor   RPB
Practical Christmas Helper, 1941   TxFS
Why We Are Here, 1936, pageant for Children's Day or church use   DLC

ETHEL HALE FREEMAN
Bill Gunn, the Fire Gun, 1935, pirate play   NPM
A Dramatization of Monsieur Beaucaire, 1916, from Booth Tarkington's   RPB
    novel
Eight Cousins, 1934, based on story by Louisa M. Alcott
Heidi, 1925, based on book by Miss Spyri (1955 edition)   FTaSU
Tommy, 1915, character play (1)   RPB

HELEN FREEMAN
The Great Way, prod. 1921, with Horace Fish

MARY ELEANOR WILKINS FREEMAN (1852-1930) AWW NAW
Eglantina, in Ladies' Home Journal, 27, July, 1910, 13-4+
Giles Corey, Yeoman, 1893, also in Harper's, 86, Dec., 1892, 20-40   RPB
The Pumpkin Giant, in Plays, 21, Oct., 1961, 61-6, adapt. by Adele Thane (1)

ANNE RICHMOND WARNER FRENCH (MRS. CHARLES ELLIS FRENCH)
(1869-1913) AWW
The Rejuvenation of Mary, 1907, 3 act comedy, by Anne Warner   RPB

NORA C. FRETAGEOT
    <u>Posey County Water Pageant</u>, 1916, celebrating Indiana's centennial,   InI
    Mount Vernon, Ind.

PEARL PAYNE FREY
    <u>The Path to Service and Happiness</u>, 1926, simple candlelight service   RPB
    for young people

FLORA M. FRICK
    <u>The Black Cat's Frolic</u>, 1928, spooky drill   RPB
    <u>Christmas Window</u>, 1928, pantomime for young people, with Mayme   RPB
    Christensen
    <u>The Coming of Easter</u>, a play, and <u>The Bunnies' Quarrel</u>, a drill, 1933   DLC
    <u>Stunts for Fall</u>, 1929   RPB
    <u>Stunts for Spring</u>, 1932
    <u>Stunts for Summer</u>, 1930, especially for camps   RPB
    <u>Stunts for Winter</u>, 1931   RPB

ETHEL L. FRITZ
    <u>Mother Goose's Thanksgiving Dream</u>   LNP

ANNA EASTMAN FROST
    <u>The Mansion Garden</u>, 1914, masque, Wallaston, Mass.
    <u>Pageant of the Charles River</u>, 1914, Newton, Mass.
    <u>Pageant of the Trees</u>, 1914, festival, Wellesley, Mass.

EUGENIA BROOKS FROTHINGHAM (1874- ?)
    <u>Mock Legislative Hearing: "Senate Bill 575,"</u> 1920, "a bill to prohibit   RPB
    child labor; for citizenship classes," pub. by Committee on Education
    for Citizenship of the Boston League of Women Voters (1)

DOROTHY WHIPPLE FRY (1897- ?)
    <u>The Rescue of Silver Bell</u>, 1927, fairy play for children   RPB

EMMA VIOLA SHERIDAN FRY
    <u>In Far Bohemia</u>, 1900? prod. 1898, with Evelyn G. Sutherland   RPB
    <u>Po' White Trash and Other One Act Dramas</u>, 1900, with Evelyn   RPB
    Greenleaf Sutherland and Percy Wallace Mackaye
    <u>Rohan the Silent</u>, 1900, prod. 1896, romantic drama written in   RPB
    collaboration with Evelyn Greenleaf Sutherland (1)

SARA BANCROFT FRY
    <u>That Ranch of Hers</u>, 1928-9

ALICE COOK FULLER
    <u>The Bonnie Color Bearers</u>, 1913, drill for girls
    <u>The Boston Tea Party</u>, 1913   RPB
    <u>The Christmas Idea</u>, 1913 (1)   RPB
    <u>Dramatized Stories, Myths and Legends</u>, 1913, one-acts
    <u>The Gifted Givers</u>, 1914, Christmas (1)
    <u>Hatchets and Canes</u>, 1914, Washington pantomime and drill   RPB
    <u>Hatchet March and Drill</u>, 1899, for Washington's birthday   MB
    <u>Joy of the LV</u>, 1914   RPB
    <u>Joyous Christmas Chimes</u>, 1916   RPB
    <u>Little Grandmother's March and Drill</u>, 1908   NcD
    <u>The Man Without a Country</u>   FFP
    <u>November's Crown</u>, 1898, pub. with Louise Koogle's <u>Thanksgiving in</u>   RPB
    <u>Brownieland</u>

ALICE COOK FULLER (continued)
Petertown Proposal, 191? farce (1)   RPB
Uncle Peter's Visits to the School, 19?? farce (1)   RPB
Under the Stars and Stripes, 1915, patriotic pageant   RPB

CAROLINE MACOMBER FULLER
The Old Songs, 1905, musical comedy (1)   RPB

ETHEL K. FULLER
The Area Door, 1933, puppet play (1)   RPB
The Dream Canal Boat, 1928, fantasy in two scenes, a Jr. League play   RPB
The Pageant of Quequechan, 1930, Fall River, Mass., for Mass.   RPB
   tercentenary

EUNICE FULLER
The Visit of Obadiah, 1907, with Margaret Currier Lyon, farce for   RPB
   females

IDA MAY FULLER
Love's Victory, 1914, pantomime in 3 scenes   RPB

MABEL B. FULLER
Knight of the Golden Crest, 19?? operetta for upper grammar grades   RPB

THELMA FULLER
It Makes a Difference, 1930, health play, with Thelma Kittredge and   RPB
   others (1)

MAUD(E) FULTON
"The Brat," 1926, prod. 1917 (RPB has 1934 ed.) adaptation of novel by   RPB
   Nathaniel E. Reeid, comedy
Cinderella of the Storm, 1928, 3 act comedy drama, with Louis Weslyn   RPB
Enter Mary Jones, 1929, 3 act comedy   RPB
The Humming Bird, prod. 1923
Miss Baxter, 1928   NHP
Sonny, 1929, 3 act comedy drama   RPB

EDITH ELLIS FURNESS (See EDITH ELLIS)

GRACE LIVINGSTON FURNISS
A Box of Monkeys, 1899, parlor farce in 2 acts   RPB
A Box of Monkeys and Other Farce Comedies, 1891   RPB
Captain of His Soul, n.d., typescript   NN
A Colonial Girl, c1902, with Abby Sage Richardson, typescript   NN
The Corner Lot Chorus, 1898? farce for females (1)   RPB
A Dakota Widow, 1915, comedy (1)   DLC
Father Walks Out, 1928, comedy
The Flying Wedge, 1896, football farce (1)   RPB
A Gentleman of France, dram. of a novel
Greta Green, prod. 1903, romantic comedy, microfilm   CU, DLC
His Unbiased Opinion, in Cosmopolitan, 15, Oct., 1893, 674-6   PTS-VIII
The Jack Trust, 1891, 3 acts   RPB
The Man on the Box, 1915, prod. 1905, based on novel by Harold   RPB
   McGrath, comedy
The Man on the Case, 1931, prod. 1907, 3 act dram. of a novel
Mrs. Jack, prod. 1902, typewritten copy (also microfilm at CU)   NN
The Nyutalops or Nyctalopia or a Nyctalops, or Myctalops, 1891, 3 acts. DLC

GRACE LIVINGSTON FURNISS (continued)
    Perhaps, 1915, comedy (1)   RPB
    The Pride of Jennice, prod. 1900, dram. of a novel, with Abby Sage
        Richardson
    "Robert Sicily," romantic drama, typewritten copy   MH
    Second Floor Spoopendyke, 1892, 2 act farce   RPB
    Tulu, 1891   RPB
    The Veneered Savage, 1891   NN

IRENE FUSSLER
    Ever' Snitch, 1930-1, in Carolina Play-Book, IV, June, 1931, 43-58,   KCC
        comedy of Carolina fisher folk (1)
    In the Shadow of the Cross, Yesterday and Today, 1938   RPB
    King, Queen, and Joker, 1932 (1)
    The Last Two Shots. 1931-2, mountain tragedy (1)
    Love an' Likker, 1931
    Treasures, 1931-2 (1)

ELIZABETH FYFFE
    The Nativity, 1922, mystery play for voices, with Linda Ekman   RPB-M

ROSE FYLEMAN (1877-1957)
    After All, 1939 (1)
    Cabbages and Kings, 1925 (1)   PTM
    Eight Little Plays for Children, 1925
    Happy Families, 1933, comic opera   NN
    In Arcady   JTF
    Nine New Plays for Children, 1934
    Red Riding Hood, 1949, children's operetta, music by "Will Grant" (pseud.)
    Seven Little Plays for Children, 1928   RPB
    Six Longer Plays for Children, 1936   NN
    The Spanish Cloak, 1939 (1)

G

MARY L. GADDESS

The Crowning of Christmas, 1911, musical for children, with Stanley   RPB
Schell
A Dream of Fair Women and Brave Men, 1891, tableau vivants   IU
The Ivy Queen, 1891, for girls, and The Revels of the Queen of May and   RPB
Her Fairies, both cantatas, both in Greek Costume Plays for School or
Lawn Performance, 1914 (Both also pub. separately.)

GRACE LEE GAFFNEY

Jolly Juvenile Minstrels, 1930   RPB
Juvenile Minstrel Capers, 1937   Or, DLC
Peggy's Patter and Lovely Lillian, 1928, monologues   IU
Sophie from Sandysville, 1929, comedy (1)   RPB
Winifred and the Talking Prince, 1936, monologue for a child   RPB

RUTH GAINES-SHELTON

The Church Fight, in Crisis, 32, May, 1926 (1)   HSB

FRANCES ORMOND JONES GAITHER (1889- ?)

The Pageant of Columbus, "within a masque of I. I. & C.; written for   RPB
the class of 1915 of Mississippi Industrial Institute and College,"
interpretive dances written by Emma Ody Pohl
The Shadow of the Builder, 1921, centennial pageant of the University   RPB
of Virginia (about Thomas Jefferson)
Shores of Happiness, 1919, "pageant whereof Odysseus is hero"   ViU, DLC

ESTHER E. GALBRAITH

The Brink of Silence, 1917 (in Literature and Living III) (1)   SSV, MRO,CSP-1
Plays Without Footlights, 1945 (She was editor.)

MARY J. GALBRAITH

contributor to Christian Endeavor Playlets, ed. by Henrietta Heron, 1928 RPB
and More Christian Endeavor Playlets, ed. by E. W. Thornton, 1929

ELIZABETH GALE

Aunt Maggie's Will, 1910, 3 act comedy
Boosting Bridget, 1918, comedy (1)
A Corner of the Campus, 1913
Just a Little Mistake, 1916, comedy (1)   RPB
Miss Molly, 1914, 2 act comedy   RPB
Mrs. Coulson's Daughter, 1912, for girls   OCl
Not Quite Such a Goose, 1925 (Also in Jacob M Ross, Ed.   RPB,PJB,GJY
Adventures in Literature, 1936) comedy (1)
The Rag Carpet Bee, 1911, entertainment (1)   RPB
The Reformer's Reformed, 1912, comedy   OCl
The Romance Hunters, 1917, 3 act comedy   RPB

JUNE WINSOR GALE

Victoria, in Poet Lore, 26, New Year, 1915, 78-110, 3 act comedy

RACHEL E. BAKER GALE
    After Taps, 1891, 3 act drama, from notes and unfinished ms. of George   RPB
        M. Baker
    Bachelor Hall, 1898, with Robert M. Baker, 3 act comedy   RPB
    The Chaperon, c. 1889, 3 act comedy for girls   RPB
    The Clinging Vine, 1889, comedy (1)   RPB
    Coats and Petticoats, 1910, comedy (1)   RPB
    Her Picture, 1894, for females (1)   PWP
    A King's Daughter, 1893, 3 act comedy   RPB
    Mr. Bob, 1894, 2 act comedy   RPB
    The New Crusade, 1908, 2 act comedy   RPB
    No Men Wanted, 1889, sketch (1) (1903 ed. at RPB)   RPB
    Rebellious Jane, 1915, 3 act comedy   RPB
        (Some of these plays have different dates in NUC)

ZONA GALE (1874-1938) AWW NAW NWAT
    The Appreciators: A Wooing, in Smart Set, 14, December, 1904, 105-7
    The Clouds, 1932   RPB, NPW
    Evening Clothes, 1932 (Also in Literature and Life, III) (1)   RPB
    Faint Perfume, 1934, dram. of her novel   RPB
    Grandma, 1932
    Miss Lulu Bett, 1921, prod. 1920, Pulitzer prize 1921   RPB, BAW,CCP
    Mr. Pitt, prod. 1924, pub. 1925 (dram. of her novel Birth)   RPB
    The Neighbors, 1914 (Also in Tom Cross and others, Eds., Good   RPB, DWP
        Reading for High School, 1931)   EMR, KFA
    Papa La Fleur, 1933 play??
    Uncle Jimmy, 1922 (Also in Ladies Home Journal,   RPB, PTM,HSP
        38, Oct., 1921) (1)

ELLEN M. GALL
    And the Doctor Said, 1933, for women (1)   RPB
    Banner Anthology of One-Act Plays by American Authors, 1929,   RPB
        editor with Leslie Carter
    "Blitz" Hits for the Entertainment Program, 1943, comp. by Carter, ed.   DLC
        by Gall
    Crossed Wires, 1926, with Leslie Carter, comedy (1)   RPB
    The Good Bad Man, 1937, by Howard Reed, ed. by Gall
    Gridiron Heros, 1935, farcical pantomime   MiD, DLC
    A Home Run, with Leslie Carter
    Her House of Memories, 1937, comedy for women (1)   An-C-VU
    My Wild Days Are Over, 1931, "musical mock wedding to be done as a   RPB
        pantomime or as a pianologue" (1)
    Now Trixie, 1925, mystery comedy for women, with Leslie Carter (1)   RPB
    Peekaboo Lady, 1928, 3 act farce, with Leslie Carter   RPB
    The Pepp and Pepper Steppers, 1931, "red hot minstrel," with Leslie   RPB
        Carter
    Something Like a Pipe, 1933, "shadow-pantomime adapt. from an old   RPB
        Norse tale"
    Stray Cats, 1925, 3 act farce, with Leslie Carter   NN
    Surprise Attacks in Bits and Skits, 1942, by various authors, editor with   RPB
        Carter   RPB
        (Check Leslie Carter)

HELEN GALLEHER
    Herald of the Restoration, "dramatization of the Prophets," in Fearless Men

HAZEL V. GAMBLE
Little Fish, in Drama, 14, Feb., 1924, 185-7 (1)
Punch, 1923, farce (1)   RPB

MARY ROLOFSON GAMBLE
Aunt Columbia's Dinner Party, in Ladies Home Journal, 34, June,
    1917, 28 (1)

MRS. JOHN GAMBREL
The Jewel Red Cross Workers, 1918, exercise for 12 children   RPB
The Missionary Mother Goose and Her Children, 1918, playlet for   RPB
    children

NOREEN ELLERS GAMMILL
Characteristic Monologues and Readings, 1927
More Character Sketches, 1936, mimeographed copy   WaU
New Character Monologues for Stage and Radio, 1948   RPB
Open Windows, 1930 (1)   RPB
Sketches from an Old Album, 1933   MiU

MARGARET PLANK GANSSLE
The New Day, 1918, masque of the future, patriotic ritual, Dakota   RPB
    Playmakers rural community pageant, St. Thomas, N. D.
A Pageant of the Northwest, Pembina County, N. D. (She was one of
    the writers.)
The Selish, 1919, Indian pageant-masque, pub. by Un. of Mont., written   RPB
    by students of the State Un. of Mont. (She was director.)

CORA DICK GANTT
Our Masters, 1918, 3 acts, c. under title The Choice of a Superman,   NN
    typescript
The Tavern, 1933, prod. 1920, by George Cohan, from a play by Gantt   RPB
    titled, The Choice of a Superman, c. 1918, burlesque of melodrama

"JANICE GARD" (See JEAN LEE LATHAM)

BECKY GARDINER
Damn Your Honor, prod. 1929, with Bayard Veiller

MARGARET DOANE GARDINER
Universal Neurasthenia; or, The House of Rest, 1907   RPB

DOROTHY GARDNER
Eastward in Eden, 1949, the love story of Emily Dickinson, 4 act opera,   RPB
    music by Jan Meyerowitz
"The Gods Condescend," 1929, 2 act comedy for high school and college,   RPB
    under direction of Gardner, Mary A. Davis and Helen Reilly
New Plymouth Cantata, 1953, music by Jan Meyerowitz

FLORA CLARK GARDNER
Famous Mothers and Daughters, 1931, pageant and pantomime   DLC
Good Health in the Land of Mother Goose, 1925   RPB
Let's Get Acquainted, 1921, suitable for community or farm bureau   RPB
    organization
Little Plays Requiring Little Rehearsal, 1931, with Margaret Frances   RPB
    Gardner

FLORA CLARK GARDNER (continued)
Living Pictures from Our Church Album, 1929, pantomime   RPB
Merry Christmas by Aeroplane, 1930   RPB
Primary Plans for Thanksgiving, 1928   RPB
Twelve One-Act Christmas Plays, 1930, with Margaret Gardner   RPB
Up-to-Date Christmas Programs, 1930, with Margaret Gardner   RPB
Up-to-Date Community Programs, 1930, with Margaret Gardner   RPB
Up-to-Date Ten Minute Plays, 1931, with Margaret Gardner   RPB

MARGARET FRANCES GARDNER (See above—Flora Clark Gardner—
        some items)

MARY GARDNER
Dramatic Reader, the land of make believe, a world for little actors,   RPB
        1923 (first pub. 1911)
Work That Is Play, 1908, dramatic reader based on Aesop's fables

MARY ELKINS GARDYNE
The Antsisters of Widdy Maloney, 1922, humorous Irish dialect verse   RPB
        entertainment

LOUISE AYRES GARNETT (? -1937)
Adestes Fideles, 1936, Christmas processional, music by Mack Evans   RPB
Belshazzar, 1932, cantata, music by Henry Hadley   RPB
The Courtship, 1920, based on a poem by Longfellow   RPB
The Fairy Wedding, 1931, cantata, music by Henry Kimball Hadley
Hilltop, in Drama, 11, May, 1921, 277-83, and in Three to Make Ready
Master Will of Stratford, 1916, "midwinter's night dream in 3 acts"   RPB
Mirtil in Arcadia, 1927, pastoral, music by Henry Hadley
The Pig Prince, in Drama, 12, April, 1922, 240-6, also in Three to Make Ready
Three to Make Ready, 1923   RPB

MARJORIE GARNETT
The Coward   OPW

THEODOSIA PICKERING GARRISON (1874-1944)
An Hour of Earth, in Smart Set, 9, March, 1903, 153-7 (1)
At the Sign of the Cleft Heart, in Smart Set, 4, July, 1901, 91-6 (1) JPM, PTS-VI
The Literati, in Smart Set, 13, May, 1904, 149-50 (1)

ELEANOR F. GARTLEY
Little Sister, 1929, 3 act comedy   RPB

LILLIAN MELANIE GARTNER
The Love Pirate, 1908   RPB

AMY ASHWOOD GARVEY (MRS. MARCUS GARVEY)
Hey! Hey! prod. 1926, musical

OLIVE WHITE GARVEY
Captain Washington, historical play (1)   SGW
His Old-Time Sweetheart, 1933, comedy (1)   RPB
Lobster Salad, 1931, "sketch especially for Rotary Anns"   RPB
Marrying Martin, 1935, 3 act comedy   RPB

ALICE GARWOOD
Himself, 1923, prod. by Pasadena Comm. Players
Redleaf, 1920, prod. by Pasadena Comm. Players

HELEN GERTRUDE GASKILL
The Most Foolish Virgin, symbolic fantasy (1)   ETP

CATHERINE BELLAIRE GASKOIN
The Lumber Room and Other Plays, 1914, one-acts   RPB

(MARY) ELEANOR GATES (1875-1951) AWW (MRS. FREDERICK MOORE)
(MRS. RICHARD W. TULLY)
Bird of Paradise, prod. 1912, with Richard Walton Tully
The Darling of the World, 1922, prod. 1918-9, at Northampton Mass.
   Municipal Theatre
Fire, 1927
Fish-Bait, 1928, 3 act farce, typescript   NN
Memories, 1933, with Laughton George
Out of the West, 1924
The Poor Little Rich Girl, 1916, prod. 1913, " play of fact and fancy in   RPB
   3 acts"
"Swat the Fly!" 1915, fantasy, propaganda for medical experiments on   RPB
   animals
The Twinkling of an Eye, 1934
The Waiting Soul, "drama of the twilight sleep" (1)
"We Are Seven," 1915, prod. 1913, 3 act whimsical farce   RPB

BEATRICE GAULE
Bicentennial Pageant in Honor of George Washington

BERTHA GAUS
Fairies of Today, 1915, entertainment in 3 scenes   RPB

LOUISE FALLENSTEIN GAUSS
A Dragon, a Hero and a King, 1945, about Perseus, by Louise Gauss   RPB
The Golden Ball, 1945, 3 act comedy based on a folk tale of the middle   DLC
   ages
Little Helpers, 1915 (also pub. in Christmas Plays for Children, 1916) (1) RPB

MARY GAVIN
The Curtains, in Poetry, 16, April, 1920, 1-11, with Cloyd Head (1)

ALLISON GAW
Pharaoh's Daughter, 1917, with Ethelean Tyson Gaw, winning   RPB, GPD
   Biblical play in 1927 Pasadena Playhouse contest
Pharaoh's Daughter and Other Biblical Plays, 1928, with Ethelean Tyson Gaw

ETHELEAN TYSON GAW
A Chinaman's Chance, 1931, comedy for men (1)   RPB
   (See above—Allison Gaw)

HELEN GAYLORD
The Gayrusans' Legacy, by S. S. G. Entertainment Co., 1910, with Luzetta RPB
   R. Sanders and Cora A. Sanders, 3 act drama
The Newrich Reception, 1910, with Luzetta R. Sanders and Cora A. Sanders
The Pokeyville Rally, 1913, drama, with Luzetta R. Sanders and Cora A.   RPB
   Sanders
Six Sharps, One Flat, 1907, with Luzetta R. Sanders and Cora A. Sanders   RPB
Snapshots, 1909, first pub. as a one-act, 1906, with both Sanders   RPB
Union Depot for a Day, 1905, with Luzetta R. Sanders and Cora A.   RPB
   Sanders

MAURINE GEE
   The Delicate Child, 1926, with Helen McIntyre, won First Samuel   RPB
      French Prize in the national contest of the General Fed. of
      Women's Clubs, 1926 (1)

MYRTLE GARRISON GEE
   Plays from American History, 1925, by Francis O'Ryan and Anna   RPB
      Wynne O'Ryan, adapted for elementary grades by Gee

EDNA GEISTER
   Four Humorous Pantomimes
   The Fun Book, 1923, stunts for every month in the year   NcGU
   Wild Nell, the Pet of the Plains; or, Her Final Sacrifice, 1928, pantomime   RPB

MINA GENNELL
   The Only Girl, 1907, 4 act comedy drama   RPB

HELEN GENTRY
   Derby, 1922 (1)   PCW

ALVA GEORGE
   The Reformation of a Liar, 1900, 3 act comedy   RPB

ANNA PRITCHARD GEORGE
   Prohibition Mother Goose, 1921   RPB

DOROTHY THOMAS GEORGE
   A Soul Made Clean, comedy (1)   HUW-3

GRACE GEORGE (1895- ?)
   Domino, adapted 1932
   Mademoiselle, 1932, adaptation of French farce
   Matrimony Pfd., prod. 1936, with James Forbes
   The Nest, adaptation of play by Paul Geraldy
   She Had to Know, 1925, adaptation of play by Paul Geraldy
   To Love, 1922, adaptation of play by Paul Geraldy

ROBERTA T. GERAGHTY
   Humanity's Cause, 1918, patriotic service of story and song, music by   RPB
      various composers

FLORENCE GERALD
   For Love and Honor, 1906, dramatic sketch   RPB

ELIZABETH SEARS GERBERDING
   Scissors or Sword, 191? (about women's clubs and suffrage)

MARGARITA SPALDING GERRY (1870—1939)
   An Interruption, in Harper's Bazaar, 40, May, 1906, 398-403

EMILY GOLDSMITH GERSON
   A Delayed Birthday, 1910, Hanukah play (1)   RPB
   The Matzoh Shalet, 1911, Passover sketch   RPB
   The Purim Basket, 1914   RPB
   The Years After, 190? Purim play   RPB

ALICE (ERYA) GERSTENBERG (1885-1972) AWW NWAT
Alice in Wonderland, 1915, musical   RPB, FON,MTP
Beyond (also in Ten One Act Plays)   MRO
Captain Joe, 1908, prod. 1912, comedy, college play for 11 girls   NN, MH
    (also in A Little World) (typed copy at MH) (1929 ed. at NN)
The Class Play, 1908, for 12 girls (Also in A Little World)
The Class President, 1929, college play for girls (also in A Little World) RPB
Comedies All, 1930, collection of short plays   RPB
Ever Young, in Drama, 12, Feb., 1922, 167-73 (1) (also in Four   STW, SBO
    Plays for Four Women
Find It, 1937
Four Plays for Four Women, 1924   RPB
Fourteen, in Drama, 10, Feb., 1920, 180-4 (1) (also in Ten One Act Plays)
Glee Plays the Game, 1934, 3 acts for women (c. 1933 as Deep Desire)
The Hourglass, 1955
The Land of "Don't-Want-To," 1928, based on novel by Lilian Bell,   RPB
    3 acts
A Little World, 1908, collection of college plays for girls   RPB
London Town (1728-1776-1780) "a new composite comedy of 3 successes NN
    of the 18th century," prod. at the Arts Club of Chicago, 1937, typescript
The Magic of Living, 1969
On the Beam, 1957, 3 act inspirational comedy
The Opera Matinee, 1925, prod. 1915, social satire (1)   RPB
    (also in Comedies All)
Our Calla, 1956
Overtones, 1929, prod. 1915 (Also in ,   RPB, SHP,STW,CCT-3,WSP, FCP
    A. P. Dickinson, Drama 1922; J. B. Hubbell and J. D. Beatty, An
    Introduction to Drama, 1927; and in Ten One Act Plays) (3 act version
    in 1922 with Lorin Howard)
A Patroness, 1917, monologue, typescript   NN
The Pot Boiler, 1944, in Little Theater Tournament 1923 (Also in   KTP, SCO
    Ten One Act Plays)
The Promise, (See Something in the Air) 1929
The Queen's Christmas, 1939 (1)
Sentience, 1933 (also titled Tuning In) comedy (1)   RPB
Something in the Air, 1942 (pub. 1920 as A Grain of Mustard and 1929 RPB
    as The Promise) with Maude Fealy
The Sound Effects Man, 1940   MWS
Star Dust, 1931   DSS
Ten One Act Plays, 1921   RPB
Time for Romance, 1941, 3 act comedy for women   RPB
The Trap (1)   ETP
Try Your Number
Tuning In (See Sentience) (1)   MRO-1937
The Unseen (Also in Ten One Act Plays) (1)   GOP
Victory Belles, prod. 1943, with Henry Adrian, farce, typescript   NN
The War Game, with Rienzi de Cordova
The Water Babies, 1930, prod. 1929, adapt. of story by Charles Kingsley RPB
When Chicago Was Young, 1932, with Herma Clark
Where Are Those Men? 1912, sketch for girls (1)   RPB
Within the Hour, 1934

MARGARET COLBY GETCHELL (See MARGARET C. GETCHELL PARSONS)

FRANCES GUIGNARD GIBBES (MRS. OSCAR L. KEITH)
Dawn in Carolina, 1946, 3 acts   RPB
The Face, 1924, 3 acts (about the painting "Mona Lisa")   RPB

FRANCES GUIGNARD GIBBES (continued)
Hilda, 1923, 4 act tragedy   RPB
The Strange Woman   ScU
Up There! 1932, 3 acts   RPB
Weapons   ScU

ALACE ZARA GIBBS
Ain't She Cute, 1930, mimeographed copy   RPB
Airplane Romance, 1930, mimeographed copy   RPB
The Fifth Hand at Bridge, 1931, monologue   RPB
Run Quick Rosie! 1919? mimeographed copy   DLC
Sarah's Birthday Gift, 1929   play?   DLC
Von Leetle Minute, 1929   play?   DLC

EMILY M. GIBSON
English-class Plays for New Americans, 1927   RPB

THELMA HARDY GIBSON
The Ideal Spot, 1928, farce (1)   IaU

BONNIE GILBERT
May Madness (1)   SPG

HELEN GILBERT
The Good Saint Anne, in Poet Lore, 35, 1924, 576-86 (1)
The Spot on the Porch, in Poet Lore, 42, Spring, 1933, 81-91

JEANETTE LEONARD GILDER (1849-1916)
dram. of Quo Vadis, prod. 1900

JOSEPHINE GILES (All plays written with William Giles)
Advice Wanted, 1915, vaudeville sketch (1)   RPB
A Bachelor's Elopement, 1913, 3 act comedy   RPB
Bill Jones, 1914, duologue   RPB
A Child of the Slums, 1910, sketch   RPB
Gabe's Home Run, 1910, comedy (1)   RPB
He Who Came Back; or, Here Comes the Bride, 1933?   RPB
The Hoosier School, 1910, farcical sketch (1)   RPB
A Hurricane Wooing, 1916, 3 act comedy
It Was the Dutch, 1910   RPB
Jake and His Pa, 1917, comedy (1)   RPB
Just Like a Woman, 1909, farce (1)   RPB
News From Home, 1917, comedy (1)   RPB
Rube and His Ma, 1908, "merry rural comedy drama in 3 acts"
Rube's Family, 1914, monologue   RPB
The Rural Post Office, 1910, sketch   RPB
Tickled to Death, 1916, vaudeville sketch (1)   RPB
Tom and Jerry, 1917, vaudeville sketch (1)   RPB
The Trusted Friend, 1910   RPB
Uncle Josh's Folks, 1909, 3 act drama   RPB
Uncle Si's Predicament, 1911, 3 act drama   RPB
Where Bill Goes Home, 1911, comedy (1)   RPB

BERTHA GILLESPIE
Black Wing, 1929

FANNIE B. GILLESPIE
Scene in Waiting Room, 1926, humorous entertainment (1)   RPB

CHARLOTTE PERKINS STETSON GILMAN (1860-1935) AWW NAW
Something to Vote For, in The Forerunner, 2, June, 1911, 143-53   FOV
Three Women, in The Forerunner, 2, May, 1911, 115-23, 134 (1)
The Yellow Wallpaper, 193? (Wetmore Declamation Bureau)   RPB

ALICE F. GILMORE
Our Library, "a Dewey Decimal Play," Wilson Library Bulletin, 5, Nov.,
          1930, 186-91 (1)

ANNELLA SLAUGHTER GILMORE
When Santa Claus' Pipe Went Out, 1918, monologue   RPB

CAROLYN DRAPER GILPATRIC
Character Studies in One Act, 1937, collection   RPB
Forty Miles an Hour, 1925 (1)   RPB
Moving Day, 1925, "calamity in one act"   RPB
O'Keefe's Circuit, 1920, entertainment (1)   RPB
Patty Makes Things Hum, 1919, 3 act comedy   RPB
Please Stand By, 1926, radioleta   RPB
Sandra Speaks, 1925, comedy (1)   RPB
Sardines, 1925 (1)   RPB
The Second Puncture, 1924, 3 act comedy   RPB
Sixty Miles an Hour, 1925 (1)   RPB

ROSE ADELE GILPATRICK
A School Pageant—the progress of civilization, by students of Coburn   MB
          Classical Institute, Waterville, Maine, in The School Review, 23,
          Dec., 1915, 704-7
The Torch of Learning, the Colby Centennial pageant, 1920, Waterville,   RPB
          Maine, directed by Lotta Alma Clark

HELENE GINGOLD (? -1926)
Abelard and Heloise, 1906   RPB
Looking for Trouble, 1913, 3 act farce   NN, DLC

RUTH GIORLOFF
Circumstances Alter Cases, 1930, comedy (1)   MPP
Highness, 1931, drama (1)   RPB
Jazz and Minuet, Little Theatre Tournament 1927, comedy (1) RPB, ETP,SSH-I
"Lavender and Red Pepper," 1932, comedy for women (1)   NPW
Maizie, 1929 (1)   OPS-V
Night Shade, 1926
The Way Out, 1932, tragedy (1)   OPS-VII

HELEN M. GIVENS
The Bull Terrier and the Baby, in Ladies' Home Journal, 23, Oct., 1906, 15+ (1)
Improving Husbands, in Ladies' Home Journal, 24, March, 1907, 10+ (1)

GENEVIEVE GIVINS
The Favorite Coach, 1929, for boys of jr. high school or high school   RPB

SUSAN KEATING GLASPELL (1876?-1948) AWW NAW NWAT
Alison's House, 1930, won Pulitzer prize in 1931   RPB, CCP, SP
Bernice, 1920, prod. 1919 (in Plays) 1st pub. in Theatre Arts Magazine,
   3, Oct., 1919, 264-300
The Big Bozo
Chains of Dew, 1922, 3 act comedy, typescript   DLC
Close the Book, prod. 1917 (in Plays) (1)
The Comic Artist, 1927, prod. 1933, with Norman Matson, tragedy   RPB
Inheritors, 1921   RPB
The Outside, prod. 1916? (in Plays) (1)   RPB, FCP,CSP-1
The People, prod. 1917 (in Plays) (1) typescript   NN
The People and Close the Book, Two One-Act Plays, 1918   RPB
Plays, 1920   RPB
Six Plays, 1933
Springs Eternal, typescript   NN
Suppressed Desires, 1917, prod. 1915, with   RPB, CSP,MRO, WTP,CCT-3
   George Cram Cook (in Plays) Also in Jerry M. Weiss, Ed., Ten
   Short Plays, 1963
Three Plays, 1924
Tickless Time, prod. 1918, with George Cram Cook   RPB, STC,SCO, HTM
   (in Plays) Also in Catharine Bullard, Ed., One-Act Plays for Junior High
   School, 1937
Trifles,   RPB, PTM,CNA, MPP,KFA, SLC,BAW,LAM,CCT, PDP,KWD, GTP ,
   prod. 1916 (in Plays) Also in Donald Fitzjohn, Ed., English One-Act
   Plays of Today, 1962; Mary Anne Ferguson, Ed., Images of
   Women in Literature, 1977; John Sweet and Kenneth Lynn, Eds.,
   Designs for Reading: Plays, 1969; L. Phillips and T. Johnson, Eds.,
   Types of Modern Dramatic Composition, 1927; R. W. Pence,
   Dramas by Present-Day Writers, 1927; and C. M. Martin, Ed., Fifty
   One-Act Plays, 1934
Trifles and Six Other Short Plays, 1926
The Verge, 1922, prod. 1921   RPB
Woman's Honor, prod. 1918 (in Plays) (1)

ANNE AND ELIZABETH GLEASON
Signal Service, n.d., comedy   RPB

CHARLOTTE GLEASON
Judas Iscariot, 1922   RPB

ORISSA W. GLEASON
The Annual Picnic of the Muggsville Sunday School, 1907   RPB
The Creole Belles; or, Female Minstrelsy Up to Date, 1903,   RPB
   entertainment
How the Club Was Formed, 1909   RPB
How the Ladies Earned Their Dollar; or, Mrs. Toploft's Scheme, 1922 (1)   RPB
How the Story Grew, 1908, entertainment for women's clubs (1)   RPB
A Modern Sewing Society, 1906, for females (1)   RPB
Rummage Donations, 1923   RPB
Trouble in Santa Claus Land, 1905   RPB

EVA M. GLEN
Arrested for Speeding, 1925, 2 act comedy   RPB

LYDIA M. GLOVER (See LYDIA MAY GLOVER DESEO)

NAN G. GLOVER
    The Shadow, 1925, won the Pearl B. Broxam prize in a contest held by   RPB
       Iowa State Federation of Women's Clubs, romantic fantasy

HELEN P. GLOYD
    Mr. Loring's Aunts, 1917, 3 act comedy   RPB

MOLLIE MOORE GODBOLD (1877- ?)
    The Flapper Grandmother, 1924, with Hetty Jane Dunaway   RPB
    Gun-shy, 1930, 3 act comedy   RPB
    Help Yourself, 1926, 3 act musical comedy   TxU
    The Love Cure, 1926, comedy (1)   RPB
    The Microbe of Love, n.d., 3 act comedy   RPB
    Polly Tickks
    "The Raw Edge," n.d., typescript   NN
    Rosetime

FELICIA GODDARD
    On With the New, dialogue, in Smart Set, 9, Feb., 1903, 83-5 (1)
    What Society is Coming To, in Smart Set, 12, Oct., 1903, 55-7 (1)

MILLY JUNE GOELITZ
    Everybody Calls Me Gene, 1926, comedy (1)   RPB

BERTHA GOES
    The Dowry of Columbine   JNS
    Every Bite, 1918, with Ruth Mary Weeks, patriotic burlesque   RPB
    Freshmen at Arden, 1931 play?

ELEANOR GOLDEN
    A Puppet Play, Little Theatre Tornament 1926
    Spring Dance, 1936, with Eloise Barrangon, adapt. by Philip Barry, 3 act
      comedy

GRACE DELANEY GOLDENBURG
    Claribel Capers, 1929, comedy (1)   RPB
    Cousin Gene, 1916, 3 act comedy   RPB
    My Maid on the Bamboo Screen, 1909, Chinese fantasy, music by   PBa
      William Smith Goldenburg

DR. LUBA GOLDSMITH
    Who Cares? 1925, health fantasy (1)   RPB

SOPHIE L. GOLDSMITH
    Wonder Clock Plays, 1925, dram. of Howard Pyle's Wonder Clock   RPB
      Stories, young

FRANCE GOLDWATER
    Washington Danced (1)

FRANCES PUSEY GOOCH
    Gerry's Awakening, 1916, 3 act romantic drama   RPB

MRS. E. H. GOODFELLOW
    Easy Entertainments for Young People, 1920   RPB
    Money Making and Merry Making Entertainments, 1926, first pub. 1903, RPB
      with Lizzie J. Rook

MRS. E. H. GOODFELLOW (continued)
Tiny Tot's Speaker for the Wee Ones, 1910, first pub. 1895, with Lizzie   RPB
    J. Rook
Vice Versa, 1896, first pub. 1892, 3 acts   RPB, EEY
Young Doctor Devine, 1925, first pub. 1896, farce for women   RPB

MABEL RAY GOODLANDER
Fairy Plays for Children, 1915, collection of one-acts
A Halloween Pantomime   SH
The Visit of the Tomter, in Woman's Home Companion, 41, Dec.,
    1914, 66 (1)

BLANCHE GOODMAN (EISENDRATH)
A Change of Heart, 1919? first pub. 190?   RPB
Checkmating Miss Fanny, 1913?   RPB
The Famous "Viney" Sketches, 1928 or earlier, black monologues
On Matrimony, 1918? first pub. 190? a Viney sketch   RPB
Rechristening Cornell, 190?   IU
Rockbottom and Miss Sally Baker, 190?   IU, OU
Uncle Zeke's Cemetery, 1917? first pub. 190?   RPB
Viney at the Moving Pictures, 191? first pub. 190?   RPB
Viney on Club Doings, 1918? first pub. 190?   RPB
Viney on Conservation, 1918? first pub. 190?   RPB
The Viney Sketches, 19?? (1918 ed. at RPB)   RPB, NN

FRANCES GOODRICH (1890- ?)
"Ah Wilderness!" scenario of O'Neill's play, 1935, with Albert Hackett   NN
Bridal Wise, prod. 1932, with Albert Hackett
Diary of Anne Frank, 1956, with Albert Hackett   RPB,FBP-IV
The Great Big Doorstep, 1943, with Albert Hackett, from novel by E. P.   RPB
    O'Donnell, 3 act comedy
Up Pops the Devil, 1933, prod. 1930, with Albert Hackett (also titled   RPB
    Let's Get Married) 3 act comedy
The Virginian, 1945, screenplay with Albert Hackett   NN
Western Union Please, 1942, prod. 1937, with Albert Hackett (also titled   RPB
    Father's Day) 3 act comedy

ELIZABETH FULLER GOODSPEED
The Land of Oz, 1928, dram. from story by L. Frank Baum   RPB
The Wizard of Oz, 1928, dram. from story by L. Frank Baum

DOROTHY ROSE GOOGINS
The Bellman of Mons   TAJ

"JULIEN GORDON" (See JULIE GRINNELL CRUGER)

MINNIE E. GORDON
Columbia's Awakening, 1918, patriotic play for young people   RPB

BESSIE M. GORSLENE
"In the Beginning," 1924, Biblical drama   RPB

MYRTLE WARNER GOSHORN
Over the Back Fence, 1929, blackface farce for women (1)   RPB

SARA ELIZABETH GOSSELINK (1893- ?)
The Light of the Cross, 1925, sacred drama   RPB
The Paramount Children's Day Book, 1923, with others   RPB
The Paramount Christmas Plays, 1925, with Pearl Holloway   RPB
The Paramount Easter Book, 1923, with others   RPB
Unto the Least of These, 1925, 3 act missionary play   RPB
When the Missionary Came, 1923, 3 act comedy   RPB
The Winning of Mrs. Bard, 1930, missionary play   RPB

ALICE GOULD
The Merchant of Venice, 1929, burlesque operatic version   RPB

ELIZABETH LINCOLN GOULD
The "Little Men" Play, 1900, dram. from Louisa Alcott, also in   RPB
    Ladies' Home Jounral, 18, Dec., 1900, 3-4+
The "Little Women" Play, 1900, dram. from Louisa Alcott, also in   RPB
    Ladies' Home Journal, 18, Jan., 1901, 3-4+
What It Means to a Woman, 1913, with Frances Whitehouse, 4 acts,   NN
    typed copy

ZINITA GRAF
The Ultimate City, 1916, pageant, Yankton, S. D.

LOUISE M. GRAFF
The Spirit of Peace, 1929, pageant of the Nativity   RPB

MANTA S. GRAHAM (1883- ?)
Angels and Stars, typescript   IaU
The Blusterbuss, typescript   IaU
A Book or a Ring, typescript   IaU
Call It a Day, pub. in Comedies Seven, 1933
A Candle to Burn, typescript   IaU
Concord Street, typescript   IaU
An Energetic Constitution, typescript   IaU
Finesse, c. 1924, won first prize from Iowa Fed. of Women's Clubs,   IaU
    typescript
A Hospital Fancy, adapt. of R. L. Stevenson story   YSP-II
In the Cupola, typescript   IaU
Inaction, typescript   IaU
Islands of Security, typescript   IaU
Know Your Town, typescript   IaU
Light Weights, 1921, collection of 5 one-act plays   RPB
A Lovesome Thing, typescript   IaU
The Magic Word, c. 1929, typescript   IaU
Meanwhile, typescript   IaU
A Narsty Half Hour, c. 1920, typescript   IaU
Nick Nollen, typescript   IaU
Niklas X and the Robber Baron
O People of Israel (earlier titles: A Decisive Half Hour and A Pincher of   IaU
    Sycamore Fruit) typescript
1001 Sons of God, c. 1920, typescript   IaU
The Other Half Dozen   YSP-1
Pennies for Understanding, typescript   IaU
A Piece of Land, c. 1939, typescript   IaU
Pilgrims, incomplete typescript   IaU
A Place for the Gold, typescript   IaU
The Poorest Boy in the World (earlier title: Better to Give) incomplete   IaU
    typescript

MANTA S. GRAHAM (continued)

Pork, c. 1922, typescript   IaU
Posada, typescript   IaU
The Prescription, c. 1927, typescript   IaU
Present Perfect, typescript   IaU
The Promotion—Washington Play, in The Instructor, 62, Feb., 1953, 33
Rest in Peace, c. 1940, typescript   IaU
The Scream, typescript   IaU
The Search, incomplete typescript   IaU
A Silk Gown, typescript   IaU
Sixty-Three, c. 1922, typescript   IaU
Still the Waters, typescript   IaU
The Supreme Gift, typescript   IaU
Ten: Twenty-one (earlier title: Eighteen: Twenty-two) typescript   IaU
Thank You Mr. Anonymous, typescript   IaU
The Tinderbox, 1936, typescript   IaU
Transplanting the Flowers, typescript   IaU
The Treasure Chest, 1931, 3 act comedy   RPB
Two's Company, printed copy c. 1919, typescript   IaU
Wakefield, typescript   IaU
Why, c. 1929, typescript   IaU
A Worthington Woman, typescript   IaU

MARY GRAHAM

Idyll, in Drama, 16, April, 1926, 255-6 (1)

SHIRLEY GRAHAM (DUBOIS) (1907-1977) AWW

Coal Dust, 1930 (1)
Dust to Earth, 1941, drama
Elijah's Ravens, 1930, 3 acts
I Gotta Home, 1939
It's Morning, 1940, tragedy
Little Black Sambo, 1937, for children, music by Charlotte Chorpenning
The Swing Mikado, 1938, jazz adapt. of Gilbert and Sullivan
Tom Tom, 1932, musical
Track Thirteen, 1940

CORA DE FOREST GRANT (MRS. ERNEST R. GRANT)

King Good Health Wins, 1919, modern Health crusade, with Alberta   DLC
    Walker

ETHEL WATTS MUMFORD GRANT (1878-1940)

John Wendham's Experiment
Just Herself, prod. 1914
A Legend of Granada, 1904, cantata, music by Henry Hadley   RPB-M
Merlin and Vivian, 1907, lyric drama   RPB-M
The Nightingale and the Rose, 1911, cantata, music by Henry Hadley   NN
Out of the Sea, 1940, operetta for children, music by Lily Teresa   RPB-M
    Strickland (1)
The Princess of Ys, 1903, cantata, music by Henry Hadley   NN, MB
Scenario (1)
Sick-a-Bed, prod. 1919, 3 act farcical comedy   RPB
Star Over Bethlehem, 1936, Christmas cantata   Or, OrP

ALEXANDRA ETHELDRED GRANTHAM (VON HERDER) (1867- ?)

Jesus of Nazareth, 1913, poetical drama in 7 scenes   RPB

CLOTILDE INEZ MARY GRAVES ("RICHARD DEHAN")
(1863-1932) (may be Brit.)
Death and Rachel, 18?? dramatic duologue   NN
The Lover's Battle, 1902, heroical comedy in rhyme, based on Pope's   RPB
    "Rape of the Lock"
A Mother of Three, 1909, 3 act farce
A Tenement Tragedy, prod. 1906 (1)

ETHEL COOPER GRAY
The Call to Citizenship, 1925, pageant for class day
Marionettes Go to School, 1929 (includes two plays)   RPB
Some Teachers of Life and Literature, 1925, pageant for high school   RPB

EUNICE T. GRAY
Case of Spoons; or, The Baroness Sorato's Garden Party, 1909, Japanese   OCl
    farce
"The Varsity Coach," 1912, college play
The Winning of Fuji, 1909, Japanese play (1)   RPB

FRANCES GRAY (BATTON)
The Beaded Buckle, 1923-4, "comedy of village aristocracy" (1)   KCF-II
Out of the Past, 1924-5, "romance of college life at Carolina in '61" (1)

ISABEL MC REYNOLDS GRAY
Florizel, 1901 play?   DLC
Jimmy's Little Sister, 1929, farce (1)   RPB
A Mad Breakfast, 1929, farce (1)   RPB

AUGUSTA GREELY
Penal Law 2010, prod. 1930, with Alexander Gerry

CLARA S. GREEN
Mother Goose Opens Her Door   BPC

CORA MAE GREEN
Jumpin' the Broom (1)   OPS-V

ELIZABETH ATKINSON LAY GREEN (1897- ?)
Balanced Diet, 1928, comedy (1)   RPB
Blackbeard, Pirate of the Carolina Coast, 1921-2, with Paul Green (1)
The Hag, prod. 1916, comedy of folk superstition (1)
Trista   KCF-II
When Witches Rode, 1918-9, play of folk superstition, pub. in The   KCF-I
    Magazine, Un. of N. C., April 1919

ERMA GREEN
Fixin's, 1923-4, with Paul Green, tragedy of a   RPB,KCF-II,SSH-IV
    tenant farm woman (1)

GOLDIE GREEN
Taking a Club to Father, and A Cure for Mr. Pessimism, 1925   RPB

MARY WOLCOTT GREEN
The Women Who Did, 1911, dramatic entertainment for women,   RPB
    historical and patriotic

RUTH GREENE
The Magic Vase, 1929, pageant of the history of pottery, created by the   RPB
    Art Dept. Kosciuszko School, Hamtramck, Mich., with Mary B.
    Ingraham and others

MARJORIE GREGG
Close Prisoners, comedy (1)

RITA GREIG
And the Meeting Came to Order, 1930, comedy, "dedicated to all   RPB
    aspiring parliamentarians"

MARY GREY
More Christian Endeavor Playlets, 1929, Ed. by E. W. Thornton, a   RPB
    contributor

ANNA HELENA GRIFFIN
Margarethe von Randau, 1901, dram. of German story   RPB

CAROLINE STEARNS GRIFFIN   (1868- ?)
The Headless Horseman, 1906, based on Washington Irving's poem   RPB
Villikins and His Diniah, 1906, "in shadow pantomime and   RPB
    Hallowe'en fun," arranged by Griffin

MRS. O. W. GRIFFIN
Recitations and Dialogues, 1904   RPB

ALICE MARY MATLOCK GRIFFITH
Westward the Course of Empire, 1924, "the history of Texas from   RPB
    exploration to annexation in a sequence of one-act plays"
Whither, in Poet Lore, 35, 1924, 140-7 (1)

ELEANOR GLENDOWER GRIFFITH
The House the Children Built, health play   HDC, SSH-IV
The Little Vegetable Man, health play   HDC
The Magic Oat Field, health play   HDC
The Wonderful Window, 1922, health play   MB, DLC

HELEN SHERMAN GRIFFITH   (1873- ?)
An Alarm of Fire, 1911, comedy (1)   RPB
A Borrowed Luncheon, 1899, farce (1)   PU
The Burglar Alarm, 1899 (1)
A Case of Duplicity, 1901 farce (1)   RPB
The Dumb Waiter, 1902 farce (1)   RPB
A Fallen Idol, 1900, farce (1)   RPB
For Love or Money, 1903, 3 act comedy   RPB
A Game of Old Maid, 1919 (1)   NN
Getting the Range, 1918, Great War play (1)   RPB
Help Wanted, 1908, 2 act comedy
Her Service Flag, 1918, Great War play (1)   RPB
The Knitting Club; or, Just Back from France, 1918, comedy (1)   RPB
The Ladies Strike, 1921, farce on servant problem, for females (1)   RPB
A Large Order, 1902 (1)   RPB
Maid to Order, 1907, farce on boarding school life, for females (1)   RPB
A Man's Voice, 1908, 2 act comedy for females   RPB
The Merry Widow Hat, 1909, farce for females (1)   RPB

HELEN SHERMAN GRIFFITH (continued)
The Minister's Wife, 1901, farce for females (1)   RPB
The Over-Alls Club, 1920, farce (1)   RPB
A Psychological Moment, 1903, farce for females   RPB
Reflected Glory, 1909, farce for females (1)   RPB
The Scarlet Bonnet, 1904, 2 act comedy   RPB
The Sewing Society, 1901 (1)   RPB
Social Aspirations, 1903, comedy   RPB
The Wrong Miss Mather, 1905, comedy for females (1)   RPB
The Wrong Package, 1906, comedy for females (1)   RPB

ELIZABETH BERKELEY GRIMBALL
The Flag of the Free   CD
The Hope of the World, 1918, pageant, Montevallo, Ala., unpub.   NN
    program
"Lest We Forget," n.d., program for celebration of Armistice Day,   MiD, Or
    typed copy
A Message from the Stuart, 1916? dramatic episode of Queen   NN
    Elizabeth's reign
The Sleeping Beauty, n.d., adapt. of Grimm's fairy tale, typescript   NN
The Snow Queen, 1920, young
Snow White and Rose Red, n.d., adapt. of Grimm's fairy tale, typescript   NN
The Torch Bearers of the Western World, 1920, pageant of S. America   NN
Under the Stars and Stripes, n.d., festival of citizenship   NN
The Waif, 1923, "Christmas morality of the 20th century"   RPB

KATHERINE ATHERTON GRIMES
The Light of the Ages, 1919, dramatic Christmas cantata, music by   RPB
    J. S. Fearis

ANGELINA WELD GRIMKE (1880-1958) NAW SBAA
Mara   DHU
Rachel, 1920, prod. 1916 by Nathaniel Guy Players at Myrtle Miner   RPB, HSB
    Normal School, Washington, D. C.

HAZEL GRIMM
Milady's Style Review, 1926, stunt for a group of 10 to 20 girls   RPB

GRACE GRISWOLD (? -1927)
Billie's First Love, 1921, comedy (1)   RPB
The Haunted Chamber, 1921, romantic comedy (1)   RPB
His Japanese Wife, 1921, comedy (1)   RPB
The Main Line, prod. 1924, with Thomas McKean

VIRGINIA A. GRISWOLD
The Christmas Story, 1921   RPB

ALICE GROFF
Freedom, 1904, 4 acts   RPB

CLARE M. GRUBB
The Magi's Gift, 1927, Christmas operetta, music and lyrics selected   RPB-M
    from Fifty Christmas Carols by Eduardo Marzo, with original
    incidental music by Bryceson Treharne
The Outlaw King, 1929, Robin Hood operetta, libretto by Grubb; lyrics by
    Iris Decker; music by Decker and Louis Malone

DOROTHY A. GRUNDY
The Charming Hobo, 1929, 3 act comedy   RPB

VIRGINIA RUDDER GRUNDY
Recitations and Plays for Special Days, 1930   RPB

SUZANNE CARY GRUVER
The Book of the Pageant of Brockton, 1921, Brockton, Mass., also pub.   RPB
    in Warren Prince Landers, Ed., Brockton and Its Centennial, 1921,
    pp. 107-76
Daughters of Wisdom, 1917, pageant of famous women, Brockton Mass   MB

BELLE WILLEY GUE
George Washington, 1924   RPB
Washington, the Pioneer, 1928, 4 acts   RPB
Washington, the Statesman, 1928, 4 acts
Washington, the Warrior, 1928, 3 acts

DOROTHY C. GUINN
Out of the Dark, 1924, pageant for high school   RMP

(MARY) FRANCES GUNNER
The Light of the Women, 1930, ceremonial for use of negro groups   RMP
    for jr. and senior high school (1)

ELIZABETH FRANCES EPHRAIM GUPTILL (1870- ?)
Answering the Phone, 1914, farce   RPB
April Fool; or, The Clown Drill, 1914, exercise for small boys   RPB
At the Court of St. Valentine, 1910   RPB
Aunt Sabriny's Christmas, 1912, for girls   RPB
Best Author's Christmas Plays, 1909, with others   RPB
Bo Peep's Christmas Party, 1914, Mother Goose play   RPB
A Brave Little Tomboy, 1912, play of the revolution   RPB
Bright Ideas for Christmas, 1920, with Ema S. Hunting and others,   RPB
    one-acts
Bright Ideas for Hallowe'en, 1920, with others
The Brownie's Vacation, 1908, for boys   RPB
Cabbage Hill School, 1906, for children   RPB
The Changed Valentine and Other Plays for St. Valentine's Day, 1918   RPB
Christmas at the Cross Roads, 1909, humorous Christmas play for h. s.   RPB
    pupils
Christmas at McCarthy's, 1916   Or
Christmas at Punkin Holler, 1916   Or
Christmas at Santa Claus' House, 1906   RPB
Christmas at Skeeter Corner, 1905   RPB
A Christmas Budget, 1904   RPB
A Christmas Dream, 1905, play in rhyme   RPB
Christmas for All Nations, 1905, play in rhyme   RPB
A Christmas Joke, 1905   RPB
A Christmas Mystery, 1916, for boys   RPB
Christmas Plays and Comedies, 1925, with others   RPB
The Complete Hallowe'en Book, 1915, one-acts
The Complete Valentine Book, 1917   RPB
The Contest of the Nations, 1918, music by Archibald Humboldt   RPB
Crowning the May Queen, 1906   RPB
The Doll's Symposium, 1911, "captivating play for children"   RPB
Dot Entertains, 1924 or earlier

ELIZABETH FRANCES EPHRAIM GUPTILL (continued)

Fun at Five Point School, 1912, burlesque	RPB
The Goblins and the Ghostly Glide, 1914	RPB
Going to School in Mother Gooseland, 1914	RPB
Gold, Frankincense and Myrhh, 1914, music by "Fred B. Holton"	RPB
The Golden Goose, 1916	RPB
Guptill's New Christmas Book, 1915	RPB
Guptill's New Year Book, 1915, one-acts	RPB
The Holiday's Carnival, 1904	RPB
In Santa Claus Land, 1901, Christmas play in rhyme	RPB
In the Wake of Paul Revere, 1906	RPB
The Last Day at Mud Hollow School, 1914, burlesque	RPB
Little Acts for Little Actors, 1916, with Edyth M. Wormwood	RPB
A Little Heroine of the Revolution, 1906, "historical play for all ages"	RPB
Little Jack's Christmas, 1913	RPB
The Lost Prince, 1905, Christmas play in rhyme	RPB
The Magic Word, 1926, young	RPB
Mother Goose's Gosling, 1903	RPB
The New Teacher at Mud Hollow, 1914, burlesque	RPB
Original Christmas Dialogues, 1905	RPB
The Pinkies and the Winkies, 1913	RPB
Red White and Blue, 1912, patriotic entertainment for schools	RPB
Santa's Rescue, 1914	RPB
The School at Mud Hollow, 1914, burlesque	RPB
The Search for Mother Goose, 1910, Christmas play for children	RPB
The Shirkers, 1908, young	RPB
Silver Stars, 1914, young	RPB
Spring's Welcome to Easter, 1916	NN
The Stars and Stripes Jubilee, 1906, music by "Archibald Humboldt"	RPB
Taking the Census, 1914, farce	RPB
Thanksgiving in the Schoolroom, 1937, with others	RPB
A Topsy Turvy Christmas, 1916	RPB
A Trip to Storyland, 1908, musical play for children	RPB
A Troublesome Flock, 1916, Mother Goose play for children	RPB
Turning the Tables, 1911, for girls	RPB
Twelve Plays for Children, 1916, one-acts	RPB
The Twins and How They Entertained the New Minister, 1914, farce	RPB
An Uninvited Member, 1912, for girls	RPB
The Waif's Thanksgiving, 1911	RPB
Wanted—a Daddy, 1913, Mother Goose play for Christmas	RPB
Wanted: a License to Wed, 1912	NN
The Whirling Dervishes, 19??	RPB

EMILY GURGEN

Bombs and Balloons, 1907, musical comedy, book by Gurgen, Ruth Ashmore, Gillian Barr and others; music and lyrics by Grace Hollingsworth	NBuG

ELIZABETH W. GWYNNE

Mrs. Murphy's Contribution, and Hash, 1925, monologues	RPB
Murphy's Little Joke, and Concentratin', 1925, monologues	RPB

H

ETTA WEAVER HADEN
The Realty Deals, 1925, 3 acts   RPB

KATHRIN P. HADEN
The Passover, 1911, cantata, music by E. W. Ashford   RPB

LIZZIE M. HADLEY
A Program for Washington Celebration

S. GERTRUDE HADLOW
Pageant of Trade, 1915, Cleveland, Ohio
Pageant of Twinsburg, 1917, Twinsburg, Ohio.   MB

LIDA HAFFORD
The Red Cross Nurse, 1917, with Sue Froman Matthews, "giving the   RPB
    actual experience of an American girl"

AUDREY HAGGARD
The Double Axe, 1929, romance of ancient Crete   NN, PSt
Little Plays from Greek Myths, 1929

ELIZABETH F. HAGUE
The Making of the Constitution, 5 acts
Nathan Hale, with Mary Chalmers, 2 acts

MRS. MALVINE HAHN
"Her Mother," c1908, 3 act drama   RPB

MARGARET H. HAHN
Sorepaw and Fells Indoor Circus, 1921, with Margaret S. Bridge   RPB

GENEVIEVE GREVILLE HAINES
Hearts Aflame, c1901, prod. 1902, 4 acts, founded on novel by   CU, DLC
    Louise Winter, microfilm copy of typewritten ms.
"Once Upon a Time," 1904, prod. 1905, Andalusian romance in 3 acts   RPB

ANNA MARCET (HALDEMAN) HALDEMAN-JULIUS
        (MRS. EMANUEL HALDEMAN-JULIUS)
Embers, 1923, with Emanuel Haldeman-Julius (1)   RPB

LOUISE CLOSSER HALE (1872-1933)
The Other Woman, in Smart Set, 34, June, 1911, 107-13, prod. in early   OCl
    1920's (typescript at NN) (1)
Paste Cut Paste, in Smart Set, 36, Jan., 1912, 125-32 (1)

ALMA L. HALL   RPB
The Thane of Cawdor, 1914, mock grand opera in 5 acts, with Helen D.
    Brewer, Pine River School, Pine River, Minn.
    (listed at RPB under Brewer.)

BERTHA PARKER HALL
Ducky Daddles and the Three Bears, 1921, "make-believe" play   RPB
Ducky Daddle's Party, 1918   play??   DLC
Henny and Penny, 1922   play??   DLC

MARY LEORA HALL
Story Plays for Little Children, 1917, with Sarah Elizabeth Palmer   RPB

MAUDE L. HALL
The Scrubtown Sewing Circle's Thanksgiving, 1910, "old ladies'   RPB
   sociable"

MARY M. HALLIDAY
Santa Claus in Mother Gooseland, 1920, musical playlet for children   RPB-M

GRACE TABOR HALLOCK (1893- ?)
Dramatizing Child Health, 1925, collection   RPB
May Day Festival Book, 1927, 1926, ed. by Hallock
The Riddle, 1925, young (in Dramatizing Child Health)   RPB

MRS. HENRY A. HALLOCK
The Packing of the Home Missionary Barrel, 1910, entertainment in   RPB
   one scene

ELEANOR HALLOWELL
Millo Make-Believe, with Abbott Coburn

NANCY S. HALLOWELL
The Nurse's Drill, 1920   RPB
A Red Cross Drill, 1918   RPB
A Semaphore Flag Drill, 1918 (also in Lieutenant Clifton Lisle, Ed., RPB
   Boy Scout Entertainments, 1918)

DORIS FRIEND HALMAN (1895- ?)
Ceiling, 1943, in Plays, 2, Feb., 1943, 54-64 (typescript at NN) (1) MPD
The Closet, 1921 (also in Set the Stage for Eight) fantasy (1)   PTM
Famine and the Ghost, (1)   JMP
How Not to Write a Play, 1927, painless demonstration in one act and a   RPB
   foreword
Honk! a Motor Romance, 1926 play?   GU, DLC
It Behooves Us, 1918, comedy of conservation   RPB
Johnny Pickup, 1920 (pub. in William I. Kaufman, ed., The Best
   Television Plays, 1954, Vol. 3, 155-82)
The Land Where Lost Things Go, 1918, 3 acts (Drama League patriotic RPB
   play prize)
Lenna Looks Down, (1)   OPS-IV
The Playroom, fantasy   (also in Set the Stage for Eight) (1)   BPW
The Rocking Horse, 1952, in The Best Television Plays, 1950/51
Rusted Stock
Set the Stage for Eight, 1923, collection of one-acts   RPB
The Voice of the Snake, 194?, comedy (typescript at NN) (1)   OPS-III
We, the Tools, in Plays, 2, April, 1943, 59-65 (1)
Will O' the Wisp, c1916, fantasy, Little Theatre   KPC, MRO,CSP-I
   Tournament, 1923 (1)(also in Set the Stage for Eight)

JESSIE HALTON
Before the Dawn, (mentioned in Harriot Stanton Blatch's Challenging
   Years.)

BERNICE LADD HALVORSON
    In Pursuit of Her Heritage, n.d., with Katherine Buxbaum, in 3   RPB
       episodes

ANNETTE MASON HAM (1873- ?)
    Angels in the Garden, 1933, Easter mystery play for children   RPB-M
    A Christmas Dream, 1954, nativity play for young people   RPB-M
    There Was One Who Gave a Lamb, 1925, Nativity play with   RPB-M
       traditional carols, for children
    The Vision at Chartres, 1941, nativity play with traditional carols, for RPB-M
       children

AGNES HAMILTON
    The Straw Hat, prod. 1926, with Paul Tulane

EDITH HAMILTON (1867-1963) AWW, NAW
    The Klubwoman, 1925, comedy (1)   RPB

HELEN HAMILTON (may be Brit.)
    The Modern Mother Goose, 1916, "being the first of a series of dramas RPB
       for young people"

MARGARET PORCH HAMILTON (1867- ?)
    The Federal Convention, 1921, dramatization of the U. S.   RPB
       Constitutional Convention of 1787

MARY P. HAMLIN
    Burnt Offering, 1933, about Jephthah's wife, peace play (1)   RPB
    Certain Greeks, 1935 (1)
    Hamilton, 1918, prod. 1917, with George Arliss   RPB
    He Came Seeing, 1928, religious drama (1)   RPB, ETO,
                                                    AGW
    The Rock, 1921, about Simon Peter, prize play of Drama League, (in RPB
       Religious Dramas. I)
    The Separatist, 1934 (1)   RPB
    Stung, n.d., vaudeville play (1)   NN
    The Style's the Thing, 1919, vaudeville sketch   NN
    The Trouble with the Christmas Presents, 1931, comedy (1)   RPB

INA HAMMER (MRS. IRA A. HARDS)
    Billy Binks, script   NNC
    Introduce Me to Peachy, with Jasmine Van Dresser, script   NNC
    Samantha Boom-de-ay, script   NNC

ELEANOR PRESCOTT HAMMOND (1866-1933)
    Susanna Shakespeare, 1916, 4 act romantic comedy   RPB

JOSEPHINE HAMMOND (1876- ?)
    Everywoman's Road, 1911, "morality of woman creator, worker,   RPB
       waster, joy-giver, and keeper of the flame," morality play of
       woman's progress

KATHRYN WIRE HAMMOND (1877- ?)
    Aunt Elzena's Wild Ride, 1930, monologue   RPB
    Parking Place for Papa, 1934, with Harriett N. Connell, 3 act comedy for RPB
       women
    Terry the Terrible, 1931, with Harriett N. Connell, 3 act comedy-drama RPB
    Well, Did You Ever, 1929, with Harriett N. Connell   RPB

VIRGINIA MAYE HAMMOND
It's Alla Matter of Dress, 1929, comedy (1)   BAO

LAURA VERNON HAMNER
Sump'n Walked Across My Grabe, 1929, "Negro dialogue that barely   RPB
escapes being a monologue"

ESSE HAMOT
Eden, 1928-9, with Druzilla Mackey

CORA MC WHINEY HAND
His Friend's Widow, 1926, 3 acts   RPB

GERTRUDE HAND (1886- ?)
Historical Stories in Dramatic Form, 1914   RPB

ELIZABETH HINES HANLEY
A Festival of Freedom, 1942? "a review of the nation's patriotic   CD,NBuG
songs in chronological sequence," arr. by Hanley
The Gifts They Brought, n.d., "pageant of many peoples in one   MiD
nation," typed copy
The Magic Path, 1930?, fairy play (also in National Recreation Assoc.,   Or
Silver Bells and Cockle Shells, 1936)
A Mother's Day Program, n. d.   CD
Now All Together, 1952? festival of fellowship   OrCS
Pageant of Historic Monroe, 1926, Monroe, Mich.   MiD
The Perfect Gift, n.d., community Christmas pageant, Moultine, Ga.,   MiD
typed copy
The Pilgrim's Pride, 192? pageant, typewritten copy   MiD, NN
Stunts of Fun and Fancy, 1925   RPB
Who Left the Cupboard Bare? 1928, Mother Goose mystery play   RPB

ELIZABETH HEMING HANNA
The Court of Juno, 1903, 2 act lyrical drama   RPB

NELLIE HANNA
The Brightville Indoor Chautaqua, 1921, with Bessie Baker   RPB
(listed at RPB under Baker)

TACIE MAY HANNA (REW) (Some plays pub. under Hanna; some under Rew)
Clipped, 1930, comedy (1)   RPB
Exclusively Yours, 1940, 3 act comedy drama   OU, DLC
The House Beautiful, 1930, also in Drama, 15, Feb., 1925, 112-4 (1)   RPB
Hyacinths, 1935, also in Drama, 12, Sept., 1922, 338-41 (1) won   RPB, RCT
1st prize in S. Calif. Tournament of One-acts at Santa Ana, Calif., 1934
and 2nd prize in L. A. County Drama Assoc. Tournament at Beverly
Hills, 1934 (listed under Rew at RPB)
Pals, 1930, 4 act high school play   RPB
Their Tomorrows, 1920, written for Boys Work Committee of the   RPB
Rotary Club, San Bernardino, Calif.
Upon the Waters, 1923, in Drama, 14, Nov., 1923, 58-62+ (1)   NN, OCl
When Stars Shine, 1938, 3 act comedy drama

BEATRICE HANSCOM
Light, 1909   RPB

MAMIE B. HANSON
  Behind the Curtain, 1928   RPB
  Prisoner of Flight, 1928   RPB

JOSEPHINE WILHELM HARD
  Pandora's Box, 1915, masque from Hawthorne's Wonder Book   RPB

MARY EMILY HARDEN
  Humorous Recitations for Children, 1927, with Edith Hadley   RPB
    Butterfield, Ruth Adkinson, Bessie Ford and others

MABEL TRAER HARDING
  The Rose-shaded Lamp, 1927, comedy (1)   RPB

BERNICE HARDY
  Mono-dramas; the new platform art, 1930, monologues   RPB
  The Sour Grapes Club, 1933, 3 act collegiate comedy   RPB

MAUD CUNEY HARE (See MAUD CUNEY-HARE)

FRANCES HARGIS
  Hero Worship, 1928, winner of Samuel French Prize in Little Theatre   RPB
    Tournament, 1928 (1)

EUSTACE HARGRAVE
  The Island Sea Dream (1)

LIZZIE ALLEN HARKER (1863-1933)
  "Marigold," 1928, Arcadian comedy, with F. R. Pryor   RPB

ANNA JANE WILCOX HARNWELL (1872- ?)
  The Alabaster Boy, c1926, with Isabelle J. Meaker (in Religious   RPB
    Dramas, II)
  An Episode Near Bethlehem   SSC
  At the Spanish Court, for Columbus Day   SPA
  Before Fort Duquesne (1)   SGW
  Blessings in Disguise, comedy (1)   SPE
  The Easter Rabbit, Easter fantasy for little children   SPS-2
  From Hand to Hand, with Isabelle J. Meaker, for Christmas (1)   SSC
  Her Name Was Ann   SLP-1
  Holly and Cypress, 1930, with Isabelle J. Meaker, for Christmas
  The Knife, with Isabelle J. Meaker (1)   SSH-II
  Locks to Pick; Key at Rear, 1909, book of charades   RPB
  Minerva Makes a Suggestion, peace fantasy   SPP
  Pocahontas and John Smith, historical play (1)   SPS
  The Pranks of Puck, "for Midsummer's Day or Halloween or all times   SPS-2
    when spirits are visible"
  She Who Will Not When She May, (1)   SGW
  The Sin of Ahab, 1922, drama (1)   RPB
  Sojourners, with Isabelle J. Meaker, also in Drama, 10, July-Sept., 1920, SSH-II
    357-64 (1)
  The Star in the East, 1921, Drama League Biblical drama prize   RPB
  To Vote—or Apple Butter?, comedy for election day (1)   SPC
  The Trial of John and Jane, 1920, "a near tragedy," Christmas and   WaPS
    children's festival operetta; music by Daniel Protheroem, (1)
  The Well, pioneer play (1)   SPA
  Youth Is Served, modern play for Thanksgiving Day   STP

GENEVIEVE HARPER
The Magic Word, 1928, with Mary Drescher, 3-scene playlet based on   RPB
    "Ali Baba and the Forty Thieves"

LUCY LOWREY HARPER
The Baby Specialist, 1927, commencement play   RPB
Bargains, 1926, 2 act farce   RPB
"Dat Meliniel Line," 1927, "histrionic stairway pageant"   RPB

EVALINE HARRINGTON
What Mamie Learned, 1922 (1)   RPB

HELEN HARRINGTON
Outwitting the Weasels, and New-fangled Notions, 1924, two plays for   RPB
    children, adapted from stories by Clara D. Pierson
The Red Flower, 1920, "play of Armenia today"   RPB

ADA LEONORA HARRIS
Cupid in the Kitchen

ALLENA HARRIS (ALLENA KANKA)
The Delinquents, 1926, with Katherine B. Miller, 4 act comedy drama   RPB
Help Yourself, 1926, with Katherine Browning Miller, 3 act comedy   RPB
Just Boys, prod. 1915, with Katherine B. Miller (Allena Kanka (Harris?)
The Last Straw   ETP
Old Walnut, 1926, comedy, also in Scholastic, 21, Jan. 7, 1933, 9-11 (1)   RPB

ANNIE ELIZABETH HARRIS
Hale Merrills Honey Quest; how one girl made the best of things,   MB, DLC
    1918, play?
Play's the Thing, 1925, manual of drill games
A School Boy's Dream, 1916, 2 acts   RPB

CLAUDIA LUCAS HARRIS (CLAUDIA HARRIS)
Adorable, 1936, 3 act comedy of youth   RPB
At the Mouth of the Mine
The Boy o' Dreams, prod. 1923 by Pasadena Community Players
Chill Billy Stuff, 1937, "refrigerated farcical romance in 3 acts"   DLC
Easter Pilgrimage, 1936, pageant   RPB
Hermit's House, 1934, 3 act mystery play   RPB
The Howling Dog, 1935, 3 act mystery drama   RPB
It's Spring, in Drama, 11, April, 1921, 245-50, fantasy (1)
Jack-in-the-Pulpit
Latch Keys for Ladies, 1934, comedy for women   RPB
The Man Who Couldn't Say No, (1)   SBO
Paging John Smith, 1935, comedy for men   RPB
Sittin' Pretty, 1936, comedy for men   RPB
"The Spirit of Christmas Giving," 1933   RPB
The Sporting Passion
There's a Man in the House, 1935, comedy   OCl, DLC
Trailer Romance, 1930, 3 act comedy   RPB
Young Mr. Santa Claus, in Drama, 12, Oct.-Nov., 1921, 42-7, Christmas
    fantasy (1)

EDNA MAY HARRIS (1900- ?)
Windblown, in Poet Lore, 38, 1927, 426-34, fantasy (1)

FRANCES HELEN HARRIS
Eight Plays for the School, 1913   RPB
Plays for Young People, 1911, for school entertainments and home theatricals

HAZEL HARPER HARRIS
When a Man Wanders, in Poet Lore, 40, 1929, 602-9, for women (1)

JANE YANCEY HARRIS
Thoroughly Tested, 1907, 6 act drama   RPB

KATHRYN R. HARRIS
Lovers of All Ages, 1906 "spectacular play"   RPB

LILLIAN HARRIS
Coast to Coast, n.d., farce   NN
Marriage is So Difficult, in Poet Lore, 38, 1927, 452-63 (1)
Publicity, in Poet Lore, 38, 1927, 590-602 (1)

LUCY HARRIS
Maud Muller, 1903, pantomime of poem by John G. Whittier   RPB

MAY HARRIS
The Open Door, in Smart Set, 20, Oct., 1906, 60-7 (1)
A Poet's Wife, in Smart Set, 44, Oct., 1914, 55-9 (1)

MAY PASHLEY HARRIS
An Inauguration Pageant for George Washington's Birthday, 1931?,
     mimeograph copy several places
Kip's Bay Historical Community Pageant, 1920
Labor Day Program
Marguette, pageant of its people, Marquette, Mich.   MiD, Mi
Pageant of Inauguration of President George Washington   JWA
Pageant of Play, 1924, typewritten copy   CD, MiD
Program for Mayday; Robin Hood legends adapted to May Day
     celebrations, 1921
The Resurrection of Our Lord, 1923, Protestant miracle play of the16th   OrP
     century
The Spirit of the Dunes, pageant
The Spirit of the Sanet, pageant
A Tribute to Labor   CD

MILDRED WILLIS HARRIS
Co-Respondent Unknown, prod. 1936, with Harold Goldman
Troupin' in the Sticks, 1927 (1)   RPB

ROSA S. HARRIS
Saving the Situation, 1924, "comedy of family life" (1)   RPB

CONSTANCE CARY HARRISON (MRS. BURTON HARRISON)
             (1843-1920)   AWW, NAW
Alice in Wonderland, 189?, young   RPB
Behind a Curtain, c.1892, monologue (in Short Comedies) (1)   RPB
The Mouse Trap, 1892 (in Short Comedies) (1)   RPB
A Russian Honeymoon, 1883, 3 act comedy, adapted from French of   RPB
     Eugene Scribe
Short Comedies for Amateur Players, 1889   RPB

CONSTANCE CARY HARRISON (continued)
  Tea at Four O'Clock, 1892, drawing room comedy (1)   RPB
  Two Strings to Her Bow, 1892, 2 act comedy (in Short Comedies)
  The Unwelcome Mrs. Hatch, 1901, "drama of everyday"   RPB

EDITH WADE HART
  Flyin', 1928, "aeronautics comedy," won first prize in one-act play   RPB
    contest of State Federation of Women's Clubs, California

ELIZABETH HARRIET HART
  Pan's Princess, 1909, masque, Freshman play at Wellesley   RPB

ELIZABETH STREET HART
  Nancy's Niece, 1916, 3 act musical comedy-drama   RPB

MARY T. HART
  The Enchanted Chimney, in Woman's Home Companion, 37, Dec., 1910,
    46-7 (1)

ZOE HARTMAN(N)
  The Christmas Bazaar,1932, by Zoe Hartmann (may be a different   RPB
    person) operetta in one act for unchanged voices; libretto and lyrics
    by Hartmann; music by Harold Wansborough
  The Chronic Kicker, 1928, 3 act comedy drama   RPB
  Cockroaches in the Basement, 1943, reproduction of typed copy (1)   RPB
  Conspiracy for Two, 1948, comedy (1)   MiD
  Indian and Famous Scout Plays for Boys' and Girls' Camps and Upper   RPB
    Grammar Grades, 1943, with Walter W. Anderson and Frances L. Fox
  Ma Nosey and Pa Gossip, 1929, comedy (1)   RPB
  Marrying Off Father, 1926, comedy (1)   RPB
  Pinch-hitting for Santa, 1945, Christmas (1)   Or
  Santa Claus Behind the Times, 1924, "fantastic comedy in 2 acts"   RPB
  Santa Claus' Busy Day, 1924 (1)   RPB
  Sitters in Revolt,1947, comedy (1)   RPB
  A Tempest in a Hat Shop, 1925, comedy (1)   RPB
  Tuning Up for the Wedding, 1924   RPB
  What's the Matter with Mother? 1931, comedy (1)   RPB

IRENE V. HARTWELL
  The New Hat, 1930, pub. by American Farm Bureau Federation   RPB

DELLA SHAW HARVEY
  An Easter Miracle (1)   BPP

EDITH MARY HARVEY
  Hansel and Gretel, 1915, with Jane Minerva McLaren, adapted from the RPB
    opera by Humperdinck

KATE HARVEY (may be British)
  Courage, (1)   BHP
  Won, (1)   BHP

MARION (MARIAN) HARVEY
  (many others by Harvey listed in NUC, but may not be plays)
  Footsteps, 1931 "breathtaking mystery play", with Nancy Bancroft   RPB
    Brosius (listed at RPB under Brosius)
  The Inner Circle, 1930, 3 act mystery thriller   RPB

ELIZABETH (LOUISE) SEYMOUR HASBROUCK (ZIMM) (1883- ?)
Elizabeth's Young Man, 1917, farce, (dram. of her story in Harper's,   RPB
    Oct., 1910)

HARRIET HOLMES HASLETT
The Board Meeting, 1932, comedy for women (1)   RPB
Dolores of the Sierra and Other One Act Plays, 1917   RPB
The Flying Grandmother, 1931, comedy for women (1)   RPB
His Chorus Girl, 1925, comedy (1)   NN
Trial Marriage, 1920, 3 act satiric comedy   RPB
The Trained Nurse, 1926 or earlier, drama (1)

"BEE HASTINGS" (See NANCY B. WEST)

FRANCES HASTINGS
The Choir Invisible, 1901, dram. of story by J. L. Allen   RPB

FRANCES ROSINA HASWIN
The Old Brigadier, 1902, drama, also in The Philosopher, 11, no. 5,   RPB
    May, 1902, 129-49 (1)

ADELAIDE WESTCOTT HATCH
Dance of the Butterflies, 1910, drill and a dance   RPB
Fairs, Fetes and Festivals, 1902   ICJ, DLC
The Fairy Star and Bell Drill, 1910   InU, NcD
A Flock of Turkeys, 1910, humorous drill   RPB
A Flower Fantasy, 1903, drill   NBuG
The Handkerchief Drill, 1904   NcD
Hints, Vol. 1, May,. 1899, "devoted to plays, entertainments, socials, fairs,
    recitations, monologues—for the use of colleges, schools, churches,
    societies, clubs, and the home circle." (She was editor.)
The March Winds, 1902," spectacular drill"
The Minuet, 1904, arr. by Hatch   RPB
Money Making Socials, 1901, "collection of novel, original and   DLC
    attractive social affairs"
A New Flag Drill, 1903   InU, NcD
The Owl and the Pussycat Drill, 1902, "nonsense comedy-song drill   RPB
    and pantomime
The Revel of the Goblins, 1910   RPB
The Rock-a-by Lady, 1910, the poem of Eugene Field arranged as a   RPB
    pantomime
Sailor Drill, 1910
Snowball Fantastics, 1903, children's drills and marches   NN
Yankee Doodle Drill, n.d.   NN
The Zobo Patriotic Drill, 1901   ICJ

KATHARINE HATCH
Off With His Head, 1924 , comedy (1)   RPB

MARY R. PLATT HATCH (1848-1935) AWW
The Dreamer, 1913, prod. by Harvard Woman's Club
Mademoiselle Vivine, 1927, vaudeville sketch   RPB
Mrs. Bright's Visitor, 1927, comedy (1)   RPB

BESSIE HATFIELD
The Golden Wish, in Drama, 11, June, 1921, 327-9, dance pantomime
    and pageant

ESSE VIRGINIA HATHAWAY (1871- ?)
Des Moines Pageant, 1914, Des Moines, Iowa
The March of the Nations, 1929, pageant for tenth anniversary of   RPB
     League of Nations
Mr. Sneeze-in-the-Open , 1924, good health play for children (1)   RPB
A Wise Woman at the Court of Hygeia, n.d., issued by the Women's   RPB
     Foundation for Health (1)

BESSIE HATTON
Before Sunrise, 1909 suffrage   (probably British)

FANNY COTTINET LOCKE HATTON (1869-1930)
          (All her plays co-authored with Frederic Hatton)
"The Blue Devil," pub. 19?? 3 act comedy, typed copy   NN
Brimstone and Hell Fire, prod. 1915, satire, typescript (1)   NN
The Checkerboard, prod. 1920
The Dancing Partner, prod. 1930, adapted from work by A. Engel and A.
     Grunwald
The Fatal Woman, prod. 1930
The Great Lover, prod. 1915, also with Leo Dietrichstein
Her Unborn Child, scenario
His Majesty's Car, prod. 1930
The Indestructible Wife, prod. 1918
Lombardi Ltd, 1928, prod. 1917, 3 act comedy   RPB
Long Island Love, prod. 1930
Love, Honor and Betray, prod. 1930
Madame Milo, prod. 1921
Mastery of Kats, "society comedy in 3 acts," typescript   NN
"Playthings," prod. 1925, typewritten copy   NN
The Songbird, pub. 1915, 4 acts
The Squab Farm, 1916, prod. 1918, typescript   DLC
The Stork is Dead, prod. 1932, an adaptation
Synthetic Sin, 1927   NN
Tonight or Never, prod. 1930, , novelized by Lewis Allen Browne from
     David Belasco's stage success by Lily Hatvany, adapt. by the Hattons
"Treat 'em Rough," 1930, prod. 1926, comedy   RPB
Upstairs and Down, prod. 1916, 3 act comedy, prompt book   NN
The Walk-Offs, 1918   NN
We Girls, 1937, prod. 1921 (about flaming youth, Freud) prompt book   NN
Years of Discretion, 1913, prod. 1912, 3 act comedy, typed copy   NN

EMMA BELL HAUCH
Stanley Takes the Business, 1930, "good play with a business lesson"   RPB

MATTIE LEE HAUSGEN
Love Story of Uneeda Ad, 1912, romantic comedy in 2 scenes   RPB

ONA (WINANTS) HAVERKAMP (See ONA WINANTS BORLAND)

JEAN C. HAVEZ
The Girl from Brighton, prod. 1912, with Aaron Hoffman, music by
     William Backer

WINIFRED HAWKRIDGE
At Slovisky's
The Florist Shop, 1926, c. 1915, also in Smart Set, 47, Oct.,   RPB, KSP,BPH
     1915 103-19,under title of The Price of Orchids, sentimental comedy (1)

RUBY HAWTHORNE
What She Saw at the Game, 1920, monologue RPB

RUTH WARREN HAWTHORNE
Mrs. Partridge Presents, 1925, with Mary Kennedy, 3 act comedy drama RPB
Queen Bee, prod. 1929, with Louise Fox Connell, 3 acts, typescript NN

DAISY BAKER HAY
Jazzy Justice, 1928, "ten-minute stunt for male actors" with Flora RPB
    Campbell Woodruff
Mammy Explains Hallowe'en, 1927 RPB

BERTHA MARIE BRECHET HAYDEN
Diamonds, 1931 (1) RPB
Home Trade, 1931, comedy (1) RPB
Jealous Little Fool, 1930, mimeographed copy (1) RPB
Lovin' Hearts, 1931 Christmas (1) RPB
Santa's Gold Stars, 1930, mimeographed copy (1) RPB
The Silver Gleam, 1930, mimeographed copy (1) RPB

BRIDGET T. HAYES
Winter Bloom, in Poet Lore, 30, 1919, 385-411.

KATHERINE M. HAYES
Rival Debating Clubs, 1912, playlet for grammar school pupils RPB

MILDRED A. HAYES
A Christmas Dream BPC

FRANCES HAYS
Pageant of Universal Peace, 1914, Bellingham, Washington

GRACE HAYWARD
The CCC Murder Mystery, 1936, 2 act comedy drama, mimeo. playscript KU
Graustark; or, Love Behind a Throne, 1926, c. 1902, modern romantic RPB
    dram. of a novel by George Barr McCutcheon
Lend Me Your Baby, 1936, 3 act farce
Little Women, n.d., dramatization of Alcott novel, typescript NN
Our (local) Murder Mystery, 1937, 2 act comedy drama, (c. 1936 under RPB
    title, CCC Murder Mystery)
St. Elmo, 1909, dramatization of novel by Augusta Evans Wilson, NN
    typescript
Some Girl, 1928, 3 act comedy
Truxton King, 1912, suggested by story by George Barr McCutcheon, NN
    typescript

ALVIRA HAZZARD
Little Heads, in Sat. Evening Quill, April, 1929, 42-4, play of Negro life (1)
Mother Liked It, in Sat. Evening Quill, April, 1928 (1)

MARGUERITE HAZZARD
The Children for God, 1929, Christmas pageant RPB

EDITH HEAL (BERRIEN) (1903- ?)
Into the Everywhere, "Play for the Mind's Eye," in Poet Lore, 38, 1927,
    466-72

ALBERTA POWELL HEALD
  The Patriot's Pageant of Peace, 1919, originally for grammar grades   RPB

LUCY HEALD (1872- ?)
  Love in Umbria, 1912, "drama of the first Franciscans," pub. by class of   RPB
    1895, Smith College

FRANCES HEALEY
  Abu Achmet and the Eggs, 1926   RPB
  A Christmas Mystery Play, 1933   RPB
  The Copper Pot, 1919 (1)   RPB,WWT
  Creeds, 1928 (1)   SFM

ANNA LENINGTON HEATH
  The Game Kid, 1934, monologue   RPB
  Planning the Husband's Banquet, 1930, comedy for women (1)   RPB
  Two Too Many, 1944, comedy (1)   RPB

FLORENCE E. HEATH
  An Island Idyl, 1902, operetta with Grace Hollingsworth   RPB, MH

MARIE ARMSTRONG HECHT
  Such Is Life, prod. 1927, with Peter Glenny
  Three Little Girls, 1930, adaptation with Gertrude Purcell from an original
    script by H. Feiner and Hardt-Warren; music by W. Rolls

BERTHA HEDGES
  The Dead Saint, in Drama, 12, June-Aug., 1922, 305-9 (1)

MARION HAWTHORNE HEDGES
  The Beloit Pageant, 1916, "from the turtle to the flaming wheel," with   MB
    Theodore Lyman Wright, Beloit, Wisconsin

MARTHA HEDMAN
  For Valor, prod. 1935, with Henry Arthur House
  What's the Big Idea? prod. 1926, with Henry Arthur House

THERESA HELBURN (1887-1959) NAW
  Allison Makes Hay, 1919, 3 act comedy, prod. 1918 under title Crops   RPB
    and Croppers
  Crops and Croppers, prod. 1918, comedy about farmerette during war
  Denbigh, 1927, typescript   NN
  Enter the Hero, 1918, Flying Stag Plays,   RPB, SLC,KTP, FSP,GLL-II + III
    No 4, prod. by Washington Square Players (1)
  A Hero is Born, prod. 1937, 2 act extravaganza, based on story by   NN
    Andrew Lang, typed copy
  Little Dark Horse, prod. 1941
  Other Lives, 1921, with E. Goodman
  A Wayward Quest, n.d. play??

ELOISE HEMPHILL
  Little Red Riding Hood, 1908, musical play arranged by Hemphill   RPB M

AGNES HENDERSON
  That Dream, 1916, soliloquy   RPB

ALICE CORBIN HENDERSON (1881-1949)
Adam's Dream and Two Other Miracle Plays for Children, 1909,   RPB
    one-acts

GERTRUDE MEVIS HENDERSON (1888- ?)
    Cheery Comedies for Christmas, 1915, with Edith Maie Burrows and   RPB
    others

GLADYS SIGLER HENDERSON ("PENELOPE DICKERSON")
    (Most of her plays were pub. under name of Penelope Dickerson)
    The A.B.C. Fairies   FWP
    Aunt Daisy on the Links, 1930   RPB
    Billy is Invited Out, 1928   RPB
    By the Sweat of Her Brow, 1931   RPB
    The Children's Program, 1929
    Dotty Drives a Bargain, 1931   RPB
    Dotty Takes a Hand, 1935   RPB
    In the Doctor's Waiting Room, 1930   RPB
    Janice Entertains Her Sister's Beau, 193?   RPB
    Janice Gets Ready for Sunday, 1927   RPB
    Janice Takes Care of the Baby, 1927   RPB
    Janice Wanted a Watch, 193?   RPB
    Johnnie Hears the Contest, 1929   RPB
    The King's Son, 1928, dramatic reading   RPB
    Little Sister Comes Up With Hers! 1931   RPB
    Little Sister of the Shiek Attends a Concert, 1928   RPB
    Lucy Chooses   FWP
    A Mother Goose Mutiny, 1923, by G. S. Henderson, costume play   RPB
    The Passers-by, 1928, religious (1)   RPB
    Pink Ice Cream, 1930   RPB
    Rats!   FWP
    She Wanted a Cat, 1935   RPB
    Tattered Tillie of Toy Town, 1929, musical playlet   RPB
    Twenty Dialect Monologues, 1928, with Peggy Reece and Gracia Stayton

GRACE VAN SCHOEN DER WOERT HOGEBOOM HENDERSON
    (GRACE VAN WOERT HOGEBOOM-HENDERSON)
    The Pardon, 1927 (1)   RPB

JESSIE E. HENDERSON
    Borrower's Day, 1916, rural comedy (1)   RPB

MINA LOUISE HENDERSON ("MINA LOUISE")
    And They Lied Like Gentlemen, 1929   RPB
    When Women are Jurymen, 1930, comedy by "Mina Louise" (1)   RPB

RUTH EVELYN HENDERSON
    Here We Come! (1)   SOP-1
    When Floods Come   SPC

SARA HENDERSON
    A Bunch of Keys, 1923, comedy-drama   RPB
    Court Day in Dogdom, 1925, lesson play for children   RPB
    Cupid Mixes Things, 1922, valentine comedy (1)   RPB
    Dolly Has the "Flu," 1923, playlet for young   RPB
    Easter Eggs, 1923, playlet   RPB
    First Aid for Kitty, 1926, playlet   RPB

SARA HENDERSON (continued)
Flippetyflop, 1925, doll-play   RPB
Flowers for Flossie, 1925, comedy   RPB
From Frowns to Smiles, 1922, good health playlet   RPB
The Lineman, 1923, farce (1)   RPB
Tommy and the Calories, 1923, good health comedy   RPB
Too Many Wives, 1922, domestic comedy (1)   RPB
A Toothbrush Fantasy, 1923, good health playlet   RPB
Where's My Toothbrush? 1922   RPB
Woman the Silent Sufferer, 1925, satire   RPB

ADELINE HENDRICKS
The Night Call, prod. 1922, melodramatic mystery

ANNE HENLEY
Cinderella, 1913, with Stanley Schell, young, illustrated play in 4 scenes   RPB
Mayanni, 191? young   RPB

GRACE R. HENRY
Gentleman Jack, musical comedy, book by Henry; music by R.   RPB-M
    Batchelder; lyrics by Sabra and Rosamund Batchelder, given by Spence
    Alumnae Society, 1917
Kits and Kelts, 1909, musical comedy, book by Henry; music and lyrics by
    Grace Hollingworth
La Belle Chasseuse; or, Hearts and Hounds, 1908, musical comedy, book   MH
    by Henry and Katharine W. Tweed
Tags and Tatters, 1912, musical comedy, music and lyrics by Grace   RPB-M
    Hollingworth

EVA HERBST
Ruth, 1921, harvest pageant   RPB

BEATRICE HERFORD
Beatrice Herford's Monologues, 1937
The Bride's Christmas Tree, in Ladies' Home Journal, 28, Dec., 1911 (1)
Monologues, 1908, collection   RPB

ETHELLE MANNING HERMES
A Thanksgiving Day Movie, 1929, "picture show of Puritan Days"   RPB

ALICE HERNDON
Hell's Alley, 1930, with Alvin Childress

JULIE ADRIENNE HERNE
Between the Acts, 1904 (1)   RPB
The Outsider, 1915, 4 acts, prompt book   NN
Richter's Wife, prod. 1905

HENRIETTA HERON
Christian Endeavor Playlets, ed. by Heron, 1928   RPB
Christmas, 1922, fifteen minute pageant   RPB, HPY
Pageants for the Year, 1928, compiled by Heron

CHARLOTTE HERR
Her People, 1928-9

NANON LEE HERREN
The Romance of the Salads and Two Other Plays, 1929   RPB

GERTRUDE HERRICK
The Full of the Moon, Irish Play, in Poet Lore, 31, Autumn, 1920, 379-92 (1)

ELIZABETH GUION HESS
Silhouettes, 1924, monologues, sketches and bits of verse   RPB

FRANCES LEEDOM HESS
Readings and Monologues of Distinction, 1925, she was compiler and   RPB
   contributor
The Talk-a-day-World, 1926, eight original readings   RPB

LENORE HAZEL HETRICK ("NOEL FLAURIER") ("HELEN STARR")
   (H-Hetrick; F- Flaurier; S-Starr)
Best Primary Plays, 1930, with others (F)   RPB
Big Book of Thanksgiving Entertainments, 1941, with Lenore K. Dolan
   and others (F)
Children's Day Treasure Book, 1937 (H)   DLC
The Christmas Entertainment Book, 1925 (F)   RPB
The Christmas Festival Book, 1944 (H)
Christmas in the Primary Grades, 1926 (F)   RPB
Christmas in the Schoolroom, 1926, with others (F)
Christmas Plays and Comedies, 1925, with others (F)   RPB
The Christmas Treasure Book, 1927 (F)   (filed under Flaurier at RPB)   RPB
Closing Day Gayety Book, 1928 (F)
The Commencement Treasure Book, 1928 (F)   RPB
The Easter Treasure Book, 1935 (H)
Everyday Dialogues, 1926 (F)   RPB
A Fall Day (F)   FWP
Five Hours to Go, 1926, 2 act comedy (F)   RPB
The Giant Assembly Book, 1936, for high schools (H)   RPB
The Giant Christmas Book, 1934 (H)   RPB
The Giant Christmas Book, No. 2, 1936 (H)
The Giant Closing Day Book, 1934 (H)   RPB
The Giant Halloween Book, 1934 (H)
The Giant Patriotic Book, 1934 (H)
The Giant Recitation Book, for all grades, 1936 (H)
The Giant Stunt Book, 1938 (H)
The Giant Thanksgiving Book, 1935 (H)   RPB
The Good Habits Book, 1939 (F)
The Grade Assembly Book, 1939 (F)
High School Assembly Plays, 1941 (S)
The High School Christmas Book, 1941 (S)
Junior High Assembly Plays and Skits, 1964, with others (S)   RPB
Junior High Variety Book, 1949 (S)   OrP
The Last Day of School in the Primary Grades, 1928, collection (F)
The Modern Health Book, 1938 (F)
The Night Cry, 1927, 3 act comedy-drama (F)   RPB
Nobody Home, 1940, mystery (H)
On Ione's Trail, 1928, 3 act comedy (F)   RPB
Patriotic Plays for Schools, 1942 (S)   RPB
Peephole Shows for Little People, 1940 (H)
Pirates and Pearls, 1928, 2 act comedy (F)   RPB
Plays With a Purpose, 1939 (H)
Puppet Plays and Peephole Shows, 1938 (H)
Radio Miniatures, 1955, collection (S)   RPB
Recitations o' Pep and Humor, 1926 (F)
Rose of the Rileys, 1927, comedy (F)   RPB

LENORE HAZEL HETRICK (continued)
The Royal Gift (F)   FWP
Saint Patrick's Day Treasure Book, 1935 (H)
The Seven Star Primary Christmas Book, 1938 (F)   RPB
Snappy Humorous Monologues, 1927 (F)
Special Patriotic Programs, 1940 (F)   RPB
Star Comedies for Junior High School, 1941 (S)   RPB
The Street Fair (F)   FWP
The Thanksgiving Primary Book, 1938 (F)   RPB
The Thanksgiving Treasure Book, 1928 (F)   RPB
Those Jangling Christmas Bells, 1934, monologue (H)   RPB
Tiny Tots' Christmas Book, 1941 (H)
The Trial of Freshman Hartnett, 1938, mock trial for junior and
    senior h. s. (H)
The Visit of the Raindrops (F)   FWP
Welcome Miss McGregor, 1927, comedy (F)   RPB
Winning Plays and Dialogues, 1930, with others (F)   RPB
The Workers (F)   FWP
The Young Folks Christmas Book, 1940 (F)   RPB

ELIZA E. HEWITT
The Christmas Sky, 1914, with Grant Colfax Tullar, Christmas service   RPB-M
He Is Risen, 1906, with Thoro Harris and James Rowe, Easter service   RPB-M
The King Wonderful, 1912, "connective and constructive service for   RPB-M
    Christmas," music by Broughton Edwards
The Ladder of Life, 1913, scriptural service for Children's Day,   RPB-M
    music by Grant Colfax Tullar and I. H. Meredith
The Spirit of Christmas, 1909, with W. A. Post, Lizzie De Armond and
    James Rowe, Christmas service
Welcoming the King, 1902, with J. E. Burnard, W. A. Post and C. H.   RPB-M
    Gabriel, Christmas service

ESTELLE SIMMS HEWSON
The Love Experiment, 1922, Home and Foreign Missionary program,   RPB
    with Gertrude Simms Hodgson, Christmas playlet
A Pageant of Service, 1921, commemorating the 100th anniversary of   MB
    the Indiana yearly meeting, Richmond, Indiana

IRENE DALE HEWSON ("JEAN ROSS")
The Corn Bringers, 1924, for girl scouts, campfire girls, schools etc. (1)   RPB
Halloween Pumpkins, 1923, young (1)   RPB
The House of Hearts, 1922, Valentine's Day   RPB
The Magic Chest, 1922, Halloween (1)   RPB
Miss Iva Newway's School, 1924, pantomime play   RPB
Queen Loving Heart, 1921, young (1)   RPB
The Saint and the Fairies, 1924, St. Patrick's Day (1)   RPB
Trouble in Our Campfire, 1923, monologue   RPB

LILLIAN P. HEYDEMANN ("LILY CARTHEW")
The American Idea, 1918, play of Jewish life (1)   RPB
Common Sense and Calories, 1931, monologue   RPB
Home Sweet Home, 1932, monologue   RPB
I Bought a Bed, 1927, monologue   RPB
Lily Carthew's Monologues, 1919   RPB

GRACE HEYER
Lusmore, prod. 1919, with Rita Olcott
The Small World, 1909   RPB

DOROTHY HARTZELL KUHNS HEYWARD (1890-1961) AWW
   Babar the Elephant, 1953, children's opera, libretto by Heyward; lyrics by
      J. Randal; music by N. Berezewski (1)
   Cinderelative, prod. 1930, with Dorothy De Jagers, pub. as Little Girl Blue
   The Dud (See Nancy Ann)
   Jonica, prod. 1930, with M. Hart, music by Joseph Meyer; lyrics by William
      Moll
   The Lighted House, 1925, typescript   NN
   Little Girl Blue, 1931, prod. 1927, with Dorothy De Jagers, romantic   RPB
      comedy
   Love in a Cupboard, 1926, comedy (1)   RPB
   Mamba's Daughter, 1939, with Dubose Heyward   RPB
   Nancy Ann, 1927, prod. 1924, winner of the Richard Herndon prize,   RPB
      Harvard, 1924 (copyright under title, The Dud, 1912 by Dorothy
      Hartzell Kuhns)
   New Georgia, 1944
   Porgy, 1927, with Dubose Heyward, also in Theatre Arts, 39,   RPB, TGA,FBP
      Oct., 1955, 35-64
   The Pulitzer Prize Murders, 1932   play??
   Set My People Free, 1941, prod. 1948, typescript   NN
   South Pacific, prod. 1943, with Howard Rigsby, typescript   NN
   Three-a-day, 1930   play??

DELIA A. HEYWOOD ("POLLY ANN PRITCHARD")
   Pritchard's Choice Dialogues no. 1, 1896   RPB
   The Red Entertainment Book, 1941 (she was a contributor)   RPB
   The Visiting Smiths, 1920, 3 act farce   RPB

GERTRUDE A. HICKMAN
   The Spirit of Sauk-e-Nuk, 1930, pageant, Rock Island, Illinois   RPB

MAUDE HICKS HICKMAN
   The Cotton Goat, 1934, 3 act play for boys   RPB
   A Dollar Down, 1938, comedy (1)   DLC
   Free Silver, 1933, Iowa Federation of Women's Clubs prize play (1)   RPB
   Magnolia's Magic, 1937, church play (1)   OO, DLC
   Signs of the Times, 1937, community play   DLC
   Soup, sand and sagebrush, 1927, 3 act missionary play   RPB
   A Southern Tonic, 1926   RPB
   The Very Idea, 1932, mystery (1)   RPB

EVELYN HIGENBOTHAM
   A Man's Right, 1925, for National Woman's Party

AILEEN CLEVELAND HIGGINS (1882- ?)
   Thekla, 1907, drama   RPB

JOY HIGGINS
   The Beacon, 1930, "dramatic spectacle to picture and symbolize the   MB
      founding of Boston," with Elizabeth Higgins Sullivan, mimeo. copy

KATHARINE ELIZABETH CHAPIN HIGGINS
      (MRS. MILTON PRINCE HIGGINS) (1847-1925)
   The Children's Message, 1916   RPB

WILHEMINA HIGGINS
   Democracy Triumphant, 1918, patriotic pageant, with Marjorie Hope   RPB
      and others

LAURENE HIGHFIELD
Hail to the Victor, 1934, Easter pageant, music by Nevin and others   RPB-M
Hope for the Ages, 1933, Christmas pageant-service, music by Nevin   RPB-M
    and others
Immanuel, 1929, sacred Christmas pageant, music by Nevin and others   DLC
The Jolly Tars, n. d., nautical opera, music by Irving Gingrich (1)
The Usurper Overthrown, 1915, temperance cantata, music by Fred B.   RPB-M
    Holton

MARY HIGHT
Police Matron, with Carl Glick (1)
A Shakespearean Fantasy, 1927   RPB

ALINDA M. HILAND
In 1849, 1909, melodrama in 7 acts   RPB

FRANCES P. HILL
The Worm Turns, 1930, domestic extravaganza   (1)   RPB

MARGARET F. HILL
The Lost Village, 1916, 18th and 20th century contrast, for high school   RPB

RUTH HILL
John Joseph Pershing, 1919, story and a play, young   RPB
Robert E. Lee, 1920, story and a play, young   RPB

STELLA RICHMOND HILL
Michigan Peaches, 1906, 3 act pastoral drama with music   RPB
The Real Thing, 1907, drama   RPB

MARJORIE HILLIS
Respectability, 1928, 3 act comedy   RPB

RUTH ELLIOTT HILLS
Come, dine with us, 1920, playlet for use in Home Ec. classes to show   RPB
    proper table service

MARY W. HILLYER
Yuletide in Other Lands, 1927, Christmas pageant   RPB

ARLINE VAN NESS HINES
Her Honor, the Mayor, prod. 1918, typed copy   DLC

ELEANOR HOLMES HINKLEY
Dear Jane, prod. 1932
A Flitch of Bacon, 1920, 18th century comedy (1)   BPW

LAURA HINKLEY
Another Man's Shoes, prod. 1918, with Mabel Ferris, comedy

MARTHA L. HINMAN
The Wise Turkey (Thanksgiving)   WPP

ESTELLE HINTON
A Pumpkin Play   WPP

CHARLOTTE TELLER HIRSCH (1876- ?)
Hagar and Ishmael, vignette, in Crisis, May, 1913

MARY S. HITCHCOCK
At the Turn of the Road, 192?   RPB
Follow Thou Me, 1929, Biblical drama   RPB
I'm Not Jane, 1932, comedy (1)   RPB
One of the Nine, 1926, 3 act Biblical drama   RPB
The Slave Maid of Israel, 1930, 3 act Biblical drama   RPB
Whatsoever Ye Sow, 1928, 3 act Biblical drama   RPB

EMILY FLORENCE ALGER HOAG (SAWTELLE) (1890- ?)
The Mountain Maid, 1916, given by the citizens of Asheville   MB

WINIFRED A. HOAG
Best Primary Recitations, 1915   DLC
Thanksgiving Dinner   SBT

DOTY HOBART
Every Thursday, n.d., comedy, typescript   NN
"That's My Hat!" 1927, farce (1)   RPB

MARGARET JEFFERYS HOBART
Inasmuch as Ye Have Done it Unto the Least, pub. in Voices from
    Everywhere, 1914, missionary play (1)

MARIE ELIZABETH HOBART (1860-1928)
        (?? same as Margaret Jefferys Hobart??)
Adeste Fideles, 1919, Christmas play   IU, DLC
Althanasius, 1911, mystery play   RPB
The Angels of Magdalena, 1933, mystery play   OCl
Conquering and to Conquer, 1917, mystery play   RPB
The Great Trail, 1913, Indian mystery play   RPB
Lady Catechism and the Child, 1905, mystery play   RPB
The Little Pilgrim and the Book Beloved, 1906, mystery play   RPB
Rebekah, 1920, Old Testament mystery play   CtY
The Sunset Hour, 191?, out-of-doors play for young juniors   DLC
The Vision of Saint Agnes' Eve, 1907, mystery play   RPB

LUCY EDITH HOBBS
A Woman's Privilege; or, Democracy in Dress, 1918   RPB

MABEL FOOTE HOBBS
May Day in the Schools, pub. in Community Drama
Ruth and Naomi, with Helen Miles (1)   SOP-1
Six Bible Plays, 1924, with Helen Miles, young   RPB

VALINE HOBBS
Sparks, 1926, fire prevention rhymes, stories and playlets, she was   RPB
    editor

IRENE HOBSON
Meet Me in Syracuse, 1908, comedy (1)   RPB

MABEL HODENFIELD
Purple at the Window, Orange at the Window, 1927, "fantastic   RPB
    comedy" (1)

LAMMIE BLACKWELL HODGES
A Romance in Feathers; or No Gold in Her Crown, 1916   RPB

LEIGH MITCHELL HODGES (1876-1954)
Bird Guardians, 1915, masque for bird protection   RPB

ELIZABETH HODGKINSON
The Pilgrim's Progress, 1920, musical miracle play based on   RPB-M
    allegory of John Bunyan, music by Edgar Stillman Kelley

ADELAIDE HODGSON
The Minerva Club, 1927, club burlesque   RPB

GERTRUDE SIMMS HODGSON
The Love Experiment, 1922, Home and Foreign Missionary program,   RPB
    with Estelle Simms Hewson
Thirteen as One, 1922, pageant of united friendly service   DLC

MARI (MARIE) RUEF HOFER (1866- ?)
Camp Recitations and Pageants, 1927
The Children's Messiah, 1902, music by Miles Birket Foster, Niels W.   RPB
    Gade and others, arranged and compiled by Hofer
Christmas in Merrie England, 1915, with old carols, dances and a masque
Christmas in Peasant France, 1926, compiled and arranged by Hofer,
    incidental music by H. Courtland Cobb
Christmas Plays, Pantomimes and Dances, 1919   RPB
Daphne and Apollo, n.d., woodland idyl adapted to the Carnival by   OCl
    Tschaikowsky
Festivals and Civic Plays from Greek and Roman Tales, 1926   RPB
A Greek Frieze, 1921   OCl
Harvest Festival, 1916   Or
Seasonal Festivals and Pageants, 1916   RPB
The Story of Bethlehem, 1912
Summer Camp Entertainments, 1925

PHOEBE HOFFMAN (1894- ?)
About Face, 1924, comedy for women (1)   RPB
The Advantage of Being Shy, 1927, comedy (1)   RPB
Alien, 1937, "Playable Short Plays" by Glen Hughes (1)   RPB
In Mrs. Saturday's Shop, 1932, prod. 1935 (c. 1932 under title Zest)   TP
The Lady of Destiny, 1925, comedy for women (1)   RPB
A Man of Ideas, 1927, phantasy (1)   RPB
The Man of the Moment   JTF
Martha's Mourning, 1923, also in Drama, 8, Feb., 1918, 111-21 (1)   RPB, MRO
Mary Finds a Mother, 1940, (Also in Twenty Short Plays on a Royalty
    Holiday, Vol II. ed. by Margaret Mayorga)
Mrs. Leicester's School, adapted from story by Charles and Mary Lamb NPW
The Triumph of Mary, 1927, country comedy (1)   RPB
A Turn of a Hair, 1929, farce (1)   RPB
Undertones, 1925, comedy (1)   RPB
The Wedding Dress, 1926, costume play of Colonial days (1)   NAB-I
When It's Spring, 1924, comedy (1)   RPB

MRS. JULIAN D. HOGATE
Pageant of Hendricks County, 1924, Danville, Ind.   InI

PEARL HOGREFE
Every Senior, 1916, morality play (1)   RPB

ANNA D. HOKE
    The Flannigans Walk-Again, 1922, monologue   DLC

AMELIA WEED HOLBROOK
    Friday Afternoon at a Village School, 1909, farcical entertainment in   RPB
        one scene
    Jack, the Commodore's Grandson, c. 1893, typewritten copy   NN
    The Rejuvenation of Miss Semaphor, 192? dramatization of story by   NN
        Hal Godfrey, typed copy
    The Terror, c.1899, typewritten copy   NN

FLORENCE HOLBROOK (1860-1932)
    Dramatic Reader for Lower Grades, 1911   RPB
    Hiawatha, 1902, dramatization of Longfellow's "Song of Hiawatha"   RPB
    Peace Pageant, Chicago, 1913

MARGARET LOUISE HOLBROOK
    His Heroine, 1906, farce (1)   RPB

MARION HOLBROOK
    Backwoods, about George Washington (1)
    Brandywine, about George Washington (1)
    In the Hearts of His Countrymen, about George Washington (1)
    The Little General, about George Washington (1)
    Mount Vernon, about George Washington (1)

LOUISA EMMA HOLLAND
    Almost Married, 1936, comedy-drama   DLC
    Amateur Robbers, 1936   DLC
    The Answered Prayer; or, A Slip Between the Cup and the Lip, 1927,   RPB
        "heart interest drama"
    The Baby Mixup; or, The Little Canoeist
    The Charming Independent Widow; or, the Determined Suitor, 1927, RPB
        "giggle drama"
    Cigaretta's Beau; or, A Chip of the Block, 1936, comedy   DLC
    Did She Kill Him? or Free as the Winds that Blow
    Listen Lottie; or, It Never Rains but what it Pours
    The Meeting of the Two Dead Men, 1935, mystery   DLC
    The Midnight Surprise; or, the Long Lost Sister, Christmas playlet
    The Misleading Leading Lady; or, the Boss' Favorite, 1929, "romance   RPB
        and comedy"
    The Poodle Dog Club; or, Missing Her Children 1936, comedy-drama, DLC
        "heart interest comedy"
    Rosie's New Teacher, 1936 "heart interest drama"   DLC
    She Changed Her Mind, 1928   DLC
    Side Money; or, Fussy Husbands and Fussy Wives, 1928,   DLC
        comedy-drama
    Where is My Lily? or, Battling with the Ocean Waves, 1934,   RPB
        "heart interest comedy"

MARIETTA HOLLEY (1836-1926) NAW, AWW
    An Allegory on Woman's Rights, 1910
    Betsey Bobbett, 1880, by "Josiah Allen's wife"   PU, DLC
    Josiah's Secret, 1910, 3 acts, by "Josiah Allen's wife"   RPB
    Woman's Rights, 19??, adapted from her My Opinion and Betsey   RPB
        Bobbitt's

GRACE HOLLINGSWORTH

An Island Idyl, 1902, operetta, with Florence E. Heath   RPB-M,MH
Bombs and Balloons, 1907, musical comedy, music and lyrics by   NBuG
    Hollingsworth; book by Ruth Ashmore, Gillian Barr, Emily Gurgen
    and others
Kits and Kelts, 1909, musical comedy, music and lyrics by   MH
    Hollingsworth; book by Grace R. Henry
La Belle Chasseuse; or, Hearts and Hounds, 1908, musical comedy,   MH
    music and lyrics by Hollingsworth; book by Grace Henry and
    Katharine W. Tweed
Tags and Tatters, 1912, musical comedy, music and lyrics by   RPB-M
    Hollingsworth; book by Grace Henry

DOROTHY HOLLOWAY

The Steadfast Tin Soldier, 1928, 3 acts, young   RPB

PEARL HOLLOWAY (1888- ?)

Beginnings, 1937, pub. by WCTU play??   Or
The Children of the Book, 1937, collection of Drama Guild plays   RPB
Christmas for Others, 1923, playlet in 3 parts   NN
The 4-H Club Tackles Father, 1938, modern rural play (1)   RPB
From Jerusalem to Jericho, 1930? religious drama (1)   NN
Great Aunt Jennie, 1943, with Helen Hausner, 3 act comedy   RPB
The Hightones Buy a Car, 1929   RPB
The Holidays' Christmas Party, and Christmas in Mother Goose Land,   RPB
    1923, two Christmas playlets for Sunday school
Let's Put on a Play, 1937, six one-act plays   RPB
Life Begins on the Farm, 1938, 4-H club play (1)   RPB
Nine Timely Programs for Elementary School, 1949   RPB
Oh, Worship the King, 1929, Christmas pageant   Or, MiD
One Clear Bright Star, 1946, Christmas   RPB
The Paramount Children's Day Book, 1923, a contributor   RPB
The Paramount Children's Day Book, No. 4, 1930   RPB
The Paramount Christmas Book, 1922, a contributor   RPB
The Paramount Easter Book, 1923, a contributor   RPB
The Paramount Missionary Book, 1926, a contributor
The Paramount Mother's Day Book, 1941, a contributor   RPB
The Paramount Parents Day Book, 1932, a contributor
The Paramount Special Day Book, 1924 ,a contributor   RPB
Point of View, 1938, modern rural play (1)   RPB
Prize Winning Percy, 1943, with Helen Hausner, comedy (1)   RPB
The Spy, 1937, adaptation of novel by J. F. Cooper   DLC
Telling the Christmas Story, 1931, complete program in 2 parts   RPB
Two Paramount Christmas Plays: ("To Have and to Give; or, To Give   RPB
    and to Have," and "Following the Star"), 1925, with Sara E. Gosselink
Uncle Abner on Commencement, 1935   DLC
"You Never Can Tell," 1936 (1)   RPB

DORIS CAMPBELL HOLSWORTH

The Leaves of the Tree, 1934, pageant, Wethersfield, Conn.   RPB
    (program at NN)
Pathways to the Light, 1930, pageant, Windsor, Conn.   RPB
When the Sun Stayed in Bed, 1922 (by Doris Holsworth, may be   RPB
    different person) (1)

FLORENCE TABER HOLT
They the Crucified, and Comrades; Two war plays, 1918, one-acts   RPB

LAURA DAVIES HOLT
The Christmas Angel Choir, 1927 (1)   RPB
The King of the Jews, 1926   RPB

HELEN WALKER HOMAN (See HELEN WALKER)

INA HOME
A Dream on Christmas Eve, 1911, young (1)

FRANCES HOMER
Beauty and the Beast of Loreland, 1936, 3 act comedy   DLC
Cinderella, 1934, "a modern 3-act version of the beloved fairy tale"   RPB
Heart Attack, 1939, comedy (1)   OCl, DLC
Jack's Beanstalk in Loreland, 1936, 3 act comedy   DLC,ViU
No Orchids, 1940, comedy (1)   RPB
Over the Rainbow, 1936, 3 act comedy   RPB
A Prince to Order, 1929, 3 act comedy   RPB
The Sleeping Beauty of Loreland, 1935, 3 act comedy   WU, DLC
The Winning of a Satin Gown, 1932, 3 act costume play   RPB

MAURINE E. HONEYCOMB
The Surprise Bag, 1929, operetta for grade children based on tunes in   RPB
     Churchill-Grindell songbooks

MILDRED OLIVE HONORS
Mother Nature's Carnival, 1928, operetta for May Day   RPB

REBECCA L. HOOPER
Alice in Wonderland Continued, operetta, music by Mabel Wheeler
     Davis, prod. at Radcliffe
A Copper Complication, 1900, operetta, music by Mabel Daniels,   RPB-M
     prod. at Radcliffe
The Court of Hearts, 1901, operetta, music by Mabel Daniels, under   RPB-M
     auspices of class of 1900, Radcliffe

HELEN P. HORNBECK
Mary Ann, 1916, comedy (1)   RPB, NN,PU

FLORENCE ISBELL HOPE
The Advent of Spring, with Myrtle B. Carpenter, in Normal Instructor
     and Primary Plans, 34, April, 1925, 76
Mabel's Aunt, 1926, with Myrtle Barber Carpenter, comedy (1)   RPB

MARJORIE HOPE
Democracy Triumphant, 1918, patriotic pageant in 1 scene, with   RPB
     Wilhemina Higgins and others

WINIFRED AYRES HOPE
Friends in Bookland, 1921, about books for children (1)   RPB
Horizons, 1926, "pageant play in interest of international amity"   RPB
Lysistrata, 192?, adapted by Hope
The Masque of Psyche; or, the Seven Ages of the Soul, 1915, arr. of   MB
     scenes from seven Shakespearean plays

EMMA B. HOPKINS
 The Long Road to To-Morrow, 1917, pageant written and presented by   RPB
  the classes in history and English in Miss Hopkins' School, N. Y.,
  under direction of Hopkins and Elinor Murphy

HESTER A. HOPKINS
 The Anybody Family on Sunday Morning, 1918 (1)   RPB

MARGARET SUTTON BRISCOE HOPKINS (See MARGARET SUTTON
BROSCOE)

MRS. ARTHUR HOPKINSON
 Women's Votes, 1911 (1)

ELLEN P. HORNBECK
 Mary Ann, 1916, comedy (1)   RPB

ALICE MERRILL HORNE
 Columbus, Westward ho!, 1922   RPB

MARY BARNARD HORNE (1845- ?)
 The Book of Drills, 1896, collection   RPB
 A Carnival of Days, 1887   DLC
 The Darktown Bicycle Club Scandal, 1897, colored sketch for lady   RPB
  minstrels (1)
 The Four-leaved Clover, 1890, 3 act operetta   RPB
 The Great Moral Dime Show, 1892, entertainment in one scene   DLC
 Gulliver and the Lilliputians up to Date, 1903 (1)   RPB
 Jolly Joe's Lady Minstrels, 1893, with "Mrs. H. M. Silsbee"
 Ladies of Cranford, 1899, based on novel by Mrs. Gaskill   RPB
 The Last of the Peak Sisters; or, the Great Moral Dime Show, 1892 (1) RPB
 The Other Fellow, 1903, 3 act comedy   RPB
 The Peak Sisters, 1887
 Plantation Bitters, 1892, "colored fantasy in 2 acts for men"
 Prof. Baxter's Great Invention, 1891, "unclassified entertainment" (1) RPB
 A Sevres Cup; or, A Bit of Bric-a-Brac, 1886, 3 act comedietta   DLC
 A Singing School of Ye Olden Times, 1922, specialty   RPB

ELIZABETH WEST HORNER
 Betty in Bookland, 1929, 3 act children's play   RPB

LAURA HORNICKEL
 Part-time Job, 1930, comedy (1)   RPB

MINNIE B. HORNING
 Lessons in English, 1919, Americanization play with Helen Horning   RPB
  Walsh

EVELYN GRANT HORNSEY
 Denial, 1927, religious drama   RPB
 The Gallant Pilgrims, 1930, religious drama (1)   RPB
 Some Of Us Are Like That, 1931, comedy   OCl

KATE HORTON
 Ballyhoo, prod. 1927
 Harvest, prod. 1925
 Ride a Cock Horse, 1933, 4 acts, typescript   NN

RUTH HORTON
  Who is Queer?, in Everyland, 5, March, 1914, 87 (1)

ELLEN EVANS HOUGH
  First Love, 1929, "a humorous and effective reading"   RPB

CAROL HOUGHTON
  Idiosyncrasies, 1930, humorous reading   RPB
  Little Miss Busybody, 1937, little girl monologue   RPB
  Open Wider, Please, 1930, humorous reading   RPB
  Your Name, Please? 1937, humorous reading   RPB
  You're Next, 1935, humorous reading   RPB

ANNIE S. HOWARD
  The Travelers; or, the Perfect Gift, 1925, allegorical playlet   RPB

FLORENCE HOWARD
  And So I Turn My Clouds About, 1926, illustrates tasks of the Home   RPB
    Bureau
  On the Banks of the River Styx, 1926, for women (1)   RPB
  The Spirit of Girlhood, 1922, girl scout pageant   OCl, DLC

KATHARINE HOWARD (1858- ?)
  Candle Flame, 1920, play for reading only   RPB
  Two Plays, and a Rhapsody, 1916 ("The House of the Future," "The   RPB
    House of Life," and "A Rhapsody") mystical plays

LEOPOLDINE "POLLY" BLAINE DAMROSCH HOWARD
  At 8:45, with Gretchen Damrosch Finletter   CU
  Gypsy Number   CU
  If Men Went to Matinees as Women Do, with Gretchen Damrosch   CU
    Finletter
  Papa Haydn   CU
  Transatlantic, with Gretchen Damrosch Finletter   CU
  The Woman Who Pays to Advertise, with Gretchen Damrosch Finletter   CU

MARGARET HOWARD
  When Betty Saw the Pilgrims, 1921, young (1)   RPB

MRS. H. W. HOWE
  Doll, dialogue, 1910?   RPB
  Excellent Entertainment, 191?   RPB
  Lincoln Entertainment, 1901, she was compiler   RPB

MANTHEI HOWE
  The Fire Imps, in Sparks, Fire Prevention Rhymes, Stories and Playlets, RPB
    ed. by Valine Hobbs, 1926 (first appeared in Normal Instructor and
    Primary Plans)

MARIE JENNEY HOWE (MRS. FREDERIC C. HOWE)
  An Anti-suffrage Monologue, 1912   NN, NRU,FOV, DLC
  The Perfect Lady (1) (suffrage)

CORRIE CRANDALL HOWELL
  The Forfeit, in Poet Lore, 36, Spring, 1925, 126-41

FLORENCE HOWELL
  Jane Wogan, (in Prize One-Act Plays, London, 1934)   PWP

JOSEPHINE HOWELL-CARTER
Hilarion, in Poet Lore, 20, Summer, 1915, 374-92 (1)

(HELEN) HELLEN MORRISON HOWIE
After the Matinee, 1908, comedy (1)   RPB
His Father's Son, 1900, farce (1)   RPB
The Reformer Reformed, 1899, comedy   RPB
Those Dreadful Drews, 1910, comedy (1)   RPB
Too Much Bobbie, 1914, farce (1)   RPB

EVELYN HOXIE
Advertising for a Husband, 1932, comedy (1)   RPB
Betsy Ross Making the Flag, 2 acts
For Lincoln's Birthday   JEL
The Good Times Christmas Book, 1929, collection   RPB
Hints and Ha'nts for Halloween, 1930, collection   RPB
It's All Over Town, 1930, gossip entertainment (1)   RPB
John Smith Solves the Problem, 1927   RPB
John's Aunt Mehitable, 1928, dramatic comedy   RPB
Jolly Dialogues and Plays, 1924   DLC
Just For Fun Dialogues, 1925   DLC
Little Folks Stories and Story Plays, 1927   DLC
Patriotic Programs for Patriotic Days, 1926   RPB
Seven Dialogues for Adults, 1925   RPB
Seven Snappy Entertainments for Adults, 1926   RPB
The Strike Mother Goose Settled, 1922 (1)   RPB
Thirty-two Schoolroom Dialogues, 1926   RPB
When Uncle Abner Proposed, 1927   RPB

EDITH L. HOYLE
Crowfeather's Christmas, 1926, with O. W. Stephenson   RPB

ELEANOR HOYT
A Misdemeanor of Nancy (1)

ELLA M. HOYT
Hello Zentral! 1928, Jewish monologue   RPB

ELISE M. HUBACHEK
From Our House to Your House, 1929, Christmas (1)   RPB

CHARLOTTE AMELIA HUBBARD (1879- ?)
Poor Richard's Dream, 1930, written by ninth grade class of Hubbard   RPB
    and edited by her

ELEANOR(E) HUBBARD
Citizenship Plays, 1922, young, one-acts   RPB
Little American History Plays for Little Americans, 1919   RPB
Plays on the Old World Backgrounds of American History, 1936, young   RPB

FRANCES VIRGINIA THOMAS HUBBARD
The Manger Babe, 1934, Christmas pageant-service, music by Thomas RPB-M
    and others
The Prince of the House of David, 1929, sacred Christmas pageant   DLC
The Sign in the Sky, 1929, sacred Christmas pageant   DLC
The Witch of Fairy Dell, 1916, light opera, music by   RPB-M
    Frederick W. Mills

LOUISE HUBBARD
The Lullaby

LUELLA M. HUFF
A Plan That Failed, for two boys   SCC

RUTH WEBB HUFFMAN
For the Love of Mike, 1924, 3 act comedy   RPB

DOROTHY HUGGINS
Brushing Up on Art, 1915, 3 act musical comedy, lyrics by Huggins   RPB-M
    and Marguerite Samuels; music by Ethylene Mather and others,
    Wellesley College

BABETTE PLECHNER HUGHES (HALL) (1906- ?) (MRS. GLENN HUGHES)
Aladdin's Wife, romantic comedy (1)   HUW-3
Angelica (1)   OPS-VIII
Backstage, 1929   CCO
Because It's June, 1940, comedy (1)   RPB
The Black Scarab, by Babette Plechner (1)   HUW-2
Bound for Mexico, 1926, melodrama (1)   RPB
The Calf That Laid the Golden Egg, 1931   HSP
Columbine in the Country, 1930, fantasy (1)   RPB
Daisy Won't Tell, 1937, farce (1)   RPB
Early Victorian, 1938, romantic comedy (1)
The First White Woman,   NPW
Fit as a Fiddle, 1936 (1)   OAT-II
Greek to You, 1938, farce (1)   OPS-IX
Harmony, 1933, comedy, trans. from French of Henry Duvernois, with RPB
    Glen Hughes (1)
If the Shoe Pinches, 1937, farce (1)
The Lady Who Came to Lunch, 1942, comedy for women (1)   RPB
The Liar and the Unicorn, 1928 (1)   SFM
Life With Mother, 1942, comedy (1)   RPB
The March Heir, 1932 (1)   OPS-VII
Maurice Sand's Plays for Marionettes, 1931, trans with Glenn Hughes RPB
Money for Jam, 1928, farce (1)   RPB
Monsieur Perrichon's Excursion, 1931, comedy, trans. from French of RPB
    Labiche and Martin, with Glenn Hughes
Mrs. Harper's Bazaar, farce (1)
Murder! Murder! Murder! Murder! 1933 (1)   OPS-VI
No More Americans (1)   OPS-V
One Egg, 1934, farce (1)   OPS-X,NAB-I
Please Do Not Pick the Flowers   YSP-I
Safety-pins First, 1932, comedy (1)   RPB
Sisters Under the Skin, (1)
Spring Scene, 1939, comedy (1)   RPB
The Surprise Party, 1941, comedy (1)   Or, DLC
Three Men and a Boat (1)   NPM
Three Players, a Fop, and a Duchess (1)   OPS-IV
Too Many Cakes, 1934, farce (1)   RPB
While the River Flows, 1930, comedy, trans. from French of Marcel   RPB
    Pays, with Glenn Hughes (1)

DOROTHEA M. HUGHES
The Spirit of Poland, 1917, 3 acts   RPB

ELIZABETH HUGHES
Women for Votes, 1912, farce in 3 acts   RPB

MARJORIE HULICK
The Medicine Show, 1926   RPB

HELEN ROSE HULL (1888-1971) AWW
The Idealists, in Touchstone, 1, Sept., 1917, 457-63 (1)
Release, in Touchstone, 6, Dec., 1919, 122-7

SARAH WATERS MONROE HUMASON
Masks and Men, 1921 (in Vassar Series of Plays, ed. by Gertrude Buck)   RPB
    historical romance (1)

MARGARET HUMMEL
Simon the Cyrenian, 1927 Easter   RPB

MAUD(E) HUMPHREY (1868- ?)
Immersion, 1926 (1)   BYP
Why Girls Stay Home, 1923, satiric comedy (1)   RPB

ESTELLE HUNT
Woof, Woof, prod. 1929, with Sam Summers and Cyrus Wood, music and
    lyrics by Edward Pola and Eddie Brandt

KATHERINE E. HUNT
A Midnight Fantasy, 1927, (c. 1913), for two girls (1)   RPB

LAURA HUNT
Good English Comes to Town, 1924, short sketch for high schools   RPB

AGNES MONK HUNTER
The Spirit of the South, 1926, pageant, Montgomery, Alabama, with   RPB
    Esther Janett Simon, program

MINERVA HUNTER
Ethel's Sunday-school Class, 1922   RPB

OLIVIA M. HUNTER
An' de Walls Came Tumblin' Down, 1926, with Lillian W. Voorhees,   LNarc
    dram. of poems and stories of Paul Laurence Dunbar
Hiawatha, 1927, with Lillian W. Voorhees, musical drama in 5 scenes   LNarc

EMA L. HUNTING
The Real American Girl, 1916, entertainment "recommended for high   RPB
    school, Washington's birthday and groups interested in colonial history"

EMA (EMMA) M. HUNTING
Betty's Ancestor, 1913, "recommended for high schools, Washington's   RPB
    birthday and groups interested in colonial history" (1)

EMMA (EMA) SUCKOW HUNTING
Bright Ideas for Christmas,1920, collection, with others   RPB
A Dickens Revival, 1914   RPB
Double Dummy, 1917, comedietta (1) (Ema S. Hunting at RPB)   RPB, JMP
Her Superior Intelligence, 1914, comedy   RPB

ADA L. HUNTINGTON
The Arrival of Billy, 1917   RPB
The Bride Arrives, 1927, 2 act comedy   RPB
A Double Proposal, 1916, comedy   RPB
Miss Fry Co-operates in Extension Work, 1929, monologue   RPB
No Tips Accepted, 1929 (1)   RPB

FRANCES HUNTLEY
Bachelor's Choice, 1936? play?   DLC
Boots and Her Buddies; or, When Man Plays Maiden, 1909, 3 act farce   RPB
Whistling in the Dark, n.d., 3 act comedy   NcD

CLARA J. H. HURD
Hunker's P.O., 1900, farce (1)   DLC
Slabtown Organizes an Aid Society, 1904, farce (1)   RPB

MARGARET STRICKLAND HURLEY
Cured   ECO

JANE HURRLE
Yes, Yes! Go On, 1928, with Eulalie Andreas, 3 act comedy   RPB

FANNIE HURST (1889-1968) AWW NAW
Back Pay, prod. 1921, melodrama of fallen woman, (story in   NN
   Cosmopolitan, 67, Nov., 1919, 35-40) incomplete prompt book
Back Street, prod. 1930-1 (1941 shooting script and film)   NN
For Daughters, 1941, play by Frank Vreeland based on her story   RPB
Humoresque, prod. 1923, pub. in Readings, Plays, Entertainments   RPB
   (story in Cosmopolitan, 66, March, 1919, 32-9) pub. 193? a reading
   from the book
It Is to Laugh, prod. 1927
The Land of the Free, 1919, prod. 1917, with Harriet French Ford
Lummox, 1923, with music

ZORA NEALE HURSTON (1901?-1960) AWW NAW
Color Struck, in Fire, I, no. 1, Nov., 1926 (1)
Fast and Furious, 1931, with Clinton Fletcher and Tim Moore
The First One, 1927, pub. in Johnson, Ebony and Topaz (1)
Great Day, 1927
Mule Bone, 1930, with Langston Hughes, excerpts pub. in Drama Critique,
   Spring, 1964
Polk County, a comedy of Negro Life on a Sawmill Camp, 1944, with   NN
   Dorothy Waring, typescript

BERTHA HURWITZ
The Adopted Son, 1920, 4 act allegorical drama   RPB

EUNICE G. HUSSEY
Newsy Wins, 1918, "burlesque on current fads in reading" (1)   RPB

MARGARET L. HUTCHINSON
Uncle Sam's Thanks Reception   CPE
When Woman Rules: A Merry Comedy for Girls in 2 acts; music by
   Lionel Elliot, 1908 (libretto only)

AGNES HYDE
Frances the Suffragette, 1914, 3 act comedy   RPB
The Vegetable Brownies on a Frolic, 1922, extravaganza (1)   RPB

DOROTHY GILLETTE HYDE
Ding-dong-bell, 1930, 3 acts, young, prize winner in Junior League   RPB
    Playwriting Contest

FLORENCE ELISE HYDE
Captain of the Host, The Supreme Test, 2 plays, 1916   RPB

SARAH ELLIS HYMAN
The Seventh Heart, prod. 1927

I

BERTHA L. ILES
  Better American Speech Pageant, Chicago, 1918   RPB

IRMA B. IMHOFF
  Christian Endeavor Playlets, 1928, a contributor   RPB
  The Downfall of King Alcohol, "In the Interest of Prohibition"   HPY
  The Great Omission, "A Plea for the Use of the Bible in the Public HPY
    Schools"
  More Christian Endeavor Playlets, 1929, a contributor   RPB
  Mother's Dream, pageant for Mother's Day   HPY
  Though Your Sins Be as Scarlet, "In the Interest of Evangelism" HPY

MAUDE ELIZABETH INCH
  The Bo'sn's Bride, 1914, "nautical yarn in 2 acts," music by William   RPB-M
    Rhys-Herbert
  Bulbul, 1911, comic operetta, music by William Rhys-Herbert   RPB-M
  The Drum Major, 1912, operetta, with Edward F. Johnston   RPB-M
  A Nautical Knot; or, the Belle of Barnstapoole, 1909, music by William RPB-M
    Rhys-Herbert
  Sylvia, 1906, operetta, music by William Rhys-Herbert   RPB-M

LAURA INGALLS
  Arlington Pageant, 1913, Arlington, Mass., with Vittoria Dallin,   MB
    programme
  Will o' the World, 1916, pageant, Wellesley. Mass.

LULA E. INGALLS
  The Town Meeting at Killingsworts, 1909, arr. from Longfellow's poem   RPB

HELEN FRANCES INGERSOLL (1878- ?)
  The Birds' Christmas Carol, 1914, with Kate Douglas Wiggin   RPB

PATSY GREY INGERSOLL
  Troupers, 1929, prod. 1928   NHP

MARY B. INGRAHAM
  The Magic Vase, 1929, pageant of the history of pottery, created by the   RPB
    Art Department, Kosciuszko School, Hamtramck, Michigan, with
    Ruth Greene and others

MARIE IRISH ("EVELYN SIMONS")
  Abel Adams' Happy Christmas, 1927, for intermediate grades   RPB
  The Adoption of Bob, 1922, for 6th grade   RPB
  Adventurous Ann, 1931, 3 act comedy   RPB
  And the Curtain Fell, 1931, pantomime   RPB
  Assembly Book for Intermediate Grades, 1934, with others   RPB
  Aunt Jane's Accident, 1926   RPB
  Barlow's Borrowing, 1926   RPB
  Best Christmas Pantomimes, 1922   RPB
  Best Commencement Stunts and Ceremonies, 1924
  The Best Drill Book, 1898   RPB
  Best Recitations and Monologs, 1926, by "Evelyn Simons"   DLC
  The Boys' Entertainer, 1908   RPB
  The Brown's Merry Christmas, 1925, comedy (1)   RPB

MARIE IRISH (continued)

Calling the Police, 1928	RPB
Catchy Comic Dialogues, 1905	RPB
Catchy Primary Dialogues, 1928	RPB
Catchy Primary Recitations, 1922	DLC
Cheery Christmas Entertainments, 1933, with others	
Children's Comic Dialogues, 1905	RPB
Choice Christmas Dialogues and Plays, 1922, one-acts	Or, DLC
Choice Christmas Entertainments, 1922	Or, DLC
Choice Dialogues for Rural Schools, 1923	DLC
Choice Thanksgiving Entertainments, 1923	
Christmas at Crane's Corners, 1926	RPB
Christmas at Dinky Flats, 1925, comedy	RPB
Christmas at Joyville Junction, 1925, comedy	RPB
Christmas at the Pines, 1935	DLC
Christmas at Stebbinses', 1916	RPB
The Christmas Entertainer, 1919	RPB
Christmas for Little Lads and Lasses, 1931	Or, DLC
A Christmas Lesson	SBC
Christmas Merrymakers, 1920	Or, DLC
Christmas on Crutches, 1926	RPB
Christmas Plots	SBC
The Christmas Program Book, 1931, with others	Or, DLC
Christmas Speakin' at Skagg's Skule, 1921	RPB
The Christmas Spirit	CJB
A Christmas Stocking (1)	HPC
Clackville Choir's Christmas Carols, 1928	RPB
Closing Day Celebrations, 1922	Or, DLC
Closing Day in the Primary Grades, 1923	NcC, DLC
Clothes-line Gossip, 1925	RPB
Colonial Dames' Tea Party, for girls	SWD
Community Games, Stunts and Entertainments, 1926, by "Evelyn Simons"	RPB
Dandy Drills and Dances, 1929, with Olive Burt	
The Dashing Darkies, 1923	RPB
The Daughters of Rebecca, 1923	RPB
The Days We Celebrate, 1904	RPB
Dinah's Reason, 1925	RPB
District School Dialogues for Children of All Ages, 1915	RPB
Easy Christmas Shopping, monologue	SBC
The Family Meets the Wife, 1933	RPB
The Fatal Dose, 1928	RPB
Father Improves His Memory, 1928	RPB
The Favorite Christmas Book, 1917	RPB
Favorite Song Pantomimes, 1909	NIC
Fellowship Drills, 1931	MiD
Fifty Humorous Monologues, 1926	WaT, DLC
Fond Fathers, 1928, 3 act comedy	RPB
Fooling the Folks, 1926	RPB
For Ladies Only, 1936, 4 entertainment specialties for women only	DLC
The Glad Time Thanksgiving Book, 1932, with Lenore K. Dolan	RPB
Good Things for Christmas, 1907	RPB
Good Things for Washington and Lincoln Birthdays, 1914	RPB
The Grade School Play Book, 1929	RPB
The Graduates Own Book, 1940, with Clara J. Denton plays??	
Grandma Brady's Christmas Guests, 1932	RPB
Grandma's Christmas Escapade, 1927	RPB

MARIE IRISH (continued)

Hallowe'en Fun, 1927	
Hallowe'en Hilarity, 1924	OrU, DLC
Halloween Merrymakers, 1930	Or, DLC
Happy Days on the Farm, 1923	RPB
Harmless Scandal, 1933, comedy	RPB
Have I Taken Poison? 1927	RPB
He Didn't Propose, 1933, comedy	RPB
Henry Hires the Cook, 1926	RPB
Hiring a Schoolma'am, 1923	RPB
How Grandma Caught the Christmas Spirit, 1925, comedy (1)	RPB
Humorous Dialogues for Children, 1919	RPB
Humorous Drills and Acting Songs, 1918	DLC
A Husband for Harriet, 1933	RPB
In Honor of Mother, 1928, collection of material for Mother's Day	RPB
It Happened in Bethlehem, 1931 (1)	RPB
Jim Jencks Gets a Jolt, 1927	RPB
John Speaks for Himself, 1934, "modern version of the famous story of	RPB
John Alden and Priscilla"	
Jolly Junior Dialogues, 1925	DLC
Joyous Programs for Springtime Celebrations, 1934, with others	RPB
The Junior-Senior Banquet Book, 1928	RPB
Lessons in Love Making, (1)	CPR-1
Little Folks' Christmas Entertainments, 1928, with others	NBuG
Little People's Plays, 1913, one-acts	RPB
Making Christmas Presents, monologue	SBC
Mamma's Boy, 1923	RPB
Mattie Discovers a Merry Christmas, 1928	RPB
The Men Give In, 1926	RPB
The Merry Makers	CJB
Miss Prim's Christmas Shopping, monologue	SBC
Mr. Boskins Escapes the Law, 1923	RPB
The Modern Pirates (1)	CPR
More Than He Bargained For, 1928 (Catchy loose-leaf play series)	RPB
A Mother for Mary, 1936	DLC
Mother Goose's Christmas	SBC
Murder in the Air, 1933	RPB
The Mystery at Mapleton, 1927, 3 act comedy	RPB
Newsboy Tim, pantomime	SBC
Novel Notions for Nifty Entertainments, 1925	
Now Take It From Me (1)	CPR-1
Old Time Songs and Pantomimes, 1922	
One Hundred Choice Monologues, 1925	DLC
Out to Win, 1927	RPB
Patriotic Celebrations, 1910	RPB
Patriotic Entertainments for Children, 1923	RPB
Patsy Dugan's Christmas; or, Santa from Clausville, 1922	RPB
Paw Decides to Leave, 1926	RPB
Paw Gets "Took," 1923	RPB
Plays and Comedies for Little Folks, 1912, one acts	
Pleasing Pantomimes and Tableaux, 1929, with O. E. Young and others	
Plymouth's First Thanksgiving and two Other Thanksgiving Plays, 1931	RPB
Poinsetta Drill, 1921, for girls	RPB
Practical Dialogues, Drills and Marches, 1900, one-acts	DLC
The Primary Christmas Book, 1922	RPB
The Professor's Daughter, 1928	RPB
Proposing to Polly, 1928 (also in Catchy Primary Dialogues)	RPB

MARIE IRISH (continued)

Pumpkin Pie Eater, 1921, Thanksgiving play for intermediate grades	RPB
The Reunion at Pine Knot Ranch, 1922	RPB
Sarah Ann and the Confidence Man, 1927	RPB
Seven Surprise Plays for 6th, 7th and 8th Grades, 1936	DLC
Shamrocks for St. Patrick's Day, 1932	RPB
Short Plays for the Grades, 1935	DLC
Six Christmas Plays for High School Assembly Programs, 1934	RPB
The Six Who Kept Christmas, 1934	RPB
Snappy Drills and Marches, 1923, by "Evelyn Simons"	DLC
Snappy Humorous Dialogues, 1922	DLC
Spooky Hallowe'en Entertainments, 1923, by "Evelyn Simons"	
Squire Hawley's Christmas	SBC
St. Patrick's Day Plays and Pieces, 1932, with Willis N. Bugbee	RPB
Sunshine Plays and Dialogues, 1929, collection with others	RPB
The Surprise Drill Book, 1903	
Susan Gregg's Christmas Orphans, 1916, 2 act comedy	RPB
Tableaux and Scenic Readings, 1906	RPB
Thanks for the Interview, 1933	RPB
A Thanksgiving Conspiracy, 1921, for grammar and high schools	RPB
Thanksgiving Days and Ways, 1931	RPB
That 'ere Line Fence (1)	CPR-1
Thirty Christmas Dialogues and Plays, 1940, with others	RPB
Thirty New Christmas Dialogues and Plays, 1909, with others	
This Way to Christmas, 1934, for high school girls (1)	RPB
This Way to Matrimony, 1934, collection of mock weddings, with NcC, DLC	
Arthur Landis	
The Tip-top Christmas Book, 1927, with Willis N. Bugbee	
The Tip-top Thanksgiving Book, 1930	
The Tip-top Valentine Book, 1929	
To Be or Not To Be Married, 1933	RPB
A Tragedy of Bargain Day, 1926	RPB
Trouble in Santa Claus Land	SBC
A Twentieth Century Cinderella, 1905	RPB
Uncle Abner's Will, 1933	RPB
Uncle Caleb's Quiet Christmas, 1925, comedy (1)	RPB
Uncle Mel's Merry Christmas, 1926	RPB
Up-to-date Commencement Helps, 1932	
Valentine Gayety Book, 1930?	
The Van Dorn's Merry Christmas, 1923	RPB
Washington and Lincoln Celebrations, 1924, by "Evelyn Simons"	DLC
What Pa Needed, 1928 (also in Catchy Primary Dialogues)	RPB
The Whatnots and the Reporter, 1928 (also in Catchy Primary	RPB
Dialogues)	
When Greek Meets Greek, 1928 (also in Catchy Primary Dialogues)	RPB
Who Is That Man? 1923	RPB

THEODORA URSULA IRVINE

Fanny Squeer's Tea-Party (scene from Dickens' Nicholas Nickleby), PTS-VII	
arr. by Irvine	

BESSIE IRWIN

The Good Samaritan, 19?? adaptation from Dorothy Elderdice,	GEU
"dramatic service telling the story of the hospital movement of the	
Methodist Episcopal Church, Atlanta, Ga."	

GRACE LUCE IRWIN
  Brass Buttons, 3 act comedy
  A Close Call, 1901, farce (1)   RPB
  Drawing Room Plays, 1903, collection of one acts   RPB
  Our New Governess, 1904, 2 act comedy   RPB
  A Spoiled Darling, 1903, 3 act comedy   RPB

MARGARET IRWIN
  The Three Visitors, in Bermondsey Book, 3, Sept., 1926, 81-93 (1)

BYRNA RACKEL ISAACS
  The Gods Are Wise, Little Theatre Tournament, 1930

SUSIE E. ISENBARGER
  Betty Jane's Christmas Dream, 1921, with Glen H. Isenbarger (1)   RPB

ROSALYN IVAN
  The Fantastic (Fantasie) Impromptu, in Drama, 11, April, 1921, 233-6 (1)

ALICE EMMA IVES (1876-1930)
  The Arrival of Miss Hammond, 1907 (originally titled, A Woman's   NN
     Way), typescript
  "Aunt Eliza," 19?? comedy, typescript (1)   NN
  Calanthy's Mistake, n. d., comedy, typescript (1)   NN
  Mary's Manoevres, prod. 1913, suffrage sketch (1)
  Meow! 1914, with Fannie Cannon, comedy (1)   RPB
  The Sweet Elysium Club, 1902, comedy, written for and produced by   RPB
     the Professional Woman's League (1)
  A Very New Woman, in The Woman's Column, 9, no. 11, March 14,   FOV
     1896, 2-3
  The Village Postmaster, 1894, with Jerome H. Eddy, 4 act domestic   RPB
     drama

CORA SEMMES IVES
  Queen Floradine of Flower Land, 1900, fairy tale arranged as a play for   RPB
     children

J

CORA JACKSON
Mother's Day, 1928, comedy (1)   RPB

FRANCES MITCHELL JACKSON
Sallie-For-Keeps, 1921 (Vassar series of plays, ed. by Gertrude Buck) (1) RPB

INEZ JACKSON
The Senior, 1906, "moral play modeled on 'Everyman,'" presented at   RPB
Cedar Rapids High School, Iowa

MARIA JACKSON
Female Masonry a' la Lease, 1908, (1st pub. 1894) "easy and laughable RPB
farce," presented by Order of Eastern Star, Spirit Lake, Iowa

MAUDE JACKSON
Pageant of Industries, 1916, Tacoma, Washington

PAULA JACOBI (JAKOBI)
Chinese Lily, in Forum, 54, Nov., 1915, 551-66 (1)

EDITH ROEDER JACOBS
Spring; or the Queen of Youth, 1925, pageant, 1st prod. at Parsons   RPB
College, Fairfield, Iowa, 1923, typed copy

ELLA JACOBS
Honor His Name   FPP

JANIE JACOBSON
Belshazzar, 1911, Scriptural play in 4 acts   NN, PU
Chanukkah Eve; or, Jacob Mendoza's Dream and What Came Of It,   OCH
1909, 4 acts
Esther, 1912, Scriptural play in 5 acts
For Liberty, 1903, for Chanukah, founded on Jewish patriotism   RPB
Joseph and His Brethren, 1905, Scriptural play in 4 acts   NN, PU
A Maid of Persia, 1905, Purim play in 4 acts   OCH
Ruth, the Moabitess, 1910, Scriptural play in 3 acts; Jephthah's Vow, NN, PU
Scriptural play in 2 acts

KATHLEEN de JAFFA (See KATHLEEN DE JAFFA)

MINNIE SUCKERBERG JAFFA (MRS. RUDOLPH COFFEE) (1886- ?)
In Walked Jimmy, 1920, prod. 1916, "American comedy of optimism"   RPB
The Trick, 1927, "comedy in 3 acts with a serious purpose"   DLC
"Undertow," 1927, "melodramatic mystery in 3 acts"   DLC

ALICE ARCHER (SEWALL) JAMES (1870- ?)
The Torch, 1922, "pageant of light from the early history of   RPB, SPN
Urbana, Ohio"

ANNETTE L. JAMES
Getting a Marriage License, 1924, comedy   RPB
Just As You Say, Mama, 1924, comedy   RPB
She Couldn't Stay a Minute, 1924, comedy   RPB

MARY A. JAMES
Papa's Daughters, 1930, burlesque skit   RPB

MAY F. JAMES
Weighed in the Balance, 1916, 4 act drama, anti-war   RPB

LORENA LUCILE JAMISON
A Pageant of Woman's Progress, 1917, with Wylla Jamison Viley   RPB

ELSIE JANIS (1889-1956)
Elsie Janis and Her Gang, prod. 1919, revue
It's All Wrong, prod. 1920
Puzzles of 1925, 1925, revue
A Star for a Night; A Story of Stage Life, prod. 1911, typescript   NN

ANNA LINTON JANUARY (1879- ?)
His Soul Goes Marching On, 1930, pageant of slavery   RPB

MYRA WILLIAMS JARRELL (1867-1937)
The Case of Kantsey Know, 1933, playlet, also in Drama, 12, March, 1922,
   210-12 (1)
"Hungry All the Years," 1935, comedy (1)   Or,IU,DLC
Meg, of Valencia, 1905   play??   MoKU

ETHEL REED JASSPON
The Open Highway, 1927, with Beatrice Becker   RPB
Ritual and Dramatized Folkways, 1925, with Beatrice Becker, for use in   RPB
   camp, club, religious assembly, settlement and camp

MARGARET JAY
The Basket Man, 1923

BEATRICE W. JEFFERSON
Right About Face, 1922, 3 act operetta for Wellesley Barnswallows, lyrics
   and libretto with Lucile J. Barrett, Hildegarde E. Churchill and others;
   music by Mary Zweizig, Rebecca Stickney and others

HESTER DONALDSON JENKINS (1869-1941)
Five Playlets, 1915, written for the Dept. of Social Betterment,   RPB
   Brooklyn, N. Y.

LUCY D. JENKINS
The Brownies' Flirtation, 1898   RPB
Juvenile Fantastics and the Butterfly, 1901, 2 entertainments for   RPB
   children

RUTH L. JENKINS
Being Like Washington   WPP

AMABEL JENKS
Dinner at Seven Sharp, 1917, with Tudor Jenks, comedy (1)   RPB
The Drifting Cloud, 1914 (1)   GP

MARY JENNESS (? -1947)
"Our Lamp of Life," 191?, service for Children's Day   RPB

EULORA M. JENNINGS
Die Prinzessin von Barnhoff (1)
Dinner at the Club, 1906 (1)   RPB
Mrs. Oakley's Telephone, 1904, comedy for women (1)   RPB
Tom's Fiancee, 1906, 3 act comedy

MARIE JENSEN
The Soldier of the Cross, 1923, "stirring missionary play"   RPB

EDITH M. JENSON
Rosemary's Garden, young

MARGIE A. JERAULD
Uncle Sam to the Rescue; or, Saving Santa's Job, 1917 "patriotic   RPB
     Christmas play for children" (1)

ELLEN JESS
Birth of a Nation's Flag, 1916, "excellent school play" (1)   RPB

ELIZABETH S. JEWELL
Through the Sweet Briars, 1915, 3 act drama   RPB

LOUISE ROGERS JEWETT (? -1914)
Mt. Holyoke Pageant of Progress, 1912, S. Hadley, Mass.

SUSAN E. W. JOCELYN
Santa Claus or Papa? 1905, young (1)   RPB

BERNICE A. JOHNSON
A Quiet Afternoon at the Club, 1913, tabloid play, in Society, 1, no. 15,   RPB
     1913, 17-20

ELLA B. JOHNSON
Bright Ideas for Closing Day, 1926, with Ella L. Ottun   Or
Celebrating Christmas in the Grades, 1937   RPB
Christmas Joy Book, 1930, with others   RPB
The Ideal Book for Spring Entertainments, 1934   Or
The Ideal Christmas Book, 1928, with Ella L. Ottun   DLC
The Ideal Drill Book, 1931   RPB
Jolly Drills for Children, 1929   DLC

EMILY PAULINE JOHNSON (1862-1913)
Ojistoh, 1911, "illustrated Indian woman monologue," with Mrs.   RPB
     Frederick W. Pender (poem by Johnson; arr. in poses by Pender)
"Prairie Greyhounds," n.d., music by Harold Eustace Key   RPB

FLORENCE JOHNSON
A-way Out in Persia, 1919, operetta written for Barnswallows,   RPB
     Wellesley College, lyrics and book by Johnson and others; music by
     Susan Lowell Wright and others

GEORGIA DOUGLAS (CAMP) JOHNSON (1886-1966) AWW, SBAA, NWAT
Attacks
A Bill To Be Passed (about anti-lynching bill)
Blue Blood, 1926 (1)   SFM
Blue-Eyed Black Boy, about lynching, typescript in Federal Theatre
     Archives, George Mason University, Fairfax, Virginia

GEORGIA DOUGLAS (CAMP) JOHNSON (continued)
Frederick Douglass, 1935, young (1)   RMN
Plumes, folk tragedy, won first prize in Opportunity,5,   RPB, FCP,RMP, LGP
    June, 1927; also in Calverton, Anthology of American Negro Literature (1)
Safe, about lynching (1)
The Starting Point, domestic play (1)
A Sunday Morning in the South, 1925, lynching (typescript   HSB, NN
    at NN) (1)
William and Ellen Craft, 1935 (1)   RMN

HESTER N. JOHNSON
On to Victory, 1915, 2 act comedy, suffrage   RPB, FOV

MABEL P. JOHNSON
The Fashion Show, 1927 (1)   RPB

MADELINE C. JOHNSON
The Club's Husband, 1928, farce (1)   RPB
A Double Surprise (1)   SBP
The S'prise Party, (1)   SBP
What Price Presidency, 1928, for women's clubs (1)   RPB

MARGARET JOHNSON
Everybody: A Little Masque for Children   SCS

MARIE W. JOHNSON
Plays and Pageants for the Church School, 1929, compiled by her   RPB

MARY (MAMIE) THOMSON JOHNSON
America's Child, 1923, community pageant   RPB
Beauty for Calves, 1932, 2 act comedy   RPB
"Calico Cat," 1934, young   RPB
"The Christmas Ship,"1933, musical play for jr. high school   NN, Or
The Elf and the Christmas Candles, 1930, young   RPB
"Harassing Harry," 1933, for Jr. high school (1)   RPB
Inside Information, 1926, for rural schools and community clubs (1)   RPB
Last Day for Little Folk, 1930   RPB
The Little Tots' Christmas Collection, 1928
The Little Tots' Thanksgiving Collection, 1928   RPB
Maggie Becomes a Lady, 1925, playlet for rural schools or farm bureau   RPB
    programs
"My Neighbor's Children," featuring playground activities (1) and   BCC
    "Oh Rosalind," comedy (1)
New Plays for Rural Communities, 1931   RPB
On Christmas Hill, 1928, music by Gladys Leach   DLC
The Pilgrim Maiden's Dream, 1924, young   RPB
"Pinched," 1934, comedy for jr. high school (1)   NN
Popular Plays for Junior High School, 1934, ten one-act plays   RPB
Rural Community Plays, 1925   RPB
Ten Christmas Plays for the Grades, 1932, with Florence F. Smith and   RPB
    Alta E. Toepp
Ten Little Pageants, 1926, music by Gladys Hodson Leach   RPB
This Little Pig Went to Market, 1933, 2 act comedy   RPB
"Toads or Pearls," 1933, jr. high school (1)   RPB
Why Don't You Advertise? 1931, rural community play   RPB
"Yellow Bird," 1934, 3 acts, jr. high school   RPB

AGNES CHRISTINE JOHNSTON
Sweet Stranger, prod. 1930, with Frank Mitchell Dazey

ANNIE FELLOWS JOHNSTON (1863-1931) AWW NAW
The Rescue of the Princess Winsome, 1908, "for old and young"   RPB

MRS. CHESTER F. JOHNSTON
Cherry Reads the Message, 1927, one-act plays for women   RPB
The Freeing of Grandpa, 1927, with May T. Neff (1)   RPB

EMMA LOUISE JOHNSTON (1863- ?)
A Book of Plays for Little Actors, 1907, with Madalene D. Barnum   RPB

LEONORA JOHNSTON
The Fir-tree Fairy, 1949, Christmas fantasy   RPB
Ripe Watermelons, 1946 (1)   RPB
Tested Plays for High Schools, 1928, by students of the drama classes of RPB
    the Louisville girls high school (Johnston was director.)

MARY JOHNSTON (1870-1936) AWW NAW
The Goddess of Reason, 1907, prod. 1909, 5 act blank verse drama   RPB

AGNES HAMILTON JONES
The Straw Hat, prod. 1926, with Paul Tulane, adapted from French play by
    Labiche

ANN VAN NARTER JONES
Which Shall Be King? 1916 (1)   SNB

ELEANOR BRODIE JONES
California, the land of dreams, 1921, pageant, with Grace Atherton   RPB
    Dennen and others, presented at 20th annual convention, Calif. Fed.
    of Women's Clubs

GLADYS OLIVIA JONES
The Discovery, 1930, 3 act comedy   RPB

GRACE LATIMER JONES (1879- ?)
A Merry Geste of Robin Hood, 1916, arranged from early English   RPB
    ballads
What Makes Christmas, Christmas, 1917, morality play (1)   *RPB

MARION JONES
Who Will She Be? 1925 (1)   RPB

SYBIL E. JONES
The Master of Shadow, prod. 1920 by Pasadena Community Players

FRANCES GRIGSBY JOPLIN
The New Testament in the Making, 1927, pageant of the Scriptures   RPB

CARINA (CARIAN) JORDAN
The Lily and the Prince, 1911
Rachel, prod. 1913

ELIZABETH GARVER JORDAN (1867-1947)   NAW
 A Confidence, in Harper's Bazaar, 43, May, 1909, 447-50, under name
    Elizabeth Jordan (1)
 The Lady from Oklahoma, 1911, prod. 1913, comedy   RPB

ELIZABETH GOODRICH JORDAN
 Christmas Customs of Many Lands, 1927, Christmas pageant for the   RPB-M
    Sunday school; music by George F. Rosche

ETHEL B. JORDAN
 What Becomes Of It (1)   SSH-IV

GRACE C. JORDAN
 The Christmas Story in Tableau, with Elva M. Rice and Clarence A.   JPP-1
    Burt

KATE JORDAN (1862-1926) AWW
 A Luncheon at Nicks, 1903
 The Masked Woman, prod. 1922, adapted from French melodrama
 Mrs. Dakan, prod. 1909
 The Pompadour's Protege, 1903
 The Right Road, 1911
 Secret Strings, prod. 1914

M. ALICE JORDAN
 Mabel: "In His Name," 1902, "military allegory and comedy drama in   RPB
    4 acts"

HELEN HAIMAN JOSEPH
 Ali Baba and Other plays for Young People or Puppets, 1927
 A Book of Marionettes, 1920
 Little Mr. Clown, 1932, adventures of a marionette
 Princesses, 1923, symbolic drama for marionettes   RPB

JEANNETTE JOYCE
 Aunt Jane Visits School, 1920, farce (1)   RPB
 In a Doctor's Office, 1920, farce (1)   RPB
 No Peddlers Admitted, 1920, farce (1)   RPB
 A Proposal in Grandma's Day, 1920, farce (1)   RPB
 The Train to Morrow, 1920, farce (1)   RPB
 An Up-to-date Proposal, 1920, farce (1)   RPB

ALICE GAY JUDD
 The Bashful Lovers, 1925, pantomimed reading   Or, DLC
 The Captain's Predicament, 1920, two act farce   RPB
 The Fickle Professor, 1922, pantomimed reading   RPB
 Mother Nature's Picnic, 1921, young   RPB
 What Happened in the Minuet, 1925, pantomimed reading   DLC

JANE JUDGE
 The Christmas Mystery, with Linwood Taft, in Drama, 11, Nov., 1920, 60-2

K

HELEN POOKE KANE (also HELEN KAINE) (1851- ?)
The Best Laid Plans, 1904, farce, under name Helen Kaine (1)   RPB
A Bundle of Matches, 1909, 2 act society comedy   RPB
Capture of Qzah, 1914, Indian play (1)   RPB
Diantha's Desertion, 1906, serio-comedy (1)   RPB
The Future Lady Holland, 1911, 3 act comedy for women   RPB
Her Nephew-in-law Elect, 1906, farce (1)   RPB
The Peregrinations of Polly, 1908, comedy for women (1)   RPB
A Russian Romance, 1907, 3 act drama for women   RPB
Under Sailing Orders, 1912, comedy (1)   RPB
The Upsetting of Jabez Strong, 1911, 3 act comedy   RPB
The White Dove of Oneida, 1907, 2 act romantic drama   RPB
Yagowanea, 1914, Indian play (1)   RPB
"Yot-che-ka, the Eire," 1914, Indian play (1)   RPB

ALLENA KANKA (See ALLENA HARRIS)

YSABEL DE WITTE KAPLAN (1877- ?)
Madonna and the Scarecrow, in Poet Lore, 34, Summer, 1923, 254-70, 3 acts
Princess Weaver of the Skies, in Poet Lore, 32, (No. 3), 1921, 267-8 (1)

HELEN FINCH KASSON
The Name They Have Forgot, 1915   RPB

HAZEL SHARRARD KAUFMAN
Little Black Sambo, 1928, for pre-school children   RPB, MRC

DOROTHY KAUSCHER
"Bos'n," in Poet Lore, 36, Winter, 1925, 583-99

MRS. HERMINIE TEMPLETON KAVANAGH
The Color Sergeant, 1903, drama (1)   RPB
Swift-Wing of the Cherokee, drama (1)   RPB

KATHARINE KAVANAUGH (ZIEGFIELD) ("KAY ZIEGFIELD") (1875- ?)
Adam's Evening, 1934, 3 act farce   RPB
Alibi Bill, 1930, 3 act farce   RPB
Ambition, 1924 (1)   RPB
A Bachelor's Baby, 1911, farce (1)   RPB
Betty, "the Girl o' My Heart," 1923, 3 acts   RPB
The Call of Youth, 1930   RPB
A Converted Suffragist, 1912, for women (1)   RPB
Corinne of the Circus, 1916, 3 act comedy drama   RPB
Countess Kate, 1912, playlet   RPB
A Couple of Heroes (1)
Dangerous Waters, 1929, 3 act comedy-drama   RPB
The Daughters of Men, 1918, drama (1)   RPB
Diamond Chip, 1924, "ranch play in 4 acts"   RPB
The Dust of the Earth, 1911, 4 act drama   RPB
Easy Terms, 1922, domestic comedy (1)
The Fire Escape, 1917, comedy (1)   RPB
The Four Adventurers, 1922, comedy for girls (1)   RPB
A Friendly Tip, 1922, playlet (1)   RPB

KATHARINE KAVANAUGH (ZIEGFIELD) (continued)

From Kitchen-Maid to Actress, 1910, farce (1)	RPB
A Gentle Touch, 1912, vaudeville sketch (1)	RPB
The Ghost Parade, 1929, 3 act farce	RPB
The Girl and the Outlaw, 1914, dramatic playlet (1)	RPB
Girl-shy, 1932, 3 act comedy	RPB
Happy Landings, 1932, 3 act farce	RPB
Hero-by-the-hour, 1930, 3 act comedy	RPB
The House Across the Way, 1910 (1)	RPB
I Like Your Nerve! 1932, 3 act comedy	RPB
In Wrong; or, the Fire Escape, 1917, comedy (1)	RPB
It Ain't My Fault, 1922, comedy (1)	RPB
It Happened in Hollywood, 1929, 3 act comedy	RPB
It Happened on Wednesday, 1934, 3 act comedy drama	
Lady Spitfire, 1935, 3 act comedy	
Let's Get Together, 1935, 3 act comedy	ViU, DLC
Lucky Winner, 1935, 3 act farce	RPB
The Man Who Came Back, 1915, playlet (1)	RPB
The Million Dollar Butler, 1933, 3 act farce	RPB
A Minister Pro Tem, 1914, comedietta (1)	RPB
Missing! One Pair! 1934	RPB
My Cousin From Sweden, 1932, comedy (1)	RPB
My Mexican Rose, 1912 (1)	RPB
No Foolin', 1936, comedy	ViU, DLC
5O Joy San, 1919, comedy-drama (1)	RPB
Oh, Professor! 1931, 3 act farce	RPB
Oh! Susan! 1924, 4 act comedy-drama	RPB
Only Sally Ann, 1929, 3 act comedy-drama	RPB
Open For Inspection, 1932, comedy for women (1)	RPB
Page Asa Bunker, 1934, 3 act comedy	RPB
The Phantom Pilot, 1930, 3 act mystery	RPB
Phillip for Short, 1933, 3 act farce, by "Kay Ziegfield"	RPB
A Point of Honor, 1906, comedy	NN, PU
The Porch Climber, 1926 (1)	RPB
The Professor of Love, 1914, comedy (1)	RPB
The Queen of Diamonds, 1915	RPB
Rose of the East Side, 1928, 3 act comedy	RPB
Second Story Peggy, 1924, 4 act comedy-drama	RPB
Settled Out of Court, 1923, domestic comedy (1)	RPB
So You're From Missouri! 1934, 3 act farce, by "Kay Ziegfield"	RPB
Some Call It Love, 1936, comedy-drama, by "Kay Ziegfield"	DLC
Speeding Along, 1931, 3 act comedy	RPB
A Stormy Night, 1931, comedy (1)	RPB
A Sweeping Victory, 1931, 3 act comedy	RPB
That Crazy Smith Family! 1939, 3 act comedy	
That Perkins Family, 1942, 3 act domestic comedy	RPB
There Goes the Bride, 1933, 3 act farce, by "Kay Ziegfield"	RPB
Three Christmas Wishes, 1931	RPB
Three Months to Live! 1938, 3 act comedy	
A Thriving Business, 1932, farce (1)	RPB
Under Blue Skies, 1913, 4 act comedy-drama	RPB
Watch My Smoke! 1924, 3 act comedy	RPB
The Wayfarers, 1912, 4 act rural play	RPB
What a Family! 1940, 3 act comedy of youth	RPB
When Jane Takes a Hand, 1924, comedy	RPB
When Kitty Eloped, 1928, 3 act comedy-drama	RPB
When the Worm Turned, 1912, comedy	RPB

KATHARINE KAVANAUGH (ZIEGFIELD) (continued)
Who Wouldn't Be Crazy! 1928, farce	RPB
Who's a Coward? 1912, comedy	RPB
The Wife Tamer; or, When the Worm Turned, 1912, comedy (1)	RPB
The Will o' the Wisp, 1923, 3 act romantic Irish comedy drama	RPB
A Woman's Stratagem, 1924, domestic comedy (1)	RPB
The Wrong Professor, 1946, 3 act comedy	RPB
You're the Doctor! 1933, 3 act farce	RPB

MOLLY DAY THACHER KAZAN (? -1963)
Blocks, 1928, by Molly Day Thacher, mimeographed copy-1933, prod. 1937 for Federal Theater	RPB, VET
The Egghead, 1958, 3 acts	RPB
Endurance Flight, 1929, with Joy Mays	
Rosemary and The Alligator, 1960, one-hour plays	RPB
The Wreck, 1929, mimeographed copy-1933	RPB, VET

PEARL M. KEATING
Historic Watertown Communitry Pageant (She was director.)	MB

ETHELYN EMERY KEAYS
His Wife By His Side, prod. 1912
A Thousand Generations and One, 1923, Little Theater Tournament

MARY GENTRY PAXTON KEELEY
Billy the Baby, n.d.	MoU
Bizarre, 1951	MoU
Christian College Prize Plays, 1934 (She was editor.)	MoU
The Kettle Singing, 1928 (1)	MoU
The Love Letters of an Englishman, 1929	MoU
The Man She Left Behind Her, c.1920	MoU
Petticoat Minded, n.d.	MoU
The Professor and the Little Gump, n.d.	MoU
The River Rat, c.1929	MoU
They Can't Have Papa, 1929	MoU
246 Green, c.1930	MoU
Vinnie Ream, 1940	MoU
What I Love I Lose, n.d.	MoU

ALICE A. KEEN
Changing Emma's Mind, 1928, comedy (1)	RPB

SARA KEENER
The Grey Switch (1)	LUU

ELIZABETH MC NEELY KEHR
The Tragedy of the Thanksgiving Feast (As the Greeks Might Have Played It), 1925	RPB

MABEL S. KEIGHTLEY
Just an Interview, 1928 (1)	RPB
The K. O. Kid, 19??, comedy, typed copy	ICU
Midnight Rose, 1928, 3 act comedy-drama	RPB
The Supreme Test, 1911, 4 act modern drama, typed copy	MH

EDNA G. KEITH
Bobby's Christmas, 1921
The Toymender, 1921

NORA KEITH
The Trifler, 1905, with Murray Carson

ELIZABETH KELLAM
The Store, 1921, one of Vassar series of plays, ed. by Gertrude Buck (1)   RPB

AIMEE T. KELLEY
Uncle Sam's Garden of Flowers, 1930, musical fantasy   RPB

ESTELLA KELLEY
The Machine Age, 1928, historical comedy   GHP

ETHEL MAY KELLEY (1878- ?)
An Impromptu Prayer, in The Booklovers Magazine, 3, Jan., 1904
Paging John Howard, in Bookman (N. Y.), 65, April, 1927, 163-6 (1)

JESSIE A. KELLEY
The Emigrants' Party, 1914, entertainment introducing folk songs and   RPB
   dances
The Employment Office, 1916, farce (1)
The Fair of the Pilgrims, 1918   RPB
Fun on the Bingville Branch, 1915 (1)   RPB
Happy School Days, 1917   RPB
Her Day of Rest, 1931, for women   RPB
Her Weekly Allowance, 1907, farce (1)   RPB
Miss Prim's Kindergarten; or, a School of Today, 1907 (1)   RPB
Mrs. Jenkins' Brilliant Idea, 1915, comedy   RPB
Our Church Fair, 1909, 2 act farce   RPB
The Pedler's Parade, 1903 (1)   RPB
A Photographer's Troubles, 1915, farce (1)   RPB
Reminiscences of the Donation Party, 1915, soliloquy of the minister's   RPB
   wife, with tableaux
The Revel of the Year, 1917 (1)   RPB
The Rummage Sale, 1916   RPB
The Rural Telephone, 1911, monologue for a lady   DLC
Santa's Surprise, 1907, Christmas exercise for giving   RPB
Scenes in a Restaurant, 1909 (1)   RPB
Squire Judkin's Apple Bee, 1905, old-fashioned entertainment (1)   RPB
The Suffragettes' Convention, 1912 (1)   RPB
Taking the Census in Bingville, 1911 (1)   RPB
Those Husbands of Ours, 1913, farce (1)   RPB
The Tramp's Convention, 1912, for males (1)   RPB
The Village Post-office, 1907   RPB

LAURA FRANCES KELLEY
Mrs. Sullivan in Politics, 1924, comedy (1)   RPB
Mrs. Sullivan's Seance, 1922, comedy (1)   RPB
Mrs. Sullivan's Social Tea, 1920, comedy (1)   RPB

(MINNIE) MAY KELLEY ("MAY SHELDON") (Kelley may be married name,
   since NUC lists Sheldon as real name, not pseud.) (RPB lists her as Sheldon)
A Dollar Down, 1929, 3 act comedy, by "May Sheldon"   DLC
Do Unto Others, 1938, 3 act comedy, by May Kelley   DLC
The Ghost Chaser, 1930, 3 act mystery comedy by "May Sheldon" and   RPB
   Loring Kelley

(MINNIE) MAY KELLEY (continued)
<u>"Major" Jones</u>, 1930, by "May Sheldon" and Loring Kelley   RPB
<u>Sadie Gets Elected</u>, 1931, rural comedy by "May Sheldon" and Loring   RPB
   Kelley
<u>That Watkins Girl</u>, 1937, 3 act comedy drama, by "May Sheldon"

ELIZABETH ROCKEY KELLOGG (1870- ?)
<u>Merry Christmas!</u> 1910, farce "written once upon a time for the College   RPB
   Club"

AMY RUTH KELLY (1878- ?)
<u>Ye Geste of Hynde Horn</u>, presented at Lake Erie College, Painseville,   RPB
   Ohio, in Feb., 1903, by the class of 1905; arranged with variations from
   the ancient ballad of "Hynde Horn" by Kelly, 1903

KATHERINE C. KELLY
<u>Frail Ferdinand</u>, 1930
                                                                                       RPB

KATHERINE WICK KELLY (MRS. FREDERICK C. MC CONNELL) (1887-1937)
<u>Forever</u>, manuscript   OrU
<u>Just Another Girl</u>, manuscript   OrU
<u>Perfection</u>, manuscript   OrU

"MOLLIE KELLY" (NUC lists as real name)
<u>Grandma's Love Seat</u>, 1946, comedy (1)   RPB
<u>Just Like Us</u>, 1934, comedy for women (1)   RPB
<u>Madame Handles a Customer</u>, 1930   RPB
<u>More Than a Million</u>, 1933, comedy, in <u>Scholastic</u>, Nov. 24, 1934,   RPB
   5-7+ (1)
<u>Teddy Bear Stays Off Relief</u>, 1938, young (1)   DLC
<u>The Terrible Candy-eater</u>, 1937, "candy store fantasy for children" (1)   DLC

SALLIE KEMPER
<u>An Old Chester Secret</u>, 1924, adapt. of book by Margaret Deland (1)   BTG
<u>Blood Will Tell</u>, 1923, comedy for women (1)   RPB, HQC
<u>Four Cents</u>, 19??   NN
<u>Moth Balls</u>, 1918 (1)   RPB

MARTHA G. KENDALL
<u>When Santa Claus Went to the Front</u>, 1918, with Ethel E. Reed   RPB

MARIETTA C. KENNARD
<u>The Flight of the Herons</u>, 1934, in <u>Drama</u>, 14, Dec., 1923, 97-8+ (1)   WU

ANNA R. KENNEDY
<u>Bible Plays Out of the East</u>, 1929   RPB
<u>The Pearl Merchant</u>, 1941, Christmas   DLC
<u>The Virgin's Tree</u> (1)   SSL

HARRIET L. KENNEDY
<u>The Lion's Mouth</u>, 1924, adapted from "The Sleeping Sickness" by   RPB
   George Madden Martin

MARION KENNEDY
<u>Programs for Special Occasions</u>, 1929, for primary grades
<u>Special Day Pageants for Little People</u>, 1929, with Katharine Isabel   RPB
   Bemis

MARY KENNEDY (MRS. DEEMS TAYLOR)
Captain Fury
Jordan
Mrs. Partridge Presents, 1925, with Ruth Hawthorne, 3 act comedy   RPB
A Surprise to the Children, 1933, music by Deems Taylor

GAIL KENT
The Parson's Greetings, 1912, 2 act romantic comedy   RPB

SOPHIA MORRIS KENT
The Wickedest Witch, 1930, 3 acts, young   RPB

BERNICE LESBIA KENYON (1883?-1935)
The Alchemist, 1923, for men (1)   RPB, STM

DORIS MARGARET KENYON (1898- ?)
Doris Kenyon's Monologues, 1929   RPB
Humorous Monologues, 1924   RPB
Monologues, 1929, first pub. 1920   PP

FRANCES S. KENYON
Up To Freddie, 1903, 2 act farce, especially designed for girls' schools RPB

FLORENCE KERIGAN
The Daughter of the Duke of Ballyhoo, 1928, 3 act comedy   RPB
The Eyes That See, 1926 (1)   RPB
The Lady of the Lilacs, 1926, dramatic novelty in 4 scenes   RPB

JANE KERLEY
Marsyas, the Faun, 1925, music by Eleanor Marum, Little Theatre
     Tournament
Miniature Music Dramas, 1929
One Night in a Nursery, 1922, "operetta dreamed by Jane Kerley about   NN
     the music of 'Six Pieces for Children'"

ROSIALEE KERLEY
The Wedding Guest, in Poet Lore, 33, Summer, 1922, 232-8 (1)

HELEN KERR
Everybody Happy? 1930, comedy (1)   RPB

VANDA E. KERST
Victory Through Conflict, 1920, with Mary W. Brownson, pageant of   RPB-M
     striving humanity, for 50th anniversary of Penn. College for Women

NELLE F. KERSTING
The Wages of Sin is Death, 1912, drama (1)   RPB

KATHARINE E. KESTER
Alleluia, 1939, Easter choral play   RPB
Bargains, comedy (1)   JMS
Boundless as the Sea, 1938, comedy (1)   DLC
The Christmas Child Comes In, 1925, based on story by Zona Gale   RPB
Give Me a Ring, 1933 (1)   OCl
Gloria, 1934, Christmas choral play
Headliners for the Campus, 1935, collection of 6 one-act plays   RPB
Headliners for School Assembly, 1934, collection of 5 one-act plays   RPB

KATHARINE E. KESTER (continued)
The Land of Forgetfulness, 1918, young, 3 acts   RPB
Love and Lather, "scintillating farce" (1)   JMS
Penny a Flower, 1932, fantasy, also in Drama, 15, Dec., 1924, 59-63 (1)   RPB
A Psalm of Thanksgiving, 1938 (1)
Rondo Capriccioso, in Poet Lore, 37, Autumn,1926, 458-67 (1)
Sing Nowell, 1940, Christmas choral-picture
The Steeplejack, 1932 (1)   RPB
Two Bouquets, 1951, based on the short story by Herbert   WU, OrCS
   Gutterson (1)

EMILIE KEYES
Gwendolyn's Getaway, 1928, "funny shadow-graph for 4 boys and   RPB
   2 girls"

MARY WILLARD KEYES
Red Cap, 1916, 2 acts, young   RPB

LUCY STEARNS KEYS
Up-to-date Anne, 1915, 2 act domestic comedy   RPB

MARGARET KIBBE
Is Santa Coming?   CLP-1
Little Plays for Christmas, 1928, with others   RPB
A Surprise for Christmas   CLP-1

MARY FRIX KIDD
Emily's Dream, 1921, geographical pageant for young   RPB
The Man Who Made Cotton King, 1931   RPB
Nature's Child, the Voice of Cotton, 1931, community pageant, prod.   MB
   by the Concord Woman's Club, Concord,. N. C.

AUGUSTA RAYMOND KIDDER (? -1939)
All By His Lonesome, 1917, with Edward Kidder, "rollicking rattling   RPB
   college play"
The Bridge Party, 1927, with Edward Kidder, "kindly social satire" (1)   RPB
The Bungalow Bride, 1926, with Edward Kidder, comedy (1)
A College Cinderella, 1915, with Edward Kidder   RPB
His and Hers, 1926 (1)   RPB
Hollyhock House, 1928, with Edward Kidder, "tale of a pretty typist"   RPB
Stage Struck, 1926, with Edward Kidder, "breezy comedietta of these   RPB
   times" (1)
Uncle Sam's Daughters and What They Have Done, 1915, "pictorial   RPB
   phantasy"

ADELE KILPATRICK
Progress of Civilization, 1915, pageant, Waterville, Maine

ANNA MAY KIMBALL
Making the Flag (1)

ASTRID KIMBALL
The Infanta's Birthday

KATHRYN KIMBALL

After the Senior Play, 193?	RPB
Apple Blossoms, 1933	RPB
The Blue-eyed Sheik, 1928	RPB
The Blue-eyed Sheik Prefers Blondes, 1930	RPB
The Bottle of Dreams, 193?	RPB
Brother at the "Pitcher" Show, 1928	RPB
Brother Makes a Cake, 1930	RPB
Cinderella in Red, 193?	RPB
Crimson Rambler, 1932	RPB
Daddy Doc, 1927	RPB
A Forgotten Witness, 1928	RPB
Glory For Sale, 1931	RPB
God Remembers, 1927	RPB
Holly Hogs, 193?	RPB
I an' Columbus, 193?	RPB
I Bet I Ain't Gonna Git to Go, 193?	RPB
In the Cafeteria, 1928	RPB
"King Midas in a Mix-up," 193?	RPB
The Lilac Lady, 1930	RPB
"Liquish" and Lions, 193?	RPB
Little Boy Blue, 1929	RPB
Little Dub, 1928	RPB
The Little King Finds Peace, 1932	RPB
A Mysterious Peep, 1928	RPB
The Penitent, 193?	RPB
Putting on the Senior Play, 193?	RPB
Taking Joy Home, 1931	RPB
A Truant Musician, 1928	RPB
Wives at Jamestown, 193?	RPB

ROSAMOND KIMBALL

Abraham Lincoln, the Boy (1)	SSL
America's Call, 192? pageant on the League of Nations	NN
The Coming of the Mayflower, 1920, pageant, written by a youth group, based on her story	RPB
The Making of the Flag (1)	SSL
The Nativity, 1916, Christmas service	RPB
Patriotic Pageants of Today, 1918, collection with Josephine Thorp	RPB
The Resurrection, 1917, Easter service	RPB
The Wooing of Rebecca and Other Bible Plays, 1925	
You and I and Joan, 1924, for girls	OCl, DLC

RUTH PUTNAM KIMBALL

Another Easy Christmas Book, 1947 (She was ed.)	RPB
As I Was Saying, 1956, collection of monologues for women	RPB
Blind Date, 1948, comedy (1)	RPB
Daisy's Ball, 1970? based on Alcott's Little Men	RPB
Easy Plays and Programs for Hallowe'en, 1946, (She was ed. with Theodore Johnson.)	RPB
Five Little Peppers and How They Grew, 1947, dram. of story by Margaret Sidney	RPB
Lydia; or, the Seller of Purple, 1928, Easter pageant	RPB
Martin Hyde, the Duke's Messenger, 1935, based on a novel by John Masefield	RPB
Pan Dowdy, 1930, 3 act comedy-drama	RPB
Parody Pictures, 1932, collection of "Get-'em-up-quick" stunts	RPB

RUTH PUTNAM KIMBALL (continued)

The Purple Monkey, 1930, 3 act comedy	RPB
The Treasure Hunters; or, The Tiger Earl, 1924, 3 act extravaganza	RPB
Treasure Island, 1927, dram. of Stevenson's book	RPB
The Whispering Room, 1935, 3 act mystery comedy	RPB

GRACE KINER

Wedding Clothes, 1928, rural N. Y. State play	RPB

BEULAH BROWN KING (1892- ?)

The Bachelor of Gray Crags, 1925, comedy for women (1)	RPB
Blame It On Sandy, 1928, 3 act farce	RPB
Blimmer's to Blame, 1927, 3 act farce	RPB
The Brush Peddler, 1937 (1)	RPB
Can You Beat It? 1929, 3 act comedy	RPB
Chintz Cottage, 1929, 3 act comedy	RPB
Clarence Decides, 1920, 3 act farce	RPB
Fashions in Men, 1931, 3 act comedy	RPB
Getting Rid of Eppie, 1927, 3 acts	RPB
The Ghostly Lover, 1931, comedy (1)	RPB
The Gorgeous Cecile, 1920, 3 acts	RPB
The Haddon Hall Mystery, 1923, comedy-drama	RPB
Happiness at Last, 1922, 3 act comedy	RPB
Henry Where Are You?, 1920 (1)	RPB
Her Husband's Watch, 1925, mystery comedy for women (1)	RPB
His Sisters, 1920, farce (1)	RPB
How Very English! 1932, 3 act comedy	RPB
The Importance of Mary, 1926, comedy (1)	RPB
The Importance of Pam, 1921, 3 act comedy	RPB
In Search of Carolyn, 1922, 3 act comedy	RPB
The Indifference of Jeremy, 1921 (1)	RPB
Keeping Up Appearances, 1935, 3 act farce	RPB
The Knight's Mare, 1925 (1)	RPB
Love in a Fog, 1936, 3 act comedy	RPB
The Maid, 1914, comedy (1)	RPB
Merely Anne Marie, 1921, 3 act comedy	RPB
Miranda's Jane, 1929, 3 act farce	RPB
The Misfortunes of Arabella's Fortune, 1924	RPB
Miss Marmaduke's Reign, 1920, 2 acts for women	RPB
A Nephew in the House, 1929, for women (1)	RPB
The Paper Cavalier, 1921, 2 act comedy	RPB
Poor Dear Uncle James! 1920, 3 act farce	RPB
Poverty Preferred, 1926, 2 acts	RPB
The Purple Pig, 1927, 3 act comedy	RPB
The Remarkable Mrs. Dana, 1925, 3 act farce	RPB
The Rev. Peter Brice, Bachelor, 1919, for women (1)	RPB
Romance Everywhere, 1938, 3 act comedy	RPB
Romantic Melisande, 1926, comedy (1)	RPB
Ruffs and Pompons, 1924 play??	DLC
Spoon Fed, 1932, 2 act comedy for women	RPB
Tommy's Present, 1933, Christmas story play	
Two Girls and a Fellow, 1927, 3 act comedy	RPB
What's In a Name! 1921 (1)	RPB

FLORENCE KING

Woman of the Hour: Sufrage Play in Three Acts, 1910, with Eugene
and Mary Isabel Quirk

FRANCES ROCKEFELLER KING
    Fluffy Ruffles, 1907 (1)   RPB

GEORGIANA GODDARD KING (1871-1939)
    Comedies and Legends for Marionettes; a Theatre for Boys and Girls,   RPB
       1904
    The Legend of St. Dorothy   WWY
    The Play of the Sibyl Cassandra, 1921, Christmas

GRACE ELIZABETH KING (1852-1932) AWW NAW
    A Splendid Offering, in Drama, 16, March, 1926, 213-5,135-7, comedy for
       women (1)

MARY PERRY KING (1865- ?)
    Daughters of Dawn, 1913, lyrical pageant, with Bliss Carman   RPB
    Earth Deities and Other Rhythmic Masques, 1914, with Bliss Carman   RPB

SARA KINGSBURY (1876- ?)
    The Christmas Guest, in Drama, 8, Nov., 1918, 455-6l, young (1)
    The Crowning of Spring, 1924
    Our Christ Liveth, 1930, 3 act Easter play   RPB
    The Rich Young Man, 1924, 3 acts
    The Voice of Montezuma   BPD

MARY F. KINGSTON
    My Son Arthur, 1916, comedy (1)   RPB
    The Trials of a Hostess, 1915, 3 act comedy   RPB

ARLIE KINKADE
    That Fellow From Arizona, 1927, comedy-drama (1)   RPB

MRS. C. F. KINNAMAN
    In a Spider's Web, 1900, with C. F. Kinnaman, 3 act musical farce   RPB

GRACE V. KINYON
    "All on a Winter's Day," comedy (1)   BCC
    Bob's Dorothy, 1931, play of modern life (1)   RPB
    Bright Comedies for Junior High Schools, 1932   RPB
    Daring Daughters, 1930, play of modern life for women   RPB
    "Gold Dust," 1932, 3 act comedy   RPB
    Merry Comedies for Junior High School, 1934   RPB
    "No Such Friend," suitable for patriotic occasions (1)   BCC
    The Open Window, 1931, missionary play   RPB
    "A Silver Lining," 1934   RPB
    "The Treasure Hunt," 1938, for Armistice Day (1)

FLORENCE KIPER (See FLORENCE KIPER FRANK)

HARRIET GRISWOLD KIRBY
    Barbesiev; or, The Troubadour, 1913, libretto   RPB
    Christmas Gift, 1933, young   RPB
    Old Hickory, He Lived It — "From birth, 1776, to election as President   DLC
       and the death of Rachel in 1828," 1935, skeleton plot for scenario

SARA E. KIRK
    In Betsey Ross' Time (1)   FFP

KATHERINE KIRKER
The Lady Compassionate, in Poet Lore, 33, Summer, 1922, 239-45 (1)

KATHLEEN KIRKWOOD
Gas: Murder, two dramas, 1924   RPB

ALINE KISTLER
"Prologue to the Pageant of the Pacific," in Overland, n.s. 84, June,
    1926, 1689

ANNETTE KITTREDGE
The Day Before the "J Hop"; or, A Mix-up in Men, 1903? farce (1)   RPB

THELMA KITTREDGE
It Makes a Difference, 1930, health play, with Thelma Fuller and   RPB
    others (1)

AMY JOSEPHINE KLAUBER
The Exile, in Poet Lore, 33, Summer, 1922, 246-54 (1)

ALICE COLE KLEENE
Kirstin, 1913, 4 acts, version of story by Hans Christian Andersen   RPB

YETTA KLEIN
Our Children's Stage, 1928, collection with Florine Schwarz   RPB
Plays for School Children, 1930, with Florine Schwarz   RPB

JULIA M. KLINCK
Queen o' the May, 1907, children's cantata   RPB

DOROTHEA M. C. KLUGE
Orpheus and Eurydice, in The English Journal, 4, Dec., 1915, 664-8,
    love masque

VIRGINIA DARE KNAUER
A Crafty Crook, 1927, comedy   RPB
Donated by the Ladies' Aid, 1926   RPB

EMMA KNAUSS
Wide Open Windows, 1925, with Frances Perry, pageant for h. s. girl   RPB
    reserves written for Girl Reserves Conference, Kansas, 1924
The World Circle,1925 with Mary L. Carr, YWCA girl reserve pageant   RPB
    for h. s. students (under name Carr at RPB)

GERTRUDE KNEVELS (1881- ?)
The Arrow-maker's Daughter, 1913, with Grace E. Smith, campfire   RPB
    play, adapt. from "Hiawatha"
David, a Biblical Play, 1937   DLC
Don't Count Your Chickens, 1936, black-face comedy (1)   DLC
Dragon's Glory, 1924, Chinese comedy   OCl, DLC
The Fairies' Child, 1915 (1)   RPB
A Little Excitement, 1921, 3 acts for girls   RPB
Minnetoska's Dream, 1915 (1)   RPB
Octagon House, 1925
The Peddler of Hearts, 1917, folk play, young   RPB
Skyboy, 1915, young (1)   RPB
Twelfth Night at Moulderby Hall, 1936, with Marie Norton Van Doren   RPB

VERA KNICKERBOCKER
    Book of the Words. A Pageant of Wichita, 1915? Wichita, Kansas, with   MB
        others

MARIETTA KNIGHT
    Dramatic Reader for Grammar Grades, 1910   RPB

AVA BEATRICE KNOWLES
    The Beginning of the Church, 1924, religious pageant, typed copy   RPB
    The Prodigal Son, 1924, religious pageant, typed copy   RPB
    The Saint, 1936, won contest sponsored by the N. Y. Federation of   RPB
        Churches (1)

ANNIE ROGERS KNOWLTON
    Why Jessica! 1918, comedy (1)   RPB

(BERNICE) BEATRICE KNOWLTON
    "The Way the Noise Began," with Don Knowlton, in Drama, 12,   JAB
        Oct-Nov., 1921, 20-1, comedy (1)

ETHEL L. KNOX
    Twelfth Night Festivals (1)   SSH-II

FLORENCE CLAY KNOX
    Butterflies and Balsam, 1948, for women (1)   RPB
    The China Guinea Pig, Drama League prize
    A Face at the Window, 1939, Christmas (1)   RPB
    For Distinguished Service, 1918, duologue for two women (1)   STW, JMS
    Many Happy Returns of the Day, 1929, comedy (1)   RPB
    The Matrimonial Fog, 1918, comedy (1)   RPB

GERTRUDE LEVERICH KNOX (WILLIS)
    Child of the Promise, 1908, with Adam Geibel and Mrs. R. R.   RPB-M
        Forman, Sunday school service
    The Lost Locket, 1925, patriotic sketch, music by Mrs. R. R. Forman
    A Rose Dream, 1915, music by Mrs. R. R. Forman, fairy operetta for
        young people

JANET KNOX
    The Shepherd of Bethlehem, 1928 (1)   RPB

JESSIE A. KNOX
    Plays with a Purpose, 1930, short sketches for presentation by home   RPB
        economic students, ed. by Knox

MARGARET KNOX (1866- ?)
    America the Beautiful, Democracy's Goal, pageant, with Anna M.   LNP
        Lutkenhaus, in St. Nicholas, 47, June, 1920, 738-44 (1)
    Aunt Jane's Story Hour (1)   LNP
    The Future of America as Our Young Folks See It , with Anna M.   LNP
        Lutkenhaus, in St. Nicholas, 47, Jan., 1920, 260-4, pageant (1)
    A Handful of Clay and Our Choice   LPS
    Story and Play Readers, 1917, with Anna M. Lutkenhaus

RUTH CRUM KNUDTEN
    Rumor, 1929 (1)   RPB

ANGELA KOELLIKER
  Doubling for Hygeia, 1927, 3 act comedy   RPB
  The Legacy, 1934, comedy, mimeographed copy (1)   RPB

ELEANOR CONSTANCE KOENIG (SHEEHAN)
  The Grave Woman, in Poetry, 32, July, 1928, 206-9 (1)
  Two Dialogues: The Shade; Two on an Old Pathway, in Poetry, 35,
      Nov., 1929, 87-91

CHARLOTTE KOHLER
  Down in Egypt's Land, 1928   VET

ERIN KOHN
  In the Light of the Bethlehem Star; or, What Luther Did for Christmas,   RPB
      1922

ADRIANA S. KOLYN
  The Book of Words of "The Pageant of Hope," presented by student   RPB
      body of Hope College on the occasion of the semi-centennial
      celebration, 1916

EFFIE LOUISE KOOGLE
  Aunt Jerusha and Uncle Josh, 1924 or earlier
  The Buzzville News, 1912, farce   RPB
  The Christmas Collation, 1909, comp. by Koogle   DLC
  Cupid's Joke, 1906, young   RPB
  Halloween Adventure, 1906, young   Or
  The Heir of Mount Vernon, 1906, colonial play   RPB
  The Knickerbockers at School, 1906, young, historical play   RPB
  Kris Kringle's Minstrels, 1912   NBuG
  Master George Washington, his Sixth Birthday Party, 1906, young   RPB
  Rastus Blink's Minstrels, 1912   RPB
  Royalty in Old Virginia, 1906, historical play   RPB
  Thanksgiving in Brownie-Land, ?1898-1905   RPB
  Uncle Sam's Brigade, 1906   RPB
  Up-to-Date America; or, the Sweet Girl Graduate's Dream, 1907   RPB
      drama-caprice" (1)
  Yankee Doodle's Trip to Dixie, 1906, young, historical play   RPB

HILDRETH KOTSCH
  Rainbow Gold, 1930, with Anna Louise Barney, "spring-time   RPB
      fantasy" (1)

HELEN KRAFFT
  Our Wives, prod. and pub. 1912, with Frank Mandel, adapt. from German

IRMA KRAFT
  The Power of Purim and Other Plays, 1915, one-acts   RPB
  "Shop Window," 19??   NN

MARY ELEANOR KRAMER
  The Old Fields at Home, 1915, music by Bertha T. Allen
  The Post-Mistress, 1915, humorous operetta, music by   RPB-M
      George F. Rosche

JOSEPHINE ELLIOTT KROHN
  Old King Cole and Other Medieval Plays, 1925   RPB
  The Queen of Hearts, 1922, operetta, music by William Lester (also in   RPB
      Old King Cole)

ERNA KRUCKMEYER
"And He Came to His Father," 1927, Drama League prize winner,   RPB
    dram. of "The Prodigal Son" (1)
There Was a Merry Prince, 1940, arr. and adapt. from Shakespeare's   RPB
    Henry IV and V

NELL KRUGER
Jamboree, 1928, skit for children (1)   RPB

CLARE KUMMER (1888-1958) NWAT (1873?-1958)
Amourette, prod. 1933
Annie Dear, prod. 1924
Banco, prod. 1922, adapt. from French of A. Savoir
"Be Calm, Camilla!" 1922, prod. 1918, "problem farce"   RPB
Bridges, 1922, prod. 1921   RPB
Chinese Love, 1922, prod. 1921 (1)   RPB
The Choir Rehearal, 1922, prod. 1916 (1)   RPB
"Good Gracious Annabelle," 1922, prod. 1916, romantic farce (first play   RPB
    by a woman to be included in Mantle and Sherwood's Best Plays)
Her Master's Voice, 1934, prod. 1932, 2 act comedy   RPB
Inspiration of the Play, "Some confessions of a woman playwright," in
    Forum, 61, March, 1919, 307-16 (1)
The Lights of Duxbury, prod. 1918
Many Happy Returns, prod. 1945
Mme Pompador, prod. 1924, book and lyrics by Rudolph Schanzer and
    Ernest Welisch, adapt. by Kummer
The Mountain Man, prod. 1921
One Kiss, prod. 1923, adapt. of French play, Ta Bouche
Open Storage, 1938, comedy (1)   OPS-IX,NBuG
The Opera Ball, prod. 1912, adapt. from German of Victor Leon and H.
    Von Waldberg; book and lyrics by Kummer and Sydney Rosenfeld;
    music by Richard Heubergen
Papers, 1927 (1)   OPS-III
Pomeroy's Past, 1926, prod. 1922 by Pasadena Comm. Players, 3 act   RPB
    comedy
The Rescuing Angel, 1923, prod. 1917, 3 act comedy   RPB
The Robbery, 1921 (1)   OPS I, MRO 1937
Rollo's Wild Oats, 1922, prod. 1920, Collier's, 66, Dec. 25, 1920, 3 act   RPB
    comedy
Roxy, (or Roxie) prod. 1919
Selected Plays, c. 1922-1934   FU
So's Your Old Antique, 1920 (1)   OPS-IV
Spring Thaw, 1937, prod. 1938, 3 act comedy   NN
A Successful Calamity, 1922, prod. 1917, 2 act comedy   RPB
Three Waltzes, prod. 1937, musical with Rowland Leigh, based on play
    by P. Knepler and A. Robinson, music by J. Strauss Sr., J. Strauss Jr.
    and O. Strauss
The Torch Bearers

EDITH KUNZ
How Prince Joy Was Saved   HDC

ADRIANA KVIYN
Pageant of Hope, 1916, Holland, Mich.

L

MRS. EDMOND LA BEAUME
The Elusive Alonzo, 1905, comedy (1)   RPB
Mlle. Rossignol; Mrs. Majoribank's Musicale, 1906, musical comedy   RPB
Mrs. Brown's Tea, 1906, burlesque   RPB
The Price of Popularity, 1905, 15 minute sketch (1)   RPB
The Problem of the Hour, 1905, comedy (1)   RPB
Room Number Ten, 1906, for girls' school   RPB

KATHRYN LACE (See JOSEPHINE BACON)

ARDA LA CROIX
The Yankee Doodle Detective, 1909, founded upon the successful play   RPB
     of the same name by Jamey Kyrle MacCurdy

MAUDE WARD LAFFERTY (MRS. W. T. LAFFERTY) (1869- ?)
Pageant of Kentucky's Historic Past, 1924, Harradsburg, Ky., music   RPB
     directed by Carl Lampert

MARY HUNEKER LAGEN
The Way Out, 1905, with Cally Ryland, farce (1)   RPB

MADELINE LAMBERT
"Count the Cost," 1923? "symbolical play in 3 acts, dealing with the   RPB
     cost of universal suffrage in America and the cost of indifference
     which threatens America at the present time."

EVA G. LAMBERTON
Timothy Cloverseed in the City, 1902   RPB

GRACE LAMKIN
Shakespeare Pageant, 1916, Shelleyville, Ind.

NINA B. LAMKIN (or LAMBKIN)
America Yesterday and Today, 1917, pageant   RPB
Around America With the Indians, 1933, plays based on Indian   RPB
     legends, with M. Jagendorf, music by Anne Church Collins, young
Camp Dramatics, 1935
Christmas and the New Year, 1934   RPB
Class Day Programs, 1937, with Edna Keith Florence
Community Days and Evenings, 1925, mimeographed copy   Or
Dances, Drills and Story-plays for Everyday and Holidays, 1916   RPB
Easter and the Spring, 1935
The Gifts We Bring, 1919, Christmas pageant for boys and girls or   RPB
     grown-ups
Good Times for All Times, 1929, "cyclopedia of entertainment"
Great Patriot's Days, 1935
Greek Pageant, 1916, Kirkwood, Mo.
Hallowe'en and Thanksgiving, 1935
Historical Pageant of Upper Michigan and Marquette County, by   MiD
     Charles J. Johnson, adapted for production by Lambkin, Lake
     Marquette, Mich., 1920
The Passing of the Kings, 1920, pageant   RPB
Shakespeare Pageant, presented several places in 1916
Traverse City Pageant, 1916, Traverse City, Michigan

KATHARINE LAMONT
  The Smugglers, 1916, 2 act musical comedy, book by Lamont,   RPB-M
    music by James M. Beck Jr., lyrics by Lamont and Paul Hyde Bonner,
    presented by Miss Spence's school society

MRS. W. H. LAMPORT
  Historic Pageant of St. Joseph County, 1916, South Bend, Ind.   MiD

FLORENCE E. LANDERS
  The Trial of Jimmy Slang, 1929, grammar play for jr. high school (1)   RPB

BERTHA PALMER LANE
  Lad and Other Story Plays for Children to Read or to Act, 1926   RPB

CHRIS LANE
  A Country Visitor, 1903, farce (1)   RPB
  "A Happy Mistake," 1907, "page of vaudeville history"   RPB
  A Lunatic Pro Tem, 188? (c1903 in NUC)   RPB
  Two Irish Heroes, 1906, comedy   RPB

ROSE WILDER LANE (1886-1968) NAW AWW
  *The Dog Wolf, 1932?   RPB
  Good Roads, 1929, play by Louise Van Voorhis Armstrong, based on   RPB
    story by Lane (1)
  *Yarbwoman, 193?   RPB
      *(Both Wetmore declamation readings)

EDITH LANG
  A Christmas Story, 1917, with music (1)   NN, DLC

MARION LANGDON
  Pageant of Thetford, 1911, Thetford, Vt., with William Langdon and   VTml
    Virginia Tanner, unpub. text

HELEN LANGHANKE
  The Doll Shop, 1920, with Lois Cool Morstrom, Christmas (1)   RPB

FANNIE MYERS LANGLOIS
  Suite B, 1911 (1)   RPB

MARION FLORENCE LANSING (1883- ?)
  Dramatic Readings for Schools, 1914, practice book in dramatics   RPB
  Quaint Old Stories to Read and Act, 1912   RPB

MARY LARCOMBE
  The Made-over Dress, 1928, humorous monologue with Maude   RPB
    Niedermeyer
  Mrs. Widdell at the Band Concert, 1928, "good encore reading," with   RPB
    Maude Niedermeyer

MARGARET LARKIN (1899-1967)
  El Cristo, 1926, winner of Belasco cup prize, Little Theatre   RPB, EMR
    Tournament, 1926 and Samuel French prize, 1926, in The Laughing
    Horse, 12, Aug., 1925 (1)

MARY LARRIMER
  Plays With a Prologue, 1925   RPB

"LIDA LARRIMORE" (see LIDA LARRIMORE TURNER THOMAS)

EMMA MAURITZ LARSON
The Christmas of the Little Pines, 1931, in Woman's Home   RPB
    Companion, 44, Dec., 1917, 29
The Christmas Sheaf, 1931   RPB
Chug's Challenge, 1931, Christmas   RPB
May Baskets New, in Woman's Home Companion, 45, May, 1918, 39 (1)
Top of the World, in Woman's Home Companion, 46, Dec., 1919, 43+

MARY AUGUSTA LASELLE (1860- ?)
Dramatizations of School Classics, 1911, dramatic reader for grammar   RPB
    and secondary schools

JEAN LEE LATHAM ("JANICE GARD") ("JULIAN LEE") (1902- ?) AWW
The Alien Note, 1930, comedy for 10 girls (1)   RPB
All on Account of Kelly, 1937, safety play   OCl
And Then What Happened? 1937, book appreciation play (1)   DLC
Another Washington, 1931, pageant by "Julian Lee," comedy (1)   RPB
The Arms of the Law, 1940, 3 act mystery   RPB
The Bed of Petunias, 1937, comedy (1)
Big Brother Barges In, 1940, by "Julian Lee," comedy (1)   RPB
The Blue Teapot, 1932, comedy (1)   RPB
Broadway Bound, 1933, 3 act comedy   RPB
The Children's Book, 1933, by "Julian Lee," with Harriette Wilburr and   RPB
    Nellie Meader Linn, contains recitations, songs, drills, exercises and plays
The Christmas Carol, 1931, dramatized by "Julian Lee"   RPB
Christmas For All, 1932, by "Julian Lee," contains recitations, songs,   RPB
    drills and plays
The Christmas Party, 1930, dram. of story by Zona Gale   RPB
Christmas Programs for the Lower Grades, 1937, by "Julian Lee," with   RPB
    Ann Clark
Christopher's Orphans, 1931 (1)   RPB
Crinoline and Candlelight, 1931, comedy (1)   RPB
Depend on Me, 1932, by "Janice Gard," 3 acts   RPB
Earl Derr Bigger's the House Without a Key, 1942, "Charlie Chan   RPB
    mystery play in 3 acts," dramatized from the novel
A Fiance for Fanny, 1931, by "Julian Lee," for 5 boys (1)   RPB
The Ghost of Lone Cabin, 1940, comedy by "Julian Lee" (1)   RPB
The Ghost of Rhodes Manor, 1939, mystery play for girls
The Giant and the Biscuits, 1934, comedy, young (1)   RPB
Gray Beard, 1941, drama (1)   DLC
Have a Heart! 1937, 3 act farce   MiD, DLC
He Landed from London, 1935, by "Julian Lee," 3 act comedy   ViU, DLC
A Health Play in One Act: Mickey the Mighty, 1937   DLC
Here She Comes! 1937, 3 act farce
I Will! I Won't, 1931, by "Julian Lee," 3 act comedy   RPB
Just for Justin, 1933, farce, by "Julian Lee" (1)   RPB
Just the Girl for Jimmy, 1937, 3 act comedy
Keeping Kitty's Dates, 1931, by "Julian Lee," farce (1)   RPB
A Lady to See You, 1931, 3 act farce   RPB
Lincoln Yesterday and Today, 1933, by "Julian Lee," songs, poems,   DLC
    readings and exercises
Listen to Leon, 1931, by "Janice Gard," 3 act farce   RPB
Lookin' Lovely, 1930, by "Janice Gard," 3 act comedy   RPB
The Master of Solitaire, 1935, drama (1)   DLC
Minus a Million, 1941, 3 act comedy   RPB

JEAN LEE LATHAM (continued)
The Nightmare, 1955, 3 acts, suspense drama	RPB
Nine Radio Plays, 1940	RPB
Old Doc, 1940, 3 act comedy drama	RPB
People Don't Change, 1941, Christmas comedy	DLC
Playmaking vs. Playwriting, 1933, suggestions for training beginning	RPB
playwrights, mimeographed copy	
The Prince and the Patters, 1934, comedy (1)	RPB
Senor Freedom, 1941, drama (1)	
A Sign Unto You, 1931, Christmas	RPB
Smile for the Lady, 1937	
Thanks Awfully, 1929, comedy (1)	RPB
Thanksgiving For All, 1932, by "Julian Lee" and Genevieve and Elwyn	RPB
Swarthout	
Thanksgiving Programs for the Lower Grades, 1937, by "Julian Lee"	RPB
They'll Never Look There! 1939, comedy (1)	
Tiny Tim, 1933, Christmas play for children, by "Julian Lee"	RPB
Tommy Tomorrow, 1935, commencement play	ViU, DLC
Washington For All, 1931, songs, recitations, drills, plays and a tableau	RPB
Well Met by Moonlight, 1937, 3 act comedy	
What Are You Going to Wear? 1937, comedy (1)	DLC

CLARA ELIZABETH LAUGHLIN (1873-1941)
Entertainments and Games, 1910	DLC

MARIE LAUGHTON
Pageant of Womanhood, 1917, Boston. Mass.	

ALICE ELIZABETH LAVELLE
Puppets of Fate, 1914, drama	RPB

LUCILLE LA VERNE
Ann Boyd, prod. 1913, dram. of novel by Will N. Harben	

LILLIAN BEATRICE LAWLER (1898- ?)
Easy Latin Plays, 1929, for high school	
The Gifts of Mother Lingua, in Classical Journal, 19, Oct., 1923, 36-9 (1)	
In the Kitchen of the King	JOP
Latin Playlets for High Schools, 1925	
Rex Helvetiorum, in Classical Journal, 15, March, 1920, 365-7 (1)	
Two Latin Playlets, 1923	RPB

ANNABAL LAWRENCE
Ruth, 1916, 3 act Biblical drama	RPB

DIANTHA FITCH LAWRENCE
Forty Winks, 1920, musical fantasy prod. by the Spence alumnae	RPB-M
society; music by Reva Marie Tonnele	

ETHEL G. LAWRENCE
Building Tomorrow's House, 1937, temperance play (1)	MiD
Standing By, 1931, missionary play (1)	RPB
Waitin' Fer Sun-Up, 1930, play of mountain life (1)	RPB

ISABEL LAWRENCE
Frolic of the Toys, 1928, pantomime or drill for primary children	RPB

LILLIAN NIXON LAWRENCE
Little Dramas for Primary Grades, 1913, with Ada Maria Skinner   RPB

ANNA CANTRELL LAWS (? -1929)
A Twice Told Tale, in Drama, 8, Aug.,, 1918, 400-13 (1)

ANNIE M. LAWTON
Christmas Holly Drills, 1905, drill for 8 girls   Or
Proserpina, 1905, operetta for children   RPB
Who Is Santa Claus? 1905, young   RPB

ELIZABETH ATKINSON LAY (See ELIZABETH ATKINSON LAY GREEN)

EULALIE CROSS LAYER
The Story of Towser, 1920, boy's monolog   RPB

PAULINE H. LAZARON
Fraternity, 1921, written for the Baltimore Hebrew congregation   RPB
      sisterhood

FANNY HEASLIP LEA (1884-1955) AWW
Crede Byron, 1936   RPB
Lolly, prod. 1929
Round-About, prod. 1929
Wooing Jane, 1907, society play by George March Otis, adapted from
      story by Lea

GLADYS HODSON LEACH
Busy Bees, 1925, rural community play   RPB
On Christmas Hill, 1928, musical play with Mary Johnson, music by Leach
Pictures from Bookland, 1927, playlet   RPB
School at Pudding Lane, 1926, Mother Goose school play by Mary   RPB
      Sharpe, music by Leach (listed under Sharpe at RPB)
Ten Little Pageants, 1926, music by Leach

LILY M. LEAMAN
The Child Moses, 1919, Biblical play   RPB

DOROTHY LEAMON
Barabbas   FRD-II

AGNES RAND LEE (1868-1939)
The Asphodel, 4 acts, in North American Review, 182, May, 1906, 770-6
The Blunted Age, in Poetry, 19, Nov., 1921, 71-3 (1)
Eastland Waters, in Poetry, 7, Feb., 1916, 234-5 (1)
Red Pearls, in International, 10, Oct., 1916, 310 (1)
The Sharing, 1914, two dramas and poems reprinted in part from various
      periodicals (also in Poetry, 3, Dec., 1913, 95-9) (1)
The Silent House, in Poetry, 1, March, 1913, 173-8 (1)

JENNETTE BARBOUR PERRY LEE (MRS. G. S. LEE) (1860-1951)
The Symphony Play, 1916, 4 acts   RPB

MARY CAROLINE LEE
The Birth of the Flag, 1921, novelty in 3 acts   RPB

MARY ELIZABETH LEE
The Black Death; or, Ta-Un, Persian tragedy, in Poet Lore, 28, Winter,
    1917, 691-702 (1)
The Honor Cross, in Poet Lore, 27, Winter, 1916, 702-6 (1)

MRS. R. W. LEE (See AMICE MAC DONNELL)

VALERIE ROBERTSON LEHMAN (1895- ?)
The Bell Maker of Nola, 1941, drama of bells and Christmas   OrP, DLC
The Call of Vacation, 1926, closing day pageant, young   RPB
The Child He Called, 1941, 2 act Children's Day drama   DLC
Fires of Yuletide, 1932, pageant-play for Christmas, music by I. H. RPB
    Meredith
Gold of the Wise Men, 1934, program of song and story, music by   RPB
    Norman Lighthill
The Great Dawn, 1939, 2 act Easter drama   OCl, DLC
The King Comes, 1931? dramatic service of worship for Christmas   DLC
The Living Christ, 1934, sacred pageant for Easter, music by I. H.   RPB
    Meredith
Santa a-la-mode, 1941   DLC
Sign of Peace, 1936, pageant of the Christmas message, music   RPM-M
    by I. H. Meredith
Song Over the World, 1952, Christmas pageant, music by Rob Roy   MiD
    Peery
The Temple of Childhood, 1933, incidental music by I. H. Meredith   RPB
The White Pearl, 1941, Christmas   DLC
Worship the King, 1924, sacred play for Christmas, incidental music by RPB
    C. Austin Miles

ETTA VERONICA LEIGHTON (1880- ?)
The Dawn of Freedom   JGH

GRACE R. LEIGHTON
Solemn Pride, 1925-9? (1)

ISABEL LEIGHTON
Marie-Adelaide, 193?, with Bertram Bloch, typescript   NN
Mercenary Mary, prod. 1925, music by William B. Friedlander
The Sapphire Ring, 1925
Spring Again, 1942, with Bertram Bloch, comedy, pub. under title   RPB
    Indian Summer in 1941

ADELINE M. LEITZBACH
Dora Mobridge, prod. 1930
Faded Orange Blossoms, n.d., "original melo-drama founded upon real   NN
    life facts," typescript
The Life of George Washington, 1914, typed scenario   NN
A Life's Mistake, 19?? 5 act romantic drama, based on Hal Caine's   ICU
    novel, The Manxman
Success, prod. 1918, with Theodore A. Liebler Jr., typed copy   NN
William Massarene, 19??, with C. W. Chase, comedy-drama based on   NN
    Ouida's novel, The Massarenes, typed copy
A Woman of Mystery; or, Such Things Have Happened, 19?? 4 act   NN
    melodrama, typescript

EMILY LELAND
Maw Moseley's Courtin' Lamp, 1915 (1)   GP-No.2

WINIFRED LENIHAN
Blind Mice, prod. 1930, with Vera Caspary

EVANGELINE M. LENT
Love in Idleness, 1903, comedy (1)   RPB
A Rag Doll, 1902, in Smart Set, 28, May, 1909, 100-10 (1)   RPB
Squaw of Bear Lake (1)
Wasula, 1908, Indian monologue for a woman   RPB
The White Silhouette and Other Acting Monologues, 1908   NN

EMMA JANE CARR LEONARD (MRS. C. HARRIS LEONARD) (1851- ?)
Flora's Review, 1912, arranged by the Ursulines of New Rochelle,   RPB
    young

MARTIA LEONARD
The Dream of Wings, 1918   NjP
The Immortal Beloved, 1927, winner of Samuel French prize, Little   RPB
    Theatre Tournament, 1927, "fantastic possibility in one act"
Lysistrata, 1912, adaptation   RPB
The Masque of Manhattan, 1909   RPB
A Tale Retold, 1928, Little Theatre Tournament, 1928

RUTH LEONARD
The Apple of Discord, 1904, with LeRoy Arnold and Lilian Garrow,   RPB
    given by the class of 1904

ISIDOR LERNER
The Mysteries and Secrets of Coney Island, 1914, motion picture   RPB
    scenario

OLGA LESH
When the Moon's Three Quarters Full, 1926 (1)   RPB

RUTH A. LETCHWORTH
Galahad, pageant   JPP-1
The Star of Bethlehem   JPP-1

LYNNE L. LEVEGOOD
A Landlord and His Tenants; or, Dispensing (with) Justice, 1927,   RPB
    comedy, mock trial

RUTH E. LEVI (LEVY)
Chanukah Sketch, 1921 (1)   RPB
A Festival of Feasts, 1923, Purim fantasy   OCl
The King's Choice, 1910, Purim sketch (1)   RPB
Miriam's Purim Play, 1914   PPDrop

ELMA EHRLICH LEVINGER (1887-1958)
At the Gates, 1925, Jewish theme (1)   RPB
The Burden, 1918 (1)   RPB
Chanukah Entertainments, 1924, collection   RPB
A Child of the Frontier, 1925, about Abraham Lincoln (1)   RPB
The Cow With Wings, domestic comedy   CNA
Entertaining Programs for the Assembly in the Jewish Religious
    School, 1930
The Golden Staff, 1923, Succoth operetta, music by Samuel Goldfarb
The Great Hope, in Stratford Journal, 5, Oct.-Dec., 1919, 321-5 (1)

ELMA EHRLICH LEVINGER (continued)

How Succoth Came to Chayim, 1923 (1)	
In the Night Watches, n.d., for High School (1)	MB
Israel's Arrow, 1924, Lag B'omer fantasy in verse	RPB
It Is Time, 1936, peace play (1)	RPB
Jephthah's Daughter, 1921, Drama League prize play (1) RPB, TAJ,FON, CJP	
Jewish Festivals in the Religious School, 1923, handbook for	
entertainments	
"Let There Be Light," 1920? pageant for religious schools	OCH
The Light of Israel, 1923, Chanukah play, 4 acts	
Out of Egypt, 1923, Passover play for senior students, 3 acts	
The Pageant of Esther, 1923, Purim pageant play	MB
Passover Entertainments, 1924	NBuG
A Present for Mr. Lincoln	JEL
A Program on Social Justice for High School, 192?	OCH
Purim Entertainments, 1924	NBuG
The Return of the Prodigal, 1927, first prize in religious drama contest	RPB
of Drama League (1)	
Ruth, 1924, little play for Shabuoth	RPB
Ruth of Moab, 1923, springtime play (1)	
Shabuoth Entertainments, 1924	NBuG
A Sick Purim, 1923 (1)	
The Silver Cup, 1923, Passover folk play (1)	
The Star of Judah, 1923, Purim play, 5 acts	
Succoth Entertainments, 1924	NBuG,MiD
The Tenth Man, 1931, also in Drama, 19, April, 1929, 204-6+ (1)	RPB
Through the School Year, 1925, collection for holidays	RPB
The Unlighted Menorah, 1923, Chanukah fantasy of the time of Felix	
Mendelssohn (1)	
The Young Defender, 1922, short sketch for Hanukka	RPB

MARJORIE RICE LEVIS

Blackouts, 1932, fourteen revue sketches, ed. by Levis (includes her	RPB
"What Price 'Grand Slam'?")	
"Don't Believe Everything You Hear!" 1925, revues	NRB
Revue Sketches, 1931	RPB
Ten Snappy Revue Sketches, 1936	RPB

EDITH M. LEVY

At the End of the Rope (1)	SCT

ALICE NORRIS LEWIS (or NORRIS-LEWIS)

Betty's Paris Hat, 1924, 2 act comedy	RPB
Bob's General Manager, 1925	RPB
The Campaigner, 1927, comedy	RPB
Exemption, 1918, Great War playlet (1)	RPB
Prisoners in Millersville, 1921, 4 act farcical drama	RPB
The Spy at St. Agnes, 1918, patriotic play for girls	RPB
Those Fraternity Blues, 1932, for high school or college (1)	RPB

CAROLINE LEWIS

The Only Girl in Sight, 1928, 3 act comedy	RPB

CARRIE BULLARD LEWIS (1865- ?)
The Captivity, 1939, cantata, text adapted from Oliver Goldsmith   DLC
Christmas With the Brownie Chimney Sweeps, 1923, young   RPB
The Parson's Sociable, 1928 or before, song or musical recitation
The Queen of the Garden, 1914, operetta for children, with Frederick   DLC
    H. Martens
The Rose and the Ring, 1934, operetta extravaganza in 2 acts, based on
    Thackeray, with Mary W. Kingsley

ELIZABETH MAY LEWIS
Uncle Sandy, Detective; or, the Flame that Lights the World, 1923,   RPB
    comedy

EMILY SARGENT LEWIS
A Dream of Brave Women, 1912, verses to be read to tableaux of women
    famous in American History, prod. at Republic Theatre, N.Y.C. by
    Women's Political Union
Election Day, 1912, suffrage play   RPB, FOV

JUSTINA LEWIS
The Eternal Megalosaurus, prod. 1918 Neighborhood Playhouse,   NN
    typescript (1)

LILA IRENE LEWIS
A Peace Pageant, in The Industrial Arts Magazine, 6, June, 1917, 231-2

LILLIAN LEWIS
Protesilaus and Laodania, 1925, 2 act poetic play   RPB

MARGARET LEWIS (See MARGARET CAMERON)

RENA LEWIS
A Hanukka Surprise, 1922   RPB

ROSA LEWIS
Hobo Drill, 1918, drill for boys   RPB

"VILLA LEWIS" (See JANE TUPMAN)

IRENE LEWISOHN (1892-1944) NAW
The Arab Fantasia
A Burmese Pwe, prod. 1925-6 at Neighborhood Playhouse
Israel, 1928, symphony for orchestra, with Ernest Bloch, arranged for   NN
    the stage by Lewisohn, typescript
A Pagan Poem, 1929-30, symphonic poem by Charles Martin Loeffler,   NN
    after Virgil, stage version by Lewisohn, typescript
Quatuon a cordes
Ritornelle, dance romance
The Salut au Monde
Sooner and Later, 1925, dance satire, music by Emerson Whithorne
Tone Pictures, stage version of Charles T. Griffes
The White Peacock, stage version of Charles T. Griffes

IRMA LICCIONE (See MILDRED CORELL)

FRANCES LIGHTNER
Puppets, prod. 1925, melodrama and puppet show

FLORENCE LINCOLN
Barbara, prod. 1917
The End of the Bridge, 1911, won the John Craig Prize, Harvard
A Piece of Ivory, in Harvard Monthly, 52, April, 1911, 56-7 (1)

MAUD MC KNIGHT LINDSAY (1874- ?)
The First Christmas Morning   CP

CAROLYN CROSBY WILSON LINK (also CAROLYN WILSON)
What Can I Do? in St. Nicholas, 45, May, 1918, 599-603

NELLIE MEADER LINN
Aunt Mary's Blunder, 1931 (1)   RPB
Bill's Rummage Sale, 1932, farce (1)   RPB
The Children's Book, 1933, collection of songs, recitations, drills, RPB
    exercises and plays, with "Julian Lee" and Harriette Wilburr
Henry's "Tux," 1930 (1)   RPB
Nice Bossy, 1937 (1)   DLC

FANNIE BARNETT LINSKY
American and the Jew, 1923, pageant for Thanksgiving
Americans All, 1929 (1)   RPB
A Bit of Scandal, 1921, 2 act comedy for females   RPB
The Box From the Attic (1)   FMM
The Counting of the Days, 1929, Lag b'Omer cycle
Cupid and Calories, 1923, 3 act comedy for women   RPB
The End of the Story, 1928, Hanukkah play
Forest Acres, 1921, 3 act comedy   RPB
Frills and Furbelows, 1926, "two-act comedy of facts and figures for RPB
    female characters"
Happy New Year, 1929 (1)   RPB
The Hut, 1922, 3 act comedy   RPB
In-laws and Outlaws, 1926, 3 act comedy for females   RPB
A Memorial Day Fantasy (1)   FMM
Norah Mixes In, 1926, 2 act comedy for females   RPB
Old Gems in New Settings, 1926, three plays written especially for RPB
    schools and camps
Old Pictures in New Frames, 1929, group of tableaux for any holiday RPB
The Pageant of the Law, 1930, Sh'vuos program   RPB
The Paper Hat, 1924, for Purim, 2 acts
Party Day, 1927, young   RPB
Patsy, 1921, 2 act comedy for females   RPB
Pictures From the Book of Exodus for Passover, 1930   RPB
A Purim Fantasy, 1929 (1)
The Sabbath Angel, 1929, 2 acts   RPB
Sammy. 1929, 3 act comedy   RPB
The Set-the-Table Lady (1)   FMC
Sundown, 1935 (1)   RPB
Threescore Years and Ten, 1924? pageant, typed copy   NN
The Way of a Maid; or, Dear "You," 1924, 3 act comedy   RPB

CLARA LIPMAN (MRS. LOUIS MANN) (1869- ?)
Billy With a Punch
Children of Today, 1926, prod. 1913, with Samuel Shipman, satirical RPB
    comedy-drama
Elevating a Husband, prod. 1912, with Samuel Shipman, typed copy MH,ICU
Flames and Embers, with Samuel Shipman

CLARA LIPMAN (continued)
The Head of the House, with Samuel Shipman
His Protege
House of Evil, 1954, with Michael Lipman   play?   DLC
It Depends on the Woman, with Samuel Shipman
Julie Bonbon, prod. 1906
The Lady from Westchester
Nature's Nobleman, prod. 1921, with Samuel Shipman
The Royal Maid, with Samuel Shipman
The Temperamental Girl

EMMA GERBERDING LIPPARD
Why We Are Thankful, 1928, exercise for children   RPB

MARION W. LIPPINCOTT
The Mysterious Valentine, 1926, romantic comedy   RPB

JULIE MATHILDE LIPPMAN (1864- ?)
Cousin Faithful, 1908 (1)   RPB
The Facts in the Case, 1912, farce (1)   RPB
A Fool and His Money, 1913, 2 act comedy   RPB
Martha by-the-day, 1919, 3 acts, "optimistic comedy," adapted from her   RPB
    novel

BESS LIPSCHULTZ
Marriages Are Made, prod. 1918 by Actors' and Authors' Theatre Inc.

MRS. M. A. LIPSCOMB
Ladies of Athens, 1905, Greek comedy (1)   RPB

LYDIA WARREN LISTER
The King of Spades, n.d., comic opera   C
The Speeders, 1929, with Henry B. Lister and Marie E. Coe, 3 act comedy RPB

GRACE DENIO LITCHFIELD (1849- ?)
The Nun of Kent, 1911, 5 act medieval tragedy   RPB
Vita, 1904, allegorical drama   RPB
Women as Advocates, in Independent, 55, July 9, 1903, 1627-30 (1)

THERESE LITTEL
Mansions, 1929, 3 act comedy for young women   RPB

MRS. W. S. LITTLE
The Historical Pageant, State Normal School, Bridgewater, in Mass.   MB
    State Normal School, Bridgewater, 75th Anniversary, 1915, 79-87,
    directed by Lotta Clark

ETHEL LIVINGSTON
A Difference in Clocks, 1900, sketch in one scene   RPB

MYRTLE ATHLEEN SMITH LIVINGSTON (1902- ?)
For Unborn Children, in Crisis, 32, July, 1926, 122-4 (1)   HSB

RUBY ERWIN LIVINGSTON
In Review, 1920-9?
Steal Away Home, 1929, dramatic reading of the Sunny South   RPB

ANNE GLADYS LLOYD (GLADYS LLOYD) ("SOMPLE") (1889- ?)
A.B.C. Capers, by Gladys Lloyd, young, (by "Somple" at RPB) (1)   RPB
Bonnie Highlanders, 1930, Scotch drill   RPB
The Children's Armistice Day Book, 1926   RPB
The Children's Closing Day Book, 1929   Or, DLC
The Children's Halloween Book, 1926   RPB
The Christmas Book, 1931, by Gladys Lloyd   RPB
Commencement Specialties, 1926, for jr. h. s., by Gladys Lloyd   NcC
The Complete Christmas Book, 1923, by "Somple"
The Complete Social Book, 1930   RPB
Drill of the Bright Examples, in Florence Signor, Ed., Health Plays and
    Dialogues
Easy Parodies for Popular Singing, 1939, by Gladys Lloyd   RPB
Easy Recitations and Dialogs, 1932, by Gladys Lloyd   RPB
Economical Abbie, 1924, comedy, by "Somple"   RPB
The Favorite Closing Day Collection, 1929   Or, DLC
The Favorite Halloween Collection, 1928   RPB
Graduation Days, 1926
Halloween Frolics for Little Folks, 1927, by Gladys Lloyd   RPB
The Happy Christmas Book, 1924, by "Somple"   NN, DLC
Here Comes the Groom! 1924, farce, by Gladys Lloyd (1)   RPB
The House that Jack Built, 1922, by "Somple" (1)   RPB
Jack-in-the-box, 1924, Christian dialog, by "Somple"   RPB
Jingle Bells, 1930, singing musical piece for any number of children, by   RPB
    "Somple"
Johnny and His Pa, 1930, farce   RPB
The Kiddies' Christmas Book, 1925, by Gladys Lloyd, with Carolyn   RPB
    Freeman and others
Merry Christmas for Young Folks, 1938, by Gladys Lloyd   RPB
Merry Christmas in the Primary Grades, 1932, by Gladys Lloyd   RPB
Mr. Massey Makes a Fourth at Bridge, 1930, farce (1)   RPB
More Stunts, 1931   RPB
Mother Goose Dramatized, 1923, collection of one-acts   NN, DLC
Of Course! 1930, farce by "Somple"   RPB
One Madding Day and Knight, 1924, by "Somple"   RPB
The Santa Claus Package, 1928 (1)   RPB
Sleighbell Capers, 1930, drill   RPB
Spring Victorious, 1928, by "Somple," young   RPB
Stunts for Everybody, 1930   RPB
Ten One-Act Humorous Plays for High School and Adults, 1932, by
    Gladys Lloyd   RPB
The Thanksgiving Program Book, 1931, by Gladys Lloyd   DLC
Thanksgiving School Programs, 1927, by Gladys Lloyd   RPB
Tip-Top Halloween Book, 1925   WaT
Up on the Housetop and Other Plays for Christmas, 1931   RPB
Vacation, 1923, closing day play, by "Somple"   RPB
Wanted: a Private Secretary, 1931, pantomime   RPB
The Wedding of Rudy and Nanette, 1931, pantomime   DLC

ELIZABETH ERWIN MILLER LOBINGIER (1889- ?)
The Dramatization of Bible Stories, 1927, "experiment in the religious   RPB
    education of children"
Dramatization in the Church School, 1923, "training course for   RPB
    leaders"
Informal Dramatization in Missionary Education, 1930   NcD, DLC
William Tyndale, 1925   OO

JOYCE E. LOBNER
The Golden Eagle   BAO

HELEN BEATRICE LOCHLAN
Irene Ashton; or, the Stolen Child, 1911, 5 act melodrama   RPB
The Spirit of Christmas, 1893, "prelude to the distribution of presents   RPB
    on Christmas Eve at the Independent Liberal Church, Greenwich, Mass."

BELLE MARSHALL LOCKE ("NELLIE M. LOCKE")
Belle Marshall Locke's Original Monologues and Sketches, 1903   RPB
Breezy Point, 1898, 3 act comedy for women   RPB
The Great Catastrophe, c.1895 (1913 ed. at RPB), by "Nellie M. Locke,"   RPB
    2 act comedy
A Heartrending Affair, 1911, by "Nellie M. Locke," monologue for a   RPB
    lady
The Hiartville Shakespeare Club, 1920, farce (1)   RPB
Humorous Monologues and Dramatic Scenes, 1908   RPB
Marie's Secret, 1894, duologue   RPB
Miss Fearless and Co., 1905, 3 act comedy for females   RPB
Mr. Easyman's Niece, 1908, 4 act comedy   RPB
Original Monologues and Sketches, 1903
A Victim of Woman's Rights, 1896, monologue, by "Nellie M. Locke"   RPB

CECILIA LOFTUS
The Lancers, 1908, with George Spink, musical version of a play by Daly

ELMA M. LOGIE
An Old Maid's Venture, 1916, comedy (1)   RPB

GRACE E. LONERGAN
The Doormat   ECO

LILY AUGUSTA LONG (? -1927)
The Masque of the Year, 1887, music arranged by Sarah D. Chapin   RPB
Pageant of Minnesota, 1911, St. Paul, Minn.
Radison, the Voyageur, 1914, 4 act verse drama   RPB

EDNA B. LONGNECKER
The Day of Rest, 1932, 3 act comedy   RPB
Hands Up, 1926 (1)   RPB
The Lingerie Shop, 1928, comedy (1)   RPB
The Orchid, 1926   RPB
The Passing of Mr. Peal, 1926, comedy (1)   RPB
References, 1928, 3 act comedy-drama, "prize winning play" in   RPB, PP-2
    Penn Pub. Co. contest

CAROLINE JUDKINS LONGYEAR
Spring, 1928, 3 act medieval romance   RPB

HELEN LEA LONSDALE
Blind Dates, 1927   RPB
Cupid's Assistant, 1928   RPB
Every Rose Has Its Thorn, 1928   RPB
A Startling Discovery, 1928   RPB
(All part of Wetmore declamation bureau, Readings, plays,
    entertainments, v. 19)

BARBARA LOOK
  Pageant of Martha's Vineyard, 1911, West Tisbury, Mass.

ANITA LOOS (1888?-1981) AWW NWAT
  The Amazing Adele, prod. 1955, musical based on a play by Pierre   NN
    Barrillet and Jean-Pierre Gredy; lyrics and music by Albert Selden,
    typescript
  Biography of a Bachelor Girl, 1934, filmscript
  Blossoms in the Dust, 1940, screenplay with Ralph Wheelwright and   CLSU
    Dorothy Yost, mimeograph copy
  Calico Vampire, filmscript
  Cheri, 1959, dramatization of novel by Colette, typescript   NN
  The Fall of Eve, prod. 1925, with John Emerson
  Gentlemen Prefer Blondes, prod. 1926, with John Emerson, (musical   NN
    version 1949, with Joseph Fields) typescript; filmed 1928 and 1953,
    musical version filmed 1949 and 1974
  Gigi, 1952, prod. 1951, dramatization of a novel by Colette, pub. in   RPB
    Theatre Arts, 36, July, 1952, 41-69
  Gogo Loves You, prod. 1964, musical
  Happy Birthday, 1947, prod. 1946   RPB
  His Picture in the Papers, 1916, filmscript
  Information Please, with John Emerson
  Lorelei, 1974, version of Gentlemen Prefer Blondes
  The New York Hat, 1912, filmscript
  Nine Fifteen Revue, prod. 1930
  Red-Headed Woman, 1932, filmscript
  San Francisco, 1936, screenplay   RPB
  The Social Register, prod. 1931, with John Emerson
  Something About Anne, prod. 1966, translation and adaptation of play,
    "The King's Mare," by Jean Canolle, musical
  The Whole Town's Talking, 1925, prod. 1923, with John Emerson,   RPB
    3 act farce
  Wild Girl of the Sierras, filmscript
  The Women, 1939, filmscript

GRACE K. LOOSLEY
  "The Inner Urge," 1930, pageant compiled and adapted for the Illinois   RPB
    State Nurses' Assoc., typed copy

HELEN TUCKER LORD
  Mrs. Jones' Afternoon Tea, 1907   RPB

KATHARINE LORD
  At Midnight, 1934 (1)   RPB
  *The Day Will Shakespeare Went to Kenilworth, 1916   RPB
  *The Greatest Gift, 1915, Christmas   RPB
  The Lark, 1916   RPB
  The Little Play Book, 1920, collection of one-acts   RPB
  *The Minister's Dream, 1916, in The Delineator, 80, Nov., 1912, 358-9   RPB
  Pageant of the Evolution of Industry, 1912, in The Playground, 5,
    March, 1912, 407-10
  Plays for School and Camp, 1922, young   RPB
    *Also in The Little Playbook)

CARRIE LORENZ
  Mother Blessing's Job, 1926, "to be given near Mother's Day" (1)   RPB

EMILIE BAKER LORING
  Where's Peter? 1928, 3 act comedy, prize winner Penn   RPB, PP-2
    Pub. Co. contest

LINA LORING
  Hallow-e'en, 1930, juvenile operetta   RPB-M
  Washington's Birthday, 1929, juvenile operetta   RPB-M

"MINA LOUISE" (See MINA LOUISE HENDERSON)

KATHERINE LOUNBERG
  The Flamingo Feather, in Glints in the Sand, South H. S., Minneapolis,
    Minn., 1924

GRACE CONSTANT LOUNSBERRY
  Delilah, 1904, 3 act poetic drama   RPB
  The Picture of Dorian Gray, 1913, 3 act dram. of novel by Oscar Wilde

CLARA M. LOVE
  George Washington Does Not Go to Sea (1)

HARRIET LOVE
  The Coontown Wedding, 1925, mock marriage in black face   RPB

MARY CATHERINE LOVE
  The Thrill to Power, 1929, drama   RPB

CAROLINE C. LOVELL
  Prince Charming's Fate, in St. Nicholas, 30, Feb., 1903, 350-9, 3 acts
  The Swayam-Vara, 1916
  The War Woman, in Drama, 13, Oct., 1922, 23-6 (1)   RCT
  Wuthering Heights, 1914, drama of the novel

LUCILE LOVELL
  The Voices of the Trees, 1909, masque   RPB

LUCILE LOVEMAN
  The Snow Queen, prod. at Peabody House, Harvard 47 Workshop play

MABEL F. LOVING
  The Airship, 1906, romantic opera   RPB

LUCY LOWE
  The Bitterly Reviled, in Poet Lore, 33, Summer, 1922, 300-7 (1)

EDITH LOWELL
  Camp Fidelity Girls, 1920, 4 act comedy, based on a story by Annie   RPB
    Hamilton Donnell
  Moment Musical, 1931, poetical play to be given with incidental music RPB
    by Schubert
  Moment Pathetique, 1931, poetic play to be given with incidental music RPB
    by Tschaikovsky
  A Portrait of Mankind, 1925 (1)   RPB
  The Power of Suggestion, 1933, monologue   RPB
  Runaway Robots (The Three Strange Visitors), 1931   RPB
  A Score of Sure-fire Monologues, 1929   RPB

EDITH LOWELL (continued)
Tell a Woman, 1928, 15- minute sketch for two women   RPB
Tickets for the Sheffield Choir, 1921, dramatization of story by   RPB
   Elizabeth Weir, comedy (1)
Twenty-one Good Monologues, 1933, with Olive White Fortenbacher,   RPB
   Mildred W. Baker and others
Varnish, 1927, comedy (1)   RPB

MINA LOY (1882-1966)   AWW
The Pamperers, in Dial, 69, July, 1920, 65-78 (1)

IDA LUBLENSKI (See IDA LUBLENSKI EHRLICH)

HELENE ELISE LUCAS
Tiger Blood and Nine Other One-Act Plays, 1928   RPB

ALETHEA LUCE
The Gift, prod. 1924, with Julia Chandler
The K Guy, prod. 1928, with Walter De Leon

GRACE A. LUCE
Brass Buttons, 1900, 3 act comedy for females   RPB

HELEN GILMAN LUDINGTON (ROTCH)
A Lunch in the Suburbs, 1906 (under Rotch) farce for women (1)   RPB
The Suffragette, 1909, comedy (1)   NN

ADELE LUEHRMANN
"Butting In" in French, in Smart Set, 31, Aug., 1910, 125-7 (1)
Disciples of the Art, in Smart Set, 33, Feb., 1911, 57-9 (1)

ANNA MAY (IRWIN) LUETKENHAUS (1874- ?)
America the Beautiful, Democracy's Goal, pageant, with Margaret   LNP
   Knox, in St. Nicholas, 47, June, 1920, 738-44 (1)
Education's Progress (1)   LNP
The Future of America as Our Young Folks See It, with Margaret Knox,   LNP
   pageant, in St. Nicholas, 47, Jan., 1920, 160-4 (1)
Master Skylark, 1914, dramatization of the book by John Bennett   RPB, LPS
A Modern Knight, Theodore Roosevelt (1)   LNP
New Plays for School Children, 1929, ed. by Luetkenhaus   RPB
Plays for School Children, 1915, ed. by Luetkenhaus   RPB
The Rainy Day Book for Boys and Girls, 1924, with Margaret Knox, plays?
Story and Play Readers, 1917, with Margaret Knox, 3 volumes
Theodore Roosevelt—a Great Soldier (1)   LNP
Tommy's Dream of Christmas Night (1)   LNP

ELIZA O'BRIEN LUMMIS
The Dear Saint Elizabeth, 1913, tragic romance of true history   RPB

EMMIE ANTOINETTE LUQUES (1854- ?)
The Snow Image and Other Plays, 1914, one-acts for children suitable   RPB
   for stage or schoolroom

PEARL LUSK
Her First Trip, 1925, monologue   RPB
Our Automobile, 1925, monologue   RPB

GRACE WELSH LUTGEN (1888- ?)
Mrs. Haynes Joines (sic) the Club, 1930, for women, "written especially   RPB
  to promote interest in Community service" (1)
Mrs. Jones Entertains Strange Callers, 1935 (1)
Pageants for Schools, Clubs and Civic Groups, 1943   RPB

MABEL LYMAN
Holliston Historical Pageant, 1724-1924, Holliston, Mass.   MB

FRANCES LYNCH
He Understood Women, prod. 1928, with Michael Kallesser

BEULAH LYON
The Pouter Pigeon, 1928, 3 act comedy   RPB

CLARA O. LYON
The Campus   APS

MARGARET CURRIER LYON
The Pledging of Polly, 1909, with Abby Bullock, 2 act farce   RPB
The Visit of Obadiah, 1907, with Eunice Fuller, farce for females   RPB

HARRIET LYONS
Exit the Villain, 1924, operetta presented by Barnswallows, Wellesley   RPB-M
  College; music by Lydia Green and others

M

PAULINE ARNOUX MAC ARTHUR
The Apocalypse, 1919, dramatic oratorio in a prologue and 3 parts,   RPB
    text drawn mainly from the Book of Daniel and the Apocalypse, with
    Henri Pierre Roche

VENITA RICH MC BURNEY
Pigtail Days, 1929   RPB
Underweight, 1929, monologue   RPB

ESTHER B. MC CABE
Evening Belles, 1924, comedy (1)   RPB

HARRIET A. MC CABE
The Charity Bazaar, 1916, 2 act entertainment   RPB

HAZEL G. MC CABE
Pa Goes to Court, 1931, 3 act comedy drama   RPB
The Path Between, 1929 (1)   BAO

MAEBELLE MC CALMENT
An Old Magazine, 1927, whimsey for 3 girls   RPB

GRACE DIETRICH MC CARTHY
Plays From the Wonder-book and Tanglewood Tales, 1910,   RPB
    dramatization of Hawthorne's version of the classic myths

LILLIAN GAYTON MAC CARTHY
Fine Clothes, 1928-9

CLARICE VALLETTE MC CAULEY
The Conflict, 1930, also in Vagabond Plays, 1921, series 1   RPB,STW,STC,SCO
Dinah, Queen of the Berbers, 1920, 3 act religious drama   RPB
The Queen's Hour, in Drama, 10, June, 1920, 295-300, "springtime morality
    play" (1)
A Return (1)
The Seeker, 1920, pageant, music by William J. Kraft   RPB
Sons of Strangers, 1924, "masque for friendly souls"   RPB
The Threshold, 1920   SFM

SUSAN AUSTIN (ARNOLD) MC CAUSLAND (1839- ?)
Did Lucifer Laugh? and other photoplays, 1924   RPB

KATE WISNER MC CLUSKEY
    (She did the following arrangements:)
Armgart, by George Eliot   PTS-II
The Balcony Scene, from Cyrano de Bergerac   PTS-II
Confessions, by A. Conan Doyle (from A Duet)   PTS-II
Cured, from The Tenor, by H. C. Bunner   PTS-III
The Examination, (from Bonaventure) by George W. Cable   PTS-II
The Falcon, by Tennyson   PTS-II
In Trust, (the library scene from Romola by George Eliot)   PTS-II
A Midsummer Night's Dream   PTS-II
A Misdemeanor of Nancy, by Eleanor Hoyt   PTS-II

KATE WISNER MC CLUSKEY (continued)
The Mothers of Edward, from story by Myra Kelley, in Ladies Home   PTS-II
    Journal, October, 1906
A Nanny's Cottage, from The Little Minister by J. M. Barrie   PTS-II
School Scene, from Hard Times by Charles Dickens   PTS-II
The Temptation, from Edmond Rostand's The Princess Faraway   PTS-II
Topsy, from Uncle Tom's Cabin   PTS-II
Two Gentlemen of Verona   PTS-II
The Will, from The Lane That Had No Turnip by Gilbert Parker   PTS-III

ELSIE MALONE MC COLLUM
In Grandma's Chest, 1897, monologue for a lady   NN
Pieces and Plays for All Ages, 1929

EDITH R. MC COMAS
Brasstacks, 1928, 3 act comedy drama   RPB

GENEVIEVE KNAPP MC CONNELL (1876- ?)
The Bone of Contention, 1918, fairy melodrama (1)   RPB

EDNA WAHLERT MC COURT
Jill's Way, in Seven Arts, 1, February, 1917, 328-35 (1)
The Truth, in Seven Arts, 1, March, 1917, 475-92 (1)

MARJORIE MC CREARY
A Christmas Revolt, 1928, young   RPB

JUNIE MC CREE (1866-1918)
The Happiest Night of His Life, prod. 1911, with Sydney Rosenfeld
Mamma's Baby Boy, prod. 1912, musical farce, music by Hans S. Linne
    and Will H. Becker
"Moving Pictures," 19?? "peep behind the doors of a moving picture   NN
    studio," typed copy and prompt book

JENNIE VAN HEYSON MC CRILLIS
Milk Fairies, 1919, good health play   RPB

CATHARINE WAUGH MC CULLOCH
Bridget's Sisters; or, the Legal Status of Illinois Women 1868, 1911 FOV

MAUDE WHEELER MC DANIEL (MRS. LEX MC DANIEL)
Are You Enlisted? 1928, written for the "Kate Cox White Circle,"   RPB
    Calvary Baptist Church, Kansas City, Mo.

ANNA SPRAGUE MC DONALD
Florian's Wife, prod. 1923, adapt. of Pirandello
Fortunate, prod. 1917-8, adapt. of Quinteros
Guiber, 1919, miracle play of Our Lady from the Old French   RPB
Ivan the Daring

DORA MARY MAC DONALD
The Advice Doctor, 1932, better English play   RPB
The American Way, 1941, patriotic play (1)   RPB
An Old English Christmas, 1938, play pageant   RPB
Apple Pie, 1947, comedy (1)   RPB
Applicants, 1913? better English play   NBuG
Assembly Programs, 1941, collection of 15-minute skits

DORA MARY MAC DONALD (continued)

Autograph Anne, 1931	RPB
The Award, 1932? "play in 2 scenes to stress courtesy in school"	RPB
The Baby Sitter, 1948, comedy (1)	RPB
The Ballyhoo, 1932	RPB
Bell Hop, 1935	DLC
The Blue Jeans Girl, 1947, comedy (1)	RPB
Butch, 1946, comedy (1)	Or, MiD
Carnival Capers for Schools, 1932, amusements	
The Christmas Miracle, 1947 (1)	RPB
"Chums," 1932, 3 act comedy	RPB
Clever Plays for Junior High Schools, 1932	RPB
The Cornhusk Doll, 1934	
For the Love of Mike, 1947, comedy (1)	RPB
"Fore!" 1934	BCC
Fred Outwits the Enemy, 1942 (1)	RPB
Goin' Modern, 1935, 3 act farce	RPB
The Great Joanne, 1937, comedy (1)	RPB
Hard-boiled, 1939 (1)	RPB
Her Adopted Land, 1941, patriotic drama (1)	RPB
Hired Girl, 1945, comedy (1)	MiD
His Personal Armistice, 1938, Armistice Day play (1)	OrCS, DLC
Honorary Colonel, 1942, patriotic (1)	DLC
"Hot Dogs!"	BCC
"In a Radio Studio," 1931, novelty skit (1)	NN, MiD
Jimmie's Wife, 1945, comedy (1)	MiD
Judy Takes Over, 1947, comedy (1)	RPB
Let Nothing Ye Dismay, 1938, Christmas (1)	RPB
The Little Patriot, 1942, "timely one-act play,"	DLC
The Mislaid Princes, 1946, comedy (1)	MiD
The Mouse and the Marquis, 1946, comedy (1)	MiD
Murder in the Family, 1948 (1)	MiD
Novelty Stunts, 1932, collection of skits and stunts	
Oh, Gloria! 1932, comedy for women (1)	RPB
Orchids for Thanksgiving, 1938, comedy drama (1)	RPB
Patriotic Plays for Our National Holidays, 1932	RPB
Pat's Pin, 1932, 3 act comedy	RPB
The Perfect Mother, 1947, comedy drama (1)	RPB
Pledges, 1932? play stressing good manners	RPB
Purpose Plays for High School Assemblies, 1932-1940	RPB
The Senior Activities Book, 1940	Or, DLC
A Sense of Values, 1946 (1)	MiD
She Gets Her Man, 1932? allegorical playlet to teach good health	RPB
Shock Treatment, 1949, comedy (1)	RPB
So That Was War! 1937, for Armistice Day or any occasion	DLC
"Sorority House," 1938, 3 act comedy	RPB
Spring Is Here, 1945, comedy (1)	MiD
Susan Gets a House, 1948, comedy (1)	MiD
Tell Tale Television, 1937 (1)	DLC
Thanksgiving, family style, 1938, comedy drama (1)	RPB
There Comes a Time, 1946, comedy (1)	Or, MiD
They Teach English, 1930	RPB
Too Many Maskers, 1932, 3 act comedy	RPB
"Uncle Santa Claus," 1932	RPB
Who Told the Truth? 1931, comedy (1)	RPB
Yankee Girl, 1943, "timely one-act play"	RPB
Ye Olde Photograph Album, 1931, novelty pantomime in one scene	

LAETITIA MC DONALD (IRWIN) (1890- ?)
Lady Alone, prod. 1927

LUCILLE MC DONALD
Fairy Facts, in Chrysalid, Sisters of Mercy, Mt. Mercy Academy, Grand
Rapids, Michigan, 1927

MRS. M. C. MC DONALD
The Message, 1908, dramatic sketch   RPB

ZILLAH (ZELLAH) KATHERINE MAC DONALD (1885- ?)
Circumventin' Sandy, in Drama, 16, May, 1926, 291-3; reprinted with
    corrections in Drama, 17, Feb., 1927, 145-6, 157-9, comedy (1)
The Feather Fisher, Keeper of Pure Water, in Touchstone, 3, June, 1918,
    229-36 (1)
L'ami
Light Along the Rails, in Touchstone, 3, June, 1918, 229-36 (1)
The Long Box, in Drama, 14, Feb., 1924, 180-2+ (1)
Lost! Strayed! Stolen! Santa Claus, won the All American Drama League
    prize, (with Estelle H. Davis?)
Markheim, dramatization of R. L. Stevenson story (1)   MP
Our John, 1925
Two Gentlemen of the Bench   YSP-II

AMICE MAC DONNELL (LEE) (MRS. R. W. LEE) (under Lee in NUC)
The Enterprise of the "Mayflower," 1913, 4 acts, young   RPB
Historical Plays for Children, 1909
The Name on the Rock, 1933, 3 acts
The Production of School Plays, 1934
Robin Hood, 1928   RPB
The Sacred Fire, 1924, morality play for the League of Nations (1)   NN
Saint George, and Beowulf (2 plays), 1913   MH
The Way of the Heart, 1913   NN

CHARLEEN MC DOWELL
The Prodigal Daughter, 1926, with Clifton E, Johnson   RPB

MARIAN GRISWOLD (NEVINS) MAC DOWELL
(MRS. EDWARD MAC DOWELL) (1857-1956)
Peterborough Pageant, 1910, Peterborough, N. H.   RPB, MB

MARGARET JULIA MC ELROY (1889- ?)
Heart's Ease and Rue, n. d., program for Decoration Day   MiD
King of the Elves, n. d., young (1)   MiD
Little New Year, 1922, pageant of the seasons, a dramatic and musical   MiD
    program
The Mother Speaks, n. d., school program for all grades   MiD
On a May-day Morning Early, 1922, out-of-door spring pageant for   MiD
    school grades
On Christmas Eve, n. d., dramatic carol service for school grades   MiD
St. Valentine's Picture Book, 1928, dramatic and musical program   RPB
    for school grades
The Shut-up Posy, 192? dramatic and musical program for school   RPB
    grades, spring pageant
Soul of Priscilla, 1920, school entertainment for all grades   MiD

ALICE MC EWEN
Masque of Arcadia, 1910, Detroit, Michigan

ELIZABETH APTHORP MC FADDEN (1875-1961)
Beggarman, Thief
The Boy Who Discovered Easter, 1926, adaptation of a story by   RPB
   Raymond MacDonald Alden (1)
The Chimes or Why the Chimes Rang, 1915, from a story by   RPB
   Raymond McDonald Alden (1)
Double Door, 1934, prod. 1933, 3 act melodrama   RPB
If Liberty Dies Here, 1944 (1)   RPB
Knights of the Silver Shield, 1929, from a story by Ramond   RPB
   McDonald Alden (1)
The Man Without a Country, 1918, with Agnes Crimmins,   RPB
   dramatization of a story by Edward Everett Hale
The Palace of Knossos, 1931, play of Theseus and the Minotaur   RPB, DSS
The Product of the Mill, 1912, won the John Craig prize, Harvard   RPB
A Salute to the Fourth, 1939, series of one-act plays for children dealing with
   freedom and democracy
A Selected List of Plays for Amateurs and Students of Dramatic Expression
   in Schools and Colleges, 1908, compiled by McFadden and Lilian E. Davis
Signature, prod. 1945
Tidings of Joy, 1933, Christmas (1)   RPB, ETO
Why the Chimes Rang, 1915 (1)
Why the Chimes Rang and Other Plays for Church and School, 1929

ANNE MAC FARLANE
Slippers, in Poet Lore, 32, Autumn, 1921, 425-30 (1)
When the Little Old Lady Spoke, 1928 or earlier, missionary play, by Anna
   McFarlane

LYDIA A. MC GAUGHEY
An International Incident, 1931, Japanese play   RPB
A Pair of Boots and Robert Joins the A.H.T.A., 1914, monologues   RPB
Rousing Roberta, 1930 play?   DLC

GRACE WINIFRED MC GAVRAN (1896- ?)
Joy and Gladness Bringing, 1942, Christmas   DLC
The Shepherd Who Stayed Behind, 1927   RPB
Star Child, 1938, play of India for intermediate grades   DLC

MARY DAVID MC GEEHEE
For the Love of Mike, 1927, 2 acts   RPB

DAISY MC GEOCH
"Collaborators," 1904, duologue   OCl, ICU
Concert Cameos, 1922, collection of one-acts   DLC

SUSIE G. MC GLONE
A Virginia Heroine, 1908, 3 act comedy   RPB

MILDRED CRISS MC GUCKIN (1890- ?)
Wild Flower, 1922, poetic fantasy (1)   RPB

ELIZABETH JELLIFFE MAC INTIRE
Four Fairy Plays, dramatization and translation of Finnish tales by Z.
    Topelius, in Poet Lore, 28, 1917, 567-99
The Ivory Tower, with Colin Clements, in Poet Lore, 30, Spring, 1919,
    127-37 (1)

HELEN MC INTYRE
The Delicate Child, 1926, with Maurine Gee, won Samuel French prize in   RPB
    contest by General Federation of Women's Clubs

CRESSY MACK
A Bit of Gossip, 1925, comedy (1)   RPB

VIRGINIA WOODS MACKALL
The Fairy Rose, 1920, 2 act operetta for children, music by Eliza   RPB-M
    McCalmont Woods
The Runaway Song, 192?, musical fantasy for young folks, music by Eliza
    McCalmont Woods (an ad is at RPB)
In Tennie Weenie Land, n.d., musical pantomime for little children, with RPB
    Margaret Severn; to be acted to the music of Max E. Oberndorfer to
    be found in "The Tennie Weenie Music Book for Piano"

CONSTANCE D'ARCY MACKAY
Abraham Lincoln, Rail-splitter   SSH-III
America Triumphant, 1926, pageant of patriotism, commemorating   RPB
    signing of Declaration of Independence, also in Woman's Home
    Companion, 52, Oct., 1925, 10-1
Ashes of Roses, in Russell Sharp, et.al., High School Anthology,
    Literary Types
The Beau of Bath   WWO,GLL-II
The Beau of Bath and Other One Act Plays, 1915   RPB
Benjamin Franklin: Journeyman   LMS, WWS,WWY
The Boston Tea Party, in Woman's Home Companion, 38,   WWS, WWY
    June, 1911, 13, 55-6 (1)
Children's Theatres and Plays, 1927
The Christmas Guest, 1909, young   RPB, TAJ
Counsel Retained   PDP
Daniel Boone   FON
"Daniel Boone, patriot," 4th of July pageant for boys, in Delineator, 78, July,
    1911, 69-70
A Day at Nottingham, festival   CD
The Elf Child, 1909   OCl
The Enchanted Garden, 1909, young   RPB, TAJ
The Festival of Pomona, in Drama, 17, Feb., 1915, 161-71 (1)
The First Noel, in St Nicholas, 56, Dec., 1928, 108-9+ (1)
The Forest Princess and Other Masques, 1916   RPB
Franklin, 1921   LMS, WWS
The Gooseherd and the Goblin, in Drama, May, 1920.
Hawthorne Pageant, 1912, Tyringham, Mass.
Historical Pageant of Portland, Maine, 1913   MB
A Hosting of Heroes, n.d., pageant, patriotic community   MiD, OrP
    celebration, typed copy
The House of the Heart, 1925? young   RPB
The House of the Heart and Other Plays for Children, 1909   RPB
How to Produce Children's Plays, 1915
In the Days of Piers Ploughman, in Scholastic, 13, Nov. 3, Nov. 17, 1928,
    6-7, 10: 6-7 (1)

CONSTANCE D'ARCY MACKAY (continued)

Ladies of the White House, 1948, chronological play for a feminine cast   RPB

List of Plays, pageants, tableaux, recitations, ceremonials, and music   MB
   suitable for the celebration of the Pilgrim tercentenary, 1920? typed ms.

A Little Pilgrim's Progress, in St Nicholas, 37, Nov., 1909, 60-3 (1)

The Little Theatre in the United States, 1917   RPB

Masque of the Moon Princess, 1914, S. Hadley, Mass.

Memorial Day Pageant, 1910, arranged for communities and schools,   RPB
   pub. in Today's Magazine and The Popular Education

Memorial Day Pageant, 1915, N. Chillicothe, Ill.   MB

Midsummer Eve, 1929, outdoor fantasy   RPB

Nimble-Wit and Fingerkin, 1909   MRC

A Norse Festival, n.d., pageant, mimeograph copy   OrP

On Christmas Eve, 1909, young   SCS

Pageant of Concord, 1914, Concord, Mass.

A Pageant of Hours, 1909, young   NN, LU

Pageant of Patriots, 1911, Brooklyn, N. Y.

Pageant of Portland, 1913, Portland, Maine, programme text   NN

Pageant of Schenectady, 1912, Schenectady, N. Y. (She was director)   RPB

Pageant of Sunshine and Shadow, 1916, New York, programme text   NN
   (also called The Child Labor Pageant, for Nat. Child Labor Committee)

The Patriotic Christmas Pageant, 1918

Patriotic Drama in Your Town, 1918, manual of suggestions   RPB

Patriotic Plays and Pageants for Young People, 1915   RPB

The Pilgrims, pageant of progress, in Woman's Home Companion, 47, April,
   1920, 24-5

Play Production in Churches and Sunday Schools, 1921   ViU

Plays and Pageants for Young People, 1912

Plays of the Pioneers, 1915, historical pageant plays   RPB

The Prince of Court Painters   WWT

The Princess and the Pixies, 1909   RPB

Rural Drama Bibliography, n.d.   PP

The Silver Lining, in M. E. Haggerty and Dora V. Smith, Readings,   SSP,SSV
   and Literature Book III, 1928

The Silver Thread, 1921, 3 act Cornish folk play   MTP

The Silver Thread and Other Folk Plays, 1910   RPB

The Snow Witch, in The Delineator, 77, Feb., 1911, 161-4; in Jacob M. Ross,
   Adventures in Literature, 7B, 1928; and in W. L. Harvey, Junior Literature,
   7A, 1929 (1)

The Spirit of Christmas Joy, in The Delineator, 78, Dec., 1911, 514-6 (1)

Suggestions for the Dramatic Celebration of the 300th Anniversary of the NN
   Purchase of Manhattan, 1926

The Three Wishes, in Elmer R. Smith, et.al., Invitation to Reading I and
   in JacobM. Ross, Adventures in Literature, 7A

The Victory Pageant, 1918, for neighborhood prod., in Delineator, 94, June,
   1919, 78-9

William of Stratford, 1916, Baltimore, Md. (also called Baltimore
   Shakespeare Pageant)

Young Michelangelo, in E. A. Cross, Appreciating Literature, 1943 and in
   Horn Book, 5, Aug., 1929, 3-13 (1)

Youth's Highway and Other Plays for Young People, 1929   RPB

KATHERINE MACKAY

Gabrielle; A Dream from the Treasures Contained in the Letters of Abelard
   and Heloise, in North American Review, 176, April, 1903, 610-33

KATHRYN C. MC KAY
    Soul Mates, in Six One-Act Plays, MIA Book of Plays, Salt Lake City, 1929

LILIA MACKAY-CANTELL (See LILIA MACKAY CANTELL)

HAZEL MACKAYE (1880-1944)

The Awakening: Ten Tableaux on War and Peace, 1915, unpub. text	NhD
Caliban, 1917, Cambridge, Mass (She was director.)	
The Challenge, YWCA pageant	NhD
The Counsel, YWCA pageant	NhD
A Dream of Freedom, 1914, Cleveland, Ohio	
The Enchanted Urn, 1924, fantasy pantomime	NhD
Euclid in Wood (1)	NhD
Forward Into Light, Inez Milholland Pageant	NhD
Garden of the Gods, 1923, 75th anniversary of Equal Rights Meeting	NhD
Good Will, the Magician, n.d., peace pageant for children for Good Will Day	RPB, SPP
In Spirit and in Truth, 1920, convocation service for the YWCA	NhD, DLC
Inez Milholland Memorial Pageant	
Jubilee Pageant, 1916, New York, for 50th anniversary of YWCA	
Liberation: The Triumph of Reason in Religion, Unitarian pageant	NhD
The Magic of the Deed, YWCA pageant	NhD
Masque of Saratoga	NhD
The New Altar, YWCA pageant	NhD
The New Vision: A Masque of Industry, 1916, Buffalo, N. Y.	NhD
A Pageant for Peace, 1915, unpub. text	NhD
Pageant of Athens, 1915, masque, Poughkeepsie, N. Y.	
Pageant of Susan B. Anthony, 1915, Washington, D. C., text	NhD
Pipes of Pan, 1914, masque, Peterborough, N. H.	
Portals of Light, 1916, New York	
The Quest of Youth, 1924, pageant for schools, about history of education, see biblio. U. S. Bureau of Education Bulletin, 1924	RPB
Sanctuary, 1913, Buffalo, N. Y., masque (She was director)	
Six Periods of American Life, 1914, suffrage pageant	NhD
Suffrage Allegory, 1913, Washington, D. C., program	NhD
Susan B. Anthony	NhD
Through the Centuries, YWCA pageant	NhD
Uncle Sam's Birthday Pageant, 1913, Independence Day program, Washington, D. C., program	NhD
The Urn, 1914, pantomime play to music	NhD
Vassar's Fiftieth Anniversary Pageant	
War and Woman's Awakening, 1915, Washington, D. C.	
Woman and the Nations: A Pageant for Peace, 1915, unpub. text	NhD
Woman in America, 1914, New York, program	NhD
Zanetto (1)	NhD

    (Many miscellaneous writings are at NhD)

MARY KEITH MEDBURY MACKAYE (MRS. STEELE MACKAYE)

Pride and Prejudice, 1906, dramatization of Jane Austen's novel	RPB

MADRA (or MARDA) MAC KENDRICK

Short Plays for Adult Foreigners, 1928	RPB
The Tea-time Topic, 1933, comedy for 6 women (1)	RPB

EDNA I. MAC KENZIE

As Our Washwoman Sees It, 1920, monologue	RPB
Ask Ouija, 1920, monologue	DLC
Bill and the Radio, 1926, monologue	RPB
The Country Cousin Speaks Her Mind, 1920, monologue	RPB
The Dearest Thing in Boots, 1922, comedy (1)	RPB
Family Hold Back, 1923, comedy	RPB
Gladys Reviews the Dance, 1922, monologue	RPB
Good Morning Mr. Keepintab, 1923, comedy	RPB
How Bobby Puts It Over, 1926, 2 act grammar grade comedy	RPB
I'm Engaged, 1922, monologue	RPB
Leave It to Phyllis, 1924 or earlier, comedy (1)	
The Maiden Vain of Dress, 1926	RPB
Paying the Piper, 1923, comedy	RPB
She Says She Studies, 1926 or earlier, monologue	
Snowbound for Christmas, 1921	RPB
The Strike of the Ladies' Aid, 1926, 2 act novelty entertainment for women	RPB
Susan Gets Ready for Church, 1920, monologue	RPB
That Awful Letter, 1924 or earlier, comedy (1)	
The Unexpected Guest, 1920 (1)	RPB
Waking the Christmas Spirit, 1925	RPB

MARGARET MAC KENZIE

The Young Visitors, 1936, prod. 1920, with Mrs. George Norman from a
   book by Daisy Ashford

DRUZILLA RUTH MACKEY (1885- ?)

Eden, 1928-9, with Essee Hamot

IDA SCOTT (TAYLOR) MC KINNEY

Around the World with Santa Claus, 1903, Christmas cantata, libretto by Ida Scott Taylor; music by Thomas Martin Towne	RPB-M
Beautiful Christmas Gifts, 1905, Christmas exercise, music by Ira B. Wilson	RPB-M
Bethlehem Echoes, 1905, Christmas service for the Sunday schools, music by Thomas Martin Towne	MnHi
King Immanuel, 1895, Christmas program for Sabbath schools, with Alfred A. Beirly, by Ida Scott Taylor	RPB-M
Santa Claus and His Elves, 1896, Christmas cantata for Sunday school, music by George F. Rosche	PP
While Shepherds Watched, 1904, Christmas exercise by Ida Scott Taylor, music by J. S. Fearis and others	RPB-M

ISABEL MC KINNEY

Mud, in Poet Lore, 30, Autumn, 1919, 417-27 (1)

ELIZABETH MAC KINNON

Smocks, 1923

MARY MC KITTRICK

The Gate of Montsalvat, 1928, "romance of love and quest of the Grail"	RPB
Where Fairies Fail, 1923, young (1)	RPB

FANNIE MOULTON MC LANE
Behind the Khaki of the Scouts, Girl Scout pageant, in St. Nicholas, 50, Feb.,
   1923, 386-9 (1)
A Pageant of Our Flag, in The Century Church Bulletin, Jan.-Feb.,   RPB
   1926, 5-15 and St. Nicholas, 52, July, 1925, 974-9

FANNY B. MC LANE
My Lady, 1922, prod. by Pasadena Community Players

JANE MINERVA MC LAREN
Hansel and Gretel, 1915, adapted from the opera by Humperdinck,   RPB
   with Edith Harvey

MARGARET MAC LAREN (See MARGARET MAC LAREN EAGER)

LAURA MC LAUGHLIN
The Hospitality of Don Jose, 1928-9

KATE L. MC LAURIN (MRS. FREDERICK CALVIN) (1885-1933)
The Alien Breed, n.d., typescript   NN
Caught, prod. 1925
A Discussion with Interruptions, in Smart Set, 26, Dec., 1908, 125-7 (1)
It All Depends, prod. 1925
The Least Resistance, 1916 play?   DLC, ViU
The Six-Fifty, prod. 1921
When We Are Young, prod. 1920
Whispering Wires, 1934, prod. 1922, mystery (typescript at NN) from   RPB
   novel by Henry Leverage

ANNIE SUSAN MC LENEGAN
The Masque of Columbus, 1908, pageant of American history,   RPB
   written for the Senior Class Day, 1906, Beloit H. S., Beloit, Wisconsin

MRS. A. L. MC MAHAN
No One Knows What a Woman Will Do, 1930, comedy (1)   RPB

SARA C. MC MAHON
Such a Little Swede, 1927 (1)   RPB

MARY SIMPSON MAC MANUS (MRS. R. D. MC MANUS)
   ("POLLY MAC MANUS")
Between Trains, 1929, for women, by "Polly MacManus" (1)   RPB
Detour Ahead, 1930, play of farm life, By Mrs. R. D. McManus (1)   RPB
Heels, 1934 (1)   RPB
Oececeo, 1929, camp fire play, by "Polly MacManus" (1)   RPB
Salvation Preferred, 1934, Christmas, by Polly Simpson MacManus (1)   RPB
The Toy Heart, 1930, by "Polly MacManus" (1)   RPB

ISABELLA (MC LENNAN) MC MEEKIN (1895- ?)
The Goblin and the Princess, 1929, 2 acts   RPB
Thanks to Johnny Appleseed, 1929, 3 acts   RPB

MARY LANE MC MILLAN
Bringers of Gifts, pageant, in Pictorial Review, 30, Dec., 1928, 18-9
Gifts of Time, in Pictorial Review, 33, Dec., 1931, 8-9

MARY LOUISE MAC MILLAN (1870- ?)
A Fan and Two Candlesticks, 1922, prod. by Portmanteau Theatre (1)   RPB
The Gate of Wishes, in Poet Lore, 22, Winter, 1911, 469-76 (1)
Her Doll, 1927 (1)   RPB
More Short Plays, 1917   RPB
Pan or Pierrot, 1924, masque   RPB
The Pioneers, 1917   LMS
Plenty of Time, 1928, comedy (1)   RPB
The Shadowed Star, 1908, written for Consumers League,   RPB, SSP,
    presented by College Club in Cincinnatti, 1907 (1)   SKS, SLC
Short Plays, 1913 (includes The Futurist, about suffrage)   RPB
Third Book of Short Plays, 1922   RPB

VIRGINIA MC MILLAN
The Raymond Center Store, 1926, 4 act comedy, "experiment   RPB
    in feminism"
A Tourist's Romance, 1928, 3 act comedy   RPB

DOROTHY E. MC MURRY
Jessie, the nymph of the foot-hills, 1908, 25 minute play   RPB

IRENE CARMAN MC MURTREY
After Effects, pub. with Myrtle Giard Elsey's Five or Six Hundred, 1925, RPB
    monologue

IRENE TAYLOR MAC NAIR
The Color Line, 1928, "play of present day China" (1)   RPB, EMR

MARGARET MAC NAMARA
Elizabeth Refuses, 1926, miniature comedy from Jane Austen's   HTM
    Pride and Prejudice
Enjoying the Business, 1924, dramatic demonstration for women's   DLC
    institutes, clubs, adult school classes, etc.
I Have Five Daughters, 1947, "morning-room comedy in 3 acts,"   RPB
    based on Jane Austen's Pride and Prejudice
In Safety, 1924, "incident of the War of American Independence" (1)   RPB
Light Gray or Dark, 1920 (1)
Live (or Love)-fibs, 1920, rustic comedy (1)
A Masque of Fashion, 1926   DLC
Mrs. Hodges, 1920, comedy of rural politics   NN, DLC
Mrs. Jupp Obliges, 1925, small domestic comedy (1)   NN, DLC
Mum's the Word, 1939, tragi-comedy (1)   DLC
A Penny for the Guy! 1928 (1)   NN, MiU
The Witch , 1920, "for 5 women players and a lighting expert" (1)
Wives and Daughters, 1948, intimate comedy   NNC
Yesterday, 1926, historical comedy

EMMA MC NINCH
Roses of Love for Altar of Service
The Spirit of Washington, pageant

ADA S. MACOMBER
Daylight Saving Time, 1925, comedy (1)   Or
Romantic Molly, 1919, comedy, orig. prod. by Central Village   RPB
    Improvement Society of Westport (1)

ELVIE KIMBALL MACOY
Patriotic Scenes Old and New, 1917, entertainment   RPB

JANNEY MC PHERSON
This Is So Sudden (1)

EVA ANNIE MADDEN (1863- ?)
A Noble Spy, 1907 (1st pub. 1899) historical play for boys   RPB

(MRS.) GEORGE MARTIN MADDEN
The Lion's Mouth, 1920

MARTHA MADISON
The Night Remembers, prod. 1934
Subway Express, prod. 1929, with Eva Kay Flint, mystery, typed copy   NN
The Up and Up, prod. 1930, with Eva Kay Flint

MARIE MADISON-BROTMAN
Mrs. Snob at the Milliners, 1907, monologue   RPB
Mrs. Snob at the Opera, 1907, monologue   RPB
Mrs. Snob at the Races, 1907, monologue   RPB

ELVA COOPER MAGNUSSON
Three Plays, 1928   RPB

EMILY E. MAGOR
"The Chate," 1918, burlesque   RPB

EMMA M. MAGUIRE
Story Plays for Little Ones, 1910, handbook for teachers   RPB

"JEANNE MAIRET" (See MARIE HEALEY BIGOT)

CLARE TREE MAJOR
Playing Theatre, 1930, collection

ANNIE MALER
The Sandman, 19??, fairy operetta for the grades   RPB

JENNIE A. MALLETTE
Pilgrims, pageant, in Woman's Home Companion, 50, Oct., 1923, 42-4

LOUISE MALLOY
His Daughter's Father, 1905, playlet   RPB
The Player Maid, 1905? romantic comedy   RPB

MISS H. E. MANCHESTER
Mock Trial for Breach of Promise, n.d., with Mrs. Charles A. Doremus   RPB

ALICE SOLIS MANDEL
Dickenson, B.S., 1934, 3 act comedy   NN
"Enter Joan!" 19?? 3 act comedy   NN
I Have Four Parents, 193? 3 act comedy, based on an article by   NN
     Maude Parker
The Lady Killer, prod. 1924, with Frank Mandel

DOROTHY MANLEY
The Stigma, 1927, with Donald Duff and Doralyne Spence

MARYA MANNES (1904-   ) AWW
Cafe, prod. 1930
Dance Me a Song, revue, prod. 1950
She Stoops to Conquer, prod. 1968, the play by Oliver Goldsmith with a
new epilogue by Mannes
(She also did translations of plays by Snitzler)

MARIE MANNING (1873-1945) AWW
Nervous Prostration, in Harper's, 125, Sept., 1912, 641-4 (1)

BEATRICE CAMERON MANSFIELD (1868- ?)
The Quality of Mercy, 1925 (1)   RPB

ELLA STRYKER MAPES (1870- ?)
Montriveau, 1901, 4 acts, adapted from French of Balzac   RPB

ANNIE RUSSELL MARBLE (1864-1936)
Faith of Our Fathers, n.d., pageant, in Drama, 10, July/Sept., 1920, 373-7,
2 acts commemorating the coming of the Pilgrims
Founders of the Faith, 1923, pageant adapted from the Acts   OCl, OO
of the Apostles
Life and the Children's Garden, 1930? pageant for Children's Day   Or
Merchants of Life, 1931, pageant, Worcester, Mass.   MWA
Pageant: The Children's Quest, 1920   RPB
Pageant: For Home and Country, 1924, Worcester, Mass., patriotic Or, DLC
and historical pageant
Pageant: Heroines of Literature, 1915, Worcester, Mass.   RPB
Pageant: Holly Berries and Christmas Cheer, 1929, Worcester, Mass. RPB

HELEN DOROTHY MARCH
The Pomegranate Seeds, 1922, for children, dramatized from   RPB
Hawthorne's Tanglewood Tales

MARY EDNA (TOBIAS) MARCY (1877- ?)
A Free Union, 1921, drama of "free love" (1)   RPB

FRANCES MARION (1888-1973) NAW
Anna Christie, 1930, adaptation of the play by Eugene O'Neill   CtY
The Beloved Adventuress, 1917, scenario, typed copy   CLU
The Big House, 1930, scenario
The Cup of Life, 1930, prod. 1925   NHP
Dinner at Eight, 1933? screenplay   NN

"PAUL MARION" (Pseud. for Pauline Phelps and Marion Short as co-authors)

CATHARINE MARKHAM
How Christmas Was Saved; or, the Sorrows of Santa Claus, 1916, 2 SNB
acts, also in St. Nicholas, 36, December, 1908, 153-7

CHARLOTTE MARKHAM
The Man Who Married the Moon

JEANNETTE AUGUSTUS MARKS (1875-1964) AWW
The Deacon's Hat, also in Three Welsh Plays (1)   LCO, SBO
Dragon, in Double Dealer, 2, Aug.-Sept., 1921, 54-66 (1)
The Happy Thought, in International, 6, July, 1912, 36-8 (1)

JEANNETTE AUGUSTUS MARKS (continued)
The Merry Merry Cuckoo, in Three Welsh Plays, and in   SSP, MRO
    Metropolitan, 36, July,1912, 45-7, and in The Dramatist, 4, October, 1912,
    291-300 (1)
The Merry Merry Cuckoo and Other Welsh Plays, 1927
The Sun Chaser, 1922, 4 acts   RPB
Three Welsh Plays, 1917   RPB
The Three Wise Men and the Star, 1932, with Maxinne McBride, in   PLP
    Plays, v. 1, 1932, 123-44
Welsh Honeymoon, in Three Welsh Plays, and in Smart Set, 38,   LCO, COP
    Nov., 1912, 135-41 (1)

JOSEPHINE PRESTON PEABODY MARKS
(See JOSEPHINE PRESTON PEABODY)

JULIE J. MARQUIS
The Victim of Jealousy, 1928, "true life drama in 3 parts"   RPB

MARJORIE MARQUIS
The First Christmas, 1930, also in Ladies' Home Journal, 47, Dec., 1930,
    14-5+ (1)

PHYLLIS MARSCHALL
George Washington, the Spirit of Americanization

ALICE LOUISE MARSH
The Bishop's Candlesticks (Les Miserables) 1924, young   RPB

ELIZABETH H. MARSH
Body and Soul, 1920, poetic drama   RPB
The Kaiser's Reasons, 1918, 3 act drama   RPB
Lawful Prey, n.d., typescript   NN

FLORENCE ANNE MARSH
The Boston Tea Party, 1924   DLC
Christmas at the Manor Hall, 1924, young   RPB
Plays for Young People, 1931, editor

HARRIET ANNE MARSH (1848-1933)
Capt. Smith and Pocahontas, 1924, in Florence Marsh, Plays for Young People
Rumpelstiltskin, 1924, also in Florence Marsh, Plays for Young People   RPB

MARIE LOUISE MORE MARSH
Snow-White
Tonsils

ABIGAIL MARSHALL
The Accomplice, dramatization of her own story which appeared in   STM
    Smart Set and which won first prize at Plays and Players Club (1)
Dad and Mother (1)

MRS. JAMES WALLER MARSHALL
The Patchwork Girl of Oz, 1930, 2 acts dram. from story by   RPB
    L. Frank Baum

LAURA MARSHALL
Green Shadows, 1928, comedy (1)   RPB
Winter Sunshine, 1925-9? in Fifteen One-Act Plays ? (1)   BAO

RACHAEL MARSHALL
The Traffic, prod. 1914, with Oliver D. Bailey

FLORENCE J. MARTIN
Christmas Eve in Santa's Workshop   WPP

HELEN REIMENSNYDER MARTIN (1868-1939) AWW
A Mennonite Maid, prod. 1924, with Frank Howe Jr., 4 act comedy

JULIA M. MARTIN
Barbara the Great, 1922, for boys (1)   RPB
The Critical Utterance (1)
For Greater Eras, 1927, drama of Columbus and the New World   RPB
The Keepers of the Declaration, 1923   RPB
On Salem Road, 1923, young   RPB
The Other Sentinel, 1923, young   RPB
The Quest of Christmas, 1922 (1)   RPB
The Thanksgiving of Praisgod Plenty, 1921 (1)   RPB
When Heroes Come, 1925   RPB
When Polly Orders Lunch, 1925, good health playlet   RPB
When the Reindeer Played Out, 1923   NN

LENA PRATHER MARTIN
Aunt Fannie's Miracle, 1925, church entertainment   RPB
Aunt Sophy Takes Charge, 1927 (1)   RPB
Christmas Eve at the Poor Farm, 1927 (1)   RPB
A Christmas That Was Different, 1930, for girls and women   RPB
Judith of the Mountains, 1928, "strong drama in 3 acts"   RPB
The Lost Coin, 1929, with Letitia W. Wood   RPB
Miss Molly's Girl, 1929, 3 acts, young   RPB
Phyllis Makes Whoopee, 1929, 3 act comedy   RPB
The Sixth Hat, 1928, farce (1)   RPB
Thoughtless Giving, 1926, comedy   RPB

NINA MARTIN
On His Honor, 1930, Wetmore declamation and readings   RPB

MARY (MAY) MARTINDALE
Gamblers All, 1916, melodrama

DOROTHY MARTYN
Grove Eden, 1912, farce (1)   RPB

CAROLINE ATWATER MASON (1853-1939)
Jesus Christs' Men; a Progress, 1810-1826, 1914, "dramatic   RPB
    presentation of early Baptist missions"

EDITH HUNTINGTON MASON
The Unwilling Burglar, 1902, with Elmer Stevens, 2 act farce   RPB

MARY L. MASON
The Awakening of Zion, 1921, "unfolding of the A.M.E. Zion   RPB
    church in picture, song and story"

DOROTHEA MASSEY
Las Rurales

"JANE MAST" (See MAE WEST)

HELEN GENEVA MASTERS
The Bozeman Trail, in Scholastic, 12, March 31, 1928, 6-8+ (1)
"The King of Culture," 1924, farce, typed copy (1)   RPB

KATE MASTERSON (1870- ?)
A Man to Order, in Smart Set, 4, May, 1901, 155-7 (1)

ALICE L. MATHEWS
Yellow Roses, 1927

FRANCES (FANNIE) AYMAR MATHEWS (c1855-1923) AWW
All For Sweet Charity, 1907, comedy   RPB
American Hearts, 1907, comedy   RPB
The Apartment, 1907, comedy   RPB
At the Grand Central, 1907, comedy for females (1)   RPB
Bigamy, 1881, with E. Henderson, 5 act society play
Both Sides of the Counter, 1907, comedy   RPB
A Charming Conversationalist, 1907, comedy   RPB
The Courier, 1907, comedy   RPB
Cousin Frank, 1896, farce for females (1)   RPB
En Voyage, 1907, comedy   RPB
Finding a Father for Flossie, 1906
A Finished Coquette, 1907, comedy (1)   RPB
The Honeymoon Fourth Quarter, 1907, comedy   RPB
Joan of Arc, 1898
A Knight of the Quill, 1907, comedy   RPB
My Lady Peggy Goes to Town, prod. 1903
Lady Jane's Highwayman, in Harper's Weekly, 47, Dec. 12, 1903, 15-17 (1)
The New Professor, 1903, comedy for ladies (1)   RPB
On the Staircase, 1907, comedy (1)   RPB
Paying the Piper, 1907, comedy (1)   RPB
Pretty Peggy, 1902, prod. 1903
The Proposal, 1907, comedy (1)   RPB
The Silent Partner, monologue
Six to One; or, the Scapegrace, 1895, comedietta, later pub. as   RPB
     The Scapegrace
Snow-bound, 1907, comedy   RPB
Tea Cups, 1907, comedy   RPB
The Title and the Money, 1907, comedy   RPB
To-Night at Eight, 1889, comedies and comediettas   RPB
Up Yonder, 1906
War to the Knife, 1907, comedy   RPB
The Wedding Tour, 1907, comedy   RPB
A Woman's Forever, 1907, comedy (1)   RPB
Wooing a Widow, 1895, comedy (1)   RPB

JUNE MATHIS
The Four Horsemen of the Apocalypse, 1921, adaptation   RPB
The Spanish Cavalier, 1923, film story in photo-dramatic form,   DLC
     based on play by Don Caesar de Bazan and Adophe D'Ennery

JUDITH MATLACK
The Two Prisoners   SCT

ADELAIDE MATTHEWS (1886- ?) AWW
An Errand for Polly, 1926, with William C. Duncan, 3 act character comedy
The First Mrs. Chiverick, 1930, with Martha Stanley (prod. 1920   OCl, DLC
    as Scrambled Wives)
Heart's Desire, 1916, with Anne Nichols
Innocent Anne, 1930, with Martha Stanley
It Never Happens Twice, 1938, 3 act comedy   RPB
Just Married, 1929, prod. 1921, with Anne Nichols (copyright under   RPB
    title, What's Your Number, 1917) 3 act comedy
Marrying Anne, 1930, 3 act comedy   RPB
Nearly Married, prod. 1929, with Anne Nichols
Nightie Night, 1929, prod. 1919, with Martha Stanley, 3 act farce   RPB
Puppy Love, 1927, prod. 1926 by Anne Nichols, with Martha Stanley,   RPB
    3 act comedy
Scrambled Wives, prod. 1920, with Martha Stanley
Sunset Glow, 1929, with "Lucille Sawyer," 3 act comedy drama   RPB
The Teaser, prod. 1921, with Martha Stanley, comedy
The Wasp's Nest, 1929, prod. 1927, with Martha Stanley (copyright   RPB
    1926 under title, The House in the Woods) 3 act mystery comedy
What's Your Number? 1917, with Anne Nichols (prod. 1921 as
    Just Married and1929 as Nearly Married)
Where Innocence Is Bliss, 1929, with Martha Stanley, 4 act comedy   RPB

CECILIA M. MATTHEWS
The Life Everlasting, 1907, church cantata for Advent or Easter.   RPB-M
    Words selected from the Holy Scriptures by Matthews; music by H.
    Alexander Matthews

EDITH VIRGINIA BRANDER MATTHEWS
At the Eleventh Hour, in Harper's Bazaar, 38, March, 1904, 232-9
Six Cups of Chocolate, 1897, "piece of gossip in one act, freely   RPB
    Englished from a Kaffee Klatsch of E. Schmithof"

ELVA DE PUE MATTHEWS (See ELVA DE PUE)

SUE FROMAN MATTHEWS
The Red Cross Nurse, 1917, "play in 6 scenes, giving the actual   RPB
    experiences of an American girl," in collaboration with Miss Lida Hafford

VIRGINIA PARK MATTHIAS
The Brownie's Dream, 1924, for Brownies or Girl Scouts   RPB
The First of May, 1922, Girl Scout play with music   RPB

ANNE FONTAINE MAURY
May Day in Canterbury, 1925, Chaucerian festival, arranged by Maury,   RPB
    celebrated at Wheaton College

MINA ROSENTHAL MAXFIELD
The Eyes of Faith, 1931, with Lena Eggleston, Easter drama   MiD, DLC
    for women
Gallant Queen, 1944, story of Esther   DLC
Ruth of Moab, pastoral of Canaan   GPD
Shrouds on the Candle, 1928-9
The Wet Parade, 1932, with Lena Eggleston, from the novel by Upton Sinclair

ELSA MAXWELL
Melinda and Her Sisters, 1916, with Mrs. O. H. P. Belmont,   RPB, FOV
    about suffrage (1)

VIRGINIA MAXWELL
Alias Billy Nix, 1927, with Ted Maxwell, 3 acts   RPB
Cinderella O'Reilly, 1926, with Ted Maxwell, 3 act Irish comedy   RPB
The Cross-eyed Parrot, 1926, with Ted Maxwell, 3 act   RPB
    melodramatic comedy
The Heart Cry, 1928, with Ted Maxwell, 3 act comedy drama   RPB
The Humbug, 1928, with Ted Maxwell, 3 act farce   RPB
The Key Note, 1927, with Ted Maxwell, 3 act mystery   RPB
Mary-gold, 1929, with Ted Maxwell, 3 act comedy drama   RPB
Rainbow Trail, 1936, with Ted Maxwell, 3 act comedy
The Runaway Bride, 1926, with Ted Maxwell and Josephine Shively,   RPB
    3 act comedy drama
Windy Willows, 1928, with Ted Maxwell, 4 acts   RPB

EVELYN LOUISE MAYBERRY
Miss Becky's Christmas Tree, 1929, monologue   RPB

MABEL MAYHEW
The Archeologist and the Lady

CORA MAYNARD
The Measure of a Man, prod. 1906
The Watcher, prod. 1910

GERTRUDE MAYNARD
Their Trees   BPC

"MARGARET MAYO" (LILLIAN SLATTEN)
(MRS. EDGAR SELWYN) (1882-1951) AWW
The Austrian Dancer
Baby Mine, 1911, prod. 1910 (1924 ed. at RPB) 3 act farce   RPB
Be Careful Baby, prod. 1918, with Salisbury Field
Behind the Scenes
Being Fitted
Commencement Days, 1908, with Virginia Frame Church, 3 act play   RPB
    of college-girl life
Cyprienne Divorcons, 1941, adaptation of French play by V. Sardou
The Debtors, prod. 1909, adaptation of German play by Fritz von Schoenthan
The Flirt
Heads Up, prod. 1929? with Zellah Covington
His Bridal Night, prod. 1916, by Lawrence Rising, revised by Mayo
The Jungle, adaptation
The Love Thief, 1926, scenario   NN, MH
Loving Ladies, prod. 1926? with Aubrey Kennedy
The Marriage of William Ashe, 1905, dram. of story by Mrs. Humphrey Ward
Nip and Tuck
Pettie Darling
Polly of the Circus, 1908 (1st pub. 1905) prod. 1907, 3 act comedy drama   RPB
    prepared by Nathaniel Reeid (typescript at NN) (1933 ed. at RPB)
The Poor Simp, 1935, 3 act comedy by Zellah Covington, revised by   RPB
    Mayo and Nathaniel Edward Reeid
Prisoner of the World
Rock-a-Bye-Baby, prod. 1918, (adaptation of her Baby Mine) book by   RPB-M
    Mayo and Edgar Allen Woolf; lyrics by Herbert Reynolds; music
    by Jerome Kern
Seeing Things, prod. 1920, with Aubrey Kennedy
Twin Beds, 1913, prod. 1914, with Salisbury Field, farce (1931 ed. at RPB) RPB

"MARGARET MAYO" (continued)
 Under Two Flags, 1913, adaptation of story by Ouida
 The Wall Street Girl, 1908, prod. 1912, book by Mayo and Edgar   NN
  Selwyn; lyrics by Otto Harbach; music by Karl Hoschna, typescript
 The White Way
 The Winding Way

JOY MAYS
 Endurance Flight, 1929, with Mollie Day Thacher

ADELAIDE B. MEAD(E)
 Doors of Happiness, 1933, program for Rally Day, with   RPB
  Emma Gary Wallace
 Gifts of the Loving Heart, 1925, "pageant of giving and gratitude   RPB
  and growth," with Emma Gary Wallace
 Glad Tidings to All People, 1928, with Emma Gary Wallace
 Theresa's Fairy Friends, "For Domestic Science Classes or Groups   HPY
  of Younger Girls," with Emma B. Wallace
 Why Photographers Go Mad, 1925, with Emma Gary Wallace   NN

E. LOUISE MEADE
 Girls of Today, 1923, pantomime   RPB

CONSTANCE MEADNIS
 Soup, 1929

KATHERINE MEAGHER
 French Frocks, 1929, with Rowena Arthur Mills, 3 act comedy   RPB

ISABELLE JACKSON MEAKER (also MEEKER)' (1874- ?)
 The Alabaster Boy, 192?, with Anna J. Harnwell (Religious Dramas, II)   RPB
 From Hand to Hand, with Anna J. Harnwell   SSC
 Holly and Cypress, 1930, "Christmas play with pageantry," with Anna J.
  Harnwell
 The Knife, with Anna Harnwell (1)   SSH-III
 My Lady's Yuletide, 1914, with Eleanor Ellis Perkins, won 3rd   MH, PP
  prize in contest by Drama League of Chicago
 Sojourners, with Anna J. Harnwell, in Drama, 10, July-Sept., 1920,   SSH-II
  357-64 (1)
 Spinet to Saxophone, 1927, "dramatic musicale in 5 chords"

LOTTIE M. MEANEY
 Pay-day, prod. 1916, with Oliver D. Bailey
 A Stitch in Time, prod. 1918, with Oliver D. Bailey

FLORENCE CRANNELL MEANS (1897- ?) AWW
 The Black Tents, 1926, "Junior play of life among the Bedouins in Syria" RPB
 Pepita's Adventure in Friendship, 1929, "play for Juniors about   RPB
  Mexicans in the U.S."
 Tara Finds the Door to Happiness, 1926, "for Juniors"   RPB

ROSE CHARLOTTE MEBLIN
 Dowry and Romance, 1923 (1)   DPP

MARTHA MEDMAN
 What's the Big Idea, prod. 1926, with Henry House

MRS. JETHRO C. MEEK
  Decatur County Pageant, 1916, Greensburg, Ind., with Mrs. Oscar Miller   InI

ISABELLE MEEKER (See ISABELLE JACKSON MEAKER)

CORNELIA LYNDE MEIGS (1884-1973) AWW
  Helga and the White Peacock, 1922, 3 acts, young   RPB
  Primrose Lane, in St. Nicholas, 46, May, 1919, 641-7 (1)
  The Steadfast Princess, 1916, won Drama League prize in 1915, young   RPB

VIRGINIA MELICK
  Fur and Warmer, 1925, comedy (1)   RPB

EVELYN EMIG MELLON
  The China Pig, 1920, by Evelyn Emig, in Poet Lore, 33, Autumn, 1922,   STW
    439-50 (1)
  How the Princess' Pride Was Broken, 1932, dramatization of   RPB
    H. C. Andersen's "The Swineherd," young
  The Old Order, 1919, by Evelyn Emig, in Poet Lore, 32, Winter, 1921,
    586-95, won University Prize at George Washington Un. (1)
  Trains, in Poet Lore, 41, Autumn, 1930, 424-32, award in International
    Settlement Play Contest (1)
  Two Prize Plays and Four Others, 1929, one acts   RPB
  Wars of the Sea, 1922, won Hollywood Community prize (1)

DORIS M. MELTON ("MILTON REYNOLDS")
  Dad Comes Across, 1930, pub. by Am. Farm Bureau Federation   RPB
  Epilogue, 1931, "dramatic fantasy," by "Milton Reynolds" (1)   MoU

ELLA HERRIMAN MELVIN
  Their Golden Wedding, 1915, church entertainment (1)   RPB

PAULA MENDEL
  Journey's End in Lovers' Meeting, with Arthur Guiterman, in Ladies
    Home Journal, 19, Feb., 1902, 9 (1)

ABBY S. MERCHANT (1882- ?)
  The Bride's Rival, 1923 (1)   RPB
  The Evergreen Lady, prod. 1922
  His Women Folk
  Irish Dew, 1920, ms.   MNS
  The New Englander, prod. 1924, ms.   MNS
  A New Frock for Pierrette, 1933, "dramatic revue and fashion show"   RPB
  The Unbent Twig, 1940   MNS
  Your Loving Son, prod. 1941, 3 act comedy, microfilm of typescript   CU

MARGUERITE MERINGTON (1860-1951) AWW
  An Everyday Man, 1895, comedy, "modernized from same play   NN
    written for and produced by Sol Smith Russell, typescript
  At Parting, n.d., comedy dramatized from sketch by the late Albert   NN
    Morris Bagby
  Bonnie Prince Charles, 1897
  Booth Episodes, 1944, based on life of Edwin Booth, typescript   NN
  Captain Lettarblair, 1891? (1906 ed. at RPB), 3 act comedy   RPB
  The Castaways, n.d., "one act sketch for singing quartet," typescript   NN
  The Court of Ferrara, n.d., dialogue, typescript   NN
  Cranford: A Play, 1905, based on novel by Mrs. Gaskell, 3 acts, in   RPB
    Ladies Home Journal, 18, Feb., 1901, 5-6+

MARGUERITE MERINGTON (continued)
Daphne; or, the Pipes of Arcadia, 1896, "3 acts of singing nonsense"
A Dish o' Tea Delayed, 1937, for high school girls, "founded on a true
   incident when the republic U.S.A. was young" (1)
Drum and Fife Parade, n.d., typescript   NN
The Elopers, 1913
Fairy Tale Plays, 1916 (1925 ed. at RPB)   RPB
Father Time and His Children, in St Nicholas, 36, Jan., 1909, 236-40 (1)
Festival Plays, 1913, one acts
Festive Plays, 1923, one acts for holidays   RPB
The Gibson Play, 1901, based on the cartoons of C. D. Gibson, "A   RPB
   Widow and Her Friends," also in Ladies Home Journal, 18, March,
   1901, 7-8+, 2 act comedy
"Goodbye!" 1893, "story of love and sacrifice," typescript   NN
Grouse Out of Season, comedy in Harper's Bazaar, 37, Nov., 1903, 1018-27 (1)
Holiday Plays, 1910, one acts   RPB
The Island, n.d., founded on the novel Foul Play by Charles Reade   NN
   and Dion Boucicault, typescript
The Key to the House, n.d., typescript   NN
Kindly Light, n.d., modern morality play, typescript   NN
The Lady in the Adjoining Room, 1905
The Land of Sally Lunn, 19??, 2 act musical fantasy, music by Percy Lee   NN
   Atherton, typescript
Late Dyal & Co., 19??, 3 act farce, typescript   NN
Love Finds the Way, 1898, typescript   NN
A Lover's Knot, in Harper's Bazaar, 44, June, 1910, 384-6, comedy (1)
More Fairy Tale Plays, 1917   RPB
The Musical Isle, n.d., typescript   NN
Oh, Belinda, 1892
Old Orchard, 1900 (called Rose Valley in Chicago prod.) prompt book   NN
One Life to Give, n.d., drama in verse founded on the story of   NN
   Nathan Hale, typescript
Pepilia, n.d., comedy, typescript   NN
Picture Plays, 1911, collection based on famous paintings   RPB
The Right Ending, n.d., sketch in blank verse, typescript (1)   NN
Scarlet of the Mounted, 1906
Snow White and the Seven Dwarfs, 1905, typescript   NN
The Testing of Sir Gawayne, 1913   MTP
That Little Shabby Gentleman, n.d., comedy, typescript   NN
The Turn of the Tide, 1905
The Vicar of Wakefield, 1909, based on Goldsmith
Washington's Birthday Pageant, in Holiday Plays, N.Y., Duffield Co., 1910

SUSAN MERIWETHER
Flight, 1928, with Victor Victor, typescript   NN
The Playbook of George Washington, 1928   DLC

MADELINE MERLI
The Mormon Wife, prod. 1901, with Howard Hall

LILLIE FULLER MERRIAM
Aunt Abigail and the Boys, 1913, college play, farce (1)   RPB
Yuletide at the Court of King Arthur, 1934, music by Stuart Bliss Hoppin RPB

GRACE F. MERRILL
Mother Goose's Thanksgiving Party   SBT

JENNY BIGGS MERRILL
  A Pageant of the Earth, in The Kindergarten Primary Magazine, 26, June, 1914

MARGARET M. MERRILL
  The Soul of the Violin, 193? (Wetmore declamations and readings)   RPB

MARIE G. MERRILL
  The Home in the Shoe, 1930, health play for children   RPB
  The Lost Sheep, n.d., play?
  The Wise Owl's School (1)   SOP-1

RUTH EARL MERRILL
  The Dismissal of the Grecian Envoys, 1918, by Jan Kochanowski, trans.   RPB
      from Polish by George Rapall Noyes and done into English
      verse by Merrill

EFFIE WOODWARD MERRIMAN (FIFIELD) (1857- ?)
  The Bachelor's Club, 1901, farce for men (1)   RPB
  Comedies for Children, 1898, one-acts   RPB
  Deacon Jenkins Choir Meeting, 1924, "fantastic entertainment," by Effie   RPB
      Woodward Fifield
  Diamonds and Hearts, 1897, 3 act comedy drama   RPB
  The Drunkard's Family, 1898, young (1)   RPB
  The Emerson Club, 1901, comedy (1)   RPB
  A Girl's Secret, 1901, 3 acts   RPB
  The Great Plummer, 1902, breach of promise case, mock trial   RPB
  The Hypnotist, 1901, comedy (1)   RPB
  In Klondyke, 1898, young (1)   NN, CtY
  Marian's Wish, 1898, young (1)   RPB
  Maud Muller, 1891, burlesque entertainment   RPB
  Modern Entertainments, 1898   MH, DLC
  The Mysterious Guest, 1898, young (1)   NN
  A Pair of Artists, 1892, 3 act comedy   RPB
  The Rehearsal, 1909, novel social entertainment   NN, PU
  The Rigmaree, 1898, young (1)   RPB
  The Silent Detective, 1901, 3 act drama   RPB
  Socials, 1891, amusements   RPB
  The Stolen Cat, 1898, young (1)   RPB
  Their First Meeting, 1899, comedy (1)   RPB
  Through a Matrimonial Bureau, 1898, comedy (1)   RPB
  Tompkins Hired Man, 1914, 3 acts   NN, OCl
  A Twentieth Century Proposal, 1902, 3 act comedy   RPB
  Uncle Ben Drake, 1926, comedy drama, by Mrs. J. C. Fifield   RPB
  What Ailed Maudie, 1898, young (1)   NN

LORINE MERRIN
  Meet the Husband, 1927, comedy (1)   RPB

MILDRED PLEW MERRYMAN (1892- ?)
  Encores and Extras, 1920, collection of monologues by Merryman,   RPB
      Crane and others
  The Seven Leagued Boots, in American Poetry Magazine, 1, Sept., 1919,
      19-24 (1)
  Woof! Woof! 1929, young (1)   RPB

NELLIE STEARNS MESSER
  The Minute Man, 1918, patriotic sketch for girls of high school age   RPB
  A Pageant-drama of Salem, 1926, Salem, Mass.   RPB

ELIZABETH TYREE METCALFE
    The Perennial Border, 1917, with James S. Metcalfe   RPB

FELICIA LEIGH METCALFE (1889- ?)
    All Night Long, 1929, 3 act mystery comedy   RPB
    Angel Unawares, 1936, 3 act comedy   ViU, DLC
    Are You Mr. Butterworth? 1938, 3 act mystery comedy   DLC
    Aunt Cathie's Cat, 1943, mystery comedy   RPB
    Auntie Up, 1932, 3 act comedy   RPB
    Come Easy, 1933, 3 act comedy
    Dear Papa, 1946, 3 act comedy
    Excuse Me Please, 1950, 3 act comedy   RPB
    Grandad Steps Out, 1944, farce   RPB
    Not Everybody's Crazy, 1949, 3 act comedy   RPB
    Off the Track, 1948, 3 act comedy   RPB
    One For the Money, 1950   ViU
    Papa Says No! 1945, 3 act comedy   RPB
    Quit Your Kidding, 1948, farce   RPB
    Shooting High, 1939, 3 act comedy   RPB
    The Skeleton Walks, 1945, 3 act mystery comedy   RPB
    Take Your Medicine, 1945, 3 act farce   RPB
    Three Days of Gracie, 1936
    Three Fingers in the Door, 1949, 3 act mystery comedy   RPB
    The Whippersnapper, 1934, 3 act comedy   RPB
    Willie's Weekend, 1947, 3 act farce   RPB

MARGARET METZGER
    Salt and Pepper, 1921, 3 act operetta, lyrics and libretto by Metzger   RPB
        and others; music by Virginia French and others;
        prod. by Barnswallows, Wellesley College

ANNIE NATHAN MEYER (1867-1951) AWW NAW
    The Adventurers, n.d., typescript   NN
    The Advertising of Kate, 1914, prod. 1922
    Black Souls, prod. 1932, about lynching   RPB
    Dinner of Herbs, prod. 1909, comedy
    The District Attorney, prod. 1921
    The Dominant Sex, 1911, 3 acts   RPB
    The Dreamer, 1912, 3 acts   RPB
    My Park Book, 1898
    The New Way, 1925, prod. 1923, 3 act comedy   RPB
    Robert Annys, Poor Priest, 1901
    P's and Q's, 1921, farce (1)
    The Scientific Mother, in Bookman (New York), 5, July, 1897, 381-2 (1)
    The Spur, prod. 1914

JOSEPHINE AMELIA MEYER (1884- ?)
    The Red Cloak, prod. 1916 by Washington Square Players, with Lawrence
        Langner
    To Be Perfectly Frank, in Smart Set, 65, June, 1921, 69-79 (1)

MARGARET MICHAEL
    Fifty-fifth Ltd., prod. 1919, 3 act farce, with William Lennox; music   NN
        and lyrics by Leon De Costa, musical version of William Gillette's
        All the Comforts of Home, typescript

MIRIAM MICHELSON (1870- ?)
Bygones, in Smart Set, 51, March, 1917, 81-92 (1)
The Curiosity of Kitty Cochraine, in Smart Set, 37, May, 1912, 133-42 (1)
Help Us to Help Ourselves, about suffrage

HETTIE LOUISE MICK
The Frog Prince
Little Red Riding Hood
The Maid Who Wouldn't Be Proper, puppet play, in Drama, 12,   LMS
    Sept., 1922, 351-7 (1)

ELIZABETH MIELE (1900- ?)
Am I Intruding? prod. 1932, comedy, typescript   NN
An Angel Comes East! n.d., typescript   NN
Anybody's Game, 1933, prod. 1932, 3 act comedy   RPB
The Big Shot, prod. 1932 (also called Ever So Happy) typescript   NN
Brains of the Family, prod. 1932, comedy, typescript   NN
The City Haul, prod. 1929, comedy, typescript   NN
Did I Say—No? 1934, prod. 1931, 3 act comedy (typescript at NN)   RPB
High Hat 'em, n.d., "smart society musical comedy," typescript   NN
Hit the Trail, prod. 1954, lyrics by Miele; book by Frank O'Neill; music
    by F. Valerio
Politics, 1929, 3 acts, typed copy   DLC
The Red-Checker, n.d., typescript   NN

ELLA STERLING (CLARK) MIGHELS (1853-1934)
Society and Babe Robinson; or, The Streets of Old San Francisco, 1914   RPB

RUTH LINING MILAM
Old Man Rabbit's Thanksgiving   WPP

ELIZABETH PALMER MILBANK
The Radio Window, 1927, vaudeville sketch (1)   RPB

NAN LANGDON MILDREN (1874- ?)
Brownie Night, in Ladies Home Journal, 30, Oct., 1913, 106 (1)
Hiawatha, in Ladies Home Journal, 30,, March, 1913, 93

ANNIE M. MILES
The Magic Trunk, 1913, pub. by Drama League of Chicago (1)   Or, PP

HELEN MILES
Ruth and Naomi, with Mabel Hobbs (1)   SOP-1
Six Bible Plays, 1924, with Mabel Foote Hobbs   RPB

INEZ MILHOLLAND (BOISSEVAIN) (1886-1916) NAW
If Women Voted, 191?

MILDRED MILLAR
Fluke, 1920

EDNA ST. VINCENT MILLAY ("NANCY BOYD")
    (1892-1950) AWW NAW NWAT
Adventures in Radio, 1945, ed. by Margaret Cuthbert, radio scripts   RPB
    by Millay and others
Aethelwold, the King's Henchman, 1927, lyric drama, (galley proofs   MH
    for the first Harper ed. of The King's Henchman)

EDNA ST. VINCENT MILLAY (continued)

Aria da Capo, 1920, prod. 1919, in   RPB,CSP,GTP, SLC,KFA,CCT-3,AAP
    Little Theater Tournament, 1925, also inThree Plays; in The Chapbook
    (London), #14, Aug., 1920, 1-24; in V. W. Church, Curtain! A Book
    of Modern Plays, 1932; and in Reedy's Mirror, St. Louis, Mo.,
    Vol. 29, No. 12, 1920, 199-202
Distressing Dialogues, 1924, by "Nancy Boyd"   RPB
The King's Henchman, 1927, 3 acts (in 1928 it became a lyric   RPB, TMA
    drama with music by Deems Taylor)
The Lamp and the Bell, 1921, 5 act drama, also in Three Plays,   RPB, STW
    commissioned byVassar College Alumnae Assoc. for its 50th
    anniversary celebration
Launzi, prod. 1923, adapt. of Molnar
The Princess Marries the Page, 1932, prod. 1918, music by   RPB
    Deems Taylor (1)
Three Plays, 1926   RPB
Two Slatterns and a King, 1921, also in Three Plays, moral   RPB, SCO,STC
    interlude (1)
The Walls of Dominoes, in Vassar Miscellany, May , 1917

AGNES MILLER

The Finding of the First Arbutus, in St. Nicholas, 47, April, 1920, 550-3 (1)
The First Thanksgiving Day, 1916, also in St. Nicholas, 40, Nov., 1912,   SNB
    61-4 (1)

ALICE DUER MILLER (1874-1942) AWW NAW

The Charm School, 1922, prod. 1920, 3 act comedy, with Robert Milton   RPB
Come Out of the Kitchen, 1921, prod. 1916, 3 act comedy by A. E. Thomas,
    based on story by Miller
Follow the Dream, 1951, with Florence Ryerson, 2 act comedy   RPB
June Days, prod. 1925, musical based on play by Miller and Robert Milton;
    book by Cyrus Ward; lyrics by Clifford Grey; music by J. Fred Coots
Little Scandal, 1951, with Florence Ryerson, 3 act comedy   RPB
Magnolia Lady, prod. 1924, musical based on Come Out of the Kitchen,
    book and lyrics by Anne Caldwell; music by Harold Levy
The Rehearsal, prod. 1915-6, orig. draft   NN
Roberta, prod. 1933, musical by J. Kern and O. Harbach based on novel
    by Miller
Sky High, 1950, prod. 1925?, with Florence Ryerson
The Springboard, 1928, prod. 1927, 3 act comedy   RPB
Unauthorized Interviews, 1917   FOV

EMILY CLARK (HUNTINGTON) MILLER (1833-1913) AWW NAW

The Little Lad of Bethlehemtown, 1911, nativity play in blank verse   RPB

ESTELLE MILLER

Uncle Sam's S.O.S., 1918, pageant, with Edith Bristol   RPB

FLORENCE MARIA MILLER (1872- ?)

Historical Pageants, 1911   MB, DLC
Making of the First American Flag, 3 acts   FFP
The Man Without a Country, 1917   DLC
Single-Handed McAuley   FFP

FRANCESCA FALK MILLER (1888- ?)

He Didn't Like Spinach, 1935, comedy (1)   RPB
It's Smart to Be Different, 1938, temperance play (1)   DLC

FRANCESCA FALK MILLER (continued)
A Light on Beacon Hill, 1937, Christmas play (1)
The Line Is Busy, 1932 (1)   RPB
Making Rosie a Cook, 1929   RPB
Marked Corners, 1954, 3-acts about young Abraham Lincoln in Indiana,   RPB
     1816-1830
One Way Out of It, 1937 (1)   DLC
Treasures in Heaven, 1937 (1)   RPB

HARRIET M. MILLER (1831-1918)
A Vision of Moses, 1924   RPB

HELEN LOUISE MILLER
Aladdin's Garden, 1930, pageant play for commencement, with   RPB
     Beulah M. Bradley
The Court of Revelry, 1930, pageant of fun and frolic for 4th of July,   RPB
     with Beulah M. Bradley
The Dream Peddler, 1937, pageant play for graduation,   DLC
     mimeographed copy
Easy Plays for Boys and Girls, 1963   RPB
First Plays for Children, 1960   RPB
Gold Medal Plays for Holidays, 1958   RPB
Holiday Plays for Teen-agers, 1952   RPB
The Missing "Linc," 1946, in Plays, V. 5, No. 4, Jan., 1946   RPB
Modern Plays for Special Days, 1965, for teenagers   RPB
On Stage for Teen-agers, 1948   RPB
The Open Sesame, 1934, pageant play for commencement, with   RPB
     Beulah Bradley, mimeographed copy
Plays for Living and Learning, 1955   RPB
Prize Plays for Teen-agers, 1956   RPB
The Quest, 1932, pageant play for commencement, mimeographed   RPB
     copy, possibly with Beulah M. Bradley
Through the Portals, 1930, pageant play for commencement, with   RPB
     Beulah M.Bradley
The Tinder Box, 1938, pageant play for commencement, with
     Beulah M. Bradley

HELENA MILLER
Purple and Fine Linen, with Anita B. Fairgrieve, the "Lend a Hand
     Smith College prize play"

JANE TAYLOR MILLER
The Christmas Story, 1915, group of tableaux based on the first 10   RPB
     chapters of Ben Hur
Trespassing, 193? With Marian de Forest??

KATHERINE BROWNING MILLER
The Delinquents, 1926, with Allena Harris, 4 act comedy drama   RPB
Help Yourself, 1926, 3 act comedy   RPB
Just Boys, prod. 1915, with Allena Kanka, juvenile court play
The Street of a Thousand Shadows, prod. Pasadena Playhouse, 1926-9?
     with Euleta Wadsworth

LAURA MILLER
It Took a Woman   YSP-II
The Joke-ative Man, prod. by Portland Civic Theater under   YSP-III
     title Hill Woman
     (Both plays won James Kerr prize from Civic Theater of Portland)

LAURA A. MILLER
Mrs. Toorich Comes to College, 1925   RPB

LEILA W. MILLER
"The Loveliest Thing," service for children's day   JPP-I

LOUISE WINIFRED MILLER
Gifts   ECO

MADELEINE SWEENY MILLER (MRS. J. LANE MILLER) (1890- ?)
The Alabaster Cruse, 1935, Easter
Children of the Book, 1935, Biblical drama for children's day or any other
    festival day of the church year
The Children's Crusade, 1919, centenary pageant for the Sunday   RPB
    school suitable for indoor or open-air production
Church Pageantry, 1925, handbook for amateur producers of   RPB
    educational dramatics
A Daughter of the Dawn, 1933, drama of early Methodism in 4 episodes. RPB
    Inspired by the life of Barbara Heck
The Easter Pilgrims, 1922, pageant   RPB
The Finding of the King, 1935, "for Christmas, historical, religious, romantic"
The Fruits of Peace, 1925, pageant for young people   RPB
Supplement. The World's Christmas Mail, 1922, service of Nativity   RPB
    scenes, carol singing, and world-offerings
The World's Christmas Fireplace, 1920, pageant for Christmas relief to OO
    the women and children of Europe
The World's Christmas Mail, 1922, "service of Nativity scenes, carol   RPB
    singing and world offerings"

MARION MILLS MILLER (1864- ?)
The Picture of Dorian Gray, 1931, dramatization of novel by Oscar Wilde RPB
The Return of Odysseus, 1917, Greek choric play   RPB

MAUDE BARNES MILLER
The Betti-attitudes, 1924, mother and daughter sketch in 4 scenes   RPB

MAY MILLER (MRS. JOHN SULLIVAN) SBAA
The Bog Guide, 1925, prize winner in Opportunity contest (1)
Christopher's Daughter, 1935   RMN
The Cussed Thing, 1926, honorable mention in Opportunity contest
Freedom's Children on the March, 1943 play??
Graven Images, 1929, young (1)   HSB
Harriet Tubman, 1935 (1)   RMN
Negro History in Thirteen Plays, 1935, edited with Willis Richardson   RPB
Nails and Thorns, 1933, "3rd prize winner in S. Un. contest"
Riding the Goat, for high school and college   RMP
Samory, 1935 (1)   RMN
Scratches, in Carolina Magazine, 59, April, 1929 (1)
Sojourner Truth, 1935 (1)   RMN
Stragglers in (of) the Dust (Dusk), 1930
Within the Shadow, 1920, first prize winner of the Howard Un. Drama award

NELLIE BURGET MILLER (1875- ?)
The Blue Moon, 1926, dream play (1)   RPB
In the Tents of the Shepherd Prince, 1950, folk play   RPB
The Land Where the Good Dreams Grow, 1921, dance fantasy for   RPB
    children, also in Theater Magazine, 36, Dec., 1922.

NELLIE BURGET MILLER (continued)
The Living Drama, 1924, drama of the drama, historical development   RPB
and modern movements visualized

MRS. OSCAR MILLER
Decatur County Pageant, Greensburg, Ind., 1916, with   InI
Mrs. Jethro C. Meek

PAULINE MILLS
The White Totem, 1930, pageant, operetta in pantomime, adapted   RPB
from story by Emma-Lindsay Squier, music by Frances Harland

ROWENA ARTHUR MILLS
French Frocks, 1929, 3 act comedy, with Katherine Meagher   RPB
"Molly," 1938, comedy (1)   RPB

JO MILWARD
Life Is Like That, prod. 1930

KATHARINE MINAHAN
The Infidel, 1904, 4 act romantic tragedy, "romance of Old Spain"   RPB

MAYE C. MINARD
Fat and Happy   CPR-1
The Kelly's Friendship Thanksgiving Dinner   CPR-1

NYDIA E. MINCHIN
The Birthday Cake   JPP
Cold Cream, 1927   ECO
The Jester's Purse, in Jacob M. Ross, Adventures in Literature, 8A   JPP
The Jester's Purse and Other Plays for Boys and Girls, 1926, ed.   RPB
by Minchin

ELAINE INGERSOLL MINICK
The Fourth Rehearsal, 1922, comedy   RPB

ELIZABETH MINOT
The Rose of Old Seville, 1904, a play and poems   RPB

AGNES E. MITCHELL
When the Cows Come Home, (poem), in Patigan, Haig, Semi-   RPB
centennial High Jinks, July 28, 1922, San Francisco

ANNE M. MITCHELL
Mistletoe, 1920, from a story by Alice Brown (1) Playmaker   RPB, DPP
Plays, Series E, No. 2
Peg's Little Sister, 1920, farce, Third Arneberg Prize Play,   RPB, DPP
Playmaker Plays, Series E, No. 8

BERNICE MITCHELL
A Morning in a Superintendent's Office, 1929, comedy (1)   RPB

ELEANOR EARLY MITCHELL
The Twelve Gifts, 1929, Christmas pageant   RPB

FANNY TODD MITCHELL
Angela, prod. 1928, adaptation of A Royal Family by Robert Marshall
Boom Boom, prod. 1929, adaptation of play by Verneuil; lyrics by Mann
 Holiner and J. Kiern Brennan; music by Werner Janssen; book by Mitchell
Music in May, prod. 1929, adaptation of the original by Heinz Merley and
 Kurt Brever; music by Emile Berte and Maury Rubens; lyrics by J.
 Kiern Brennan
Wonderful Night, prod. 1929, adaptation of Die Fledermaus by J. Strauss

FAYE L. MITCHELL
Ellen Meets the Committee, 1929 (1)	RPB
The Flowers Teach Tommy a Lesson	HPP
Pauline of Paris, 1930	RPB
Pitch in His Hair, 1954 play??	
Soft Shoulders, 1929, comedy (1)	RPB
Two Flower, with Jessie B. McCurrach	HPP
Wanted—a Slogan, 1929	RPB
When the Darbys Dieted, 1930, farce (1)	RPB

JULIA D. MITCHELL
Demons and Fairies, 1931, project play , young (1)	RPB
Sleeping Beauty, 1924, 3 acts, young	RPB

MARY M. MITCHELL
Perspectives

MINNIE BELLE (ALEXANDER) MITCHELL (1860- ?)
The Way There, 1914, 4 act morality play, with John Fowler Mitchell Jr.   RPB

NORMA MITCHELL (189?-1967)
Autumn Hill, prod. 1942, with John Harris	
Buy, Buy Baby, prod. 1926, with Russell Medcraft, based on a play by	
Francis R. Bellamy and Lawton MacKall	
Cradle Snatchers, 1931, prod. 1925, with Russell Medcraft	
I Can't Bear It, with R. Medcraft, based on a play by F. Bellamy and	NN
L. MacKall, typescript	
Post Road, 1935, prod. 1934, with Wilbur Daniel Steele	RPB
When Hell Froze, prod. 1930, with Wilbur D. Steele	

RUTH COMFORT MITCHELL (1882- ?)
Beau Trevisor, 193?	RPB
A Modern Girl, prod. 1914, with Marion Fairfax	
My Son, 1915, comedy drama based on German play by Larrongel (1)	DLC
The Sweetmeat Game, 1916 , Chinese play (1)	

ADA MIXON
Peace on Earth, in Poet Lore, 28, New Year's, 1917, 65-77

HELEN L. MOBERT
The Owl's Feather, 1917, Irish fairy play presented by graduating	RPB
class of 1917 at Mt. Holyoke	
The Singing Pool, in Poet Lore, 30, Summer, 1919, 275-88 (1)	

MAMIE HARRIS MOBLEY
Better Than Gold, 1931	RPB
"The College Hobo," 1930	RPB
"Deestrick Skule Up-to-Date," 1931	RPB

MAMIE HARRIS MOBLEY (continued)
Follow Me, 1929	RPB
'44 Flappers, 1928	RPB
Ghosts of Tomorrow, 1930	RPB
High Flyers, 1929	DLC
"Jo-the-Dynamo," 1931	RPB
"Joker's Jubilee," 1929	RPB
"Keepers of the Gates," 1931, mimeographed copy	DLC
Member Honey; or, the Conjurer, 1929	RPB
"The Rosy Pathway," 1931	RPB
"Uncovered," 1930, mimeographed copy	RPB
The Zander-Gump Wedding (comic section), 1928	RPB

MARGARET MOCHRIE
Bill's Day in Court, 1928	RPB
The Fire Ghost	SPE, SH
Magic Gold Pieces, 1924, Girl Scout play (1)	RPB
The Mystery Boy, 1928	RPB
A Twentieth Century Fair, 1926, comedy (1)	RPB

VIRGINIA MOFFAT
The Nativity Story, 1920, Christmas program for children of all grades	RPB

MARY L. MONAGHAN
Country School Dialogues, 1915, especially suitable for the last day of school, for all ages	RPB
Dialogues for Closing Day, 1923	RPB
Dialogues for District Schools, 1939	RPB
Dialogues for Rural Schools, 1920	RPB
Good Things for School Programs, 1925	RPB

ISABEL MONCRIEFF
A Modern Magdalen, 1901, 3 act drama	RPB

HARRIET MONROE (1860-1936) AWW NAW
After All, in Poet Lore, 12, July-Sept., 1900, 321-6, also in The Passing Show	
The Passing Show, Five Modern Plays in Verse, 1903, one-acts	RPB

HARRIET EARHART MONROE (1842- ?)
The Pageant of Protestantism, 1917, celebrating the quadricentennial of the Reformation	MB

HELEN ALBEE MONSELL (1895- ?)
Black Shadows, 1931, 3 act mystery drama	RPB
Blue-ribbon Pie, 1934, 3 act comedy for women	RPB
Flying High, 1924, 3 act rural comedy drama	RPB
His Just Desserts, 1934, comedy (1)	RPB
It's a Ming! 1930, 3 act farce for girls	RPB
The Keepsake, 1928, 3 act farce	RPB
Moon Shy, 1931, 3 act farce	RPB
The Mystery of the Masked Girl, 1931, 3 acts for girls	RPB
The Other Ghost, 1932, 3 act mystery	RPB
Powder Puff Girl, 1938, 3 act farce for women	RPB
Solo Flight, 1933, 3 act comedy	RPB
Three Moss Roses, 1933, 3 act comedy	RPB
The Witch's Doll, 1933, 3 act mystery	RPB

EDITH MONTGOMERY
The Brownies and the Butterflies, 1916   RPB

ELIZABETH MONTGOMERY
The Light of the Star of Peace, in Ladies Home Journal, 35, Dec., 1918, 87 (1)

LUCY MAUD MONTGOMERY (1874-1942)
Anne of Green Gables, 1908   RPB
Mrs. Skinner's Romance, 1908   RPB
Vanity and Vexation of Spirit, 1908   RPB
The Way of Transgressors, 1908   RPB
    (All Wetmore declamations and readings)

VICTORIA MONTGOMERY
Blind Alleys, prod. 1924, with Alice Fleming Sidman

CAROLINE H. MOOAR
Why We Celebrate Washington's Brithday   FPP

ANNE KING MOODY
Blue Beard's Bride; or, the Last Leap Year in Fairyland, 1904   RPB

GRACE MOODY
The Bargain Counter, 1910, 3 act farce for females   RPB

LUCIA M. MOONEY
The Original Thirteen   FPP

ANNE MOORE
Self Defense, prod. 1915

BESSIE COLLINS MOORE
On Bayou La Barre, in Poet Lore, 37, Winter, 1926, 576-83 (1)

DAISY M. MOORE
How Can Nations Practice the Golden Rule? (1)   TMC
More Christian Endeavor Playlets, ed. by E. W. Thornton,   RPB
    1929, a contributor
Why Pray for Others? (1)   TMC

FLORENCE BRADLEY MOORE
A Tale from India, masque   JNS

JESSICA MOORE
Betsey Ross; or, the Origin of Our Flag, 1933, historical operetta;   NBuG, OU
    music by George L. Spaulding
A Joke on the Toy Maker, 1909, music by George L. Spaulding,   RPB-M
    young (1)
Lost, a Comet, 1918, musical play for young people, music by   RPB-M
    George L. Spaulding
Mother Goose Island, 1917, musical play for children   MiD
Nearly a Honeymoon, 1925, music by George L. Spaulding (1)   RPB-M
The Spirit of Christmas, 1912, music by George L. Spaulding (1)   RPB-M

LIDIAN RUTH MOORE
Christmas at the Gables, 1937, comedy (1)   DLC
Like As a Father, 1931? (1)   NN
The Mantuan, 1930, 3 acts, winning play in Vergil contest   RPB

MINET BLACKWELL MOORE
George Washington's Dream (1)

MABEL M. MORAN
Jane Is Psychic, 1934, comedy (1)　　　　　　　　　　　　　RPB
The Shakespeare Garden Club, 1919, fantasy (1)　　　　　　RPB
Why Move to Town? 1938, comedy for women (1)

FLORENCE E. MORE
Revising a Geography, 1929, young (1)　　　　　　　　　　　RPB
Sportsmen, beware! 1937, 30 minutes of fun for actors and　　OrCS
　　audience, young

AGNES MORGAN (1879-1976) NWAT
Grand Street Follies of 1925, music by Lily Hyland
Grand Street Follies of 1927, music by Max Ewing
Grand Street Follies of 1928, music by Max Ewing, Lily Hyland and
　　Serge Walter
Grand Street Follies of 1929, music by Arthur Schwarts and Max Ewing
The Legend of the Dance, prod. 1925, medieval interlude
The Little Clay Cart, adapt. from Hindu of King Shudraka, young
Sudraka, 1934, adaptation of a Hindu drama
The Suicide of the Rue Sombre, prod. 1921-2, based on story by
　　Leonard Merrick

AGNES BANGS MORGAN
In April '75
In the Reign of King James
The Orange Girl (1)
　　(All produced at Radcliffe)

ANNA MORGAN (1851-1936) NAW
The Great Experiment, 1909 Shakespearean fantasy, with　　　　RPB
　　Alice Ward Bailey
Selected Readings, 1928, "designed to import to the student an　　RPB
　　appreciation of literature in its wider sense," compiled by Morgan

MRS. EDWARD NASH MORGAN
Terence, prod. 1904, based on a novel by Mrs. B. M. Crocker

CATHERINE A. MORIN
The Mushroom Meadow (1)　　　　　　　　　　　　　　　　BHP

M. JOSEPHINE MORONEY
Fair Play　　　　　　　　　　　　　　　　　　　　　　　　FWP
The First Thanksgiving　　　　　　　　　　　　　　　　　SBT
A Hoover Thanksgiving　　　　　　　　　　　　　　　　　SBT
Our First Flag, 1921, cantata, music by Elmer Samuel Hosmer　　RPB-M
The Pilgrims of 1620, 1920, cantata, music by Elmer Samuel Hosmer　RPB-M
A Real Thanksgiving　　　　　　　　　　　　　　　　　　SBT
The Silly Isles, 1925, operetta, music by Elmer Samuel Hosmer　　RPB-M

DELLA MORRELL
Things Not Seen, in Six One-Act Plays, MIA Book of Plays, 1929

ALICE MORRILL
A Gift to Santa Claus, 1923　　　　　　　　　　　　　　　RPB

BELLE CHAPMAN MORRILL
Christmas Preparatory Services, 1925					RPB

ANGELA MORRIS
Dorinda Dares, 1924, adapted from story by "Marjorie Bowen" (1)			BTG

ELIZABETH WOODBRIDGE MORRIS (1870-1964)
The Christmas Conspiracy, in St. Nicholas, 39, Dec., 1911, 163-9, 2 acts		SNB
The Crusade of the Children, 1923, Religious Dramas, I				RPB
The Summoning of the Nations, 1934, short pageant of the changing			RPB
   world, written under the auspices of the League of Nations

GRACE MORRIS
Youth and Old Age, 1909 (1)							RPB

HILDA MORRIS
The Book Children's Christmas (1)						CPO

"MARION MORRIS" (See VERNA WHINERY)

ANNE MORRISON (189?- ?)
Jonesy, 1929, 3 act comedy based on short stories by John Peter Toohey		RPB
Pigs, 1924, with Patterson McNutt, 3 act comedy (copyright 1923			RPB
   under title, Johnny Jones Jr.)
Their First Anniversary, 1934 (1)					OPS-VIII
Wilbur
The Wild Westcotts, 1926, prod. 1923, 3 act comedy				RPB

HONORE´ (MC CUE) WILLSIE MORROW (1880?-1940) AWW
Benefits Forgot, 1917, Wetmore Declamation reading				RPB

MARTINA MORROW
The Prophets, 1902, Biblical representation					RPB

KATHERINE DUNCAN MORSE (1888- ?)
Goldtree and Silvertree, 1925, fairy plays to read and act, music by		RPB
   Marion E. LeBron
The Nativity, in Poetry, 37, Dec., 1930, 126-9
On the Road to Parnassus, 1922, 2 scenes					RPB
The Shop of the Perpetual Youth, 1922 (1)					RPB

LAURA M. MORSE
Charity Higgins' Vocal Organ, 1910, amusing entertainment			RPB

LOIS COOL MORSTROM
The Doll Shop, 1920, with Helen Langhanke					RPB

LILLIAN MORTIMER ("NAILLIL REMITRON") (? -1946) AWW
An Adopted Cinderella, 1926, 3 act comedy drama				RPB
The Bride Breezes In, 1926, 3 act comedy drama				RPB
Bunco in Arizona
Cabbages or Dollars, 1931, 3 act comedy drama				RPB
The City Feller, 1922, 3 act comedy of rural life				RPB
Closed Lips, 1932, 3 act comedy drama					RPB
The Eighteen Carat Boob, 1929, 3 act comedy drama				RPB
The End of the Lane, 1925, 3 act comedy drama				RPB
Eyes of Love, 1925, 3 act comedy drama					RPB

LILLIAN MORTIMER (continued)

The Gate to Happiness, 1930, 3 act comedy drama	RPB
George in a Jam, 1931, 3 act comedy drama	RPB
The Girl of the Streets	
The Girl Who Forgot, 1927, 3 act comedy drama	RPB
A Girl's Best Friend	
Go Slow Mary, 1925, 3 act farce	RPB
Happy Valley, 1930, 4 act comedy drama	RPB
He's My Pal, 1927, 3 act comedy drama	RPB
Headstrong Joan, 1927, 3 act comedy drama	RPB
The Heart of the Plains	
His Irish Dream Girl, 1928, 3 act comedy drama	RPB
Jimmy, Be Careful! 1931, 3 act comedy drama	RPB
Kate Barton's Temptation	
Little Miss Jack, 1922, 4 act comedy drama	RPB
Lonely Little Lizalou; or, Two Brides, 1928, 3 act comedy drama	RPB
Love's Magic, 1928, 3 act comedy drama	RPB
Mamy's Lil' Wild Rose, 1924, 3 act comedy drama of the Sunny South	RPB
A Man's Broken Promise, 1906	
A Manhattan Honeymoon, 1929, 3 act comedy drama	RPB
Mary's Castle in the Air, 1926, 3 act comedy drama	RPB
Mother in the Shadow, 1936, 3 act drama of mother love	DLC
Mother's Moment, 1933, 3 act comedy drama	RPB
Nancy Anna Brown's Folks, 1926, 3 act comedy drama	RPB
No Account David, 1929, 3 act comedy drama	
No Mother to Guide Her, 1905 (typed copy at ICU) also in The	CLP-VIII
Great Diamond Robbery & Other Recent Melodramas, Edited by	
Garrett H. Leverton, Princeton Un. Press, 1940	
Nora, Wake Up, 1927, 3 act comedy drama	RPB
The Open Window, 192?, by "Naillil Remitron," typescript	NN
The Path Across the Hill, 1923, 3 act comedy drama	RPB
Paying the Fiddler, 1929, 3 act comedy drama	RPB
The Road to the City, 1923, 4 act comedy drama	RPB
Ruling the Roost, 1926, 3 act comedy drama	RPB
The Shadow of the Gallows	
The Simon-Pure Simpleton, 1932, 3 act comedy drama	RPB
Six Wives on a Rampage, 1934, 3 act comedy drama	RPB
That Terrible Kid, n.d., 4 act comedy drama, typescript	NN
That's One on Bill, 1924, 3 act youthful comedy	RPB
Two Brides, 1928, 3 act comedy drama	RPB
Up the Hill to Paradise, 1935, 3 act comedy drama	RPB
A Wild Flower of the Hills, 1929, 3 act comedy drama	RPB
The Wild Oats Boy, 1930, 3 act comedy drama	RPB
The Winding Road, 1927, 3 act comedy drama	RPB
The Winning of Joy, 1925, 3 act comedy drama	RPB
Yimmie Yonson's Yob, 1923, 3 act comedy drama	RPB

FRANCES MC KINNON MORTON

The Three Friends, in St. Nicholas, 51, March, 1924, 530-3

MARGUERITE W. MORTON

The Blind Girl of Castel-Cuille, 1892, tableau of poem by Longfellow	RPB
Ideal Drills, 1926, collection of drills, marches and motion songs	RPB
Poison, 1895, farce in 1 scene for 4 females, adapt. by Morton	RPB
Prize Drills and Dances, 1911	
The Red, White and Blue Drill, 1919	RPB
Scene from "The Last Days of Pompeii," 1909, arranged by Morton	RPB

MARGUERITE W. MORTON (continued)
 The Spanish Gypsy, 1905, based on poem by George Eliot   RPB
 The Two Roses, 1894, 2 act farce   RPB

MARTHA MORTON (1865-1925) AWW NWAT
 A Bachelor's Romance, 1897, (pub. 1912) 4 act romantic comedy   RPB
   (typescript at NN)
 "Brother John," 1893, typescript   NN
 The Diplomat, prod. 1902
 "A Fool of Fortune," prod. 1896, typescript   NN
 A Four Leaf Clover, 1905
 Geoffrey Middleton,Gentleman, 1892
 Helene Buderoff; or, A Strange Duel, 1889   DLC
 Her Lord and Master, 1902 (1912 ed. at RPB)   RPB
 His Wife's Father, 1895, prod in London as The Sleeping Partner, 1897,   NN
   typescript
 The Illusion of Beatrice
 The Merchant, prod. 1891, a Wall Street drama, won 1st prize in N. Y. World
   playwriting competition
 The Movers, 1907, typescript   NN
 On the Eve, prod. 1909, from German of Leopold Kampf
 The Senator Keeps House, prod. 1911, prompt book   NN
 A Strange Duel; or, Helene Buderoff, 1895   DLC
 Three of Hearts, prod. 1915, based on a story, "Hearts and Masks," by
   Harold McGrath
 The Triumph of Love: The Merchant, 1891, won N. Y. World playwriting
   competition, also The Theatre Magazine playwriting competition in 1904
 The Truth Tellers, 1905
 Val Sinestra, 1924

KATHARINE PRESCOTT MOSELEY
 Daggers and Diamonds, 1921, "travesty in one act"   RPB, PTM

ESTELLE M. MOSES
 Hunger, 1926, comedy (1)   RPB

GRACE CELESTE MOSES
 The Tree of Memory, 1924, Armistice Day pageant   RPB,SSH-III

HARRIET CALHOUN MOSS
 The Drama Class of Tankaha Nevada, with Mary Aldis, in Aldis,
   Plays for Small Stages,1915 (1)

F. ETHEL MOULD
 The Trimming of the Tree, in Ladies Home Journal, 36, Dec., 1919, 143-4 (1)

HOPE H. MOULTON
 Aunt Julia's Pearls, 1927, 3 act comedy   RPB
 Hamlet, 1927, burlesque (1)   RPB
 It's Up to You, 1931, 3 act comedy   RPB
 Let's Get Married, 1929, 3 act comedy   RPB
 Marry the Boss's Daughter, 1932, 3 act comedy   RPB
 Othello, 1927, burlesque (1)   RPB
 The Platitudinous Pose, 1934, comedy (1)   RPB
 Romeo and Juliet, 1927, burlesque (1)   RPB

MARIE MUGGERIDGE
The Rest Cure, 1906 (1)   NN

HELENE MULLINS (1899- ?)
The Truth About Liars, in Poet Lore, 34, Spring, 1923, 145-51, comedy (1)

ETHEL WATTS MUMFORD (See ETHEL WATTS MUMFORD GRANT)

CARABEL LEWIS MUNGER
The Goose Creek Line, 1916, 2 act comedy   RPB
Just Like a Woman, 1912, comedietta (1)   RPB

HELEN WAITE MUNRO
A Day Off at the Old Ladies' Home, 1930, for women (1)   RPB
Faith of Our Fathers, 1939, service for churches and Sunday schools   DLC
The Fourteenth Veteran, 1930, Memorial Day play for elementary schools RPB
Jean's Dream Christmas, 1932   RPB
Oldville Has a New Minister, 1938, with Carrie W. Ladd   RPB
The Return of the Christmas Special, 1929   RPB
Settin' Up With Wilhemina, 1930, Dutch comedy (1)   RPB
The Soldier City, 1951, for Memorial Day   RPB
What Is a King? 1936, fantasy (1)   DLC

LELIA MUNSELL
The Gifts, a pageant for Rally Day   HPY
Let There Be Peace, "Suitable for Armstice (sic) Day or Any Other   HPY
     Patriotic Occasion. Also for Christmas"

JANE MURFIN
Daybreak, prod. 1917, with Jane Cowl, typescript   NN
Information Please, prod. 1918, with Jane Cowl
Lilac Time, prod. 1917, with Jane Cowl
Mr. Grant, 1935, screenplay of play by Arthur Goodrich   NN
Prince Gabby, comedy, based on story, "The Talkative Burglar," by   NAB-II
     Edward Wallace (1)
Smilin' Through, 1924, prod.1919, with Jane Cowl, melodramatic   RPB
     romance, original author listed as Allan Langdon Martin
Stripped, prod. 1929

ELEANOR J. MURPHY
Colonial Times   WPP

ELINOR MURPHY
All's True, 1917, pageant written under her direction by English class   RPB
     at Miss Hopkins' School, N. Y.
Dream Pictures, 1917, pageant written and presented by a class in   OCl
     history at Miss Hopkins' School
I'll Try, in St. Nicholas, 48, Jan., 1921, 256-60, young (1)
The Long Road to Tomorrow, 1917, pageant written under her   RPB
     direction by the English class at Miss Hopkins' School, N. Y.

ETHEL ALLEN MURPHY
The Victory of the Gardens, 1919, pageant for the U. S. school   MB
     garden army

HELEN AGNES MURPHY
No Lantern for Wu Lee, 1924, missionary play of China   NN, NcD

KATHERINE C. MURPHY
The New Managing Editor, 1909 (1)   RPB

LOUISE BOYCE MURPHY
A Frat Initiation, 1909, college sketch   RPB
The Mother Goose Comedy, 1907   ViU

MARGUERITE MURPHY
Father's Day On; or, Mother's Day Off, 1926 (1)   RPB
Lucky Moon, 1924, young   RPB
Protecting Peg Jane, 1924, 3 act comedy drama   RPB

ANNE MURRAY
No Other Way, 1922, prod. by Pasadena Community Players
Run, hero, run! 1937, comedy
Zee-Zee, 1927, 3 act comedy, winner of 2nd prize in Penn. Pub.   RPB, PP-1
   Co. contest

JOSEPHA MARIE MURRAY
A Dream Lesson, 1916, fairy play for girls (1)   RPB
Her Son's Sweetheart, 1915, 2 act comedy for females   RPB
Playing the Game, 1916, 2 act comedy for females   RPB

MABEL HAY BARROWS MUSSEY (1873- ?) (See MABEL HAY BARROWS)

MARY M. MYERS
Patriotic Characters   FPP

MARY V. MYERS
The Squirrels' Thank You   SBT

TRACY DICKINSON MYGATT
The Aino Puku, in World Outlook, 4, June, 1918, 20-1 (1)
Bird's Nest, 1922, fantasy (1)   RPB
Children of Israel, 1922, 3 acts
Crystal's Career, before 1922
Friendly Kingdom, 1921, pageant play for girl reserves, typed copy   MiD
Good Friday, 1919, "Passion play of Now" (about World War I)   RPB
Grandmother Rocker, 1922, costume play (1)   RPB
His Son, in Poet Lore, 39, 1928, 605-31 (1)
"The New Star," typescript   NN
The Noose, prod. 1918-9 by Neighborhood Players, in Drama, 20,
   Nov., 1929, 42-8 (1)
Seventy-three Voted Yes, in World Outlook, 4, Sept., 1918, 18-9
The Sword of the Samurai, Religious Dramas, II, peace play   FRD-II
Watchfires, 1917, 4 acts   RPB

ETHEL MYHAND
The Modern Spinsters' Association, 1923, farce   RPB

N

ADELE NATHAN
The Song of Solomon, pantomime
We Hold These Truths, 1943, pageant, by Adele (Gutman) Nathan   NN

MAY ROSE NATHAN
Foothills of Fame, 1922, farce (1)   RPB
"Poor Me," 1921, with Elsie West Quaife, comedy   RPB

ELEANOR F. NAUGHTON
As We Like It, 1930, with Belle Barsky, "play on manners"   RPB

NANCY NAUMBURG
The Adoption, 1930, based on a story by de Maupassant

MRS. VINCENT NEALE
Maids and Bachelors; or, Employers Beware, 1914, 3 act farce   RPB

MAY T. NEFF
The Freeing of Grandpa, 1927, with Mrs. Chester F. Johnston (1)   RPB

ALICE DUNBAR NELSON (See ALICE RUTH MOORE DUNBAR-NELSON)

FAUNIE MULLVAIN NELSON
The Chief's Thanksgiving Invitation, 1930, young (1)   RPB
The Land of Lost Illusions, 1926, young (1)   RPB
Over the Rainbow Bridge, 1926, young (1)   RPB
Rainbow's End, 1929 (1)   RPB
The Smile Maker, 1926, young (1)   RPB
A Timely Shower, 1930, for Mother's Day   RPB

HOPE NELSON
The Story of George Washington   FPP

LUCY H. NELSON
Jephthah's Daughter, 1909, 3 act Biblical drama   RPB

MARION LAWRENCE NELSON
Spirals, 1928, written for Northwestern Un. and Drama Club   RPB
    of Evanston (1)

ELSA BEHAIM NESSESSON (1877-1969)
In the Secret Places, in Drama, 17, November, 1926, 43-5+

EVA THOMAS NETTLETON
Uncle Sam's Council, 1912, young (1)   RPB

KATHERINE S. NETZORG
Hiawatha Dramatized, 1915, with L. P. Kellenbarger   RPB

SARA NEUMANN
The Old Order, in Drama, 11, February, 1921, 147-50 (1)   NN

GERTRUDE NEVILS (See GERTRUDE KNEVELS)

MARY ROSS NEVITT
Rostof Pearls, 1912, social incident (1)   RPB

BERTHA NEWBERRY
The Toad, prod. 1911 at Forest Theater, Calif.

MAUD CHRISTINE NEWBURY (1883- ?)
The Gifts of Nations, 1923, pageant for rural schools   RPB

CLARA NEWCOMB
Pageant of New London, 1911, New London, Conn.

ETHEL L. NEWMAN
Wally and the Widow, 1905, duologue (1)

HELEN L. NEWMAN
The Service the Fairies Did   WPP
Unthankful Thankful, 1922, "a little girl who lost her name for a year"   RPB

CAROLINE NEWNES
Under the White Flag, in Smart Set, 7, July, 1902, 159-60 (1)

VIDA NEWSOM
Bartholomew County Pageant, in celebration of the Indiana Centennial   InI

ADELAIDE NICHOLS
At the Gate of Stars, 1918, patriotic masque   RPB
The Children of the Pilgrims, 1920, "pageant for the use of schools and   RPB
    societies in celebration of the landing of the Pilgrims at Plymouth in
    1620," music arranged by Andra S. Wavle
The Floating Bridge, 1932, "four plays of gods and men in the   RPB
    Japanese form"
The Haunted Circle and Other Outdoor Plays, 1924   RPB

ANNE NICHOLS (1891?-1966) AWW NWAT
Abie's Irish Rose, 1924, prod. 1922   CCS
Down Limerick Way, 1920, prod. 1919
The Gilded Cage, prod. 1920, typescript   NN
The Happy Cavalier, 1918
Heart's Desire, 1916, with Adelaide Matthews
Her Weekend, prod. 1936 under title Pre-Honeymoon
Howdy, King, 1926
Just Married, 1929, prod. 1921, with Adelaide Matthews, 3 act comedy   RPB
The Land of Romance, 1922
Linger Longer Letty, prod. 1919, with Bernard Grosman, music by Alfred
    Goodman
A Little Bit Old Fashioned, 1918
Love Dreams, prod. 1921, lyrics by Oliver Morosco, music by Werner
    Janssen or Jensen)
The Man from Wicklow, 1917
Marry in Haste, 1921
Nearly Married, prod. 1929, same as Just Married, with Adelaide Matthews
Pre-Honeymoon, prod. 1936, with Alfred Von Ronkel (first titled
    Her Weekend)
Puppy Love, 1926
Sam Abramovitch, 1927
Seven Miles to Arden, 1919
Springtime in Mayo, 1919

CONTENT S. NICHOLS
   Everychild, School Morality Play, in St. Nicholas, 42, February, 1915,
      358-9 (1)

DAISY D. NICHOLS ("DORA DEANE")
   A True Heroine, 1905, with Jane Tupman, 4 act musical comedy drama   RPB

DOROTHY E. NICHOLS
   Campus Cavalcade, 1939, pageant of Stanford   CSt
   A Child Is Born, 1931, modern nativity play (1)   RPB
   Hickory Dickory, 1934, 3 act modern comedy
   Lost Children, 1931, Christmas play for children   RPB
   Seven Spinsters and a Song, 1933, fantasy for Junior high schools (1)   RPB
   Sounding Brass, 1931, miracle play in a medieval setting   RPB
   When to Laugh, 1928, 3 act comedy   RPB
   Who Picked Mrs. Flower?, 1947, with Dorothy Wyman, pub. in   RPB
      Twenty Short Plays on a Royalty Holiday, 1942

EDNA PHYLLIS NICHOLS
   The Fixer, 1928, comedy (1)   RPB

MARY EUDORA NICHOLS ("EVE BROWN") (1901- ?)
   Hula on Broadway, 1929, by "Eve Brown," musical comedy   RPB

ANNE NICHOLSON
   The Magic Horn, with Charlotte Chorpenning

MEREDITH NICHOLSON (1866-1947)
   Honor Bright, 1923, with Kenyon Nicholson, 3 act comedy   RPB
   Rosalind at Red Gate, 1910, play by George Middleton, based on   MH
      story by Nicholson, typed copy
   Tell Me Your Troubles, 1928, with Kenyon Nicholson, 3 act farce   RPB

RUTH ARNOLD NICKEL
   Christmas Everywhere, 1924, young   RPB
   The Greatest of These; a feast of lights, 1924, "pageant for the joint   RPB
      use of the Light brigade, the Young Women's and the Women's
      Missionary Societies"

MAUDE NIEDERMEYER
   The Made-Over Dress, 1928, with Mary Larcombe, humorous   RPB
      monologue
   Mrs. Widdell at the Band Concert, 1928, with Mary Larcombe,   RPB
      "good encore reading"

MINNIE A. NIEMEIER
   New Plays for Every Day the Schools Celebrate, 1928 (1936 ed. at RPB)   RPB

LILLIAN EDITH NIXON
   Fairy Tales a Child Can Read and Act, 1912   RPB

KATE WOODWARD NOBLE
   A Colonial Tea, 1915, published by the D.A.R. (1)   RPB

"ROSE NOEL"
   The Path of True Love, 1929, 3 act comedy   RPB

CATHERINE WILSON NOLEN
   Being Married, 1929-30, domestic comedy (1)
   The Family, 1928-9, episode of the American home (1)
      (Both are Carolina plays)

JEANETTE NORDENSHIELD
   Don't Do That, 1913, comedy (1)   OCl

FRANCES NORDSTROM (188?- ?)
   All Wrong, 1919
   Her Market Price, 1924
   It Pays to Flirt, 1918, with Joseph McManus
   Lady Bug, 1935, prod. 1922, 3 act comedy
   Little Doctor Love, 1935 (1)   OCl, DLC
   Music Box Revue, prod. 1921, with Irving Berlin and others
   On the Ragged Edge, 1919
   Room 44, prod. 1912
   The "Ruined" Lady, prod. 1920, typescript   ICU
   Snapshots of 1921, prod. 1921, with Glen MacDonough and others
   Some Lawyer, 1919

"MRS. GEORGE NORMAN" (See MELESINA MARY BLOUNT)

LOUISE NORMANN
   The Day of Judgment, 1929   RPB

KATHLEEN THOMPSON NORRIS (1880-1966) AWW NAW
   The Kelly Kid, 1926, with Dan Totheroh, comedy (1)   RPB, PTM, CCO
   Perfect Service, 1934, also in Harper's Bazaar, Sept., 1930, 82-3+,   RPB
      "rollicking little one act farce, bright as a gold piece"
   Victoria, 1934   RPB

ALICE WHITSON NORTON (1897- ?)
   A Barrel of Fun; or, It's Good Enough for the Missions, 1924,   RPB
      playlet for girls
   A Basket of Beautiful Things   FWP
   Choosing a Doll   CLP-I
   Christmas Eve on the Trolley Car   CLP-I
   Christmas Time at Santa's Headquarters   CLP-I
   The Fairies and a Christmas Tree   CLP-I
   Home for the Holidays, 1926 (1)   NN, IU
   Little Plays for Christmas, 1928, with others   RPB
   The Night of Nights, 1934, 2 act Christmas play   DLC
   The Paramount Children's Day Book, No. 4, 1930, a contributor   RPB
   The Paramount Mother's Day Book, 1941, No. 2, a contributor   RPB
   A Suitor for Sallie, 1926, 2 act comedy   RPB
   The Toy Shop Mix-up   CLP-I
   The Wisest Wish   FWP

ELEANOR NORTON
   The Triumph of Earth, in Poetry Review, 10, March-April, 1919, 89-95 (1)

IDA G. NORTON
   Club Stunts, 1922, five entertaining stunts for women's clubs, high   RPB
      schools, and other organizations

LOUISE NORTON
  Little Wax Candles, 1914, farce (1)   RPB

MARY NORTON
  A Cure for Discontent   TDF

ELISE RIPLEY NOYES
  The Gypsy's Prophecy, 1927, "mid-Victorian episode" (1)   RPB

MARION INGALLS OSGOOD NOYES (1859- ?)
  Little Plays for Little People, 1910, with Blanche H. Ray   RPB

MAY GERTRUDE GAFFNEY NUNNEY (MRS. GEORGE F. NUNNEY)
    (1877- ?)
  A Complete Holiday Program for First Grade, 1911, with Nancy   RPB
    M. Burns

JULIA K. NUSBAUM
  Golden Gifts, 1922 (1)   RPB

O

PAULINE EATON OAK
The Dearest Wish, 1922, outdoor pageant for children   CD

VIOLET OAKLEY (1874- ?)
The Book of the Words, 1909, Westchester County Historical Pageant   RPB
Cathedral of Compassion, 1935, dramatic outline of the life of Jane Addams
Pageant of Westchester, 1909, Bronxville, N. Y., with E. P. Oberholzer,   NHi
    programme text
Philadelphia Historical Pageant, 1908

EUNICE M. OBENSCHAIN
The Dance of the Fairies, 1908, exhibition drill for girls   RPB

AGNES O'CONNOR
For the Colleen
Lilacs
(She won the Un. Prize in Dramatic Compositon, Un. of N. D., Dakota
    Playmakers)

KATHERINE OFFICER
All Soul's Eve, in International, 7, Jan., 1913, 14-5 (1)

JANET OGDEN
Going to School in China, in Everyland, 5, 112-3 (1)

OLIVE OGLE
The Bellman of Mons, 1928?, adaptation of play by Dorothy Sherrill   RPB

DELLA (or DELLE) HOUGHTON OGLESBEE
The Ten Fingers of Francois, in Drama, 14, Nov., 1923, 65-9,   SSH-I
    Christmas play of old Provence (1)

RUTH O'HANLON
In My Day (1)   SCT

CONSTANCE MARIE O'HARA
Enter the Champion, 1930, comedy (1)   RPB
Exit the Grand Duchess, 1926, comedy (1)   RPB
The Years of the Locusts, 1935, 3 acts   RPB

KATE RICHARDS O'HARE (CUNNINGHAM) (1877—1948) NAW
World Peace, 1915, 3 act spectacle drama, with Frank P.   RPB

ANNA G. WILLIAMS O'HIGGINS
The Holdup, 1930, with Harriet French Ford, comedy (1)   RPB

ESTHER KATHLEEN O'KEEFE
An Historic Pageant of the Story of Marshall County, Indiana, n.d.   InI

MARION R. O'KEEFE
The Literary Club, 1916, comedy (1)   RPB

RITA OLCOTT
Lusmore, prod. 1919, with Grace Heyer

VIRGINIA OLCOTT
Everyday Plays for Home, School and Settlement, 1925, young   RPB
Holiday Plays for Home, School, and Settlement, 1930, orig. pub. 1917,   RPB
    young
Household Plays for Young People, 1928   RPB
Industrial Plays for Young People, 1928   RPB
International Plays for Young People, 1925   RPB
Little Lost Aster, 1928, "play of a Flower Child who Forgot her   RPB, SSL
    Name and Home"
The Night Before Christmas   SCS
Patriotic Plays for Young People, 1918 (1934 ed. at RPB)   RPB
Plays for Home, School and Settlement, 1916   RPB
World Friendship Plays for Young People, 1929   RPB

AMY OLIVER
Hicks at College, 1909, with Sara Preston and Ralph E. Dyar,   RPB
    3 act comedy

MARGARET SCOTT OLIVER
The Hand of the Prophet, 1913, Arabian play in 4 episodes   RPB
The King's Son, in Drama, 16, May, 1926, 297-8 (1)
The Seige of Alhambra, 1926, cantata, music by Clarence K. Bawden   NBuG
Six One Act Plays, 1916
Tea & Little Rice Cakes, and Other Plays, 1926   DLC
The Turtle Dove, 1913, Chinese play, comedy   RPB, KPC, SSV

"TEMPLE OLIVER" (See JEANNIE OLIVER DAVIDSON SMITH)

MARIE OLLER
Little Plays from Greek Myths, 1928, with Eloise K. Dawley   RPB

ESTHER E. OLSON (1901- ?)
Altering at the Altar, 1931, romantic comedy   RPB
Beside a Garden Wall, 1931, revue of old and modern times within   RPB
    the garden
Billy's First Date, 1941, comedy (1)   Or, DLC
Christmas Memories, 1931, "recalling the much loved Christmas   RPB
    hymns in a home of today"
Conclusions, 1931, comedy (1)   RPB
Cottage for Sale, 1941, comedy (1)   RPB
A Date With a Dream, 1950, 3 act comedy   RPB
Four Shorts for High Schools, 1939   RPB
Giving Thanks Today, 1930, Thanksgiving play, young   RPB
Glamour Boy, 1949, 3 act comedy   RPB
Green Shudders, 1947, 3 act mystery play for women   RPB
The Hallowe'en Party, 1930, young (1)   RPB
I'm a Family Crisis, 1952, 3 act comedy   ViU, OrCS
Let's Make Up, 1941, comedy (1)   RPB
Lighting the Way, 1930, Christmas play (1)   RPB
The Man Higher Up, 1928, 3 act comedy   RPB
Meddlin', 1930, comedy (1)   RPB
Mister Co-ed, 1952, 3 act comedy   RPB
Moon Winks and Other Dramatic Themes, 1929, arranged for platform
    and radio presentation
No Man's Paradise, 1929, for females, 3 acts   RPB

ESTHER E. OLSON (continued)

No Room at the Inn, 1928, "telling the story of the crooked   RPB
   mouth lamp" (1)
October Gave a Party (1)   JGH
On the Way Home (1)   JPM
Parlor Tricks, 1928, "for women but of interest to men" (1)   RPB
A Peach of a Family, 1930, 3 act comedy   RPB
Prom King, 1941, 3 act comedy   DLC
A Proposal by Proxy, 1935, novelty (1)   DLC
A Question of Figures, 1939, comedy (1)
Red Shoes at Plymouth, 1929, Thanksgiving play   RPB
Right Around the Corner, 1930, comedy (1)   RPB
A Senior and His Day, 1929, complete program for Class Night exercises RPB
Seventeen Is Terrific, 1947, 3 act comedy   RPB
Some Little Fixer, 1928   RPB
Spark Plugs, 1927, comedy for teenagers (1)   RPB
A Summer Day Dream (1)   JGH
Sweetheart Revue, 1929, "evening's entertainment built around the RPB
   sweetheart theme and embodying the popular sweetheart songs"
Swing Fever, 1940, 3 act comedy   NBuG, DLC
They Say, 1927, for 5 ladies (1)   RPB
This Thing Called Love, 1931, 3 act comedy   RPB
Tuning In With Youth, 1940, collection of radio plays
Two's Enough, 1929 (1)   RPB
Under the Spreading Christmas Tree, 1947, for girls   RPB
Up in the Air, 1928, for 5 women (1)   RPB
Valiant Hector, 1929, 3 act comedy of youth   RPB
The Wallflower Cuts In, 1943, comedy (1)   RPB
Why We Give Thanks, 1931, Thanksgiving play for children   RPB

BILLIE ONEAL (MRS. BEN G. ONEAL)

The Inspiration, prize play of Woman's Forum of Wichita Falls   OPW
Prize-winning One Act Plays, 1930, she was compiler   RPB

ROSE MELLER O'NEIL

Three Wonder Tales, prod. 1910, adapt. from Hawthorne's The Wonder Book

"ANNE O'NEILL" (See MRS. JACOB S. RANDALL)

SISTER M. AGATHA O'NEILL

Unified by the Spirit of Prayer. The Life of George Washington

SISTER MARY EDWIN O'NEILL (1867- ?)

The Christmas Candle and Other One-act Plays, 1930   RPB
The Coming of the Light: St. Patrick at Tara, 1925, 3 acts   RPB

MARY O'REILLY

Evangeline Entertainment, 1905, arranged in 5 acts for school   RPB
   exhibitions and private theatricals, with music

CLARA BEATRICE ORWIG

Back Home Again, 1925, 3 act comedy   RPB
Black and Blue, 1926, 3 acts   RPB
Clearing Skies, 1936, with J. C. McMullen   RPB
Gentlemen Prefer Bonds, 1926 (1)   RPB
High Hattie, 1928, comedy (1)   RPB
In Abraham's Boudoir, 1928, comedy (1)   RPB

CLARA BEATRICE ORWIG (continued)
Poison Ivy, farce (1)   DLC
The Runaway Detective, 1931, 3 act mystery comedy   RPB

ANNE WYNNE O'RYAN
Angel Cake, 1928, 3 act comedy   RPB
Just Because, prod. 1922, with Helen S. Woodruff, music by
    Madelyn Sheppard
Plays from American History, 1925, with Francis O'Ryan   RPB
Things, 1923, 3 act comedy
What's In a Name? prod. 1920, with John Murray Anderson and Jack
    Yellen, music by Milton Ager

INNIS GARDNER OSBORN
An Easy Mark, 1910, farce (1)   RPB
O.K. Phipps, 1937, 3 acts   RPB
A Taking Way, 1914, farce (1)   RPB
Up Against It, 1911, farce (1)   RPB

LYNN OSBORN
Easy Money, 1926, farce (1)   RPB
The Isle of Smiles, 1926, farce (1)   RPB
Moonshine, 1926, farce (1)   RPB

HELEN OSGOOD
Helen Osgood's New Monologues, 1929   RPB
Helen Osgood's Successful Monologues, 1925
Monologues and Character Sketches, 1934

MONICA BARRIE O'SHEA
The Rushlight, in Drama, 7, Nov., 1917, 602-15 (1)

SUSANA CLAYTON OTT (1877- ?)
The Good Night at San Gabriel, 1947   RPB
A Masque, 1915, story of the nativity for the Commonwealth of   RPB
    Los Angeles

ELLA L. OTTUN
Bright Ideas for Closing Day, 1926, with Ella B. Johnson   Or
Christmas Joy Book, 1930, a contributor   RPB
The Ideal Christmas Book, 1928, with Ella B. Johnson   DLC

MARY ELIZABETH OVERHOLT
The Door of Success, 1926, young (1)   RPB

GRACE SLOAN OVERTON
Drama in Education, 1926, theory and technique
Dramatic Activities for Young People, 1927
A Mother's Tomorrow, 1933, 2 acts   RPB

GWENDOLEN OVERTON
First Love—and Second, in Smart Set, 3, Jan., 1901, 141-6 (1)

MARY WHITE OVINGTON (1865-1951) AWW NAW
The Awakening, 1923, 4 acts (1972 ed. at RPB)   RPB
Hazel, in The Crisis, 1913
Phyllis Wheatley, 1932, based on her letters

GRACE ARLINGTON OWEN
 Engaged by Wednesday, 1912, 3 act farce   RPB
 The Wonderful Story of Illinois, 1918, pageant   RPB

IDA MAY OWEN
 Sir Richard Serves His Queen   JPP

MARIE BANKHEAD OWEN (1869-1958)
 The Acting Governor, 1913, 4 acts   AU
 Alabama Centennial Commission Series of Children's Plays in
  Commemoration of the close of a century of statehood, 1919,
  Montgomery, Alabama, Paragon Press, collection of one acts, all pub.
  individually also
 Alabama; or, the Making of a State, 1919, historical play, third in RPB
  the series
 At Old Mobile, 1919, historical play, second in the series   DHEW
 The Battle of Maubilla, 1919, historical play, first in the series RPB
 De Soto and the Indians, 1919, first in a series of children's plays RPB
 The Extra Plate, 1937, 4 act comedy   NcD, DLC
 How Alabama Became a State, 1919, third in a series of children's plays RPB
 How Bienville Saved Mobile, 1919, second in a series of children's plays RPB

RUTH BRYAN OWEN
 Bethlehem, children's pageant of Christmas, in Woman's Home
  Companion, 50, Dec., 1923, 22-3

P

FANNY HANCE PACKARD
    The Man Who Understood Women, 1924, comedy   RPB
    Mrs. Gray of Lonesome Mountain, 1925, church entertainment (1)   RPB

MRS. WILLIE DAY PADGITT
    The Womanless Divorce Case, 1927? (1)   RPB

ELLA FLORENCE PADON
    In Charge of the Consul, 1915   RPB
    Her Little Sister, 1901 play?

EDITH M. PAFFENBERGER
    Mother Sudds of Tenement Court, 1925, playlet   RPB

KATE (KATHERINE) STEARNS PAGE (1873- ?)
    Robin Hood, 1921, with music, for children   RPB

MARY SHAW PAGE
    Training Mary, 1921, comedy (1)   RPB

JOSEPHINE PAGE-WRIGHT (See JOSEPHINE PAGE WRIGHT)

JENNIE E. PAINE
    The Oxford Affair, 1924, with Josephine H. Cobb, 3 act comedy   RPB

EDITH F. A. U. PALMER PAINTON (1878- ?)
    As a Woman Thinketh, 1914, "comedy of the period"
    The Blue Entertainment Book, 1930, a collection with Lillian Stain   RPB
        Schreiner, Laura Rountree Smith and J. A. Baxter
    A Burns Rebellion, 1913, "conference of the best-known character   RPB
        creations of Robert Burns"
    The Class Ship; or, Launched But Not Anchored, 1914, dram. of   RPB
        Longfellow's "The Building of the Ship" (1)
    Clubbing a Husband, 1915, 3 act comedy for women's clubs   RPB
    The Commencement Manual, 1915, collection of miscellaneous items   RPB
    The Crimson and the Blue, 1912, class play in 4 acts and an epilog   RPB
    The Dear Boy Graduates, 1912, 4 act farce   RPB
    Dialogues and Plays for Entertainment Days, 1917, one-acts
    En Masque, 1904, monologue for a woman   RPB
    A Forest Carnival, 1906, "spectacular entertainment in 2 acts"   RPB
    The Graduates' Choice, 1914, commencement playlet (1)   RPB
    The Healing Touch, 1914, 4 act drama   RPB
    Just Plain Dot, 1912, commencement playlet for children   RPB
    The Lady of the Library, 1917, 3 act comedy-drama   DLC
    The Laughing Cure, 1916, 2 act comedy   RPB
    A Mere Man, 1915, "study in feminine color" (1)   RPB
    Polly in History Land; or, Glimpses of Washington, 1917, 4 acts   RPB
    A Prairie Rose, 1913, comedy-drama of the Kansas prairies in 4 acts   RPB
    The Prize Essay; or, "Boy Wanted," 1916, 2 act comedy for girls
    Sister Angela, 1912, drama for female characters only   RPB
    Some Class, 1917, commencement play in 4 acts and an epilogue   RPB
    Specialty Entertainments for Little Folks, 1917, one-acts
    Star Bright, 1915, 3 act comedy drama   RPB

EDITH F. A. U. PALMER PAINTON (continued)
The Triumph of the Cross, 1905, Easter cantata   RPB
The Value of X, 1916, commencement play in 3 acts and prologue   RPB
The Vision of the Graduate, 1914, commencement play
Wanted! a Cook, 1916, comedy (1)   RPB
The Winning Widow, 1916, 2 act parlor comedy   RPB

CARLA L. PALM
The Perplexing Pirandello, in Drama, 15, Feb., 1925, 102-4, comedy (1)
Schnitzleresque, in Drama, 14, March-April, 1924, 210-2+, satire (1)

ANNE PALMER
Hat at the Theatre (1)

ANNE BUZBY PALMER
Hanging Out the Wash, 1918, with Katharine E. Smedley, Negro farce (1) RPB

ANNE M. PALMER
At the Depot, 1915, character play (1)   RPB
Buying a Suit for Jimmy (1)

ANNIE D. PALMER
The Rescue, 1927, "Improvement Era prize play" (1)   RPB
"Sazy," 1922, 3 act social service drama   RPB

BELL ELLIOTT PALMER (MRS. JAMES ALLERTON PALMER) (1873- ?)
The Anti-Gossip Club, 1925, novelty entertainment for women (1)   RPB
Aunt Billy from Texas, 1923, farce   RPB
The Bluners from Blue Ridge, 1924, 3 act comedy-drama   RPB
Bob Upsets the Calendar, 1923, young   RPB
Can't You Listen a Moment? 1927 (1)   RPB
Christmas at the Old Folks' Home, 1926   RPB
Christmas Truants, 1928 (1)   RPB
Dodging an Heiress; or, His Uncle's Choice, 1918? 2 act comedy   RPB
The Easter Song Bird, 1924 (1)   RPB
Easy Plays for Women, 1933   RPB
Fidgets, 1932, special entertainment for 10 women   RPB
Fighting It Out at the Cheer Club, 1924 (1)   RPB
Her Blessed Boy, 1923, young   RPB
The Home of Confusion, 1924, 3 acts   RPB
The Hoot-Owl, 1923, 2 act comedy   RPB
In the Garden of Life, 1924, Easter (1)   RPB
It Can't Be Done, 1925, comedy (1)   RPB
Just Carrying On, 1926, "for all patriotic occasions," for women (1)   RPB
The Love Flower, 1921 (1)   RPB
The Meddlesome Mrs. Mars, 1929, for women (1)   RPB
Men Not Wanted (1)
The Menu Committee, 1931, specialty entertainment for 10 women   RPB
Miss Hope Hall's Sale, 1926, Colonial play for women (1)   RPB
Mrs. Santa Claus, Militant, 1914, Christmas comedy (1)   RPB
The Necktie Hero, 1925, comedy (1)   RPB
"Not So Turribul," 1925, sketch   RPB
Out of Town, 1907, 3 act comedy   RPB
Paint Pots, 1927, monologue   RPB
The Point of View, 1906, comedy sketch   RPB
The Professor's Truant Gloves, 1906, comedy sketch   RPB
Rest a Bit, Mother, 1925, 3 act play for church or school use   RPB

BELL ELLIOTT PALMER (continued)
Setting the Nation Right, 1924   RPB
A Social Crisis; or, Almost a Tragedy of Tongues, 1918? comedy (1)   RPB
Such As We Can't Use, 1926, Christmas, for women   RPB
They Do Say, 1924, entertainment for women's clubs or societies   RPB
Tilton, the Uplifter, 1924, 3 act comedy   RPB
The Tree of Golden Fruit, 1929, for Mother's Day (1)   RPB
The Truth Party, 1925, entertainment for women   RPB
Truthful Husbands, 1924, comedy for Washington's birthday (1)   RPB
The Umbrella Man, 1926, 3 act comedy   RPB
The Very Idea, 1932, for women (1)   RPB
Virginia Opens the Door, 1927, 3 acts   RPB
We Never Gossip, 1932, comedy for women (1)   RPB
What Can We Do With Aunt Sally? 1922, 2 act comedy   RPB
What's the Use? 1926, 3 act comedy   RPB

FANNY PURDY PALMER (1839-1923)
Three Plays, 1928 ??   RPB

HELEN M. PALMER
A Man and a Maid, 1907, farce (1)   RPB
New Year's Day, in Harper's Bazaar, 35, May, 1901, 43-8, comedy (1)

JOSEPHINE LUDLOW PALMER
The Lighting of the Christmas Tree, 1921, with Annie L. Thorp adapted   RPB
    from "The Christmas Guest" by Selma Lagerlof, Vassar play (1)

KATE B. PALMER
The Spirit of Woman in Bohemia, 1913   RPB

MARTHA ROYLE PALMER
The Best Seller, 1913, for amateurs (1)   RPB

MAUDE G. PALMER (MRS. GEORGE T. PALMER)
His Old Sweethearts, in Ladies Home Journal, 26, Nov., 1909, 13+ (1)

MAY MC KINNEY PALMER (1865- ?)
Three Short Plays, 1925, young   RPB

ROSE AMELIA PALMER
Caponsacchi, 1927, prod. 1923, with Arthur Goodrich, based on "The   RPB
    Ring and the Book" by Robert Browning, 3 acts

SARAH ELIZABETH PALMER
Story Plays for Little Children, 1917, with Mary Leora Hall   RPB

MARJORIE BARTHOLOMEW PARADIS
Just as Good, 1931?
The New Freedom, 1931, prod. 1930, 3 act comedy   RPB
None But the Fair, 19??, reprinted from Plays, the drama magazine   WU
    for young people (1)
One Act Plays for All-Girl Casts, 1952   RPB

EMILY SEABER PARCHER
Hey Dickie! 1932   RPB
"Hey, Ma!" 1928   RPB
Life Is Bitter, 1931   RPB

EMILY SEABER PARCHER (continued)
    Mrs. Jones at the Wheel, 1929   RPB
    On the Shelf, 1930   RPB
    Robert Makes Love, 1932   RPB
    Ronny Drives the Car, 1931   RPB
    A Ten Cent Ride, 1932   RPB
        (All are Wetmore Declamation Bureau readings, plays, entertainments)

AMY MINCHER PARISH
    Blood Ties, 1927, drama (1)   RPB

REBECCA M. PARISH
    Saul in the Desert   HPY

JULIA E. PARK
    Trial for the Murder of the King's English, 1919 (1)   RPB

CHARLOTTE BLAIR PARKER (See LOTTIE BLAIR PARKER)

DOROTHY ROTHSCHILD PARKER (1893-1967) AWW NAW NWAT
    After Such Pleasures, 1934, by Edward F. Gardner, revue based on her novel
    Big Broadcast of 1936, 1935, with Alan Campbell, screenplay
    Candide, 1957, prod. 1956, book by Lillian Hellman; lyrics by Parker
        and others; music by Leonard Bernstein
    Close Harmony; or, the Lady Next Door, 1929, prod. 1924, with   RPB
        Elmer Rice, 3 acts (c. 1924 under title Soft Music)
    The Coast of Illyria, prod. 1949, with Ross Evans, based on life of
        Charles Lamb
    The 49ers, prod. 1922, revue (She was a contributor.)
    Here We are, 1931 Also in R. David Cox and Shirley Cox, Eds.,   CCT
        Themes in the One-Act Play, 1971 (1)
    The Ladies of the Corridor, 1954, prod. 1953, with Arnaud d'Usseau   RPB
    The Little Foxes, 1941, with Alan Campbell, screenplay
    Mr. Skeffington, 1944, with Alan Campbell, screenplay
    Round the Town, 1924, she did lyrics for the revue
    Shoot the Works, 1931, revue (She was a contributor.)
    A Star Is Born, 1937, with Alan Campbell, screenplay
    Sweethearts, 1938, with Alan Campbell, screenplay

LOTTIE BLAIR PARKER (CHARLOTTE BLAIR PARKER)
    (1858-1937) AWW
    Lights of Home, 1903
    The Redemption of David Corson, prod. 1906, from a novel by Charles
        Frederic Goss
    Under Southern Skies, prod. 1901, typescript   NN, MH
    Way Down East, 1900, prod. 1898, pastoral drama (typescript at NN)   RPB
        elaborated by Joseph R. Grismer, based on play by Parker
    White Roses, won a play contest sponsored by N. Y. Herald

LOUISE N. PARKER
    Disraeli, Little Theatre Tournament, 1927

MARY MONCURE PAYNTER PARKER
    Art Clubs Are Trumps, 1918, for females (1)   RPB
    The Back Street Driver, 1926, monologue   RPB
    Black Art, 1903, minstrel sketch (1)   RPB
    Bread, Butter and Romance, 1922, comedy (1)   RPB
    A Day at the Know-it-all-Woman's Club, 1904   RPB

MARY MONCURE PAYNTER PARKER (continued)

Driving from the Back, 1926, monologue	RPB
The End of the Journey, 1928, monologue	RPB
Funny Monologues and Poems, 1921	RPB
George Has a Grouch on Sisters, 1913, monologue	RPB
George Says Boys Don't Have Such a Snap in Life After All, 1910, monologue	RPB
The Gun and the Gospel, 1928, monologue	DLC
Happy Plays for Happy Days, 1934, 12 one-acts	RPB
Helping Santa Claus	JEP
Hot Air; or, Station P.U.N.K. Broadcasts, 1926, "take-off of a broadcasting studio program" (1)	RPB
How Mandy Got the Vote, 1910, monologue	RPB
I Swippa da Street, 1928, monologue	RPB
Jolly Monologues, 1921	RPB
Little Miss America and the Happy Children, 1918, "jingle history of the U.S., a patriotic play in one act"	RPB
Lively Monologues and Poems, 1922	RPB
"Love Behind the Scenes," 1903, comedy (1)	RPB
Love, Eet Ees Wonderful! 1928, monologue	CLSU, DLC
Maggie MacCarty Listens at the Door, 1913, Irish monologue	RPB
Mandy's Lost Opportunity, 1913, Negro monologue	RPB
Merry Monologues, 1916, "a laugh for every day in the year"	RPB
Miss Queen Jezzy-Belle an' de Grapes, 1941, monologue	RPB
Mistah Absalom an' His Ha'r, 1941, monologue	NN
Mistah Balaam an' His Mule, 1934, monologue	RPB
Mistah John Baptist an' Miss Salomy, 1941, monologue	NN
Mistah Moses an' de Calf, 1932, monologue	RPB
Mistah Noah an' de Ark, 1928, monologue	RPB
Mrs. Busby's Pink Tea, 1902, comedy (1)	RPB
Mrs. Gadabout's Busy Day, 1903, comedy (1)	RPB
Mrs. Hoops Hooper and the Hindu, 1921, comedy (1)	RPB
Mrs. Lot Gets Some Salt, 1931, monologue	RPB
Monologues for Young Patriots, 1917	RPB
Monologues, Stories, Jingles and Plays, 1917	RPB
Monosketches, 1938, new monologues	
Mostly Comics, 1923, collection of monologues, readings and poems	RPB
The Mother They Forgot, 1926, monologue	RPB
The Mother Who Served, 1930, monologue	RPB
New Monologues and Dialect Stories, 1908	RPB
The Old Oaken Bucket, 1913, 4 act rural drama	RPB
Parker's New Monologues, 1936	
Peppy Monologues, 1933	
Powder and Patches, 1902, 2 act comedy	RPB
The Princess Innocence, 1906 (1)	RPB
The Prodigal Comes Home, 1930, Biblical drama (1)	RPB
A Quiet Evening at Home, 1906 (1)	RPB
The Rehearsal, 1906, farce (1)	RPB
Shadows, 1915, "play of the South today and a dream of the past" (1)	RPB
Snappy Monologues, 1931	RPB
When Lucindy Goes to Town, 1913, monologue	RPB
When Your Wife's Away, 1902, farce	RPB

MAUD MAY PARKER

Louisiana, 1917, pageant of yesterday and today	RPB
The Missive, 1907, Biblical dramatic poem	

REBA KIDDER PARKER
Miss Neptune, 1914, 2 act comedy   RPB

JULIETTE B. PARMALEE
The Sequel of the Womanless Wedding, 1922, "mock trial for   RPB
    man characters"

KATHARINE PARRY
Cease Fire! 1921, with John R. Collins (1)   DLC

KATE PARSONS
The Commodore Marries, prod. 1929, 3 act comedy drama, typescript   NN

KITTY PARSONS
Aunt Abigail's Bomb, 1928, comedy (1)   RPB
The Better Man, 1928 (1)   RPB
Catching the 4:14, 194? (1)   RPB
The Double Honeymoon, 1928, comedy (1)   RPB
Everything Comes to Her Who Waits, 1928, comedy (1)   RPB
The Good For Nothing, 1928, comedy (1)   RPB
In a Subway Station, 1926 (1)   RPB
Just Out of the Hospital, 1928, comedy (1)   RPB
The Proxy Bridegroom, 1927 (1)   RPB

LAURA MATILDA STEPHENSON PARSONS (1855- ?)
Aunt Jerusha's Quilting Party, 1901, novelty in one scene   RPB
Colloquy of the Holidays, 1899, for children   DLC
The District School at Blueberry Corners, 1894, 1st pub. 1889, farce RPB
Jerusha Dow's Family Album, and Jerusha Dow's Album, No. 2,   RPB
    her friends and neighbors, 1892-9
Jerusha Dow's Album No. 2, her friends and neighbors, 1899   RPB
Living Pictures of the Civil War, 1894   RPB
The New Woman's Reform Club, 1902, humorous entertainment (1)   RPB
The Old Maid's Convention, 1899, entertainment in one scene   RPB
Scenes and Songs of Ye Olden Times, 1894, old folk's entertainment RPB
Scenes in the Union Depot, 1905, humorous entertainment (1)   RPB
Tableau and Pantomime Entertainments for School or Public Perfor- RPB
    mance, 1914, with Clara Ella Cooper, Bertha Currier Porter and others
A Variety Contest, 1901, humorous entertainment in one scene   RPB

MARGARET COLBY GETCHELL PARSONS (1891- ?)
Almost Rehearsal-less Plays, 1931, stunts and novelty programs   RPB
The Birthday Candles, in Woman's Home Companion, 44, Aug., 1917, 23 (1)
By the People   SPC
Christmas Greetings, 1929 ("A pattern traced") typed copy listed
    at RPB play?
Colette of the Red Cross, 1918, for Red Cross Juniors (1)   RPB
The Elfin Knight of Halloween   SSH-I
Elsie in Bookland (1)   SSL
Enemies, Peace Play for children   SPP
Fathers, for Fathers' Day   SAR
Good Turns; or, Only a Tenderfoot, 1928, 3 act Boy Scout play   RPB
Hans and Gretel (1)   SSH-I
In the Children's Playhouse, 1923, collection   RPB
Jack-i'-the-green, 1920, outdoor play for a May festival   Or
The Little Patriot and Barbara Fritchie, 1927   RPB
Massa Linkum's Sojer   SLP-1

MARGARET COLBY GETCHELL PARSONS (continued)
A Modern Thanksgiving, 1937 (1)   RPB, STP
The Mothers They Forgot (1)   SSH-IV
The New Holiday (1)   SSL
Off the Old Block, 1935, comedy for women (1)   OCl, DLC
One Night Stand, 1942, five one-act plays for young people
Only Your Father, Christmas (1)   SSC
The Prophecy, 1931, for boys (1)   JPG
Proposal Number Seven, 1918, 2 act comedy   RPB
Rainy Day Plays, 1920, mimeographed copy   Or
Red Letter Day Plays, 1921, one-acts   RPB
The Rummage Sale, 1927, for females (1)   RPB
Scoops, 1930, 3 act comedy for females   RPB
Spruce, Cone and Bunchberry, 1916, "about an unpleasant family   RPB
    which becomes pleasant when the Camp Fire spirit enters the home"
Ten Stirring Bible Plays, 1927   RPB
The Woman's Club Playbook, 1935, collection   RPB

MIRA CLARK PARSONS
Santa's Predicament, 1909   RPB

EDNA PASCHALL
Enter Elinore, 1923, 3 acts, written for and given by Dramatic Club of   RPB
    the Springfield, H. S.
Under Contract, 1924 or earlier, 3 act comedy drama

HELEN PASCHALL
The Tempestuous Tale, 1916, presented by the class of 1916, Mt.   RPB
    Holyoke; plot suggested by Dorothy Towle; written by Helen Paschall;
    words and music by Ruth Elms

HATTIE PASHLEY
Pageant of Palos Park, 1916, Palos Park, Illinois

KATHERINE PATRICK
Die Keppel, 1929
Hammer Beat, 1930

CORA MEL PATTEN (1869- ?)
Pageant of Illinois, 1909, with Thomas Wood Stevens, Evanston, Illinois
Peace Pageant, 1915, programme text   MB
A Peace Pageant for Children and Young People, 1915, with   MB
    Elma C. Ehrlich
Plays for Children, 1923, compiled by Patten

ADA PATTERSON
The Bonfire, 1927, with George Nelson, 3 act comedy drama, typescript   NN
Love's Lightning, prod. 1918, with Robert Edeson

ANNE VIRGINIA SHARPE PATTERSON (1841- ?)
The Lady of the Green Scarf, 1910, "entertainment exercise for schools   RPB
    embodying the need for conserving our country's natural resources"

ANTOINETTE DECOURSEY PATTERSON
Disposing of Polly, 1925, comedy   RPB
Flop Goes the Flapper, 1924, comedy   RPB
For the Love of Kitty, 1924, comedy (1)   RPB

ANTOINETTE DECOURSEY PATTERSON (continued)

The Kill-joy, 1924, comedy	RPB
The Knock Out, 1925, comedy	RPB
Managing Clarence, 1925, comedy	RPB
Melissa Makes Good, 1924, comedy	RPB
Room for Argument, 1925, comedy	RPB
Shocking Mrs. Simpkins, 1924, comedy	RPB
Thirty Comic Dialogues, 1925	DLC
What Ails Maria? 1925, comedy	RPB

EMMA PATTERSON
One Raisin Too Much, 1925

LOIS B. PATTERSON
Amos Putnam, Match-Maker, 1930, pub. by Am. Farm Bureau Fed.   RPB

MARJORIE PATTERSON
Pan in Ambush, 1921, "spring phantasy" (1)   VP

KATE HOLLAND PATTON

At the Railway Station, 1930, monologue	RPB
Just Before the Wedding, 1929, comedy (1)	RPB

NANETTE BAKER PAUL (1866-1928?)
Dramatic Sketches in the Life of Susan B. Anthony, 1926, for   RPB
    National Woman's Party

SUSAN PAXSON
Two Latin Plays for High School Students, 1911   RPB

MARY PAXTON

Little Vinnie Ream, n.d., with Henry Lancaster, typescript	NN
The Kettle Singing, 1929 (1)	RPB

ELIZABETH STANCY PAYNE

Harem Scarem, 1924, 2 act farce	RPB
The Purple Rim, 1935 (1)	OCl. DLC

FANNY URSULA PAYNE (1875- ?)

God's Creatures, 1922, short drama written for the Am. Soc. for the prevention of cruelty to animals	RPB
A Pageant of Girlhood, 1928, prepared by Community drama service	Or
The Parted Sisters, 1914, allegorical play (1)	RPB
Plays and Pageants of Citizenship, 1920, one-acts	RPB
Plays and Pageants of Democracy, 1919	RPB
Plays for Any Child, 1918, one-acts	RPB
Two War Plays for Schools, 1918, one-acts	RPB
Winning an Heiress, 1915, farce	RPB

LILIAN HARRIS PAYNE
May Queen, 1926, 1st pub. 1923, carnival extravaganza   RPB

FRANCES M. PAYSON

Down Among the Fairies, 1929, operetta, libretto and lyrics by Payson and Vane Kendrick; music by Henry S. Sawyer (1)	RPB-M
Elma, the Fairy Child, 1889, operetta	DLC

STELLA T. PAYSON
   Burglar-proof, 1925, 3 act comedy   RPB
   The Christmas Spirit, 1922   RPB
   Mechanical Dolls, 1925, young, Christmas (1)   RPB
   The Society Column, 1922 (1)   RPB

ELEANOR LANE PEABODY
   The Evolution of the English May Day, 1924, pageant presented at   RPB
      Wheaton College

JOSEPHINE PRESTON PEABODY (MRS. LIONEL MARKS) (1874-1922)
      AWW NAW NWAT
   The Chameleon, 1917, 3 act comedy   RPB
   The Collected Plays of Josephine Preston Peabody, 1927   RPB
   Fortune and Men's Eyes, 1900, also in Dickinson, Ed., Drama,   RPB, COP
      Garden City, N. Y., 1922, 87-135 (1)
   Marlowe, 1901, 5 act drama   RPB
   Pan, 1904, choric idyll, music by Charles Harris   RPB
   The Piper, 1909, won Stratford play contest, 1910; also in   RPB,MRA,DCC-2
      Thomas H. Briggs, et.al, Romance, 1932, also one scene in PTS-VI
   The Portrait of Mrs. W., 1922, about Mary Wollstonecraft, 3 acts   RPB
      and epilogue
   The Wings, 1917, prod. 1912, also in Harper's Magazine, 110, May, 1905, RPB
      947-56 and in Poet Lore, 25, Vacation, 1914, 352-69 (1)
   The Wolf of Gubbio, 1913, about Francis of Assisi, 3 acts   RPB

LILIAN J. PEARSON
   The Christmas Chain, 1921   RPB
   How the Christmas Was Found, 1921 (1)   RPB

MRS. ELIA WILKINSON PEATTIE (1862-1935) AWW
   Castle, Knight and Troubadour, 1904, in an apology and 3 tableaux RPB
   The Great Delusion, 1932, drama (1)   RPB
   The Love of a Caliban, 1898, romantic opera (1)   RPB
   Thunder, prod. 1919, with Pearl Franklin
   Times and Manners, 1918, pageant, pub. by Chicago Woman's Club
   The Wander Reed and Seven Other Little Theatre Plays, 1923   RPB

MARY GRAY PECK
   Germelshausen, 1904, 4 act drama, with Carl Schlenker and   RPB
      Frances B. Potter

ANITA PEDIGO
   Si's First Basketball Game, 1930, Wetmore declamations   RPB

MS. (?) PEEL
   Pageant of Atlanta, 1914

KATHARINE V. PEIRCE
   Old English Plays Her Part, 191? Americanization pageant   RPB

LILLIAN SUTTON PELE'E
   At the Little Pipe, in Poet Lore, 31, Autumn, 1920, 422-31, Hungarian folk
      play (1)
   Stringing Beads, in Poet Lore, 39, Summer, 1928, no. 2, 295-305 (1)
   Ties of Blood, in Poet Lore, 32, Winter, 1921, 572-80 (1)
   The Trigger, 1927, 3 act mystery farce   RPB
   Wives on Strike, 1920, 3 act satirical comedy   RPB

NETTIE H. PELHAM
> The Baby Show at Pineville, 1904, musical play for children   RPB
> The Belles of Blackville, 1897, Negro minstrel entertainment
> The Christmas Ship, 1888, Christmas entertainment   RPB
> The Matrimonial Exchange, 1905, 2 act eccentric comedy   RPB
> A Musical Bouquet, 1901, 2 act novelty   RPB
> The Old Fashioned Husking Bee, 1891, old folks' entertainment
> The Realm of Time, 1890, pageant for young people and children   RPB
> The White Caps, 1891, for children   RPB

MAY PEMBERTON
> Christmas Plays for Children, 1914, one-acts

MRS. FREDERICK PENDER
> Ain't It Awful, Mabel?, 1911, humorous verse monologue   RPB
> His Exceptional Mother-in-law, 1905 (1)   RPB
> Ojistoh, 1911, with Emily Pauline Johnson, illustrated Indian   RPB
>   woman monologue

MARY LUCY PENDERED (1858-1940)
> Hymen a' la Mode, in Smart Set, 32, Sept., 1910, 127-30 (1)
> William Penn, 1922

SUSIE B. PENDLETON
> Freemasonry Outdone; or, the Up-to-date Order of Goosie Girls, 1905, RPB
>   mock initiation for all female characters in one scene

ANNA PENLAND
> The Obedient Princess (1)   RSS

MARGARET PENNEY
> Elusive Cynthia, prod. 1923, Pasadena Comm. Playhouse
> The Falcon and the Lady, 1924, romance (1)   RPB
> Other People's Husbands, 1924, comedy (1)   RPB

CAROLINE de F. PENNIMAN
> Three Christmas Wishes, 1926   RPB

JULIE HELENE PERCIVAL
> The Bully, prod. 1924, with Emmett Corrigan, typed copy   NN

"LOTTA X. PERIENCE"
> "Mr. Wright Gets in Wrong," 1928, "drama of trade and commerce   RPB
>   in one act and a half"

ANNIE STETSON PERKINS
> Arctic Hospitality; or, Queen Summer at the Pole, 1905   RPB

ELEANOR ELLIS PERKINS (1893- ?)
> Daybreak, 1918, missionary pageant, prepared for the golden jubilee RPB
>   celebration of the Woman's Board of Missions of the Interior
> Moon Magic, c1931, masque for Midsummer's Eve   DSS
> My Lady's Yuletide, 1914, with Isabelle J. Meaker, won 3rd prize   MH, PP
>   in contest by Drama League of Chicago
> The Scotch Twins, 1930, for children, from the book by   RPB
>   Lucy Fitch Perkins

ELEANOR ELLIS PERKINS (continued)
    Shakespeare's Lovers in a Garden, 1927, flower masque, written for   RPB
        Drama League of America, for its tercentenary celebration of
        Shakespeare's birthday, by Alice C. D. Riley, re-edited in 1927,
        prologue and epilogue by Perkins
    Thy Brother's Keeper, 1919, morality play   RPB

ELIZABETH A. PERKINS
    The Child in the Midst, 1919, child welfare life-play   RPB

EVELYN M. PERKINS
    The Coming of Joseph, 1930   RPB

LOUISE SAUNDERS PERKINS (See LOUISE SAUNDERS)

MRS. MAX PERKINS
    The Woodland Princess

SOPHIE HUTH PERKINS
    The Colored Ladies' Political Club; or, The Colored Suffragettes, 1910,   RPB
        female minstrel afterpiece
    Mirandy's Minstrels, 1934   RPB
    Walk This Way, Please, 1917, satire on shopping   RPB

FRANCES PERRY
    Wide Open Windows, 1925, with Emma Knauss, pageant for high   RPB
        school students

LOUISE SUBLETTE PERRY (1901- ?)
    Devil's Lane, 1928, modern morality play (1)   RPB
    One Fine Day   YSP-II
    Saturday Market   YSP-I

LUCIA PERRY
    King Tutankhamon's Ruin, in Bookman (New York), 58, Jan., 1924, 604-5 (1)

JULIA MOOD PETERKIN (1880-1961) AWW
    Box-Chillen, 1932   OPS-VII
    Scarlet Sister Mary, 1930, with Daniel Reed, based on her story,   NN
        typescript

VIRGINIA PETERSEN
    Confetti, 1928, harlequinade

AGNES EMELIE PETERSON
    A Bed of Hay, Christmas   YSP-III
    Briar Rose, 1929, opera fantasy, music by Louis Woodson Curtis   RPB
    Christmas Gift, 1938   YSP-IV
    The Christmas Lamb, 1941   RPB
    Creaking Stairs, 1935, mystery play for younger players   WaPS, DLC
    The Eyes of Tlaloc, 1936, 3 act mystery
    Gilt-Edged, 1929, Christmas comedy   HSP
    In the Light of the Star, 1935, in Drama, 21, Nov., 1930, 19-20+ (1)
    Joan of the Nancy Lee, 1931, 2 act comic opera, music by
        Louis Woodson Curtis
    La Posada, 1938, Christmas (1)
    Madonna of the Roses, 1937, comedy drama (1)

AGNES EMELIE PETERSON (continued)
The Marriage of Nannette, 1923, 3 act comic opera, music by
   Louis Woodson Curtis
The Merry Hares, 1939, 3 act comedy   OCl, DLC
Mocha Cake, 1938, 1st pub. 1933, comedy (1)   RPB
The Necklace Is Mine, 1937 (1)
A Pageant in Honor of Vergil Bi-millennium, 1930, music by   CSmH
   William Hartshorn, mimeograph copy
Penel'pe, 1938 (1)
Roads, 1927, pastoral comedy, Drama League prize   GHP
Shelter for a Wanderer, 1952, Christmas (c. as La Posada, 1939) (1)   RPB
Star On the Trail   YSP-V
The Wind, in Drama, 15, May, 1925, 174-7+ (1)
Words and Music by Pierrot   YSP-III

CLARA BELLE PETERSON
The Coming of Summer, with Gertrude Porter Driscoll   JPP

OLGA PETROVA (1886- ?)
The Ghoul, 1925 (1)   RPB
Hurricane, 1924, "four episodes in the story of a life"   RPB
What Do We Know? 1930, prod. 1927
The White Peacock, 1922, 3 act romantic tragedy   RPB

EMMA PETTY
The Gift of Jehovah   DPC
Savannah Postpones Her Ascension, 1921   RPB

HELENA A. PFEIL
Bill Perkins' Proposin' Day, 1910, rustic comedy (1)   RPB

ELIZABETH STUART PHELPS (See ELIZABETH STUART PHELPS WARD)

PAULINE PHELPS ("PAUL MARION") ("PRISCILLA WAYNE")
The Adolescent Young, 1927, satirical farce (1)   RPB
The Adventures of Tom Sawyer, 1941, 1st pub. 1936, 3 act adaptation   RPB
As Molly Told It, 1909, by "Paul Marion," with Marion Short, RPB
   romantic comedy
As the Moon Rose, 1907, dramatic romantic Revolutionary war NN
   recitation and monologue
Au Revoir Sally, 1928, with Marion Short   RPB
Aunt Elnora's Hero, 1900, humorous monologue for a woman   NN
Aunt Polly from Peru, 1947, 3 act comedy   RPB
Aunt Sarah on Bicycles, 1899, humorous monologue for a woman NN
The Average Boy, 1905   NN
The Bad Boy Comes Back, 1935, 3 act comedy, with Marion Short RPB
The Belle of Philadelphia Town, 1925, 4 act colonial comedy , with RPB
   Marion Short
Betsey Holden's Burglars, 1906, comedy monologue for a woman NN
Billy's Animal Show, 1907, humorous recitation for a boy   NN
The Birds' Christmas Carol, 1942, dram. of story by   RPB
   Kate Douglas Wiggins (1)
The Bishop and the Convict, 1939, based on an incident in   RPB
   Les Miserables (1)
Black Gold, 1932, 3 act dramatic comedy, with Marion Short   RPB
The Blue Ribbon Hat, 1930 (1)   RPB
"Borrowed Tails," 1937, comedy (1)   RPB

PAULINE PHELPS (continued)

A Box of Powders, 1906, comedy, with Marion Short (1)   RPB
Burlesque Pantomime of Shakespeare's "Seven Ages of Man," 1903   NN
"The Christmas Rose," 1938, comedy (1)   RPB
The Confederates, 1906, romantic comedy, with Marion Short (1) RPB
The Cook, 1903, "humorous monologue in Irish dialect for a lady" NN, IU
Cozy Corners, 1922, 4 act comedy, with Marion Short   RPB
County Fair at Punkinville, 1912, with "Paul Marion," farce   RPB
Courting the Widow, 1909, romantic comedy, with "Paul Marion" RPB
Cousin Ann, 1938, comedy (1)   RPB
A Cyclone for a Cent, 1894, farce (1)   RPB
Daisy's Music Practice Hour, 1907   IU
Deacon Slocum's Presence of Mind, 1904, monologue for a woman
Dialect, 1899, Werner's readings and recitations, No. 21   RPB
    (She was compiler.)
"The Dormitory Dub," 1936, comedy (1)   RPB
Dramatic Selections, 1898, Werners readings and recitations, No. 10 RPB
    (She was compiler.)
"Dumb Dora," 1932, comedy (1)   RPB
A Dumb-waiter Difficulty, 1906, monologue for a woman   RPB
Edith Economizes, 1932   RPB
A Family Plate, 1904, comedy, Irish dialect monologue for a woman NN
Firetown's New Schoolhouse, 1903, monologue, "As told by   NN
    the Deacon's wife"
The Flour Girl, 1927, 3 act comedy, with Marion Short   RPB
Food Conservation Club Meeting, 1928, humorous monologue   RPB
    for a woman
The Girl from Out Yonder, 1929, 4 act comedy drama, with Marion Short RPB
"Glass Dishes," 1938, 3 act comedy   RPB
A Grand Army Man, prod. 1907, by Harvey O'Higgins, based on play
    by Phelps and Marion Short, prod. by David Belasco??
Her Cuban Tea, 1902, humorous monologue for a woman
The Hidden Guest, 1926, 3 act comedy, with Marion Short   RPB
His First Shave, 1936, comedy (1)   RPB
Home From College, 1915, sketch for 4 males, with Marion Short (1) RPB
Home Sweet Home, 1929, comedy (1)   RPB
The Hoosier Schoolmaster, 1940, comedy adapted from book by Edward
    Eggleston   RPB
Huckleberry Finn, 1940, 3 act adaptation   RPB
Humorous Readings and Recitations, 1899, Werner's readings and RPB
    recitations No. 20 (She was compiler.)
I Know George Washington, patriotic play (1)   RPB, NPW
The Impatience of Job, 1932, 3 act character comedy, with Marion Short RPB
In Washington's Day, 1932, play of Revolutionary times, with   RPB
    Marion Short
Jack's Brother's Sister, 1916, sketch, with Marion Short (1)   RPB
Jane Eyre, 1941, adaptation   RPB
A Jolly Brick, 1903, monologue   NN
Junior Buys a Car, 1937, comedy (1)   RPB
Just Commonplace, 1903   NN
Kit's Caller, 1908, humorous monologue for a woman   RPB
"The Leading Lady," 1936, comedy (1)   RPB
The Little Minister, 1940, based on book by J. M. Barrie   RPB
Little Women, 1939, 3 act dramatization   RPB
"The Lost Letter," 1938, comedy (1)   RPB
"The Lost Ring," 1938, Thanksgiving (1)   RPB
"Love in Bloom," 1935, comedy (1)   RPB

PAULINE PHELPS (continued)

Lucky Lucy, 1938, comedy (1)	RPB
Madame Butterfly, 1954, dram. of story by John Luther Long	WaSp
The Man Without a Country, 1941, adapt. of story by Edward Everett Hale (1)	RPB
A Merry Christmas, 1940 (first scene from Little Women) (1)	RPB
A Midnight Courtship, 1903, monologue (1)	NN
A Millinery Melee, 1904, comedy monologue for a woman	NN
A Million Dollar Joke, 1934, 3 act comedy	RPB
Minister's Black Nance, 1899, monologue	NN
Miss Minerva and William Green Hill, 1939, comedy from the book by Frances Boyd Calhoun	RPB
Mr. Price's Pressed Pants, 1936	RPB
Mrs. Moneymade's Fitting, 1928, with Marion Short	RPB
The Moon and the Moonstruck, 1930 (1)	RPB
Nancy Pretends, 1927, 3 act modern comedy, with Marion Short	RPB
The Night Club Girl, 1932, with Marion Short (1)	RPB, NPW
No Wedding Bells for Me, 1937, by Charles George, based on a play by Phelps and Short	RPB
The Old Fifer, 1907, dedicated to the Sons of the American Revolution	NN
Only Me, 1924, 3 act modern play, with Marion Short	
"Orchids for Marie," 1935, comedy (1)	RPB
Overalls Bridget, 1928, monologue	RPB
The Patched Coat, 1937, comedy (1)	RPB
Pawnshop Granny, 1935 (1)	RPB
Pease and Beans, 1928, satirical farce (1)	RPB
Pride and Prejudice, 1941, adaptation	RPB
The Quilting Bee at Bascomb's, 1932, comedy (1)	RPB
The Reverend Mr. Tuffscrappen, 1906	NN
Rosalind's Surrender, 1901, monologue	RPB
The Ruggleses in the Rear, 1942, suggested by a story by Kate Douglas Wiggins	RPB
The Ryerson Mystery, 1933, 3 acts, with Marion Short	RPB
Saint Cecilia, 1908 (1)	
Scorching versus Diamonds, 1903, monologue	NN
A Shakespearian Conference, 1901	
Shameless Sarah, 1932, colonial comedy (1)	RPB
Shavings, 1930, prod. 1920, 3 act comedy from a story by Joseph C. Lincoln, with Marion Short	RPB
Sister Sally, 1933, 3 act farce	RPB
Sixteen Two Character Plays, 1906, one -acts with Marion Short	RPB
A Spinster from Choice, 1929, comedy (1)	RPB
Spinster Thurber's Carpet, 1903	NN
The Sprightly Widow Bartlett, 1930, colonial comedy (1)	RPB
Stop! Go! 1930, 3 act comedy drama, with Marion Short	RPB
A Story of Hard Times, 1903	NN, IU
Sweet Clover, with Marion Short	
The Sweet Girl-graduate, 1900, humorous monologue for a woman	RPB
A Telephone Romance, 1900, monologue for a woman	RPB-micro
The Tell Tale Heart, 1939, based on Poe's story (1)	RPB
That Boy Jimmy, 1941, 3 act comedy	RPB
Tom Sawyer Wins Out, 1940, dram. of incident from the book (1)	RPB
A Trial Performance; or, the Stage Struck Maiden, 1903 (1)	RPB
"Tub Trouble," 1938, comedy (1)	RPB
Uncle Peter and the D.D.S., 1935, farce (1)	RPB
What a Masquerade Did? 1906, society monologue for a woman	NN

PAULINE PHELPS (continued)
Where's Grandma? 1932, 3 act comedy, by "Priscilla Wayne" and
  Wayne Sprague
Who Said Quit? 1932, 3 act comedy, with Marion Short   RPB
The Wistful Widow, 1932, 3 act comedy, with Marion Short   RPB
Witches' Hour and Candlelight, 1922, with Marion Short (1)   RPB

THE FOLLOWING ARE PLAYS FOR WHICH PHELPS PROVIDED THE TEXT
AND STAGE BUSINESS:

A Backward Child, 1906, by Harriet Louise Childe-Pemberton, child and RPB
  governess farce for 2 females, with Marion Short
Crystal Gazer, 1906, by Leopold Montague, with Marion Short   RPB
Fast Friends, 1906, by R. E. Henry, comedy for 2 females,   RPB
  with Marion Short
A Happy Ending, 1906, by Bertha Moore, romantic pathos play   RPB
  for 2 females, with Marion Short
He, She and It, 1906, by William Muskerry, matrimonial comedy,   RPB
  with Marion Short
Husbands in Clover, 1906, by H. C. Merivale, comedy,   RPB
  with Marion Short
A Love Suit, 1913, by W. Gordon Smythies, romantic comedy,   RPB
  with Marion Short
A Morning Call, 1906, by Charles Dance, romantic comedy,   RPB
  with Marion Short
"The Nettle," 1906, by Ernest Warren, comedy, with Marion Short   RPB
A Show of Hands, 1906, by W. R. Walkes, farce, with Marion Short   RPB
Those Landladies, 1906, by Ina Leon Cassilis, boarding house   RPB
  comedy for two females, with Marion Short
Two Jolly Girl Bachelors, 1906, by Edward Martin Seymour,   RPB
  with Marion Short
Villain and Victim, 1906, by W. R. Walkes, farce, with Marion Short   RPB
The Violin Maker of Cremona, 1940, by Francis Coppee (called Fennel)   RPB

ALICE EVELYN PHILIPPS
The Enchanted Lake, 1924, sylvan play   RPB
Oddments, 1938, book of plays   RPB

BETTINE K. PHILLIPS
Aunt Dinah's Quilting Party, 1903, original entertainment in 1 act   RPB
  and 1 scene

MARGUERITE KREGER PHILLIPS
The Boy Who Found the King, 1929, Christmas play, adapt. of   RPB
  story by Raymond McDonald Alden
The Christmas Image, 1930, Christmas play and pageant for young folks RPB
The Christmas Spirit of Swift Deer, 1930 (1)   RPB
Christmas Trimming   YSP-III
A Family Affair, 1951, 3 act comedy   RPB
Grandma and Mistletoe, 1931, Christmas (1)   RPB
A Halloween Frolic, 1931   RPB
Hospital Zone, 1964, comedy (1)   RPB
Mary Wasn't Here, 1949, comedy (1)   RPB
Mrs. Hall's Club Paper, 1931, comedy for women's clubs (1)   RPB
Once in a Palace, 1931, 3 act comedy   RPB
People Are Funny, 1950, 3 act comedy   RPB
Pink Geraniums, 1931, drama (1)   RPB
Rockabye Baby, 1950, 3 act comedy   RPB

EDNA PHILLPOTTS
  Angel in the House, 1915

MAY E. PHIPPS
  Alice in Wonderland, 1927, dance pantomime, with Marjorie Van Horn   RPB
  A Christmas Book, 1925, Christmas playlet for children,   RPB
    with Marjorie Van Horn

ELIZABETH PICKETT
  Ivania, 1918, 3 act operetta, libretto by Picket and others; music by   RPB-M
    Caroline Bergheim and others; prod. by Barnswallows, Wellesley College

ALICE PIERATT
  Day's End, 1927-8, drama of a mountain woman, also in   KFA, CNA
    Carolina Play-Book, Sept., 1931
  Let's Be Somebody, 1932, 3 act comedy   RPB
  Sigurd, the Mountain Boy, 1932 (1)   RPB

CLEO PIERCE
  The Great Gold Penny, 1928, "little thrift play"   RPB

GRACE ADELE PIERCE
  One Night in Venice, 1916, "dramatic poem arranged for readings and   RPB
    other dramatic renditions"

JESSIE PALMER PIERCE
  And the Lamp Went Out, 1913, pantomime   RPB

ELDA M. PIERO
  The Daughter of Jairus, 1930, drama of Eastertide   DLC
  The Temple of Praise, 1922, missionary thank-offering pageant   RPB

DOROTHY FISKE PIERSON
  Magic in the House, 1928, young   RPB

HARRIET H. PIERSON
  The Bridal of Pennacook, 1913, entertainment in tableaux and   RPB
    pantomime, illustrating an Indian legend, adapted from a poem
    by J. G. Whittier
  School Dialogues and Entertainments for Grammar Grades, 1910,   RPB
    with others

"M. S. PINE" (See SISTER MARY PAULINA FINN)

DELIA DELIGHT DORRANCE PINNEY
  The Floral Addenda, 1914   RPB

MAI PIPES
  The Boy They Turned Away, 1929, Christmas play for children   RPB
  The King's Wish, 1915, 3 act drama   RPB
  The Master's Voice, 1915, 3 act drama   RPB
  "The White Wolf," 1915, 2 act fairy play   RPB

MRS. FREDERICK J. PITT (See SADA COWAN)

AGNES ELECTRA PLATT
  Camera Clicks, 1913, acting monologue for a woman   RPB
  Helping Father in a Business Deal, 1906, comic monologue for a woman   RPB
  Model Growl, 1912, "store window wax-figure comedy" (1)   RPB
  The Racing Lion, n.d., typescript   NN
  When Women Rule, 1913, farce (1)   RPB

ELSIE HAWLEY PLATT
  The Bones of Our Ancestors, 1915, dram. of novelette by   RPB
    Constance Fennimore Woolson

LILLIAN PLEASANT
  Their Godfather from Paris, 1905, comedy (1)   RPB

HUBERTA MARIANNE PLUM-WOEHNING (See HUBERTA MARIANNE
    PLUM WOEHNING)

PEGGY POE
  A Gypsy Love Moon, 1924, with music   RPB
  The Land of the Slowpokes, 1926, folk play of Dixie (1)   RPB
  Little Ginger Snap's Birthday Party, 1924, folk play   RPB
  Mr. Lafayette Green Smells Ham, 1926, monologue   RPB
  Mr. Put-it-off, 1927   RPB
  Sambo, Li'l Sal and the Pancake Party, 1924, folk play of Dixie (1)   RPB

EDITH POFFENBERGER (probably same as Edith M. Paffenberger)
  The Strike at Warren's, 1927, 3 acts   RPB

EMMA POHL
  Pageant of Columbus, 1915, Columbus, Miss.

KATE A. JACOBY POHLI (MRS. EMIL POHLI)
  Professor Bernhardi, 1913, adaptation of comedy by Schnitzler   RPB

HILDA SATT POLACHECK
  The Walking Delegate, 1912, prod. at Hull House Theater, adapt. of   ICIU
    novel by Leroy Scott

MIRA POLER
  The Pageant of Southampton, 1930, Southampton, Mass.   MB

ALICE LEAL POLLOCK
  Cleopatra's Night, 1920, 2 act opera, music by Henry Hadley   RPB
  The Co-respondent, prod. 1916, with Rita Weiman, typescript   NN
  The Resemblance, with Aura Woodin Brantzell, in Smart Set, 33, Feb., 1911,
    127-34 (1)
  Wireless, "modern episode," in Smart Set, 24, March, 1908, 96-103 (1)

MADELINE POOLE
  The Elf That Stayed Behind and Other Plays for Children, 1918, one-acts RPB
  A Lady to Call, 1918, by Carl W. Pierce, based on her story

AGNES PORTER
  The Man with the Book, in Four Full Length Plays, 1928

BERTHA CURRIER PORTER
Gadsby's Girls, 1909, 3 act farce   RPB
Lucia's Lover, 1907, 3 act farce   RPB
The Luck of Santa Claus, 1918, young   RPB
The Mishaps of Minerva, 1910, 2 act farce   RPB
The Mother of Santa Claus, 1908, young   RPB
Pictures in the Fires, 1905, tableau entertainment   RPB
The Syndicated Santa Claus, 1908, young   RPB
Tableau and Pantomine Entertainments for School or Public   RPB
    Performance, 1914, with Clara E. Cooper, Laura M. Parsons and others
The Village Postmistress, 1912, 3 act rural comedy   RPB
The Voice of Authority, 1913, 3 act farce for women   RPB

ELEANOR HODGMAN PORTER (1868-1920) AWW NAW
Her Old Sweethearts, in Ladies Home Journal, 27, April, 1910, 17+ (1)
Miss Billy, 192? comedy based on her story, typescript   NN
Pollyanna, the Glad Girl, 1915, 4 act comedy by Catherine Chisholm
    Cushing, based on book by Porter

JESSE PORTER
Betty at Bay, 1918, prod. 1919

LAURA SPENCER PORTER
"The Light of Other Days," in Ladies Home Journal, 23, Dec., 1905, 20,
    based on her story, "The Christmas Dance at Red Oaks" (1)

OLIVE PORTER
The Ringmaster, prod. 1909

KATHERINE J. POSTLE
The Palace of Dreams, 1918, Christmas fantasy, music by F. Lester Price   RPB

DOROTHY POTTER
Under the Eagle: Three Plays with a Prologue and Epilogue, 1916,   RPB
    one-acts

FRANCES B. POTTER
Germelshausen, 1904, 4 act drama, with Mary Gray Peck and   RPB
    Carl Schlenker

GRACE POTTER
About Six, prod. 1918 at Provincetown

MARIE JOSEPHINE WARREN POTTER
The Winged Soul, 1925, festival for the 50th anniversary of the   RPB
    founding of Wellesley College

GENEVIEVE POTTER-CASE
Beautiful California, 1914   RPB

ANNIE E. POUSLAND
A Thanksgiving Pageant   JPP-I

CAROLINE MARGUERITE POWER
Madame Delphine, 1928
Short Plays from Great Stories, 1928, with Roland English Hartley   RPB
The Two of Them, with Roland English Hartley, in Golden Book, 21,
    April, 1935, 355-8 (1)

BEULAH POYNTER
Lena Rivers, 1906, dram. of book by Mary J. Holmes, typed copy   NN
Molly Bawn, 1907, dram. of the novel, typescript   NN
One Way Street, prod. 1928, mystery melodrama about drug addiction
The Unborn, prod. 1915 by Sociological Fund of Medicine, Review of Reviews

JULIA PRATT
Pageant of Social Science, 1916, Buffalo, N. Y.

MARY PRATT
A First-class Hotel

RACHEL BROOK PRATT
The Way of the World, 1921

BERTHA G. PRENTICE
"Tony," 1922, 3 act dramatic comedy   RPB

JANET PRENTISS
Inasmuch, in Everyland, 5, Dec., 1913, 29-35 (1)
Just Plain Peter, 1913   RPB

EFFA ESTELLE PRESTON (1884- ?)
Alex the Great, 1939, class play for 8th grade and jr. h. s.   RPB
All Out for Uncle Sam, 1942, patriotic pageant for grammar grades   RPB
America Preferred, 1942, patriotic pageant for grammar grades   RPB
The Angel in the Window, 1952, drama (1)   RPB
The Bamboo Princess, 1945, 2 act Chinese operetta for h. s. or college,
    music by Henry S. Sawyer
Bandana Junior Minstrel, 1933, music by Harold Wansborough   RPB-M
The Black Cat Entertains, in Primary Educator, 45, Oct., 1927, 112-3+
Blah, blah, Black Sheep, 1931, 2 act play for upper grammar grades   RPB
Buster Brownie's Night Out   FOA
By Cold Wave, 1935   Or, DLC
The Cavalcade of Columbia, 1941, pageant for h. s. and adults   RPB
The Children's Christmas Book, 1926   RPB
The Christmas Dolls' Revue, 1951, for intermediate grades (1)   RPB
The Christmas Gayety Book, 1924   DLC
The Christmas Program Book, 1931, with others
A Christmas Strike, 1930, comedy (1)   RPB
The Circus Comes to Town, by E. E. Preston, in Frances Signer, Ed., Plays
    for School Days, 1921
The Closing Day Program Book, 1953, with Beatrice Marie Casey
The Coat of Many Colors, 1939, Biblical pageant   RPB
The Cobbler of Fairyland, 1934, 3 act junior operetta, music   RPB-M
    by Carol Winston
Danger at the Crossroads, 1929, mystery   RPB
Danger at the Door, 1933, jr. h. s. (1)   RPB
David and Jonathan, 1939, Biblical pageant   RPB
The Dolls on Dress Parade, 1922 (1)   RPB
Efficiency Phillip Manages Christmas, 1927   RPB
First Floor Front, 1929, 3 act mystery comedy   RPB
The Flag Works a Miracle, 1941, patriotic play (1)   RPB
A Fountain of Peace, 1938, peace play (1)   DLC
Freedom Rings, 1941, patriotic play (1)   RPB
Fun with Stunts, 1956   RPB
Funny One-Act Christmas Plays, 1935, with others   RPB

EFFA ESTELLE PRESTON (continued)
Gabby Gets in Step, 1944, patriotic pageant   RPB
Getting Gracie Graduated, 1939, class play for 8th grade and jr. h. s.   RPB
The Ghost Walks, 1927, pantomime   RPB
Good Things for Closing Day, 1953, with others
A Greene Christmas, 1929, comedy (1)   RPB
The Gumps in Grammar Land, 1928, good English play for   RPB
    grammar grades
The Gypsy Troubadour, 1931, 2 act operetta for H. S., colleges and
    glee clubs, music by Donald Wilson
Halloween Celebration, 1925   Or, NBuG
High School Assembly Plays, 1937, with others   RPB
Holly Tree Inn   FOA
Home of the Free, 1944, patriotic pageant
Homer on the Range, 1937, 3 act mystery comedy for jr. h. s.   RPB
Immediate But Not Temporary, 1942, comedy (1)   RPB
In Days of Washington   FPP
In a Toy Shop (1)
Jack Horner's Christmas Pie   FOA
The Kidnapping of Santa Claus, 1928, Christmas operetta for   RPB-M
    elementary school, music by George M. Wilmot
The Knight Before Christmas, 1933, comedy (1)   RPB
Little New Citizen, 1941, patriotic (1)   RPB
Meet Mr. Santa Claus, 1934, 2 act Christmas operetta, music   RPB-M
    by George M. Wilmot
Miss Liberty's Light, 1941, patriotic pageant   RPB
Modern Entertainments for Churches, 1939, with Maud C. Jackson   RPB
Modern Pantomime Entertainments, 1938   RPB
The Modern Stunt Book, 1945, with Beatrice Plumb and   RPB
    Herry W. Githens
Mother Goose Celebrates, 1926, pageant for primary schools   RPB
Mother Goose Enlists, 1942, patriotic play for primary grades   RPB
Mother Goose's Family   FOA
Mrs. Chester's Christmas Carol, 1943, Christmas play for women (1) DLC
Mrs. Santa's Saucepan   FOA
Our United States, 1926, patriotic pageant   RPB
A Party in Mother Goose Land, 1922 (1)   RPB
Peace Rules the Day, 1938 (1)   DLC
Plays for Special Occasions, 1934, for grammar, intermediate and jr. h. s. RPB
Polite Priscilla and Gertie the Goop, 1927   RPB
The Popular Commencement Book, 1931   RPB
Punchinella Puppet Plays, 1936   RPB
Santa Claus on the Air, 1930, comedy (1)   RPB
Santa's Air Line, 1926, Christmas operetta, music   RPB-M
    by George W. Wilmot
Santa's Ups and Downs, 1928 (1)   RPB
The Second Thanksgiving, 1938, for upper grammar grades (1)   RPB
The Skywayman, 1949, 2 act operetta, music by Harold Wansborough RPB-M
Star of Wonder, 1952, Christmas (1)   RPB
Station U.S.A., 1942, patriotic pageant for grammar grades   RPB
A Strike in Santa Land, 1922 (1)   RPB
Ten Clever Plays for Children, 1927   DLC
Thank you, America, 1943, patriotic pageant for a large group   DLC
Thankful for What? 1938, Thanksgiving play for intermediate   RPB
    and grammar grades (1)
A Thanksgiving Dream, 1922, primary grades (1)   RPB
A Thanksgiving Prodigal, 1938, comedy drama (1)   RPB

EFFA ESTELLE PRESTON (continued)
Uncle Lemuel Looks at Life, 1940, patriotic play (1)   RPB
Uncle Sam's Right Arm, 1918, patriotic exercise, young   RPB
The Upper Grades Closing Book, 1940   RPB
Vacation Days, 1925, for grade children   RPB
The Voice That Failed, 1952, drama (1)   RPB
Washington's Birthday (1)
The Way to the Wishing Gate, 1923, allegorical playlet   RPB
What, No Angel Cake! 1933, 2 acts, for jr. h. s. and h. s.   RPB

IDA REID PRESTON
Getting Sandy, 1927, 3 act comedy   RPB
"Here Comes Aunt Sarah," 1935, comedy (1)   RPB

MARY FRANCES JOHNSON PRESTON
The Banqueteer, 1928   RPB
Novel Stunts, 1930   MiD, NcC

SARA PRESTON
The Braino Man, 1907, 3 act comedy with others, senior class play,   RPB
    Un. of Minn.
Hicks at College, 1909, with Amy Oliver and Ralph E. Dyar,   RPB
    3 act comedy

MRS. W. H. PRESTON
Uncle Sam's Flower Garden, 1915, allegorical temperance   RPB
    play for children (1)
Ye Tea Party of Ye Olden Times, 1913   RPB

CLARA B. PRICE
A Colonial Tea, 1900, with Alonzo Price, musical comedy, libretto   NN
The Song of the Seashell, 1903, comic opera with Alonzo Price   RPB-Lyrics

OLIVE M. PRICE
American History in Masque and Wig, 1931   RPB
Angelica, Inc., 1937, romantic comedy drama for girls and young women
Announcing Antonia, 1941, 3 act all-girl play   DLC
Ask for the Moon, 1942, 3 act comedy for an all-girl cast   OCl, DLC
The Boy in Blue, 1927, for Memorial Day (1)   RPB, SSH-II
Butterfly Wings, 1927, young, "play for June time"   RPB
Debutante Plays for Girls 12 to 20, 1936   RPB
Family Tree, 1943, 3 act comedy for women   RPB
Freshman Bill, 1941, comedy of adolescence in 3 acts   DLC
From Picture Book Towne, 1931, George Washington pageant
    play for children
The Gateway of Tomorrow, 1929, Americanization play   RPB
Gifts of the Gods, 1927, for Valentine's Day (1)   RPB, SSH-I
Glass Mountain, 1954, play?   DLC
Holiday Hill, 1940, 3 act comedy for jr. h. s.   Or, DLC
Lantern Light, 1925, play of New England witchcraft   OCl
The Master Washington Marches On, 3 acts
Out of the Mist, 1953, 3 act comedy drama   RPB
Plays from American History and Literature, 2 vols.
Plays of Belles and Beaux, 1937, seven short plays for jr. and senior h. s.   RPB
Plays of Far Places, 1936   RPB
The Redbud Tree, 1931, George Washington pageant play for children

OLIVE M. PRICE (continued)
The Sandman's Pack o' Dreams, 1927, for   RPB, JWA
    Washington's birthday (1)
Short Plays from American History and Literature,   RPB
    for classrooms—4 volumes: I-1925; II-1928; III-1933; IV-1935
Singers in the Dark, 1927   RPB
Sparkling Sixteen, 1947, 3 act comedy   RPB
Stage-struck, 1946, 3 act comedy   DLC
Star Eternal, 1940, Christmas (1)
Sub-Deb Sue, 1942, 3 act comedy   RPB
Washington Marches On, 1931, play of the life of George Washington   RPB
When the Bough Breaks, 1945, 3 act comedy   ViU
The Young May Moon, 1939, comedy of adolescence in 3 acts   OCl, DLC

FANNIE E. PRICE-WILSON
Massa Washington at Home (1)

MARY ELIZABETH PRIEST (1868- ?)
Recitations and Dialogues for Special Days in the Sunday School, 1911   RPB

OLGA PRINTZLAU
Back Here, prod. 1928
The Jay Walker, prod. 1926
The Ostrich, prod. 1930, typescript   NN
Window Panes, 1932, prod. 1927, 3 act drama

"POLLY ANN PRITCHARD" (See DELIA A. HEYWOOD)

DORCAS PROCTOR
Mother Baker's Christmas, 1926, 2 act play for upper grades   RPB
Uncle Joe's Minstrels, 1925   RPB

LUCY SOUTH PROUDFOOT
The Festival of Days, 1927   RPB
Two Water Pageants, 1924, "fairy water play without words"   OrU

SARAH SHERMAN PRYOR
The Rut, 1923, in Little Theatre Tournament

FAY PULSIFER
Black Vengeance, 19??, with C. D. Woodyatt, typescript   NN
Circus Set, 193? with Lyle Leverich   NN
Go West Young Man, prod. 1923, with Cara Carelli

GERTRUDE PURCELL (189?-1963)
Just Fancy, prod. 1927, with Joseph Stanley, lyrics by Leo Robin; music by
    Joseph Meyers and Philip Charig; based on a play by A. E. Thomas
Luckee Girl, prod. 1928, adaptation of French play by A. Barde and M. Yvain
The Madcap, prod. 1928, with Gladys Unger; adaptation of French of
    Regis Gignous and Jacques Thery; lyrics by Clifford Grey;
    music by Maurice Rubens
Tangletoes, prod. 1925, typescript   NN
Three Little Girls, prod. 1930, adaptation by Purcell and Marie A. Hecht
    from an original script by H. Feiner and Hardt-Warden; music by W. Rolls
Voltaire, prod. 1922, with Leila Taylor
Wolf! Wolf! prod. 1925

JULIE HELENE PURCIVAL
  The Bully, prod. 1924, with Calvin Clark

NANNIE SUTTON PURDY
  Hafed the Persian, 1920, 4 acts   RPB

NINA SUTHERLAND PURDY (1889- ?)
  The Heritage   JOP

LULA M. PUTNAM
  Ourselves and Others, 1922, Christmas program and playlet   RPB

NINA WILCOX PUTNAM (1888-1962)
  Deliver the Goods, 19?? with Ethel Watts Mumford, typed prompt book   NN
  Orthodoxy, 1914, also in Forum, 51, June, 1914, 801-20 (1)   RPB

ROSALIE B. PUTNAM
  Grandma Gay Slips Into High, 1927, comedy (1)   RPB

Q

EDITH M. QUACKENBUSH
 The Amateur Fireman, 1929, for children from 5th to 8th grade for fire RPB
  prevention week

ELSIE WEST QUAIFE (1870- ?)
 Aunt Polly Basset's Singin' Skewl, 1927 RPB
 Carrie Lee Lumpit, 1924 RPB
 Dinner Out, 1940, farcical melodrama (1) DLC
 The Emancipated Ones, 1917, comedy (1) RPB
 French's Oral Readings for Moderns, 1938, chosen and edited by Quaife
 In a Bookshop, 1941, comedy for women (1)
 The Knitting Girls Count One, 1918, patriotic play (1) RPB
 Mennemen Inn, 1910, 3 act comedy RPB
 Monologues of Every Day, 1931, with Ernest Nehring
 Monologues of To-day, 1915
 The Natural Incentive, 1918 RPB
 "Poor Me," 1921, with May Rose Nathan RPB
 Three Girls from School, 1910, music by William ICU, PU
  Marchall Hutchison
 Two Little Rebels, 1907, 2 acts ICU

SUSAN QUINN
 Esther Investigates, 1928, 3 acts RPB
 Miss De Vergne Goes Camping, 1929, 2 acts RPB
 The Village Improvement Society, 1929, 2 act entertainment RPB

PAULINE BROOKS QUINTON
 The Locust Flower and The Celibate, 1916, two plays RPB

MARY ISABEL QUIRK
 Woman of the Hour; Suffrage Play in Three Acts, 1910, with
  Eugene Quirk and Florence King

R

KATE MILNER RABB
Pageant of Spencer County, Rockport, Ind., 1916   InI

MARGARET RABE
The Princess' Choice, in Quarterly Journal of Speech Education, 5,
    May, 1919, 279-86 (1)

MARTHA RACE
At the Door of the Inn, 1924, Christmas pantomime   Or, GEU
Missionary Marionette Plays, 1927
The Palm Branch, 1932, Easter pantomime with reading and music   RPB
Rummage, 1917, comedy with musical numbers (1)   RPB
They Who Weave. Gold, silver and precious stones; "portraying in   NN
    dramatic form the religious contribution of the home to the life
    of the child," 1926
Uncle Sam, P. M., 1917, musical sketch (1)   RPB
What Child Is This? Christmas pageant   CP
Why the Chimes Rang, 1922, Christmas pantomime, from story by
    Raymond MacDonald Alden

RUBY LORRAINE RADFORD
The Good Luck Idol, 1936, comedy   DLC
Magic Gifts, 1927, 2 act play for children, music by Karin   RPB
    Sundelof Asbrand

ANNA RADKE
A Fair Exchange, 1930, with Edna Buttimer, 3 act comedy   RPB

MAGDELENTE CRAFT RADKE
Celestine Hangs On, 1923, comedy (1)   RPB
Killarney, 1927   RPB
The Thirteen Colonies, 1926, patriotic pageant   RPB
The Wise Young Generation, 1923, 3 act comedy   RPB

SARAH S. RAFTER
Winona, the Indian Girl, 1901   RPB

ANNA RAMSPACHER
"The Agitator," 1908, Greek tragedy in 4 acts and seven scenes, written RPB
    and edited by Ramspacher
Goosey Island, 1909, 3 act comedy   RPB

HELEN RAND
Pageant of Peace and War, 1915, Valley City, N. D.

ETHEL CLAIRE RANDALL
The Great American, 1932, George Washington Pageant, with   DLC
    James K. Knudson
The Waves of Torre

GERTRUDE BLANCHARD RANDALL
Kismet: Fate, 1907, dramatic sketch (1)   RPB

MRS. JACOB S. RANDALL ("ANNE O'NEILL")
The Farmer's Saturday Night, 1930   RPB
New Rugs of Old Rags, 1930, by "Anne O'Neill"   RPB

MADELINE I. RANDALL
Gifts of the Month, for last day   HPP
Peace Masque, 1916, St. Johnsbury, Vermont
The Weatherman   HPP

ANNIE EDITH KEELING RANDLE (1888- ?)
"The Blood Calls Out," 1928, 3 act drama   RPB
"The Voice on the Wire," 1919   DLC

EDITH RANDOLPH
Lamma's Eve, in Poet Lore, 32, Summer, 1921, 288-306, fantasy (1)

JUTTA MORDT BELL RANSKE
The Temple Dancer, 1918, opera, music by John Adam Hugo (1)   RPB-M

ALICE RAPHAEL
An Interlude in the Life of St. Francis, in Drama, 11, Nov., 1920, 37-40 (1)
Dormer Windows, in Drama, 11, Aug./Sept., 1921, 418-20 (1)

ISABEL NANTON RAWN
Pageant of Southern Highlands, 1916, Mt. Berry, Georgia

BLANCHE H. RAY
Little Plays for Little People, 1910, with Marion Ingalls Osgood Noyes   RPB

PATRICIA RAYBURN
She, 'n Her Daughter, 'n Her Daughter, 1926   RPB

FLORENCE R. RAYFIELD
The Chicken Lifters' Convention, 1933, blackface farce (1)   RPB
The Ten Good English Commandments, 1928, for intermediate   RPB
    grades or jr. h. s.

ANNA REARDEN
The Partheneia, 1912, masque of maidenhood, presented at Un. of Calif.   RPB

OLIVE IRENE REDDICK
The New Minister at Muncie, 1917, tithing sketch in 4 acts   RPB

JENNIE REE
Hosannah to the King, 1904, Christmas service, with   RPB-M
    Charles H. Gabriel

PEGGY REECE
Bashful Bachelor Beaux, n.d.   DLC
A Buth-day Present for 'Rastus, 193?   RPB
By de Photo-grapher's, 1930   RPB
Don't Tell Me No Gossip; I Won't Listen   RPB
Eph'um at the Drugstore, 1936   RPB
Jimmie, the Unafraid! 1927   RPB
Jimmie's Big Fish Story, 1927   RPB
Juvenile Plays and Readings, 1929

PEGGY REECE (continued)
    Lena and "Yellercution by de Schoolhouse," 1927   RPB
    Lena by de Football Game, 1930   RPB
    Lena Chooses a Hat, 1927   RPB
    Lena Practices for the T'eatre Stage, 1927   RPB
    Lucindy and the Ha'nts, 193?   RPB
    Lucindy on a Diet, 193?   RPB
    Madame Cherry Tre Spills the Beans (1)
    Maw, What Did Dad Say? 1927   RPB
    Oscarina and the Cakes, 1927   RPB
    The Runaway Jack-in-the-box, 1929   RPB
    Sambo and the Circus, 1935   RPB
    The Silly Stork, 1927   RPB
    Tige an' the Lick'rish Whip! 1927   RPB
    Twenty Dialect Monologues, 1928, with Gracia Stayton and
        Penelope Dickerson
    When We Grow Up! 1930   DLC

DENA REED
    Kiddie, 1933, 3 act comedy   RPB
    The Three Graces, 1925, with Kenyon Nicholson, 3 act comedy   RPB

ETHEL E. REED
    When Santa Claus Went to the Front, 1918, with Martha G. Kendall   RPB

ETHELYN REED
    The Intruder, in Smart Set, 36, March, 1918, 133-8 (1)

MARY KATHARINE REELY (1881- ?)
    Bringing Up Nine, 1929, adaptation of a play by Miss Reely, in   SSM
        Wisconsin Library Bulletin, June, 1923, under the title "Uncle Sam
        Brings it to Your Door" (1)
    Cave Stuff, 1928, "play in 2 episodes, a variation on the theme that   RPB
        woman is the more primitive sex"
    Daily Bread, 1924 (1)   RPB, SSH-IV
    Daily Bread; A Window to the South; The Lean Years, 1919, one-acts
    Early Ohios and R. I. Reds, 1921, awarded 1st prize in Minneapolis   RPB
        Woman's Club Contest, comedy (1)
    Flittermouse, 1927, also in Drama, 14, Dec., 1923, 104-7, farce (1)   RPB, GPF
    The Greatest Is Curiosity, 1927 (1)   RPB
    The House Can't Build the Barn, 1927, drama (1)   RPB
    The Lean Years, 1924 (1)   RPB, PTM
    "Let Every Heart," 1936, modern Christmas play (1)
    They Just Won't Talk, peace play (1)   SSA
    They're Not What They Used To Be, 1929, comedy (1)   RPB
    Three One-Act Plays, 1924   RPB
    To Be Dealt With Accordingly, 1928, "social adjustment play" (1)   RPB
    Trails, 1928, "play of contrasts in 2 episodes"   RPB
    A Window to the South, 1924 (1)   RPB

ROSEMARY REES
    Her Dearest Friend, 1910 (1)

LULU T. REESE
    Winnowing, 1911, 5 act drama   RPB

RHODA OTTMAR REBAY REICHEL (1878- ?)
    Modern Justice, 1906, 5 act drama   RPB

CAROL MC MILLAN REID
Amusin' Susan, 1928, rural comedy   RPB
Joan's Ark, 1931, comedy (1)
Locked Windows, 1933 (1)   YSP-IV, Or, OCl
Mollie Durkie's Harvest, 1930, pub. by Am. Farm Bureau Federation   RPB

EDITH GITTINGS REID (1863- ?)
Florence Nightingale, 1922, drama   RPB

LOUISA REID
The Fighting Corporal, 1918-9, Negro comedy, Carolina folk play (1)

CATHERINE F. REIGHARD
Garden Rivals, 1921
Plays for People and Puppets, 1928   RPB

"NAILLIL REMITRON" (See LILLIAN MORTIMER)

CAROLYN RENFREW
The Last of the Strozzi and The Lure, 1923, two plays   RPB
Plays, 1943, 6 poetic dramas   RPB

MARION RENFREW
His Father's Gone South, 1929, "short 3 act business comedy with no   RPB
     change of scenery"

EMMA RENNIE
"Some One to Welcome Me," 1925, vaudeville sketch   RPB

TACIE MAY HANNA REW (See TACIE MAY HANNA)

BEATRIX REYNOLDS
Everychild, 1914, fairy music play (1)   RPB

HELEN M. REYNOLDS
Mothering Day   BPC

NINA RHOADES (1863- ?)
The Girl Who Paid the Bills, 1909, comedy (1)   RPB

BEATRICE E. RICE
The Matchmakers, in Werner's Magazine, 27, July, 1901, Halloween comedy

BEVA E. RICE
Womanless Divorce, 1929   RPB

CAROLYN FRANCES RICE
The Charity Pupil, 1912, with Marion Spring Clark, 4 acts, "boarding   RPB
     school episode for females"
More Time Out (1)

ELVA M. RICE
The Christmas Story in Tableau, with Grace C. Jordan and   JPP-1
     Clarence A. Burt

ETHEL M. RICE
Do You Remember? 1929, "old-fashioned photograph album, done   RPB
    as a rhymed specialty"

KATHARINE MC DOWELL RICE
Charley's Country Cousin, 1905, 4 act comedy   RPB
The Christmas Spirit of Jane Haskins, 1913, monologue   MB
Dr. Hardhack's Prescription, 1908, young, 4 acts   RPB
Good As Gold, 1902, 4 act comedy   RPB
Good King Wenceslas, 1907, young, Christmas, 2 acts   RPB
Mrs. Bagg's Bargain Day, 1904, 2 act comedy   RPB
Mrs. Tubb's Telegram, 1904, also in St. Nicholas, 32, Feb., 1905, 344-55,   RPB
    comedy (1)
A Successful Stratagem, 1902, comedy (1)   RPB
Uncle Joe's Jewels, 1908, 3 act comedy   RPB

REBECCA RICE (1899- ?)
The Christmas Eve Prince   CLP-1
Evelyn's Christmas Lesson   CLP-1
The Fairies' Christmas Party   CLP-1
The Ghost of Deepdens, 1934, mystery play for girls   RPB
Hildegard Lilian   CLP-1
The Light in the Window   CLP-1
Little Plays for Christmas, 1928, with others   RPB
Mrs. Santa Claus' Reception   CLP-1
A Present for Joy   CLP-1
Putting on the School Play   CLP-1
Tabby's Thanksgiving Doll   BPC

CAROLINE RICHARDS
Mary Ann's Books, 1924, lesson play   RPB

IRMAGARDE RICHARDS
"It Came Upon the Midnight Clear," 1924, Holy Night play   RPB

LAURA ELIZABETH HOWE RICHARDS   (1850-1943) AWW NAW
Acting Charades, 1924, collection   RPB
Captain January, 1890   RPB
Fairy Operettas, 1916, holiday plays for children   RPB
The Pig Brother Play-Book, 1915, collection   RPB
Seven Oriental Operettas, 1924   RPB
The Troubling of Bethesda Pool, 1917, by Mrs. George F. Bancroft,
    2 act comedy, based on a story by Richards

ABBY SAGE RICHARDSON   (1837-1900)
A Colonial Girl, 1902, with Grace Livingston Furniss
Donna Quixote, 1890, dramatic idyl of the 18th century   MH
The Pride of Jennico, prod. 1900, with Grace L. Furniss, partial text   NN
The Prince and the Pauper, 188? dram. of book by Twain   CSmH

ANNA STEESE SAUSSER RICHARDSON   (1865-1949)
Big Hearted Herbert, 1934, with Sophie Kerr, 3 act comedy based on   RPB
    story by Kerr
Chin Chin, 1934, with Sophie Kerr
Christmas Conspiracy, in Woman's Home Companion, 37, Dec., 1910, 25+ (1)
Let's Scrap It, 1935, comedy (1)   OCl
The Love Leash, prod. 1913, with Edmund Breese, comedy

ANNA STEESE SAUSSER RICHARDSON (continued)
"Mlle. Mystic," midsummer comedy, in Woman's Home Companion,
37, Aug., 1910, 8+ (1)
The Maid from Mars, 1901   RPB
"A Man's a Man," 192? with Henry Leslie Fridenberg, 4 act drama,   NN
typed copy
Miss Mosher of Colorado; or, A Mountain Psyche, 1899, comedy drama

DORSIE GILLIS RICHARDSON
The Power of Song; or, The Wandering Boy Returning, 1923   RPB

GRACE RICHARDSON
Awake! Thou that Sleepest! 1918, war play for girls   RPB
Duck in Exile (1)   JGH
The Gingerbread House (1)   JGH
Puck in Petticoats and Other Fairy Plays, 1915   RPB
The Ring of Salt (1)   JGH
Sonny Santa Claus, 1928, young   RPB
Summer Snow and Other Fairy Plays, 1916   RPB

ISLA PASCHAL RICHARDSON (1886- ?)
The Canceled Debt, 1934 (1)   RPB
Doughnuts, 1929, 2 act comedy   RPB
Just Another Day, 1935 play?   DLC
The Message, 1949, Easter (1)   DLC
The Prominent Author, 1929, for women (1)   RPB
That's What They All Say, 1928, comedy (1)   RPB
Too Much Static, 1936, comedy (1)
Uncle Bob's Bride, 1934 (1)   RPB

GENEVIEVE RICHEFIELD
Rosemary's Engagement, 1926, 3 act comedy   RPB

GRACE LOUISE SMITH RICHMOND (1866-1959) AWW
Honor and the Girl, in Ladies Home Journal, 10, Feb., 1903, 13 (1)
The Perfect Church, in Ladies Home Journal, 38, June, 1921, 115 (1)
When the Boys Came Home, in Ladies Home Journal, 35, Sept., 1918, 13-4+ (1)

LILLIAN RICKABY
The Christmas Spirit, 1921, with Franz Rickaby, 2 act poetic fantasy   RPB
Waiting at the Church, 1923, with Franz Rickaby   RPB
Who Kissed Barbara? 1921, with Franz Rickaby, farce (1)   RPB

JEAN RIDGE
What's Keeping Laura? 1924   RPB
Wilt Thou, Mabel? 1924, comedy   RPB

EDNA RIESE
"Our Career," 1913, comedy (1)   RPB

HELEN RIESENFELD
Lorenzo the Magnificent, 1924, play in 25 episodes, from the   RPB
Vassar Review, June, 1924, 3-17

KATHLEEN B. RIGBY
The Gauge of Youth, 1927, for women (1)   RPB

GRETCHEN RIGGS
Pierrot in the Clear of the Moon, pantomime

ALICE CUSHING DONALDSON RILEY (1867-1955)
Blossom Time, 1905, entertainment of verse, song and music for children DLC
The Blue Prince, young
The Brotherhood of Man, 1924, pageant of international peace, for   RPB
    pageantry class, Drama League Institute, 1921, also in L. Taft, Ed.,
    Pageants With a Purpose
The Bubble Peddler, sequel to Red Riding Hood story
Christmas Time, 1905, entertainment of verse, song and music for   OrP
    children
The Evolution of Social Ideals, "modern drama course arranged to compare
    certain significant plays in their bearing on world processes in social
    evolution" (Study Course No. 10 of the Drama League courses—in
    Drama League Monthly, Vol I, no. 6,1917, 256-67
Harvest Time, 1905, verse and song entertainment for children   RPB
Her Sable Coat, 1941, comedy for 4 women (1)   Or, DLC
The House That Jack Built, 1919, (1st pub. 1902) 2 act children's operetta, RPB
    music by Jessie L. Gaynor
Let's Pretend, 1934, collection of 4 half hour plays for children   RPB
Little New Moon, 1929, "fantasy in the Chinese manner"   RPB
The Lost Princess Bo Peep, 1931   RPB
The Lover's Garden, 1915, flower masque, arranged from   NjR
    Shakespeare for the Tercentenary, in Drama, no. 20, Nov., 1915
The Mandarin Coat, 1923, prod. 1922, in Drama, 13, Jan.,   NN, ICU
    1923, 132-5+ comedy (1)
The Mandarin Coat and Five Other One-Act Plays for   RPB
    Little Theatres, 1925
On Plymouth Rock, 1908, operetta, music by Jessie L. Gaynor   RPB
The One-Act Play, study course No. 18 of the Drama League Course,
    in Drama League Monthly, Vol 2, No. 8, 617-29; no. 9, 639-46; Vol. 3,
    no. 1, 8-13, 1918
The Play's the Thing for Children, 1932, collection   RPB
The Rival Peach-Trees, 1929, "short fantasy somewhat in the   DSS
    Chinese manner"
Shakespeare's Lovers in a Garden, 1927, flower masque for   RPB
    Drama League of America
The Sponge, 1921, prod. 1924, comedy (1)
A Star Shone, 1935, Christmas, 3 acts   RPB
Taxi! 1927, in Drama, 16, Feb., 1926, 177-8, comedy (1)   RPB
Ten Minutes by the Clock (1)   MRC
Ten Minutes by the Clock and Three Other Plays for Outdoor and   RPB
    Indoor Production, 1923, one-acts
Their Anniversary, 1922, in Drama, 12, Feb., 1922, 157-62, comedy (1)
The Toy Shop, 1931, music by Jessie L. Gaynor   RPB
Uplifting Sadie, 1927   NPW
Valentines, 1927, fantasy   RPB
The Weathervane Elopes (1)   OPS-III
Welcome Spring! 1909, spring or Easter program for Sunday or   OrP
    Day schools for primary or intermediate grades
The World Applauds, prod. 1936 for Federal Theater

MARY ROBERTS RINEHART (1876-1958) AWW NAW
The Avenger, 1908, with Mr. Rinehart
Bab, 1925, 4 act farce, by Edward Childs Carpenter based on   RPB
    story by Rinehart

MARY ROBERTS RINEHART (continued)
The Bat, 1932, prod. 1920, with Avery Hopwood, 3 act   RPB, CCS, CCF
  comedy mystery
The Breaking Point, 1932, prod. 1923
Cheer Up, prod. 1913
The Double Life, 1908, prod. 1906, by "Rineharts and Roberts"
Seven Days, 1931, prod. 1909, with Avery Hopwood, 3 act farce   RPB
Spanish Love, prod. 1920, with Avery Hopwood
A Thief in the Night, prod. 1920, with Avery Hopwood
Tish, 1939, by "Alice Chadwicke" (Wilbur Braun), based on her stories   RPB

LINA BARBARA TAYLOR RING (BARBARA RING) (1879-1941)
Aesculapius, 1930 (1)   RPB
North Flies South, 1941, Pan American comedy (1)   RPB
Simon Bolivar, the Liberator, 1934, pageant drama, shortened form of
  pageant presented on Pan American day by the city of Miami, 1932
The $100,000 Club Paper, 1918, comedy for clubwomen (1)   RPB
Three Plays Under Three Flags, 1928   RPB
Whom Dreams Possess, 1939, with Rudolph Elie Jr., for Federal Theater

BELLE MAC DIARMID RITCHEY ("ELIZABETH WEIR")
At the Sacred Well, with Mabel Hubbard Johnson   YSP-III
His Blue Serge Suit, 1934, farce (1)   RPB
His Blue Serge Suit and Other Plays, 1924
Hurry Henry, 1938, with Mabel Hubbard (Johnson?) 3 act comedy   DLC
A Little Change   YSP-II
The Middle Years, 1931, 3 act comedy   RPB
Never Ain't, 1931 (1)   RPB
The Pryde Pearls, 1934, 3 act mystery comedy, from Prydehurst, a   RPB
  novel by Hammel Johnson, mimeographed copy
Soul Vibrations, dram. of a story by Mabel Hubbard Johnson   YSP-I
There Is a Lad Here, 1925, religious   RPB
They Clean the Attic   SCS-l, NN
Three Who Met at Banbury Cross, 1934, with Mabel Hubbard Johnson,   RPB
  Christmas (1)

DICIE M. RITTENHOUSE
Christian Endeavor Playlets, ed. by Henrietta Heron, 1928, a contributor   RPB
Good Resolutions, pageant for the New Year   HPY
More Christian Endeavor Playlets, ed. by E. W. Thornton, 1929,   RPB
  a contributor
Teacher's Christmas Book, 1951, for primary and intermediate grades   RPB
Thanksgiving Day, pageant and pantomime   HPY

AMELIE RIVES (See AMELIE RIVES CHANLER TROUBETZKOY)

ESTELLE HARRIET ROBBINS
A Comedy in the Woods (animated botany) 1930, 3 plays   RPB

INA BREVOORT DEANE ROBERTS (1874- ?)
A Pleasant Disappointment, 1928 (1)   RPB

MARY ELIZABETH ROBERTS
Ben Takes a Hand, 1925, comedy (1)   RPB
Family Jars, 1935, comedy (1)   RPB
Little Church of Hidden Valley, 1934 (1)   RPB
Marrying Off Brother Samson, 1926, comedy (1)   RPB

MARY ELIZABETH ROBERTS (continued)
Mister Arithmetic Steps In, 1934 (1)   RPB
Moon Signs, 1935, comedy (1)   RPB
The Mystery of Cedar Grove, Halloween (1)   BCC
Mystery of the Tapping Keys, 1931   RPB
Oh, These Hard Lessons, 1935, comedy (1)   RPB
The Old Home Place, 1929   RPB
Select Plays for Junior High School, 1935, six one-acts   RPB
A Thankful Halloween, 1934 (1)   RPB
What Became of the Cat, 1935, comedy (1)   RPB
What Gold Cannot Buy, 1934, for Mother's Day (1)   RPB
Who Knocks? 1935 (1)   RPB

OCTAVIA ROBERTS
The Happy Day, 1915, farce (1)   RPB

MARJORIE FREELAND ROBERTSON
When Toys Talk, 1928, musical play (1)   RPB

MATTIE CARRUTH ROBERTSON
The Big Nose, 1927   RPB
Cat Got His Tongue, 1927, "dialog for 3 little girls"   RPB
Frog in His Throat, 1927, playlet   RPB
(All Wetmore Declamation Bureau readings, entertainments and plays, v. 23)

ANNE GLENN ROBESON
Betty and Scarlet Bunny, 1932, 3 act fairy play, adapt. of story by W. A.   RPB
    Lillycrop
A Pageant of Time   BPC

DORIS ISABELLE ROBIDOUX
The Children's Recital Book, 1928, humorous monologues for youngsters RPB
Mirth Provoking Monologues, 1929   RPB

ELIZABETH ROBINS (MRS G. R. PARKES) (1862-1952) AWW
Votes for Women, 1907, prod. 1909, 3 acts   RPB

HELEN JOSEPHINE ROBINS (1871- ?)
The Scholars and the Children, 1918, Christmas   RPB
The Triumph of Saint Tharsicius, acolyte and martyr, 1933   NN

MRS. FRED ROBINSON
Do Missions Pay? missionary play

HAZEL M. ROBINSON
The Original Two Bits, 1920, 2 act farce   RPB

MARY CLOSE ROBINSON
A Daughter of the Dons, 1908, 5 act military drama   RPB
In Dixie, 1907, 3 acts   RPB
Miss Conover's Vocation, 1907, 2 acts   RPB
The Primrose Path, 1909, merry interlude of the time of Good Queen Bess RPB

MARY LOUISE ROBINSON
The Knight in Poverty, 1925, 3 act operetta, for Barnswallows, Wellesley   RPB
    College; book by Robinson; lyrics by Mary C. Brown and others; music by
    Margaret Bixler and others

VIOLET ROBINSON
    Home Sweet Home
    Household Gods

ELEANOR ROBSON (See ELEANOR ROBSON BELMONT)

ETHEL HEDLEY ROBSON
    In Colonial Days   FPP

MAY ROBSON (1858-1942) NAW
    "Her Night Out," 1911, 3 acts, with Charles T. Dazey (orig. title, The   NN
        Three Lights; prod. under title A Night Out) prompt book

ETHEL GESNER ROCKWELL
    "All We Like Sheep," 1936, peace play (1)   RPB
    I Am Come, 1929, Biblical drama   RPB
    It Is I, 1927, Biblical drama   RPB
    Magda, 1924, Biblical drama   RPB
    Me for You, 1930, musical comedy with fashion review, by Helen   Or
        Durham, revised by Rockwell
    Pat's Society Circus, 1930, revised from Helen Durham's Circus   RPB
    The Way, 1927, Christmas pageant of peace   RPB

ETHEL THEODORA ROCKWELL (1884- ?)
    The Apostles of Light, 1923, religious pageant drama of the   DLC
        centenary movement, Nashville, Tenn.
    The Book of Words of the Pageant of William Woods College, 1915,   RPB
        Fulton, Mo.
    The Centennial Cavalcade of Wisconsin, 1936, pageant
    Children of Old Carolina, 1925, pageant, Dunn, N. C.   RPB
    Children of Old Wisconsin, 1935, pageant   RPB
    The Freeport Pageant of the Black Hawk Country, 1915, Freeport, Ill. RPB
    The Lincoln-Douglas Debate, being the 3rd episode in "The Pageant   SPN
        of the Blackhawk Country"
    Milton Memories, 1955, dedicatory pageant of Milton House,   WHi
        Milton, Wisc., with Winnie Saunders
    Pageant of Beloit, 1916, Beloit, Wisc.
    Pageant of the Black Hawk Country (or Pageant of Freeport) 1915,   IFSchs
        Freeport, Ill., unpub. program text
    Social Center Pageant, 1914, Sauk City, Wisconson
    Star-Spangled Banner Pageant, 1914, Madison, Wisc.   RPB, SPN
    Williams Woods College Pageant, 1915, Fulton, Mo.
    (She also published several bibliographies of plays, edited collections of
    plays, and wrote drama reference books in her capacity as Chief of the
    Bureau of Dramatic Activities at University of Wisconsin)

ALICE RODEWALD
    The Muse and the Movies, 1927, comedy of Greenwich Village

SYLVIA AMANDA RODGERS
    Ousting the Pastor, 1920, 4 act comedy drama   RPB
    The Welcome Guest, 1928, drama   RPB

MARTINA B. RODNEY
    The Key to Health, 1927, written and presented under direction of   RPB
        Martina Rodney at Jefferson Jr. H. S., Rochester, N. Y.
    Three Splendid Plays for Junior High School, 1927, with Gertrude   RPB
        Ermatinger Taylert

MARY E. ROE
    The Count of Elsinore; or, Valdemar, the Baltic Rover, 1901, drama   RPB

ORPHA V. ROE
    The Better Speech Fairy, 1926   RPB
    Friday Afternoon, with A.R.G.   FWP
    The Hollanders   FWP
    Hunting for Spring   FWP
    "Just As I Please,"   FWP
    The Lady Fair, "for Younger Girls in the Interest of Health"   HPY
    The Last Study   FWP
    Little Girl Confessions   FWP
    The "Mind Your Mother" Club   FWP
    Neighborly Neighbors   FWP
    Their Choice   FWP
    Where Are the Flowers and the Birds?   FWP
    Willie's Success   FWP

FRANCES LOUISE ROGERS
    Pylgrym Cronycles, 1923, "adapt. from original sources, especially   RPB
        Bradford's History of Plymouth Plantation, and done into dramatic
        episodes for modern readers"

GERTRUDE ROGERS
    The God and the Maid, 1907, cantata, music by Alexander von Fielitz   RPB-M

JULIA ANNE (or ANNIE) ROGERS
    Charge It to George, 1951, comedy (1)   RPB
    Mademoiselle Spectacles, 1915, 3 act comedy with incidental songs   RPB

GERTRUDE MARTIN ROHRER (1875- ?)
    The Toy Shop, 1916, Christmas   RPB

LILLIAN ROLLE
    The New Country Woman

KATHERINE METCALF ROOF
    Christmas Tryst, in Touchstone, 6, Dec., 1919, 83-9+ (1)
    The Edge of the Wood, in Drama, 10, Feb., 1920, 196-9 (1)
    Man Under the Bed, 1924, farce   RPB
    The Mirror, 1924 (1)   RPB
    The Secret, in Smart Set, 19, Aug., 1906, 108-11 (1)
    The Stone Venus, in Poet Lore, 37, Spring, 1926, 124-52
    Three Dear Friends, 1914, "feminine episode" (1)   RPB
    The Wanderer, in Smart Set, 23, Nov., 1907, 130-3 (1)
    The World Beyond the Mountain, in International, 7, Nov., 1913, 322-4 (1)

JUANITA E. ROOS (1878- ?)
    The Bells of Capistrano, 1928, 3 act operetta; book and lyrics with   RPB-M
        Charles O. Roos; music by Charles Wakefield Cadman
    Drama from the Yellowstone, 1921, text with Charles O. Roos; music   RPB-M
        by Thurlow Lieurance
    The Far Horizon, 1934, "cantata of Chinese character"   RPB-M
    The Ghost of Lollypop, 1927, 2 act operetta, libretto with Charles O.   RPB-M
        Roos; music by Charles Wakefield Cadman
    Princess Ting Ah Ling, 1930, 2 act operetta, with Charles O. Roos

IVY ASHTON ROOT
  The Greatest Love, prod. 1906

EMMA ROSCOWER
  A Day in a District School, 1911, 2 act comedy   RPB

MABEL J. ROSEMON
  The Christmas Wish, 1953, Christmas play   Or
  The Dawn Immortal, 1914, Easter service of story and song   RPB-M
  In Quest of the King, 1912, Christmas service of story and song, . RPB-M
    music by I. H Meredith and Fred W. Peace
  The Star of Glory, 1914, service of story and song for Christmas

CARLA F. ROSENTHAL
  The Little Shakeresses, 1923, young   RPB
  Our Family Picnic, 1928, monologue   RPB

ROSA ROSENTHAL
  The Realist (1)   SCT

"JEAN ROSS" (See IRENE DALE HEWSON)

JEANIE QUINTON ROSSE
  The Egyptian Princess, 1899, 2 act romantic operetta, music by   RPB-M
    Charles Vincent
  The Japanese Girl (O Hanu San), 1912, 2 act operetta, music by   RPB-M
    Charles Vincent

ALICE ROSTETTER
  The Queen's Lost Dignity, 1923, "for merry marionettes"   CJP
  Which Is Witch: or, Mable and Maisie, young (1)   JOP
  The Widow's Veil, 1920, prod 1918 (1)   RPB, FSP

HELEN GILMAN LUDINGTON ROTCH
  (See HELEN GILMAN LUDINGTON)

AGNES EDWARDS ROTHERY (1888- ?)
  Miss Coolidge, 1927, comedy (1)   RPB

ADRIENNE ROUCOLLE (1875- ?)
  Bridget's Trials, 1908, monologue   RPB
  A Half-hour of Madness, 1908, monologue   RPB
  Her Cowboy Lover, 1908, monologue   RPB
  The Jealous Wife, 1908, monologue   RPB
  The Letter, 1908, monologue   RPB
  The Victim, 1913, 3 acts   RPB
  Waiting for the Verdict, 1908, monologue   RPB

ESTHER ROUSH
  Death Comes to Sonia, play of the Russian Revolution, in The Carolina Play-
    Book, III, June, 1930, 53-9, winner in the high school play tournament

AURANIA ELLERBECK ROUVEROL (1885-1955)
  All in Marriage, prod. 1936, pub. under title, Love Isn't Everything
  Andy Hardy, 1953, 3 act comedy   RPB
  The Great American Family, 1947, comedy adapted from novel by   RPB
    Lee Shippey

AURANIA ELLERBECK ROUVEROL (continued)
Growing Pains, 1934, prod. 1933, comedy of adolescence   RPB
It Never Rains, 1930, prod. 1929, 3 act comedy of young love   RPB
Just Folks, 1923, Pasadena Community Players
Love Isn't Everything, 1937, 3 act comedy with Emile Littler   DLC
Money, 1939
Places, Please, prod. 1937
The Price of Love, in Drama, 16, March, 1926, 219-20+
Skidding, 1925, prod. 1928, won 1st prize Pasadena Drama   RPB
     League contest
When's Your Birthday? 1924, based on Paradise, a novel by Alice Brown RPB
Where the Heart Is, 1941, (originally titled Money in 1939) 3 acts   RPB
Young April, 1940, sequel to Growing Pains, with William   RPB
     Spence Rouverol
Young Man of Today, 1944, 3 acts   RPB

GRACE ROWE
Old Fashioned Roses, comedy of rural life, in Wise, ed. Missouri Plays

ADELAIDE CORINNE ROWELL (1887- ?)
The Beggar Maid (1)   SOP-I
Beloved It Is Morn, in Poet Lore, 36, Spring, 1925, 101-25, fantasy (1)   SPG
Hail the Conquering Hero, 1921, 3 act comedy   RPB
The High Heart, 1930, "based upon the final incident in the career   SSH-III
     of Sam Davis, famous Confederate scout," also in Drama, 17,
     March, 1927, 173-6+
The Last Frontier, in Drama, 15, April, 1925, 157-60+ (1)   SOP
The Little Fir Trees (1)   SSL
Pizen Song, prod. 1936, Federal Theater
The Silly Ass, in Drama, 12, Sept., 1922, 344-50, comedy (1)
Unto the Least of These, in Drama, 18, Nov., 1927, 43-6+,   SNC-2
     miracle play (1)

IDA M. ROWEN
Sir Richard Serves His Queen   JPP

REZIA ROWLEY
Spelled Backwards, 1925

BERTA RUCK (AMY ROBERTA RUCK OLIVER)
     (MRS. OLIVER ONIONS) (1878- ?)
G. For George, in Pearson, Plays for Amateur Actors, 1921

CLARA RUGE (1856- ?)
On the Road, 1905 (1)   NN

AGNES CLEMENTINE RUGGERI (1881- ?)
A Day and a Night, 1912, 2 act comedy for women   RPB
Reception Day at the Settlement House, 1913, entertainment for girls (1) RPB

CHARLOTTE RUMBOLD
St. Louis Pageant and Masque, 1914 (She was director.)

MARGARET RUMPLE
The Boys' Literary Conference, 1904, school play for 6 boys   RPB

BERTHA RUNKLE
The Helmet of Navarre, prod. 1901, with Lawrence Marston

ADA KELLOGG RUNNER
Say It With Flowers, 1924   RPB

ALMA RUPNOW
There Is a Way, 1927, pageant of Christian endeavor, with Martha Boese RPB

MARGARET DANA RUSH
The Radio Mystery, 1929, 3 act farce, by Dana Rush and John   RPB
    Milton Hagan, reprod. of the original professional performance by
    Nathaniel Edward Reeid

AMY REQUA RUSSELL
Poor Columbine, 1929 (1)   RPB

BERTHA M. RUSSELL
The Feast of Faith, 1930 (1)   RPB
The Thornless Crown, 1931 (1)   RPB

MARY C. RUSSELL
Penelope's Affinity, 1905, for women's clubs (1)   RPB

MARY MC SORLEY RUSSELL (1881- ?)
At the Inn, 1938, Christmas (1)   RPB
Christmas Magic, 1963, comedy for women (1)   RPB
Drama as a Factor in Social Education, 1924 (contains some plays)   RPB
Dramatized Bible Stories for Young People, 1921, one-acts   RPB
Dramatized Missionary Stories, 1930   RPB
A Fashion Revue; or, Styles Old and New, 1959   RPB
Her Answer, 1935, social problem play (1)   RPB
Holy Night, 1932, Christmas   RPB
How to Dramatize Bible Lessons, 1924, includes 12 dramatized stories RPB
How to Produce Plays and Pageants, 1923, includes plays   RPB
Just What the Patient Ordered, 1967, for women (1)   RPB
Mothers on Parade, 1962, for women (1)   RPB
Mrs. Maloney's Affliction, 1936, play?   DLC
One Way Out, 1935, social problem play (1)   RPB
The Pact, 1935, social problem play (1)
Pageants for Special Days in the Church Year, 1928   RPB
The Price of a Party, 1935, social problem play (1)   RPB
Producing Your Own Plays, 1931
A Puritan Style Show, 1933, pageant   RPB
The Right Word, 1935, social problem play (1)   RPB
Three Sons, 1941, 3 acts, Easter   RPB
The Three Women of the Nativity, 1960   RPB
Why Nancy Understood, 1935, social problem play (1)   RPB

NELLIE STUART RUSSELL
The Curing of Dad, 1928, comedy (1)   RPB
The Sun Is Coming Out, 1931, play of rural life (1)   RPB
The Surprising Bride, 1926, study in heredity   RPB

OLIVE RUSSELL
Semiramis, prod. before 1921 at Cleveland Playhouse, pantomime

GRACE DORCAS RUTHENBURG (1897- ?)
Alas Dear Goliath (1)   SAR
The Birthday Gift (1)   SSL
The Children
Crowns Off, about Colonial Revolution   SAP
The Death of Anulis (1)   SOP
The Frog with the Gold Crown   SPE
The Girl Who Climbed the Sky
The Gooseberry Mandarin, 1928, semi-tragedy for puppets, in   GMO, IPA
     Theatre Arts, 12, July, 1928, 501-4 (1)
Hans Bulow's Puppet, 1930? fantasy (1)   RPB, BYP
Hans Bulow's Last Puppet, in Scholastic, 20, March 5, 1932, 17-8+ (1)
Harlequin Breaks a String, Christmas   SNC-2
The King Was in His Counting House, Thanksgiving   STP
The Loyal Deserter, in Elmer R. Smith, et.al, Invitation to Reading,
     Book I, 1945 (1)
The Moon for a Prince, 1931, fantasy   DSS
Moses Was an Oyster Man, 1927 (1)   OPS-VII
Mothballs and Mushrooms
O Bright Flame Lifted, peace play (1)   NPW, SPP
The Pink and Beautiful Bird, Christmas, 1932   SSC
Retreat (1)   OPS-VIII,SSC
Rip Van Winkle, 1935   SPS
Solomon, in Poet Lore, 36, Winter, 1925, 600-9, by Grace Hutchinson
     Ruthenburg
The Talking Chair, 1932   RPB, MRC
The Tree Inclined   SLP-1
The Tubercle Tumbles   SPC
Very Good Friday   SPS-2
The Wearing of the Green, in The DePauw Magazine, March, 1920   SPS-2
     under title of The Apotheosis of Bill
The Witch Girl, young   SNP
The Wolf at the Door, 1930   RPB
The Year That Wouldn't Be New   SPA

LUCILE RUTLAND
Lafitte, 1899, with "Rhoda Cameron"   DLC
Light o'Love, 1906 (1)   RPB

ESTELLE L. RYAN (1890- ?)
Historical Plays of Colonial Days, 1912, with Louise E. Tucker,   RPB
     one acts for 5th year pupils

HELEN P. RYAN
What Our Flag Stands For   LNP

FLORENCE WILLARD RYERSON (CLEMENTS) (1894?-1965)
Albuquerque Ten Minutes, 1951, comedy (1)   RPB
All On a Summer's Day and Six Other Short Plays, 1928, with   RPB
     Colin Clements
Angels Don't Marry and Other One Act Plays, 1938, with Colin Clements RPB
A Cup of Tea, 1927, farce (1)   NAB-II
The Devil on Stilts, 1937, comedy, with Colin Clements (1)
The Divine Flora, 1947, with Colin Clements   RPB
Double Date, 1951, comedy (1)   RPB
Ever Since Eve, 1942, with Colin Clements, 3 acts   RPB

FLORENCE WILLARD RYERSON (continued)

<u>Farewell to Love</u>, 1938, with Colin Clements, also in Mayorga,	RPB
Margaret, Ed., <u>The Best One -Act Plays of 1938</u> and in <u>One-Act</u>	
<u>Play Magazine</u>, 1, Nov., 1937, 579-96, comedy (1)	
<u>Fine Feathers</u>, 1937, with Colin Clements, comedy (1)	CSdS
<u>First Person Singular</u>, 1937, monologues, with Colin Clements	RPB
<u>Follow the Dream</u>, 1951, with Alice D. G. Miller, 2 act comedy	RPB
<u>Gallant Lady</u>, 1938, with Colin Clements, comedy drama (1)	RPB
<u>Gay Ninety</u>, 1934, with Colin Clements (1)	RPB, SPS-2
<u>Glamour Preferred</u>, 1941, with Colin Clements, 3 act comedy,	RPB
(c. under title, <u>Morality Clause</u>)	
<u>Going! Going! Gone!</u> 1951, comedy (1)	RPB
<u>Harriet</u>, 1943, with Colin Clements, 3 acts	RPB
<u>Her Majesty, the King</u>, 1938, with Colin Clements (1)	RPB
<u>Hit or Miss</u>, 1929, with Colin Clements, farce (1)	RPB
<u>Hot Lemonade</u>, 1929, with Colin Clements (1)	OPS-V
<u>Isn't Nature Wonderful?</u> 1938, monologues, with Colin Clements	RPB
<u>Jilted</u>, 1928, with Colin Clements, comedy	RPB
<u>June Mad</u>, 1939, with Colin Clements, 3 act comedy based on	RPB
their novel, <u>This Awful Age</u>	
<u>Ladies Alone</u>, 1937, with Colin Clements, 8 comedies	RPB
<u>Last Night</u>, 1938, a duologue, with Colin Clements, also in <u>Emerson</u>	
<u>Quarterly</u>, 19, Feb., 1939, 15-6	
<u>Letters</u>, 1928, in <u>Drama</u>, 16, April, 1926, 253-4 (1)	SOP
<u>Little Scandal</u>, 1951, with Alice D. G. Miller, 3 act comedy	RPB
<u>The Littlest Shepherd</u>, 1929, with Colin Clements, Christmas	RPB, SSL
interlude (1)	
<u>The Loop</u>, 1928, with Colin Clements, "an experiment in lights and	JDC
shadows," also in <u>Emerson Quarterly</u>, 10, Jan., 1930, 15-7	
<u>Love Is Like That</u>, 1928, with Colin Clements	
<u>Materia Medica</u>, 1937, with Colin Clements, comedy (1)	
<u>Men Folks</u>, 1928, with Colin Clements	
<u>Miss Sydney Carton</u>, 1937, with Colin Clements, comedy (1)	RPB
<u>Movie Mother</u>, 1937 (1)	GMO
<u>Needlework</u>, 1951, comedy (1)	RPB
<u>Never Too Old</u>, 1937, with Colin Clements, comedy (1)	RPB
<u>Oh, Susanna</u>, 1948, with Colin Clements, musical based on songs of	RPB
Stephen Foster; music and lyrics by Ann Ronell	
<u>On the Lot</u>, 1928, with Colin Clements, "fantastic comedy," also in	SSH-I
<u>Drama</u>, 19, Nov., 1928, 46-7 (1)	
<u>On the Other Side of the Wall</u>, 1930, with Colin Clements, for	SSP
Armistice Day	
<u>Perfect Ending</u>, 1934, with Colin Clements (1)	RPB, OAT-III
<u>A Romantic Interval</u>, 1928, with Colin Clements (1)	
<u>Sky High</u>, 1950, with Alice D. G. Miller, 3 act comedy	RPB
<u>Spring Green</u>, 1944, with Colin Clements, 3 act comedy	RPB
<u>Star Song</u>, 1951, Christmas (1)	RPB
<u>Star Song and Other One-Act Plays</u>, 1951	RPB
<u>Star-struck</u>, 1937, with Colin Clements, comedy (1)	ICU, DLC
<u>Stick 'em Up!</u> 1929, with Colin Clements, comedy (1)	RPB
<u>Storm</u>, 1928, with Colin Clements	
<u>Strange Bedfellows</u>, 1948, prod. 1945, with Colin Clements, 3 act comedy	RPB
<u>Sugar and Spice</u>, 1938, with Colin Clements, comedy (1)	An-C-VU
<u>The Tenth Word</u>, 1937, with Colin Clements, comedy (1)	RPB
<u>That's Hollywood</u>, 1940, with Colin Clements, comedy (1)	
<u>The Third Angle</u>, 1928 (1)	SFM
<u>Through the Night</u>, 1940, mystery, with Colin Clements	RPB

FLORENCE WILLARD RYERSON (continued)
The Triumph of Job, 1951, pageant (1)   RPB
The Wicked Witch, 1920, with Colin Clements (1)   SSL
The Willow Plate, with Colin Clements   SPG, OPS-VI
Winnie Weeks, 1940, with Colin Clements, monologues   RPB
Write Me a Love Song, 1938, with Colin clements, comedy (1)   NN, OCIW
Years of the Locust, 1941, with Colin Clements, 3 acts   NN

THE FOLLOWING ARE BASED ON STORIES BY RYERSON, ARRANGED AS
CONTEST SELECTIONS BY OLIVE FORTENBACHER:
Anna the Absolute, 1930   RPB
Babs and the Little Gray Man, 1930   RPB
Bargain Days for Babies, 1930   RPB
Discarded: One Superfluous Wedding, 1931   RPB
The Truthful Lies of Jimsie, 1930   RPB
Willie the Worm, 1931   RPB

CALLY THOMAS RYLAND (1871- ?)
The Way Out, 1905, with Mary Huneker Lagen, farce   RPB

MADELEINE LUCETTE RYLEY (1868-1934)
The Altar of Friendship, prod. 1902, typed copy   MH
An American Citizen, 1895, prod. 1899, 4 act comedy   RPB
An American Invasion, prod. 1902
Christopher Jr., 1889, 4 act comedy   RPB
A Coat of Many Colors
The Grass Widow
Mice and Men, 1903, prod. 1902, 4 act romantic comedy   RPB
Mrs. Grundy, 1924, 4 acts   DLC
My Lady Dainty, 1900, prod. 1901, typescript   NN
Richard Savage, prod. 1901, based on Dr. Johnson's biography of Savage
    in Lives of the Poets
The Sugar Bowl, 1904, 4 act comedy   NN

ANITA RYTTENBERG
Rosamund at the Tracks, "philosophical melodrama with Albert
    Weinberg," in Poet Lore, 39, Autumn, 1928, 436-48 (1)

S

LILLIAN KEAL SABINE (1880- ?)
The Rise of Silas Lapham, 1927, dram. of novel by Howells, Theatre   RPB
    Guild Play, 4 act comedy

MARY PARMLY KOUES SACHS (1882- ?)
The Twelfth Disciple, 1946, prod. 1930   RPB

CLARA ELIZABETH SACKETT
The Shining Goddess, 1920, pageant
Through the Portals, n.d., festival for children, typed copy   MiD, OrP

WINIFRED ST. CLAIR
The Snubbing of Fanny, 1914 (1)   NN

ADELAIDE ST. CLAIRE
The Iron Ann, with Arthur Grahame (1)

FELICITAS SALESKI
A Christmas Pageant, 1916   RPB

M. ELIZABETH SALOIS
The Boys' George Washington

FRANCES A. F. SALTONSTALL
The Butlers, 1922, 2 acts   RPB
A Dangerous Experiment, 1922, farce in 2 scenes   RPB
"Not So Bad," 1926, 2 act comedy   RPB
Unto the Third Generation, 1926 (1)   RPB

GAIL ELIZABETH SAMPSON
Elizabeth's Ad, 1923, in The Forge, 17, no. 3, Cincinnati, 1923 (1)   RPB

GLADYS B. SAMPSON
The Hardscrabble Town Meeting, 1929   RPB
Sally of the Music Store, 1927, musical play (1)   RPB

JESSIE ETHEL SAMPTER (1883-1938) NAW
Candle Drill for Hanukka, 1922, "for 9 girls whose ages do not   RPB
    matter, but whose sizes are important"
The Last Candles, 1918, dramatic sketch for Chanukah   RPB

CORA A. SANDERS
The Gayrusans' Legacy, 1910, by S.S.G. Entertainment Co., with   RPB
    Luzetta R. Sanders and Helen Gaylord, 3 act drama
The Newrich Reception, 1910, with Luzetta Sanders and Helen Gaylord
The Pokeyville Rally, 1913, drama in one scene, with Luzetta   RPB
    Sanders and Helen Gaylord
Six Sharps, One Flat, 1907, with Luzetta Sanders and Helen Gaylord   RPB
Snapshots, 1906, with Luzetta Sanders and Helen Gaylord, "2 act drama   RPB
    representing incidents and happenings in a photographer's studio"
Union Depot for a Day, 1905, with Luzetta Sanders and Helen Gaylord   RPB

LUZETTA SANDERS (See CORA A. SANDERS)

MABELLE P. SANDERS
　　Lily Ling's First Christmas, 1930, for girls　　　　　　　　　RPB

MARGARET WEBB SANDERS
　　Spring's Heyday, 1924, fantasy (1)　　　　　　　　　　　　RPB

VIRGINIA SANDERSON
　　Long Ago in Judea, 1925, Christmas　　　　　　　　　　　RPB

EMILY WHITE SANDFORD
　　Sub Rosa, 1929, comedy (1)　　　　　　　　　　　　　　RPB

SARA A. SANDT
　　Dinner at the Dinsmore's, 1929, character monolog　　　　　RPB

AMELIA SANFORD
　　The Advertising Girls, 1909, "masque of very fly leaves in 2 scenes"　RPB
　　The Automatic Servant Girl, 1906, farce (1)　　　　　　　　RPB
　　A Commanding Position, 1909, farce for women　　　　　　　RPB
　　A Corner in Strait-Jackets, 1904, farce (1)　　　　　　RPB, BCF
　　The Ghost of an Idea, 1914, first pub. 1898, comedy (1)　　　RPB
　　Maids, Modes and Manners; or, Madame Grundy's Dilemma,　　RPB
　　　　1911, first pub. 1903
　　A Stew in a Studio; or, Cabbage vs. Rose, 1910, 3 act comedy　RPB

ANNE PUTNAM SANFORD
　　　　　Collections of plays edited by Sanford:
　　American Patriotic Plays, 1937　　　　　　　　　　　　RPB
　　Armistice Day, 1927　　　　　　　　　　　　　　　　RPB
　　Assembly Room Plays, 1936　　　　　　　　　　　　　RPB
　　Christmas Plays, 1932　　　　　　　　　　　　　　　RPB
　　George Washington Plays, 1931　　　　　　　　　　　　RPB
　　Lincoln Plays, 1933
　　Little Plays for Everybody, 1932, for grammar and high schools　RPB
　　Little Plays for Little People, 1929, with Robert Haven Schauffler　RPB
　　The Magic Book; an Anthology for Book Week, 1941, first pub. 1929,　RPB
　　　　with Robert Schauffler
　　New Plays for Children, 1936　　　　　　　　　　　　RPB
　　New Plays for Christmas, 1935　　　　　　　　　　　　RPB
　　One Act Plays for Women, 1934　　　　　　　　　　　RPB
　　Outdoor Plays for Boys and Girls, 1930　　　　　　　　RPB
　　Pageants of Our Nation, 1929
　　Peace Plays, 1932　　　　　　　　　　　　　　　　RPB
　　Plays for Autumn and Winter Holidays, 1938　　　　　　RPB
　　Plays for Civic Days, Citizenship Plays for Community Centers, 1931　RPB
　　Plays for Graduation Day, 1931　　　　　　　　　　　RPB
　　Plays for Spring and Summer Holidays, 1938　　　　　　RPB
　　Plays of Story and Legend, 1937　　　　　　　　　　RPB
　　Thanksgiving Plays, 1935　　　　　　　　　　　　　RPB

　　　　　Plays written by Sanford:
　　The Birthday Party (1)　　　　　　　　　　　　　SSH-IV
　　Brother Musicians (1)　　　　　　　　　　　　　SSH-IV
　　The Jewels of Isabella (1)　　　　　　　　　　　SSH-IV
　　The Night at the Inn　　　　　　　　　　　　　　SSC

MARGARET ELIZABETH SANGSTER (1894- ?)
The Littlest Orphan and the Christ Baby, 193?   RPB
The Ninepin Club: or, Flora the Queen of Summer, with Caroline A.   HBP
  Creevy (1)
A Thanksgiving Dream, with Caroline Creevy (1)   HBP

ANNA MERCHANT SAPIRO
Yiddish Mock Trial, 1926   RPB

MARIE ANTOINETTE SARLABOUS ("JEAN BART")
The Man Who Reclaimed His Head, 1932, (1935 scenario based on   NN
  her play, with Samuel Ornitz at NN)
The Squall, 1926
A Woman Denied, 1931

HILDA SATT
The Walking Delegate (written for Hull House Playhouse)

ANNA ELIZA HICKOX SATTERLEE (1851- ?)
Found: a Young Nobleman, 1916, temperance   RPB

CATHARINE IRVINE SAUNDERS (1872- ?)
Oh Canada! 19??, 3 act comedy, typed copy   An-C-VU
The Theorist, 1927, comedy (1)   RPB

FLORENCE WENDEROTH SAUNDERS
Mrs. De Brie Says, 1909, "series of brilliant monologues"   RPB

LILLIAN SAUNDERS
The Bee, in Drama, 14, Feb., 1924, 170-2+ (1)
The Good Hope, 1928, trans. by Saunders and Caroline Heijermans-
  Houwink of drama by Herman Heijermans, prod. at Civic Rep. Theater
Night Brings a Counselor, in Drama, 13, April, 1923, 251-3 (1)
Sob Sister, in Drama, 11, July, 1921, 354-7 (1)

LOUISE SAUNDERS (1893- ?)
Figureheads, fantasy (1)   GOP, LAM
The Grim Truth, 1903, pub. in The Seminary Yearbook, Plainfield   RPB
  Seminary, 1904 (1)
The Knave of Hearts, 1925, fantasy, in S. A. Leonard, Junior   RPB, LAM,
  Literature, Book II, 1930 (1)   FDD
Magic Lanterns, 1923, collection   RPB
Our Kind, in Smart Set, 64, Feb., 1921, 73-84, comedy (1)   NN
Poor Maddalena   KSP, KTP
The Woodland Princess, 1909, operetta for young people, music by   RPB
  Alice Terhune (1)

WINNIE SAUNDERS
Milton Memories, 1955, dedicatory pageant of Milton House, Milton,   WHi
  Wisconsin, with Ethel Theodora Rockwell
Mother Goose's Christmas Party, 1911 (1)   RPB

DOROTHY SAVAGE
Ion, tragedy (1)   PJB

ETTA SAVIER
Sammy Leyman's Cow and the Liar's Contest, 1928 or earlier, readings

MONICA SAVORY
    The Little Scarlet Flower, 1932, 3 act operetta, music by   IU, PPT
        Bryceson Treharne
    The Magic Bowl, 1932, 3 act operetta, music by Bryceson Treharne   RPB
    The Toymaker, 1929, 3 act operetta for jr. h. s., music by   RPB-M
        Bryceson Treharne

LUCY M. SAWYER ("LUCILLE SAWYER")
    If I Were You, 1929, 3 act comedy
    The Strugglers, prod. 1911, with H. M. Horkheimer
    Sunset Glow, 1929, with Adelaide L. Matthews, 3 act drama   RPB

RUTH SAWYER (MRS. ALBERT C. DURAND) (1880-1970) AWW NAW
    The Awakening, prod. 1918
    The Christmas Apple, 1939, by Margaret D. Williams, adapt. of   RPB
        story by Sawyer
    The Sidhe of Ben-Mor, in Poet Lore, 21, July/Aug., 1910, 300-10,   RPB
        Irish folk play (1)

CAROL SAX
    Questions, in Touchstone, 5, May, 1919, 111-4, with Morris Christie (1)

AMELIA F. SCARDEFIELD
    Settled for Life, 1908, 4 act romantic comedy   RPB

EVA WINIFRED SCATES
    The Historic Pageant of Fort Fairfield and the Aroostook Valley,   MB
        1916, Fort Fairfield, Maine (She was director.)

EILEEN SCHAAF
    Luck of the Dutch, 1925, 5 act comedy   RPB

ETHELINDA SCHAEFER
    Alcibiades, 1904, 4 acts   RPB

BARBARA LOUISE SCHAFER
    A Book of One-Act Plays, 1922 (She was compiler.)   RPB

LUCILLE SCHAMBERGER
    The Spirit of Liberty, 1918, with Jessie M. Webb, "patriotic play   RPB
        especially suitable for use in the schools" (1)

DOROTHY SCHENCK
    The Little Princess Who Travelled Far to Worship the King, 1928   RPB

MARIE BATTELLE SCHILLING
    Who Trimmed the Christmas Tree? (1)   BMC

ELLEN SCHMIDT
    A Dramatic Reader, Book 3, 1916   RPB

GLADYS SCHMIDT
    Merry-go-round, 1929, recitations for children, with Edwin   RPB
        Lewis Peterson

FRANCES HOMER SCHREINER
    Betty's Butler, 1921, comedy (1)   RPB
    Cin'm' Buns, 1920, comedy (1)   RPB

LILLIAN STAIR SCHREINER
The Blue Entertainment Book, 1930, with Edith F.A.U. Palmer   RPB
  Painton, Laura Rountree Smith and J. A. Baxter
Dolly Travers' Inheritance, 1915, 4 acts   RPB
Heavenly Twins, 1899, 3 act farce   PU
In the Days of '76, 1913, 4 act romantic drama   RPB
Jack's Visitors; or, the School Boy's Dream, 1904, patriotic and   RPB
  historical play (1)
Miss Poinsetta, 1916, Christmas play for young folks (1)   RPB

ELEANOR ALLEN SCHROLL
Christmas in Mother Goose-ville, 1915 (1)   RPB
Heralds of the King, 1928, with J. H. Fillmore, musical service   RPB
  for Children's Day
The Highway Robbers, 1908, for boys (1)   RPB
The Lost Doll, 1934, Christmas operetta, music by William M. Schmitt (1) RPB
A Star in the Sky, 1928, with J. H. Fillmore, Christmas service   RPB
  for young people
Why Santa Claus Comes in December, 1909, first pub. 1901   RPB

OLEDA SCHROTTKY
Everybody's Affair, 1925, 2 act Girl Scout play   RPB
A Pot of Red Geraniums, 1924, 2 acts, Christmas   RPB
Why the Rubbish? 1924, Girl Scout play   RPB

EMMA SCHULZ
Favorite Dramatizations, 1920, with Blanche Fisackerly   RPB

HELEN MERCI SCHUSTER
Awakening of Galatea, 1906, illustrated romance of statue scene   RPB
  from the play, Pygmalion and Galatea, by W. S. Gilbert, arranged and
  posed under direction of Schuster

ESTHER DRESDEN SCHWARTZ
Three Souls in Search of a Dramatist, in Drama, 16, April, 1926, 247-8+
  farce (1)

FLORINE SCHWARZ
Our Children's Stage, 1928, with Yetta Klein, 12 plays for children   RPB
  in the lower grades
Plays for School Children, 1930, with Yetta Klein   RPB

CHARLOTTE SCOONES
The Heart of the Valley, 1925, "story of how the territory of the   RPB
  Miss. Valley came under the flag of the U.S.A."

EVELYN SCOTT (1893-1963) AWW
Love, prod. 1921 by Providence Players (AWW lists prod. 1930)

FRONA SCOTT
The Christian Soldier, 1916, Children's Day service, music by   RPB
  Ira B. Wilson

MRS. JAMES E. SCOTT
The Gifts of Autumn   WPP

MARGARETTA (or MARGRETTA) SCOTT
The Bag o' Dreams, in Drama, 11, Jan., 1921, 131-2, young (1)
The Heart of Pierrot, in Drama, 10, Feb., 1920, 200-2 (1)   SBO
Three Kisses, in Drama, 10, Oct., 1919, 15-21 (1)
The Tragedy, in Poet Lore, 53, Autumn, 1947, 195-213

NATALIE VIVIAN SCOTT (1890- ?)
Zombie, in Theatre Arts, 13, Jan., 1929, 53-61   IPA

LIZZIE B. SCRIBNER
Beresford Benevolent Society, 1906, with Emma E. Brewster, farce (1)   RPB
Parlor Varieties, 1886 ed. with Emma E. Brewster; 1903 ed. with   RPB
     Brewster and Clara J. Denton

ELLA SCRYSMOUR (SEE ELLA SEYMOUR)

ANTOINETTE QUINBY SCUDDER (1898- ?)
The Cherry Tart and Other Plays, 1938   RPB
Five One Act Plays, 1934   RPB
The Henchman of the Moon, 1934, 5 act poetic drama   RPB
The Maple's Bride and Other One-Act Plays, 1930   RPB
The Masque of Our Lady in Egypt, 1933   RPB
The World in a Matchbox, 1949, collection   RPB

EDNA DRAKE SCUDDER
That Crucial Affair, 4 acts

EFFIE SEACHREST
Egyptian Photoplays, 1921
Greek Photoplays, 1916, children's plays   RPB

THELMA W. SEALOCK
Saturday's Lamb, 1928, for older children (1)   RPB

CLARA SEARLE
The Tale of the Griffin, 1908, musical comedy presented by   RPB-M
     the class of 1909, at Mt. Holyoke College; music by Marion Osborne;
     lyrics by Searle and Elizabeth Cole

KATHARINE SEARLE
Caterina, dram. from George Eliot's "Mr. Gilfil's Love Story"
Moving Out, prod. at Radcliffe, comedy (1)
Three War Sketches, 1916, one-acts   RPB
Two Plays, 1920 ("Roderick's Career," drama, and "Game," comedy)   RPB

MARGARET CASSIE SEARLE
Bad Debts, 1921, Vassar play (1)   RPB

ZELDA SEARS (1873-1935)
The Clinging Vine, prod. 1922, music by Harold Levey, typescript   NN
Cornered, with Dodson Mitchell
Home-made Happiness, 1922, music by Harold Levey   NN
"Lady Billy," prod. 1920, music by Harold Levey, typescript   NN
Lollipop, prod. 1924, music by Vincent Youmans; lyrics by Sears and
     W. DeLeon; book by Sears

ZELDA SEARS (continued)
A Lucky Break, 1926, prod. 1925, 3 act farce (also titled Broke)   RPB
  reproduction of the original professional performance by Nathaniel
  Edward Reid
The Magic Ring, prod. 1923, music by Harold Levey
Once Upon a Time, 1922, music by Harold Levey   NN
The Pathway to Paradise, 1922, music by Harold Levey   NN
The Scarlet Woman
Undertow

ELIZABETH FERGUSON SEAT
The Stockings' Revolt, 1910, Christmas (1)   RPB

MARION WEBSTER SEAVEY
Little Boy Blue, 1914, pantomime (stage director's book at RPB)   RPB

MARTHA M. SEAVEY
Judith of Tyre, 1924, 3 act drama   RPB
Miss Tabitha's Garden, 1925, comedy (1)   RPB
Theodore's Aunt, 1924, comedy (1)   RPB

MOLLY ELLIOT SEAWELL (1860-1916) AWW
Maid Marian, 1893, dram. of her story
The Sprightly Romance of Marsac, prod. 1900, with William Young

ANNA PHILLIPS SEE
Love and Tea, 1915, 2 act comedy drama of colonial times, written   RPB
  for the DAR
When Women Vote, 1911, 2 act farce   RPB

WINIFRED SEEGER
My Divinity, 1911, 3 act musical comedy   RPB

CLOVER HARTZ SEELIG
The Choice, 192? peace pageant   RPB

CLARA LEWIS SEEMAN
Alberta at the Beach, 1930   RPB
Archie Masters Diving, 1931   RPB
At the Accident, 1931   RPB
At Bedtime, 1930   RPB
At Grandma's, 1927   RPB
At Mother's Request, 1929   RPB
At Our School on Decoration Day, 1929   RPB
At the Skating Rink, 1928   RPB
At the Swimming Pool, 1927   RPB
Aunt Katie Lends a Helping Hand, 1932   RPB
Benny Boggle's First Date, 1932   RPB
Codfish Deliriums, 1930   RPB
*The First Day at the Kindergarten , 1932, comedy contest selection OrCS
Freddie's Installment Plan, 1932   RPB
Freshie's Big Game, 1932   RPB
In Case of Fire, 1930   RPB
Little Brothers Are That Way, 1932   RPB
Now Abideth Faith, 1927   RPB
Sally Lou Has Lost Her Teeth, 1931   RPB
Tobias at the Oil Station, 1925   RPB

CLARA LEWIS SEEMAN (continued)
Tommy Stearns at the Lib'ary, 1925   RPB
Tommy Stearns Scrubs Up, 1925   RPB
Tommy Stearns Turns Dentist, 1931   RPB
All but * are listed as Wetmore Declamation Bureau readings, plays and
    entertainments.

CLARETTE L. SEHON
Here, There and Everywhere, 1926, "play that shows the various   RPB
    types of work carried on by YWCA here, at home and in other countries"
Little Prince Hansa, 1927, "how a Roumanian lad found the road to   Or
    health and happiness, story and pantomime"

JENNY HOPKINS SEIBOLD
The Mover's Daughter, 1914, 3 acts, adapted by Edward Elsner   RPB
    (also titled The Girl from "Somewhere")

MARJORY (or MARJORIE) ALLEN SEIFFERT
Noah's Ark, "play for toys," in Poetry, 37, April, 1928, 1-14 (1)
The Old Woman, in Poetry, 13, Jan., 1919, 204-8 and Poetry, 15, Nov., 1919,
    111-3

GWENDOLEN LOGAN SEILER
The Princess and Mr. Parker, 1934, 3 act comedy for children and others
The Princess and the Swineherd, 1930, comedy for young and old   RPB
    in 3 acts; lyrics and incidental music by Conrad Seiler

GARA SELDEN
Gerda and the "Maycrobes,"193?   RPB
Oley Gives Up Golf and 'Rastus as "Valey," 1928, 2 monologues   DLC

ETTA SQUIER SELEY
Beans for Dinner, 1936, comedy   DLC
Juvenile Monologues and Recitations, 1927   RPB
Two Good Monologs, 1924   NN, DLC
Useful Dialogues for Young Folks, 1928   RPB

ANNE SELLECK
The Black Knight, 191? with Helen Ward Banks, from Scott's Ivanhoe   RPB

IRMA PEIXOTTO SELLERS
The Adored One, in Drama, 14, May-June, 1924, 153-61

RUTH SELMAN
The Doll's Playhouse   BPP

EDITH SELTER
Cinderella at Home, 1930, good 4-H Club play   RPB
Mrs. O'Grady's Girl, 1931, 3 act comedy   RPB

PEARL SETZER
The Black Rooster, in The Southern Ruralist, April, 1924, comedy   NcU
    of country folk (1)
The Building of Catawba, 1925? historical pageant,   NcU, NcD
    Hickory, N. C., text
Nancy's Commencement Dress, 1924

PEARL SETZER (continued)
Raleigh, a Tercentenary Pageant and Drama
Visions Old and New, 1924, historical pageant of Gaston   NcU
  County, N. C., text

MARGARET SEVERN
In Tennie Weenie Land, n.d., musical pantomime for little children,   RPB
  with Virginia W. Mackall; to be acted to the music of Max E.
  Oberndorfer to be found in "The Tennie Weenie Music Book for Piano"

GRACE SEVRINGHAUS
The Kingmaker's Choice, 1927, music by Lyman R. Bayard   RPB

EDNA BELLE SCOTT SEWELL (MRS. CHARLES W. SEWELL)
  (1881-1967) NAW
Farm Bureau Wins and Weds Indiana Agriculture, 1924, 2 acts   RPB

ELLA MAY SEXTON
California at Christmas Tide, 1902   RPB

ETHELYN SEXTON
Bernstein Tries 'Em Out, 1925 (1)   RPB
A Busy Day in Bangville, 1922, comedy (1)   RPB
The Dance of the Red, Red Rose, 1930 (1)   RPB
The Delay of the Overland Flyer, 1923   RPB
First Aid to Santa, 1921, 2 acts   RPB
Just Around the Corner, 1928, 3 act comedy drama   RPB
March On, Michigan, 1934, pageant of the making of a state   DLC
Miss Burnett Puts One Over, 1921, comedy for girls (1)   RPB
Mistletoe and Holly, 1927, collection   RPB
School Spirit, 1928, novelty for a "fill-in" (1)   RPB
Shakespeare Up-to-Date, 1916, class day play for girls' schools (1) RPB
Talking Trees, 1935, for Arbor Day   DLC
We Aim to Please, 1929, novel fashion show   RPB

ALTA HALVERSON SEYMOUR (1893- ?)
Going to the Fair, 1932, juvenile operetta, lyrics and music by   RPB-M
  Helen Wing (1)
The Inn of the Golden Cheese, 1929, juvenile operetta, lyrics and   RPB-M
  music by Helen Wing (1)
The Lemonade Stand, 1934, juvenile operetta, lyrics and music by   RPB-M
  Helen Wing
Mulligan's Magic, 1931, juvenile operetta, lyrics and music   RPB-M
  by Helen Wing (1)

MRS. ARTHUR T. SEYMOUR
A Campfire Cinderella, 1918, Campfire play (1)   RPB
The Mystic Seven; or, The Law of the Fire, 1918, Campfire play (1)   RPB
The Protest of the Trees and Flossie's Alphabet Lesson, 1918,
  two Bluebird plays
The Unselfish Violet, 1918, Bluebird play for very little girls (1) RPB

ELLA SEYMOUR (Also SCRYSMOUR)
Bridge of Distances, prod. 1925, with John S. Seymour

EMMA CARTER SEYMOUR
The Final Rehearsal, 1909, musical sketch (1)   RPB

MARY SEYMOUR
A Daughter-In-Law, comedy (1)   BCF

MAYCE F. SEYMOUR
The Fairies, 1926, drama   RPB

MILDRED D. SHACKLETT
The Land of No Fences, 1927, young   RPB
The Town that Santa Forgot, 1927 (1)   RPB

SARAH SHADE
Strictly Business, 1926 or earlier

ALMA MATER WILSON SHAFER
King Winter's Court and the Miss Springtime Company, 1922, "can   RPB
    be given by a dramatic or dance school" (1)

ELEANOR SHALER
Loose, 1925, with Thurston Macauley   NRB

(MARTHA) MATTIE BAYLY SHANNON ("MARTHA BAYLY")
    ("BARBARA STUART") (1885- ?)
The Angelic Song, 1941, Christmas drama   DLC
Angels of Christmas, 1930, candle light pageant   MiD, WaSp
Barabbas, 1934, Easter   RPB
The Bearer of the Cross, 1937, Easter   NcD
The Blessing of Christmastide, 1924, pageant   RPB
The Child Divine, 1942, Nativity pageant, music by various composers   Or
Choice Dramas for Children's Day, 1939
A Christmas Blessing, 1948?   Or
The Christmas Child, 1940   RPB
Christmas Flowers, 1938 (based on poem, "Legend of   Or
    the Christmas Rose")
The Christmas Message, 1933, story cantata dramatized   RPB-M
A Christmas Pageant: The Abiding King, 1932   DLC
The Christmas Story Hour, 1934, Christmas pageant for little   RPB-M
    children, by "Martha Bayly"; incidental music by Arthur Grantley
Christmas Surprises, 1924, 3 acts   RPB
The Conquering Sign, 1944, Easter program of song and story, music by
    "Stewart Landon" (pseud.)
Dramas and Pageants for Christmas, 1939
Eureka Christmas Recitations, 1939   Or
Eureka Plan and Program Book for All Occasions, 1934
Finding Christmas, 1944, pageant, by "Martha Bayly"   DLC
Friends of Jesus, 1943, pageant service for Children's Day   RPB
A Garden of Praise, 1942, pageant for children's day and general use,   DLC
    by "Martha Bayly"; music by Arthur Grantley
The Gift, 1943, chancel play with music for children's day and general   DLC
    use, by "Martha Bayly," music by Arthur Grantley
The Gift of Life, 1935, dramatic pageant for Easter   RPB
God's Candles, 1931, Easter pageant with music   RPB-M
God's Family, 1936, children's day dramatization   DLC
A Great Inheritance, 1938, 3 act Easter drama   RPB
Hail! King of Glory, 1939, Easter cantata, music by Lawrence Keating
The Happiness Way, 1929, 2 act Christmas play   RPB
The Heart of Christmas, 1928, story cantata dramatized for choir   RPB-M
    and Sunday school, music by Adam Gebiel

(MARTHA) MATTIE BAYLY SHANNON (continued)

The Holy Advent, 1938, Christmas cantata, music by "Lee Rogers" (pseud.)

The Home Beautiful, 1939, by "Martha Bayly," for Mother's Day (1)   RPB

In the Bethany Home, 1940, religious drama for Easter, by   DLC
   "Martha Bayly" (1)

Joyful and Triumphant, 1940, Christmas pageant   DLC

Keeping Christmas, 1935, Christmas pageant for young, by   DLC
   "Martha Bayly"

The Kingdom of Eternal Life, 1941, Easter, by "Martha Bayly" (1)   DLC

A Legend of the Christmas, 1940, religious drama   RPB

Life Eternal, 1930, Easter cantata for choirs, music by "Fred B.   RPB-M
   Holton" (pseud. for Ira Bishop Wilson)

A Little Child Shall Lead Them, in Elsie Duncan Yale, ed., Four Plays for RPB
   Children's Day,1936

The Little Shepherd, 1942, Christmas dram. for juniors, primaries and
   beginners, by "Barbara Stuart"

The Lowly King, 1941, religious drama for Lenten season (1)   RPB

The Monarch Divine, 1939, Christmas cantata, music by Lawrence Keating

Mothers of All Time, 1931, Scriptural service   DLC

A Mother's Tribute, 1935, for Mother's Day   RPB

The Music of Bethlehem, 1943, "an S.A.B. Christmas choir cantata,"
   music by "Fred B. Holton" (pseud. for Ira B. Wilson)

No Gift in Return, in Elsie Duncan Yale, ed., New Christmas Dramas, 1941RPB

Noel Book of Christmas Hymn Pantomimes and Christmas   Or
   Monologues with Lesson Talks, n.d.

O Holy Night, 1946, Christmas service, music by Isaac H. Meredith   Or

An Original Christmas Entertainment, 1924, for children, music   RPB
   by M. Isabelle Ritter

Our Heritage of Faith, 1941, "pageant of holy women for Mother's   DLC
   Day and general use"

Out of Darkness, 1937, religious dramatization for Christmas   RPB

Possessions, 1935, modern missionary play in prologue and one act   RPB

The Promised One, 1943, pageant of the first Christmas

Religious Dramas for Worship and Service, 1938, ed. by Shannon   RPB

The Search for a King, 1933, Christmas   RPB

Shining Candles, 1944, Christmas pageant, music by Ellen Jane Lorenz   MiD

"A Sign Unto You," 1936, Christmas   DLC

So Great a Faith, n.d., religious drama for Easter, by "Martha Bayly"   NcD

The Songs of Christmas, 1941, with carols and tableaus   RPB

There Is No Death, 1939, religious drama for Easter (1)   RPB

The Triumph, 1932, pageant of the resurrection and triumph of   RPB-M
   Jesus, by "Martha Bayly"

The Truth About Christmas, 1936   DLC

An Unshadowed Cross, 1927, pageant play with music for Easter;   RPB
   also in Elsie Duncan Yale, Ed., Four Easter Dramas, 1939

The Uplifted Cross, 1930, pageant for Easter with familiar music   RPB

The Way of the Cross, 1941, Easter, by "Barbara Stuart"   DLC

The Way of Peace, 1934, Christmas, by "Martha Bayly," music by   RPB-M
   Forrest G. Walter

When Christmas Really Came, 1936, Christmas pageant for   RPB-M
   young, by "Martha Bayly"; incidental music by Arthur Grantley

Yuletide Blessings, 1946, with I. H. Meredith   Or

MATHILDE SHAPIRO

Made In Heaven (1)   SCT

MARGARET SHARPE
Jimmy Jenkins' Halloween, 1928, young   RPB
A Royal Girl Scout, 1928, 2 acts   RPB

MARY G. SHARPE
Aunt Nan Goes Traveling, 1924, monologue   DLC
At the Doctor's Office, 1924, monologue   RPB
Dorothy Dumb's Christmas Shopping, 1931   RPB
The Land of Play   BPC
School at Pudding Lane, 1926, Mother Goose school play, music by   RPB
     Gladys Hodson Leach
To Make 'em Laugh, 1928, collection of humorous readings   RPB
Two Funny Ones for the Reader, 1931, two monologues   RPB
Two Snappy Dialect Recitations, 1931, two monologues   RPB
Windows and Other Humorous Monologs, 1948

FRANCES WELLS SHAW (1872-1937)
A Garden Drama, 1926, for children and grown-ups   RPB
In the Pasha's Garden
The Person in the Chair, in Drama, 11, Feb., 1921, 171-4 (1)

MARY SHAW (1854-1929) NAW NWAT
The Parrots' Cage, 1914, pro-feminist allegory (1)   RPB, FOV
The Woman Of It; or, Our Friends, the Anti-Suffragists,   RPB, FOV
     1914, satire (1)

LILLIAN SHEAROUSE
Redbeard the Pirate   APS

MRS. RENA CARY SHEFFIELD
Osceola, Chief of the Seminoles, 1926, pageant   RPB

ANN SHELBY
Gold Braid, prod. 1930

ALICE SHELDON (See ALICE BRADLEY)

MARY ABBY MERRIAM SHELDON ("MRS. CHARLES M. SHELDON")
     (1864- ?)
Fifty-fifty, 1925   RPB

"MAY SHELDON" (See MINNIE MAY KELLEY)

RUTH GAINES SHELTON (See RUTH GAINES-SHELTON)

EDNAH SHEPARD
Management, 1924
The Ticket Punch, 1923

ELIZABETH LEE SHEPARD
The Red Carnation, 1905

ESTHER SHEPHARD
Jet, 1921 (1)   HUW-1
Pierrette's Heart, 1924 (1)   NN, OCl
A Venetian Hour   YSP-I
The Wife, 1925

EMMA SHERIDAN
The Wind and Lady Moon, in Drama, 12, June-Aug., 1922, 314-8 (1)

ELLEN BURNS SHERMAN (1867- ?)
The Soldier's Dream, n.d., reprinted from The Herald of Peace, Jan.,   RPB
    1928, mimeograph copy

HELEN HOYT SHERMAN
The Lady from Philadelphia, 1912, orig. pub. 1901, farce (1)   RPB

SYLVIA SHERMAN
The Pipes o' Pan, 1916, "a wood dream"   RPB

DOROTHY SHERRILL
The Bellman of Mons, 1928? first pub. 1924 by Sherrill, adapted   RPB
    from play of Sherrill by Olive Ogle

EDNA SHERRY
Inspector Kennedy, prod. 1929, with Herbert Gropper

LAURA CASE SHERRY
    Ambition
    Just Livin'
    The Mask, in The Playbook, 2, Feb., 1915, 3-26, tragedy (1)   ICU
    On the Pier, 1920 (1)   DWP
    Romance

ANNIE SHERWOOD
Prices, 1904, "panoramic melodrama, romance imaginary, act first,   RPB
    scene fourth, ...fifth, ...sixth ...seventh"

CARRIE POTTER SHERWOOD
The New Parson, 1923, 3 act comedy   RPB

JOSEPHINE SHERWOOD
    The Orientals, operetta with K. C. Berry
    Princess Perfection, 1899, operetta   RPB-M
    (Both produced at Radcliffe)

MARGARET POLLOCK SHERWOOD (1864-1955)
Vittoria, in Scribner's, 37, April, 1905, 497-504, 5 acts   MH

HATTIEBELL SHIELDS
The Palace of Carelessness, 1928, 2 act operetta, with Ivine Shields   RPB-M
    and Laurene Shields
Station Cloudville, 1931, 2 act operetta, with Ivine Shields and   RPB-M
    Laurene Shield

IVINE SHIELDS (See work with Hattiebell Shields)

LAURENE SHIELDS (See work with Hattiebell Shields)

EVA BECKER SHIPPEE
Leave It to Dad, 1926, 3 act comedy for mixed characters   RPB

ELIZABETH BLOUNT SHIPPEN
"The Nativity" and "The Consecration of Sir Galahad," 1923, two   RPB
    pageants for the church, with Eugene Rodman Shippen

JOSEPHINE SHIVELY
A Christmas Eve Dream, 1929 (1)   RPB
The Runaway Bride, 1926, 3 act drama with Ted and Virginia Maxwell   RPB

BLANCHE W. SHOEMAKER
Three Compromises of the Constitution (1)

DORA ADELE SHOEMAKER
A Fighting Chance; or, For the Blue or the Gray, 1900, 3 acts   RPB
The Girls of 1776, 1905, 3 act drama for females   RPB
A Patron of Art, 1901, farce (1)   RPB

RACHEL WALTER HINKLE SHOEMAKER ("MRS. J. W. SHOEMAKER")
(1838-1915)
Choice Dialogues, 1914   (She was editor.)   RPB
Choice Dialogues for School and Social Entertainment, 1889   RPB
   (She was editor.)
Classic Dialogues and Dramas, 1888 (She was compiler.)   RPB
Delsartean Pantomimes, 1893   RPB
The Elocutionist's Annual, Nos. 5-12, 14, 15, 17, comprising new   RPB
   and popular readings, recitations, declamations, dialogues, tableaux,
   etc., 1873-89 (She was compiler of 8-17.)
Little People's Speaker, 1896 (She was compiler.)   RPB
Shoemaker's Dialogues, 1885 (She was editor.)   RPB
Shoemaker's Best Selections for Readings and Recitations, 1891—   RPB
   19 vols. (She compiled 8-19.)
Young Folks' Readings and Recitations, 1884 (She was compiler.)   RPB
Young Folks' Recitations designed for young people of fifteen years,   RPB
   1897 (She was compiler.)

VIOLA BROTHERS SHORE (1891-1970)
Fools Rush In, prod. 1934
Is This a Father? prod. 1935, with Jack Hayden, prompt book   NN
New Faces, prod. 1934, with Nancy Hamilton
Piper Paid, prod. 1934

MARION SHORT ("PAUL MARION")
As Molly Told It, 1909, by "Paul Marion," with Pauline Phelps, romantic RPB
   comedy for 2 females
At the Second Show, 1929   RPB
Au Revoir Sally, 1928, with Pauline Phelps   RPB
Aunt Sally and the Crime Wave, 1936, 3 act comedy   ViU, DLC
Background, 1929   RPB
The Bad Boy Comes Back, 1935, with Pauline Phelps, 3 act comedy   RPB
The Belle of Philadelphia Town, 1925, with Pauline Phelps,   RPB
   4 act colonial comedy
Betty Engaged, 1928, 3 act comedy   RPB
Billy Goes Haywire, 1935, comedy (1)
Black Gold, 1932, with Pauline Phelps, 3 act dramatic comedy   RPB
The Blossoming of Mary Anne, 1915, 4 acts   RPB
A Box of Powders, 1906, with Pauline Phelps   RPB
Boyfriend, 1942, comedy (1)   RPB
The Confederates, 1906, with Pauline Phelps , romantic comedy (1)   RPB
County Fair at Punkinville, 1912, by "Paul Marion," with Pauline   RPB
   Phelps, farce
Courting the Widow, 1909, by "Paul Marion," with Pauline   RPB
   Phelps, romantic comedy

MARION SHORT(continued)

Cozy Corners, 1922, with Pauline Phelps, 4 act comedy	RPB
Cupid Throws a Monkey Wrench, 1933, comedy (1)	RPB
The Deception Committee, 1931, dialect sketch (1)	RPB
The Flour Girl, 1927, with Pauline Phelps (c. 1920 under title, Hot Pancakes) 3 act comedy	RPB
The Getaway, 1929, comedy (1)	RPB
The Girl From Out Yonder, 1929, with Pauline Phelps, 4 act comedy drama	RPB
The Golden Age, 1919, with Sidney Toler, 4 act comedy of youth	RPB
Golden Days, 1922, with Sidney Toler, 4 act comedy	RPB
A Grand Army Man, 1907, with Pauline Phelps	
"Grandpa Goes Hunting," 1934, comedy (1)	RPB
Her Alienated Affections, 1932, mock trial (1)	RPB
The Hidden Guest, 1926, with Pauline Phelps, 3 acts	RPB
Home From College, 1915, with Pauline Phelps	RPB
The Honor of the Stars and Stripes, 1918, 4 act patriotic play	RPB
The Impatience of Job, 1932, with Pauline Phelps, 3 act character comedy	RPB
In Washington's Day, 1932, with Pauline Phelps, "play of Revolutionary times," 3 acts	RPB
Information Wanted, 1937, 3 act comedy	
Jack's Brother's Sister, 1916, with Pauline Phelps, sketch (1)	RPB
The Jade Necklace, 1929, modern 3 act comedy	RPB
Jealous? Certainly Not! 1931, comedy (1)	RPB
Lady Luck, 1932, comedy (1)	NPW
The Lights of Happyland, 1922 (1)	
The Little Terror, 1937, 3 act comedy	
Madam Magnificent, 1936, 3 act comedy	
Managing Mother, 1936, comedy (1)	Or
Marindy Gets "Assurance," 1931, blackface sketch	RPB
Miss Somebody Else, 1918, 4 act comedy mystery	RPB
Mrs. Moneymade's Fitting, 1928, with Pauline Phelps	RPB
The Mysterious Mrs. Updyke, 1932, 3 act comedy	
Nancy Pretends, 1927, with Pauline Phelps, modern 3 act comedy	RPB
The Nervous Miss Niles, 1931, 3 act comedy	
The Newspaper Bride, 1934, 3 act comedy	
The Night Club Girl, 1932, with Pauline Phelps (1)	RPB, NPW
No Wedding Bells for Me, 1937, by Charles George, based on a play by Short and Phelps	RPB
Nobody Is Home, 1931, 3 act comedy	
Only Me, 1924, with Pauline Phelps, 3 act modern play	
Pauline Pavlovna, 1914, dramatic romantic play or recitation by Thomas Bailey Aldrich, arranged as a play by Short	RPB
Peach Tree Road, 1930, 3 act modern comedy	RPB
'Rastus Gets Discussed, 1931, Negro dialogue for 2 women, blackface sketch	RPB
The Return of Hi Jinks, 1916, 4 act comedy based on farce by J. H. Rortz	RPB
The Return of Mr. Benjamin, 1933, mystery (1)	RPB
Rose of the Southland, 1924, 3 act comedy	RPB
The Ryerson Mystery, 1933, with Pauline Phelps, 3 acts	RPB
Shavings, 1930, prod. 1920, with Pauline Phelps, 3 act comedy from a story by Joseph C. Lincoln	RPB
She Wouldn't Stay Put, 1933, modern comedy (1)	RPB
A Short Short Story, 1935, comedy (1)	OCl, DLC
Sixteen Two Character Plays, also encores, 1906, with Pauline Phelps	RPB
Sparks, 1929, "an in-between play," by F. W. Erdman, ed. and rev. by Short (1)	RPB

MARION SHORT(continued)

Stop! Go! 1930, with Pauline Phelps, 3 act comedy drama	RPB
Sweet Clover, with Pauline Phelps	
They Will Grow Up, 1934, 3 act comedy	
Thirteen Diamonds, 1935, 3 act comedy	
Thrills, 1932, comedy (1)	RPB
The Touch-Down, 1913, 4 act comedy	RPB
The Trailer Man, 1938, 3 act comedy	ViU, DLC
The Varsity Coach, 1921 or earlier, 3 act play of college life	
Who Said Quit?, 1933, with Pauline Phelps, 3 act comedy	RPB
The Wistful Widow, 1932, with Pauline Phelps, 3 act comedy	RPB
Witches' Hour and Candlelight, 1922, with Pauline Phelps (1)	RPB

      (FOR PLAYS FOR WHICH SHORT AND PHELPS PROVIDED TEXT
      AND STAGE BUSINESS SEE PAULINE PHELPS)

EMMA SHOUDY

My Lord the Count, 1900, society drama	RPB

SARA VENORE SHRINER

At the Theatre, 1918, monologue	RPB

EVELINE SPOONER SHULTZ

A Poor Magdalene; or, The Crowning of Love, 1902	RPB
Queen Esther at the Palace, 1902, 20 living pictures with recital	CLSU, NN
or explanation	
Twentieth Century Temperance Socials, 1902 (contains two plays—	RPB
"The Power of Love; or, Can She Reform Him?" and "Adam's Fall," farce)	

LUCY C. SHUMWAY

The Grange in the Community, 1923, "pageant for an indefinite num-	RPB
ber of characters. Designed for use in Pomona or subordinate granges."	

CELIA E. SHUTE

Jerry; or, A Family Resemblance, 1924, comedy (1)	RPB

SALLY SHUTE

The Burglary at Browns, 1927, 3 act comedy	RPB
By Candlelight, 1935, 2 acts	RPB
Cynthia's Candlesticks; or, Heirlooms, 1929, 3 act comedy	RPB
Down Fido! 1926, for girls (1)	RPB
Fickle Fortune, 1926, 3 act comedy	RPB
June Time, 1926, 3 act comedy	RPB
The Minister Comes to Tea, 1926, for females (1)	RPB
Miss Todd's Vampire, 1920, comedy (1)	RPB
My Lady's Charm, 1937, 3 acts	RPB
The Old Pinter Place, 1935, comedy (1)	RPB
Paradise, 1927 (1)	RPB, GJY
Ragging Bob, 1927, 2 acts	RPB
Theodore Jr., 1920 (1)	RPB, JET
Welcoming the New Minister, 1946, for women (1)	RPB

ELLEN SHYNE

The Man Without a Country, 1918, tabloid in 4 scenes for 8th grade	RPB
pupils, based on the story by Edward Everett Hale, pub. with Jessie A.	
Kelly's, The Fair of the Pilgrims	

ALICE FLEMING SIDMAN
Blind Alleys, prod. 1924, with Victoria Montgomery

CLAIRE GINSBURG SIFTON (1897- ?)
Blood on the Moon, with Paul Sifton, manuscript   DLC
The Doctors, with Paul Sifton, manuscript   DLC
Ernie, in One-Act Play Magazine, 3, Jan., 1940, 19-28 (1)
Give All Thy Terrors to the Wind, 1937, with Paul Sifton, in William
    Kozlenko, Ed., The Best Short Plays of the Social Theatre, 1939 (1)
In the Meantime, 1930, with Paul Sifton, 3 acts, mimeograph copy   DLC
Kate Larsen, with Paul Sifton, in One-Act Play Magazine, 2, June-July,
    1938, 161-75
Midnight, prod. 1930, with Paul Sifton, typescript   NN
1931—a play, 1931, with Paul Sifton   RPB

FLORENCE RAE SIGNOR
Christmas Plays and Recitations, 1923 (She was compiler.)
Health Plays and Dialogues, 1923, "combining entertainment with the   RPB
    teaching of practical health lessons," compiled by Signor
Japanese Entertainments, 1924, recitations, plays, music and suggestive RPB
    programs, compiled and edited by Signor
Plays for School Days, 1921, for intermediate and grammar grades   RPB
    (She was compiler.)

LOUISE M. SILL
The Captain of the Gray Horse, 1903, with Rachel Crothers, founded   MH
    on a novel by Hamlin Garland, typed copy

GRACE VERNE SILVER (1889- ?)
Socialist Dialogues and Recitations, 1913, compiled with   RPB
    Josephine R. Cole

ALTHEA OSBER SILVERMAN
The Riddle of the Ages, 1936, 3 scenes   RPB
The Romance of Judas Maccabeus, 1924, hist. romance of the   RPB
    Maccabean War

MATTIE FRANCES SIMMONDS
Grown-up Children, in Poet Lore, 36, , Autumn, 1925, 434-40 (1)

EVELYN SIMMS
Christopher's Aunts, 1909, monologue   NN
The Conspirators, 1910, 2 act comedy for girls   RPB
Divided Attentions, 1915, comedy (1)   RPB
Her Ladyship's Niece, 1905, 4 act comedy   RPB
Hidden Harmonies, 1917, comedy (1)   RPB
The Lodging Housekeeper, 1909, monologue   RPB
Love and a Way, 1904, 3 act comedy for females   RPB
Maidens All Forlorn, 1901, 3 act comedy for women   RPB
Marjorie's Mischief; or, Playing Gooseberry, 1909, society comedy (1)   PU
A Packet for Popsey, 1910, farce (1)   RPB
Playing Gooseberry, 1909, society comedy (1)   RPB
The Romance of Phyllis; or, Love & a Way, 1904, 3 acts for women   PU
The Unexpected, 1909, monologue   NN
A Vision of Consolation, 1916, drama (1)
Ze Aftairnoon Tea, 1909, monologue   RPB

ESTHER JANETT SIMON
"The Land of Happiness," 1923, health pageant of Michigan   DLC
    Tuberculosis Assoc., typed copy
Randolph County Historical Pageant, n.d.   InI
The Spirit of the South, 1926, historical pageant of Alabama   RPB

ROWENA SIMON
Marmaduke and Gwendolyn; or, Shakespeare Was Right about the   RPB
    Course of True Love, 1930, pantomime

"EVELYN SIMONS" (See MARIE IRISH)

SARAH EMMA SIMONS (1867- ?)
Dramatization, 1913, selections from English classics adapted in
    dramatic form
A Shakespeare Festival, 1916, "being a fantasy of mockery and mirth   RPB
    composedof scenes from various plays, presented by
    5 companies of players before Queen Elizabeth and her court"

LILLIE SIMPSON
By Unanimous Vote, 1929, "little play with a big lesson"   RPB

MABEL P. SIMPSON
What's the Use? 1927, civic drama written for the Young People's RPB
    Department of the Better Government Assoc. of Chicago
    and Cook County

MAUDE B. SIMS
A Pan of Fudge, before 1912, boarding school sketch

MARJORIE SINCLAIR
Her Son, prod. 1917-1926? by Pasadena Community Players

FRANCES D. SINGLER
The Drum, 1929, Christmas (1)   MiD
The Dustman, 1934, first pub. 1930, drama (1)   RPB
The Extra Plate, 1930, farce, with Marion Vincent Dailey,   RPB
    mimeograph copy
Fandango Laughs, 1930, tragedy, mimeograph copy (1)   RPB
Is A Dor Knob, 1930, mimeograph copy, winning play in 1929   RPB
    Un. of Minn. contest (1)
Manitou of Who Dances in the Fire, 1931 play?   DLC
With Eyes of the Heart, 1930, drama, mimeograph copy (1)   RPB

INA DUVALL SINGLETON
Untrue to Type, 1921 (1)   RPB

LUCILLE SISSMAN
The Three Wishes   FWP

ADA MARIA SKINNER (1878- ?)
Children's Plays, 1919, one-acts, with Eleanor L. Skinner   RPB
Christmas Stories and Plays, 1926, ed. by Skinner   RPB
Dramatic Stories for Reading and Acting, 1914
Little Dramas for Primary Grades, 1913, with Lillian Nixon Lawrence   RPB
Little Folks' Christmas Stories and Plays, 1915, ed. by Skinner   RPB
The New Year, in St. Nicholas, 45, Jan., 1918, 257-62 (1)
Storyland in Plays, 1915, dramatic reader

CONSTANCE LINDSAY SKINNER (1877-1939) AWW NAW
David, prod. 1910 at Forest Theatre, Calif. (by Constance Skinner)
Good Morning, Rosamond! prod. 1917
Over the Border, n.d., 4 act romantic comedy, with Herbert Heron,   MH
    typed copy

CORNELIA OTIS SKINNER (1901-1979) AWW NWAT
Captain Fury, prod. 1925
Edna His Wife, prod. 1937, adapt. from a novel by Margaret A. Barnes,   NN
    promptbook
Family Circle, 1950, 3 act comedy, by Anne Coulter Martens,   RPB
    dram. of book by Skinner
Mansion on the Hudson, prod. 1935
One Woman Show, 1974, collection of monologues written and performed
    by Skinner
Opening Night, 1952, by Roland F. Fernand, adapt. from story   RPB
    by Skinner, comedy (1)
Our Hearts Were Young and Gay, 1946, by Jean Kerr, from book   RPB
    by Skinner and Emily Kimbrough
Paris '90, prod. 1952
The Pleasure of His Company, 1959, prod. 1958, "rueful comedy,"   RPB
    with Samuel Taylor; also in Kronenberger, Louis, ed., Best Plays of
    1958-1959; and in Theatre Arts, 44, April, 1960

ELEANOR LOUISE SKINNER (1872- ?)
Children's Plays, 1918, with Ada M. Skinner   RPB
Tales and Plays of Robin Hood, 1915   RPB

FLORENCE W. SKINNER
America's Future, 1929, thrift pageant   RPB
A Commencement Dilemma, 1924, class day or commencement play (1) RPB
The Hope of the World, 1926, pageant (1)   RPB
The Nurse's Dream, 1924, health play, "In effect, it is a pageant of RPB
    all sorts of women and children illustrating the necessity of hygienic
    personal practices"
Pennies and Nickles and Dimes, 1929, thrift play   RPB
Pie, Pickle and Ham, 1924, health play (1)   RPB

IRENE SKINNER
Scenario for the Henry County, Indiana, Centennial Pageant, 1916   InI

MAUD SKINNER
Pietro, prod. 1920, with Jules Eckert Goodman

LILLIAN SLATTERN (See "MARGARET MAYO")

LUCILE CRITES SLIGH (See LUCILE CRITES)

EUDORA HOLLINSHEAD SLOCUMB
The Woman's Convention, Punkville, U.S.A., 1915, "inconsistent   RPB
    brochure of fun and folly" (1)

KATHARINE E. SMEDLEY
Hanging Out the Wash, 1918, Negro play, with Anne Buzby   RPB
    Palmer, farce (1)

ALICE MARY SMITH (1879- ?)
    Short Plays by Representative Authors, 1920 (She was editor.)   RPB
    The Strength of the Weak, prod. 1906, with Charlotte Thompson

ANNETTE L. SMITH
    Bright Ideas for Grange Lecturers, 1925   RPB
    The Last Day at Center Ridge School, 1922   RPB

BESS FOSTER SMITH
    Cooperation on the Farm, 1929, pageant dealing with cooperative   RPB
        marketing (1)
    The Country Woman, 1929, pageant (1)   RPB
    Father and Sons, 1929   RPB

BESSIE BLAIR SMITH
    A Considerable Courtship, 1923, farce (1)   RPB
    Parted by Patience, 1904, farce (1)   RPB

BUELAH SMITH
    Christmas Shopping, 1904, comedy for children (1)   RPB

DORA VALENTINE SMITH (1893- ?)
    A Case of Lese Majesty, 1923, better speech play by the students of the   RPB
        University High School, Minneapolis

DORIS SMITH
    Rosario, the Pageant of the Rose, 1925, Portland, Oregon   RPB-M
    The Spirit of Frances Willard, 1923, pageant   DLC

DUCKIE SMITH
    The Pink Scarf, 1912, "bright little sketch"   RPB

ETHEL M. SMITH
    The Independence Day Pageant, Washington, D. C., in Drama, 13,
        February, 1914, 118-30

FLORENCE F. SMITH
    Doctoring Old Daddy World, 1930, "young people's church society"   RPB
    The Gossip's Eliminator, 1932, comedy   RPB
    Ladies' Aid Beauty Parlor, 1929, shadow play   RPB
    A Spell of Christmas Joy, 1930   DLC
    Ten Christmas Plays for the Grades, 1932, with Mary T. Johnson   RPB
        and Alta E. Toepp

GENEVIEVE THOMPSON SMITH
    Frail Emma, prod. 1928, partial typed script   OrHi
    Lady Hamilton, c.1920, prod. 1922 by San Diego Community   OrHi
        Players, typed script
    The Rage Breakers, c.1920, farce, typed script (1)   OrHi

GRACE E. SMITH
    The Arrowmaker's Daughter, 1913, with Gertrude Knevels, campfire   RPB
        play, adapted from "Hiawatha"

GRACE JERVIS SMITH
    Where Women Rule the Court, 1929, mock trial (1)   RPB

HARRIET D. SMITH
  Mother Sets the Stage, in Script, ed. by L. F. Brown and Fay P. LeCompt, RPB
    anthology of literature produced by students of the College of
    William and Mary, Richmond, 1930

HARRIET E. SMITH ("ELIZABETH WHITEHILL")
  Lohengrin, 1907, "musical burlesque for wax figures"   RPB
  The Rummage Sale at Hickory Hollow, 1909, by "Elizabeth Whitehill" (1) RPB

HYACINTHE STODDART SMITH
  Cordia, in Poet Lore, 19, Summer, 1908, 165-92, 3 acts

JEANIE OLIVER DAVIDSON SMITH ("TEMPLE OLIVER") (1836-1925)
  The Seal of Hellas, 1915, classical drama   RPB

JENNIE S. SMITH (See S. JENNIE SMITH)

JESSICA BELLE WELBORN SMITH ("MRS. L. WORTHINGTON SMITH")
  The Lamp of Heaven, 1919, Chinese play (1)   RPB

JUSTINA SMITH
  History of Texas, 1915, pageant, Denton, Texas
  Pageant of American Costumes, 1914, Denton, Texas
  Shakespeare Pageant, 1916, Denton, Texas

LAURA ROUNTREE SMITH (1876-1924)
  The Blue Entertainment Book, 1930, with others   RPB
  Bright Ideas for Halloween, 1920, with Elizabeth Guptill and others
  Christmas Candles, young   SCC
  Christmas in the Land of Make Believe, 1924   RPB
  The Circus Book, 1913, story with dramatizations   MeBa
  Community Plays for Various Days, 1921   NN, NBuG
  Drills and Plays for Patriotic Days, 1918   RPB
  Fairy Tale Pageant, in Musician, 20, May, 1915, 197-8
  Fan Dialog and Drill for Twelve Little Girls   TDF
  The Favorite Halloween Collection, 1938, with Ann Gladys Lloyd
  Games and Plays for Children, 1911   RPB
  The Gingerbread Boy and Joyful Jingle Play Stories, 1930   PP
  The Green Entertainment Book, 1930, with others (1941 ed. at RPB)   RPB
  Harvest Time, 1905, Thanksgiving play   RPB, STE
  Helps and Hints for Halloween, 1920, one-acts
  A Jack o' Lantern Drill   TDF
  A Japanese Reception, 19??, "tableau by a sister of the Visitation" NN
  The Lost Reindeer   SCC
  Puppet Plays for Special Days, 1919   RPB
  The Real Santa Claus   HPC
  Robinhood's Party, 1910   NN
  Special Day School Exercises, 1907, with Thomas Bryan Weaver   DHEW
  Thanksgiving Long Ago   SBT
  Thirty Christmas Dialogues and Plays, 1940, with others   RPB
  Thirty New Christmas Dialogues and Plays, 1909, with others
  Three Drills and a Farce by Teachers Who Have Used Them, 1901,   RPB
    with others
  Vacation Time. Game of Cloud and Sunbeam, 1910, young   RPB
  A Woodland Musical Pageant, in Musician, 21, May, 1916, 305-6

LENA R. SMITH
  The Lady Shore, 1905, with Mrs. Vance Thompson

LILIAN SMITH
The Witches' Curse; or, What Happened to Macbeth, 1929, burlesque   RPB
      operatic version

LILLI HUGER SMITH
Daddy, 1912, 3 act comedy   RPB
A Rank Deception, 1899, 2 act farce   RPB

MARGARET HOLBROOK SMITH
A Pair of Frauds, 1905, also in Werner's Magazine, Feb., 1902, comedy (1) RPB

MARIA WILKINS SMITH
Exitum Caesaris, in Classical Journal, 16, December, 1920, 157-64
      (in Latin) (1)

MARIAN (or MARION) SPENCER SMITH (See MIRIAM SPENCER SMITH)

MARY BRAINERD SMITH (1871- ?)
Christmas Folks, 1920, Christmas Eve dream for Sunday schools and   RPB
      day schools
The Quest, 1926, missionary pageant   RPB
The Time Family's New Year Resolutions, 1919, young   RPB

MARY STAFFORD SMITH (1859?-1934)
Penny Wise, prod. 1919, with Leslie Vyner

MAUDE SUMNER SMITH
The Busy Christmas Fairies, 1922, operetta for kindergarten or first grade RPB
From Footlights to Foothills, 1930, 3 act comedy   RPB
The Low-boy Wins, 1930 (See Susan Sumner Smith)   DLC

MILDRED KATHARINE SMITH
It's Human Nature, 1935, with Madeline Blackmore, 3 act comedy

MIRIAM (or MARIAN, or MARION) SPENCER SMITH
An American Grandfather, in Poet Lore, 35, 1924, 443-55 (1)
Good Night, in Drama, 16, February, 1926, 174+ (1)
The Hamburger King, in Drama, 15, March, 1925, 125-7+ (1)
Slow But Sure, in Drama, 17, February, 1927, 138-40, comedy (1)
The Wedding Anniversary, in Drama, 17, April, 1927, 206-7 (1)

MYRTLE HARRIS SMITH (MRS. CHAUNCEY PALMER SMITH)
The Acid Test, 1925, comedy (1)   RPB
The Grapes Hang High, 1925, comedy for women's clubs (1)   RPB
What Would You Do? 1926, domestic comedy (1)   RPB

NORA ARCHIBALD SMITH
Action Poems and Plays for Children, 1923   RPB
A Christmas Festival Service for Home, Kindergarten and
      Sunday School, 1893
Christmas in the Mousehole, by N. A. Smith, in American Childhood, 15,
      December, 1929, 30-1+
Christmas in Old England, in St. Nicholas, December, 1905
The Crowning of Peace, pageant   SSA
Plays, Pantomimes and Tableaux for Children, 1917   RPB
What Happened to the Tarts? in St. Nicholas, 47, August, 1920, 936-40

NORA DEL SMITH
The Cave and The Woman's Masquerade, 1911, 2 college comedies   RPB

ORA L. SMITH
Henpeck Holler Gossip, 1925, comedy (1)   RPB

PEARL MILLER SMITH
The Spirit of Spring, 1928, pageant of the wild flowers   RPB

PHRONIA ECKES SMITH
Will India Wait? 1923   RPB

RITA CREIGHTON SMITH
The Rescue, 1916, prod. by Provincetown Players (1)   BPH

S. JENNIE SMITH (also JENNIE S. SMITH)
Doctor Cureall, 2 act comedy   EEY
A Free Knowledge-ist; or, Too Much for One Head, 1893, 2 act comedy   RPB
The Home Guard, 1904, comedy for females (1)   RPB
Not a Man in the House, 1914?, 1st pub. 1897, comedy (1)   RPB
A Perplexing Situation, 1916, 2 act comedy   NN
Trying It on Beldon, 1904, 2 act comedy   RPB

SUSAN SUMNER SMITH (See MAUDE SUMNER SMITH)
The Low-boy Wins, 1930, comedy (1)   RPB

MRS. W. J. SMITH
The Comic Sheet Wedding, 1928   RPB

WINIFRED SMITH (1879- ?)
Lelia and Isabella, with Windsor P. Daggett, "commedia dell'artes"

CAROLYN FRANCES SMITHWICK
The Female Muster, n.d., comedy (1)   RPB

ROSINA K. SMYTH
Jimmie's Magic Whistle, 1930, Christmas playlet for children   RPB
    under twelve

MINA SLOANE SNELL
Does Mr. Jones Live Here? 1932, comedy (1)   RPB
Pea-green Cats, 1930, comedy (1)   RPB
Peter, Be Careful! 1941, farce (1)   DLC
The Shutter, 1931 (1)   RPB
Stormy Weather, 1935 play?   DLC

IDA SNOW
The Goddess of Peace and the King of War, 1916   RPB

LAURA E. V. SNOW
A Puzzled Detective, 1904, 3 act farce   RPB

KATHRYN SNYDER
At an Irish Wake, 1925, monologue   RPB
The Jewish Saleslady, 1925, monologue   RPB
The Joys of Ill Health, 1925, monologue   RPB

MAE STEIN SOBLE (MRS. JOHN J. SOBLE)
Bible Plays for Children, 1919, one-acts   NN, DLC

JUDITH KATRINA SOLLENBERGER (1901- ?)
The Call
The Marriage Gown, 1922   IPP
Sunrise

SELINA SOLOMON (S)
The Girl from Colorado; or, The Conversion of Aunty Suffridge, 1906

"SOMEPLE" (See ANNE GLADYS LLOYD)

CORNELIA SORABJI (1866-1954)
Gold Mohur Tune: "To Remember," 1930, 5 acts, also in Nineteenth Century,
    106, July, 1929, 133-42

HETTY LOVEJOY SORDEN
The Bag of Fresh Air Dreams   HDC

GRACE SORENSON
The Christmas Orphans, 1936 (1)   RPB
Christmas Plays for Boys and Girls, 1937   RPB
The Elusive Aunt Laura, 1933, 2 act mystery comedy   RPB
Holiday Plays for Young Actors, 1950   RPB
The Human Christmas Gift, 1934 (1)   RPB
Humorous Plays for Children, 1925   RPB
Juvenile Comedies, 1926   RPB
Lively Plays for Boys and Girls, 1934, one-acts   RPB
Merry Little Plays for Children, 1931   RPB
The Mysterious Friends, 1928, for upper grades and jr. h. s., 2 acts   RPB
The Mysterious Guest, 1935, play?   DLC
Peppy Plays for Boys and Girls, 1939   RPB
The Precious Manuscripts, 1939, 2 acts for jr. h. s.   RPB
Thanksgiving Plays for Boys and Girls, 1938   RPB
The Traveling Cousin, 1939, 2 act comedy for jr. h. s.   RPB
An Unselfish Christmas, 1935, play?   DLC
Wise Freshmen, 1944, comedy (1)   Or, DLC

WINIFRED SOTHERN
A Doorstep Dialogue   PTS-V

MINNIE SHEPHERD SPARROW
What Will Barbara Say? 1918-9, romance of Chapel Hill (1)
Who Pays? 1919-20, tragedy of industrial conflict, Carolina play (1)

MARGARET A. SPAULDING
Horses, 1927, stunt   RPB

DOROTHY SPEARE (1898-1951)
Romeo and Juliet, in Bookman (New York), 57, March, 1923, 7-17

FLORENCE LEWIS SPEARE (MRS. M. EDMUND) (1886-1965)
The Bride and the Burglar, 1922, comedy (1)   RPB
Jones Versus Jones, 1922, modern comedy (1)   RPB
The Star Gleams, 1922, community Christmas choral   RPB

DORALYNE SPENCE
The Stigma, 1927, with Dorothy Manley and Donald Duff

EULALIE SPENCE
Being Forty
Brothers and Sisters of the Church Council, 1920
Episode, in The Archive, April, 1928
Fool's Errand, 1927, won Samuel French prize in National Little Theatre RPB
    Tournament (1)
Foreign Mail, 1926, won second prize in Crisis contest (1)
Help Wanted, in Saturday Evening Quill, April, 1929
Her, 1927
Hot Stuff, 1927
The Hunch, won second prize in Opportunity play contest 1927; also in The
    Carolina Magazine, May, 1927 (1)
La Divina Pastora, 1929
The Starter, comedy of Harlem life, Opportunity prize play (1)   LGP
Undertow, 1929, in Carolina Magazine, 49, April, 1929 (1)   HSB
The Whipping, 1932, screenplay, 3 act comedy based on novel by
    Ray Flannagan

MARY C. SPENCE
Blind, 1929 (1)   RPB

FRANCES PEMBERTON SPENCER
Dregs (1)   MRO

LILIAN WHITE SPENCER
Pageant of Colorado, 1927, Denver, Colo., epic drama, music by Charles   RPB
    Wakefield Cadman
Sun-bride, 1935   CoD
The York Pageant, 1927, how the American Federation was founded,   MB
    York, Penn., with adaptation to the field by Percy Jewett Burrell
    and Alice Kraft

BELLA COHEN SPEWACK (1899- ?) AWW NWAT
Boy Meets Girl, 1937, prod. 1935, with Samuel   RPB, GTB, CCS-2, FP
    Spewack, comedy; also in Bennet Cerf, Ed., Sixteen Famous
    American Plays, won the Roi Cooper Megrue Prize
Boy Meets Girl; Spring Song, 1936, two plays (screenplay for Boy   RPB
    Meets Girl, 1938, with Samuel Spewack)
The Cat and the Fiddle, 1933, with Samuel Spewack, screenplay
Clear All Wires, 1932, with Samuel Spewack, 3 acts (screenplay, 1933)   RPB
Enchanted Nutcracker, 1963, teleplay
The Festival, 1955, with Samuel Spewack, 3 act comedy   RPB
Golden State, 1951, prod. 1950, with Samuel Spewack
Kiss Me Kate, 1951, prod. 1949, with Samuel Spewack, music and   RPB-M
    lyrics by Cole Porter, in Theatre Arts, 39, Jan., 1955, 34-57
Leave It to Me, 1938, musical adaptation of Clear All Wires, music by   NN
    Cole Porter, typescript
Miss Swann Expects, prod. 1939, with Samuel Spewack, prompt book   NN
My Favorite Wife, 1940, with Samuel Spewack, screenplay
My Three Angels, 1953, with Samuel Spewack, 3 act comedy, based on   RPB
    book by Albert Husson; also in Theatre Arts, 38, June, 1954, 34-61;
    in John Gassner, Ed., Twenty Best European Plays on the American
    Stage; in John Chapman, Ed., Theatre 1953
The Nuisance, 1933, with Samuel Spewack, screenplay

BELLA COHEN SPEWACK (continued)
  Out West It's Different, prod. 1940, with Samuel Spewack
  The People vs. Benito Mussolini, 1943, with Samuel Spewack, presented   CtY
      under auspices of Council for Democracy, No. 2, radio script
  Poppa, 1929, prod. 1928, with Samuel Spewack, 3 act comedy
  Rendezvous, 1935, with Samuel Spewack, screenplay
  Should Ladies Behave? 1933, with Samuel Spewack, screenplay
  The Solitaire Man, 1934, prod. 1926, with Samuel Spewack, melodrama
  Spring Song, 1936, prod. 1934, with Samuel Spewack   RPB
  Three Loves Has Nancy, 1938, with Samuel Spewack, screenplay
  Trousers to Match, 1941 (copyright 1937 under title, I've Got a Book, RPB
      and prod. 1939 as Miss Swann Expects), with Samuel Spewack,
      3 act comedy
  Vogues of 1938, with Samuel Spewack, scenario   NN
  The War Song, prod. 1928, with Samuel Spewack and George Jessel
  Weekend at the Waldorf, 1945, with Samuel Spewack, screenplay;
      novelized by Charles Lee
  Woman Bites Dog, 1947, prod. 1946, with Samuel Spewack, 3 act comedy RPB

(LADY) LEONORA von STOSCH SPEYER (1872-1956) AWW
  Holy Night, 1919, paraphrase in English of Yule-tide masque by   RPB
      Hans Travsil
  Love Me, Love My Dog, in Smart Set, 58, 1919, 73-82

DOROTHY GLADYS SPICER
  The Sleeping Princess, 1929, "May Day masque from many lands"   RPB
  The Song of the Coffee Bird, n.d., "play of a Dervish who loved the   RPB
      King's daughter"
  Yuletide Wakes, Yuletide Breaks, 1927, "holiday revel of many lands"   RPB

SARAH V. SPILLARD
  Thanksgiving Then and Now   SBT

HELEN BURNHAM SPLANE
  You Tell 'em, 1928, comedy (1)   RPB

HARRIET ELIZABETH PRESCOTT SPOFFORD (1835-1921) AWW NAW
  The Changeling, in St. Nicholas, 26, April, 1899, 501-12
  The Fairy Changeling, 1911, flower and fairy play   RPB

AGNES WRIGHT SPRING (1894- ?)
  The Price of Justice, 1928, 3 act comedy drama   RPB

BESSIE WREFORD SPRINGER
  Gassed, 1920, comedy (1)   RPB
  A Girl to Order, 1914, 2 act comedy   RPB
  Slats, 1913, 2 act college comedy drama
  The Two Dicks, 1911, 2 act comedy   RPB

FLETA CAMPBELL SPRINGER
  Where's Your Wife? prod. 1919, with Thomas Grant Springer and
      Joseph Noel

BEULAH GREENE SQUIRES
  The Angels' Court, 1930, 3 act Christmas play   RPB
  A Crown of Stars, religious pageant, missionary play
  The Halo of the Cross, 1931, pageant for churches   RPB
  Twelve Playlets About the Apostles, 1949   NN

EDITH LOMBARD SQUIRES (1884-1939)
And I Don't Mean Maybe, 1931	RPB
The Christmas Shadow, 1931, 3 acts	RPB
Eleven Plays for Little Children, 1931	RPB
Four In a Box, 1930	RPB
The Fourth Hand, 1934, mimeograph copy (1)	DLC
Queen Jezebel, in Poet Lore, 40, 1929, 615-26	
Six Little Plays of Early Quaker Life, 1932	RPB
Straight Through the Western Gate, 193? "dealing with 3 episodes	SPN
in the life of George Rogers Clark"	
Ten Little Plays for Little Tots, 1930	RPB
The Topaz of Ethiopia, 1939, with Elizabeth H. Emerson, for Christmas	RPB
Turning the Corner, 1931, 3 act comedy	RPB
Who Said Pie? 1930	RPB

MRS. JOSEPH L. STACY
White Gifts for the King, 1918, Christmas service	RPB-M

KATHERINE STAGG
The Star-Spangled Banner, 1907, war episode in the Civil War (1)	RPB

CLARA INGLIS STALKER
The Student's Dream, 1918, school masque, "written to commemorate	RPB
Illinois' one hundred years of statehood"	

M. LIZZIE STANLEY
Spirits of Days Gone By, young	SWD

MARTHA M. BURGESS STANLEY (1879- ?)
The First Mrs. Chiverick, 1930, with Adelaide Matthews, comedy	
Innocent Anne, 1930, with Adelaide Matthews, 4 act comedy	OCl, OrCS
Let and Sublet, 1930, comedy of youth (c. 1927 under title, Bad	RPB
and Glad of It)	
My Son, 1929, prod. 1924	
Nightie Night, 1929, prod. 1919, with Adelaide Matthews, farce	RPB
(c. 1919 under title, Oh, How Could You?)	
Puppy Love, 1927, prod. 1926, with Adelaide Matthews, 3 act comedy	RPB
Scrambled Wives, prod. 1920, with Adelaide Matthews	
The Teaser, prod. 1921, with Adelaide Matthews	
The Wasp's Nest, 1929, prod. 1927, with Adelaide Matthews, 3 act	RPB
mystery comedy (c. 1926 under title, The House in the Woods)	
Where Innocence Is Bliss, 1929, with Adelaide Matthews, 4 act	RPB
comedy (c. 1921 under title, Long Live the Queen)	

EMILIE BLACKMORE STAPP
The Holly Wreath, 1922, with Eleanor Cameron (1)	RPB
The Little Gray Lady, 1922, with Eleanor Cameron (1)	RPB
The Lost Firewood, with Eleanor Cameron (1)	RPB
Mr. February Thaw, 1922, with Eleanor Cameron (1)	RPB
Mollie's New Year's Party, 1922 (1)	RPB
The Tadpole School, 1922, with Eleanor Cameron (1)	RPB
(All are listed as Baker's series of Happyland's Fairy Grotto Plays)	

LYNN STARLING (1891- ?)
"Beverly Hills," 1940, with Howard J. Greer, 3 acts, typed copy	NN
The Climax, 1944, from the screenplay by Starling and Curt Siodmak	
The First Apple, 1934, 3 act modern comedy	RPB

LYNN STARLING (continued)
For Heaven's Sake, 194? (about WW II) typescript   NN
In His Arms, 1925, prod. 1924
Meet the Wife, 1926, prod. 1923, 3 act comedy   RPB
Skin Deep, prod. 1927
"Weak Sisters," 1925, typed copy   ·   DLC
Women of Glamour, 1936, screenplay by Starling and Mary C.   CLSU
    McCall; based on a play by Milton Herbert Gropper, mimeograph copy

MAUD STARLING
Historical Plays for Children, 1912, with Grace E. Bird   RPB

AUGUSTA M. STARR
Damn it, Matilda, 1930, comedy, mimeograph copy   RPB

"HELEN STARR" (See LENORE HAZEL HETRICK)

GRACIA STAYTON
Alice Scraps Her Slang, 1928, "funny encore reading"   RPB
At the Lace Counter, 1931   RPB
Chris'mus Presents, 1927   RPB
Gwendolyn Meets the Dentist, 1931   RPB
A Hostess of the Hills, 1927   RPB
How George Washington Became the "Father of His Country," 1927   RPB
The Lady Who Had Been to New Yawk, 1927   RPB
Mr. Mishkowsky und de "younk leddy," 1928   RPB
Mr. Schnickelfritz und der Vise-crackniks, 1930   RPB
Mrs. Schnickelfritz und de Four O'clock Train, 1928   RPB
The Oo-la-la Hat, 1931   RPB
Paw Rents a Modern Apartment, 1928   RPB
Twenty Dialect Monologues, 1928, with Peggy Reece and Penelope Dickerson
"Who Lost the Latchkey?" and "Mrs. Jack Advises," 1928, two readings   RPB
    (Most are Wetmore Declamation Bureau readings, plays
    and entertainments)

ADELAIDE STEDMAN
The Substitute Bride, in Smart Set, 35, October, 1911, 129-36 (1)

EVELYN AGNES STEEL
The Awakening of Everymaid, 1913, being the second Partheneia   RPB
    performed at Un. of Cal.

ASA MANCHESTER STEELE
A Cure for Hypnotism, 1919, farce (1)   RPB
Greater Than War, 1918, war-time play (1)   RPB
Madamoiselle (sic) de Maupin, 1903, comedy founded on novel by   NN
    Theophile Gautier, typed copy
Pettycoats and Bayonets, n.d., 4 acts   RPB

GERTRUDE STEIN (1874-1946) AWW NAW NWAT
Code for Stein collections:
    SW   Selected Writings of Gertrude Stein
    LOP   Last Operas and Plays
    SOP   Selected Operas and Plays
    G+P   Geography and Plays
    GSF   The Gertrude Stein First Reader
    GSF+ The Gertrude Stein First Reader and Three Other Plays

GERTRUDE STEIN (continued)

Brewsie and Willie, 1955, by Ellen Violett and Lisabeth Blake,   RPB
    adaptation from book by Stein (1)

Byron a Play, 1933 (LOP)

Circular Play, 1920 (SOP)

Daniel Webster, Eighteen in America: a Play, 1937, pub. in Spearhead: Ten
    Years' Experimental Writing in America, New Directions, 1947

Dr. Faustus Lights the Light, 1938 (prod. 1951) (LOP, SOP) also in   RPB
    Margaret Mayorga, ed., Best One-Act Plays of 1949-1950

An Exercise in Analysis, 1917 (LOP)

For the Country Entirely, 1916 (SOP and G+P)

Four Saints in Three Acts, 1927-8, music by Virgil Thomson   RPB
    (LOP, SOP, SW) also in Transition, 16-7, June, 1929, 39-72

Geography and Plays, 1922   RPB

The Gertrude Stein First Reader and Three Other Plays, 1946   RPB

Gertrude Stein's First Reader, new musical   RPB

An Historic Drama in the Memory of Winnie Elliot, 1930 (LOP)

In a Garden, prod. 1950, opera, music by Meyer Kupferman (1) (GSF) RPB-M

In Circles, prod. 1967

In Savoy; or, Yes is for a very young man, 1946, prod. 1949, play of the   RPB
    resistance in France

It Happened, a Play, 1913

Ladies Voices, 1922 (SOP, G+P)

Last Operas and Plays, 1949   RPB

Listen to Me, 1936 (LOP)

Look and Long, prod. 1955, (GSF+, SOP) also in Lowell Swortzell, ed.,
    All the World's a Stage: Modern Plays for Young People, 1972

Lucretia Borgia, 1968, first pub. in Creative Writing, 1, no. 8,   RPB
    October, 1939

The Maids, prod. 1955 (GSF+)

A Manoir (LOP)

The Mother of Us All, 1946, prod. 1947, music by Virgil   RPB-M, FCP
    Thomson, scenario by Maurice Grosser

Operas and Plays, 1932   RPB

Paisieu, 1928 (LOP)

Photograph, 1920 (LOP)

A Play Called Not and Now, 1936 (LOP)

A Play of Pounds, 1932 (LOP)

Play I, 1930 (LOP)

Sayin With Flowers (SOP)

Scenery and George Washington, n.d., "a novel or a play," in Hound   NNC
    & Horn, 5, No. 4, July-Sept., 1932, 606-11

Selected Operas and Plays of Gertrude Stein, 1970, ed. by John   RPB
    Malcolm Brinnin

Short Sentences, 1932 (LOP)

The Tavern, prod. 1920

They Must Be Wedded to Their Wife, 1931 (LOP, SOP)

Third Historic Drama, 1930 (LOP)

Three Sisters Who Are Not Sisters, 1946, prod. 1955 (SOP, GSF)

Turkey and Bones and Eating and We Liked It, 1922 (SOP, G+P)

A Village, are you ready yet not yet, 1928, 4 acts   RPB

A Wedding Bouquet, 1938, ballet, music by Lord Gerald Berners   RPB

What Happened, 1913 (SOP, G+P), also in Michael Benedikt, Theatre
    Experiment, 1967; and in Albert Poland and Bruce Mailman, eds.,
    The Off-Off Broadway Book, 1972

Will He Come Back Better, Second Historic Drama, In the Country,
    1930 (LOP)

Yes is for a very young man, 1944-5 (LOP, SOP) mimeo copy   TxCM

GEORGIA STENGER
Above All Else, Liberty, 1927, play of colonial Virginia   RPB
The Bitter Bites and the Bitter Bits (1)   SOP-1
A Legend of Old Manhattan, 1927, harvest play for young people   RPB
On the Road to Bethlehem, 1930, young   RPB
The Spirit of '76, 1925, colonial play in one scene   NN
This-a-way and that-a-way (1)   SOP-1

LEONA STEPHENS
The Morning After, prod. 1925, with Len (or Lon) D. Hollister

NAN (ANN) BAGBY STEPHENS
Black Sheep
Charivari, 1928, in Theatre Arts, 12, Nov., 1928, 814-22 (1)   IPA
The Cure-All
Glory, 1932   play?
The Green Vine, 1939, 3 act comedy
John Barley Corn
Lily, 1940 (1)   RPB
Roseanne, prod. 1923-4, "about colored people"
Six Little Plays of Old New Orleans
Tares
Unto Caesar

ANN STEPHENSON (may be Britishj)
Life's Little Sideshows, for a "he" and a "she," 1925, with   CaOTP, DLC
   Allan Macbeth
Pulling the Show Together, 1928, collection

CORA BENNETT STEPHENSON
A Lover's Knot, 1916, opera, music by Simon Buchhalter (1)   RPB-M

DAISY D. STEPHENSON
The Boy Washington   FPP
February's Famous Men   FPP

"LYDIA STEPTOE" (See DJUNA BARNES)

ADA STERLING (1870-1939)
Mary Queen of Scots, 1921, verse drama   RPB
Nica, prod. 1926
Show Folks; or, The Happiness Makers, 1918, 4 act comedy drama, NN
   typescript

SARA HAWKS STERLING
The Christmas Star, 1924, 3 acts   RPB
Hamlet's Brides, 1900, Shakespearean burlesque (1)   RPB

CAROLYN H. STERN
Making of America, pageant, with Charles Hanson Towne, in Delineator,
   100, July, 1922, 7

BEATRICE M. STEVENS
Motion Picture Dramatization of "Hats Off!"   FFP

CAROLINE D. STEVENS
Elopements While You Wait, in Drama, 13, Feb., 1923, 184-7, farce (1)

DANA J. STEVENS
A Christmas Highwayman, 1927 (1)   RPB
Eliza Gets Kissed, 1929, farce (1)   RPB
Old Acre Folk, 1903, 2 act rustic drama   RPB
Plain People, 1910, 4 act rural play   RPB
The Sawdust Queen, 1910, 3 act circus play   RPB

ELIZABETH STEVENS
Old Growler's Christmas Eve, 1923, comedy   RPB

ELIZABETH M. STEVENS
Rocking Chair Row, 1926, comedy for 6 ladies (1)   RPB

MARGARET TALBOTT STEVENS
The Birth of a Railroad, 1927   RPB

SOPHIE S. STEVENS
Building a Character   LNP
Fairy Gifts   LNP

AUGUSTA STEVENSON
An Indian Boy's Pet and Other Plays, 1939
The Black Pearl and Other Plays, 1938   NBuG
Children's Classics in Dramatic Form, 1909-11, 4 volumes   RPB
Dramatic Reader, no. 1-5
Dramatized Scenes from American History, 1916   RPB
The Hole in the Dike and Other Plays, 1938   RPB
Plays for the Home, 1913 (first pub. as Children's Classics in   RPB
   Dramatic Form)
The Puppet Princess; or, The Heart that Squeaked, 1915, Christmas   RPB
   play for children
The Red Shoes and Other Plays, 1938   RPB
Romantic Indiana, 1916, pageant   RPB
Scenes from American History, 1938
The White Canoe and Other Plays, 1938, young   RPB

CHRISTINE WETHERILL STEVENSON
The Pilgrimage Play, prod. 1920, story of Christ

FERN STEVENSON
Old Home Town and How It Grew, pageant, in Playground, 17, Oct.,
   1923, 391-2

MABEL B. STEVENSON
The Brown Mouse, 1921, 4 act rural play, adapt. of novel by   RPB
   Herbert Quick

MARGARETTA STEVENSON
Two Dollars, Please! 1922   IPP

ANN STEWARD
Cupid's Choice, 1929, little play in rhyme for primary and   RPB
   intermediate children
Getting a Permanent Wave, 1927, comedy   RPB
The Interrupted Wedding, 1927, young (1)   RPB

ANNA BIRD STEWART
The Belles of Canterbury, 1912, Chaucer tale out of school, for girls (1)   RPB
The Jekyl and Hyde Woman, 19?? (1)   NN
The Laughabet, 1918, operetta for children's voices, music by Harold   IU
    Vincent Milligan (1)
A Midsummer Dance Dream, 1916, fantastic comedy based on   RPB
    Shakespeare (1)
This Way to Fairyland, 1931 (1)   RPB

ELLEN STEWART
Pleasantly Purple, 1931
A Very Pale Pink Angel, 1930-1, whimsical satire (1)

JANE STEWART
Exercise for February 28th   FPP

JANE AGNES ꞨTEWART
A Notable Pageant on the Green, in Journal of Education, 76, Sept., 1912, 326

LILA STEWART
Cincinnati Pageant, 1914, Cincinnati, Ohio

MARY STEWART (? -1943)
The Land of Punch and Judy, 1922, book of puppet plays for children   RPB

LAURA JEAN LIBBEY STILWELL
The Abandoned Bride, c1908, 4 acts   NjR
Another Man's Treasure, c1908   NjR
Could She Forget—Or Forgive? c1908, 4 act "drama of intense   NjR
    heart interest"
Do You Love Me Dear? c1908, 4 acts   NjR
Don't Judge Her Too Harshly, 'Till You Know Her Sad Love Story, c1908 NjR
Estranged—But They Still Loved, c1908, "thrillingly intense comedy   NjR
    drama of heart throbs and hearty laughter," 4 acts
The First Kiss, c1908   NjR
The Heart of Saucy Susalyn   NjR
In a Moment of Temptation, c1908, 4 acts   NjR
In an Unguarded Moment, c1908, "romantic drama of intense   NjR
    heart interest," 4 acts
Jolliest Little Maid in Town, c1908, "drama of intense heart   NjR
    interest," 4 acts
Knowing All—But Trusting Him Still, c1908   NjR
Look Before You Leap, c1908   NjR
Love Me—And I Am a King, c1908   NjR
Love or Honor? c1908, 4 acts   NjR
Lovers Once But Now We're Parted   NJR
Madge Darling   NjR
Only a Flirtation, c1908   NjR
A Political Plot; or, The Widow of Monte Carlo, 1902, 4 acts
A Poor Girl's Love, c1908, 4 acts   NjR
Pretty Dorothy's Honor c1908, 4 acts   NjR
The Pretty Little Flirt, c1908, 4 acts   NjR
The Price of a Young Girl's Heart, c1908   NjR
Riches; or, A Poor Young Man   NjR
The Sad Love Story of a Pretty Village Belle, c1908   NjR
A Sudden Betrothal, c1908, 4 acts   NjR
Sweethearts Once But Now We Have Parted, c1908, 4 acts   NjR

LAURA JEAN LIBBEY STILWELL (continued)
An Unhappy Love, c1908   NjR
The Waifs of Rag-pickers Alley, c1908
When His Love Waned, c1908   NjR
When Love Is True, c1908, 4 acts   NjR
When Love Takes Wing, c1908   NjR
When True Hearts Meet, c1908, 4 acts   NjR
When You Meet the Right One, c1908, 4 acts   NjR
A Young Girl's Fatal Error, c1908, 4 acts   NjR

ELEANOR STINCHCOMB
A Goose and Some Geese, 1908, Mother Goose play   RPB

LOUISE STITELY
The Hope of the Springarns, 1928, comedy (1)   RPB

ELEANOR BANG STOCK
God's Quest, 1928   RPB

DOROTHY STOCKBRIDGE (TILLETT) (1896- ?)
Jezebel (1)   STC, SCO
The Mistletoe Bough, 1923, in Little Theater Tournament

STELLA PRINCE STOCKER
Ganymede, prod. 1902
Sieur du Lhut, 1916, 4 act historical play, with Indian pageant features and
    Indian melodies

HELEN STOCKING
Historical Community Pageant of San Jose, 1917, music by Ruth   RPB
    Cornell; song verse by Clarence Urmy; directed by Garnet Holme
Why Not? 1921, typescript   NN

DORA H. STOCKTON
The Golden Wedding, 1914 (1)   GP-I

ERMA M. STOCKWELL
The Girl from Weepah, 1929, with Myrtle B. Carpenter, comedy   RPB
    for women (1)

ALTHENE S. STODDARD
Path of a Century, 1825-1925; a pageant, Crawfordsville, Ind.   InI

ANNE GLEN STODDARD (1880- ?)
A Book of Marionette Plays, 1927, with Tony Sarg   RPB
Don Quixote, 1926, with Tony Sarg, written for marionettes   NN, MH
The Tony Sarg Marionette Book, 1921, text by F. J. McIsaac, with   RPB
    two plays for home marionettes by Anne Stoddard

ROSE PASTOR WIESLANDER STOKES (1879-1933) AWW NAW
In April, prod. 1915, Washington Square Players
The Woman Who Wouldn't, 1916   RPB

LILLIAN STOLL (See LILLIAN STOLL BEAZLEY)

"JANE STONE" (See JANE DRANSFIELD)

"JANE STONE" (See JESSIE TRIMBLE)

MARY IRENE STONE
 Plays from Bible Stories, 1927   NcD, DLC

SELMA B. STONE
 The Call of the Nirvana, 1924, by Rudolph Broda, English version with RPB
  the collaboration of Selma B. Stone

MABEL RUTH STONG (1905- ?)
 Brain Dust, 1937, drama (1)   OrCS, DLC
 Tombs, prize play of the Texas Federation of Women's Club   OPW
  One-Act Play Contest
 Yaller Squares, 1936, comedy for 6 women (1)   RPB

ALICE PARRY STOOPS
 Pageant of Petersburg and Pike County, Indiana, n.d.   InI

KATHLEEN STOTT
 The Triumph of the Cross, 1930, Easter   RPB

EDITH J. STOUFFER
 The Romance of the Pumpkin, 1920, pageant   RPB

CLARA STOW
 The Party of the Third Part, in Drama, 15, Feb., 1925, 110-1, comedy (1)

EDITH STOW (1875- ?)
 Wives a-plenty, 1926, 3 act comedy with music   RPB

EDNA HIGGINS STRACHAN
 The Caravan   YSP-II
 The Chinese Chest, 1935, 3 act comedy   RPB
 The Chinese Water Wheel, 1931, in Drama, 21, Oct., 1930, 15-6+ OPS-VI
 Fifty-fifty, 1932, farce (1)   RPB
 The McMurray Chin, 1932, 3 act comedy drama
 Romany Chi   YSP-IV
 Stuffed Owls   YSP-I
 This Genius Business, 1937, 3 act comedy
 Three Potatoes for Mary   YSP-I
 A Unicorn and a Fish   YSP-III
 A Weakness for Nurses   SCS-1
 Wienies on Wednesdays   YSP-I

LILIAN HOLMES STRACK (1886- ?)
 Buzz-z-z Means the Line Is Busy, 1932, contest selection   RPB
 Captain Marcy's Last Run, 1929, contest selection from a story by DLC
  Philip Curtiss
 Contest Winners for Prize Speaking, 1925, from the stories of popular RPB
  writers, arranged by Strack
 A Convert to Santa Claus, 1930, contest selection from story by RPB
  Roy Rolfe Gilson
 The Extra Pound, 1925, contest selection from story by   RPB
  Dorothea Canfield Fisher
 Gun Shy, 1926, by R. G. Kirk, arranged by Strack   RPB
 Hiney Bloss—champeen, 1925, contest selection from story by   CLSU
  G. W. Ogden

LILIAN HOLMES STRACK (continued)

Human Beings Being Human, 1934, acting character monologues	RPB
John Jackson's Arcady, 1928, contest selection from story by F. Scott Fitzgerald	
The Johnny Graham Shift, 1931, contest selection	RPB
Nails, 1932, contest selection	RPB
Only Skin Deep, 1932, contest selection	RPB
Platform Readings, 1925	RPB
The Play's the Thing, 1932, contest selection	RPB
The Prize Group, 1933, monologue	RPB
Reading, 'riting and 'rithmetic, 1932, contest selection	RPB
Selected Readings from the Stories of Juliet Wilbor Tompkins, 1925, arranged by Strack	
"Steve Carter Who Won the War," 1925, contest selection from story by Bruce Barton	RPB
The Strack Platform Readings, 1925, from the stories of Ellis Parker Butler	RPB
Strack Selections from Booth Tarkington's Stories, 1926	
Views and Previews, 1931, contest selection	RPB
Wilkie's Unforgivable Sin, 1929, contest selection from story by Homer Croy	DLC
Winning Monologues for Contests and Public Speaking, 1923	RPB

EMILY STRANG

Pageant of Oxford, 1913, Oxford, Mass.

JOANNA GLEED STRANGE

Today? in The Survey, 36, June 10, 1916, 287-9	NN

"MICHAEL STRANGE" (See MRS. BARRYMORE TWEED)

ANNA REESE STRATTON

The Inward Light, 1919, with Allan Davis, 4 act drama	RPB

RITA STRAUSS

In Bells and Motley; or, the May Queen (1)	BHP
The Wooden Shoe; or, St. Valentine's Day (1)	BHP

MRS. ERIC STREATFIELD (See KITTY BARNE)

ALICE M. STREHLE

"Faith of Our Fathers," 1929, historical pageant for Centennial celebration of Presbyterian Church, Danvers, Illinois	RPB

NETTINA LOUISE STROBACH

Plays for Schools and Little Theatres, 1930 comp. by Strobach with Frederick Koch	RPB
Pompons, fantasy (1)	HUW-2

GRACE COOKE STRONG

The Girl and the Undergraduate, 1912, comedy (1)	RPB
Marrying Belinda, 1912, farce (1)	RPB
The Templeton Teapot, 1912, farce (1)	RPB

MARION RAE STROSSMAN (1884- ?)

Centennial Pageant of Illinois, 1918, Aura, Ill., typed ms.	MB
The Spirit of Christmas, 1919, adapted from Dickens' A Christmas Carol	RPB

FRANCES STRUNSKY
Water and Wine, 1928, mimeograph copy, story of Theseus   RPB, VET
    and Ariadne

REBECA STRUTTON
Best Primary Plays, 1930, "30 dramas for little folks," with   RPB
    Noel Flaurier and others
Christmas Plays and Comedies, 1925, with others   RPB
The Doll Shop (1)   SBP
The First Rehearsal (1)   SBP
The Queen of Roseland (1)   SBP
Spirits of Autumn, Spring, Summer, Winter, four one-acts   SBP
A Visit to Fairyland (1)   SBP
The Week Family (1)   SBP
Wild Flowers (1)   SBP

MARIA HALSEY STRYKER
Health Fairy Playlets, 1921   RPB
Queen of the Harvest, 1922, health pageant   RPB

"BARBARA STUART" (See MATTIE BAYLY SHANNON)

RUTH MC ENERY STUART (1856 or1849-1917) NAW
The Snow-cap Sisters, 1901, burlesque   RPB

ALICE STUBBS
A Pageant of American Citizenship, 1925   RPB

REBECCA FORBES STURGIS
One War Babe, Great War tragedy (1)   SLP

RUTH SUCKOW (1892-1960) AWW NAW
What King Christmas Brought, in Bright Ideas for Christmas, 1920

ELIZABETH HIGGINS SULLIVAN (1874- ?)
The Beacon, 1930, with Joy Higgins,"dramatic spectacle to picture and   MB
    symbolize the founding of Boston," mimeo copy
The Strongest Man (1)   BPW

MAUDE J. SULLIVAN
Victory Divine, 1907, sacred cantata , the words taken from the   RPB-M
    Scriptures and arranged by Sullivan; music by J. Christopher Marks

DOROTHY LEHMAN SUMERAU
Bearers of Light, 1935 play?   DLC
Choice Dramas for Children's Day, 1939
Christmas Feast of Lights, 1933, sacred drama for Christmas   RPB
The Christmas Gifts, 1959 (1)   RPB
The Christmas Miracle, 1932   RPB
Christmas Stars, 1938, musical pageant by Phoebe Whittier?, music by
    various composers
Commencement Is Here! 1959, collection of material for senior and   RPB
    jr. h. s.
A Drop in Christmas, 1936   Or, DLC
The Easter Revelation, 1945, cantata-drama, music by Charles Francis Lane
Emmanuel, 1931, mythical Christmas story of the child and the chimes   RPB
Gold, Frankincense and Myrrh, 1943, story and song service   DLC
    for Christmas

DOROTHY LEHMAN SUMERAU (continued)

The Great Light, 1930, Christmas pageant	RPB
I Beheld His Glory, 1935, Christmas pageant	RPB
Jake Snyder's Christmas, 1931, young	RPB
The King's Garden, 1942, Children's Day pageant	DLC
Let the Little Ones Come, 1930, Children's Day play	DLC
Let Us Give Thanks, 1943, Thanksgiving story and song service	DLC
Magnificent Motherhood, 1942, modern Mother's Day play	DLC
Make His Name Glorious, 1958, "dramatic service of worship on the life and work of Lottie Moon"	RPB
The Miracle of Christmas, 1944, pageant for primary and junior children	DLC
Out of the Easter Garden, 1934, children's pageant	RPB
The Pilgrims' Thanksgiving, 1924, pageant	RPB
The Shepherd Who Came Late, 1934, Christmas	RPB
Through Other Eyes, 1939, Christmas (1)	DLC
With the Bethlehem Shepherds, 1936 play?	DLC

CLAIRE SUMNER

Hail the King, 1908, Christmas service, with Charles H. Gabriel, Lizzie De Armond and James Rowe	RPB

KARIN SUNDELOF-ASBRAND ("KARIN ASBRAND")

Bright Dummy, 1948, 3 act mystery comedy	RPB
Charity Begins at Home, 1930, comedy drama, "adapted from the Boston Post prize story" (1)	RPB
Christmas Jewels, 1933, play with music for children	DLC
Children of Other Lands, 1952, 5 plays for young folks by Karin Asbrand	RPB
Children Seen and Heard, 1955, by Claribel Spamer, Eva M. Quinlan and Karin Asbrand, platform readings for young folks	RPB
The Children's Program Book, 1958, by Karin S. Asbrand	RPB
Come Ye That Mourn, religious pageant	
Easy As Pie, 1953, by Karin Asbrand, teenage play (1)	RPB
Easy Bible Story Dramatizations for Children, 1939, with Mrs. Stanley Ross Fisher	RPB
Easy Church Plays for Women and Girls, 1955, by Karin Asbrand	RPB
Easy Easterettes, 1949, by Karin Asbrand, book of short programs for Easter for people of all ages,	RPB
Easy Programs for Church Holidays, 1953, by Karin S. Asbrand	RPB
Easy Sunday School Entertainments, 1939	RPB
Engaged for the Month, 1927, by Karin Asbrand, comedy (1)	RPB
Flag of the Free, 1941, by Karin Asbrand, patriotic play for the grades	RPB
Follow the Star, 1929, Christmas pageant	
The Forgotten Gift, 1939, Christmas, with music	DLC
Foster's Formula, 1969, by Karin Asbrand, teenage comedy (1)	RPB
The Fourth Wise Man, 1951, by Karin Asbrand, 2 act Christmas play	RPB
Gallantly Streaming, 1941, patriotic playlet for the grades	DLC
Gifts of Myrhh, 1931, Christmas play adapted from prize story in Boston Post	RPB
God So Loved the World, 1938, passion play in 3 episodes	RPB
Good and Faithful Servant, 1962, by Karin Asbrand, humorous missionary play	RPB
Hark the Little Angels Speak, 1959, by Karin Asbrand, Christmas plays, exercises, recitations for youngsters	RPB
Honor Thy Mother	CTM
The Image of Christmas, 1958, by Karin Asbrand, "living pictures of the Christmas season"	RPB

KARIN SUNDELOF-ASBRAND (continued)

It's Time for Remembering, 1956, by Karin Asbrand, Memorial	RPB
Day play for the grades	
Joy to the World, 1935, Christmas	DLC
Kin to the King, 1936, Easter pageant	DLC
The Kingdom, 1929, presentation of the Easter story with music	RPB
Kitchen Kanaries, 1952, by Karin Asbrand, "spice of life variety show"	RPB
The Lights of Christmas, 1946, by Karin Asbrand	RPB
Long May It Wave, 1941, patriotic play for the grades	DLC
Merry Christmas to the World, 1941, pageant of good will for the grades	DLC
Message from the Manger, 1942, patriotic pageant for Christmas	DLC
Midnight Son, 1948, by Karin Asbrand, 3 act mystery comedy	RPB
Mrs. Wigglesworth Gets Religion, 1928, 2 act comedy	RPB
Mother's Day Treasure Book, 1937, recitations, songs, pageants,	RPB
exercises, plays	
Much Ado Over Nancy, 1929, 3 act farce	RPB
A New Kind of Old-Fashioned Girl, 1929, 3 act comedy of youth	RPB
The Old District School, 1949, by Karin Asbrand	RPB
On the Road to Moonlight Town, 1928	DLC
One Night in Bethlehem, 1941, by Karin Asbrand, pageant play	RPB
One Starry Night, 1950, by Karin Asbrand, Christmas pageant	MiD
Polly and the Pages, 1929, patriotic pageant for juniors	DLC
The Portal, 1935, Easter	DLC
The Promise, 1932, Easter	RPB
The Queer Duck, 1927, by Karin Asbrand	RPB
Readings for Young Readers, 1963, by Karin Asbrand	RPB
Readings for Young Stars, 1953, by Karin Asbrand and Claribel Spamer	RPB
Rehearsal-less Easter Collection for Children, 1950, by Karin Asbrand	RPB
Rehearsal-less Fun, 1958, by Karin Asbrand	RPB
The Sailors Come Home	CTM
Santa's Shadow, 1933, 2 act Christms play	RPB
The Silver Lining, 1928, by Karin Asbrand, 3 act comedy drama	RPB
Skippy Sees Things Through, 1928, 3 act comedy drama	RPB
So It's Christmas Again, 1956, by Karin Asbrand, young	RPB
Star of Light, 1946, by Karin Asbrand, candlelight pageant for Christmas	RPB
Still Shines the Star, 1940, by Karin Asbrand, Christmas pageant	MiD
This Is Our America, 1941, patriotic play for the grades	DLC
The Third Day, 1931, pageant of the resurrection	RPB
Tidings of Peace, 1952, by Karin Asbrand, Christmas pageant	RPB
United We Stand, 1942, patriotic pageant for the grades	DLC
Valentine Box, 1956, by Karin Asbrand, young	RPB
The Way of the Cross, 1928, Easter	RPB
The Week Before Christmas, 1958, by Karin Asbrand, pantomime	RPB
in 2 parts	
What About Marcelline? 1929, 2 act comedy	RPB
What So Proudly We Hail, 1941, patriotic pageant for the grades	RPB
Where a Mother Waits for You	CTM
Whoa, Auntie, 1947, by Karin Asbrand, 3 act comedy	RPB
Winning the Peace, 1943, patriotic pageant for the grades	DLC
Witches' Brew, 1956, by Karin Asbrand, for Halloween	RPB

MARJORIE CHASE SURDEZ (See MARJORIE CHASE)

EVELYN GREENLEAF SUTHERLAND (1855-1908)

At the Barricade, n.d., "episode of the commune of '71,"	RPB
romantic tragedy	
Boy O'Carroll, 1902, with Beulah Marie Dix	

EVELYN GREENLEAF SUTHERLAND (continued)
The Breed of the Treshams, 1902, with Beulah Marie Dix
Collected Works, 1900
A Comedie Royall, 1900?, "being a forgotten episode of   RPB, SSV
   Elizabeth's day"
The End of the Way, 1900, drama (1)   RPB
Fort Frayne, 1902, with Gen. Charles King
Galatea of the Toy Shop, 1899?, fantasy (1)   RPB
His Own, script   NNC
In Aunt Chloe's Cabin, 1925, first performed in 1899, "Negro comedy   RPB
   sketch in one scene for female minstrels"
In Far Bohemia, 1900, with Emma Sheridan Fry   RPB
In Office Hours and Other Sketches, 1900, for vaudeville and   RPB
   private acting
Joan of the Shoals, prod. 1902, history
The Lilac Room, 1907, prod. 1902, with Beulah Marie Dix
Matt of Merrymount, 1902, with Beulah Marie Dix
Monsieur Beaucaire, prod. 1901, with Booth Tarkington
Po' White Trash, 1900?   RPB
Po' White Trash and Other One-Act Dramas, 1900, with   RPB
   Emma Sheridan Fry and Percy Wallace MacKaye
A Quilting Party in the Thirties, first performed 1899 in connection with
   pageant, "Our New England," "outline sketch for music in one scene"
The Road to Yesterday, 1925, prod. 1906, with Beulah Marie Dix,   RPB
   comedy of fantasy
Rohan the Silent, 1900, romantic drama, with Emma Sheridan Fry (1)   RPB
A Rose o' Plymouthtown, 1908, prod. 1902, 4 act comedy, with   RPB
   Beulah Marie Dix
The Story of a Famous Wedding, first performed 1899, "novelty admirably
   suited for Colonial societies, Daughters of the Revolution, and so on," in
   connection with pageant, "Our New England"
Young Fernald, 1902, with Beulah Marie Dix

VIDA RAVENSCROFT SUTTON (1880- ?)
At the Sign of the Boar's Head, play of the War of Independence (1)   SGW
The Betrothal of Mai Tsung, 1924, missionary play of China today,   RPB
   with Kyung Shien Sung
Christ Is Born in Bethlehem, 1924   RPB
In 1864, 1924, Civil War (1)   SLP-1, Or
In the Forest of Domremy, 1924   play?   Or
The Mantle of the Virgin, in Drama, 12, Dec., 1921, 71-99+, miracle play (1)
A Masque of the Seventeenth Century, 1927   RPB
A Pageant of the Fifteenth Century, 1924, songs by Kate V. Thompson,   RPB
   music by Adele Baldwin
A Pageant of the Women of the Sixteenth Century, 1927   RPB
The Pilgrim's Holiday, 1920 (1)   RPB
Wooing and Witches, 1925, Shakespearean medley   RPB

ANNA CANADA SWAIN (1889- ?)
Chee Moo's Choice, 1929, missionary play
The Glorious Light, 1928, pageant
Jelizabeta: Maid in America, 1929, missionary play
Rocks and Reefs and Mud Flats, 1929, drama on race prejudice
Susanna of the Parsonage, 1930
Ten Missionary Dramatizations for Boys, 1927

CORINNE ROCKWELL SWAIN
Christmas Babes in the Woods (1)   SNB
A Maeterlinkian Moving Day, in Smart Set, 37, June, 1912, 117-20 (1)

MABEL M. SWAN
Mousme´ of the Japanese Toy Shop, musical play in 3 scenes   BPP

LAURA C. SWARTZ
Christmas on Time, 1929, collection   RPB
The Holiday Clock, 1929, Christmas   RPB

JUNE SWENARTON
Bubbles, 1916, 3 act comedy   RPB

ELIZA MORGAN SWIFT
Converting Mrs. Noshuns, 1922   RPB

PHYLLIS MC NEAL SWINTON
Plays for Classroom and Auditorium, 1929   DLC

ADELAIDE BANGS SYMONS
The Beer Garden   RUM-III

NETTA SYRETT (probably British)
The Fairy Doll and Other Plays for Children, 1922, one-acts
The Old Miracle Plays of England, 1911   DLC
Robin Goodfellow and Other Fairy Plays for Children, 1918, one-acts
Six Fairy Plays for Children, 1904, one-acts   RPB
Two Domestics, 1922, for women (1)   DLC

T

GLADYS LEONA BAGG TABER (or TABOR) (1899-1980) AWW
La Gitana, 1920, 3 act operetta written for Wellesley College,   RPB
    Barnswallows; lyrics and book by Taber and others; music by Marjorie
    Perkins and others
Lady of the Moon, 1928, 3 act romantic comedy (under Tabor at RPB)   RPB
Miss Manda, in Poet Lore, 38, 1927, 412-21 (1)

GRACE ELLIS TAFT
Chimalman and Other Poems, 1916, coll. of plays and poetry on   RPB
    Aztec themes

GLADYS TALBOT
The Book of the Patriotic Pageant, 1918? Elendale, N. D.; text with
    Mrs. F. W. Leamer, Dorothy Smith and others

HANNAH LINCOLN TALBOT
At Miss Penhallow's, 1904, boarding house scenes   RPB

JENNIE (or JEANNIE) TALLADAY
Aunt Hannah's Quilting Party, 1891 play?   DLC
The Little Country Store, 1894 (1)   RPB
Stumpville Sewin' Circle, 1907, 2 act comedy   RPB
Uncle Sam's Relation, 1904, 2 act comedy   RPB

JANE DARROW TALLMAN
The Pompion Pie, 1923, 2 act Pilgrim play   RPB

MARIANA M. BISBEE TALLMAN
Choice Monologues, 1924   RPB

VIRGINIA TANNER (1881- ?)
Brooklyn Historical Pageant, 1915, text by Martin Weyrauch (Tanner was
    director.)
Greek Pageant, 1912, Baltimore, Maryland
Historical Masque of Rockport, 1914, Rockport, Mass.   MB, DLC
Masque of Endymion, 1915, Rockport, Mass.
Pageant and Masque of Technology and Power, 1916, with Ralph Cram   MB
A Pageant at Bennington, 1927, Bennington, Vermont   RPB
A Pageant for Albany's Tercentenary or The Founding of the City of   RPB
    Albany, 1924
The Pageant of the Little Town of X, 1914   MB
The Pageant of the Machias Valley, 1913, pageant of the lumber   MB, PBL
    lands, Machias, Maine
Pageant of the Odyssey, 1913, Millbury, Maine (1915, Casco Bay, Maine)
Pageant of Patriotism, 1911, with Ralph Davol, Taunton, Mass.
A Pageant of Portsmouth, 1923, Portsmouth, N. H.   RPB
A Pageant of Quincy, 1925, for tercentenary of Quincy , Mass.   MB
A Pageant of the State of Maine, 1928, Bath, Maine   RPB
Pageant of Thetford, 1911, Thetford, Vermont, with William   VTml
    and Marion Langdon, unpub. text (Tanner was dance director.)

RUTH TATROE
  Bobbie's Big Day, 1930   RPB
  Mrs. Cohen at the Amusement Park, 1929, Wetmore Declamation   RPB
    and Reading

VIVA TATTERSALL
  Ritzy, prod. 1930, with Sidney Toler

GERTRUDE ERMATINGER TAYLERT
  Three Splendid Plays for Junior High School, 1927, with   RPB
    Martina B. Rodney

EDITH TAYLOR
  Miss Gulliver Travels, 1931, with George Ford
  The Woman from Nod, by Edith F. Taylor (may not be same woman)   DPC

HELEN LOUISE TAYLOR (1908- ?)
  Angelus, 1929   OPS-V

IDA SCOTT TAYLOR (See IDA SCOTT TAYLOR MC KINNEY)

KATHARINE TAYLOR
  The Shady Hill Play Book, 1928, with Henry Copley Greene   RPB

KATHARINE HAVILAND TAYLOR (1888- ?)
  The Family Failing, 1931, "melodramatic comedy of domestic   RPB
    tyrannies and adjustments" (1)
  From the Back Seat, 1932   RPB
  His Folks, 1931   RPB
  Keeping Him Home, 1927, tragic comedy (1)
  Mix Well and Stir, 1930, comedy (1)   RPB
  A Mother's Influence, 1929, "comedy of many errors" (1)   RPB
  Rest and Quiet, 1932, "comedy of complications and jangled nerves" (1) RPB
  Simply a Matter of Love, 193?   RPB
  The Taming of the Crew, 1928, with Hadley Waters   RPB
  Who Can Cook? 1934, "comedy of frustration and fulfillment" (1) OCl, DLC

LAURETTE TAYLOR (1884-1946) NAW
  "At Marian's," 1933, typescript, 3 acts   NN
  The Dying Wife, 1925   OPS-I

LEILA TAYLOR
  Voltaire, prod. 1922, with Gertrude Purcell

MARY G. TAYLOR
  Something for Nothing, 1920, entertainment, with Hazel Bacon (1)   RPB

NELLIE ROSILLA TAYLOR
  A Builder of Dreams; or, The President, 1921, 3 act drama   RPB

SARA TEASDALE (1884-1933) AWW NAW
  On the Tower, in International, 4, Aug., 1911, 41-2 (1)

MARY E. TELFORD
  The Children's Christmas Dream, 1916 (1)   RPB

HERMINIE TEMPLETON (See HERMINIE TEMPLETON KAVANAGH)

ANICE MORRIS STOCTON TERHUNE
The Woodland Princess, 191? operetta for young people, book by Louise RPB
Saunders (Perkins); libretto by Terhune

MOLLIE DAY THACHER (See MOLLIE DAY THACHER KAZAN)

HELEN THOBURN
The Ministering of the Gift, 1913, pageant directed by Lotta Clark,   MB
illustrating work of YWCA

BETTY THOMAS
The New Minister Arrives, 1923, 2 act comedy   RPB

MRS. C. A. THOMAS
An Abused Little Stomach, 1925, good health playlet   RPB

EDITH MATILDA THOMAS (1854-1925) NAW
A New Year's Masque and Other Poems, 1885   RPB
The White Messenger and Other War Poems, 1915 (1)   RPB

GERTRUDE IDA THOMAS ("GAIL WHITE") (1889- ?)
(All works published under name "Gail White")
The Chimes Ring In, 1930, Christmas   RPB
Christmas at 400 Green Street, 1932, for 5 women   RPB
Crazy About It? 1933, for women   RPB
The Fate of Slim Lou, 1930, shadow play   RPB
The Great Vitaflake Contest, 1938, "comedy of questions and answers"(1) RPB
Katie Gets Adopted, 1930, Christmas pantomime   RPB
"Lulu, It's a Gift," 1933, for women   RPB
The Reign of Mrs. Buffet, 1932, "clever club comedy for 7 women"   RPB
Two Funny Shadow Plays and Two Behind-the-Curtain Dialogs, 1932   RPB

KATE THOMAS (See KATHARINE THOMAS JARBOE BULL)

LIDA LARRIMORE TURNER THOMAS ("LIDA LARRIMORE") (1897- ?)
Aunt Caroline's Pearls, 1935, by "Lida Larrimore"   play?   DLC
Betty Lou, "The Dream Girl," 1928, by Lida Larrimore Turner,   RPB-M
music by R. M. Stults, 3 act comic operetta
Cousin Julia's Jade Ear-ring, 1923, by Lida Larrimore Turner, comedy, (1) RPB
Forbidden Fruit, 1927, by "Lida Larrimore," comedy (1)   RPB
A Frock for Francie, 1927, by "Lida Larrimore," comedy (1)   RPB
The Grandfather Man, 1927, by "Lida Larrimore," comedy (1)   RPB
Last Tag! 1927, by "Lida Larrimore" (1)   RPB
Little Brother Sherlock, 1927, by Lida Larrimore Turner, comedy (1)   RPB
The Littlest Bridesmaid, 1924, by "Lida Larrimore," 3 act comedy   RPB
The Miniature Lady, 1924, 2 act operetta, music by R. M. Stults   NN
Miss Polly's Patchwork Quilt, 1928, by Lida Larrimore Turner,   RPB-M
2 act operetta, music by R. M. Stults
The Missionary Box, 1928, by "Lida Larrimore," comedy (1)   RPB
The Odd-Job Man, 1929, by "Lida Larrimore," 3 act comedy   RPB
Paris Labels, 1927, by "Lida Larrimore," comedy (1)   RPB
The Perfect Little Goose, 1925, by "Lida Larrimore," 3 act comedy   RPB
Second Fiddle, 1930, by "Lida Larrimore," 3 act comedy   RPB
The Third Floor Front, 1928, by "Lida Larrimore," 3 act   RPB, PP-2
romantic comedy
Toast and Tea, 1929, by "Lida Larrimore," for women (1)   RPB

LIDA LARRIMORE TURNER THOMAS (continued)
Winnie and the Wise Man, 1928, by "Lida Larrimore," 3 act comedy   RPB
Yesterday's Roses, 1927, by "Lida Larrimore," 3 act romantic   RPB, PP-1
    comedy, won first prize in first play contest of Penn Pub. Co.

MIRIAM THOMAS
The Lady of the Lake, 1916, with Margaret Dakin, dram. of poem by   RPB
    Sir Walter Scott

CAROLINE WASSON THOMASON
Beauty and the Beast, 1921, in English and French   RPB
Bluebeard, 1921, in English and French   RPB
Cinderella, 1921, in English and French   RPB
Plays for Children in French and English, 1922, one-acts   RPB
Red Riding Hood, 1920, in English and French   RPB
The Three Bears, 1921, in English and French   RPB

ALICE CALLENDER THOMPSON
All About Adam, 1911, 2 act comedy   RPB
An Auction at Meadowvale, 1908 (1)   RPB
Aunt Matilda's Birthday Party, 1908, for girls (1)   RPB
A Broken Engagement, 1908, comedy (1)
The Coming of Annabel, 1912, comedy (1)   RPB
The Day of the Duchess, 1911, farce (1)   RPB, JET
Fudge and a Burglar, 1907, farce for girls (1)   RPB
The Good Old Days, 1912, comedy (1)   RPB
Hannah Gives Notice, 1907, comedy (1)
Her Scarlet Slippers, 1908, comedy (1)   RPB
Honest Peggy, 1912, farce (1)   RPB
In the Absence of Susan, 1904, 3 act comedy   RPB
An Irish Invasion, 1911, comedy (1)   RPB
Just Like Percy, 1918, first pub. 1905, 3 act comedy   RPB
Katie's New Hat, 1911, farce (1)   RPB
A Knot of White Ribbon, 1910, comedy (1)   RPB
The Luckiest Girl, 1910, for girls (1)   RPB
Miss Deborah's Pocket Book, 1914 (1)   RPB
Miss Susan's Fortune, 1908, comedy (1)   RPB
Mollie's Way, 1912, 3 act comedy   RPB
Much Too Sudden, 1910, comedy (1)   RPB
Oysters, 1909, farce (1)   RPB
A Peck of Trouble, 1910, comedy (1)   RPB
Plays for Women Characters
The Red Parasol, 1913, comedy for girls (1)   RPB
The Return of Letty, 1909, comedy (1)   RPB
Romantic Mary, 1909, 3 act comedy   RPB
A Suffragette Baby, 1912, comedy (1)   RPB, FOV
Susan's Finish, 1909, comedy (1)   RPB
The Truth About Jane, 1909, comedy for women (1)   RPB
Truth, the Mischief, 1906, for girls (1)
The Wrong Baby, 1907, farce (1)   RPB

ALTA E. THOMPSON
Friar Tuck and the Black Knight (1)   SOP-1
George Washington; Midshipman (1)   SGW
Nausicaa and Her Maidens (1)   SOP-1
Rip Van Winkle for Marionettes   SPE

BLANCHE JENNINGS THOMPSON (1887- ?)
At the Sign of the Bumblebee, by B. J. Thompson, in Normal Instructor and
    Primary Plans, 36, April, 1927, 70-2, operetta
The Dream Maker, 1933, in Drama, 12, March, 1922, 197-9, fantasy (1)   RPB
The Silver Sandals, 1921, by Blanche Thompson, young   RPB

CHARLOTTE THOMPSON
The Awakening of Helena Ritchie, 1908, prod. 1909, dram. of story MH, DLC
    by Margaret Deland
Give and Take, 1909, with Fred De Gresac, 3 act comedy   RPB
Nell Gwyn
Rebecca of Sunnybrook Farm, 1932, prod. 1910, with Kate Douglas Wiggins
The Silver Mounted Harness
The Strength of the Weak, prod. 1906, with Alice M. Smith
A Suit of Sable, 1909, 3 act comedy   DLC

MRS. DEAL THOMPSON
The Old Maid's Plea, 1927, entertainment in one scene   RPB

ELOISE BIBB THOMPSON
Africannus, 1922
Caught, 1925, prod. by the Ethiopian Folk Players, Chicago
Cooped Up, 1924, prod. by the Lafayette Players, N. Y.

KATE VERNON THOMPSON (? -1927)
A Pageant of the Fifteenth Century, 1924, by Vida R. Sutton   RPB
    (Thompson did prologue and songs.)

LILLIAN BENNET THOMPSON (1883- ?)
In the Dark, 1922, with George Hubbard (1)   NN, OCl
"A Narrow Squeak," 1922, with George Hubbard, comedy (1)

LILIAN SPENCER THOMPSON (MRS. VANCE THOMPSON)
The Lady Shore, 1905, with Lena Smith

MARAVENE KENNEDY THOMPSON
Fun in a Theatrical Office, 1909, vaudeville entertainment   RPB
The Net, prod. 1919

SUE BYRD THOMPSON
The Younger, 1923-4, "comedy of the present day flapper" (1)

THEODOSIA JESSUP THOMPSON
Three Eastern Plays, 1927

MRS. VANCE THOMPSON (See LILIAN SPENCER THOMPSON)

EUNICE THOMSON
The Lost Collar Button, 1933, "Near- Greek tragedy"   RPB
The Opera Singer at Home, 1934   RPB
Stand or Stumble; or, Hector the Hired Man, 1926, "with apologies   RPB
    to Horatio Alger"

KATHYRNE THORNE
The Naughty Duchess, 1925, with "Julien Gordon," music by   NN
    Victor Englander, typescript

MRS. GUDRUN THORNE-THOMSEN
A Tramp and A Night's Lodging, 1917, pub. by Chicago School of Civics and
     Philanthropy

CLARE THORNTON
The Marriage of Dotty, also in C. Arthur Pearson, ed. Plays for   JMP
     Amateur Actors, 1921 (1)

ANNIE LONGFELLOW THORP
The Lighting of the Christmas Tree, 1921, adapt. with   RPB
     Josephine L. Palmer from "The Christmas Guest" by Selma Lagerlof (1)

JOSEPHINE THORP
At the Milestone (1)   SPG
Bonds of Liberty
The Enchanted Book Shelf (1)   SSM
A Memorial Day Pageant, n.d., typed copy   MiD, PP
Patriotic Pageants of Today, 1918, with Rosamond Kimball, one-acts   RPB
The Road to Tomorrow, 1920, pageant, typed copy   NN, MB
The Torch and Other Patriotic Pageants of Today, 1918
The Treasure Chest, 1922, children's fairy play (1)   RPB, SSH-II
When Fairies Come (1)   SSL

ALTHEA COOMS THURSTON
And the Devil Laughs (1)   LUU
The Exchange, fantasy (1)   SBO, LCO, LUU
A Pageant of Spring, 1920, in Drama, 12, April, 1922, 251-2
The Trail Blazers, pageant
When a Man's Hungry (1)

ESTHER TIELKEMEIER
Polly's Troubles, 1930   RPB

EUNICE HAMMOND TIETJENS (1884-1944) AWW NAW
Arabesque, prod. 1925, with Cloyd Head, music by Ruth White Warfield

ESTHER BROWN TIFFANY (1858- ?)
The Angel at the Sepulchre, 1889   RPB
Anita's Trial; or, Our Girls in Camp, 1889, 3 act comedy for females   RPB
Apollo's Oracle, 1897, musical (1)   RPB-M
An Autograph Letter, 1889, 3 act comedy
Bachelor Maids, 1897, comedy (1)   RPB
A Blind Attachment, 1895, comedy (1)   RPB
A Borrowed Umbrella, 1893, comedietta (1)   RPB
A Hole in the Fence, 1909, 2 act farce   RPB
A Model Lover, 1893, 2 act comedy   RPB
A Rice Pudding, 1888, 2 act comedy   RPB
The Saffron Trunk, 3 act comedy
The Spirit of the Pine, 1890   RPB
A Tell-Tale Eyebrow, 1897, 2 act comedy   RPB
That Patrick! 1886, comedy (1)   RPB
The Tocsin, 1909, drama of the Renaissance   RPB
The Way to His Pocket, 1889, comedy (1)   RPB
Young Mr. Pritchard, 1886, comedy in 2 scenes   RPB

ALICE L. TILDESLEY
The Cast Rehearses, 1921 (1)
Marrying Money, 1920, comedy (1)   RPB

DOROTHY STOCKBRIDGE TILLETT (See DOROTHY STOCKBRIDGE)

KATHERINE DAVIS TILLMAN
Aunt Betsy's Thanksgiving, 1919 (1)   RPB
Fifty Years of Freedom; or, From Cabin to Congress, 1910, 5 act drama   RPB
The Spirit of Allen, 1922, pageant of African Methodism   OWibfU
Thirty Years of Freedom, 190? 4 act drama   RPB

EDITH SANFORD TILLOTSON
Bethlehem Bells, 1932, Christmas pageant for the church school,   RPB-M
    music by George F. Rosche
The Builders, 1915, service for Children's Day, music by   RPB-M
    I. H. Meredith
Children of America, 1918, patriotic service for Children's Day,   RPB-M
    music by "Fred B. Holton" (Ira B. Wilson)
The Choir of Bethlehem, 1945, Christmas carol cantata, music by "Noel
    Benson" (Ira B. Wilson)
The Chorus in the Skies, 1943, carol choir cantata, music by "Fred B. Holton"
    (Ira B. Wilson)
Christmas Eve in Hillside Village, 1943, cantata-drama, music by "Charles
    Francis Lane" (Ira B. Wilson)
Christmas in the Heart, 1919, Sunday school service, music by   RPB-M
    Isaac H. Meredith
Christmas Memories, 1914, Christmas series, music by Ira B. Wilson   NBuG
Christmas Praises, 1909, with Charles H. Gabriel, Alice J. Cleater,   RPB-M
    and Lizzie De Armond, Christmas service
The Church Fair, 1916, musical comedy, music by Ira B. Wilson   RPB-M
Cinderella's Christmas Party, 1919, juvenile cantata for Christmas,   RPB-M
    music by I. H. Meredith
The Coming of the Conqueror, 1918, patriotic Christmas cantata for   RPB-M
    Sunday school and choir, music by "Fred B. Holton" (Ira B. wilson)
The Courtesy of Miles Standish, 1929, cantata, music by Ira B. Wilson   IU
Crown After Cross, 1945, Easter choir cantata, music by "Fred B. Holton"
    (Ira B. wilson)
Down the Chimney with Santa Claus, 1914, for Sunday schools, day   RPB-M
    schools, etc., music by Ira B. wilson
Easter, 1910, cantata, music by Ira B. Wilson   NN
The Easter Awakening, 1915, music by "Fred B. Holton"   RPB-M
    (Ira B. Wilson)
The Easter King, 1918, sacred 2-part cantata for Easter, music by   RPB-M
    I. H. Meredith
The Easter Sunrise Song, 1944, Easter cantata, music by "Fred B. Holton"
    (Ira B. Wilson)
An Echo from Bethlehem, 1934, Christmas musical play, music   RPB-M
    by George S. Schuler
The Festival of Happy Days, 1913, juvenile cantata for Sunday   RPB-M
    schools, day schools or church entertainments, music by John D. Creswell
The First Christmas, 1911, cantata, music by Ira B. Wilson   RPB-M
Flags and Wreaths, 1918, patrtiotic Christmas service   RPB-M
Following Yonder Star, 1945, Christmas cantata-pageant, music by
    Roy E. Nolte
The Frost King's Daughter, 1938, cantata, music arranged from
    Edward Grieg by Ira B. Wilson
George Washington, the Father of Our Country, 1931, cantata,.   NN, IU
    music by Ira B Wilson
The Gift Day, 1915, giving service for Christmas, music by   RPB-M
    "Fred B. Holton" (Ira B. Wilson)

EDITH SANFORD TILLOTSON (continued)

The Gift Supreme, 1912, "service telling the story and exemplifying   RPB-M
  the true spirit of Christmas"

Gifts, 1921, "connective service for Christmas," music by   NBuG
  I. H. Meredith

The Good Shepherd, 1915, cantata for church choirs, choral   RPB-M
  societies, etc., music by Ira B. Wilson

The Gospel of Easter, 1915, Easter cantata for church choirs,   RPB-M
  choral societies, etc., music by J. S. Fearis

Growing Like Him, 1919, service for Children's Day   RPB-M

Hail Messiah! 1930, Christmas cantata, music by Ira B. Wilson   RPB-M

He Rose Again, 1932, Easter cantata, music by Henry W. Petrie   RPB-M

Heroes of America, 1944, cantata, music by Ira B. Wilson

The Holy Nativity, 1924, Christmas cantata, music   NBuG
  by Henry Wildermere

A Joke on Santa Claus, 1919, humorous Santa Claus cantata,   Or
  music by Ira B. Wilson

June Praise, 1919, Children's Day service based on favorite   RPB-M
  classics, with others

June-tide Blessings, 1914, service for Children's Day, music by   RPB-M
  I. H. Meredith

June-time Blossoms, 1910, Children's Day service   RPB-M

King Christmas and His Court, 1931, Christmas pageant featuring   RPB
  well-known Christmas carols

The Legend of Sleepy Hollow, 1927, cantata, adapt. of Washington   RPB-M
  Irving, music by Ira Wilson

Life, 1915, music by I. H. Meredith   RPB-M

The Lord of the Eastertide, 1916, cantata, music by J. D. Creswell   RPB-M

More than Conquerors, 1918, music by I. H. Meredith   RPB-M

Mother Mine, 1932, Mother's Day service   RPB-M

Others, 1919, service for Children's Day, music by I. H. Meredith   RPB-M

Over the Rainbow, 1915, operetta for young singers, music   RPB-M
  by F. W. Peace

Over the Top, 1918, complete service, music by I. H. Meredith   RPB-M

Paul Bunyan and His Lumberjacks, 1941, cantata, music by
  Ellen Jane Lorenz

The Rag Sociable, 1911, old-fashioned entertainment, music by   RPB-M
  various composers

The Reign of Peace, 1910, Christmas service for the Sunday school,   RPB-M
  music by I. H. Meredith

Robinson Crusoe, 1930, children's cantata, music by Ira B. Wilson   IU, OCl

Santa at Station J.O.Y., 1927, Christmas cantata, music by   RPB-M
  Arthur Radcliffe

Santa Claus & Co., 1912, for Sunday schools, day schools, etc.,   RPB-M
  music by Ira B. Wilson

Santa Claus and the Fairy Godmother, 1915, music by Ira B. Wilson   RPB-M

Santa's Joy Factory, 1912, Christmas cantata, music by I. H. Meredith   RPB-M

Star of the Christ Child, 1938, Christmas choir cantata, music by
  Edward W. Norman

Star of the East, 1916, music by I. H. Meredith   RPB-M

The Star of Hope, 1923, Christmas cantata, music by   RPB-M
  John Sylvester Fearis

The Story of His Birth, 1947, Christmas pageant, music by I. H. Meredith   Or

The Sweetest Story Ever Told, 1907, with Charles Gabriel and   RPB-M
  Alice Jean Cleator, Christmas service

That Song of Old, 1939, Christmas cantata, music by Ira B. Wilson   DLC
  (in Priority 4 Collection at DLC)

Tidings of Joy, 1914, cantata, music by C. Harold Lowden   RPB-M

EDITH SANFORD TILLOTSON   (continued)
The Treasure Hunters, 1916, comic operetta, book by William   RPB-M
    Danforth; lyrics by Tillotson and Danforth; music by J. S. Fearis
Under Christmas Skies, 1916, Christmas exercise, music by   RPB-M
    10 authors of note
A Virginian Romance, 1905, 2 act musical comedy, book and   RPB-M
    music by H. Loren Clements; lyrics by Tillotson
A Visit from Santa, 1916, cantata, music by Ira B. Wilson   RPB-M
Washington, Chief of Our Nation, 1907, music by I. H. Meredith   MB

ALICE TIMONEY
Bottled, prod. 1928, with Anne Collins, prompt book   NN
Wilderness Road, 1930, with Anne Collins, 3 act comedy-drama   RPB

MARIAN D. TINNEY
The Chasm, 1908, with Roy S. Tinney (to be produced under the   RPB
    pen name of Janet and Hector Donald)

GLENNA SMITH TINNIN
One Night in Bethlehem, 1925, with Katharine S. Brown   RPB

BERTHA SMITH TITUS
Junior Holidays, 1921, children's pageant   RPB

BERTHA IRENE TOBIN
Dollies and Girls, Christmas dialogue for 2 girls   JEP
Recitations, Drills and Plays for Children, 1921, one-acts   RPB
Wanted—a Santa Claus, 1929 (1)   RPB

HELEN L. TODD
For His Name's Sake   DPC

MARY VAN LENNUP IVES TODD   (1849- ?)
"A Dose of Hell," 1915, comedy, "with preface and the case for equality" RPB
A Premature Socialist, 1906, "Ouida's wittiest story built into a comedy" RPB
    (based on An Altruist)
Purgatory

ALTA M. TOEPP
Children's Plays for Special Days, 1935   RPB
The Cost of Smiles, 1930   RPB
The Gib-Goblins, 1928, Halloween, young   RPB
Grandma Perkins' Party, 1930, 3 acts, young   RPB
In Memory, 1928, children's pageant for Memorial Day   RPB
Jean's Seventy-five Cents, 1928, short 3-act Christmas play for girls   RPB
Mother Forest at Witching Hollow, 1930, young (1)   RPB
Peppy Stunts and Games, 1938, with others
Ten Christmas Plays for the Grades, 1932, with Mary T. Johnson and   RPB
    Florence F. Smith

MARGARET OTEY TOMES
The Children and the Evangelists, in Drama, 11, Nov., 1920, 58-60 (1)

JULIET WILBOR TOMPKINS   (1871- ?)
For Charley, 1936 (1)   RPB
Happy Medium, 1906, 3 act musical comedy, music by Gilbert Tompkins RPB
The Millionaire, 1930, with Nathan Edward Reid, 3 act comedy   RPB, GHP

JULIET WILBOR TOMPKINS (continued)
   Once There Was a Princess, 1927, 3 act romantic comedy   RPB
   Tired, 1924, comedy, in Little Theater Tournament (1)   RPB
   The Trap, 1937 (1)

GERTRUDE FULTON TOOKER
   Everychild, 1914, 3 acts   RPB

MARY ANN TOPPING
   Blazer's Scraps; or, What the Town Crier Cried, 1901, drama adapted   RPB
      from the story

ALICE COYLE TORBERT
   Vergil, 1929, festival play   RPB

HELEN H. TORRENCE
   You Can't Joke with a Woman, 1928, ed. by Alice Gerstenberg   RPB

MRS. RUSSELL B. TOWER
   The Light of the World, Christmas pageant   JPP-1

DOROTHY TOWLE
   The Tempestuous Tale, 1916, presented by the class of 1916, Mt. Holyoke RPB
      College; plot suggested by Towle; play written by Helen Paschall;
      words and music by Ruth Elms and others

ADDIE L. TOWNE
   The Key to a Happy Home, 1924, thrift pageant play   RPB

ANNE TOWNSEND
   Bruin's Inn, 1925   RPB, SSL
   The Cracker Conspiracy, 1926, 4th of July fantasy   RPB
      (Both pub. by Ed. Div. of the National Safety Council)

BLANCH TOWNSEND
   Beyond the Alps Lies Italy, 1931, comedy (1)   RPB
   Borrowed Time, 1930, comedy (1)   RPB

MARGARET TOWNSEND
   The Passing of the Idle Rich, prod. 1913

WILLA A. TOWNSEND
   Because He Lives, 1924
   Christmas Helps, 1929, collection arranged by Townsend   MB
   A Song in the Nighttime, n.d., Christmas pageant program for   DHU
      Sunday schools

JANE TOY (COOLIDGE)
   Agatha, 1922-3, romance of plantation days, pub. in The Southern Ruralist,
      Atlanta, April 15, 1924 (1)
   Reward Offered, 1921-2, comedy of mountain characters (1)   KCC

KATE (KATRINA) NICHOLS TRASK (1853-1922) AWW NAW
   After the Battle, 1913, (Act II, Scene 2 from In the Vanguard) IU, OU
   In the Vanguard, 1914 (1922 ed. at RPB)   RPB
   King Alfred's Jewels, 1908, drama   RPB
   The Little Town of Bethlehem, 1929   RPB

KATE (KATRINA) NICHOLS TRASK (continued)

Mors Et Victoria, 1903, drama   RPB

Without the Walls, 1919, reading play   RPB

LOUISE TRAVOUS

Around the Clock to Music, 1930, stunt for readers and performers   RPB

MAY L. TREADWELL

Marse Gawge de Lubines' Man, in Florence Signor, Plays for

   School Days, 1921

Mary Grace Stirs the Apple Butter, 1923, comedy (1)   RPB

The Use in Useless, in Florence Signor, Plays for School Days, 1921

SOPHIE TREADWELL (1891?-1970) AWW NWAT—(1885?-1970)

Actress, incomplete   AzU

Andrew Well's Lady, 1931, later titled Judgment in the Morning   AzU

The Answer, 1918?   AzU

Claws, 1918   AzU

Constance Darrow, 1908?   AzU

For Saxaphone, 1934   AzU

Garry, 1954   AzU

The Gorgeous Innocent, TV drama   AzU

Gringo, prod. 1922   AzU

Guess Again (1)   AzU

Highway, 1942, prod. on TV in 1954   AzU

His Luck (1)   AzU

Hope for a Harvest, 1938 (1941 ed. at RPB)   RPB

Intimations for Saxophone, 193? typescript   NN

The Island, 1930   AzU

John Doane (1)   AzU

Judgment in the Morning, 1952 (See Andrew Well's Lady)   AzU

La Cachucha (1)   AzU

Ladies Leave, prod. 1929, satire   AzU

The Last Are First, 192? (first version of Promised Land) typescript   NN

   (1933 version at AzU)

The Last Border, 1947   AzU

Laughter , 1922? play about Chaplin's youth   AzU

Le Grand Prix, 1905, her first full length play   AzU

The Life Machine, prod. 1931

Lone Valley, 1928, prod. 1933 (had many earlier titles)   AzU

Loney Lee (Lue), 1923 (later version of Philomel)   AzU

Love Lady, 1924 (later version of Old Rose)   AzU

Loving Lost

Lusita, 1931   MB, DLC

Machinal, 1928   GTP, BAW

Madame Bluff, 1918   AzU

A Man's Own (1)   AzU

Many Mansions, 1925   AzU

Million Dollar Gate, 1930   AzU

Mrs. Wayne (later titled The Eye of the Beholder) (1)   AzU

Natalie, Inc. (also titled Women Are Terrible) TV drama   AzU

Nepenthe (about Poe) 4 acts   AzU

Now He Doesn't Want to Play, prod. 1967 at Un. of Arizona Theatre,

   comedy

Oh, Nightingale, 1922, prod. 1925 (later version of Loney Lee)   AzU

Old Rose, 1921 (later version of Claws)   AzU

Philomel   AzU

SOPHIE TREADWELL (continued)
Poe, a Play, n.d., typescript   NN
Promised Land, 1933   AzU
The Right Man, 1908   AzU
Rights, 1921 (later titled The King Passes, Mary Beaton—1938; and   AzU
   Love and Principle—1941)
The Settlement, 1911 (also titled Limelight)   AzU
The Siren, 1953   AzU
A String of Pearls, 1943-4? mystery   AzU
Sympathy (1) (her first produced play)   AzU
Three, 1936   AzU
To Him Who Waits (1)   AzU
Trance, 1918 (1)   AzU
Woman with Lilies, 1948 (had several early titles)   AzU
You Can't Have Everything, 1925   AzU

JESSIE TRIMBLE ("JANE STONE") (1873- ?)
The End of the Battle, 1913, by "Jane Stone" (1) (suffrage)   RPB
The New Man, 1913, by "Jane Stone" play?   DLC
The New Mrs. Loring, 193?, 3 acts   NN
The Wedding Day, 1909

MARTHA TRITCH
Isotta's Trump, (1)   SCT

AMELIE RIVES CHANLER TROUBETZKOY (PRINCESS TROUBETZKOY)
   (1863-1945)   AWW NAW
Allegiance, prod. 1918, with Prince Troubetzkoy
Athewold, 1893, by Amelie Rives, in Harper's, Feb., 1892, 394-424, 5 acts
Augustine the Man, 1906, dramatic poem   RPB
Blackmail, another title for The Fear Market
The Fear Market, 1920, prod. 1916, adapt. by Clara Beranger of a   CLSU
   play by Amelie Rives
Herod and Marianne, 1888, tragedy, Lippincott's Magazine,   RPB
   Sept., 1888, 305-89; also in George Alexander Kohut, ed., A Hebrew
   Anthology, Vol. 2, 1913
Love-in-a-Mist, 1927, prod. 1926, 3 act comedy drama with   RPB
   "Gilbert Emery"
November Eve, 1923
Out of the Midst of Hatred, in Virginia Quarterly Review, 2, April, 1926,
   226-37 (1)
The Prince and the Pauper, prod. 1920, dram. of Twain
Say When, prod.1928
The Sea-Woman's Cloak and November Eve, 1923, 2 plays   RPB
The Young Elizabeth, 1938

ETHEL WENDELL TROUT
Fair Exchange, 1926   RPB
If Wishes Came True, 1927, morality play for children of   RPB
   intermediate grades
Old Santa Claus Remembers, 1928, young   RPB, JEC
The Stronger Force (1)   CPR-1

MARJORIE TROWBRIDGE
A Christmas Play, in St. Nicholas, 51, Dec., 1923, 194-200

EMMA JANE VAUGHAN TRUE
    Listen Ladies! 1922, 2 act comedy for women   RPB
    The Mystery Man, 1931, comedy (1)   RPB

MARY E. TRUE
    In Moonbeams, 1915, young (1)   RPB

ANNIE ELIOT TRUMBULL (ANNIE ELIOT) (1857- ?)
    As Strangers, in Scribner's Magazine, August, 1896 (1)
    A Christmas Party, n.d.   RPB
    A Confidence Game
    From Four to Six, 1893, in her Stories of New York, 1893, by Annie Eliot   RPB
    The Green-room Rivals, 1894, comedietta by Annie Eliot   RPB
    Haman, 1907, tragedy   RPB
    Love or War, 1928, farce   RPB
    A Masque of Culture, 1893, by Annie Eliot, dedicated to   RPB
        Saturday Morning Club, Hartford
    Matchmakers, 1884, comedy by "A. E."   RPB
    Mind Cure; or, When Doctors Agree, 1896   RPB
    Problems of a Philanthropist, 1900   RPB
    St. Valentine's Day, 1892, comedy for females, by Annie Eliot (1)   RPB
    A Virginia Reel, 1888, comedietta in 2 parts   RPB
    The Wheel of Progress, 1898   RPB

JANE T. TRUMBULL
    The Early Bird Catches the Worm, 1928   RPB

ALTHEA SPRAGUE TUCKER
    The Happy Hoboes, 1928, with Harriet French Ford, comedy (1)   RPB
    Wanted—Money, 1928, with Harriet French Ford, comedy (1)   RPB

BERNICE GALLUP TUCKER
    Historic Pageant of Long Island, 1927, music by Corinne Locke Barcus   RPB

LOUISE EMERY TUCKER (1876- ?)
    Historical Plays of Colonial Days for Fifth Year Pupils, 1912, with   RPB
        Estelle L. Ryan

RUTH WILKINSON TUCKER
    The Fanatic, 1930, drama (1)   RPB
    It Must Be Love, 1930, comedy (1)   RPB

LA VERNE TUERS
    The Care of the Teeth, 1926, hygiene sketch   RPB
    Halloween in the Garden, 1924, "a tiny play"   RPB
    To-To's Alphabet, 1926, health sketch (1)   RPB

JEWEL BOTHWELL TULL
    The Bridge, 193? (Also in English Club of Cornell College,   NN, NcD
        Cornell College Chapbooks, No. 9)
    Children of the Inn, 1933, Christmas play
    Dead Men Can't Hurt You, 1933 (1)
    The Forgotten Man, 1934 (1)
    The Gorilla, 1923, 3 act melodrama, typescript   NN
    Grandpa Sits by the Fire, 1935, comedy (1)   DLC
    The Hyacinthe Garden, 1932, Easter fantasy   RPB
    The Slacker, 1917 (1)   RPB

"MAY TULLY" (MAY GERTRUDE TULLY)
Mary's Ankle, 1932, prod. 1917, farce   RPB

ELLA J. TUNNELL
Bobby and Betty Grumble, 1930, 2 act Christmas play for children   RPB
Flambo, the Clown, 1930, jr. h. s. or h. s. (1)   RPB
A Halloween Promise, 1931, young (1)   RPB
Santa's Revenge, 1932 (1)   RPB
Two Short Valentine Plays, 1931, with Helen Tuttle   RPB

JANE TUPMAN ("VILLA LEWIS")
A True Heroine, 1905, 4 act musical comedy drama, written by   RPB
    Tupman, dram. by Mrs. Daisy D. Nichols ("Dora Deane")

EDITH SESSIONS TUPPER
The Road to Arcady, prod. 1912
Thou Shalt Not Steal, in Smart Set, 27, Feb., 1909, 134-40 (1)

MARGARET TURNBULL
Classmates, prod. 1907, with William C. Douglas (or DeMille?)
The Deadlock, prod. 1914

ANNABEL TURNER
Any Evening, 1930, comedy (1)   RPB

ANNABELLE TURNER
'Liza on Suffrage, 1920, monologue   RPB

GENEVIEVE TURNER
Corn Silk; a Mandan Legend, 1914, adapted for school use by   RPB
    Turner and others

LIDA LARRIMORE TURNER (See LIDA LARRIMORE TURNER THOMAS)

HELEN TUTTLE
Two Short Valentine Plays, 1931, with Ella Tunnell   RPB

MRS. BARRYMORE TWEED (BLANCHE MARIE LOUISE OELRICHS
BARRYMORE)
        ("MICHAEL STRANGE") (1890-1950) NAW
Clair De Lune, 1921, dram. of Hugo's The Man Who Laughed   RPB
The Living Corpse, 1918, adaptation of Tolstoy
Lord and Lady Byron

KATHARINE W. TWEED
La Belle Chasseuse; or, Hearts and Hounds, 1908, musical comedy;   MH
    book by Tweed and Grace Henry; music and lyrics by
    Grace Hollingsworth

U

MARGARET ULLMANN (1882- ?)
Pocahontas, 1912, pageant   RPB

GLADYS BUCHANAN UNGER (1885 -1940) (listed as both British and
     American)
Adopted, 193? scenario for motion picture, story by Unger, typed copy   NN
African Vineyard, with Walter Armitage, prod. 1936 for Federal Theatre,   NN
     prompt book.
"All That Glitters," 193? scenario with Marjorie Leonard, typed copy   NN
"Baby Bonds," 193? scenario with Jesse Lasky Jr., typed copy   NN
Beau Brummel, prod. 1933, 2 act operetta; libretto by Unger; lyrics by   NN
     Edward Elliescu; music by H. Tierney; based on Clyde Fitch's play,
     typescript without music
Betty, prod. 1916, with Frederick Lonsdale, lyrics by Adrian Ross and
     Paul A. Rubens; music by Paul A. Rubens
"The Blonde Senorita," 1931, scenario with Marcella Burke, typed copy   NN
The Business Widow, prod. 1923? 3 act comedy, based on German of   NN
     Engel and Sassman, typescript
California Cousins, ms.   NN
Charles Dickens' Great Expectations, 1935, typed scenario   NN
The Chenerys, adaptation by Unger of Les Fresnay by F. Vandereni
Coming Out Party, 1933, with Jesse Lasky Jr., motion picture   CLSU
     scenario, from original by Unger and Becky Gardiner, mimeo. copy
Cross Your Heart, 1939? with Marcella Burke, 3 act modern comedy,   NN
     typescript
"Dear Little Girl," 1926, scenario, typed copy   NN
The Demi-Reps, 1938, with Stuart Walker, based on Harriette   NN
     Wilson's memoirs, 3 acts, typescript
The Divine Woman, 1928, based on motion picture story by Unger   MH
Double Exposure, 1928? 3 act comedy, typescript   NN
Edmund Kean, 1903
Experience Unnecessary, prod. 1931
The Fair Circassian, prod. 1921
The Goldfish, prod. 1922, "comedy of many manners in 3 acts,"
     adaptation of French play,
  L'Ecoledes Cocottes by Armont and Gerbiden, typescript   NN
Henry of Lancaster
High C, ms.   NN
In an Arab Garden, 1902
Inconstant George, 1909, adaptation of French of R. de Flers and
     A. de Caillavet
Ladies of Creation, 1932, prod. 1931, "modern comedy in 3 acts,"
     (c. 1922 as Private Life, rev. in 1928)
"Legal Murder," 193? with Cyrus Roberts, typed scenario   NN
Lemonade Boy, 1906, prod. 1907
"Little Dorritt," 19?? adaptation of Dickens, typed scenario   NN
London Pride, prod. 1916, with A. Neil Lyons
The Love Habit, prod. 1923, adaptation of farce by L. Verneuil
Love Watches, prod. 1908, adaptation of French play, L'Amourveille
     (summary and excerpt in Theatre Magazine, November, 1908)

GLADYS BUCHANAN UNGER (continued)

The Lovely Lady, prod. 1927, book with Cyrus Wood; lyrics by
  Cyrus Wood; music by Dave Stamper and H. Levey; based on French
  play, Dejeuner de Soleil

The Madcap, prod. 1928, adaptation with Gertrude Purcell from
  French of R. Gignoux and J. Thery; music by Maurice Rubens;
  lyrics by Clifford Grey

"The Madonna of the Underworld," 193? scenario with   NN
  "Leyla George" (pseud.) typed copy

The Marionettes, prod. 1911, adaptation of play by P. Wolf

The Marriage Market, prod. 1913, adaptation of play by M. Brody and
  F. Martos (Unger wrote the book for the musical.)

The Merry Countess, prod. 1912, adaptation of J. Strauss' Die Fledermaus

The Monkey Talks, prod. 1925, adaptation from play by Rene Fauchois

Mystery of Edwin Drood, 1935, scenario with John L. Balderston,   NN
  adapt. of Dickens

A Night in Athens, 193? musical comedy based on French play by Andre NN
  de Badet; music by Harry Tierney; lyrics by Raymond Egan, typescript

Nightbirds, variant title of The Merry Countess (Unger wrote book
for the musical.)

Nona, prod. 1932

An Original Radio Story, 193? typed copy (suggested titles: NN
  "House-pets," "Kind-hearted Kitty," "Polly's Protegees")

Our Mr. Hepplewhite, 1919, 3 act comedy

"Pharaoh's Flapper," 193? typed scenario   NN

The Refugee, 1922? typescript   NN

Richard Brinsley Sheridan, 190? prod. 1904, typecript   NN

"A Rose Tree in the Sudan," 193? scenario with Jessy Lasky Jr.,   NN
  typed copy

Sea Serpent, 1933, typed scenario   NN

The Secret Song, 1933, "screen story of modern Russia," typed scenario   NN

The Serf-Actress, 193? typed scenario   NN

The Son and Heir; or, The English, 1913, "original modern   NN, DLC
  comedy in 4 acts"

Starlight, prod. 1925, comedy, based on Abel Hermant's Dialogues,   NN
  typed copy

Stolen Fruit, prod. 1925, adaptation

Striking, prod. 1915, with P. Rubens

The Sultan Complex, 1930, with Walter Armitage, 3 acts, typed copy   NN

Sunshine of the World, prod. 1920, operetta with K. K. Ardaschir and
  C. Cuvillier

A Synopsis of "Babes in New York," 193? with Jesse Lasky Jr.,   NN
  typed scenario

Top Hole, prod. 1924, book by Eugene Conrad and George Dill; revised
  by Unger; music by Jay Gorney; lyrics by Owen Murphy

Toto, 1916, libretto by Unger, music by Archibald Joyce and M. Morgan;
  lyrics by A. Anderson (piano score pub. 1916)

$25 an Hour, prod. 1933, with Leyla Georgie, comedy, typed copy   DLC

Two Girls Wanted, 1926, 3 acts

The Virgin of Bethulia, prod. 1925, adaptation of Henri Bernstein's Judith

The Werewolf, prod. 1924, translation of play by Rudolph Lother
  (NN has 36 items in 2 volumes of unpublished and unproduced moving
  picture scenarios, radio and stage plays by Unger, 1925-193?)

EVA UNSELL

Stigmata, with Beulah Dix and Evelyn G. Sutherland, 4 act tragedy   OrU

GEORGIA LYONS UNVERZAGT
More Christian Endeavor Playlets, 1929, Ed. by E. W. Thornton,   RPB
a contributor
The Vision of Sir Launfall, 1928, pageant based on poem by   RPB
James Russell Lowell, with Dorothy Clark

BLANCHE UPRIGHT
The Valley of Content, 1922, prod. 1925

MINNIE LEONA UPTON
The Juvenile Recitation Book, 1928, with others   RPB

CAROLINE FOULKE URIE
A Fable in Flowers, 1918? operetta, music by Eleanor Smith and   RPB
Gertrude Modern Madeira Smith

ELIZABETH URQUHART
Suited at Last; or, Sauce Bordelaise, 1920, comedy (1)   RPB

IRENE URQUHART
Grotesquerie, mystic drama (1)   HUW-3

EDITH GWYNNE UTTERBACK
A Little Learning Now and Then, 1924, "contrast of the modern   RPB
educational methods with the 'larnin' of fifty years ago,"
"appreciation of the modern teacher and her problems"
They Who Vote Shall Read   CPE

V

MARY DE PEYSTER RUTGERS MC CREA CONGER VANAMEE
(MARY CONGER VANAMEE)
The Pageant of Woman's Opportunity, 1922, Vassar College

DOROTHY HENRY VAN AUKEN
Boastful Benny, 1927, with Arthur Henry, for 4th and 5th grades (1)   RPB
The Eagle's Feather, 1927, with Arthur Henry   RPB
Mother's Day, 1927, with Arthur Henry, 3 acts   RPB

RUTH VAN BLARCOM
The Utopians, 1913, all college operetta, Wellesley, with Marie Collins RPB-M

HELEN G. VAN CAMPEN
Life on Broadway, "Musical Comedy Rehearsal," McClure's, 41, May,
   1913, 68-74 (1)

DAISY MELVILLE VANCE
On the Road of Yesteryear, 1927, with Richard Melville (1)   RPB
Short Plays from Dickens, 1935   RPB

ELLEN VAN COLKENBURG
The Deluded Dragon, with Harriet Edgerton, puppet play

ALICE D. VANDERLAAN
The Magic Flute, 1920, for Camp Fire girls   RPB

ETHEL BEEKMAN VAN DER VEER
As the Tumbrils Pass, with Franklyn Bigelow (1)   OPS-VII
Babouscka, 1929, fantasy (1) (typed ms. at NcU)   OPS-V
The Beauty Shoppe, 1933, with Franklyn Bigelow, 3 act comedy   RPB
The Boy on the Meadow, 1928, Christmas (1)   RPB, SSH-I
The Emperor's Doll, with Franklyn Bigelow, comedy based on a   OPS-VIII
   Japanese legend (1)
The Feast of Barking Women, first prize in Drama League   OPS-IX
   contest of 1927 (1) (typed ms. at NcU)
Fernseed in the Shoe, 1929, comedy (1)   RPB
Gabriel and the Hour Book, 1934, with Franklyn Bigelow, from story   RPB
   by Evaleen Stein, 3 acts
The Lay Figure, 1936 (1) (typed ms. at NcU)   OAT-II
Let It Burn, with Franklyn Bigelow, comedy (1)   NPW
Path of Roses   SSL
The Perfect Pattern
The Romance of the Willow Pattern, 1926, "short comic-tragedy   ETP
   in the Chinese manner" (1)
St. Cyprian and the Devil, 1928, "fantasque," "founded upon   OPS-VI
   fragments of a poem by Athenais-Eudocia, Empress of
   Byzantium written about A.D. 422" (1)
Shipping Mother East, 1928, satirical comedy (1)   RPB, SSH-IV
The Six Gods, 1935, with Franklyn Bigelow, "comedy founded on a   NPM
   Japanese No dance" (1)
Sunday Supplement; or, Romance in Rotogravure, 1932, comedy (1)   RPB
When the Horns Blow, 1928, comedy (1)   RPB, SSH-II

LETTIE COOK VAN DERVEER (or VANDERVEER)
Anyday Entertainments, 1922, collection   RPB
Assembly Book for Intermediate Grades, 1934, with Marie Irish,   RPB
  Dorothy Roberts and others
A Basket of White Carnations   JEM-2
The Borrowed Suitcase, 1930, 2 act college comedy   RPB
Christmas Doings, 1920, collection   RPB
Christmas Giving, exercise for five small children   JEP
The Christmastime Book, 1931, collection   RPB
A Day at Happy Hollow School, 1910   RPB
Dossy's Pink Christmas, 1934   RPB
Father and Son Banquet   CTM
Fun Enough to Go Around, 1924, campfire play, 3 act comedy   RPB
Green Paint and Ironing Boards, 1932, comedy of country life   RPB
Halloween Happenings, 1921   RPB
He Loved Kipling, 1927, comedy with radio possibilities (1)   RPB
Joyous Programs for Springtime Celebrations, 1934, with others   RPB
The Ladies' League Trims the Tree, 1930, for females   RPB
A Lincoln Sort of Fellow   JEL
Look What You've Done! 1926, for females, 3 acts   RPB
Miss Hitty's Valentine, 1925   RPB
Mother and Daughter Banquet   CTM
My Lady Sleeps, 1931, 3 act comedy   RPB
Now Don't Laugh, 1932, comedy (1)   RPB
Plays for the Classroom, 1923   RPB
The Raggy-Tag Man, 1927, 3 act play for juveniles   RPB
Seeing Nellie Home, 1930, comedy (1)   RPB
Short Plays for Just Us Fellows, 1929, "nine peppy plays for boys"   RPB
"A Snow-bound Christmas," 1936 play?   DLC
The Spirit of '76   JPG
Thanksgiving Plays and Ways, 1927   RPB
Those Extra Days, 1935, assembly book for upper grammar grades,   Or
  with others

LILLIE H. VANDERVEER (ALBRECHT)
Doctor Foster's Patients. 1927. Mother Goose play   RPB
Etta Ket and the Goops, 1928   RPB
The Thrift Fairy's Bank, 1929, young   RPB

J. LILLIAN VANDEVERE
Far-Away Friends, 1937, operetta   MsSM
The Flower of Venezia, 1934, 2 act operetta, libretto by   RPB
  Ronald Dundas; music by Edgar Hansen (director's guide at RPB)
The French Dolls Drill, 1914, for girls   RPB
A Holiday Hook-up, 1939, "Christmas children's play consisting   DLC
  principally of songs accompanied by rhythm instruments and piano"
The Mender Man, 1930, children's play (1)   RPB
Peggy and the Pirate, 1928, 2 act operetta, libretto by   RPB
  Geoffrey F. Morgan; music by Geoffrey O'Hara (stage director's
  guide by Vandevere and Morgan)
The Princess Has a Birthday, 1932, operetta   MsSM
The Purple Pigeon, 1932, two act operetta (stage director's guide   RPB
  by Vandevere)
Wind of the West, 1937, cantata, music by Roy S. Stoughton

JASMINE STONE VAN DRESSER
Eight-Thirty Sharp, comedy, in Delineator, 99, Jan., 1922, 20-1+ (1)
Young D'Arcy, in Delineator, 99, August, 1921, 24-5+ (1)

MINA VAN DRESSER
Cobwebs, 1928-9

ANTOINETTE PRUDENCE VAN HOESEN (WAKEMAN) (1856- ?)
The Testing, 1909, by A. P. Van Hoesen   DLC

MARJORIE VAN HORN
Alice in Wonderland, 1927, dance pantomime, with May E. Phipps   RPB
A Christmas Book, 1925, Christmas playlet for children, with   RPB
    May E. Phipps

NITA VAN HOUSEN
The Gift of Gifts, 1922, school health pageant   RPB

NORA VAN LEEUWEN
Festival and Pageant of Nations, 1914, New York City, unpub.   NN
    pageant program

ANNA VAN NOORDEN
The Backwoodsmen, 1926, romance of the War of 1812   RPB

ETTA C. VAN NORMAN
Betrayal   DPC

MARY VAN ORDEN
Partheneia, 1915; The Queen's Masque, 1915, music by   RPB
    Charles Louis Seeger Jr.

KATE VAN TASSEL
From Death to Life, 1902, Easter cantata, music by James C. Bartlett   RPB-M

FAITH VAN VALKENBURGH (See FAITH VAN VALKENBURGH VILAS)

GILDA VARESI
Enter Madame, 1921, prod. 1920, with Dolly Byrne   RPB

ALICE SUMMER VARNEY
Story Plays Old and New, 1915, one acts   RPB

ADELLA F. VEAZIE
Mrs. Hydebound's Views on Economy, 1920, monologue   RPB

CORNELIA C. VENCIL
On Vengeance Height, 1920, with Allan Davis, in Little   RPB, VP
    Theater Tournament, 1924 (1)

CAROLINE VERHOEFF
The Sleeping Beauty, in St. Nicholas, 40, April, 1913, 548-52, 5 acts

KATE JORDAN VERMILYE
The Pompadour's Prote´ge´, in Smart Set, 11, Sept., 1903, 75-87 (1)
Secret Strings, 1916

VIRGINIA FOX-BROOKS VERNON (1894- ?)
Modern One Act Plays from the French, 1933, collected and   RPB
    translated with Frank Vernon
Red Rust, 1930, prod. 1929, with Frank Vernon, adaptation of play by RPB
    V. Kirchon and A. Ouspensky

FANNIE COLLINS VICE
    Brown and the Agents, 1931, comedy (1)   RPB
    Keener's Christmas Gifts   CPR
    The Live Wire Parodies, 1930, with others, plays?
    Mother Takes Up Slang, 1933   RPB
    Spending Mother's Prize Money, 1935 play?   DLC

FAITH VAN VALKENBURGH VILAS
    The Faith of Little Jotham, 1924? miracle of Christmas (1)   RPB
    "Fiat Lux" (Let There Be Light) 1922, modern mystery play (1)   RPB
    Goldilocks, 1926, two act operetta   RPB
    His Mother's Son, 1923, "human document," pub. under title, Fuel, (1)
        in The Journal of Expression's Little Theatre No.
    The Home Valley, pageant
    Let There Be Light, by Faith Van Valkenburgh (See "Fiat Lux")
    The Maker of Souls, 1924, "Oriental phantasy in 2 acts"   RPB
    The Masque of Merlin, 1916   RPB
    A Masque of Old Loves, Valentine whimsey   CD
    The May Queen, 1924, masque for May Day, typed copy   RPB
    Miracle of Christmas, n.d., typed copy play?   MiD
    Out of the West, 1920 (1)
    The Star Wife, 1924, masque of the Pocantico Valley, masque of   RPB
        Americanization; music by Elizabeth Thorne Boutelle (copy at RPB
        without music)
    Tears of Dawn, medieval fantasy, in Poet Lore, 33, Spring, 1922, 105-13 (1)
    The Three Thanksgivings, November humoresque   SSH-II
    The Trees of the Blazed Trail, 1922, prod. 1920, masque of   RPB
        Americanization, given in Westchester County, N. Y.
    White Tulips, 1919 (1)   RPB

WYLLA JAMISON VILEY
    A Pageant of Woman's Progress, 1917, with Lorena Lucille Jamison   RPB

GLADYS BRACE VILSACK
    Rosamond and Simonetta, 1925, two poetic plays by Gladys Brace
    The Unpardonable Sin, 1915 play?   DLC

ANNETTE E. VINJE
    Hay Harvest, in International Plays, 1936
    That Bridge of Sighs, 1931, short burlesque   RPB
    Tombstone or Washing Machine, 1930, comedy (1)   RPB

IRIS VINTON
    Breaking Through, for young citizens   SPC
    Buried Treasure, 1932, comedy (1)   RPB
    The Cradle, Christmas tale of Brittany   SNC-2
    Halcyon, peace play   SPP
    Just Babies, 1939 (1)   RPB, SOP
    Signal at Dawn, in Samuel Simon, comp., Thrillers! 1937
    The White Birds of Cholula   SSC
    The Zebra Dun, in Samuel Sylvan, comp., Easily Staged Plays   SPE
        for Boys, 1936

MARY C. VLASEK
    The Advent of Spiritualism; or, Great Oaks from Little Acorns Grow,   RPB
        1918, playlet

LULA (LULU) VOLLMER (LOUISA SMITH VOLLMER) (1898-1955) NWAT
The American Story, 1949, radio script
The Curse of Drink, 1916?
Dearly Beloved, prod. 1946, typescript   NN
The Dunce Boy, prod. 1925, typescript   NN
Green Stones, with G. G. Dawson-Scott
Grits and Gravy, n.d., weekly serial radio program (only first   NN
     episode at NN)
The Hill Between, 1939, prod. 1938, 3 act folk play, prepared by   RPB
     Nathaniel Edward Reeid
The Honor and the Glory, 19?? typescript   NN
In a Nutshell, prod. 1937, typescript   NN
Moonshine and Honeysuckle, 1934, prod. 1933, 3 act comedy (orig. a   RPB
     radio program)
Sentinels, prod. 1931
The Shame Woman, prod. 1923, typescript   NN
She Put Out to Go, n.d. (c1946) typescript   NN
Shining Blackness, 1932
Sun-Up, 1924, prod. 1923   RPB, QRA, TTM, TMA, LOL
Trigger, prod. 1927
Troyka, prod. 1930, adapted from Hungarian of Imre Fazekas   DLC
The Widow's Sons, (also called Her Seven Sons), weekly radio   NN
     program, 1936-7

AMALIE VON BEHR
Cartoon, 1930

JANET M. VON SCHROEDER
The Quest, 1914, pastoral play, poetical allegory   RPB

LILLIAN WELCH VOORHEES
An' de Walls Came Tumblin' Down, 1926, with Olivia M. Hunter, dram. of
stories LNarc
     by Paul Laurence Dunbar
The Free Man, n.d., from the story, "The Wisdom of Silence," by   LNarC
     Paul Laurence Dunbar, synopsis and scenario
Hiawatha, 1927, with Olivia M. Hunter, musical drama in 5 scenes   LNarC
Jimsella, n.d., comedy of Negro life, from story of same name by   LNarC
     Paul Laurence Dunbar, synopsis and scenario
The Life of the Flowers from Waking to Sleeping, March through .   LNarC
     November, 1928, dance drama

MARY MARVIN HEATON VORSE (1874-1966) AWW NAW
Wreckage, 1924, with Colin Clements (1)   RPB

MAUDE BATCHELDER VOSBURGH
The Health Champions, 1921, modern health crusade play, written   RPB
     for Mass. T. B. League (1)
The Homemakers, 1920, "play of the Pilgrims in 3 acts"   RPB
Miss Maria, 1917, dram. of a story by Margaret Deland, comedy (1)   RPB

MATHILDE A. VOSSLER
The Striking of America's Hour, 1925, with Laura S. Copenhauer and   RPB
     Katherine S. Cronk, pageant of Christian liberty

LESLIE VYNER
Penny Wise, prod. 1919, with Mary Stafford Smith

W

LEILA WADDELL
The Hippodrome Horror, in International, 12, March, 1915, 94-5 (1)

LEILA A. WADE
Plays from Browning, 1923

MARY HAZELTON BLANCHARD WADE (1860-1936)
Abraham Lincoln, 1914, story and play   RPB
Benjamin Franklin, 1914, story and play   RPB
George Washington, 1914, story and play   RPB
Ulysses Simpson Grant, 1914, story and play   RPB

NEVA MC FARLAND WADHAMS
A Fat, Jolly Old Man (1)   CPO
The Juvenile Recitation Book, 1928, with others   RPB

EULETA WADSWORTH
The Street of a Thousand Shadows, 1926-9? with Katherine B. Miller

NATALIE Z. WAGNER
The Gypsy's Secret, 1930, for jr. h. s. (1)   RPB
He Is Come! The Messiah, 1953, Christmas entertainment   MiD
The Rag Doll's Christmas Eve, 1924   RPB

BLANCHE SHOEMAKER WAGSTAFF (1888- ?)
Alcestis, 1911, poetic drama   RPB
Colonial Plays for the School Room, 1912   RPB
Eris, 1914, poetic dramatic allegory   RPB

ANTOINETTE PRUDENCE VAN HOESEN WAKEMAN
(See ANTOINETTE PRUDENCE VAN HOESEN)

DOROTHY WALDO
A Full House, 1914, farce (1)   RPB
Idowanna, 1919, young (1)   RPB
Kid Curlers, 1916, farce (1)   RPB
Sylvia's Aunts, 1914, farce for females   RPB, JET

EDITH H. WALDO
Aunt Hester's Dilemma, 1909, 2 act farce   RPB

EDNA LA MOORE WALDO (1893- ?)
For the Honor of Old Glory, 1927, "patriotic pageant designed to   RPB
   teach correct flag etiquette for Flag Day or other patriotic occasions"
Grandma Gray Comes Back to the Farm, 1931, "simple rural   RPB
   club pageant"
More Christian Endeavor Playlets, 1929, ed. by E. W. Thornton,   RPB
   a contributor
The Story of Esther, 1926, for use in church and schools   RPB
They Wanted Publicity, 1927, for 7 women (1)   RPB

GEORGIA WALDRON
Up York State, prod. 1901, with David Higgins

MARION WALDRON
Masque of the Four Schools, 1915, Pittsburgh, Pa.

AMY WALES
Rockbound, prod. 1929, with Michael Kallesser

ALBERTA WALKER (1878- ?)
Health Plays for School Children
King Good Health Wins, 1919, modern Health crusade play, with   DLC
    Mrs. Ernest R. Grant (Cora De Forest Roberts Grant)

ALICE JOHNSTONE WALKER (1871- ?)
Abe's First Fish, 1932, about Abraham Lincoln (1)   RPB, SSL
At the White House, 1863   JEL
Dolly Peckham's Clothes Line, 1928, based on events around   RPB
    Newport, 1776-8, 3 acts
In Boston, 1864   JEL
Lafayette, Christopher Columbus, The Long Knives in Illinois, 1919, RPB
    three plays
Little Plays from American History for Young Folks, 1914
Mary Muldoon's Morning, 1929 (1)   RPB
On a Plantation, 1863   JEL
The Sanctuary Knocker   SPG
The Thurday, 1931, Brittany legend   DSS

AMELIA H. WALKER
Little Scarface, 1923, based on Indian legend (1)   RPB, SOP-I

MRS. GURNSEY WALKER
Commander-in Chief, 1926, drama in 6 scenes   RPB
Janey, 1923, 2 act missionary play   RPB

HARRIET K. WALKER
"Lest We Forget," 1923, "reminder in 1 act and 5 scenes"   RPB

HELEN WALKER (HOMAN) (1893- ?)
Presenting Mrs. Chase-Lyon, 1926, includes stories and dialogues   RPB

LILLIE M. WALKER
Her Sacrifice, 1921, entertainment for churches, Sunday schools, etc. RPB

LILLIE NOLTING WALKER
That Girl, 1916   RPB

LYDIA LE BARON WALKER
Stung! 1925, 3 act comedy   RPB

MOLLIE CULLOM WALKER
Programs, Plays, Songs, Stories for Workers with Children, 1921,   RPB
    compiler

JENNIE WALL
The Wood Box, 1925, 2 acts   RPB

AGNES WALLACE
A Pageant of Vocations, 1914, for girls   RPB

BERTHA M. WALLACE
Too Busy, 1928, N. Y. rural play, ed. by Alexander Drummond and   RPB
Mary Eva Duthie

EMMA B. WALLACE (May be same as Emma Gary Wallace)
Theresa's Fairy Friends, with Adelaide B. Meade, for Domestic Science   HPY
Classes or Groups of Younger Girls

EMMA GARY WALLACE
The Beautiful Garden, 1933, Easter pageant playlet   RPB
Belles We Have Met, 1930, novelty entertainment   RPB
Doors of Happiness, 1933, with Adelaide B. Meade, program for   RPB
Rally Day
The Flag of Courage, 1913, allegorical temperance play (1)   RPB
Gifts of the Loving Heart, 1925, with Adelaide B. Meade, "pageant of   RPB
giving and gratitude and growth especially suitable for a
Christmas season"
Glad Tidings to All People, 1928, with Adelaide B. Meade   RPB
Tony, the Color Bearer, 1925, young (1)   RPB
Why Photographers Go Mad, 1925, with Adelaide B. Meade   NN

FLORENCE MAGILL WALLACE
Pageant Building, 1918 (book about pageants)
The Seven Ages of Giving, 1910, "spectacular entertainment in 2 scenes   RPB
for any time of the year"

MAUDE ORITA WALLACE
At the Court of Santa Claus, n.d., musical (1)   Or, WaPS
The Golden Apple, 1917, 4 act operetta for children   RPB-M
The Lion Tamer, 1913, 4 acts   RPB
Meet King Winter, 1946, musical playlet for children   DLC
Patty Sue's Birthday Party, 1939, operetta for elem. grades (1)   RPB-M
Peanuts and Pennies, 1927, musical play for boys   RPB-M
Regular Girls, 1918, entertainment for girls   RPB
"Uncle Sam's" Visit, 1916, musical play for children   Or
When Betsy Ross Made "Old Glory," 1920, musical playlet for the young OCl
Who Stole the Tarts? 1944, musical for elem. grades   DLC

MIRIAM LODER WALLACE
The Dream of the Little Princess
The Fairy Ring
The Masque of the Melancholy Marquis   (All are dance pantomimes)
Sleeping Beauty

SARA A. WALLACE
Mothers of Men, 1914, "pageant of noble womanhood especially   RPB
adapted to Mother's Day"

DOROTHY BRUSH WALMSLEY (See DOROTHY HAMILTON BRUSH)

MABEL WALN
Conquest of Peace, 1922, pageant   RPB

HELEN HORNING WALSH
Lessons in English, 1919, Americanization play, with Minnie B. Horning RPB

KATHERINE WALSH
Shamus O'Brien, 1903, 4 act drama   RPB

NINA WILLIS WALTER (1900- ?)
A Change of Heart   CPR

ZELIA MARGARET WALTERS
The Magic Gift, 1925, Christmas play for children   Or
Mrs. O'Brien's Birthday Cake, 1924   RPB

BESSIE REED WALTON
The Eternal Magi, 1927 (Wetmore declamation, v. 30)   RPB

EMMA LEE WALTON (1874- ?)
Dodging the Cops, 1930 (1)   RPB
The Signal, 1941, comedy (1)   DLC
Such a Quiet Evening, 1930 (1)   RPB

GEORGINA JONES WALTON
The Light of Asia, prod. 1928

REUBENA HYDE WALWORTH (1867-1898)
Where Was Elsie? or, the Saratoga Fairies, 1900 (?)   RPB

ALICE WANGENHEIM (or WANGENHEINS)
The Cave of Precious Things, in Journal of Home Economics, 11, May, 1919,
    215-20, K. W. Hinks, adapter (1)

BEATRICE WANGER
Episodes by Nadja, 1929   RPB
More Episodes by Nadja, 1930   NN, NNC

ANNETTE PERSIS WARD
Battle of Lake Erie, 1913, pageant, Cleveland, Ohio
"Lest We Forget" Oliver Hazard Perry, the War of 1812, the Battle of
    Lake Erie, 1912, centennial celebration

ELIZABETH STUART PHELPS WARD (1844-1911) AWW NAW
Within the Gates, 1900, also in McClure's, 17, May, June, July, 1901,   RPB
    35-43, 142-9, 236-50, 3 acts

LUCILE AHRENS WARD
A Question of Importance, 1929, monologue   RPB
Sounds That Pass in the Night, 1930, farce (1)   RPB
Such a Surprise, 1929, comedy (1)   RPB
Wherever the Star Shines, 1929, Christmas pageant   RPB

MURIEL WARD
On the Line, 1930, 2 acts   RPB

WINIFRED DUNCAN WARD
Babes in the Wood, in Touchstone, 5, July, 1919, 281-5

"MARGARET WARDE" (See EDITH KELLOGG DUNTON)

SHIRLEY WARDE
Queen at Home, prod. 1930, with Vivian Crosby
Trick for Trick, prod. 1932, with Vivian Crosby and Harry Wagstaff Gribble

ALICE HOLDSHIP WARE
Like a Flame Together, 1938, in Theatre Workshop Magazine, 11,   NN, OCl
   1938
Mighty Wind A'Blowin', 1936
The Open Door, 1922, pageant of Negro history, prod. by the Atlanta Players

ANNE WARNER (See ANNE WARNER FRENCH)

ELLEN E. KENYON WARNER
Nonsense Dialogues for the Youngest Readers, 1917, first pub. 1912   RPB

GERTRUDE CHANDLER WARNER
A Christmas Play   WPP

EDNA WARREN
Rights of Possession, in Little Theatre Tournament, 1930

ELGINE WARREN
Sauce for the Goslings, 1922, good speech play (1)   RPB

GLADYS EVELYN WARREN
The Cherry Blossom Princess (1)   BHP
The Paradise of Children (1)   BHP

MARIE JOSEPHINE WARREN
*The Elopement of Ellen, 1905, Roxbury Latin School Theatrical,   RPB
   3 act comedy
Endymion, 1909, 3 act comedy   RPB
Mistletoe and Holly-Berry, 1922, old English Christmas play (1)   RPB
The Substance of Ambition, 1909, drama (1)   RPB
*Tommy's Wife, 1906, 3 act farce   RPB
The Twig of Thorn, 1910, 2 act Irish fairy play, prod. by Philadelphia   RPB
   Society of Brooklyn Heights Seminary
      * (Both written for and produced by Wellesley College students)

ROSE WARREN
Rejected, in Touchstone, 1, Sept., 1917, 506-9

MILDRED BAER WASHBURN
What It Gets Down To, won prize for best play, Little Theatre of Duluth

CHARLOTTE WASSUNG
Reforming a Bad Boy   LPS
What I Would Like To Be   LNP

GRACE GREGORY WATKINS (1874- ?)
An Old Time Courtship, 1911, 3 act comedy   RPB

LOUISE WARD WATKINS
Four Short Studies and a Play, 1925 ("An Interlude,"about Charles Lamb) RPB

LURA WOODSIDE WATKINS
Buried Treasure, 1933 (1)   RPB
The Ghost Hunters, 1928, comedy (1)   RPB
The Hope Chest, 1932 (1)   RPB
The Last of the Joneses, 1928, comedy (1)   RPB
A Match for the Matchmakers, 1933, comedy (1)   RPB
A Quiet Evening at Home, 1932   RPB

MAURINE DALLAS WATKINS (1900-1968)
Chicago, 1927, prod. 1926, satiric comedy   RPB
Chicago, 1975, musical vaudeville based on the play by Watkins,   RPB-M
    book by Fred Ebb and Bob Fosse; music by John Kander; lyrics by Fred Ebb
Gesture, in Three Acts, 1926, typed copy   DLC
Marshland
Revelry, prod. 1927, based on novel by Samuel Hopkins, about life of Warren
    Harding (According to Covens based on novel by S. H. Adams)

ALICE EVELYN WATSON
The Dancing Master, 1903, farce operetta (1)   RPB

ANNAH WALKER ROBINSON WATSON (1848- ?)
The Cross of Calvary, 1922, pageant of the years   RPB
The Moon Flower, 1918, Red Cross benefit, Memphis Tenn.   DLC
The Path of Progress, 1920, "pageant drama of the nation, 1620-1920,"   RPB
    Memphis, Tenn.

CAMILLE C. WATSON
The Legend of the Juggler, 1925, medieval pantomime in 3 tableaux   RPB

EVELYN WATSON
The Convalescence of Robbie, 1911, young   RPB
The Mission of Letty, 1914, serious comedy for women, 3 acts   RPB
Our Minister's Bride (1)
Patsy from Dakota, 1914, 3 act comedy   RPB

MRS. T. E. WATSON
The Gifts of St. Patrick, 1925 (1)   NN
A Grand Evening, 1925 (1)   RPB

MRS. HOWARD L. WATTS
Ye Did It Not Unto Me, 1922, playlet   RPB

MARY STANBERRY WATTS (1868-1958) AWW
Three Short Plays, 1917   RPB

CONSTANCE E. WAUGH
Holiday Plays for Girls, n.d., one acts (may be British)   OCl

ADELAIDE SCHMIDT WAYLAND
Initiation Night at Raggedy Man's Corner, 1904   RPB

"PRISCILLA WAYNE" (See PAULINE PHELPS)   ("Priscilla Wayne" was
    also a pseudonym for Besse Toulouse Sprague, who wrote several plays
    in the 1930s)

GUSTINE NANCY COURSON WEAVER
    (MRS. CLIFFORD SELDEN WEAVER) (1873-1942)
The Cotton Doll Farm, Inc., 1932, 3 act operetta, music by Belle Biard Gober
Hop-Run and Six Other Pageants, 1927   RPB

ROSE WEAVER
The Road to Happiness   HPY

HELEN WEBB (HARRIS)
Frederick Douglas
Genifrede, 1923, Howard Un. Players

JESSIE M. WEBB
   The Spirit of Liberty, 1918, with Lucille Schamberger, patriotic play   RPB
      especially suitable for use in the schools (1)

MARGARET WEBB
   The Spirit of the Prairie, 1915, masque; words by Webb; music by   RPB
   Isabel Savage; presented under auspices of YWCA and YMCA on
   Washburn College campus

AMY L. WEBER
   Off Col'uh, Little Theatre Tournament, 1927
   Wine of Life, Little Theatre Tournament, 1928

JEAN WEBSTER (ALICE JEAN CHANDLER WEBSTER MC KINNEY)
      (1876-1916) AWW NAW
   Daddy Long Legs, 1914, dram. of her novel   RPB

EDITH M. WEEKS
   In Poppyland, 1926 or earlier, musical entertainment for children

RUTH MARY WEEKS
   Every Bite; a Patriotic Burlesque, 1918, with Bertha Goes   RPB

LAURA CHRISTINE WEGNER
   Riley Readings with Living Pictures, 1921, novelty entertainment (James RPB
      Whitcomb Riley's works arranged by Wegner)

CLAIRE I. WEIKERT
   The Know It All, 1925, "dedicated to the tent and awning industry   RPB
      and to business in general"
   Learning Is Earning, 1926, "written for the 15th annual convention of   RPB
      the National Tent and Awning Manufacturers Assoc."

ANITA WEINBERG
   The Philosophy of the Toothbrush, with Albert Weinberg, in Poet Lore, 36,
      Winter, 1925, 615 23 (1)

MILDRED WEINBERGER
   Elaine, in Poet Lore, 34, Spring, 1923, 72-110 (1)

EVELYN MAUDE WEINGARDNER
   Was It Fault or Destiny? n.d., monologue   RPB

"ELIZABETH WEIR" (See BELLE MAC DIARMID RITCHEY)

FLORENCE RONEY WEIR (1861-1932)
   Busher's Girl, 1915, 3 act comedy   RPB
   The Cuckoo's Nest, 1918, comedy (1)   RPB

MARY ETHEL WEISS
   The Story of Little Lu De, 1926, church entertainment   RPB

OLIVE M. WELD
   The Merry Travelers, 1911, 3 act comedy   RPB

RITA WELLMAN (1890- ?)
  Barbarians, 1917, prod. by Provincetown Players, war play
  Dawn, in Drama, 9, Feb., 1919, 89-102 (1)
  For All Time, 1918 (1)   SLC
  Funiculi Funicula, 1917, prod. by Provincetown Players (1)   MRO
  The Gentile Wife, 1919, prod. 1918, 4 acts   RPB
  The Lady with the Mirror, in Drama, 8, Aug., 1918, 299-316 (1)
  The Rib Person, prod. 1918 by Provincetown Players, typescript   DLC
  The String of the Samisen, prod. 1919 by Provincetown Players (1)   CSP

ANNA MARY WELLS
  Lady Bolshevik, 1925

CAROLYN WELLS (1869-1942) AWW NAW
  April's Lady, in Ladies Home Journal, 33, April, 1916, 38 (1)
  Chrissy in Christmasland, 1912
  *Christmas Gifts of All Nations, in Ladies Home Journal 29, Dec., 1912, 86+ (1)
  *The Day Before Christmas, in Ladies Home Journal, 21, Dec., 1903, 16 (1)
  Dolly Dialogue, in St. Nicholas, 34, Dec., 1906, 156-7 (1)
  The Fairest Spirit, in Ladies Home Journal, 32, June., 1915, 15+ (1)
  The Glory of the World, in St. Nicholas, 44, Dec., 1916, 151-7
  *The Greatest Gift, in Ladies Home Journal, 30, Dec., 1913, 32+ (1)
  *Is Santa Claus a Fraud? in Ladies Home Journal, 27, Dec., 1909, 9-10 (1)
  Jolly Plays for Holidays, 1914, one act plays for Christmas   RPB
  Maids of Athens, 1914, 3 act operetta, music by Ferenc Lehar   CU
  The Meaning of Thanksgiving Day, 1922, also in Ladies Home Journal, 38,
    Nov., 1921, 30+ (1)
  The-Night-Before-Christmas-Dream, in Ladies Home Journal, 33,
    Nov., 1916, 36+ (1)
  Once Upon a Christmastime, in Ladies Home Journal, 31, Nov., 1914, 75 (1)
  The Play Lovers, in Ladies Home Journal, 39, Aug., 1922, 13+ (1)
  Queen Christmas, 1922, pageant, in Ladies Home Journal, 37,   RPB
    Dec., 1920, 32+ (1)
  The Sweet Girl Graduate, 1922, commencement play, also in   RPB
    Ladies Home Journal, 38, May, 1921, 19+ (1)
    (* Also in Jolly Plays for Holidays)

CHARLOTTE ELIZABETH WELLS
  Croesus and Ione, 1902, 4 act drama   RPB
  The Riddle Woman, prod. 1918, with Dorothy Donnelly,   NN
    incomplete typescript

FLORENCE WELLS
  Miss Usa's Peach Party, 1927, young   RPB

HELEN LOUISE WELSHIMER (1901- ?)
  More Christian Endeavor Playlets, 1929, ed. by E. W. Thornton,   RPB
    a contributor
  Twins, 1935, farce (1)

GERTRUDE WELTON
  Maisie at the Movies, 1922, monologue   RPB
  Sales and Solitaire, 1918, shop-girl monologue   RPB

RUTH WELTY
  Anthony's Antics, 1932   RPB
  The Chased Lady, 1930, comedy (1)   RPB

RUTH WELTY (continued)
    Crashing the Movies, 1932, 3 act comedy   RPB
    A Hint of Lilacs, social drama   STN
    The Loves of Lionel, 1929, satirical comedy (1)   RPB
    Polishing Henry, 1931, comedy (1)   RPB
    This Hero Business, 1928, with Cecil W. Secrest, 3 act comedy   RPB
    With Privileges, prod. 1930, with Roy Hargrave

MARGARET WENTWORTH
    A Gift of Years, 1941, "play of Chinese gratitude"   RPB
    The Purchase Price, 1930 (1)   RPB

MARGARET H. WENTWORTH
    The Christian Year, 1909, Christmas mystery play   TxU, PU

MRS. MARION JEAN CRAIG WENTWORTH (or CRAIG-WENTWORTH)
    (1872- ?)
    The Blue Cape, 1940, in free verse, peace play (1)   RPB
    The Flower Shop, 1912, 3 acts   RPB
    The Golden Touch, 1927, young   RPB
    The Princess and the Goblins, 1930, dram. of story by George   RPB
        MacDonald, written by students of Elm Lea, under Wentworth's direction
    The War Brides, 1915, also in Century, 89, Feb., 1915, 527-44 (1)   RPB
    What If They Could, 1927, radio whimsey (1)   RPB

BIRDIE WEST
    The Black American, 1919, first pub. 1901, dedicated to the NAACP   RPB

EMMA ELISE WEST (1876?- ?)
    Three Girls from School, 1910, 2 act comedy with music   NN, OCl
    Two Little Rebels, 1907, 2 acts   RPB

LOUISE BRONSON WEST
    In Extremis, by Louise West, comedy (1)
    The Whole Truth, 1906, comedy (1)   RPB

MAE WEST ("JANE MAST") (1892?-1980) AWW NWAT
    Babe Gordon (variant title of Constant Sinner)
    Catherine Was Great, prod. 1944
    The Constant Sinner, 1931, based on her novel, Babe Gordon
    Diamond Lil, 1949, prod. 1928, based on her novel of the same name, "scarlet
        woman in a setting of ice" (filmed as She Done Him Wrong, 1933)
    The Drag, prod. 1926
    Pleasure Man, prod. 1928, based on her novel
    Sex, 1927, prod. 1926, incomplete typescript   NN
    Sextet, 1961
    Wicked Age, prod. 1927

NANCY B. WEST ("BEE HASTINGS")
    The Harvest, n.d., by "Bee Hastings," 3 acts   RPB

OLIVE WEST
    The Trust Versus the Common People; or, Capital vs. Labor, 1904,   RPB
        "musical comedietta, satire on modern times"

ANNETTE WESTBAY
    The Heaven Tappers, prod. 1927, with George Scarborough

EFFIE ELLSLER WESTON (1858-1942)
As Who Shall Say, n.d., prompt book   NN
The Columbine Trail, n.d., romantic drama   NN
The Flyers, n.d., adapt. of novel by George B. McCutcheon, typescript   NN
Good Ground, n.d., prompt book   NN
Hawks and Doves, n.d., typescript   NN
Heart's Byways, 19??, typescript   NN
Her Calvary, 19??, typescript and prompt book   NN
His Love Story, 19??, typescript   NN
His Official Fiance´e, n.d., based on novel by Berta Rucks, prompt book   NN
His Woman, n.d., typescript   NN
Honesty's Garden, n.d., dram. of story by Paul Creswick, typescript   NN
Jim and I, 191? typescript (1)   NN
Man and the World, n.d., typescript   NN
Miss Moccasins, n.d., based on novel by Marah Ellis Ryan, motion   NN
  picture script
"The Rosary," n.d., dram. of story by Florence L. Barclay, typescript   NN
The Substitute, in Smart Set, 31, July, 1910, 115-21 (1)
Tillie, n.d., dram. of book by Helen Martin, typescript   NN
The Turn of the Road, n.d., typescript (1)   NN
A Wolf in Sheep's Clothing, n.d., prompt book   NN

EDITH NEWBOLD JONES WHARTON (1862-1937) AWW NAW
Ethan Frome, 1936, dram. of her book, by Owen Davis and   RPB
  Donald Davis
The House of Mirth, 1981, prod. 1906, with Clyde Fitch, dram.   RPB
  of her novel (typescript at NN)
The Old Maid, 1935, dram. by Zoe Akins   RPB
Pomegranate Seed, in Scribner's, 51, March, 1912, 284-91 (1)

HARRIET MARTHA WHEELER (1858- ?)
A Consort of Heroines, 1902, "representation of literary characters   RPB
  in 3 scenes"

VERNA WHINERY ("MARION MORRIS") (1886- ?)
Bells of Bethlehem, 1935, Christmas pageant, book and lyrics by   DLC
  "Marian Morris"; music by "Anne Owen" (Ira B. Wilson)
Candles of Youth, 1936, pageant for Children's Day   DLC
Children of the Starlight, 1933, Christmas pageant   RPB-M
The Cross Beautiful, 1931, Easter pageant, music by Grant C. Tullar   DLC.
Festival of Lights, 1930, candlelight service for Easter, "miniature   RPB
  E-Z pageant"
The Hand of God, 1930, Biblical drama founded on the Book of Ruth   RPB
The Heart of Christmas, 1935, pageant   RPB-M
The King's Birthday, 1929, miniature pageant for Sunday schools   RPB
Knights of the Cross, 1930, "miniature E-Z pageant for Children's Day"   RPB
My Song and My Star, 1934, by "Marion Morris," Christmas pageant;   DLC
  music by "Miriam Lois Fisher"
The Open Tomb,1935, by "Marian Morris," Easter pageant;   OrP, DLC
  music by Jane Lorenz
The Shepherd's Trail, 1933, by "Marian Morris," Christmas pageant;   DLC
  music by "Miriam Lois Fisher"
Sound the Jubilee, 1919, "playlet for the young people's branch and   RPB
  loyal temperance legion"
The Sower, 1930, "miniature E-Z pageant for Mother's Day"   RPB
The Star, 1928, Christmas pageant, music by Grant C. Tullar   DLC

VERNA WHINERY (continued)
    Star Gleams, 1932, Christmas pageant, music by "Anne Owen"   RPB
      (Ira B. Wilson)
    The Three Wise Men, 1934, Christmas pageant, music by   RPB
      Broughton Edwards
    Tidings of Great Joy, 1929, Christmas pageant   DLC
    Who Bids? 1933, pageant for Children's Day or other occasions,   RPB
      incidental music by "Miriam Lois Fisher"
    The Wisest Wise Man, 1944, Christmas pageant, music by   DLC
      Stewart Landon

STELLA DUNAWAY WHIPKEY
    Door Mats, in Poet Lore, 40, Spring, 1929, 92-108 (1)
    Very Crude Oil, in Drama, 20, May, 1930, 237-9 (1)

JOSEPHINE W. WHITAKER
    Miss Lillian's Portrait, 1923, comedy (1)   RPB

RUTH WHITBECK
    Speaking of Exercise, pub. in Two Prize Health Plays, 1930, won first   RPB
      prize Mass. State Tuberculosis Assoc. Contest of 1928

MILDRED WHITCOMB
    Half a Loaf, 1929, 2 acts for h. s. students   RPB

CLEMATIS WHITE
    A Convert, in Smart Set, 35, Nov., 1911, 103-6 (1)

"GAIL WHITE" (See GERTRUDE IDA THOMAS)

JESSIE BRAHAM WHITE
    Snow White and the Seven Dwarfs, 1925, prod. 1912, music by   RPB
      Edmond Rickett

KATE ALICE WHITE
    The Americanization of the Canavas, 1923, Americanization play   RPB
    And Christmas Came, 1946? pantomime   RPB
    And the Ghost Walked, 1936, pantomime   RPB
    Aunt Adeline's Heirs, 1936, farce   DLC
    Behind the Scenes, 1933 (1)   RPB
    The Boy Scout Forms a Patrol, 1931, 3 acts   RPB
    Done to Death, 1934, burlesqued pantomime   RPB
    The Downfall of Poor Speech, 1920   RPB
    The Mechanical Maid, 1933, comedy   RPB
    Mose's Dilemma, 1934, farce   RPB
    Pa Goes to the Sale, 1931   RPB
    Pa's Radio, 1925, monologue   RPB
    Pete Sells His Eggs, 1922, farce   RPB
    Professor Searchem Visits Mars, 1931   RPB
    Tested Project Plays for the Grade School, 1921   RPB
    The Traveling Photographer, 1920, farce (1)   RPB
    Two Valentines   SPD
    White's Book of Monologs, 1928   DLC
    Ye Moderne Beauty Shoppe, 1936   RPB

LUCY WHITE
    The Bird Child, 1922, also in International, 8, Nov., 1914, 337-9 (1)   LGP

LULA C. WHITE
  A Boston Tea Party   FPP

MRS. WILLIAM M. WHITE
  Centennial Book, official program of ceremonies and the pageant in   InI
    celebration of Fountain County at Covington, Ind., sponsored by
    DAR, 1926

JESSE MEIGS WHITED
  When Thrones Trembled, 1920, 3 act 18th century Masonic drama   RPB

ETHEL WHITEHEAD
  A Social Problem, dialogue for 2 boys   CSS
  The Way of Happiness and Other Plays, 1911   ICN

"ELIZABETH WHITEHILL" (See HARRIET E. SMITH)

GLADYS WHITEHILL
  The Owl's Feather, 1917, with Helen Mobert, Irish fairy play written   RPB
    and presented by class of 1917, Mt. Holyoke College
  Temperament, 1917

FRANCES WHITEHOUSE
  Are You a Crook? prod. 1913, with William J. Hurlbut, farce
  What It Means to a Woman, 1913, with Elizabeth Gould, 4 acts,   NN
    typed copy

JOSEPHINE HENRY WHITEHOUSE
  Ambush, 1927, farce   NAB-II
  The Canary, by J. H. Whitehouse, in Poet Lore, 37, Winter, 1926, 589-96 (1)
  Daily Bread, by J. H. Whitehouse, in Poet Lore, 40, Jan., 1929, 129-41,
    "drama of domestic life" (1)
  Indian Summer, in Poet Lore, 39, 1928, 455-66, comedy (1)
  Jeremiad, 1926, prize in Westchester County Little Theater   RPB
    Tournament (1)

BESSIE M. WHITELEY
  Hiawatha's Childhood, 1915, operetta (1)   RPB-M

JULIA FARRELL WHITELY
  The Best of All Ways, 1927, romantic adventure (1)   RPB

FLORENCE L. WHITFIELD
  Romany Blood, 1929, plays and poems   RPB

MARY VAUX WHITFORD
  Ingenuous Grandmother (1)   SCT

ELEANOR CUSTIS WHITING
  Ashes, in Poet Lore, 33, Autumn, 1922, 423-38 (1)
  Common Ground, in Poet Lore, 32, Jan., 1921, 140-8 (1)

EVELYN GRAY WHITING (CARD)
  A Confidence Game, 1900, 2 act comedy   RPB
  Deception's Web, 1903, 2 act comedy   RPB
  The Farmerette, 1914, 3 act comedy   RPB
  A Girl in a Thousand, 1907, 4 acts for women   RPB

EVELYN GRAY WHITING (continued)
 Gone Abroad, 1904 (1)   RPB
 Mrs. Briggs of the Poultry Yard, 1905, 3 act comedy   RPB
 No Admittance, 1902, farce for females (1)   RPB
 No Trespassing, 1916, 3 acts   RPB
 Six Kleptomaniacs, 1904, farce for females, by Evelyn Whiting Card

MAISIE B. WHITING
 Mrs. Carver's Fancy Ball, 1904, comedy (1)   RPB
 The Pink Swan Pattern, 1905   RPB
 Two Aunts and a Photo, 1903, comedy (1)   RPB

MARGARET ABBOTT EATON WHITING (1876- ?)
 Plays and Pageants for Children, 1925, she was compiler

MARGOT WHITLOCK
 The King's Ward, 1926

ELEANOR WOOD WHITMAN (1875-1948)
 Amos, the Shepherd Prophet, 193? 3 act drama based on Old Testament, NN
   typescript
 Bible Parables in Pantomime, 1924   NN, DLC
 The Drama of Isaiah, 1917   RPB
 Jeremiah, 1925, 5 act Biblical drama   RPB
 Nehemiah, the Builder, 1926, 4 act Biblical drama with music   NN, OCl
 The Prophet of Love; or, "Reaping the Whirlwind," 193? drama   NN
   based on story of Hosea, the prophet, typescript

MRS. E. C. WHITNEY
 The Court of the Year   EEY

MARY ELLEN WHITNEY
 Bible Plays and How to Produce Them, 1927   NcD, DLC
 Some Little Plays and How to Act Them, 1927

ALICE L. WHITSON
 Christmas on a Day Coach, 1924 (1)   RPB
 Gaining a Member   CPE
 The Great Decision   CPE
 The Paramount Children's Day Book, 1923, a contributor   RPB
 The Paramount Christmas Book, 1922, a contributor   RPB
 The Paramount Easter Book, 1923, a contributor   RPB
 The Paramount Mother's Day Book, 1941, a contributor   RPB
 The Paramount Special Day Book, 1924, a contributor   RPB

HAZEL LOTZE WHITTAKER
 Gas, Air and Oil, 1930, comedy, mimeo copy   RPB
 Holy Night, 1930, Christmas, mimeo copy   RPB
 Key in the Lock, 1930, mimeo copy (1)   RPB
 Mr. Fixit and Company, 1930, comedy, mimeo copy   RPB
 A Slice of Life, 1930, mimeo copy (1)   RPB

MATTIE C. L. WHITTEMORE
 Maggie Interrupts, 1928, comedy (1)   RPB

PHOEBE WHITTIER
Christmas Stars, 1938, musical pageant, music by F. G. Walker and   WaSp
        Broughton Edwards
The Risen King, 1930, Easter pageant   RPB

MARY (MAY) HOYT WIBORG
Taboo, prod. 1922

J. MAE CULP WICK
A Radio Christmas; or, Christmas in Room 326, 1922 (1)   RPB

FRANCES GILLESPY WICKES (1875- ?)
A Child's Book of Holiday Plays, 1916   RPB
Stories to Act, 1915

MARY F. WICKLIFFE
A Harvest Pageant, 1924   RPB

JOSEPHINE WILHELM WICKSER
Official Program and Book of Words of the Pageant of Oswego, 1925,
        Oswego, N. Y.
A Pageant of the Garden, 1928, presented by Twentieth Century Club   RPB
The Pageant of Saratoga, "Why America Is Free," 1927, with adaptation   RPB
        to the field by Percy Jewett Burrell, Master of the Pageant, Saratoga, N. Y.
The Romance of Buffalo, 1932, pageant, with William Dodd Chenery,   NBuG
        in Buffalo Centennial, 1832-1932, 1932, Vol. 1, 15-46
The Romance of the Valley, 1926, presented at Rome, N. Y. as part of   RPB
        the Zonta girls work week program
The Spirit of Buffalo, 1923, pageant, Buffalo, N. Y.   NBuG
Three Pageants, 1936   RPB

MARGARET WIDDEMER
The Singing Wood, 1926, poetic drama   RPB

JEANNE ELIZABETH WIER
Pageant of Reno, 1914, Reno, Nevada

KATE DOUGLAS SMITH WIGGIN ("MRS. G. C. RIGGS") (1856-1923)
        AWW NAW
Bluebeard, 1914, by "Mrs. G. C. Riggs," "herein lies the story of the   RPB
        miraculous discovery in a hat box of an unpublished opera by the
        late Richard Wagner, dealing in the most unique and climateric
        manner with feminism, trial marriage, bigamy and polygamy."
        (actually, a prose spoof of an opera)
The Birds' Christmas Carol, 1914, dramatic version with Helen   RPB
        Ingersoll (1) (In 1942 Pauline Phelps did a dram. of Wiggin's story, and
        in 1943 Alden Carlow did one—both are one-acts and both are at RPB.)
Fragments of a Play, in Poet Lore, 40. 1929, 281-7
Mother Carey's Chickens, 1925, with Rachel Crothers   RPB
Mrs. Ruggles Trains Her Brood, 193?   RPB
The Old Peabody Pew, 1917, dram. from her book (1)   RPB
Rebecca of Sunnybrook Farm, 1920, with Charlotte Thompson, prod. by
        Pasadena Comm. Players, later made into a film
The Ruggles Family, 193?   RPB
The Ruggleses in the Rear, 1942, comedy by Pauline Phelps, suggested
        by some of the characters in Wiggin's The Birds' Christmas Carol

KATE DOUGLAS SMITH WIGGIN (continued)
  A Thorn in the Flesh, 1926, monologue freely adapted from the French   RPB
    of Ernest Legouve´, also in Poet Lore, 36, Summer, 1925, 191-9'

MAY WOOD WIGGINTON
  Love and Friendship, 1925, from the novel by Jane Austen, 5 acts

WILMA (or WILNA) WIGGINTON
  Three Rogues and a Rascal, in Plays, 1918-19, farce (1)   RPB

CAROL VAN BUREN WIGHT
  The Scallop Shanty; a Chatham play, 1918, written for Chatham   DLC
    branch of American Red Cross
  Sir Thomas More and Other Verses, 1925 ("Sir Thomas More" is a play.)   RPB

MARIAN WIGHTMAN
  The Dagger, prod. 1925

HELEN HANNAH CLIFFORD WILBUR ("ELENE WILBUR") (1878- ?)
  Godfather's Christmas, 1929, comedy (1)   RPB
  The Kidnapping, 1912, by "H. C. Wilbur" (1)   RPB
  The Marriage Cake, 1927, comedy (1)   RPB
  Mistletoe and Moonlight, 1929, mystery comedy (1)   BAO
  Morning Hate, prod. 1936 by Federal Theatre
  She Got Away With It, 1934, with Henry David Gray, 3 act comedy   RPB
  The Table Set for Himself, 1930, Christmas, also in Scholastic, 23, Dec. 16, RPB
    1933, 9-11+ (1)
  The Wares Never Did So, 1928, comedy drama (1)   RPB

HARRIETTE WILBURR (1891- ?)
  An Affair of State, 1908, school entertainment   RPB
  All in a Garden Fair, 1922, flower pageant (1)   RPB
  All the Year Round, 1909, collection of entertainments   RPB
  Apple Blossoms, 1908, fancy frolic
  Aunt Jerushy Wants to Jine, 1933, comedy (1)   RPB
  Autumn Leaves, 1908, fancy drill   NcD, InU
  Beau Brummel's Brigade for Twelve Boys, 1907   NcD
  Calendar Days, 1916 (1)   RPB
  Celebrating Thanksgiving Day, 1936, collection   RPB
  The Children's Book, 1933, with Jean Lee Latham and   RPB
    Nellie Meader Linn
  Choo Lee and Haru, 1910, pantomime   RPB
  The Christmas Puddings, 1913   RPB
  The Christmas Stockings, 1913   RPB
  Christmas Sugar Plums, 1916, drill   RPB
  The Christmas Toy Shop, 1922, musical play for children   RPB
  The Complete Drill Book, 1919, with others   RPB
  Costume Drills and Dances, 1931, collection   RPB
  Daisies; a Maypole dance, 1908   NcD
  The Dancing Christmas Trees, 1917   DLC
  Dandy Dialogues for Christmas, 1911, with others   RPB
  Dat Watermillyun, 1916, for 8 boys   DLC
  Drills and Entertainments for Children, 1910   MH, DLC
  Emblems of Liberty, 191? patriotic exercise for children   NcD
  Father Christmas and His Family   SBC
  Flitting Fireflies, 1931, fantasy   DLC
  Fluttering Flags, 1915, drill for children   NcD.

HARRIETTE WILBURR (continued)

Friday Afternoon Entertainments, 1914, collection	RPB
The Gang Goes to Mill, 1924 play??	DLC
George and Martha Washington, 1917	CSmH, DLC
Golden Rod and Asters, 1908, flower quadrille	
Hail to the Flag, 1918, drill for small girls	RPB
A Half Hour with Washington, 1912 (1)	RPB
The Hall of Fame, 19?? dialogue for any occasion	RPB
The Happy Christmas Book, 1924, with others	
Harriette Wilburr's Series of Flower Plays, 1908	NN
Haste Makes Waste, 1920, farce (1)	RPB
Holly, 1908, jumping rope drill	NcD, InU
Holly Wreath Time, 1922, drill and song	RPB
Keeping Thanksgiving, 1915, in Ladies Home Journal,	RPB
31, Dec., 1914, 34 (1)	
The Liberty Bells, 1917, drill for girls	RPB
The Liberty Dance, 1917	DLC
Little Plays for Little Players, 1910	RPB
The Lucky Christmas Book, 1933, collection	RPB
Merry Christmas Bells, 1917, dance for 12 girls	RPB
Mistress Mary's Garden, 1911, flower exercise	RPB
The Modern Drill and Exercise Book, 1905	DLC
Morning Glories, 1908, symbolic drill	NcD, InU
Our Country's Flag, 192? drill for children	RPB
Over Here; or, Work Enough For All, 1918, musical patriotic program	RPB
Pansies, 1908, minuet dance	NcD, InU
Parade of the Parasols, 1928, Japanese drill for 8 girls	RPB
Peppermint Sticks, 1922, drill for 10 boys	RPB
A Pilgrim's Dream, 1918?	RPB
Poppies, 1908, sleepy drill	NcD, InU
Pussy Willows, 1908, costume drill	NcD, InU.
The Red-White-and-Blue Pageant, 1917, exercise for 12 children	
Roses, 1908, bouquet drill	NcD, InU
Shamrock, 1908, staff drill	NcD, InU
Snowballs, 1908, staff drill	NcD, InU
Spring Flowers, 1908, flower festival	NcD, InU
A Stack of Black Cats, 1922, drill for boys	RPB
Sweet Peas, 1908, dainty flower play	NcD, InU
The Thanksgiving Garden, 1922, humorous costume drill and dance	RPB
for 8 children	
Thanksgiving in the Schoolroom, 1937, with others	RPB
The Thanksgiving Month, 1916, exercise for children	RPB
That Thanksgiving Dinner, 1913?	RPB
Tip-top Entertainment Book, 1925, with others	NBuG, WaSp
Uncle Sam and Columbia, 1919?	RPB
A Week in Sunbonnet Land, 1918?	RPB
The Wise Old Owl. 1918?	RPB

CONSTANCE GRENELLE WILCOX

The Blue and Green Mat of Abdul Hassan, 1925, Appleton Short	RPB
Plays, no. 5, Arabian adventure	
Egypt's Eyes, 1924, 3 acts	RPB
Four of a Kind, 1920, "play for a boat" (1)	RPB
The Heart of Frances, 1925, Appleton Short Plays no. 10 (1)	RPB
Mah-jongs, 1923, "play of one hundred intelligences" (1)	RPB
Mother Goose Garden, 1920, "fantasy for a garden" (1)	RPB
Pan Pipes, 1920, "woodland play, a fantasy" (1)	RPB

CONSTANCE GRENELLE WILCOX (continued)
  The Princess in the Fairy Tale, 1920, "garden fairy story for children" (1) RPB
  Told in a Chinese Garden, 1920, "play pageant for a garden,   RPB, FON
    a fantasy" (1) (also in The Book of Make Believe, Boston, 1932
    and in Drama, 34, May, 1919, 116-50)
  Told in a Chinese Garden and Four Other Fantastic Plays for   RPB
    Outdoors or Indoors, 1920

ELLA WHEELER WILCOX (1850?-1919) AWW NAW
  Mizpah, 1906, with Luscombe Searelle, story of Esther, 4 act poetical play RPB
  The New Hawaiian Girl, 1910
  The Supreme Victory, and Yesterday and Today, 1920, 2 plays,   NN
    lyrics by Wilcox, text by Ruth Helen Davis

GRACE WILCOX
  Translated, in Poet Lore, 36, Summer, 1930, 251-60

HELEN L. WILCOX
  Larola   FRD-I

CAROLINE S. P. WILD
  The Kettle Sings; or, The Domestic Conscience, 1917 (1)   RPB

EVA M. WILDE
  Judkin's Grocery, 1929, novelty entertainment   RPB

JESSIE WILKINSON WILDER (1871- ?)
  Playing Square, 1926 (1)   RPB
  Under the Law, 1925 (1)   RPB

MARION WILDER
  Another Man's Place, 1923   DPP

MARIAN WARNER WILDMAN
  (See MARIAN WARNER WILDMAN FENNER)

SARAH KING WILEY (1871-1909)
  Alcestis and Other Poems, 1905 ("Alcestis" is a play.)   RPB
  The Coming of Philibert, 1907   RPB
  Dante and Beatrice, 1909   RPB
  The Football Game, 1904, comedy (1)   PU, DLC
  Iphigeneia Before the Sacrifice at Aulis, 1912, cantata, dramatic scene for NN
    soprano, chorus and orchestra; music by William Henry Humiston
  Patriots, 1902, American Revolutionary comedy (1)
  Poems: Lyrical and Dramatic, 1900, includes "Cromwell," historical play RPB

ALLENE TUPPER WILKES
  The Creaking Chair, 1926, 4 act mystery
  The Spirit of Christmas, 1916   RPB

WILHEMEN WILKES
  An Outsider, 1910, college play for girls (1)   RPB

EVA WILKINS
  The Brogues of Kilavain Glen, 1911 (1)   RPB

ELLA CRANE WILKINSON
    Freddy's Great Aunt, 1904, for women (1)   RPB
    Madame De Portment's School, 1904, comedy (1)   RPB

MARGUERITE OGDEN BIGELOW WILKINSON (1883-1928)
    The Passing of Mars, 1915, modern morality play   RPB

SENORA MAE WILKINSON
    Blood Will Tell, 1924, "3 act racial and moral drama"   RPB

ELLEN MELVILLE WILLARD (1853- ?)
    The Ballad of Prudence Dean, 1904, pantomime, young   RPB
    The Favorite Book of Drills, 1907
    Fun for Little Folks; or, Children's Party Book for All Seasons, 1908   Or
    Pictured Readings and Tableaux , 1915
    Yuletide Entertainments, 1910, collection   RPB

HELEN LIDA WILLCOX (1883- ?)
    Along the Years, 1930, pageant of Methodism   RPB
    Amelida, 1925, "dramatization showing the need for schools in   NcD
        Mexican labor camps"
    America Grows Up, n.d., Americanization pageant   Or
    The Bank Job, 1926, jr. h. s.   RPB
    Bet You Don't Dare! 1940, jr. h. s.   RPB
    Bible Study Through Educational Dramatics, 1924   RPB
    The Black Bag, about prohibition
    The Cash Crop, 1937, "play of American rural life" (1)   DLC
    The Class Party, 1928, jr. h. s.   RPB
    Dawn in the West, 193?, "play of China today" (1)   RPB
    Deep Unto Deep. n.d., religious drama pageant   IEG
    Dramatic Sketches of Mission Fields, 1921   MiD, ICU
    El Dorado, 1917, "pageant of South American freedom"   RPB
    Election Day, 1916   RPB, SPC
    Findings, 1926, jr. h. s. girls   RPB
    The Heroine of Ava, 1916   RPB
    His Honor, the Owl, 1934, elem. grades   RPB
    Kanjundu; or, From Fear of the Enemy, 1913, missionary play RPB
    Kasim, 1926, play of Persia   NcD
    Keeping the Peace, 1928, jr. h. s.   RPB
    Larola, 1917, missionary play   RPB
    Lydia, Seller of Purple, 1923, 2 acts   OO, DLC
    The Magic Carpet, 1920, "program of the Near East"   IaU
    Mission Study Through Educational Dramatics, and Slave Girl   MiD
        and School Girl, 1918
    On to Oregon! 1936, "dramatic sketch on the story of   WaPS
        Marcus Whitman"
    The Pact of Paris, peace play   DFP
    The Pilgrimage; or, The Haj, 1912   RPB
    "Precious Flower and the Flies," dram. of story in The Honorable NN
        Crimson Tree by Anita B. Ferris, young
    Pueblo Pioneers, 1932, "play of Indian life in the Southwest" (1) RPB
    Rome or the Kingdom   DFP
    Slave Girl and School Girl, 1912   RPB
    The Standing Cane, Cuban theme
    The Street of Ivory, play of China, also in Ehrensperger, H. A., NN
        comp., Plays to Live By, 1934 (1)
    Sunlight or Candlelight, 1912, missionary play   RPB

HELEN LIDA WILLCOX (continued)
The Test, 1916, missionary play (1)   RPB
Tides of India, 1923, pageant play   OO, DLC
Tractored Out! 1940, about migrant crop workers (1)   RPB
Two Thousand Miles for a Book, 1913, missionary play,   RPB
    American Indian theme
The Unveiling, 1925, jr. h. s., pub. by Child Welfare Society   RPB
The Victory of Light, 1926, masque   RPB
The Wings as Eagles, 1940, missionary play on China (1)   RPB
Youth's Easter, 1920, morality play

EDITH MORGAN WILLETT
His Lordship, the Burglar, 1902, comedy (1)   RPB
Under the Black Cassock, 1907 play?   NN

ALICE STEVENS WILLIAMS (MRS. OTIS CARL WILLIAMS)
The Runaway Appetite, 1930, 3 acts, young   RPB

BERTHA WILLIAMS
Boy Blue Discovers Halloween, 1931, playlet   RPB
Hail! Stunt Night, 1930, 50 new stunts for camp frolics or   RPB
    social gatherings
A Memorial Day Pageant, by Bertha Mae Williams   HPP
The Raggedy Girl's Dream   JGH
Tested Camp and Playground Plays, 1931   RPB

CLAIRE WILLIAMS
The Best Cellar, 1926

EMILY CODDINGTON WILLIAMS (1876- ?)
Pals, 1925 (1)   RPB

EVA WILLIAMS
Good Health Fairies, 1922, 5 acts   RPB
Peter Rabbit Helps the Children, 1922, springtime playlet   RPB

GENEVIEVE MACDONALD WILLIAMS
Pageant of Dubois County, 1916, Huntington, Ind.   InI

GRACE P. WILLIAMS
Mrs. Santa to the Rescue, 1926   RPB
When Santa Came to the Orphanage, 1926 (1)   RPB

HARRIET E. WILLIAMS
Historical Pageant of Connersville, Fayette County, Ind., 1916   InI

MRS. HARRY ALSTON WILLIAMS
On the Stairway of Life in Seven Ages, 1909 (1)   RPB

HELENA V. WILLIAMS
The Champion, 1921, "especially written for presentation in   RPB
    Tiny Tim's house"
Sally, Health Crusader, 1921, for marionettes, with   RPB
    Mathurin Marius Dondo

LAURA M. WILLIAMS
At the Summer Dance Hall, 1916, monologue for a woman   RPB
Hannah Sprouts, 1916, monologue for a woman   RPB
In Granny's Time, 1916, monologue for a woman   RPB
Twenty Funny Monologues, 1924
Up-to-the-Minute Monologues, 1919   RPB

MARGERY WILLIAMS
Out of the Night, 1929, prod. 1927, with Harold Hutchinson, 3 act   RPB
    mystery comedy

SARA M. WILLIAMS
The Turkey Girl (1)   LUU

ANNA E. WILLIAMSON
Christmas Stars, 1915, in Christmas Plays for Children, Series I, 1916 (1)   RPB

HAZEL ALLIS WILLIAMSON
A Christmas Play, 1922, "dramatizing and emphasizing the Christmas   RPB
    messages—the Giving of substance, the Giving of service," 2 acts

DOROTHY WILMOT
"An American Citizen"; or, The Awakening of an American   RPB
    Citizen, 1928 (1)

BERTHA M. WILSON
The Bootblack Drill, n.d., young   NN
Chinese Wedding, 1895, "representation of the wedding   PU
    ceremony in China"
The Christmas Star, 1911, monologue   NN
Indian Sketches, 1894, "entertainment for home talent"   MH
John Brown's Ten Little Injuns, 1895, "tomahawk march and drill   NN
    for male characters"
The March of the Chinese Lanterns, 1912? first pub. 1895, "spectacular   RPB
    novelty drill for girls"
Maud Muller Drill, 1895, pantomime drill   NN
Mr. Sprigg's Little Trip to Europe, 1904, comedy (1)   RPB
Nigger Baby, 1915, monologue   NN
Playing the Society Belle; or, The Tragedy of a Slipper, 1894, comedy   RPB
    monologue for a woman
Preciosa, the Spanish Dancer, 1911, adapt. from Longfellow's   RPB
    "Spanish Student"
Raggles' Corner, 1901, farce (1)   RPB
"Seniors," 1895, "written for the class of 1895 of the S. D. state   DLC
    normal school at Spearfish," 3 acts
The Show at Wilkins' Hall; or, A Leaf from the Life of Maria Jane, 1895,   NN
    "arranged for either a lady or a gentleman in female costume"
Spring Garlands, 1895, " 'pose'-y drill and march for maids and gallants of
    ye olden tyme"
The Tragedy of Blind Margaret, 1895, adapt. of Longfellow's   RPB
    "Blind Girl of Cast'el-Cuill'e," monologue
Wilson's Book of Drills and Marches for Young People, 1895

CAROLYN WILSON (See CAROLYN CROSBY WILSON LINK)

CLARA WILSON
Who Defeated Doogan? 1924, with Fannie R. Buchanan, "study of   DLC
    election laws and a farce of election errors" (1)

DOROTHY CLARKE WILSON (1904- ?)

"And Myrrh," 1935, Christmas	RPB
The Broken Circle, 1941 (1)	RPB
The Brother, 1939, 3 act religious play	RPB
Brothers, 1933, peace play (1)	RPB
The Burden Bearers, 1938, religious play (1)	RPB
The Carpenter, 1947	RPB
C'est la Guerre! 1935 (1)	RPB
Christian Family Brown, 1936	RPB
The Empty Room, 1930, drama of the first Christmas	RPB
The Far Country, 1933, drama of youth and the great adventure	RPB
The Father, 1936 (1)	RPB
For He Had Great Possessions, 1932, religious play (1)	RPB
The Friendly Kingdom, 1940 (1)	RPB
The Gifts, 1944	RPB
The Good Soldier, 1933, drama of Christian loyalty	RPB
A Grain of Wheat, 1940, dram. of novel by Toyohiko Kagawa	RPB
High Hurdle, 1938, temperance play (1)	RPB
Into Thy Kingdom, 1936, Easter (1)	RPB
Joseph of Arimathea, 1932, Easter	RPB
The King's Son, 1934	RPB
The Light in the Window, 1933, Easter	RPB
The Lost Church, 1930, pageant drama	RPB
The Lost Star, 1931, pageant fantasy of the first Christmas	RPB
The Man Who Lived Too Soon, 1946, play of Leonardo da Vinci	RPB
The Mighty Dream, 1947, drama of Christian brotherhood	RPB
Miss Nancy's Legacy, 1934 (1)	RPB
No Room in the Hotel, 1941, Christmas	RPB
The Other Shepard, 1934, drama of the first Christmas	RPB
Peace I Give Unto You, 1932, religious drama, peace play	RPB, ETO
Peace on Mars, 1959 (1)	RPB
The Pentecost of Youth, 1932, pageant of religious education	RPB
Pilgrims of the Way, 1931, drama of the early church	RPB
Release, 1933, Lenten play (1)	RPB
Return, 1937 (1)	RPB
The Return of Chandra, 1954, "play of the new India"	RPB
Salvage, 1937 (1)	RPB
Send Out Thy Light, 1942, dramatic service of worship	RPB
Shepherds Abiding, 1933, Christmas religious fantasy (1)	RPB
Simon the Leper, 1934, drama of the Christ	RPB
Smoke, 1935 (1)	RPB
The Sorrowful Star, 1939, Christmas pageant	RPB
The Straight White Road, 1937, pageant of Christian growth	RPB
These Things Shall Be, 1932, drama of Christian education	RPB
They That Sit in Darkness, 1931, Christmas	RPB
The Things that Are Caesar's, 1937, peace play (1)	RPB
This Night Shall Pass, 1941	RPB
Twelve Months of Drama for the Average Church, 1933	RPB
The Unlighted Cross, 1933, drama of Christian education (1)	RPB
The Way of the Cross, 1934, Easter (1)	RPB
Where the Fires Are Lighted, 1939 (1)	RPB
The Whirlwind, 1934, temperance play	RPB
White Christmas, 1934, missionary play (1)	RPB
Wild Anarchy, 1938, temperance play (1)	RPB

EDNA ERLE WILSON

Good Things for Harvesttime, 1924, "up-to-date entertainment"	RPB

ELIZABETH WILSON (1867- ?)
The Spy, 1915, Revolutionary War play in 4 acts   RPB
William Fell, 1924, typed copy   RPB

GAIL WILSON
Waste, 1919, allegorical play written for the War Information Dept.,   RPB
    Woman's Committee, Council of National Defense, Illinois division

HARRIET SMIRLE WILSON
Sophronia's Wedding, 1919, "small town comedy in 3 acts of other days" RPB

LEILA WEEKES WILSON
Like Father, Like Son, "bit of domesticity in one act and a motor,"
    in Drama, 13, Feb., 1923, 188-91 (1)

LEISA GRAEME WILSON
The Lady Loses Her Hoop, "sad tale in sadder verse," in Drama, 12,   RPB
    May, 1922, 279-80 (1)
Penny Buns and Roses, 1924, musical fantasy,   RPB
    music by Charles Ripper (1)

LILLIAN P. WILSON
The Fruit of Toil and Other One-Act Plays, 1916   RPB

LOUISE LATHAM WILSON
All on Account of an Actor, 1904, farce (1)   RPB
A Case of Suspension, 1923, first pub. 1899, comedy (1)   RPB
The Fortunes of War, 1904, farce (1)   RPB
A Little Game With Fate, 1901, comedy (1)   RPB
The Old Maid's Association, 1900, farce (1)   RPB
A Parliament of Servants, 1901, comedy (1)   RPB
Priscilla's Room, 1921, farce (1)   RPB
Returning the Calculus, 1917, college comedy (1)   RPB
The Scientific Country School, 1913, first pub. 1899, farce   RPB
The Smith Mystery, 1899, comedy (1)
A Suit of Livery, 1901, 2 act farce   RPB
The Trouble at Satterlee's, 1911, farce (1)   NN, PU
Two of a Kind, 1899, comedy   RPB
Where Is Helen? 1917, 2 act farce   RPB
The Wreck of Stebbins' Pride, 1903, 2 act comedy   RPB

MARIAN WILSON
Burglar-proof, 1929, comedy (1)   RPB

MIRIAM WILSON
The Spirit of Christmas, 1916, "original fantasy in 2 short acts"   RPB

OLIVIA LOVELL WILSON
Cobbler's Bargain, with Mrs. Charles Fernald   BPP
The Honeymoon, with Mrs. Charles Fernald   BPP
The Irish Washerwoman, with Mrs. Charles Fernald   BPP
Learning Lessons, with Mrs. Charles Fernald   BPP
Left, with Mrs. Charles Fernald   BPP
Marriage of Prince Flutterby, 1886, comedy for children (1)   PU, MH
Parlor Varieties, Vol. III (See E. E. Brewster)
Plays, Pantomimes and Charades, 1887   DLC
The Power of Sons, with Mrs. Charles Fernald   BPP

OLIVIA LOVELL WILSON (continued)
  School and Temperance Dialogue, with Mrs. Charles Fernald   BPP
  School Opera, with Mrs. Charles Fernald   BPP

SUE ANN WILSON
  The Festival of the Harvest Moon, 1921, folk festival (1)   SSH-II
  The Festival of Yankee Doodle, 1923   RPB

ONA WINANTS
  The Lamentable Tragedy of Julius Caesar, 1901, in song and verse   RPB

MARIAN F. WINNEK
  Educated

MARY WINSOR
  Queen Vashti, 1923, for National Woman's Party
  A Suffrage Rummage Sale, 1913   RPB, FOV

ANNIE STEGER WINSTON
  The Blackball, 1926, comedy (1)   RPB
  The Waiting Room, 1926, monologue   RPB

ELLEN IRWIN WINTER
  Sail Right In, 1929, comedy (1)   RPB
  Sheep, 1930, drama (1)   RPB

MARY WINTER
  The Ruling Class, comedy, in Drama, 15, April, 1925, 150-2 (1)
  Where There's a Will, There's a Way; or, The Old Family Nake, 1886, OCl
    "old-fashioned Irish comedy in 3 acts," pub. in Dublin

ELIZABETH WINTERS
  Columbia, the Gem of the Ocean, 1899   RPB
  Japanese Fan Drill   TDF
  The Green Entertainment Book, 1930   RPB

MYRA PAGE WIRE'N
  The Bulwark, 1940, 3 act drama   DLC
  Most, a play, 1910, "relation of heart and soul"   DLC
  Vik, prod. 1914

CLARE TEAL WISEMAN
  The Prosecutor, 1914, with Clifford G. Roe, 4 act drama   RPB

FRANCES WITHERSPOON
  The Other Room, 1928, in Little Theater Tournament, in Poet Lore,
    38, 1927, 269-90

ANTOINETTE WITHINGTON
  Pageant of the Nations, 1914, Newburyport, Mass. (by A. Withington)
  The Purple Iris, 1929, story from old Japan (1)   RPB, SPE

MRS. ARTHUR WITHINGTON
  The Hanging of the Greens, "fantasy to precede the holiday   RPB, SSC
    season, given annually by the Honolulu Association and written
    for them," also in Mary W. Hillyer, Yuletide in Other Lands, 1927

GEORGIANA BOWEN WITHINGTON
A Children's Parade, 1915?, Little Compton, R. I.   MB

HAZEL BOND WITT
Ladies First, 1929, comedy, mimeo copy   RPB

HUBERTA MARIANNE PLUM WOEHNING (or PLUM-WOEHNING)
Montana, 1901, 3 act drama   RPB
Pausanias and Xerxa, King Xerxes' Daughter, 1904, 5 act historical drama RPB

THERESA HUNT WOLCOTT
Programs for Christmas Entertainments, in Ladies Home Journal, Dec., 1906

DAISY WOLF
We Never Learn, 1928

RUTH LEVI WOLF
Miriam's Purim Play, 1914   RPB

SARA WOLFF
The Klass and Fakultee, 1928, stunt for banquets and class meetings   RPB

ANNA WOLFROM
Albion and Rosamond, and The Living Voice, 1916, two plays   RPB
Human Wisps: Six One Act Plays, 1917   RPB

MIRIAM WOLFSON
The Spirit of Hadassah, 1927 (1)   RPB

CORA ANTOINETTE WOOD (BINNINGER) (1867- ?)
Buying Culture, 1922 (1)   RPB, BTG
Double Solitaire, 1931 (1)

FRANCES GILCHRIST WOOD (MRS. LANSING P. WOOD)
The Book of the Pageant of Ridgewood, N. J., 1915   RPB
    (She was pageant master.)

LETITIA W. WOOD
Dynamic Worship Programs for Young People, 1950
Fifteen Minute Problem Plays, 1930
The Lost Coin, 1929, with Lena Prather Martin, church play   RPB

PEGGY WOOD (1892-1978)
The Flying Prince, 1927, with Eugene Wood, fantasy (1)   RPB
Miss Quis, 1937, with Ward Morehouse, 3 acts, prod. by Federal Theater   RPB

VIVIAN ELLIOTT WOOD
Dinty, Davy and the Dinosaur, and Dinty and David Do Spring   DLC
    Poems, 1927, two monologues
Thou Shalt Not Steal, 1930, monologue   RPB
Violet of the Neckwear, 1926, monologue   DLC

ELIZABETH WOODBRIDGE (See ELIZABETH WOODBRIDGE MORRIS)

HANNAH REA WOODMAN (1870- ?)
Bess Goes to Europe, 1911, "comedy of haste in 3 acts"   RPB
Billy Ben's Pirate Play, 1912, "dress rehearsal" (1)   RPB

HANNAH REA WOODMAN (continued)

The Bobbie Bennett Plays for Children, 1922	RPB
Captain Lincoln's Way, 1928, Indian play for boys	RPB, SOP-I
The Cinder Maid, 1912, romantic comedy for little folks	RPB
The Clever Doctor, 1912, adaptation of a Grimm's tale	RPB
Dear Heart, 1930, adaptation of a Grimm's tale	RPB
For His Country, 1928, historical play for boys for	RPB, SOP-I
Washington's birthday (1)	
Galliger, 1911, 3 act h. s. comedy	RPB
General Marion's Company Dinner, 1932	NBuG, DLC
His First Commission, 1931, Washington play for little folks (1)	RPB
His Uncle John, 1908, 3 acts	DLC
The Honest Shoemaker, 1912, domestic play for little folks	RPB
The King of Nolande, 1923	RPB
The Master's Birthday, 1908, 3 acts, young	RPB
The Oaten Cakes, 1912, historical play for little folks	RPB
Preserving a Smith, 1911, 3 act burlesque of shadows	RPB
The Professor, 1907, 3 acts	RPB
Professor Grindem: his commencement, 1903, 3 acts	DLC
Professor Wright Falls in Love, 1923	RPB
The Rescue of Prince Hal, 1911, 3 act comedy of manners	RPB
She Organized a Club, 1903, 2 act farce	RPB
The Sweet Girl Graduates, 1902, "to my own boys and girls, the	RPB
class of 1902, by the author, Professor of English Literature, Drake	
University," 3 act farce	

NANCY MANN WADDEL WOODROW (MRS. WILSON WOODROW)
    (1866?-1935) NAW
    The Universal Impulse, in Smart Set, 34, June, 1911, 71-2 (1)

FLORA CAMPBELL WOODRUFF

Jazzy Justice, 1928, ten-minute stunt for male actors, with	RPB
Daisy Baker Hay	

HELEN S. WOODRUFF
    Hooray for the Girls, 1919, book by Woodruff; lyrics by Annelu Burns;
        music by Madelyn Sheppard; "presented by the sub-debs, debs, and
        super debs of N. Y. society for the benefit of the American Committee
        for Devastated France"
    Just Because, prod. 1922, with Anne Wynne O'Ryan, music by Madelyn
        Sheppard

MRS. JOHN WOODRUFF

Grand Pantomime, Jack and Jill, n.d., fantasy	RPB

ALICE WOODS
    The Devil's Glow, prod. 1917-8 by Provincetown Players

FRANCES WOODS
    Pageant of Ridgewood, 1915, Ridgewood, N. J.

MARJORIE WOODS

The Birthday Ball, 1921, about Revolutionary War (1)	RPB
The Christmas Ghost, 1929, for girls	RPB
Patriotic Pepper, 1929, Washington's birthday play for girls	RPB
Turkey Red, 1929, Thanksgiving play for girls	RPB
Why We Celebrate, 1927, holiday plays for young people	RPB

VIRNA WOODS (1864—1903)

The Amazons, 1891, lyrical drama	CStoC
Charles IX, c.1902, historical play, typed ms.	CStoC
Christopher Columbus, n.d., handwritten ms.	CStoC
Courtier and King, historical romantic drama, scenario	CStoC
Drida, Queen of Mercia, scenario	CStoC
Florine, notes and dialogue	CStoC
Griselda: The Peasant-Duchess, c.1900, romantic drama, typed ms.	CStoC
Horatius, 1899, tragedy, typed ms. draft	CStoC
Jephthah; or, As It Is Written, c.1900, tragedy, typed ms.	CStoC
King of Northumberland, 1899, historical romantic drama, typed ms.	CStoC
A Knight Errant, c.1901, 5 act heroic comedy, typed ms.	CStoC
Lalla Rookh, c.1900, 4 act romantic comedy, typed ms.	CStoC
Lord Strathmore, n.d., typed ms.	CStoC
The Mask of a King, 4 act romantic drama, typed scenario	CStoC
Miriam (1)	CStoC
Strathmore, typewritten copy	CStoC
That Affair of Brown's, incomplete typewritten copy	CStoC

EUGENIE WOODWARD

Two By Two, prod. 1925, with John Turner

RUTH M. WOODWARD

The Fortunes of War, 191? (1) typed copy	NN
The Red Geranium, prod. 1922	

BEULAH BAILEY WOOLARD

"April in Paris," 1956 play-pageant especially adapted for senior class day exercises	RPB
Beyond the Port, 1939, especially adapted for senior class day exercises	DLC
Giants of Fortune, 1929, especially adapted for Senior Class Day exercises	RPB
The Graduate's Seven Guides, 1930, especially adapted for senior class day exercises	FTaSU
The Knight Triumphant, 1934, especially adapted for Senior Class Day exercises	RPB
Let Youth Speak, 1940, especially adapted for senior class day exercises	RPB
The Open Road, 1937, especially adapted for senior class day exercises	RPB
Out of the Past, 1933, especially adapted for senior class day exercises	FTaSU, NcC
The Parting of the Braves, 1935, especially adapted for senior class day exercises	RPB
Pirate's Gold, 1933, especially adapted for senior class day exercises	FTaSU, NcC
Renovating Miss Emma, 1937, 3 acts	ViU, DLC
The Senior Follies, 1936, especially adapted for senior class day exercises	NcC
Seniors at the Bar, 1931, burlesque class trial especially adapted for senior class day exercises	FTaSU
"The Set of the Sail," 1929, especially adapted for senior class day exercises	RPB
The World Outside, 1929, especially adapted for senior class day exercises	RPB
Youth Marches On, 1937, "stirring class day play in 3 parts," with Ann Pitts Hick	RPB

OLIVE F. WOOLEY

Sara (1)	LUU

CELIA PARKER WOOLLEY (1848-1918)
The Angel at the Gate, 1919, Easter fantasy (1)   RPB

SARAH CHAUNCEY WOOLSEY ("SUSAN COOLIDGE") (1835-1905) AWW
Ginevra, 1906, monologue for a woman   RPB

MAUDE LAVON WORCESTER
The Proof of the Pudding, 1923   RPB
The Wrong Mummy, 1923   RPB

HELEN CHAFFEE WORKMAN (1868- ?)
Tested Readings for Young People, 1929   RPB

FLORINE R. WORMSER
The Portrait, in Smart Set, 28, June, 1909, 76-83 (1)

EDYTH M. WORMWOOD
The Doll That Saved an Army, 1916, historical play for   RPB, JPG
    young people (1)
The Haunted Gate, 1913, Halloween (1)   RPB
Little Acts for Little Actors, 1916, with Elizabeth Guptill   RPB
The New Woman in Mother Goose Land, 1915, young   RPB
No Girls Admitted, 1912, for 8th grade or h. s. (1)   RPB

EDNA RANDOLPH WORRELL
The Belles of Fol-de-rol, 1914, operetta   RPB
Christmas Everywhere, 1924, tableau   RPB
The Christmas Garden, 1914, with music, young   RPB
Christmas Harvest, in Ladies Home Journal, 32, Dec., 1916, 42 (1)
A Corner in Hearts, 1909, Christmas parlor play (1)   RPB
A Dream Come True, pageant of the Red Cross, in Ladies Home
    Journal, 35, Nov., 1918, 112-8 (1)
The Flag Makers, 1915, in Ladies Home Journal, 32, May, 1915, 40 (1)
Following the Doves, "pageant of peaceful American industries,"
    in Ladies Home Journal, 36, June, 1919, 155.
Gifts for the King, 1919, Christmas   RPB
Good Neighbor Plays, 1942, by Edna Worrell (may be a   Or, DLC
    different person)
The Little Boy Nobody Wanted, 1929, Christmas   RPB
The Little Stranger, 1921, "moving picture play to use with stereopticon" RPB
The Lost Violin, 1924, for h. s. boys   RPB
The Messenger Birds, in Bright Ideas for Christmas (1)   RPB
Mother Goose Bazaar, 1909, adapted from nursery rhymes   RPB
Queen of the Year, 1916, winter cantata for schools   RPB
Reaping and Giving; or, The Christmas Harvest, 1919   RPB
The Run-a-way Bear, 1908   RPB
Shouting the Battle Cry of "Feed 'em," 1917, in Ladies Home   RPB
    Journal, 34, Nov., 1917, 40, young (1)
The Toys' Rebellion, 1911, in Ladies Home Journal, 20, December, RPB
    1902, 16, Christmas parlor play for children (1)
Two Merry Wagers, 1914, farce (1)   RPB
Waiting for Dorothea, 1930, with tableaux (1)   RPB

RUTH MOUGEY WORRELL
The Kingdom of Love, 1925, "masque pageant on farm and country DLC
    migrants," pub. by N. Y. Council of Women for Home Missions
Pageant of the Red Cross, 1921   OU

RUTH MOUGEY WORRELL (continued)
The Way of Peace, 1924, pageant with Laura S. Coppenhauer and   RPB
     Katharine S. Cronk

"JENNY WREN"
Fowl Deeds, 1920, Negro comedy   RPB
The Municipal Davenport, 1926, "one word play"   RPB

ALICE MORGAN WRIGHT
Kalidasa, 1904? English version of Sakuntala; based upon Monier   RPB
     Williams' translation of the Sanskrit drama, adapted by Wright

CAROLINE WRIGHT
The Sky Scrappers, 1906, operetta, book by Wright; lyrics by Wright   RPB-M
     and Sara M. Bourke; music by Mabel Osborne, presented at
     Radcliffe College

GRACE LATIMER WRIGHT
Blind Alleys, prod. 1917 by Washington Square players

HARRIET SABRA WRIGHT
New Plays from Old Tales, 1921, arranged for boys and girls   RPB

JOSEPHINE PAGE WRIGHT (or PAGE-WRIGHT)
The Dragon of Dors, 1907, "terpsichorean romance in 3 acts"   RPB
The Harp of Ten Strings, 1906? play?   NN

LUCY WRIGHT
The Wonder Worker (1)

VIRGINIA B. WRIGHT
Clarindie Cackler's Courtship, 1902, 2 act farce   RPB

EUPHEMIA VAN RENSSELAER WYATT
Her Country, 1924, drama staged by Nathaniel Edward Reeid (1)   RPB

MINNIE E. WYCOFF
Weaving at Ripley County, 1927, pageant, Versailles, Ind., with others

ADELAIDE H. WYETH
Fun in a Photographer's Gallery, 1908 (1)   RPB
Huldah's Parin' Bee, 1908   RPB
Hunkers' Corners, 1908   RPB
Pa's Picnic, 1909, 2 act rural play   RPB

ELIZABETH HEYWOOD WYMAN
Ted's Chum, 1923, comedy (1)   RPB
Virginia Visits Santa Claus, 1923   RPB

ANNA WYNNE
The Broken Bars, 1906, modern morality play (1)
The Courtship of Then, Now and Tomorrow, prod. 1915
Maggie Brannigan on Romeo and Juliet and Other Monologues, 1906   RPB
The Night of Entertainment, 1908, 2 act comedy for college girls   RPB
On the Path of the Child, 1916, morality play (1)   RPB

X-Y-Z

ELSIE DUNCAN YALE

"All Aboard!" 1924, Christmas cantata, music by Clyde Willard   PP
All in a Christmas Garden, 1928, "pretty play for intermediate grades"   RPB
At Castle Christmas, 1934, cantata for young people, music by   RPB-M
    Clyde Willard and others
Aunt Jane's Christmas, 1933, secular Christmas cantata for   RPB-M
    young people, music by Clyde Willard
"By This Sign Conquer!" 1936, pageant play for Easter   RPB
The Call of the Star, 1944, Christmas cantata, music by Lawrence Keating
The Captain of the Guard, 1918, Easter song story, music by   RPB-M
    Adam Geibel
The Centurion, 1912, Easter song story, music by Adam Geibel   RPB-M
The Chaldean, 1912, Christmas song story, music by Adam Geibel   RPB-M
Choice Dramas for Children's Day, 1939
Christmas at Jollyville Junction, 1924   RPB
The Christmas Review, 1917, cantata, music by J. Lincoln Hall   RPB-M
A Christmas Service, 189?, music by Edward Daniel Faulkner
Christmastide, 1943, cantata-pageant
"Come Any Time," 1926, Christmas comedy for 7 girls   OCl
Come Let Us Adore Him, 1945, Christmas cantata
The Dawn of Christmas, 1950, Christmas choir cantata, music by Roy E. Nolte
A Day at Camp Killkare; or, Aunt Jane and the Campfire Girls, 1915   RPB
Dramas and Pageants for Christmas, 1939
The Easter Light, 1922, pageant   NN
The Exalted Christ, 1944, Easter choir cantata, music by Roy E. Nolte
"Fairest Lord Jesus," 1940, pageant-cantata for Easter   RPB-M
Four Christmas Dramas, 1940   RPB
Four Easter Dramas, 1939, with Mattie Shannon   RPB
Four Plays for Children's Day, 1936, with others   RPB
Four Plays for Easter, 1936   DLC
The Garden Guest, 1933, floral cantata, music by J. Lincoln Hall   RPB-M
    and others
The Garden of Joseple, 1921, story cantata for Easter, music by   RPB-M
    Adam Geibel
The Girls of Glen Willow, 1918, camp play   RPB
Gloria in Excelsis, 1943, Christmas choir cantata, music arranged by Ellen
    Jane Lorenz
The Glorious Galilean, 1943, Easter choir cantata, music by Ira B. Wilson
The Glory of the Cross, 1931, story pageant for Easter   RPB-M
Grandmother's Rose Jar, 1912   RPB
He Came to Bethlehem, 1932   RPB
He That Liveth, 1942, Easter choir cantata, music by Ira B. Wilson   RPB-M
The Holy Land, 1918, story cantata for Christmas, music by   RPB-M
    Adam Geibel
In Excelsis, 1915, Christmas cantata, music by Joseph Lincoln Hall
The Inn, 1917, song story for Christmas, music by Adam Geibel   RPB-M
The Inventor, introducing the wishing box, 1915, Christmas   RPB
Judith, 1916, Easter song story, music by Adam Geibel   RPB-M
The Light of Christmas, 1948, Christmas choir cantata, music by L. S. Clark
The Light of Life, 1914, Christmas cantata, music by Adam Geibel   RPB-M
The Light of Love Divine, 1931, Christmas pageant, music from   RPB
    ancient and modern Christmas carols

ELSIE DUNCAN YALE (continued)

Look Pleasant Please, in Mattie B. Shannon, An Original   RPB
    Christmas Entertainment, 1924
The Lookout Club, 1932, Christmas cantata for young people,   RPB-M
    music by M. Isabelle Ritter
The Minister's Aunt, 1945, musical entertainment, music by "Chas. Francis
    Lane" (Ira B. Wilson)
The Moon Maiden, 1935, comic operetta, music by Clarence Kohlmann
A Morning in the Orient, 1911? song story   RPB
New Christmas Dramas, 1941, with Mattie Shannon   RPB
A Night in the Orient, 1910, "Christmas cantata without Santa Claus,"
    music by Adam Geibel
No Room in the Inn and She Wanted to Write, in Two Christmas   RPB
    Readings, 1933 with Irene McCague Ihde
Onesimus, 1934   RPB
Pageantry for Easter, 1923   RPB
The Redeemer Liveth, 1933, Easter   RPB
Resurrection and Life, 1907, service for Easter, music by   RPB-M
    C. Harold Lowden
Risen, 1922, Easter service, music by Joseph Lincoln Hall   RPB-M
Santa's Wishing Box, 1912, Christmas cantata, music by   RPB-M
    Clarence Kohlman
Save the Wild Flowers, with Frances Duncan, in Woman's Home
    Companion, 54, May, 1927, 49 (1)
She Married the Minister! 1939   RPB
The Shepherd King, 1907, Christmas cantata, music by   IU
    Joseph Lincoln Hall
Special Dramas for Christmas, 1938, with others   RPB
Star of the King, 1914, Christmas service, music by J. Lincoln Hall   RPR-M
There Came Three Kings, n.d., Christmas cantata, music by   RPB-M
    C. Kohlman
Three Dramas for Children's Day, 1940, with Lida S. Leech   RPB
Three Dramas for Easter, 1940   RPB
Thy God Reigneth, 1944, cantata, music by Lawrence Keating
The Traveller, 1914, Christmas song story, music by Adam Geibel   RPB-M
The Triumph of the Crucified, 1944, cantata, music by Lawrence Keating
Two Beautiful Pageants for Easter, 1932   DLC
The Two Christmas Boxes, 1915, for girls   RPB
Two Christmas Readings, 1933, with Irene McCague Ihde
The Village Choir, 1934, musical entertainment, music by   RPB-M
    C. Austin Miles and M. Isabelle Ritter
We Have Seen His Star, 1941, Christmas choir cantata, music by
    "Lee Rogers" (Roger C. Wilson)
Welcome Happy Morning, 1935, "pageant beautiful for Easter"   RPB-M
The White Elephant Sale, 1928, "novelty entertainment for   RPB
    young folks' church societies"
The Wishing Well; or, The Golden Gloves, 1940, pageant cantata   RPB-M
Worship at the Manger, 1944, cantata drama for Christmas, music
    by "Noel Benson" (Ira B. Wilson)

ELIZABETH HALL YATES

The Adults, 1926, comedy (1)   RPB
Masques, 1923   play??   DLC
A New Song, in Horn Book, 14, Nov., 1938, 388-90 (1)
The Slave, in Lydia G. Deseo and Hulda M. Phipps, Looking at Life Through
    Drama, 1931
Small Plays for Small Casts, 1926   RPB

PATTY M. YATES
   Primary Plays, 1929   RPB
   Swat That Fly!   JPR

MARY (or MARTHA) YELLOTT
   Waffles for Breakfast, 1921, "comedy of newly married life" (1)

ANITA YOUNG
   A Bowl of Rice, 1930

CECILIA MARY YOUNG
   The Illinois Trail, 1918, pageant commemorating the Illinois centennial   RPB
   The Redemption Play, 1933, "depicting Christ's redemption   RPB
      of man," 3 acts

EMILY YOUNG
   Hello Alexander, prod. 1919, with Edgar Smith; music by Jean Schwartz;
      lyrics by Alfred Bryan
   Red Peppers, prod. 1922, with Edgar Smith; music by Albert Gumble and
      Owen Murphy; lyrics by Howard Rogers and Owen Murphy

ERMA YOUNG
   Mother Goose Marries Santa Claus, 1930   RPB

GLADYS I. YOUNG
   The Taming of Horrors, 1921, Girl Scout play   RPB

LILLIAN YOUNG
   Frenzied Finance   NPM

PAULINE RODGERS YOUNG
   Off the Road, in Poet Lore, 36, Summer, 1925, 300-5

RIDA JOHNSON YOUNG (1875?-1926) AWW NWAT
   "Barbara's Dilemma," 1906, monologue   RPB
   Barry of Ballymore, prod. 1911 at Academy of Music
   The Boys of Company B, prod. 1907, typescript   NN, MH
   Brown of Harvard, 1909, prod. 1906   RPB
   Buried Treasure, see Captain Kidd Jr.
   Captain Kidd Jr., 1920, prod. 1916, 3 act farce, also titled Buried Treasure RPB
   Chatterton, 1906, monologue   RPB
   Cock o' the Roost, prod. 1924
   The Dream Girl, prod. 1924, with Harold Atteridge; music by Victor Herbert
   The Front Seat, prod. 1921
   The Girl and the Pennant, 1917, prod. 1913, with Christy Mathewson,   RPB
      baseball comedy
   Glorious Betsy, prod. 1908
   Her Soldier Boy, prod. 1916, adapt. of musical by Leon Victor; music by
      Emmerich Kalman and S. Romberg
   His Little Widows, prod. 1917, with William Cary Duncan; music by William
      Schroeder
   The Isle of Dreams, prod. 1913
   John Clayton, Actor, 1906 (1)   RPB
   Lady Luxury, prod. 1914, music by William Schroeder
   The Lancers, prod. 1907, with J. Hartley Manners
   The Last of the Cargills, 1906, dramatic scene for 2 characters (1)   RPB
   Little Old New York, 1928, prod. 1920, 4 act comedy   RPB

RIDA JOHNSON YOUNG (continued)
Little Simplicity, prod. 1918, music by Augustus Barratt
Lord Byron
Lot 79, prod. in London 1918
The Lottery Man, 1924, prod. 1909, 3 act comedy   RPB
Macushla, 1920, prod. 1912, typescript   NN
Maytime, prod. 1917, with Cyrus Wood; music by Sigmund Romberg RPB-M
Mistress Betty
Naughty Marietta, prod. 1910, comic opera, music by Victor Herbert   RPB-M
Next, prod. 1911, 3 act comedy, typed copy   MH
The Rabbit's Foot, prod. 1924
Ragged Robin, prod. 1910 at Academy of Music, with R. Olcott
The Red Petticoat, 1912, music by Jerome Kern; lyrics by Paul West
Shameen Dhu, prod. 1914
Soldier Boy, prod. 1918, with E. Wallace and F. Chappelle; music by Sigmund
    Romberg
Sometime, 1946, prod. 1918, 2 act musical romance; music by R. Friml
A Successful Calamity, 1922, prod. 1917
A Wise Child, 191? 3 acts, typescript   NN

"KAY ZIEGFIELD" (See KATHARINE KAVANAUGH)

LOUISE SEYMOUR HASBROUCK ZIMM
    (See ELIZABETH LOUISE SEYMOUR HASBROUCK)

Appendix A

Provincial Dramatists

The following is a list of names and plays taken from:
Paul T. Nolan, Provincial Drama in America, 1870-1916, a Casebook of Primary
     Materials, Metuchen, N. J.: The Scarecrow Press, 1967.
Names marked with (*) are also included in my checklist.

Anna Byrne Adams, Fathma, Daughter of the Beys, 1908
Martha W. Austin, Tristram and Isolt, 1905
Mary McDougal Axelson, Life Begins
*Mrs. Bernice Babcock, Mammy, 1915
                Mary, pub. in Arkansas Progress, I, 20, Oct., 24, 1914
                The Soul of Ann Rutledge
Sallie C. Battaile, Questions and Answers and Compositions and Speeches for the
Deestrick Skule, 1911
Lena Blackburn, The Sheath Gown Girls, 1908
Frances St. John Brenon, The Intruders, 1909
Alice Brooks, Le Vipere, 1900
Anna Burgess, Money Against Money, 1909
Ellen Harrell Cantrell, Freaks of St. Valenitne, 1893
Mary Chase
Kate Chopin
Alice Kingsbury Cooley, Did She Sin? 1873
           The California, 1893
           Borrowed Till Midnight, 1898
Louise Henry Cowan, Rajah Sindl, 1910
           The Reckoning. 1913
           Belhaven, the Future City, 1906
           The Sword of Chivalry, 1907
           Yolande, 1907
           The Rajah of India: or, Marcelle, 1896
           (pub. under name Louise Henry)
Catherine Davy, Arizona Girl Bandit, 1907
Ruth Everett, Cohen's Toy Shop, 1906
*Minnie Maddern Fiske
Frances Nimmo Greene, Speaking of Adam, 1915
           The Ultimate American, 1913

Kathryn Stone Hardman, United; or, As a Woman Saw It, 1914
Mary Isabelle Hassim, The Boomers
Margaret Henry-Ruffin, The Bride, 1909
                              The Heart of a Harp, 1906
                              The Leprechaun, 1907
Sara Barton Holt, The Radish King, 1887
*Alice E. Ives, dram of Beulah, 1910
Mrs. Phillip Jackson, Bitter Fruits; or, Matrimony in Prospect, 1893
Isidor G. Jacobson, He Stoops to Conquer, 1894
Amy Laird, The Little Puritan, 1910
*Margaret Larkin, El Cristo, 1926
*Caroline Cowper Lovell, The Swayam-Vara, 1916
                              dram. of Wuthering Heights, 1914
Norma A. Lucy, The Crook, 1911
Isabel S. McLaughlin, The Question, 1911
                        My Wife's Daughter
*Marie Madison, Colonel Bob: a Western Pastoral, 1908
                        (with John Wallace Crawford)
Mrs. Wade A. Martin, Coward, 1914
Frances Morris, Arizona Bess, 1892
Lyda Nagel (Mrs. Ray A. Tidwell)
*Marie Bankhead Owen, The Acting Governor, 1913
                          The Deltan, 1908
                          The Transgressors, 1909, with M. Mayo
Elizabeth Pierce-Lyman, Tesca: Libretto of a Grand Opera, 1915
Matsy Wynn Richards, One Wonderful Dream: Mother Goose Fantasy, 1915
Lidie Auirett Rivers, Just Life Itself, 1911
                      Sour Grapes, 1913
                      Naomi, 1911
Freda Slemons Ruble, El Paso, Down by the Rio Grande, 1908
(under name Freda Slemons) Joshua Copelan's Daughter, 1903
                          Saint or Sinner: An Emotional Drama, 1903
                          The Sweetest Girl in Dixie, 1907
Leila May Smith, Out at Old Aunt Mary's; or, A Visit from the Riley Children, 1916
*Fleta Campbell Springer
Edna Sutton Stark, Via the Heart, 1912
                    Diamonds Seven, Hearts Eight, 1915
Caroline Stern, "The Queen Decides," in At the Edge of the World, 1916
Rose Strauss, Bluffing It, 1912
Eva Thatcher, Twenty Minutes Till Train Time, 1899
Anna Van Vredenburgh, The Grandest Pagan of Them All, 1905
Mary E. Waddington, Al Douglass, 1908
                      The Return, 1908
                      When Daughters Will, 1911
Cannie West, A Man's Love; or, Driven from Eden, 1913
Mary A. Wolff, Affinity and Duty; or, Evangeline and Gretchen, 1913
Martha Young, Old Turk: an Easter Drama, 1905

Appendix B

Collections
Edited by Florence R. Signor

Plays for School Days, Dansville, N. Y.: F. A. Owen Publishing Co., 1921

Aileen Schofield	The Traitor
Etta V. Leighton	How the Constitution Saved the Nation
Mary G. Reed	The First Flag
E. C. Tulip	The Toy's Celebration
Zelia Cornell Wiley	Santa's Helpers
E. E. Preston	The Circus Comes to Town
Grace M. Cole	A May Day Play
Etta M. Arnold	Rip Van Winkle
May L. Treadwell	"Marse Gawge de Lubines' Man"
Harriet Harlan	Stock
Marie Sabin	The Pilgrims in Their Three Homes
Myrtle Kaufman	"Abe" Lincoln's Neighbors
and pupils	
Clara Childs	The Courtship of Miles Standish
Mae Ihler	The Quarrel of the Days of the Week
May L. Treadwell	The Use in Useless
Bessie A. St. Clair	A Runaway Thanksgiving Dinner
Beth Harris	How "The Star Spangled Banner" Was Written

Japanese Entertainments, Dansville, N. Y.: F. A. Owen Pub. Co., 1924

Pauline More Wetzel	Her Father's Will
Elizabeth Smith Denehie	A Japanese Frolic
Nellie R. Cameron	America and Japan, a dialogue
Hallie Ives	The Little Maids of Far Japan
Ruth Angelo	The Bird's Gifts
Grace A. Lusk	Japanese Fan Drill
Harriet S. Wardell	Cherry Blossom Drill

Health Plays and Dialogues, Dansville, N. Y.: F. A. Owen Pub. Co., 1923

Maud L. Bowser	Mother Goose's Health Children
Rose M. Stack	A Model Child
Josephine Perkins	The Merry Microbe
Gail Anderson	Winning the Championship
Eva La Liberte	The Fly Union

Gladys Lloyd	Drill of the Bright Examples
Marie Thien	David's Dream
Ruth K. Duke	Billy's Dream
Clara E. Putnam	The House That Tom Built
Esther Lindeburg	The Goblin Germs
Esther Lindeburg	Fairy Health to the Rescue
Laura McIlhargey	Bernice's Fairies
Nelle Caesar	Johnny's Lesson
Helen Ambuhl	Giant Sickness
Kathryn E. Woods	The Health Charm

Minor Contributors
to Collections

Grace B. Faxon, Pieces and Plays for Washington's Birthday, Dansville, N. Y.:
    F. A. Owen Pub. Co., 1916

Susie M. Best	Eliza Cook	Alice Garnett
Hazel Dysart	Edna Dean Proctor	Abbie Farwell Brown
Hallie Ives	Alice Cook Fuller	Rose Mills Powers
Elva J. Smith	Jennie D. Moore	Anna M. Pratt
Eva May Moss	Ida B. Bassford	Mary K. D. Dingwall
Lillian M Jones	Rosemary E. Richards	Mary L. Burdick
Aliee E. Allen	Margrete L. Peterson	Nora Perry
Clara A. Nash	Bertha L. Swope	Effa E. Preston
Edith P. Mendes	Louise Schlitz	Margaret C. Fairlie
Virginia Baker	Lula C. White	Lucia M. Mooney
Mary Mapes Dodge	Daisy D. Stephenson	Mary V. Myers
Mary Bailey	Jane A. Stewart	Lizzie M. Hadley
Bertha E. Bush	Lillian H. Campbell	Hope Nelson
Daisy D. Stephenson	Ella Jacobs	Caroline H. Mooar
Margaret E. Sangster	Ethel H. Robson	

Grace B. Faxon, Many a Way for Memorial Day, a collection of recitations,
    quotations, words for familiar tunes, exercises, dialogues, and plays.
    Boston: Walter H. Baker Co., 1926 (many are poems)

Grace B. Faxon	Frances Wright Turner	Celia Thaxter
Mary B. Hosmer	Kate Putnam Osgood	Mary Ashley Townsend
Martha E. Oliver	Amelia Josephine Burr	Charlotte Holmes Crawford
Margaret Bell Merrill	Gertrude Robinson	Emma A. E. Lente
Eula Gladys Lincoln	Olive E. Dana	Etta V. Leighton
Henrietta F. Dunlap	Fannie Barnett Linsky	Constance Cottin Cook
Emma Huntington Nason	Minna Irving	

Grace B. Faxon, Many a Way for Closing Day, Boston: Walter H. Baker Co., 1926
    (many are poems)

Constance Cottin Cooke	Fannie Barnett Linsky	Emily D. Denby
Ann Augusta Gray	Anna V. M. Jones	Frances Margaret Fox
Minnie Leona Upton	Claribel Young Glen	Carolyn Wells
Alice Cromwell Hoffman	Emily Westwood	Lewis Marie Zetterberg
Marjorie Dillon	Caroline MacCormack	Annie Willis McCullough
Madeline S. Bridges	Elizabeth Lincoln Gould	Eva J. Beede
Margaret Vandegrift	Henrietta R. Eliot	Henrietta F. Dunlap
M. Elsie Wentworth	Alice E. Allen	Grace B. Faxon

Grace B. Faxon, <u>Many a Way for Closing Day,</u> Boston: Walter H. Baker Co., 1926
(continued)

Mary A Gillett	Priscilla Leonard	Alie Webster
Elizabeth Akers	Alice E. Allen	Meredith Nicholson
Ellen H. Willis	Sarah K. Bolton	Marguerite Stockman Dickson

Carolyn R. Freeman and Ann Gladys Lloyd and others, <u>The Kiddies' Christmas Book,</u> Syracuse, N. Y.: Willis N. Bugbee Co, 1925.

Ann Gladys Lloyd
Carolyn R. Freeman
Olive F. Woolley Burt, <u>The Wise Gifts</u>
Lucile Crites, <u>Santa's Gifts Plus His Suprise</u>

Selected Bibliography

Chinoy, Helen Krich and Linda Walsh Jenkins. Women in American Theatre. New York, 1981.

Chubb, Percival. Festivals and Plays in School and Elsewhere. New York, 1912.

Community Drama: Suggestions for a Community-wide Program of Dramatic Activities, 1926.

Coven, Brenda. American Women Dramatists of the Twentieth Century: A Bibliography. Metuchen, New Jersey, 1982.

The Drama Magazine. Volumes 1-21, February, 1911-June, 1931. Chicago.

The Dramatic Index, 1909-1949. Boston.

Doyle, Sister Mary Peter. A Study of Play Selection in Women's Colleges. Chapel Hill, North Carolina, 1935

Ferguson, Phyllis Marschall. "Women Dramatists in the American Theatre, 1901-1940." Ph. D. dissertation, University of Pittsburgh, 1957.

Firkins, Ina Ten Eyck. Index to Plays, 1800-1926. New York, 1927. Supplement, 1935.

Franklin, Margaret Ladd. The Case for Woman Suffrage: A Bibliography. New York, 1913.

George Washington Pageants and Plays. Washington, D. C., 1931.

Hatch, James Vernon. Black Images on the American Stage: A Bibliography of Plays and Musicals, 1770-1970. New York, 1970.

Hatch, James V. and Omani Abdullah. Black Playwrights, 1823-1977: An Annotated Bibliography of Plays. New York, 1977.

Hazeltine, Alice I. Plays for Children, an annotated bibliography. Chicago, 1921.

Hinding, Andrea, Ed. Women's History Sources: a guide to archives and manuscript collections in the United States. New York, 1979. Volume 2 edited by Suzanna Moody.

Ireland, Norma Olin and David E. Ireland. An Index to Monologs and Dialogs. Boston, 1939.

Keller, Dean H. Index to Plays in Periodicals. Metuchen, New Jersey, 1979.

Koch, Frederick, Betty Smith, and Robert Firch. Plays for Schools and Little Theatres. Chapel Hill, North Carolina, 1937.

Koch, Frederick and Nettina Strobach. Plays for Schools and Little Theatres. Chapel Hill, North Carolina, 1930.

Koster, Donald Nelson. The Theme of Divorce in American Drama, 1871-1939. Philadelphia, 1942.

Logasa, Hannah and Winifred Ver Nooy. An Index to One-Act Plays. Boston, 1924. Supplement, 1924-1931.

McCaslin, Nellie. Theatre for Children in the United States. Norman, Oklahoma, 1971.

McFadden, Elizabeth and Lilian E. Davis. A Selected List of Plays for Amateurs and Students of Dramatic Expression in Schools and Colleges. Cincinnati, 1908.

MacKay, Constance D'Arcy. The Little Theatre in the United States. New York, 1917.
MacKaye, Percy. The Civic Theatre. New York, 1910.
MacKaye, Percy. Community Drama. Boston, 1917.
Mantle, Burns and Garrison P. Sherwood. The Best Plays of 1899-1909, 1909-1919,
        then yearly to 1930-31. New York.
Merrill, E. Carolyn, comp. "Pageants and Masques (A List)." Boston Public Library
        Bulletin, Series 4, Volume 4: 101-115.
Mersand, Joseph. Index to Plays. Metuchen, New Jersey, 1966.
Miller, Elizabeth Erwin Lobingier. The Dramatization of Bible Stories. Chicago, 1918.
Miller, Elizabeth Erwin Lobingier. The Dramatization in the Church School.
        Chicago, 1923.
Nolan, Paul T. Provincial Drama in America, 1870-1916—A Casebook of Primary
        Materials. Metuchen, New Jersey, 1967.
Peace Plays for Adults. Philadelphia, 193?
Perry, Clarence Arthur. The Work of the Little Theatres. New York, 1933.
Plays for Amateurs. Chicago, 1915.
Rockwell, Ethel Theodora. American Life as Represented in Native One-Act Plays.
        Madison, Wisconsin, 1931.
Rush, Theresa Gunnels, Carol Fairbanks Myers, and Esther Spring Arata. Black
        American Writers, Past and Present: A Biographical and Bibliographical
        Dictionary. Two volumes. Metuchen, New Jersey, 1975.
Sanford, Anne Putnam. Pageants of Our Nation—Central States. New York, 1929.
Spearman, Walter. The Carolina Playmakers: the First Fifty Years. Chapel Hill,
        North Carolina, 1970.
Sper, Felix. From Native Roots, a Panorama of Our Regional Drama. Caldwell,
        Idaho, 1948.
Tackel, Martin S. "Women and American Pageantry: 1908-1918." Ph. D. dissertation
        City University of New York, 1982.
Tebbets, Ruth E. Children's Plays. New York, 1936.
Theatre Magazine. Volume 1–53, 1901-1931. New York.
Thomson, Ruth Gibbons. Index to Full Length Plays, 1895-1925. Boston, 1956.
        Volume 2—1926-1944.
Ward, Winifred. Creative Dramatics for the Upper Grades and Junior High Schools.
        New York, 1930.
Wise, Claude Merton. Dramatics for School and Community. Cincinnati, 1923.

About the Compiler

FRANCES DIODATO BZOWSKI has contributed entries on American women playwrights to the *Cambridge Guide to World Theatre* and the forthcoming *Cambridge Guide to American Theatre* and has published articles in scholarly journals. She is working on a study of themes of the New Woman in plays by women.